Municipal Management Series

Local
Government
Police
Management

Editorial Advisory Committee

Cornelius J. Behan

Noel C. Bufe

Raymond C. Davis

Herman Goldstein

Eduardo Gonzalez

George L. Kelling

Gerald W. Lynch

Charles "Bud" Meeks

Daniel N. Rosenblatt

Elsie Scott

Lawrence W. Sherman

Darrel W. Stephens

James K. "Chips" Stewart

Gary W. Sykes

Robert Wasserman

Chuck Wexler

Hubert Williams

Mary Ann Wycoff

Municipal Management Series

Local Government Police Management

Third Edition

Editor
William A. Geller

Published for the
ICMA Training Institute

By the
International
City
Management
Association

Municipal Management Series

Local Government Police Management

Effective Communication

The Effective Local Government Manager

Effective Supervisory Practices

Emergency Management: Principles and Practice for Local Government

Housing and Local Government

Management of Local Planning

Management of Local Public Works

Management Policies in Local Government Finance

Managing Fire Services

Managing Human Services

Managing Local Government: Cases in Decision Making

Managing Municipal Leisure Services

The Practice of Local Government Planning

The Practice of State and Regional Planning

Small Cities and Counties: A Guide to Managing Services

Library of Congress Cataloging-in-Publication Data

Local government police management. — 3rd ed.
    / editor, William A. Geller.
        p.   cm.   — (Municipal management series)
    Includes bibliographical references and index.
    ISBN 0-87326-084-8
    1. Police administration—United States.   2. Law
enforcement—United States.   3. Local government—
United States.   I. Geller, William A.   II. Series.
HV7935.L63   1991
352.2'0973   dc20   91-19797
                                                 CIP

Printed in the United States of America.

97969594939291
54321

Foreword

The United States is on the threshold of a new era of policing, an era in which the police function is being repositioned to make major contributions to addressing and solving the problems of drugs, crime, and violence that affect the quality of life in communities throughout the nation.

No one can deny the breadth of these problems. Cities with increasingly scarce fiscal resources are faced with crumbling infrastructure, increasing crime, drug abuse, widespread unemployment, racial tension and racially motivated attacks, and expanding levels of senseless violence. There are no easy solutions.

Today's police leaders are uniquely positioned to become a catalyst for dealing with many of these important problems. They have a historic opportunity to move policing from a largely reactionary posture into the forefront of problem solving in the neighborhoods of our cities and towns.

Just as police leadership of the 1920s and 1930s advanced policing from within, establishing a professional commitment to integrity, education, training, and quality management, today's police leadership has the opportunity to participate in shaping a vision that will sustain policing through the next fifty years.

The riots of the 1960s caused deep soul-searching about an institution that no longer was capable of being responsive to the demands of the day. As a result, policing was redirected toward protecting and serving the society in its quest for a peaceful and safe existence, free from fear and with democratic values applied equally to all Americans.

Now, with U.S. cities in crisis, with the problems of violence, crime, racial polarization, disorder, and drugs tearing at the basic fabric of our communities, police and other local government leaders must go a step further in redefining the police role in the local government structure that manages fundamental public services.

The police role traditionally has been primarily enforcement, and the nation's prisons are overpopulated as a result. Police leaders are now asking themselves whether they want their legacy to be the building of more prisons and the incarceration of record numbers of citizens.

The inmates of prisons today are predominantly poor, undereducated, low- or unskilled, unemployed or unemployable. Most are minority. We arrest them in record numbers for the crimes they commit, but the problems on our streets grow worse, not better. Why is this? It is because institutions that used to constitute society's infrastructure—family, neighborhood, schools, churches, even social service providers—have lost their capacities to socialize and give meaning and value to a large, important segment of our people.

The police find themselves dealing with the failures of these other social institutions.

People without jobs—and without the prospect of jobs—cannot and do not live well. It should not surprise us that so many of them turn to drugs for a brief respite from despair. Many turn to crime to feed their habits and to ease their pain. Recognizing this does not excuse their illegal behavior, but it does challenge leaders to search for better ways in order to make a difference.

Police leaders must keep their eyes on these broad, critical issues while they develop as skilled managers of dynamic police agencies and ever-changing operational practices. This and the earlier volumes of *Local Government Police Management* have been devoted to the development of these managers. But good management alone will not prepare police executives for the challenges of the twenty-first century. Strong and clear value-oriented leadership is critical as well, and the reader will also find inspiration here for the articulation of departmental values.

The new vision of policing described in these pages draws on many of the strengths of the professional model of policing and on examples of excellence in the private sector. More significantly, it focuses attention on the relationships of the police with the residents of neighborhoods, with other units of government, with the business community, and with colleagues in their own organizations.

Great leaders have great visions. They focus on what could be rather than what has been. They look beyond the obvious and dream of the ideal. They articulate a vision for their communities and their employees with a sense of purpose toward which they can direct their energies.

No one becomes a leader in a vacuum. Every successful leader had a mentor, an advisor, a role model. The police profession must develop a commitment to mentoring that capitalizes on the talent and expertise available in retired and current leaders and in the private sector. Mentoring becomes fruitful when it is combined with a strong vision about the future—a vision about how the individual and the organization can make a difference in the community and society at large. The next generation of police leaders will find much in this text to help them clarify their vision and develop their capacity to make a difference.

Police leaders today are increasingly equipped to rise to the challenges set for them on these pages. They are better educated and more representative of their communities than at any time in recent memory. They can draw on the emerging successes of community-focused, problem-oriented policing and carry forth that developing vision. They have the opportunity to focus on solving problems rather than merely responding to reports of incidents, and they have the benefit of an increased willingness of residents to share responsibility for community order maintenance and crime control. These efforts aim to build neighborhood capacities to directly confront many of the issues which are so important to the quality of life. Our challenge to be creative is greater than at any time in the nation's recent past. The opportunities are clear.

City managers, mayors, and local governing bodies also have a major role in reshaping American policing. First, they have a responsibility to fully understand the changing nature of the police function, so they can provide adequate support, advice, and oversight to the efforts of police leaders in meeting these new challenges. Even the most visionary police leader will be ineffectual if the chief executive or the elected council does not fully understand the importance of the police as a vital part of the total governmental service delivery structure. The police must be viewed as a resource in meeting the important needs of residents. Elected and appointed local government leaders also have a responsibility to challenge their police executives to achieve excellence as collaborators with other local agencies and with a host of other public and private groups and organizations in the community. Finally, they have a responsibility to ensure that the young men and women in the middle ranks of police departments are provided with opportunities to develop the skills, knowledge, and vision necessary to assume future leadership positions.

As individuals with a vested interest in the future of our communities, the readers of this golden anniversary edition of *Local Government Police Management* will be charged with a mission in the coming years. We will be called upon to develop new ways to deliver police services equitably, effectively, and within the context of democratic values in an environment of increasingly scarce fiscal resources. As we move ahead, our skills and creativity will surely be tested. But if we build on our proud past and develop a meaningful vision for the future, If we develop leaders who are creative, sensitive, and thoughtful, we will play an integral part in restoring to our country the values, principles, and quality of life that made it great. That includes safer streets and safer communities. That includes the basic freedoms of any democracy, especially the freedom from fear.

The challenge of today's leaders is not to leave policing in America in the same condition we inherited it, but to improve it by exercising leadership that makes a difference.

Lee P. Brown
Commissioner
New York City
Police Department

President
International
Association of
Chiefs of Police

Foreword

The importance of police management to the quality of life in a community cannot be overemphasized. The police have substantial power to intervene in residents' daily activities. They are the visible representatives of government in many sensitive and emotional situations. And they have the authority to use deadly force if need be. For these reasons, the police department is continually scrutinized by the local governing body, citizens, and the press; and police performance remains high on the agenda of city and county managers and other chief administrators.

At a time of fiscal constraints on local government, fundamental questions about policing take on new urgency. What should the police be doing? How well are they performing? And how do we know?

Because policing is so central a service of local government, ICMA has long been committed to helping police chiefs and local administrators work together to answer those questions and strengthen police management at the local level. Over the last fifty years, ICMA has published, in ten editions and under the direction of seven editors, a substantial book on local government police management.

This golden anniversary edition of *Local Government Police Management* reflects significant changes in the environment of policing over the past decade—a virtual epidemic of drug-related crime; a growing body of research that challenges our assumptions about the effectiveness of traditional police practices; mind-boggling technological advances in information systems and forensics; and the blossoming demographic diversity of the population and the work force.

At the same time, the book reflects significant changes in the philosophy and practice of policing—a shift in orientation away from incident-driven reaction and response toward prevention and problem solving; a new interest in setting and using standards of performance and professionalism in police work; and, significantly, a growing realization that effective policing requires a new partnership between police and the communities they serve. Among the names for this partnership are community-oriented, community-based, and problem-oriented policing.

Finally, this book reflects an emphasis on "values-driven" management that is finding a voice in police theory and practice in the 1990s. The book concludes with a reflective piece that is a departure from tradition for ICMA's "Green Book" series but should strike a responsive chord with its readership. In the final chapter, a scholar and a chief encourage their police colleagues to recognize and heed time-honored values and be explicit about incorporating them into departmental policies and practices.

To create this book, ICMA turned to experts in policing—those who have pondered and studied the significant questions confronting departments today and who have managed those departments in changing times. The editor, Bill Geller, assembled a roster of advisors and participants who are broadly representative of the field today. We extend special thanks to Bill for his prodigious efforts and to the members of the editorial advisory committee whose names appear opposite the title page of this book:

Cornelius J. Behan, Chief of Police, Baltimore County Police Department, Towson, Maryland; former Chief of Patrol, New York City Police Department; and Past President, Police Executive Research Forum; Noel C. Bufe, Director, Northwestern University Traffic Institute, Evanston, Ilinois; former Deputy Administrator, National Highway Traffic Safety Administration, U.S. Department of Transportation; and former Executive Director, Highway Safety Planning, Michigan State Police; Raymond C. Davis, former Chief of Police, Santa Ana, California; Herman Goldstein, Evjue-Bascom Professor of Law, University of Wisconsin Law School, Madison, Wisconsin; Eduardo Gonzalez, Deputy Director, Metro-Dade Police Department, Miami, Florida, and Past President, Hispanic American Police Command Officers' Association; George L. Kelling, Research Fellow, Program in Criminal Justice Policy and Management, Kennedy School of Government, Harvard University, and Professor, Department of Criminal Justice, Northeastern University, Boston, Massachusetts; Gerald W. Lynch, President, John Jay College of Criminal Justice, New York, New York, and President, New York City Police Foundation; Charles "Bud" Meeks, Executive Director, National Sheriffs' Association, Alexandria, Virginia, and former Sheriff, Allen County, Indiana;

Daniel N. Rosenblatt, Executive Director, International Association of Chiefs of Police, Arlington, Virginia; Elsie Scott, Deputy Commissioner of Training, New York City Police Department, and former Executive Director, National Organization of Black Law Enforcement Executives, Washington, D.C.; Lawrence W. Sherman, President, Crime Control Institute, Washington, D.C., and Professor, Department of Criminology, University of Maryland, College Park, Maryland; Darrel W. Stephens, Executive Director, Police Executive Research Forum, Washington, D.C.; former Chief of Police, Newport News, Virginia; and former Chief of Police, Largo, Florida; James K. "Chips" Stewart, Director, Justice Systems Technology Practice, Booz-Allen & Hamilton, Bethesda, Maryland, and former Director, National Institute of Justice, U.S. Department of Justice, Washington, D.C.; Gary W. Sykes, Director, Southwestern Law Enforcement Institute, Richardson, Texas; Robert Wasserman, Research Fellow, Program in Criminal Justice Policy and Management, Kennedy School of Government, Harvard University, Cambridge, Massachusetts, and Principal, St. Germain Group, Boston, Massachusetts; Chuck Wexler, Special Assistant, The President's Drug Advisory Council, Washington, D.C.; former Director of the Professional Development Division, International Association of Chiefs of Police; and former Operations Assistant to the Police Commissioner, Boston Police Department; Hubert Williams, President, Police Foundation, Washington, D.C., and former Director, Newark Police Department, Newark, New Jersey; Mary Ann Wycoff, Project Director, Police Foundation, Washington, D.C., and Tarpon Springs, Florida.

A number of ICMA staff members and other individuals also contributed to this project: Barbara H. Moore, Director of Publications, who oversaw the project; Jane E. Lewin, who copyedited the manuscript; Verity Weston-Truby and Christina A. Davis, who undertook a variety of editorial responsibilities; Dawn M. Leland, who managed production; and Mary W. Blair and Tonya L. Horsley, who provided administrative assistance.

William H. Hansell, Jr.
Executive Director

International City
   Management Association
Washington, D.C.

Preface

Much about police technology, technique, and targets has changed in the 162 years since Sir Robert Peel's "Bobbies" began to provide a prototype for what would become the American local police department—a publicly financed, publicly accountable, paramilitary, bureaucratic, twenty-four-hour, primarily uniformed force. Consider, for example, the relative ease and accuracy of information sharing then and now. News of Peel's organizational invention in 1829 at best could reach American shores in three weeks by steamship; today, police who cannot even pronounce one another's names participate in live international teleconferences on how to forge partnerships for public safety with the community, and they electronically exchange and analyze fingerprint records, DNA data, and other information in seconds. Until the advent of a workable fountain pen in 1884, police who questioned criminal suspects recorded any incriminating statements longhand using a quill; today, roughly a third of all American police agencies use videotape to document the manner and content of stationhouse confessions by serious felony suspects. (And, in an ironic symmetry, citizens sometimes use videotape to document police-civilian encounters on the streets.)

Yet, despite the technological developments, discovering the *strategic* innovations that will help police protect a free society—so that the police work in a way that promotes freedom—remains one of the most difficult challenges of local governance. As work on this golden anniversary edition began—fifty years after ICMA's publication in 1938 of the book under its previous title, *Municipal Police Administration*—our nation's police confronted a number of crises. But these are crises as understood by the ancient Orientals, whose written symbol for "crisis" is made up of the characters for "danger" and "opportunity."

The dangers are apparent. Murder rates at the beginning of this decade set new records in many American jurisdictions, frustrating and frightening neighborhoods everywhere. Drug abuse and related disorder problems continued to press into every nook and cranny of the country. As Lee Brown has observed elsewhere, "Communities too small to have double parking problems contend with crack dealers." And a generation of youth is in jeopardy. Speaking to the National Organization of Black Law Enforcement Executives, Reverend Joseph Lowery commented: "Our youth have despair for breakfast, futility for lunch, hopelessness for dinner and sleep on a pillow of desperation."

Yet, there *are* opportunities to make a difference, and steps are being taken to seize these opportunities. Our nation's communities are coming to understand that the health of a democracy depends on citizens doing their part to work with government. Whereas the police radio call "officer needs assistance" traditionally has meant "come quickly, bring guns," increasingly the police are calling for and receiving assistance on a much more diverse range of challenges and from a much wider array of public and private sources. In these unconventional alliances many see great promise for reclaiming even our most devastated and violence-torn neighborhoods.

Moreover, there is even some cause for optimism about the level of crime in America. Our legitimate outrage over the devastation of some urban neighborhoods and over rising national murder rates should not confuse us into thinking that the nation *overall* has been suffering a surge in other types of violent crime. The federal government has conducted victimization surveys that tally *all* crimes (other than homicide) committed against Americans and not just the fraction of crime that the public reports to police, the police report to the FBI, and the FBI reports to the media. These victimization surveys reveal that the number of *violent* crimes per 1,000 population in the United States was lower in 1990 than in any of the previous seventeen years, except for 1986. Furthermore, the number of police feloniously slain in America each year has been steadily declining since the mid-1970s. Half as many officers were killed in the line of duty in 1990 as in 1974; and based on the number of violent crime arrests made in the two periods, police were 300 percent *less* likely to be killed by offenders as the decade of the 1990s began than they were in the mid-1970s.

There is reason for hope at the global level as well. In our generation, emerging democracies dot the world's landscape. As American police and other local government officials watch their international colleagues struggle with the fundamental issues that confront those policing a newly emancipated society, the conclusion seems inescapable that *every* democracy, our own included, is perpetually and necessarily an *emerging* democracy. That is, with change as the only constant, if a democracy stops emerging it starts eroding. Thus, this is a book about policing in a way that nurtures democratic processes and recommits the police and all other citizens to the principles that define a democracy, even under pressure.

Most of the fundamental issues confronting America's emerging police leadership will differ little from those confronted by Peel, his mentors, and our contemporary colleagues around the globe: To whom are the police accountable in a democratic state and through what mechanisms? What role should the public have in self-policing, in collaborative efforts, and in picking the priorities and tactics of the professional police? In seeking to achieve an ordered liberty, how can the police foster order without squelching liberty? In fulfilling their "order maintenance" or peacekeeping responsibilities, how should the police distinguish between dangerous disorder and desirable diversity (especially in a multi-cultural community)? In our pluralistic society, how can the police safeguard the cultural "mosaic"—an invigorating coexistence of proud cultures, races, ethnicities, religions, and political and other preferences? In our increasingly pluralistic police organizations, what can be done to create models of interracial and intercultural cooperation and respect among officers that will set a tone for improvements in the broader community? How can the police be motivated to be physically courageous and imaginative in protecting the innocent, yet compassionate and just in handling criminal suspects and others whom the police see as adversaries? How can police leaders and managers better integrate systems and operations inside the police organization so that it has the capacity to solve the *internal* problems that could inhibit successfully addressing the *community's* difficult problems? How can police and local government managers establish a police work environment in which officials are willing to consider whether defective work—ineptness, brutality, corruption, laziness, misguided zealousness, or some other deficiency—is the product of systemic problems or of policy, supervisory, or training failures rather than solely the individual responsibility of the workers? How can we fashion a work environment that encourages police officers to be creative and gives them permission, within reason, to make mistakes in pursuit of departmental missions? Without supervisors—and the community—granting police officers appropriate "permission to fail," asking police to take risks in devising better methods sends troubling mixed messages and becomes a cruel joke. Most of these challenges and the advice about addressing them contained in this volume apply regardless of location or agency size. The problems are as great and the prescriptions as pertinent for the 79 percent of America's local police departments that employ fewer than 25 sworn officers as they are for the biggest police bureaucracies in the land.

As police search for the path to help define the responsibilities and secure the rights of citizenship in our "emerging democracy," they encounter new problems, new enemies, new allies, new visions of a better tomorrow. The book that follows offers as guideposts along this stimulating and precarious path modern principles, standards, and techniques that can facilitate the work of police leaders and managers and the efforts of appointed and elected government officials to stimulate excellence in policing. These guideposts will also help the police and other government officials provide guidance to others about how to behave in a democracy.

It is no accident that this text's practical advice for managing the full range of functions required of any modern police agency begins and ends with chapters which explore the lessons that history may hold for those readers who will lead American policing into the next century. Over the past five decades, this ICMA book has endeavored both to honor the accomplishments of the past (including painfully learned lessons) and to explore the often dimly perceptible outlines of the future. So, too, this edition—the product of writing and advice by more than two hundred of the most insightful practitioners and most "street-wise" scholars in the field—seeks to present an amalgam of the old and the new. It seeks to present a vision of ever more valuable, efficient, and equitable police work built on the solid foundation prepared by previous generations of police. It seeks to keep the best of policing's *process*-orientation (for example, methods that foster integrity and the use of legitimate, nonpartisan police tactics) and to introduce a heightened focus on obtaining *results* that benefit the service population. It seeks results obtained by harnessing satisfactory external and internal working relationships.

The "remodeling" of police organizations and police work that is being done and will need to be done in years ahead on the foundation provided by our predecessors follows the architects' maxim that "form follows function." If the focus of the police is to shift to crime prevention, fear reduction, order maintenance, and the empowerment of communities to restore informal social control systems, then the mission and culture of the police organization must be adapted. If the work of police is to include creative "problem solving," then some aspects of traditional organizational constraints will need to be altered and new support and quality control systems created. Asking some or all of a police department's officers to engage in creative community problem solving within the paramilitary, bureaucratic, risk-averse work environment that has come to characterize much of policing over the past several decades is like asking someone to tap dance in snow shoes. It looks funny and isn't very effective. At the same time, when officers need to implement tactical maneuvers requiring great discipline, coordination, and timing (such as execution of search warrants, the rescue of hostages, and certain aspects of controlling hostile or even friendly crowds), any attempt to exalt the officers' individualism could prove disastrous. Again, form must follow function.

If the forms that police organizations take and the approaches that their employees adopt in the continual process of remodeling are to be as sound as possible, the perspectives of people within and outside of police organizations must be considered. When an architect designs a structure without adequately identifying the insights and needs of those who must use it, the result is unlikely to be a happy one. Since police of all ranks and responsibilities and citizens of all walks of life are the legitimate "users" of the police structure in a democratic society, all belong in the circle of public safety "change agents" and collaborators. To be sure, the idea of police-public collaboration will produce tension for all parties at times. Some of the sources of this tension can be reduced—especially misunderstandings and disrespect between the police and the public concerning each others' responsibilities, values, and styles. What cannot be changed, however, is the duty of the police on occasion to give members of the public orders— orders enforceable, if necessary and proper, with physical coercion. An imbalance of real or perceived power—whether between friends, spouses, co-workers, or other collaborators—almost always makes

for uneasy partnerships. As Woody Allen has observed, "The lion and the lamb shall lie down together, but the lamb won't get much sleep." Nevertheless, by emphasizing the positives—the strengths, intelligence, and experience that each partner brings to the collaboration and their common interest in leaving the world better than they found it—powerful coalitions can be forged.

This preface is full of lofty talk about the capacity of the police to protect the public while "enforcing freedom," as Police Chief Neil Behan likes to put it. Such talk may seem applicable to only a small segment of modern police work. If so, I commend to the reader the discussion in the concluding chapter of this volume. It examines the Preamble of the United States Constitution and derives from that analysis practical guidance for the exercise of police discretion on such seemingly prosaic matters as the issuance of parking tickets. With this examination, the book concludes on the same note on which it begins. The experiment in ordered liberty—a "morality play" in which the police are very prominent actors—is a play whose first draft was penned by some mighty respectable writers, including the drafters of the U.S. Constitution. But this play calls upon the actors to do a substantial amount of improvisation. To be sure, the playwrights have expressed clear preferences about the ultimate shape of the play and its central themes. Just as certainly, the actors have the power to alter it for better or worse. It is to those at all levels of police organizations and their bosses and collaborators outside those organizations who must fulfill these difficult improvisational responsibilities, day to day and decade to decade, that this book is directed and dedicated.

William A. Geller
Wilmette, Illinois

Advisory task forces

1 The evolution of contemporary policing

Samuel G. Chapman, Professor, Department of Political Science; Director, Law Enforcement Administration degree program, University of Oklahoma, Norman, Oklahoma

George T. Hart, Chief of Police, Oakland, California

Norval Morris, Julius Kreeger Professor of Law and Criminology, University of Chicago Law School

Stanley E. Morris, Deputy Director, Office of National Drug Control Policy, Washington, D.C.; former Director, U.S. Marshals Service

Samuel Walker, Professor, Department of Criminal Justice, University of Nebraska at Omaha

Willie L. Williams, Commissioner, Philadelphia Police Department, Philadelphia, Pennsylvania

2 Organization and management

William J. Bratton, Chief, New York City Transit Police

G. Patrick Gallagher, Director, Institute for Liability Management, Gallagher Bassett Services, Inc., Leesburg, Virginia

Steven R. Harris, Chief of Police, Redmond, Washington; Vice President, International Association of Chiefs of Police

David J. Kelly, Chief of Police, Glenview, Illinois

Mack A. Kennedy, Captain, Criminal Investigation Division, U.S. Capitol Police, Washington, D.C.

R. Gil Kerlikowske, Chief of Police, Fort Pierce, Florida

Daniel L. Schofield, Chief, Legal Instruction Unit, Legal Division, FBI Academy, Quantico, Virginia

Norman H. Stamper, Assistant Chief of Police, San Diego, California

Elizabeth M. Watson, Chief of Police, Houston, Texas

E. L. "Bud" Willoughby, Sandy, Utah; former Chief of Police, Salt Lake City, Utah

3 The patrol function

Steven C. Bishop, Chief of Police, Kansas City, Missouri

Edward Brooks, former Deputy Superintendent of Police, Chicago, Illinois

Arthur Deutcsh, Chief of Police, Birmingham, Alabama

Drew Diamond, Chief of Police, Tulsa, Oklahoma

Thomas G. Koby, Assistant Chief of Police, Field Operations Command, Houston, Texas

George Napper, Ph.D., former Commissioner, Department of Public Safety, and former Chief of Police, Atlanta, Georgia

Ruben B. Ortega, Chief of Police, Phoenix, Arizona

Robert P. Owens, Chief of Police, Oxnard, California

Robert C. Trojanowicz, Director and Professor, School of Criminal Justice, Michigan State University, East Lansing, Michigan

4 Crime prevention, fear reduction, and the community

Sam V. Baca, Chief of Police, Lakeland, Florida; former Chief of Police, Albuquerque, New Mexico

Sidney J. Barthelemy, Mayor, New Orleans, Louisiana; Chairman, Police Policy Board, U.S. Conference of Mayors

Keith R. Bergstrom, Chief of Police, Tarpon Springs, Florida; former Assistant City Manager, Miami, Florida

Betsy Cantrell, Project Director, Neighborhood Watch Programs, National Sheriffs' Association, Alexandria, Virginia

Reuben M. Greenberg, Chief of Police, Charleston, South Carolina

Peter Hunt, Dutton, Virginia; former Executive Director, Chicago Area Project, Chicago, Illinois

Antony Pate, Director of Research, Police Foundation, Washington, D.C.

Albert J. Reiss, Jr., William Graham Sumner Professor of Sociology and Lecturer in Law, Yale University, New Haven, Connecticut

Elsie Scott, Deputy Commissioner of Training, New York City Police Department; former Executive Director, National Organization of Black Law Enforcement Executives, Washington, D.C.

Michael E. Smith, Director, Vera Institute of Justice, New York, New York

5 Criminal investigations

Terence J. Green, Program Manager, Violent Criminal Apprehension Program, National Center for the Analysis of Violent Crime, FBI Academy, Quantico, Virginia

Beverly J. Harvard, Deputy Chief, Atlanta Police Department, Atlanta, Georgia

Richard E. LaMunyon, Executive Director, Wichita Greyhound Charities, Inc., Wichita, Kansas; former Chief of Police, Wichita, Kansas

Gary T. Marx, Professor, Department of Sociology, Massachusetts Institute of Technology, Cambridge, Massachusetts

Donald W. Story, Chief of Police, Matteson, Illinois

Richard H. Ward, Vice Chancellor for Administration and Director, Office of International Criminal Justice, University of Illinois at Chicago

6 Traffic services

Russell J. Arend, Director, Institute of Police Technology and Management, Jacksonville, Florida

Don R. Derning, Past President, International Association of Chiefs of Police; former Executive Director, Illinois Association of Chiefs of Police; former Chief of Police, Winnetka, Illinois

Robert W. Landon, Management Services Coordinator, Washington Association of Sheriffs and Police Chiefs; former Chief, Montana Highway Patrol; former Chief, Washington State Patrol; Past President, International Association of Chiefs of Police

Howard P. Patinkin, Commander, Traffic Division, Chicago Police Department

William M. Rathburn, Chief of Police, Dallas, Texas; former Deputy Chief, Los Angeles Police Department

Garold Spencer, Major, Special Services, Oklahoma City Police Department, Oklahoma City, Oklahoma

Jack B. Walsh, Security Administrator, Grange Insurance Co., Columbus, Ohio; former Superintendent, Ohio State Highway Patrol, Columbus, Ohio

7 Local drug control

Francis E. Amoroso, Director, Bureau of Intergovernmental Drug Enforcement, State of Maine, Pownal, Maine; former Chief of Police, Portland, Maine

Philip B. Heymann, James Barr Ames Professor of Law, Harvard Law School, Cambridge, Massachusetts

Sterling Johnson, Jr., Special Narcotics Prosecutor, City of New York

Glenn A. Levant, Deputy Chief and Commanding Officer, Bureau of Special Investigation, Los Angeles Police Department

Susan Michaelson, Assistant Director, Program in Criminal Justice Policy and Management, Kennedy School of Government, Harvard University, Cambridge, Massachusetts

Rudolph Nimocks, Director, University of Chicago Police Department; former Deputy Superintendent, Bureau of Investigative Services, Chicago Police Department

Marty Tapscott, Chief of Police, Richmond, Virginia; former Chief of Police, Metropolitan Police Department, Washington, D.C.

Fred Taylor, Director, Metro-Dade Police Department, Miami, Florida

8 Organized crime

Robert V. Bradshaw, Chief of Police, Reno, Nevada

Richard J. Condon, Director of Administrative Services, Paine Webber, New York; former Commissioner, New York City Police Department

Patrick Fitzsimons, Chief of Police, Seattle, Washington

John J. Jemilo, Attorney; former Executive Director, Chicago Crime Commission; former First Deputy Superintendent, Chicago Police Department

Robert J. Kelly, President, International Association for the Study of Organized Crime; Professor, Department of Educational Services, Brooklyn College, Brooklyn, New York

David Margolis, Acting Deputy Assistant Attorney General for the Criminal Division, U.S. Department of Justice; former Chief, Organized Crime and Racketeering Section, Criminal Division, U.S. Department of Justice, Washington, D.C.

Lois Felson Mock, Social Scientist and Research Program Manager, White Collar and Organized Crime, Crime Prevention and Enforcement Division, National Institute of Justice, Washington, D.C.

Oliver B. "Buck" Revell, Special Agent in Charge, Dallas Division, FBI; former Associate Deputy Director for Investigations, FBI, Washington, D.C.

9 Fostering integrity

James J. Carvino, Chief of Police, Boise, Idaho; former Deputy Director, Office of Liaison Services, U.S. Department of Justice; former Chief, U.S. Capitol Police; former Chief of Police, Racine, Wisconsin

Waynette Chan, Assistant to the City Manager, City of Austin, Texas; former Chief of Staff, Office of the Chief, Houston Police Department

Daryl F. Gates, Chief of Police, Los Angeles Police Department, Los Angeles, California

Michael J. Kelly, Public Safety Director, Oakwood, Ohio

Wayne A. Kerstetter, Professor, Department of Criminal Justice, University of Illinois at Chicago and Research Fellow, American Bar Foundation, Chicago, Illinois; former Superintendent, Illinois Bureau of Investigation

Gerald W. Lynch, President, John Jay College of Criminal Justice, New York, New York

Wesley A. Carroll Pomeroy, Executive Director, Independent Review Panel of Dade County, Miami, Florida; former Executive Secretary, Detroit Board of Police Commissioners; former Chief of Police, Berkeley, California

10 Human resource management

Albert A. Apa, Executive Director, Illinois Local Governmental Law Enforcement Officers Training Board, Springfield, Illinois

Sharen E. Gromling, Personnel Director, Winchester, Virginia

James Hargrove, Assistant Police Commissioner, Personnel Bureau, New York City Police Department

Clarence Harmon, Secretary, St. Louis Board of Police Commissioners; Lt. Colonel, St. Louis Metropolitan Police Department, St. Louis, Missouri

Robert B. Kliesmet, President, International Union of Police Associations, AFL-CIO, Alexandria, Virginia

Kim Kohlhepp, Manager, Center for Testing Services, International Association of Chiefs of Police, Arlington, Virginia

John Stedman, Senior Researcher and Director, Senior Management Institute for Police, Police Executive Research Forum, Washington, D.C.

Bryce (Bill) Stuart, City Manager, Winston-Salem, North Carolina

11 Information management

Jay A. Carey, Jr., Chief of Police, Newport News, Virginia

J. David Coldren, Executive Director, Illinois Criminal Justice Information Authority, Chicago, Illinois

Bruce D. Glasscock, Chief of Police, Plano, Texas; former Chief of Police, Fort Collins, Colorado

Richard C. Larson, Professor, Operations Research Center, Massachusetts Institute of Technology, Cambridge, Massachusetts

Bishop L. Robinson, Secretary, Maryland Department of Public Safety and Correctional Services, Baltimore, Maryland; former Chief of Police, Baltimore, Maryland

Gregory A. Thomas, Uniform Crime Report Redesign Project, New York State Division of Criminal Justice Services, Albany, New York

Mack M. Vines, former Chief of Police, Dallas, Texas, St. Petersburg, Florida, Charlotte, North Carolina, and Cape Coral, Florida; former Director, Bureau of Justice Assistance, U.S. Department of Justice, Washington, D.C.

12 Research, planning, and implementation

Carol H. Duncan, Assistant Chief, Support Services Division, Alexandria Police Department, Alexandria, Virginia

Sheldon Greenberg, Associate Director of Management Services, Police Executive Research Forum, Washington, D.C.

Sarah A. Puryear, Director, Management Information Division, Winston-Salem Police Department, Winston-Salem, North Carolina; Past President, National Association of Police Planners

J. Brian Quinn, Professor, Amos Tuck School of Business, Dartmouth College, Hanover, New Hampshire

Fred Rice, Jr., former Superintendent of Police, Chicago, Illinois

Jerry Sanders, Commander, Field Operations, San Diego Police Department, San Diego, California

Fred W. Stoecker, former Chief of Police, Wilmette, Illinois

Victor G. Strecher, Professor and former Dean, College of Criminal Justice, Sam Houston State University, Huntsville, Texas

13 Personnel and agency performance measurement

Robert R. Bing, Director, Colorado Law Enforcement Training Academy, Golden, Colorado

Bertram S. Brown, M.D., Executive Vice President, Forensic Medical Advisory Service, Rockville, Maryland; former Director, National Institute of Mental Health

Gerald A. Cooper, Esq., Executive Assistant to the Superintendent, Chicago Police Department, Chicago, Illinois

James Ginger, Deputy Director for Administration, Police Foundation, Washington, D.C.

Charles Grover, Chief of Police, Prairie Village, Kansas

James Hogan, Sergeant, Newport News Police Department, Newport News, Virginia

Jerry L. McGlasson, Chief of Police, North Richland Hills, Texas; President, Texas Police Chief's Association

Ken Medeiros, Executive Director, Commission on Accreditation for Law Enforcement Agencies, Inc., Fairfax, Virginia

14 Equipment and facilities

James L. Black, President, Pro-Tech Investigative Services, Jackson, Mississippi; former Chief of Police, Jackson, Mississippi

Bruce G. Campbell, Chief of Police, Brattleboro, Vermont

John H. Cease, Chief of Police, County of Roanoke, Virginia

Frank C. Gilbert, Chief of Police, Oak Lawn, Illinois

Larry J. Joiner, former Chief of Police, Kansas City, Missouri

Robert K. Olson, Chief of Police, Yonkers, New York

Matt L. Rodriguez, Deputy Superintendent, Bureau of Technical Services, Chicago Police Department

Ray Surette, Ph.D., Associate Professor, Department of Criminal Justice, Florida International University, Miami, Florida

15 The governmental setting

Allen H. Andrews, Consultant; former Superintendent of Police, Peoria, Illinois

Camille Cates Barnett, Ph.D., City Manager, Austin, Texas

William E. Kirchhoff, City Manager, Redondo Beach, California; Commissioner, Commission on Accreditation for Law Enforcement Agencies

George Latimer, Dean, Hamline University Law School, St. Paul, Minnesota; former Mayor, St. Paul

Leonard A. Matarese, Community Manager and Director of Public Safety, Ocean Reef, Florida

William D. Miller, Chief of Police, Skokie, Illinois

James E. Montgomery, Sheriff/Director, King County Police Department, Seattle, Washington

Wayne W. Schmidt, Executive Director, Americans for Effective Law Enforcement, Chicago, Illinois

Jeremy Travis, Deputy Commissioner, Legal Matters, New York City Police Department, New York, New York

16 External resources

William C. Cunningham, President, Hallcrest Systems, Inc., McLean, Virginia

Michael T. Farmer, Manager, Security, Exploration and Producing

Division, Mobil Corporation, Fairfax, Virginia

Donald G. Hanna, Chief of Police, Champaign, Illinois

Vincent Lane, Chairman and Chief Executive Officer, Chicago Housing Authority, Chicago, Illinois

William H. Logan, Jr., Director, Department of Safety, Evanston Township High School, Evanston, Illinois; former Chief of Police, Evanston, Illinois

Michael G. Shanahan, Chief of Police, University of Washington at Seattle

Marilyn Steele, Ph.D., Consultant; former Program Officer, Charles Stewart Mott Foundation, Flint, Michigan

Cynthia G. Sulton, Manager of Security Planning, Corporate Security Department, Mobil Corporation, Fairfax, Virginia

Peter L. Szanton, President, Szanton Associates, Washington, D.C.

17 Forensic sciences

Christopher A. Crofts, Assistant United States Attorney, U.S. Department of Justice, Casper, Wyoming; former Director, Division of Criminal Investigation, Office of the Attorney General, State of Wyoming, Cheyenne, Wyoming

Barry A. J. Fisher, Director, Scientific Services Bureau, Los Angeles County Sheriff's Department

Richard S. Frank, Chief, Laboratory Operations Section, Office of Forensic Sciences, Drug Enforcement Administration, Washington, D.C.; Past President, American Academy of Forensic Sciences, Colorado Springs, Colorado

David F. Green, Field Representative, Mid-States Organized Crime Information Center, Springfield, MO; former Chief of Police, Sioux Falls, South Dakota

Ernest A. Jacobi, Chief of Police, Evanston, Illinois

H. Scott Kingwill, Publisher, Law and Order Magazine, Wilmette, Illinois

Steven R. Schlesinger, Director of Education and Training Programs, U.S. Institute of Peace, Washington, D.C.; Adjunct Professor, Department of Government, School of Public Affairs, American University; former Director, Bureau of Justice Statistics, U.S. Department of Justice

Irving C. Stone, Chief, Physical Evidence, Southwestern Institute of Forensic Sciences, Dallas, Texas

18 Arrestee and lockup management

Sherman Block, Sheriff, Los Angeles County, California

Allen F. Breed, Chairman Emeritus, Board of Directors, National Council on Crime and Delinquency, San Francisco, California; former Director, National Institute of Corrections, U.S. Department of Justice

Richard J. Elrod, Judge, Circuit Court of Cook County, Chicago, Illinois; former Sheriff, Cook County, Illinois; Past President, National Sheriff's Association

J. D. Hudson, former Director, Atlanta Department of Corrections, Atlanta, Georgia

Jess Maghan, Ph.D., Associate Commissioner for Training and Resource Development, New York City Department of Correction; former Director of Training, Police Academy, New York City Police Department

Michael Mahoney, Executive Director, John Howard Association, Chicago, Illinois

19 Practical ideals for managing in the nineties: a perspective

Charles A. Gruber, Chief of Police, Elgin, Illinois; Past President, International Association of Chiefs of Police; former Chief of Police, Shreveport, Louisiana, and Quincy, Illinois

Daniel P. Guido, Commissioner of Police, Suffolk County Police Department, Yaphank, New York; former Commissioner of Police, Nassau County Police Department, Mineola, New York

Hobart M. Henson, Director, National Center for State and Local Law Enforcement Training, Federal Law Enforcement Training Center, Glynco, Georgia

LeRoy Martin, Superintendent of Police, Chicago, Illinois

William H. Moulder, Chief of Police, Des Moines, Iowa

Dennis Nilsson, Commanding Officer, Traffic Management Bureau, Evanston Police Department, Evanston, Illinois

John E. Otto, Corporate Security Representative, Delta Airlines, Atlanta, Georgia; former Associate Deputy Director, Administration, FBI, Washington, D.C.

Charles D. Reynolds, former Chief of Police, Dover, New Hampshire; Past President, International Association of Chiefs of Police

Atkins Warren, Regional Director, Region VII, Community Relations Service, U.S. Department of Justice, Kansas City, Missouri

Special advisors

Robert M. Fogelson, Professor of Urban Studies and History, Department of Urban Studies and Planning, Massachusetts Institute of Technology, Cambridge, Massachusetts

W. Douglas Franks, Chief of Police, Tustin, California

Steve Gaffigan, President, Gaffigan & Associates, Silver Spring, Maryland

Gary J. Leonard, Chief of Police, Sandy City, Utah

Joseph D. McNamara, Ph.D., Research Fellow, Hoover Institution, Stanford University, Stanford,

California; former Chief of Police, San Jose, California

Jerome H. Skolnick, Claire Clements Dean's Professor of Law (Jurisprudence and Social Policy Program), University of California, Berkeley

William L. Tafoya, Ph.D., Supervisory Special Agent, Behavioral Science Unit, FBI Academy, Quantico, Virginia

Melvin L. Tucker, Chief of Police, Tallahassee, Florida

Reginald Turner, former Chief of Police, Pontiac, Michigan

◉ICMA

The International City Management Association is the professional and educational organization for chief appointed management executives in local government. The purposes of ICMA are to enhance the quality of local government and to nurture and assist professional local government administrators in the United States and other countries. In furtherance of its mission, ICMA develops and disseminates new approaches to management through training programs, information services, and publications.

Managers, carrying a wide range of titles, serve cities, towns, counties, and councils of governments in all parts of the United States and Canada. These managers serve at the direction of elected councils and governing boards. ICMA serves these managers and local governments through many programs that aim at improving the manager's professional competence and strengthening the quality of all local governments.

The International City Management Association was founded in 1914, adopted its City Management Code of Ethics in 1924, and established its Institute for Training in Municipal Administration in 1934. The Institute, in turn, provided the basis for the Municipal Management Series, generally termed the "ICMA Green Books." ICMA's interests and activities include public management education; standards of ethics for members; *The Municipal Year Book* and other data services; local government research; and newsletters, *Public Management* magazine, and other publications. ICMA's efforts for the improvement of local government management—as represented by this book—are offered for all local governments and educational institutions.

Contents

Part one:
The foundations
of policing

1 The evolution of contemporary policing

Policing in the United States is in a period of dramatic change. Long-standing assumptions have been undermined. The role of the police in the community has been questioned. And overwhelming social problems call for the police to develop new and flexible organizational structures and strategies.

To put these changes into perspective, it is useful to look backward for a moment and reflect on the predecessors of today's police departments and police leaders. Thus, this chapter presents a brief history of police in the United States, beginning with the early police agencies and describing the changes wrought in the 1930s under the influence of "scientific management," the political reforms introduced in subsequent decades, the effects of the social upheavals of the 1960s, and the responses to the research findings of the 1970s and 1980s. Finally, the chapter reflects on where these changes have brought us—and what they promise for the 1990s.

The roots of public civil police

The idea of a public civil police force originated in England in the eighteenth century. The idea grew as developing metropolitan areas and industrial centers, especially London, were threatened by riot, disorder, and crime—offshoots of industrialization, migration, and urbanization. Those who conceived the idea of police—England's political, legal, and philosophical elites—sought to avoid the dangers inherent both in the use of "secret" police, as had occurred in France, and in the use of military forces for domestic policing, as had occurred in England to subdue rioting. For a century, English reformers groped their way toward a police system that would reflect democratic values. As Sir Robert Peel, whose officers came to be known affectionately as "bobbies," couched it, the goal was for police "to keep peace by peaceful means."

This idea and its organizational invention—bureaucratic police departments—spread throughout the United States between 1840 and 1860. Either immediately or eventually, U.S. police resembled their English counterparts in many respects: they were organized on a quasi-military basis; they wore uniforms; they patrolled the streets twenty-four hours a day; they embodied Peel's spirit of "peace" officers; their mission was to prevent crime, disorder, and riot; and they investigated crimes.

Yet despite these similarities, U.S. police were profoundly different from their English counterparts.[1] The English police were created by national leaders who decided that police authority was to derive from both law and the crown. In the United States, the responsibility for domestic tranquility lay with local government. Not until the twentieth century, for the most part, did national and state police develop in America. State governments authorize cities to create police departments, and the cities, in turn, typically do opt to create them. Of all the factors that have shaped police development in the United States, local political control and authorization have been pivotal.

Created by local government, U.S. police departments, especially during their crucial formative years, reflected the patterns of city politics and administration.

During the last quarter of the nineteenth century, when big city administration was largely the province of "leaders of urban tribal politics, the ward bosses,"[2] police districts in most big cities were adjuncts of the political machines and were packed with cronies of the ward bosses. In tribute, police loyally "turned out the vote." Financial corruption and inequitable, discriminatory, inefficient, and brutal policing thrived.

To be sure, this portrayal of venal ward politics and corrupt police was largely promulgated by muckrakers and Progressives who had their own political axes to grind. By most historical accounts, however, it was accurate enough to justify Egon Bittner's somewhat droll conclusion: "Of all the institutions of city government in late-nineteenth-century America, none was as unanimously denounced as the urban police. According to every available account, they were, in every aspect of their existence, an unmixed, unmitigated, and unpardonable scandal."[3]

Such characterizations of U.S. police were to continue during at least the first two decades of the twentieth century. Indeed, if anything, police corruption worsened with ratification of the Prohibition amendment in 1920. Even the Boston police department, reputedly one of the least corrupt major police departments in the early part of the century, succumbed under the combined influences of the famed Boston police strike and Prohibition.

Efforts by social reformers, both in the nineteenth and early twentieth centuries, to detach the police from ward politics largely failed. Not until the 1930s were internal reformers, aligned with Progressives, able to achieve significant success in wresting control of police organizations from ward politicians. During that decade, U.S. policing as we know it began to take shape.

Scientific policing in the 1930s   In no other branch of government have such remarkable changes been made as those made in the field of police organization and administration during the last quarter of a century. One can scarcely believe that such great advances could be made in so short a time. It is a far cry indeed from the old politically-controlled police department to the modern scientifically operated organization. Under the old system, police officials were appointed through political affiliations and because of them. They were frequently unintelligent and untrained, they were distributed throughout the area to be policed according to a hit-or-miss system and without adequate means of communication; they had little or no record system; their investigation methods were obsolete; and they had no conception of the preventive possibilities of the service. In these modern organizations, high standards of admission have been established, the men move up through the ranks by highly selective processes, the personnel is distributed according to scientific formulas and principles, and communication systems have been developed to a degree where only fractions of seconds are lost between the time the message is received until it is transmitted to the men on the beat. A complete and detailed system of records has been instituted, and scientific investigative methods have been adopted. Crime prevention through scientific measures has been established in different parts of the country, and the results are proving the worth of the endeavor.

Source: August Vollmer, "Police Progress in the Past Twenty-Five Years," *Journal of Criminal Law and Criminology* 24, no. 1 (May–June 1933).

Scientific policing: The 1930s

The 1930s were a heady decade for U.S. police; the occupation had come far and its prospects were bright. August Vollmer, considered by many to be the father of modern policing, thought he saw significant improvements in the practice of policing (see accompanying sidebar).[4]

In his assessment, Vollmer emphasized the application of "scientific" principles to organization, deployment of personnel, criminal investigation, and crime prevention. This emphasis on science and objectivity can be found in several dimensions of the reforms of the 1930s: police were to be selected and promoted on the basis of such "objective" criteria as psychological tests and personnel rating schemes; and police departments were to be evaluated on the basis of such scientific, objective measures as crime, arrest, and clearance statistics (see the chapters on the patrol function, criminal investigations, human resources, and performance measurement).

Contributions of scientific policing

How should this early stress on scientific principles and measures be interpreted? First, it was clearly congruent with professional and popular thinking of the time. Rationalism and reverence for science characterized the age. Second, it was consistent with the scientific management methods of the organizational theorist Frederick Taylor, who strove to align workers with machines through elaborate measurement programs and classical bureaucratic structures. Third, science and technology had already contributed to policing: fingerprinting was used for identification, the telephone and radio were used for communication, and the automobile was used for transportation and patrol. Although use of fingerprinting had languished in the United States until the Federal Bureau of Investigation promoted its use during the 1930s and the tactical use of telephones and automobiles would not be widely adopted until the 1930s and 1940s, the potential of all three was nevertheless widely recognized.[5]

The attraction of science and objectivity, however, was much greater than these particular developments imply. Scientific structure, scientific administrative processes (personnel policies and allocation, measurement of outcome, and so forth), and scientific tactics (patrol and investigation) were not only considered valuable in their own right but were also intended as bulwarks against political influence and meddling—the nemesis of policing. Writing in 1929, reformer Bruce Smith had made this clear: "Without exceptions, all proposals for improvement of organization and control have necessarily been aimed at the weakening or the elimination of political influences."[6]

Significant innovations had been put into place by the end of the 1930s. For example, the Uniform Crime Reports (UCR), developed by Smith and Vollmer and adopted by the International Association of Chiefs of Police (IACP), was ensconced within the FBI in 1930. Thus for the first time, standardized crime-related record keeping existed on a national level. Another example was that automobiles, linked by radio communication, were promising to revolutionize patrol. (Although debates about the effectiveness of cars versus other forms of patrol lasted until the 1950s, use of automobiles for patrol began before 1910.) Third, O. W. Wilson, the strongest advocate of motorized patrol, had developed his ideas about the scientific distribution of personnel in beats by 1933. According to his plan, beats were to be constructed through the use of crime, arrest, complaint, demographic, and hazard data, thereby ensuring not only similar workloads for officers but also equitable distribution of police services across geographical areas of cities on the basis of need.[7] A fourth example involved organizational structure. During the 1930s, managerial authority was being centralized in the office of the chief; command and control concepts such as unity of command and span of control were being implemented, thereby rationalizing police departments; units were being organized functionally, rather than geographically; and special units were devised and administered centrally to provide tailored police services for special populations (for example, juveniles) or problems (for example, vice).

An early view of automobile patrol Auto patrol is fast becoming the standard in police departments throughout the country. Where radio communication is not available, the automobile may be used to get the patrolman over the streets and through the alleys with greater speed so that larger areas will be covered. This method sacrifices some of the intensiveness of foot patrol while providing reasonable protection over a broader area. At the same titme it places in the patrolman's hands a means of pursuit which is denied the foot patrolman. To be effective, the police must have offensive weapons and transportation at least as efficient as those of the criminal.

Source: O. W. Wilson, *Police Administration* (New York: McGraw-Hill, 1950), 210.

Each of these innovations had value in its own right, and each also served the vital, if not primary, purpose of insulating police departments and personnel from political interference. The UCR enabled police departments to be evaluated independently of political judgments; by offering evidence of police efficiency both over time and relative to other cities, statistics buffered police departments and administrators from judgment on the basis of political performance (for example, turning out the vote).[8] Use of automobiles for patrol not only increased the range of patrol officers but also improved the ability of police executives to monitor and control them. Further, motorized patrol may have isolated officers from the influences of citizens, especially politically minded citizens or others who police administrators believed might "persuade" patrol officers not to enforce the law uniformly. Likewise, communications systems further augmented administrative surveillance and control of officers. Data-based beat allocation systems, by facilitating equitable distribution of police services, gave police the high moral ground in the public mind if anyone, particularly politicians, attempted to force the police to allocate services on the basis of favoritism. The spread of civil service and the use of objective examinations to select and promote personnel limited the influence of politicians over personnel matters. Centralization of command and the replacement of geographical by functional organization not only increased administrative and patrol efficiency

---

Political influence: A historical perspective When the police department is controlled by the machine, political influence begins with the appointment of the recruit, rallies to save him from discipline, helps him to secure unearned wages or disability benefits, grants him unusual leaves of absence, secures an unwarranted promotion for him, or gives him a soft job. In countless ways the creeping paralysis of political favoritism spreads and fastens itself upon the force to sap its vitality and destroy its morale for the benefit of the part, at the expense both of the public and of the police force itself.

Source: O. W. Wilson, *Police Administration* (New York: McGraw-Hill, 1950), 17–18.

but also lessened significantly the influence of ward politicians. Similarly, creation of centralized special units reduced the power of precinct commanders relative to the central command staff.[9]

Foundations of police legitimacy

Pivotal to the character of U.S. policing was its source of authority or legitimacy. Before the 1930s U.S. police had received their mandate from local politicians. But U.S. urban and police reformers not only rejected police decentralization to the ward level; they also rebelled at the notion that police authority to act derived from mandates issued, and priorities set, by these politicians. In place of local political authorization, police in the 1930s, following the leadership of reformers, rallied around the idea that they were primarily, if not exclusively, enforcers of the criminal law. Law, especially criminal law, became the primary source of police authorization.[10]

Characterizing criminal law as the fundamental source of police authorization was compatible with the move by reformers to narrow police functions. This move was based on the reformers' belief that the law was to be administered in a fair and just way, not arbitrarily or as a favor. Before the reforms of the 1930s, police had been conceived of, and had operated, as a local government agency that provided a wide array of social, emergency, regulatory, and crime-related services.[11] Reformers repudiated this view, substituting the idea that police were criminal law enforcement agencies whose resources would be squandered if they were not targeted on crime, especially serious crime. The list of functions nominated for elimination from urban policing was long, comprising many regulatory functions and even traffic control.

Accenting crime was timely. In the United States of the 1930s, crime was perceived to be dramatically increasing. Stimulated by the intense publicity associated with crimes like the kidnapping and killing of Charles and Anne Lindbergh's baby, police portrayed themselves as the last bastions of defense against crime, mayhem, and rapidly deteriorating U.S. values. One of the leading portraitists was J. Edgar Hoover, who had reformed the corrupt Bureau of Investigation he had inherited (the predecessor of the Federal Bureau of Investigation) and enhanced its prestige by pursuing John Dillinger and "Pretty Boy" Floyd, creating the "Ten Most Wanted" list, and engaging in other high-visibility crime-related activities. Riding the crest of national concern over Prohibition-era lawlessness, police nominated themselves, and were accepted by local communities, as the "thin blue line." In this metaphor, they stood alone, separating good citizens from the depredations of "vermin of the worst type," "mad dogs," "human vultures," and "Public Rat Number 1"—labels given to criminals in 1934 by Hoover and Lewis J. Valentine, commissioner of the New York City police department.[12] When the crime-related functions of the police were accented and political authorization was rejected, the character of U.S. policing during the next half-century was set: police aspired to be scientific crime fighters organized and administered according to objective principles.

Vollmer's legacy

Surely it was premature for Vollmer, or other contemporary writers, to suggest that during the early 1930s most police departments looked anything like the well-organized scientific units he described in the passage quoted in the sidebar ("Scientific policing"). Most departments were underfunded and generally poorly managed, and their officers were undereducated. The claims made for policing certainly did not characterize the policing of the 1930s; barely characterized the policing of the 1950s; and, indeed, do not characterize some police departments even in the 1990s.[13]

Given the rampant corruption, continuing political abuse, and organizational inefficiency that afflicted policing during the 1920s and 1930s, how could Vollmer write as he did? Possibly he recognized that a number of powerful forces—principally the firmly entrenched Progressive Movement and public alarm about crime and the quality of policing—were enabling courageous and innovative police executives to make decisions that would permanently alter the nature of policing. As local political and police elites (some in universities) espoused the values of science, lawfulness, equity, and administrative efficiency and then implemented those values with political, legal, organizational, and administrative innovations, they were consciously repositioning policing to improve its contributions to society.

Vollmer's pronouncements did not mean that politics were totally removed from policing, that administrative inefficiencies had evaporated, or that policing had emerged as a profession. But the values and theories undergirding the ideal vision of Vollmer and other police elites were sufficiently coherent to constitute a strategy that differed significantly from the strategy pursued under the old system. In actuality, Vollmer's view of a bright new day in policing was more prescriptive than descriptive. In his enthusiasm for the destination, Vollmer celebrated the journey as if it were concluded. And the celebration was contagious. Vollmer's vision spread throughout policing.

The new model, or paradigm, that Vollmer identified was based on seven developments that came to fruition in the 1930s.

First, to one degree or another, innovative police executives were implementing the model. Wilson in Wichita (1928–1939) and William P. Rutledge in Detroit (1926–1930) were early examples, and many others followed. Vollmer's 1933 article enumerated city after city in which police reforms congruent with his model were being initiated.

Second, starting in Chicago in 1919, cities and states created crime commissions whose findings became grist for the reformers' mill. The commissions called public attention to the growing problem of crime in society; castigated the functioning of criminal justice agencies, especially police; and called for reforms. In 1929, President Hoover created the Wickersham Commission, the first national commission to deal with crime and police, a recognition of the national interest in police practices and domestic tranquility. The commission's exposure of "third-degree" practices—coercing suspects to confess—and public concern about the practices provided reformers with additional leverage.

Third, the custom of police surveys—that is, administrative studies of police departments—grew rapidly during the 1920s. One of the first, published in Cleveland in 1922, was codirected by Felix Frankfurter and Roscoe Pound, funded by the Cleveland Foundation, and conducted by Raymond Fosdick, who had just published *American Police Systems*. Smith surveyed his first police department—New Orleans—in 1924. Between then and 1955 he would study more than fifty departments. Other experts, including Vollmer, also conducted many surveys. The survey reports, regardless of author, were consistent with the new vision of policing to the point of repetition. Virtually all of them contained recommendations to "shorten the span of control, get more cops out from behind desks onto the streets, reduce the number of district stations, and to strengthen the hand of the chief."[14] And beginning with Fosdick's study of Cleveland, surveys increasingly evaluated police departments on the basis of their effectiveness in dealing with crime—representing, as noted earlier, reformers' desire to develop objective means of evaluating police departments independently of political judgments.[15]

Fourth, the FBI played several roles in the diffusion of new thinking about police. Its public relations campaigns disseminated a vision of policing. It administered the UCR. In 1930 it created its own crime laboratory. And in 1935 it created the National Police Academy, where generations of police leaders would be trained.

Fifth, during the 1930s, U.S. universities began to become involved in police programs. Although some of the programs lapsed and few flourished until the 1960s, programs were developed in the 1930s at the University of California at Berkeley (with both Vollmer and Wilson playing key roles), at the predecessor college of Michigan State University, and at Northwestern University, San Jose State College, and Harvard University.

Sixth, police departments engaged in their own public relations; and the IACP, not prepared to leave promotional efforts solely to J. Edgar Hoover, created a public relations committee in the late 1930s. The campaigns conducted by local departments and by the IACP were extensive and attempted to build a broad social consensus for reform along the lines of Vollmer's model of policing. The public relations efforts took many forms: speakers' bureaus, consultation with movie and radio producers, newspaper editorials, lectures, displays at fairs, and publicity for informal charitable activities (the articles bore such titles as "The Santa Claus in Blue" and "Penn Troopers Play Santa Claus to Eighty Needy Families").[16]

Finally, in 1938 the International City Management Association published *Municipal Police Administration*, the first in a series of volumes on police management. The first volume embodied the principles of administration that were crucial to the reform movement and broadened police thinking beyond local rules, customs, and culture. Later dubbed the "Green Monster" by thousands of police officers who studied it to prepare for civil service promotional examinations, the volume would become one of two classic police sourcebooks. Wilson's *Police Administration*, published in 1950, is the other.

Consolidation of reforms: 1940–1960

During the 1940s and 1950s, police departments nationwide had come to embrace an integrated and coherent organizational strategy that sought authority in criminal law; narrowed police functioning to crime control; emphasized classical organizational forms; relied on preventive patrol, rapid response to calls for service, and criminal investigation as its primary tactics; and measured its success by crime, arrest, and clearance data.

Moreover, having loosened the hold of politicians over their organizations in many jurisdictions, police executives established strong boundaries around their departments. So strong were these boundaries and so autonomous would most police departments become that, in 1977, Herman Goldstein could write that police departments had become the least accountable agencies of city government.[17] Indeed, with rare exception police defined themselves as *professional* organizations that should be kept out of the purview of citizens, academics and researchers, and other persons with an interest in police. Police business was just that: *police* business.

Further developments in policing during the 1940s and 1950s were largely confined to improving or tinkering with the functioning of police departments. It was thought that better personnel should be recruited, hired, and maintained; that training should be improved; and that technology should be used to strengthen existing tactics. Efficiency and officer functioning should be improved through the strengthening of command and control. In all, police reformers were confident that they had finally come into their own.

Middle-class constituency building

Having largely freed themselves from political influences in most areas of police administration and having created relatively impenetrable organizational boundaries, police still had the problem of how best to structure the relationship between police and the public. From the police point of view, the primary problem was the residual contempt middle-class citizens felt for police because of the latter's political and corrupt heritage and the fact that policing was still largely a semiskilled, blue-collar occupation.[18]

Reformers had strong views about the public's proper role vis-a-vis police. Wilson, for example, emphasized the need for public support of the police (see the accompanying sidebar), and he encouraged the police to build this support, especially within the middle class, by converting influential citizens to the police point of view and by educating the public about the proper role of police.[19] In his words, "Strong personalities within a community, if not converted to the police point of view, may likewise do much to destroy public confidence in the police, to build resentment, and to prevent the creation of a desirable rapport between police and the public."[20]

The police and the public: 1950
Public cooperation is essential to the successful accomplishment of the police purpose. Public support assists in many ways; it is necessary in the enforcement of major laws as well as of minor regulations, and with it arrests are made and convictions obtained that otherwise would not be possible. A public that observes laws and complies with regulations relieves the police of a large share of their burden. Difficult programs can be carried out. . . . Preferred techniques can be operated successfully. . . . Public commendation and praise build police morale. . . . Without public support budgetary requirements for needed buildings, equipment, and personnel are difficult to obtain. Police salaries, relief days, sick and retirement benefits, and other conditions of service are also favorably influenced by a friendly and cooperative public.

Source: O. W. Wilson, *Police Administration* (New York: McGraw-Hill, 1950), 388.

William H. Parker, chief of police in Los Angeles during the 1950s, fully articulated the position that police should use modern public relations techniques to educate citizens on proper police roles and methods. For Parker, considered one of the premier reform chiefs, suitable police practices would be developed only if there were a strong public demand for "professional law enforcement." Drawing on lessons from the private sector, Parker wrote that this demand had to be created.[21]

Adjusting to new urban migrants

Ignored during this era of strategic consolidation and middle-class constituency building were many new immigrants and urban migrants, especially blacks and Hispanics, who neither shared many conventional "middle-class" values nor were receptive to the public relations programs of police departments, which were intended to appeal to the (mainly white) middle class.

Some background is required to understand the experiences of blacks and Hispanics with police. European immigrants of the late nineteenth and early twentieth centuries—the Irish, Italians, and Germans, for example—had been largely absorbed into the urban political landscape and had therefore benefited from the political localism that characterized urban politics. Many became police officers themselves and found policing to be a good job in which avenues of mobility existed, either within the command structure or within police unions—at first through cronyism, later through more equitable mechanisms, such as civil service in departments or elections in unions. The middle and upper classes, if not necessarily enchanted with local police, nevertheless tolerated them because citizens could exert substantial influence on police by controlling media, boards, commissions, and civic groups.[22]

Moreover, political localism had enabled the European immigrant groups to deflect attempts by the middle and upper classes to control their life-style. Before the immigrant groups rose to the middle class, some elements of their life-style were considered by the middle and upper classes to be "immoral," and Progressives attempted to legislate "morality" through vice laws. But it was the local police, after all, who were charged with enforcing those laws. And German, Italian, and other European immigrants "worked out an arrangement with the police whereby they were allowed to behave as they saw fit provided they kept a semblance of public order and stayed out of upper-middle and upper-class neighborhoods."[23]

But blacks—whose parents and grandparents could still recall slavery, who experienced Jim Crow racism directly, and who understood the role played by police in enforcing both—experienced the police differently. When they and other groups, especially Hispanics, moved into cities in the 1940s and 1950s, the rules of the game were different. The machines, a source of political power and economic mobility for earlier European immigrants, were virtually dead. The "rope ladder" of opportunity no longer existed. Centralization, civil service, and other reforms ensured that the groups that had dominated police in previous periods and had been grandfathered into policing during the implementation of progressive reforms would continue to dominate it.

Further, unlike the German, Italian, Irish, and other European immigrants, blacks and Hispanics were not able to deflect attempts to control their life-styles. The "deals" cut by Irish and German immigrants, for example, were closed to these newer migrants to U.S. cities. The reform movement, at least during the 1950s and early 1960s, may even have worsened the situation of minorities. Freed from the constraints of local political influences and rallying around the ideology of "decaying American values," police were unwilling to abide by the ground rules that had earlier characterized the relationship between immigrant groups and police. "Equal enforcement of the law," a mainstay of reform values, now meant that laws targeting morality and vice would be pursued as aggressively in migrant as in middle- and upper-middle-class neighborhoods. Egon Bittner described the history thus: "The Yankee aimed at the Irishman, but the black man caught the blow."[24]

Whether or not the situation for minorities worsened during the early stages of the reform era, the effect of reform on minorities was different from what it was on the white middle class.

As dramatic as this change [from the political to the reform era] must have appeared to the white middle-class inhabitants of America's major cities, the transition to the reform era was barely noticeable to black and other minorities. Replacing politics with law as the source of police authority had many desirable aspects for those provided full protection by the law. For those who lacked both political power and equal protection under the law, however, such a transformation could have had little significance.[25]

Shocks and change: The 1960s

When blacks rioted in many cities during the 1960s, police attitudes and actions caught some of the blame for these eruptions. Postmortems noted long-festering tensions between mostly-white police departments and black neighborhoods. They reported also that excessive use of force was often the spark that set off disorders. The police were seen as sources of violent conflict as much as peacekeepers, an interpretation that tended to undermine the claims that policing was an emerging profession.

Demonstrations

The riots were only one of a series of jolts to the police that began in the 1960s, jolts that became the source of watershed changes in the way police departments were managed. The police were jolted again when middle-class Vietnam War protestors, civil rights activists, and poor people—whole segments of society—rose up in angry demonstrations. The police were ill prepared and desperate to maintain order. The first response of most police was to attempt to quell disturbances with arrests backed up by force. Public outrage at the televised presentations of these confrontations was substantial. Police tactics, once tolerated when used against perceived criminals, were denounced when used against demonstrating members of the middle class. Anti-war demonstrations brought the police into contact with a large, organized body of citizens who had close ties to the news media and other sources of influence. With seeming impunity, enraged college students and other middle-class protestors routinely called police storm troopers and—worse—"pigs," hardly terms that describe professionals. The police began to lose hope of enlarging their base of unswerving support among the educated middle class.

Court actions

Another blow to the police was the discovery that presumed allies could not be taken for granted. The Supreme Court, which police had hitherto viewed as a distinguished partner in helping to foster law and order, shocked them with a quick succession of rulings:

1961: Evidence illegally seized by police cannot be used against state-level criminal defendants (*Mapp* v. *Ohio*).

1963: Defendants in state-level felony cases have right to counsel (*Gideon* v. *Wainwright*).

1964: The accused have the right to counsel during interrogation (*Escobedo* v. *Illinois*).

1966: Suspects have the right to counsel when criminal investigations begin to focus on them; they must be informed of their right to remain silent (*Miranda* v. *Arizona*).

The Court, under Chief Justice Warren, set new rules for police conduct in criminal investigations and said the penalty for violating those rules was exclusion of evidence obtained in the breach. To act constitutionally, police had to inform suspects of their rights to counsel and subject the use of wiretaps and other investigative methods to judicial approval.

The Warren Court rulings were not the first efforts to limit police actions. For decades, reformers both inside and outside police circles had wanted to improve the lawfulness of police performance, especially in the conduct of criminal investigations and use of deadly force. In the 1930s, the Wickersham report had excoriated police for the practice of the "third degree," and serious concern about the lawfulness of criminal investigations (the area highlighted by the Wickersham report) persisted into the 1960s and beyond.

Likewise, even though during the 1950s police visionaries such as Parker in Los Angeles had established rigorous reviews of all weapon discharges, during the 1960s and early 1970s "ricocheting" bullets and "warning" shots continued to kill an unusually large number of persons, frequently minorities, throughout the United States. The killings exacerbated the chronic ill feelings that existed between the police and minority communities in many cities. (Not until 1985, however, would the Supreme Court rule that police may not use deadly force to catch fleeing felons except in severely limited circumstances involving the threat of death or injury [*Tennessee* v. *Garner*]).

The police response to the High Court's rulings of the 1960s was largely one of bitterness and outrage: criminals would have all the advantage; police would be shackled and impotent to deal with serious crime; police, just like other professionals, could and should regulate themselves. But eventually the furor subsided, and the Court, at least during the remainder of the 1960s, made no major changes in its criminal procedure rulings.

Affirmative action

The 1960s delivered still another jarring message. The goals of affirmative action collided with the reality of police departments, which, for the most part, were virtually all-white, all-male operations. Leaders of racial minorities in the inner cities asserted that police agencies made up of "white mercenaries" who lived in outlying areas of the city—or even in the suburbs—had no stake in the minority-dominated neighborhoods. They claimed that riots and other disorders, as well as faltering crime control efforts, resulted partly because the police had lost contact with, and alienated, people they did not resemble. In fact, few departments could meet tests that measured whether they were representative of the communities they served. Minorities and women succeeded in challenging entrance and promotional examinations on grounds they were culturally biased and not work related. Old-style civil service entrance examinations, once hallowed as impartial gateways to professional policing, were faulted for excluding many able citizens from police ranks.

The search for a police response

Amidst riots, anti-war and civil rights demonstrations, restrictive Court decisions, and the developing claims of affirmative action, the police in the 1960s were also struggling with the tormenting problem of crime rates that burst out of control and seemingly could not be contained. In the 1964 presidential campaign, crime for the first time became a national political issue. The federal government responded to the issues of crime, riots, and other disorders by establishing prestigious presidential commissions and starting the flow of what would be billions of dollars to state and local government through the Law Enforcement Assistance Administration.

As the police struggled to bring down crime rates, they modified their public relations programs in attempts to deal with those who were at odds with police. Heretofore the middle and upper classes, not minorities, the poor, or the disenchanted, had been the target of public relations programs. Now these programs were directed toward people who were actively hostile to the police.[26]

Popularized by President Johnson's Commission on Law Enforcement and Administration of Justice, community relations programs sprang from a variety of motives and took an assortment of forms. At their worst, community relations programs were trivial efforts to "sell" a model of policing to citizens who were largely hostile to police. In such circumstances, community relations officers— always out of the mainstream in police organizations—came to be seen as hapless "flak catchers" by citizens and as the "empty holster crowd" by "real" cops doing "real" police work: patrolling, responding to calls for service, and investigating crimes. But at their best, community relations programs were serious attempts to identify and solve neighborhood problems. Regardless, such programs remained out of the mainstream in police departments: in the minds, if not the mouths, of many police was the deep-seated belief that communities, not police, were the source of problems. "Support your local police" became a

Blue-ribbon commissions and the police   One measure of the turmoil in U.S. cities and the controversy surrounding police practices in the 1960s and early 1970s was the proliferation of blue-ribbon commissions during that period. Five national commissions were formed to examine various aspects of police services and the criminal justice process and make recommendations for reform.

The President's Commission on Law Enforcement and Administration of Justice, which published its reports in 1967 and 1968, was influenced by urban racial turmoil. Among the outgrowths of its work were the Safe Streets Act of 1968 and the Law Enforcement Assistance Administration, which provided significant funding for police-related programs.

The National Advisory Commission on Civil Disorders (popularly known as the Kerner Commission) was similarly inspired by riots and other disorders in many U.S. cities in the summer of 1967. Its report examined patterns of disorder and prescribed responses by the federal government, the criminal justice system, and local governments.

The National Commission on the Causes and Prevention of Violence was established after the assassinations of Martin Luther King and Robert Kennedy in 1968. Its report, *To Establish Justice, To Insure Domestic Tranquility*, was published in 1969.

The President's Commission on Campus Unrest was established following student deaths related to protests at Kent State and Jackson State universities in 1970.

The National Advisory Commission on Criminal Justice Standards and Goals issued six reports in 1973 in an attempt to develop standards and recommendations for police crime control efforts.

In addition to the work of these national commissions, the American Bar Association in 1973 published its *Standards Relating to the Urban Police Function*, the end product of a lengthy standard-setting effort that began in 1963.

The voluminous reports of these commissions contain insights that continue to have direct relevance to contemporary police concerns. Many of the most important recommendations in the commission reports can be seen, in retrospect, to be the seeds of important strategic, technological, and operational initiatives that will command the attention of policing into the twenty-first century.

euphemism for the underlying conviction that all would be fine if only citizens would obey the law and adopt, in Wilson's words, "the police point of view."

However strong the forces for change that were converging on the police, the 1967 report of President Johnson's crime commission reaffirmed the strategy associated with traditional police reform and professionalism. Aside from acknowledging that some police tactics were unpopular in minority communities and urging the development of community relations programs, the report endorsed the reform agenda: more police, better equipment, more education for officers, improved command and control, enhanced training of officers, expanded use of technology—in other words, continued implementation and refinement of the reform agenda. Good policing was still equated with the intuitively reasonable tactics and theories of reform.

But the often unproductive, even unsuccessful, reponses to riots and demonstrations and the seemingly ever-increasing crime rates suggested that all was not well. What the police—heirs to Vollmer's vision of scientific policing—were doing did not appear equal to the challenges at hand. The stability that had characterized the urban world in which policing had thrived from the 1940s through the early 1960s had ended, and with it some police illusions about the adaptability of their strategy and about their own professionalism.

True, the police were protected by civil service from the vagaries of ward politics, guided by a general code of ethics, and supported by a body of knowledge that was built on experience and backed by a professional organization, the IACP. However, the crises of the 1960s exposed fissures in the body of accepted police knowledge; many tactics were not productive, and there was little methodologically sound research aimed at developing new ones. Further, few police officers had had a college education—one hallmark of professionalism—and virtually no police agency required a college degree for entry and promotion.

Policing, in fact, was a craft in search of new responses to the continual challenges of a turbulent era. Some police leaders believed that police management had to change its perceptions and produce effective results or face the possibility of losing control over management decisions ranging from hiring and promotions to policies on investigations and arrests. They believed that the anger directed at police (especially about police use of force), the *Miranda* decision, and the exclusionary rule (*Mapp* v. *Ohio*) provided them with new tools for improving police organizations. Agreeing that police responsibilities included guaranteeing constitutional rights to all citizens, these leaders embraced rather than fulminated against the new Court rulings. At the same time, police leaders and scholars were arguing that the police needed a new base of reliable knowledge—knowledge derived by means of state-of-the-art social science methods—if they were to succeed in doing their job.

The advent of research: The 1970s and 1980s

During the early 1970s, stimulated in part by pioneering field work associated with President Johnson's crime commission, social scientists increasingly undertook research into policing. Police were largely hostile to research and resisted its development—perhaps less because they opposed the use of professional methods for investigating problems than because they suspected the motives of researchers. In this case, however, the decentralization of policing was an advantage: individual researchers were able to penetrate enough departments to start creating a composite picture of the police occupation, role, and organizations.[27] The most startling findings concerned the police role. Researchers found that police spent a great deal of time on efforts unrelated to law enforcement, that police activities were exceedingly diverse, and that officers exercised wide discretion. These findings shocked persons concerned about policing in America. Such insights were incompatible with the beliefs promulgated by police about police: police work was law enforcement—fighting crimes in progress—and, in the typical command and control organization, line police personnel exercised

---

Research findings: 1973   First, there is general agreement that the vastly preponderant majority of police manpower, time, and resources, is and must be allocated to activities that have either nothing, or only very little, to do with law enforcement in the strict sense of the term. Second, these activities, commonly referred to as peacekeeping, entail the methodical handling of an enormously wide-ranging variety of often highly complex and almost invariably very serious human problems. Third, policemen typically receive no instruction, no guidance, and, above all, no recognition for doing this work.

Source: Egon Bittner, "Police Research and Police Work," *Police Yearbook* (Lexington, MA: Lexington Books, 1973), 17–24.

little or no discretion. Research proved otherwise. Despite a generation of attempts to narrow police functioning and to eliminate individual decision making, the broad functioning and wide discretion of police officers had continued.

The implications of these unforeseen findings for the reform strategy were unclear. When acknowledged, the findings certainly had implications for training and supervision. Yet the problems associated with crime during the 1970s were so serious and the reputed effectiveness of patrol and rapid response to calls for service so deeply ingrained in police thinking that few, if any, alternatives to the usual tactics were considered.

Team policing was an exception. Based on Home Beat Policing in London's metropolitan police, team policing aimed at working more closely with neighborhoods; officers worked as teams rather than as individuals, and decision making was decentralized. However, team policing efforts in cities followed a predictable pattern. They would begin with a flourish and a show of enthusiasm, give early signs of success, and then—generally by the end of the second year—would vanish. The most carefully evaluated example of this pattern was in Cincinnati.[28]

Questions about the basic tactics of police, especially preventive patrol, had been raised during the late 1960s—largely by sources external to police, however. The president's crime commission noted gaps in knowledge about preventive patrol. The American Bar Association's Urban Police Function Standards raised questions about the deterrent value of preventive patrol. Interviews with prisoners suggested that fear of apprehension by police during the commission of crimes was not pronounced.[29] One researcher noted that reported crime was not consistently affected by increased levels of motorized patrol. Another reported that more than 90 percent of arrests were the result of citizens' calls to the police rather than actions initiated by police themselves.[30]

The Kansas City experiment

Although in the 1970s the early findings about the police role and the questions research had raised about patrol effectiveness were perplexing and, to many, intriguing, their effect on mainstream policing or public policy regarding police was minimal. Publicly voiced disagreements were relatively polite and unemotional. Then the Kansas City (Missouri) Preventive Patrol Experiment, funded by the Police Foundation, stirred things up. The findings are now well known, although still disbelieved in some quarters: preventive patrol was found to have little or no effect on citizen perception of police presence or personal safety or on victimization or reported crime.[31] Many, both inside and outside policing, were suspicious of the findings, and some were outraged by them. A tradition-bound belief about patrol had been challenged. The ensuing debates are also well known. How representative of the police world was Kansas City? How powerful was the research design? How faithfully was the experiment executed?

The significance of what occurred in Kansas City is far greater, however, than either the findings of the experiment or the controversy they generated. First, the Kansas City study introduced rigorous experimentation into American policing; until that time, no research conducted in policing had used an experimental or quasi-experimental design. Second, in contrast with earlier research, it was conducted *by* police, not *on* police. Although Police Foundation consultants helped the Kansas City police department design and conduct the study, the experiment grew out of questions asked inside the police department, and the department administered it from beginning to end. Findings were published with the blessings of the department, and a police officer was among the authors.

Finally, the preventive patrol experiment was developed by a task force dominated not by senior police officials but by patrol officers, street-level practitioners.

Further research efforts

Before policing could catch its breath after the preventive patrol findings, two more studies were published: one on criminal investigations by the Rand Corporation and another on response time, again in Kansas City (see the chapters on criminal investigations and the patrol function). Like the preventive patrol experiment, both studies questioned the efficacy of the police at what they saw as the core of their mission: crime control.

The significance of this explosion of research can be understood in light of observations made in 1973, before publication of the first report about Kansas City:

Of all the occupations dealing with people, the police alone have not, at any time during this century, raised serious questions about the nature of their mandate, have never moved in any sustained manner in the direction of self-scrutiny and self-criticism, and did not attempt to build into their operations a stable program of study and research.[32]

Now some police were raising serious questions about their mandate; they were moving steadily toward self-scrutiny and self-criticism; they were beginning the process of building into their operations a stable program of study and research. During the rest of the 1970s research in police departments proliferated—in San Diego, Dallas, Cincinnati, Wilmington, Hartford, Newark, Flint, Birmingham, New York City, Rochester, and in other cities. During the 1980s, the list expanded to include Los Angeles, Minneapolis, Baltimore County, Madison, Houston, Newport News, Washington, Boston, Omaha, Dade County, Chicago, and Milwaukee.

During the 1970s, research received additional support when the Police Foundation created the Police Executive Research Forum (PERF), whose membership was made up of college-educated police executives who ran large agencies (later expanded to include medium-sized agencies). PERF began almost immediately to carry out its mandate to foster research and to spur debate in an occupation notably averse to the public clash of ideas.

In one decade, policing—which had been notorious for its insulation and isolation and for its lack of self-assessment and stable program of research—began to develop into a self-analytic, research-generating occupation. To many, policing appeared on its way to becoming a true profession.

Sensing these developments in policing and committed to encouraging them, the National Institute of Justice (NIJ) embarked in new directions during the 1980s. By deliberately establishing policies to ensure collaboration between practitioners and researchers in all stages of research—conception, review of proposals, conduct, authorship, and peer review of publications—NIJ created bridging mechanisms that helped researchers and practitioners establish a firm foundation of policy-relevant research.

In one decade, policing—which had been notorious for its insulation and isolation and for its lack of self-assessment and stable program of research—began to develop into a self-analytic, research-generating occupation. To many, policing appeared on its way to becoming a true profession.[33]

Contemporary policing: Partnerships for public safety

Many research findings are presented throughout this volume, and a systematic review is beyond the scope of this chapter. It is useful, however, to close the chapter with a broad overview of where the field of policing seems to be heading.

The first round of research during the 1970s showed what didn't work. Preventive patrol seemed to prevent little; rapid response to calls for service proved largely ineffective; criminal investigations rarely improved clearance rates. During the late 1970s and early 1980s, however, this picture gradually changed. Properly used information and improved police management of criminal investigations increased police productivity in clearances and arrests. Foot patrol reduced fear, increased citizens' satisfaction with police, and improved the attitudes of police toward citizens. Alternatives existed to rapid response to calls for service. Fear could be reduced in a variety of ways. Police could play a special role in dealing with domestic violence. Programs that targeted repeat or serious offenders had the potential to prevent crime by prolonging the incarceration of those offenders.[34]

Other factors also influenced policing during the 1980s and seem likely to play a powerful role in shaping policing through the turn of the century. The police services that citizens demanded were often at odds with the services police offered. The problems that citizens wanted the police to help with were broader than those the police considered most important. The police emphasized serious crimes, especially crimes in progress; citizens were concerned, as well, about disorder. Citizens increasingly demanded foot patrol (or other tactics that increased the links between police and citizens); the police preferred motor patrol. The movement by crime victims to hold criminal justice agencies accountable to them gave police special responsibilities and opportunities to serve victims. The growing neighborhood self-help movement affected police in at least two ways: efforts by citizens to protect their own neighborhoods increased and so did demands for greater control over service providers, including police.[35] Moreover, urban fiscal realities frequently limited the growth of police departments or, in many cities, led to reductions in police personnel. Finally, private and corporate security, unobtrusively and steadily, grew in size and social import. The segments of the public that could afford the expense began to purchase security, suggesting that police were unable to provide minimum levels of protection and raising questions about the equitable distribution of public safety.

Both the trend line in police research and the changing environment of police managers were reflected in two ground-breaking articles published in the late 1970s and early 1980s. In the first, Goldstein advocated a basic restructuring of police work through a "problem-oriented" approach.[36] Rather than focusing their efforts on *incidents*, as police were organized to do with 9–1–1 telephone systems, he advocated concentrating on *problems* (of which the incidents were symptomatic).

The second article, known popularly as "Broken Windows," drew together years of research by numerous scholars and practitioners and thrust onto the nation's crime agenda an argument made in three principal steps: (1) neighborhood disorder is a primary source of citizen fear; (2) just as unrepaired broken windows signal that no one cares and can lead to more serious destruction, untended disorder signals that no one cares and can lead to more serious disorder and crime; and (3) if police are to reduce fear and disorder, they must turn to citizens for both legitimacy and assistance.[37]

Taken together, these two articles drew major attention to what had been minor themes in policing. At their best, community relations and team policing programs were precursors of problem-oriented and community policing (both discussed elsewhere in this volume). The Kansas City patrol experiment, for example, resulted from the problem-oriented deliberations of a task force that debated whether or not patrol officers could be diverted from preventive patrol to concentrate on the problems youths were creating near schools. Team policing contained most of the elements of problem-oriented and community policing.[38]

One of the likely reasons that problem-oriented and order-maintenance strategies were rapidly embraced by many police officials beginning in the 1980s was that they represented skills already in the officials' organizations. In a sense, community relations, team policing, and the occasional foot patrol unit were the "skunk work" of police organizations—outside of mainstream police activity, often staffed by organizational mavericks, and generally considered to be of marginal utility. The discrediting of earlier tactics, changing demands, and shifting urban circumstances led innovative police administrators to draw on capacities already inside their organizations to develop future strategies.[39]

Cognizant of developments in the field and of the changing nature of urban America, today's police chiefs are responsible for crafting the police strategy that could well shape policing for the next fifty years.

Today's police leaders are in a position similar to the one Vollmer was in during the 1930s. Cognizant of developments in the field and of the changing nature of urban America, they are responsible for crafting the police strategy that could well shape policing for the next fifty years. This strategy will be developed within a context of fiscal shortfalls, a seemingly permanent underclass, and the present drug crisis. Current themes—control over the police, the role of unions in the development of the profession, the role of neighborhoods in the formulation of policy, and others—are discussed elsewhere in this book. Like Vollmer's "scientific policing," the labels and metaphors police executives use to describe their strategy (for example, problem-oriented or community policing) will likely give way to other labels and metaphors. Regardless, in an atmosphere that is increasingly receptive to change, today's police leaders can help make the emerging strategy of police consistent, coherent, and socially useful.

1   For discussions of similarities and differences between U.S. and English police, see Wilbur R. Miller, *Cops and Bobbies: Police Authority in New York and London 1830–1870* (Chicago: University of Chicago Press, 1973); and Peter Manning, *Police Work* (Cambridge: MIT Press, 1979).

2   Egon Bittner, "The Rise and Fall of the Thin Blue Line," book review in *American History* (Baltimore: Johns Hopkins University Press, September 1978), 421. See also Robert Fogelson, *Big-City Police* (Cambridge: Harvard University Press, 1977); Samuel Walker, *A Critical History of Police Reform*, (Lexington, MA: Lexington Books, 1977); and Thomas Repetto, *The Blue Parade* (New York: Free Press, 1978).

3   Bittner, "The Rise and Fall of the Thin Blue Line," 422.

4   August Vollmer, "Police Progress in the Past Twenty-Five Years," *Journal of Criminal Law and Criminology* 24, no. 1 (May–June 1933). On Vollmer's stature in the evolution of modern policing, see Donal E. J. Macnamara, "August Vollmer: The Vision of Police Professionalism," in *Pioneers in Policing*, ed. Philip John Stead (Montclair NJ: Patterson Smith, 1977).

5   See Samuel Walker, *A Critical History*, 157. J. H. Haager, in *The Automobile as a Police Department Adjunct* (Louisville, KY: 1909), cited in Donald D. Dilworth, ed., *The Blue and the Brass* (Gaithersburg, MD: International Association of Chiefs of Police, 1979), had a prescient understanding of the future role of the telephone and automobile in police work.

6   Bruce Smith, "Municipal Police Administration," *The Annals* 146 (November 1929): 27.

7   On the UCR, see Thomas Repetto, "Bruce Smith: Police Reform in the United States," in *Pioneers in Policing* ed. Stead, 171–206. On crime tallies, see, for example, Bennet Mead, "Police Statistics," *The Annals* 146 (November 1929), which discusses the development of most of the measures used to evaluate police during the reform era: crime rates, clearances, clearance ratios, cost per citizen, and number of police per 100,000 population. On motorized patrol, see, for example, Stanley Schrotel, "Changing Patrol Methods," *The Annals* 291 (January 1954), 46–53. Early proponents of motorized patrol had great confidence that it would be so valuable it would enable police to eliminate city crime altogether. See, for example, Jonathan Rubinstein, *City Police* (New York: Farrar, Straus and Giroux, 1973), 20. On Wilson's patrol allocation concepts, see O. W. Wilson, "The Use of Records in Administering Police Activities," *City Manager Yearbook*

(Washington, DC: International City Management Association, 1933), 152.

8   See L. S. Timmerman, "The Annual Police Report," *The Annals*, 146 (November 1929), for an example of the importance police reformers placed on the use of crime statistics as measures of organizational efficiency. O. W. Wilson, for example, informed his mentor, August. Vollmer, about his successes in dealing with crime, comparing the performance of his department in one year with its performance in the preceding year (letter to Vollmer dated October 11, 1932, O. W. Wilson Collection, Bancroft Library, University of California at Berkeley, quoted in Gene E. Carte and Elaine H. Carte, "O. W. Wilson: Police Theory in Action," in *Pioneers in Policing*, ed. Stead).

9   Fogelson, *Big-City Police*, 176.

10 In resisting decentralization, the early reformers also opposed the idea of a single-city police department. Reformers, especially Vollmer and Smith, attempted to rally both political and police support for regional or metropolitan police. Until very recently, regionalization has been an important ingredient of police reform. For good or ill, police have not been able to muster the same support for regionalization as for centralization within a city. See, for example, Gene E. Carte and Elaine H. Carte, *Police Reform in the United States: The Era of August Vollmer, 1905–1922* (Berkeley: University of California Press, 1975), 75; and the discussion of regionalization in this volume's chapter on the governmental setting. For a detailed discussion of criminal law as the basis for police authority, see George L. Kelling and Mark H. Moore, *The Evolving Strategy of Policing*, Perspectives on Policing (Washington, DC: National Institute of Justice and Harvard University, 1989).

11 See, for example, Eric H. Monkkonen, *Police in Urban America: 1860–1920* (Cambridge: Cambridge University Press, 1981).

12 On the crime alarm of the 1930s, see K. E. Jordan, *Ideology and the Coming of Professionalism: American Urban Police in the 1920s and 1930s* (Ph.D. diss., Rutgers University, 1972); George L. Kelling, "Juveniles and the Police: the End of the Nightstick," in *The Role of the Juvenile Court*, ed. Francis X. Hartmann, Vol. 2 of *From Children to Citizens* (New York: Springer-Verlag, 1987); and Walker, *A Critical History*, 152–153.

13 For a discussion of the persistence of political influence and corruption in policing during the period 1930–1970, see Fogelson, "Second Wave of Reform," *Big-City Police*, 167–192.

14 Repetto, "Bruce Smith," 198. For discussions of the crime commissions, see *The Administration of Criminal Justice in the United States* (Chicago: American Bar Foundation, 1955); Samuel Walker, "Setting the Standards: The Efforts and Impact of Blue-Ribbon Commissions on the Police," in *Police Leadership in America*, ed. W. A. Geller (New York: Praeger, 1985); Walker, *A Critical History*; and Ralph G. Murdy, *Crime Commission Handbook* (Baltimore: Criminal Justice Commission, 1965).

15 Walker, *A Critical History*, 127.

16 For a discussion of public relations, see Jordan, *Ideology and the Coming of Professionalism*; and Kelling, "Juveniles and the Police."

17 Herman Goldstein, *Policing a Free Society* (Cambridge, MA: Ballinger, 1977).

18 Egon Bittner, "The Impact of Police-Community Relations on the Police System," in *Community Relations and the Administration of Justice*, ed. David Patrick Geary (New York: John Wiley and Sons, 1972), 369–386.

19 O. W. Wilson, *Police Administration* (New York: McGraw-Hill, 1950).

20 Ibid., 389.

21 William H. Parker, "The Police Challenge in Our Great Cities," *The Annals* 291 (January 1954), 6. Parker's innovations in Los Angles are chronicled in William A. Bopp, *A Short History of American Law Enforcement* (Springfield, IL: Charles C Thomas, 1972). They include the creation of an internal affairs unit (a procedure to insulate discipline from politics), the creation of a bureau of administration incorporating intelligence and planning and research units, establishment of a community relations program, the use of helicopters for patrol, and a firearms policy in which all discharges of firearms were reviewed.

22 Fogelson, *Big-City Police*, 257.

23 Ibid.

24 Bittner, "The Rise and Fall of the Thin Blue Line," 427.

25 Hubert Williams and Patrick V. Murphy, "The Evolving Strategies of Police: A Minority Point of View," working paper (Cambridge: Program in Criminal Justice, Harvard University, 1989).

26 Bittner, "The Impact of Police-Community Relations."

27 William H. Westley, *Violence and the Police* (Cambridge: MIT Press, 1970); Jerome Skolnick, *Justice without Trial* (New York: John Wiley and Sons, 1966); Arthur Niederhofer, *Behind the Shield: The Police in Urban Society* (Garden City, NY: Anchor, 1969); James Q. Wilson, *Varieties of Police Behavior* (Cambridge: Harvard University Press, 1968); Elaine Cumming, Ian Cumming, and Laura Edell, "Policeman as Philosopher, Guide, and Friend," *Social Problems* 12 (1965): 276–86; American Bar Association, *Standards Relating to the Urban Police Function* (New York: American Bar Association Project on Standards for Criminal Justice, Institute of Judicial Administration, March 1972).

28 A. I. Schwartz and S. N. Claren, *Evaluation of Team Policing in Cincinnati* (Washington, DC: Police Foundation, 1977).

29 Institute of Defense Analysis, "Analysis of Response to Police Deterrence" (Washington, DC, unpublished study, 1966).

30 J. S. Press, *Some Effects of an Increase in Police Manpower in the 20th Precinct of New York City*, Rand Report R704–NYC (New York, October 1971), reported on the effect of motorized patrol. A. J. Reiss, Jr., *The Police and the Public* (New Haven: Yale University Press, 1971), described the reliance of police on citizens for information leading to arrests.

31 George L. Kelling et al., *The Kansas City Preventive Patrol Experiment* (Washington, DC: Police Foundation, 1975).

32 Egon Bittner, "Police Research and Police Work," *Police Yearbook* (Lexington, MA: Lexington Books, 1973), 19.

33 This view was by no means universally held. As during the 1930s, the new vision of policing was constrained by long-standing traditions. In this case, the traditions included, among others, lack of career mobility for police executives, the con-

tinuing low status of patrol officers, the need for portable pensions, and variable educational requirements.

34 These and other research findings are discussed and cited in numerous chapters in this volume. See, in particular, the chapters on the patrol function, criminal investigation, and crime prevention.

35 See, for example, Nathan Glazer, *The Limits of Social Policy* (Cambridge: Harvard University Press, 1988); and George L. Kelling and James K. Stewart, *Neighborhoods and Police: The Maintenance of Civil Authority*, Perspectives on Policing, no. 10, (Washington, DC: National Institute of Justice and Harvard University, 1989).

36 Herman Goldstein, "Improving Policing: A Problem-Oriented Approach," *Crime and Delinquency* 25 (1979): 236–58.

37 James Q. Wilson and George L. Kelling, "The Police and Neighborhood Safety," *Atlantic Monthly* (March 1982): 29–38.

38 For a discussion of team policing and its fate in police departments, see Kelling and Moore, "The Evolving Strategy of Policing." For more on problem-oriented policing, see Herman Goldstein, *Problem-Oriented Policing* (New York: McGraw Hill, 1990); and John Eck and William Spelman, *Problem-Solving: Problem-Oriented Policing in Newport News* (Washington, DC: Police Executive Research Forum, 1987). See also the chapters on the patrol function, criminal investigations, and drug control in this volume.

39 For a discussion of strategic change, see Kelling and Moore, *The Evolving Strategy of Policing*; Henry Mintzberg, "Crafting Strategy," *Harvard Business Review*, no. 4 (July–August 1987): 66–77; and Danny Miller and Peter H. Friesen, *Organizations: A Quantum View* (Englewood Cliffs, NJ: Prentice-Hall, 1984).

2 Organization and management

A powerful tradition, rooted in principles of scientific management and the military model of command, has customarily provided the starting point for discussions of police organization and management.[1] This tradition holds that the mission and basic goals of the organization are set externally—by law, by elected officials, or simply by custom. The role of police executives is seen as finding efficient means—organizational, programmatic, and technological—for achieving those goals. Police executives are expected to do so by performing the traditional managerial functions of planning, organizing, coordinating, and controlling.

Planning—both traditionally and currently—requires police executives to translate broad policy goals into more specific, operational objectives; to identify the organizational requirements of those objectives; and to determine which parts of their organization must be expanded or contracted to meet the operational objectives.[2] Planning also requires executives to monitor the organization's environment to identify emerging problems that must be addressed. And it requires them to stay in touch with new problem-solving methods they might adopt to increase their organization's efficiency or effectiveness.

Organizing and coordinating are concerned with the detailed deployment of the organization's resources. One crucial aspect of this function is establishing the basic structure of the organization.[3] A second is defining the process of decision making so as to identify the proper level for making different kinds of decisions and to ensure that the organization has the capacity to identify and resolve important policy questions.[4] A third aspect is identifying and filling any gaps in the administrative systems that guide individual efforts and establish individual accountability. This includes, for example, having a current manual of policies and procedures.

Controlling requires executives to oversee and sanction the conduct of their employees. This includes developing accounting and information systems to keep track of expenditures, activities, and accomplishments.[5] It also means developing performance measurement systems for individual officers and for the organization as a whole. Finally, it includes developing internal investigative and disciplinary procedures to guard against misconduct (including corruption) and misuse of authority.[6]

In addition to these technical managerial functions, police executives are expected to provide inspirational leadership. This involves setting high standards of ethical conduct for themselves and their subordinates and protecting the morale of the organization.[7] Discipline must be accompanied by assurances from the top that those who perform well will be rewarded and that honest mistakes will be consistently and impartially distinguished from careless or badly motivated actions. Otherwise, police officers will feel victimized by what they view as arbitrary managerial actions.

As part of exercising leadership, top managers are also expected to shield their organization from disruptive external influences—particularly improper political pressures. Although it is always difficult to distinguish proper political oversight from political interference, executives are expected to resist demands to use the organization's assets for the particular personal purposes of politicians rather than the broader, long-term interests of the community. These expectations are felt particularly keenly among employees, who want their leaders to protect the ultimate purposes and values of the organization against arbitrary demands for change.

All this is traditionally expected of police executives. What is *not* traditionally expected is that police executives will raise questions about the basic mission of the organization or will propose new ways of using the organization to meet challenges confronting society. After all, those are matters of policy—not administration or management.

Nor is it considered good form to raise doubts about whether the organization is using the best methods for achieving its objectives. To admit to uncertainty about the best means of dealing with particular problems or to commit large portions of the organization to experimental approaches is thought to suggest professional incompetence and insufficient respect for the accumulated knowledge and traditions of the organization.

Nor are managers traditionally expected to give their subordinates discretion in developing methods of handling the particular problems they face. It is thought that that would look like a retreat from managerial responsibility for setting direction and exercising control. That would also seem to risk substantial abuse of discretion.

Finally, in the traditional view, managers are discouraged from using informal channels to seek outside advice about which problems are locally important. Instead, they are expected to limit themselves to obtaining policy guidance through central, official channels. Otherwise, it is thought, the police department could be accused of playing politics.

For at least the past decade, tradition has been challenged on a number of fronts. It would probably be an overstatement to describe the important changes now impinging on police management as a revolution, but they can certainly be called a fast-paced evolution.[8] And each step in this evolution has implications for the organization and management of police departments and the performance of managerial functions.

Forces shaping contemporary police management

Three broad forces shape current thinking about the effective organization and management of police departments. The most powerful is important changes in the environment of policing—changes that affect the tasks the police must perform and the resources available to them. Another is significant changes in managerial thought in general. A third is the accumulating knowledge about the strengths and limitations of current approaches to policing.

Changes in the environment of policing

Simply stated, the nation's communities are changing. Many jurisdictions are becoming larger and are facing a host of problems associated with growth, while others are shrinking and are facing problems that accompany decline. Inner cities are becoming poorer as middle-class residents move to suburban areas, taking with them the tax dollars that support schools and other public services and institutions. Those who remain in the inner cities are frequently poor people and immigrants, many of whom require special services.[9]

Suburban areas are changing as well. Many local administrators and police chiefs have been alarmed to find in their own communities many of the problems traditionally associated with larger places—drug dealing, homelessness, poverty, and crime, for example.

These trends are fundamentally changing the nature of police work. For one thing, there is more of it to do and fewer resources with which to do it. Police workload, reported crime, calls for service, and arrests have increased—but the resources available have not kept pace.[10] This is true in the rest of the criminal justice system as well. Indeed, the system as a whole is losing its capacity to punish, deter, incapacitate, and rehabilitate. This alone would necessitate some rethinking of police strategies. Second and more important, however, the tasks themselves that the police are engaged in seem to be changing.

One change in police tasks is that, in large and small communities, fear— quite apart from actual criminal victimization—has become a major problem.[11] It is fear that motivates people (particularly elderly people) to stay off the streets and to buy guns. It is also fear that drives small businesses to abandon neighborhoods.[12] With them go jobs for teenagers, contributions to civic groups, and rallying points for community development. The police must therefore deal not only with crime, but also with fear of crime and the effects of that fear.

In addition, the police are being drawn into social emergencies that can produce violence if left unattended. They are asked to mediate domestic disputes, to deal with youthful runaways, to force a landlord to provide heat, or to compel a tenant to live up to the terms of the lease. Indeed, much of the crime that the police handle seems to emerge from nagging disputes among people who know one another, rather than from predatory attacks by hardened offenders.[13]

As police are drawn more deeply into the social structures of communities, important questions about the police mission and role arise.

These changes in police tasks are drawing the police more deeply into the social structures of communities. As they are drawn in, important questions about the police mission and role arise. Are the calls that are prompted by fears, disputes, and minor social emergencies worth handling well, or are they distractions from the central police mission of dealing with serious predatory crime and remaining ready to deal with still more of it? Are the skills and capabilities police have developed the right ones for such "domestic" or "social" situations? What other agencies might more properly and more effectively be charged with handling these problems? Where should the police turn for guidance on these questions? In essence, the current environment—in which economic decay is a background for problems of crime, fear, and social disorder—is sharply posing the question of what the police mission should be and how they should fulfill it. The answer has important implications for the organization and management of police departments.

Changes in managerial thought

A second important change affecting policing comes from managerial thought in general. In the past, good management—in both the public and private sectors—was held to focus on developing ever more refined internal controls. It was assumed that managers faced stable and predictable environments. To the extent they did not, their task was to improve their ability to predict future events so that the organization would be ready to meet whatever new challenges arose. Effective internal administration depended on well-defined operational objectives, the development of functional specialties, and the daily exercise of tight operational control. Often the path to improved organizational performance lay in the direction of increased standardization of procedures.

This line of thinking about management has been profoundly upset by three factors: (1) the economic success of the Japanese, who have a radically different managerial philosophy;[14] (2) research findings on the managerial practices of successful private-sector organizations;[15] and (3) the growth of the service economy at the expense of the production economy. Predictable external environments and planned change have yielded, conceptually, to relentless, unpredictable competition and the need for constant innovation.[16] The doctrine of tight managerial control is being supplanted by doctrines of worker participation, total quality management, and shared commitment to excellence as the principal devices for motivating organizational performance.[17] The focus on efficient use of internal resources has been transformed into a focus on developing close connections among the organization, its customers, and its markets.

The doctrine of tight managerial control is being supplanted by doctrines of worker participation, total quality management, and shared commitment to excellence.

It is obvious that a police department is not a service organization in the same way that a restaurant or a bank is. There are important differences between public-sector organizations and private-sector organizations. Yet it is also true that when managerial philosophies change in the private sector, the public sector is affected. And it is not obviously inappropriate for public-sector executives to begin thinking about what value their organizations have for citizens of the communities they police, and about how they are positioned to serve the community. Indeed, some police executives relish the opportunity to ask that basic question about policing—the question of how best to use the assets entrusted to them to make the greatest contribution to their cities and towns—and to assume that the answer may not be already known. More particularly, the shifting conceptions of managerial excellence suggest it may be possible to decentralize police organizations, reduce reliance on rules and constant supervision, and increase reliance on selection, training, and the formal statement of values to create an organizational culture that can properly guide officer conduct.[18]

New knowledge about effective policing

In addition to having been buffeted and stimulated by broad social trends and evolving concepts of management, the field of policing has also been following a logic of its own as it learns from its own experience and develops its own ideas about how best to police the nation's communities.[19]

Crime control remains the central mission of the police, but whether it should be the *exclusive* focus is less clear.

As discussed in the first chapter in this book, a predominant force in modern U.S. policing has been the "reform strategy." That strategy (1) emphasized crime fighting as the primary, perhaps exclusive, task of the police; (2) relied primarily on the techniques of random and directed patrol, rapid response to calls for service, and retrospective criminal investigation to achieve crime-fighting objectives; (3) sought to ensure effective discipline and control through elaborate rules and close supervision; and (4) tried to guarantee the fair and impartial enforcement of the law by insulating the police from close contact with any kind of political influence. That strategy helped to create more lawful, professional, and effective police departments, but this basic conception now contains very few additional developmental possibilities.

A police department that is "more effective" is still not as effective as it could be. Although the police are better and more efficient and effective, the reform strategy has fallen short in dealing with crime problems. Research has shown that the mainstays of random and directed patrol, rapid response, and retrospective criminal investigation are not as effective as was thought. To deal fully with problems of crime, new approaches are required, including working with the community to identify and resolve problems.

As police administrators face the uncertain and rapidly changing environment within which successful policing must occur, traditional ideals and principles continue to provide important guidance. Yet, at the same time, the developments noted above are shaking the traditions of police organization and management. Crime control remains the central mission of the police, but whether it should be the *exclusive* focus is less clear.[20] The principal means of controlling crime is still law enforcement, but it is increasingly apparent that the police can bring other competencies to bear in handling particular problems.[21] It is important for police executives to demand disciplined conduct from their officers, but the best way to achieve that result is now less clear than it once was. And although the police should be insulated from political interference, they must find mechanisms for learning what citizens want from the police and for restoring their own accountability.

A new analytical framework: The concept of corporate strategy

With the field poised on the brink of new strategies and structures for policing the nation's communities, it is timely to consider an unconventional framework for analyzing the organization and management of policing. Forward-looking police executives have turned to an analytic framework that many private-sector executives have used to chart their course into an uncertain future: the concept of "corporate strategy." They have attempted to adapt elements of this framework that are useful in charting the course of police organizations.

Strategic analysis: Definitions of organizational purpose

The development of a corporate strategy has to do with "the choice of purpose [or mission], the molding of organizational identity and character, the unending definition of what needs to be done, and the mobilization of resources for the attainment of goals in the face of aggressive competition or adverse circumstances."[22] More succinctly, corporate strategy means "setting some direction for the organization based on an analysis of organizational capabilities and environmental opportunities and threats."[23] That analysis is called "strategic analysis," or sometimes "strategic planning."

Using corporate strategy in the context of public-sector organizations produces some important shifts in the traditional perspective. Rather than beginning with externally mandated objectives and then figuring out how to achieve them, as policing has traditionally done, the concept of corporate strategy begins with the question of mission. Indeed, strategic analysis is primarily a methodology for deciding what the organization's mission, or purpose, should be. Moreover, it suggests that in defining purposes, managers might be guided not simply by their traditional mandated purposes—nor simply by a technical view of the problem they are responsible for solving—but also by a sense of what their organization might usefully contribute to current problems that may or may not have been part of their original mandate. In other words, in considering the overall goals of policing, one would have to take into account current environmental challenges, what police departments have learned from their own experience, and policing's unique organizational capabilities.

Corporate strategy provides a framework in which questions of organizational purpose and management are raised; it thus opens up areas of discussion that remain closed if one thinks along more traditional lines.

In the traditional perspective, a police executive thinks not about ultimate purpose but about establishing a visible police presence, responding rapidly to calls for service, and successfully investigating crimes. From the new perspective suggested by the concept of corporate strategy, a police executive might consider instead the broader and different question of how he or she might best use a force that (1) is large, disciplined, and resourceful, (2) carries the authority of the state, (3) has access to transportation, and (4) is available on instant notice around the clock—might best use such a force to make the maximum contribution to the quality of life in today's urban and suburban communities. The executive might also ask whether the organization is doing what the citizens of the community want, and how the department is organized to learn what the community wants and needs. Finally, he or she might even consider what gives a public police force a competitive advantage over private security efforts, and how the public effort might complement private efforts. Essentially, corporate strategy, with strategic analysis, provides a framework in which questions of organizational purpose and management are raised; it thus opens up areas of discussion that remain closed if one thinks along more traditional lines.

Three tests of a public organization's purpose

For this private-sector concept to fit the public-sector environment, it must be adapted. Figure 2–1 is a diagram that might help police executives work with the concept of a "corporate strategy" for policing. The basic notion is that if a particular strategy, or statement of mission, is to be successful, it must meet the three tests symbolized by the circles in the diagram. First, the mission, or goals and objectives, must be capable of attracting continued support from political and legal officials who authorize the continuation of the enterprise. Second, it must be operationally feasible and should take advantage of the distinctive competencies and capabilities of the organization. Third, it must be considered valuable to the community. If a proposed strategy fails any of these tests, it fails as an appropriate strategy. The second test—operational feasibility and suitability—is one that the public sector shares with the private sector. The first and

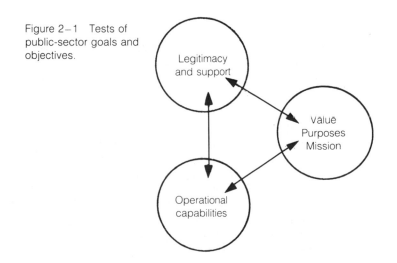

Figure 2–1 Tests of public-sector goals and objectives.

Legitimacy and support

Value Purposes Mission

Operational capabilities

third tests, however, are adaptations of the private sector's approach to corporate strategy.

In the public sector, the executive's focus on political and legal authorization is an adaptation of the private sector's focus on economic markets. In effect, the adapted model draws attention to the question of whether those who authorize the continuation of an organization—for example, elected chief executives, appointed administrators, elected representatives to legislative bodies, oversight agencies, the media, and assorted interest groups—will continue to support the organization, given its announced purposes and accomplishments. In this sense, political enthusiasm for the enterprise—built by promises of value to the community as well as by concrete performance—is considered a barometer of acceptance much as market success is for private organizations.

In the public sector, though, the "authorizing environment" of the police department supplies more than just the financial support that is implied by market success. It also supplies authority for the police to compel others to act in the public interest. Indeed, access to public authority is one of the most important differences between private- and public-sector organizations. But the public agencies that have the power to compel are responsible for using it only when justified. So both the use of public money and the use of public authority are overseen by elected and appointed officials—by the appropriations committees and budget agencies, on the one hand, and by authorizing committees of legislative bodies and the courts, on the other hand.

The other change made when the concept of corporate strategy is brought into the public sector is that attention is focused not on financial returns to the organization but on something much harder to define—the value of the organization to the public: the organization's ability to solve public problems. To a degree, the public good is defined by the political and legal mandates governing a public-sector enterprise—that is, by the official statement of the organization's mission and objectives. But there are other ways of defining public value and establishing standards for assessing it. The techniques of policy analysis, for example, can be used to identify important social problems and to propose ways for the organization to solve them,[24] or program evaluations and performance audits can be used to determine whether public-sector organizations have been effective in achieving the purposes set for them.[25] On occasion, benefit/cost analysis can be used to determine whether the public is getting its money's worth.[26] Even citizen surveys can provide a clue to the effectiveness and value of public-sector enterprises. None of these techniques gives a perfect estimate of whether the public interest has been served, but in combination they may provide some guidance.

The concept of corporate strategy requires a manager to define purposes for the organization that can sustain political and legal support and are of public value in addition to being operationally achievable.

In the public sector, then, the concept of corporate strategy requires a manager to define purposes for the organization that can sustain political and legal support and are of public value in addition to being operationally achievable. One can come to a decision about such purposes by examining the political and legal demands on the organization, exploring the environment the organization faces, and thinking through the question of how the distinctive competencies of the organization might best be used. That is the methodology employed here to reach conclusions about the effective organization and management of police departments.

The purpose of police organizations

In defining the purpose of police departments, one must ask what functions police departments are expected to—or could usefully—perform for society (the test of political and legal support). It is also relevant to know how well police departments are performing current functions (the test of value) and what the strengths and weaknesses of their current capabilities are (the test of sustainability). That information contains clues to how police departments may have to be reorganized to improve their performance and how innovative and adaptable police management will have to become. First, though, it is useful to examine the traditional view of the purpose of police organizations.

The traditional purpose: Professional crime fighting

The basic purpose of an organization can generally be summarized in a relatively simple phrase. The traditional purpose of police departments, for example, is often described as professional law enforcement (or professional crime fighting). (The reasons for the dominance of this view of policing are discussed below.) This definition of purpose for police departments can be viewed from several perspectives: political, operational, and substantive.

In the context of law enforcement, "professional" means not only technically competent but also disciplined and fair.

In *political* terms, the concept of "professional law enforcement" appeals primarily to a constituency that is interested in controlling or reducing crime. The phrase "law enforcement" signals the prominence of that task. A little less obvious, but equally important, is the promise implied by the word "professional": the promise to demonstrate the legal virtues of impartiality, nonintrusiveness, and minimal use of force.[27] In the context of law enforcement, "professional" means not only technically competent but also disciplined and fair. Indeed, it is the inclusion of this word that separates the modern era of "professional policing" from the "bad old days" of incompetence, corruption, and brutality (see the chapter on the evolution of contemporary policing). "Professional" also serves to distinguish modern public police departments from the growing ranks of private security guards, whose professionalism has been questioned on grounds of loose entry standards, limited training, and low wages. (There are exceptions to this generalization, but by and large it is valid at the beginning of the 1990s.)

In *operational terms*, "professional law enforcement" directs attention to key aspects of the organization that police administrators must manage. Because the phrase makes enforcement of the law (in an impartial way) the key task and the defining, distinctive competence of police organizations, it directs the attention of police managers to efforts to ensure that their officers are trained and equipped to perform this function. Thus, training tends to emphasize knowledge of the law and the disciplined use of force. Administrative arrangements must require that when officers deploy force to make arrests, they use it properly, and when officers stray accidentally or intentionally, they are subjected to retraining or discipline.

In *substantive* terms, "professional law enforcement" defines the most important purpose of the police as enforcing the laws that protect life and property from criminal attacks. Often, the phrase is construed more broadly to extend to enforcing the laws that protect citizens' rights not to be harassed by other citizens or by the police themselves. For the most part, however, society and police understand the phrase to mean effective action in enforcing the *criminal* laws. That is why "professional crime fighting" is, in many ways, more accurate than "professional law enforcement." Professional law enforcement is nonetheless the preferred phrase because it avoids raising the issue of the extent to which the police are obliged to enforce and protect civil liberties as they seek to keep society safe from criminal offenders.

The concept of professional law enforcement worked as a statement of the overall purpose of policing because it defined a sustainable "deal" between the organization and the rest of society, and it directed the manager's attention to the most important societal values that were to be protected or advanced by the organization's operations. The question addressed in the remainder of this chapter is whether this phrase (or its broader formulation) is the best strategic concept to guide the organization and management of police departments in the years ahead or whether more-powerful concepts are now emerging and proving their worth in the hands of innovative police leaders. The techniques to be used in answering this question are the techniques of strategic analysis. The mission of police departments is redefined and is then subjected to the three tests described above.

Strategic analysis and the crime control function

As explained above, all discussions of the functions of police departments begin with the subject of crime control. Indeed, to many people, everything else is not only secondary but also a dangerous and wasteful distraction from the primary business of the police.

There are three reasons that crime control has this status in people's ideas about policing. First, crime control is an urgent and compelling societal task. The belief that the police may succeed in reducing crime is what sustains public support for the police. The threat that crime might become uncontrollable if policing were neglected or changed is frequently used to argue against budget cuts or proposals to change the way police departments operate.[28]

Second, the police seem particularly well suited to dealing with the problem of crime. Both citizens and police see criminal law, with its capacity to deter and incapacitate offenders, as an extremely powerful instrument in dealing with crime, and they see the police as uniquely qualified to invoke that power.[29] The police are set up to be on the lookout for crimes and to respond immediately when summoned by those who witness or are victimized by criminal offenses. They are also specially trained to recognize when an arrest is appropriate or required and when and how to use force to ensure that citizens submit to the orderly process of justice.

The police response to crime is largely reactive, and police executives sense the limits of that approach.

Third, crime control is the function, or mission, that evokes the greatest enthusiasm and commitment from the police themselves. Many officers join police departments to become members of the "thin blue line" that protects decent people from predatory criminals. Their training as recruits emphasizes the skills associated with bringing force to bear on angry, resistant people. The attributes that qualify them for transfer from patrol units to detective bureaus are most closely related to their ability to make arrests. As a result, a culture forms in the police department that sees crime fighting as not only the department's most important function but also its only honorable one.

However, powerful forces have begun to undermine the notion that crime fighting is the only way to use the assets of a police department for the benefit of society. Ironically, the most powerful of these forces leading police executives to rethink their exclusive preoccupation with crime control is the executives' own accumulating knowledge and sophistication about the nature of crime and their growing awareness of the strengths and limitations of current approaches to dealing with it. The most important of the new forces are discussed in the remainder of this section.

Beyond crime control: Crime prevention

The dominant characteristic of the current approach to crime control is that it is "reactive": the police tend to wait until a crime occurs and a call for help is made before they act. This approach has some important advantages. It ensures that the police do not intrude too deeply into citizens' lives and that, when they do intrude, there is an important reason for doing so. In this sense, the reactive approach economizes on the use of state authority.[30]

The police do not rely exclusively on reactive approaches, however. (Alternative approaches are discussed at some length in the chapters on the patrol function, crime prevention, criminal investigations, local drug control, and organized crime.) Patrol operations seek to deter crimes before they happen, as well as to ensure that a car is nearby if a serious crime occurs. If directed patrol operations are well targeted, the likelihood increases that crimes will be deterred. The police have also turned to more proactive efforts with respect to such crimes as narcotics offenses and extortion: to discover offenses and prosecute the offenders, they use informants, electronic surveillance, and undercover operations. They also use these methods to deal with street crimes, such as robbery and burglary.[31]

Still, the police response to crime is largely reactive, and police executives sense the limits of that approach. The reactive approach has always made it difficult to deal effectively with so-called victimless crimes—crimes that do not regularly produce victims or witnesses who are willing and able to mobilize the police and identify the offenders. (Victimless crimes include drug dealing, prostitution, bribery, and gambling.) Increasingly, however, the limitations of the reactive approach have also come to apply to ordinary street offenses, such as robbery and burglary. Such crimes should produce victims and witnesses who request service and offer cooperation, but, in the context of today's cities, they often do not, simply because many victims and witnesses are afraid to come forward.[32]

A frontier that practitioner-researcher teams are exploring is the notion that there might be some "criminogenic" circumstances that breed crime and that could be eliminated.

Another drawback of the reactive approach is that it does not enable the police to prevent specific crimes. Instead of having to wait for a crime to occur before taking action, they would much rather be able to intervene before the crime occurs, thus avoiding another criminal victimization. In a sense, of course, the reactive approach to crime control does have some preventive effects on crime. To the extent that the prospect of arrest, prosecution, and punishment deters criminal offenders, the reactive approach prevents some crimes. Furthermore, although the reactive approach requires that one offense occur—or as many as it takes to bring the culprit to justice—the approach is effective at least in preventing future offenses by that offender. Still, police executives believe there may be a way to prevent crime that is neither as reactive as lying in wait for an offender to inflict harm nor quite as proactive as getting into "social work."

A frontier that practitioner-researcher teams are exploring is the notion that there might be some "criminogenic" circumstances that breed crime and that could be eliminated.[33] A crowded street with cash-and-carry merchants jammed up against check-cashing storefronts, for example, might be a set of conditions that unduly tempt and enable certain people to commit larcenies. A dark hallway in a largely abandoned or fear-ridden housing project might facilitate a rape that otherwise would not occur. Recreational youth activities that end after much of the public transportation has stopped running might create conditions leading to fights among the teenagers or to fear and anger among the citizens living in adjacent neighborhoods.

As police departments are usually organized, however, it is hard to discover and analyze such conditions. The police are organized to notice and respond to incidents, not to notice and respond to the underlying problems or conditions that produce the incidents.[34] If individual street-level police practitioners do notice underlying problems, traditionally they are neither expected to place them on the department's action agenda nor rewarded for trying to do so. Yet police departments are increasingly finding that if they look behind the incidents, they can identify such problems. They also are finding that plausible solutions do not necessarily lie in enforcing the law but often in making such other responses as mobilizing other city agencies to take remedial action, organizing citizens to deal with an underlying problem, or mediating a dispute without recourse to the courts.[35] Indeed, many of the calls the police receive come repeatedly from the same places (see the chapter on the patrol function). If underlying problems can be dealt with, the results might be not only the prevention of crimes likely to emerge from the dangerous circumstances but also the reduction in calls for service.[36] This is crime prevention that is neither social work nor law enforcement as traditionally conceived.

Reducing fear and enhancing security

In pursuing their crime control mission, police executives are also frustrated by finding that citizens' fears are not necessarily tied to the likelihood that they will become victims of crime. Police executives have long assumed that the best way to reduce fear is to reduce criminal victimization. Consequently, they have seen the two objectives as closely aligned. Empirical research shows, however, that people's fears are surprisingly uncorrelated with their real risks of criminal victimization.[37] The fears seem to be triggered much more often by "incivilities," such as noisy teenagers, garbage on the streets, graffiti, and a general atmosphere of decline and indifference, than by actual levels of criminal victimization. In this sense, fear is a separate problem from criminal victimization.

Fear is socially costly.

In addition to being a separate problem, fear is also socially costly. It causes citizens to spend money and time on a variety of security devices. Even worse, it causes them to stay at home, to regard their fellow citizens with suspicion, even to move to another neighborhood. Paradoxically, although such responses may make individual citizens feel more secure, they make the broader society more dangerous, for they tear apart the social networks and informal mechanisms of social control that, in a healthy society, do most of the work of crime control and fear reduction (see the chapter on crime prevention). Such responses may also undermine the community's commitment to public security efforts by shifting resources toward private ones.

The fact that, even with all their precautions, citizens still feel afraid, plus the fact that security is increasingly provided by private individuals and commercial security firms (in wealthy neighborhoods, in places of employment, in public housing complexes), signals an important shortcoming in the traditional approach to both crime control and crime prevention.

As discussed more fully in the chapter on crime prevention, research has shown that there are some things police departments can do to reduce fear. The most important is probably to be as much of a presence in the minds of the citizens as they can be.[38] The method for doing this that is getting popularity is to get out of cars and talk to people. Apparently, the response people get from a 9–1–1 system, with all its capabilities, does not provide a reassuring sense that the police are available. So far, only personal contacts sustained over time seem to produce that effect.

Taken together, all these facts about fear pose an important strategic question for police executives, namely, should fear be acknowledged and responded to as a problem in its own right. A compelling case can be made for seeing fear as an important separate problem. And, indeed, a number of police departments have programs that do independently address the problem of fear. But many police executives have lingering concerns that the resources devoted to dealing with fear might better be spent on reducing real criminal victimization. They sense that stilling fears in a world in which criminal victimization rates have remained unchanged is a cynical and dangerous shell game. A policy maker deciding to forgo spending police resources on fear reduction activities, however, would be well advised to have available some plausible methods of reducing levels of actual criminal victimization and some powerful arguments making the case that citizens' current fears have been grossly overreported.

In sum, thoughtful police executives, taking crime control as their primary if not exclusive mission and rigorously scrutinizing the logic of that enterprise in light of their experience, are beginning to understand that crime will not necessarily yield to current approaches. The reactive strategy does not reach some important crimes effectively, and does not give police broad enough opportunities to prevent crime. Nor does it reduce citizens' fear of crime. These police executives are beginning to think they should describe their mission in terms of crime prevention and fear reduction as well as crime control.

Community roles in crime control

Current thought about the police mission has also been influenced by the discovery that the police are very dependent on the community for success in controlling crime. This discovery began to emerge as the police explored how effective their current programmatic technologies were in controlling crime.

The hardest blows policing had to take in the 1970s and 1980s were research results indicating that the principal programs on which the police were relying to control crime had only a limited effect (see the chapters on evolution, the patrol function, crime prevention, criminal investigations, and local drug control). The Kansas City patrol experiment told police that varying the levels of random patrol had little effect on the levels of crime or fear.[39] Indeed, citizens did not even recognize when patrol had been increased or reduced in their areas. Additional studies in Kansas City and elsewhere suggested that rapid response to calls for service did not necessarily result in increased arrests.[40] A series of studies of the investigative process, for example, found that detectives were crucially dependent not on the rapidity of police response but on the quality of information provided by victims and witnesses: if victims and witnesses could identify the offender, the crime could be solved. If they could not, only rarely could forensic wizardry fill the gap.[41]

Although these studies have been attacked from some quarters on methodological and other grounds, over time they have helped police executives understand why crime and fear could be increasing even as more resources were being devoted to policing. Although many other factors were contributing to increasing crime rates (for example, limited capacities to prosecute, try, and punish those offenders the police caught; a bulge in the proportion of the population in crime-prone ages; and adverse social and economic trends), it becomes increasingly plausible that weaknesses in the police strategy were also at least partly to blame. That was the bad news associated with the studies.

The good news was that the studies pointed to possible improvements in the strategy of policing. Specifically, they reminded police executives of what many already knew intuitively: that the police cannot succeed in their efforts without an effective partnership with the communities they police; indeed, that the community itself is the first line of defense in controlling both crime and fear. Thus, the thin-blue-line metaphor began to yield to the metaphor of a broad blanket of community self-determination.

The police cannot succeed in their efforts without an effective partnership with the communities they police; indeed, the community itself is the first line of defense in controlling both crime and fear.

The community's central role in securing public safety became apparent once one looked closely at how the police strategy really worked. Many offenses occur far from the view of patrolling police officers, visible only to other citizens. Without the help of citizens, the reach of police patrol is thin and superficial. Unless citizens are willing and able to call the police immediately, the rapid response capability that has been so carefully constructed is of little value.[42] If the call is delayed, the police cannot prevent the crime or catch the offender. All they can do is comfort the victim—which is not without value but is hardly the full measure of desired police service. Unless citizens provide information, police can neither solve crimes nor guarantee an effective prosecution. In this sense, vigilant and motivated citizens are an integral part of police operations. If that piece of the machinery is not working well, the return on expensive investments in police capabilities is limited—like a state-of-the-art aircraft with an inadequate flight plan.

The fact that communities are the first line of defense was driven home by an important and unexpected development. In the 1980s citizens who were dissatisfied with public policing turned more and more to private self-defense. During the decade expenditures on private security rose much more rapidly than expenditures on public police. Employment in private security also grew much faster than employment in public police agencies. By 1985 private security guards outnumbered public police two to one.[43] The fact that the public police were implicitly (and sometimes explicitly) competing with private security activities for a share of the security business made many police executives rethink their role and the way they wanted to relate to the communities they policed.

If the police are operationally dependent on assistance from citizens and citizens must inevitably be the first line of defense in controlling crime, the question of what the police must do to mobilize and guide those forces becomes crucial. In the past, the answer was to be responsive to the citizenry by responding quickly to individual calls for service. That did not, however, create effective working partnerships between citizens and the police. There seem to be two reasons for this.

First, it is by no means clear that the police response to individual incidents has been very satisfactory. Citizens call the police because they want help.

Traditionally, police have arrived on the scene conveying a strong sense that they are interested only in serious crimes and that the only question that needs addressing is whether someone has broken a law. If the incident does not involve a crime, or if no arrest seems appropriate, the police have been eager to cut short the encounter with the citizen and get back "in service" to be available to be dispatched to the next call. This response does not necessarily make friends among citizens or increase their enthusiasm for calling the police next time.

Second, responding to occurrences phoned in by individual citizens focuses police attention on incidents rather than on larger and more lasting underlying problems (see the chapters on the patrol function and criminal investigations). It makes the police think of their clients exclusively as individuals rather than as both individuals and members of groups. The focus on incidents and individual victims has made it hard for the police to form partnerships with community groups.[44] Partnerships have also been inhibited by the organizational structure of police departments. The functional organization of departments implies that geographically based community groups—groups whose concerns cross functional boundaries—cannot gain convenient access to departments because few in the department share their particular perspective.

The question thus becomes to what extent the police are prepared to adapt their organization and management to strengthen their relationships with community networks and thereby strengthen their capacity to control crime. This would require deflecting their current preoccupation with crime enough to see the additional concerns that citizens bring them as worthy of consideration. The idea is that one spends time building the relationship so that it is strong when tested in dealing with crime. To try to deal with crime without developing that relationship is fruitless. Yet one cannot build the relationship by concentrating exclusively on crime. Thus, police executives are rethinking the role of the community in crime control efforts and are exploring how police-community relationships might best be developed (see the chapter on crime prevention).

Other roles of the police

The last important factor shaping police views about their mission is the simple fact that citizens call them for many purposes other than crime control. Crime fighting in the form of interrupting crimes in progress or pursuing fleeing offenders occupies far less than 10 percent of a patrol force's time. The bulk of the time is taken up with other matters—giving information to citizens, filling out reports, responding to medical emergencies, and mediating conflicts that have not yet escalated into crimes.

Crime fighting in the form of interrupting crimes in progress or pursuing fleeing offenders occupies far less than 10 percent of a patrol force's time.

When the police talk to communities at meetings with concerned citizens, the citizens are rarely concerned exclusively or even primarily with what the police regard as serious crimes. They are very interested in discussing such matters as disorderly bars, inadequate garbage collection, and poor street lighting. It is not an accident that citizens routinely use the police for help with such problems. Citizens today have many needs and fears, and the police have many capabilities beyond the ability to fight crime that are useful to citizens. Citizens see that the police officer's formal authority can be quite helpful to them in mediating a variety of disputes. They also find the stature and prestige of the officers helpful to them as they seek to organize their own neighborhood activities or to request assistance from other governmental agencies.

An important question is whether these non-crime-related services are beyond the police mandate. Police executives—with the support of the communities they serve—can answer this question in several ways. First, they can decide that these demands are distractions from their essential focus and do what they can to reduce the demands or shift them to other agencies. Second, they can decide that these demands are consistent with their basic crime-fighting mission and are therefore important. Providing these services to citizens might advance crime-fighting objectives by helping to eliminate conditions that can lead to crime and by building the types of relations with the community that help in solving crimes. Third, they can decide that these non-crime-related activities are worth doing in their own right and that the police are uniquely—or at least ideally—positioned to provide them.

Which direction a police executive takes on these questions has important implications for the definitions of the police function or mission; for the enthusiasm that citizens, political and legal authorities, and other influential segments of society feel for their police department; for the kinds of capabilities that must be developed within the department; and for the value of the police to the community. Ultimately, the challenge facing police executives is to find the best use of their department in confronting the urgent problems of their communities.

The accountability of police management

As discussed above, an organization's mission or purpose must meet the three tests of (1) support from public officials, (2) operational feasibility and suitability, and (3) value to the community. Support from public officials—and from the public generally—is a function of police accountability for use of the two main public resources entrusted to them: tax dollars and the authority to bring the power of the state to bear on individual citizens suspected of wrongdoing. (See also the subsection below on accounting internally for the use of authority.)

Recognizing the value of accountability

The current strategy of policing puts heavy emphasis on independence from political interference. Because society has learned to value the impartial administration of justice and the ideal of a professionally competent police department, the police have been insulated from some forms of improper political interference. Chiefs of police have often been protected from arbitrary firing by special civil service rules.[45] In many departments, a host of other appointments and promotions are strictly regulated by civil service rules. Police departments have fought to assign patrol resources on the basis of need rather than political power (see the chapter on the evolution of contemporary policing). Mayors and council members are frequently reluctant to intervene publicly in police affairs lest they be accused of improper political interference.[46]

The acknowledged importance of maintaining police independence from improper political interference, however, has misled some police executives (and even more police officers) into believing that the police are autonomous and that any kind of political oversight is improper. In their view, they should be allowed to enforce the law in ways they see fit, and elected officials and neighborhood associations should not attempt to influence police department operations.

The reality is that political interference and political oversight are quite distinct and that the police, like all public institutions, must remain accountable to both citizens (through their elected representatives) and the law. As discussed in the chapter on the governmental setting, the police are broadly accountable to the chief executive of the local government for which they work. They are accountable to special oversight agencies, such as civil service commissions and budget agencies. They are accountable to citizens through media coverage of their activities. And they are accountable to courts—through the courts' responses to the criminal cases they bring against criminal defendants and the civil suits filed by citizens against the police for improper conduct.

Police accountability to these agencies, to the media and the citizenry at large, and to the courts is required morally and legally. It is also necessary in practice. However much the police complain about all these forms of oversight, the practical reality is that any of the overseers can rise up in indignation at the police and force them to change their operations. To put fully into perspective the sometimes difficult position in which police administrators find themselves, it should be observed that the rank and file likewise has powerful capacities to rise up in indignation, with equally profound implications for police policy. Moreover, policing is one of the few occupations in which the individual first-line worker possesses substantial de facto power, through egregious misconduct, to "fire" his or her boss (to calm a public that is outraged by some flagrant violation of policy, the chief may—rightly or wrongly—be offered up as sacrificial lamb).

The police are accountable to public officials and the public generally for use of the two main public resources entrusted to them: tax dollars and the authority to bring the power of the state to bear on individual citizens suspected of wrongdoing.

The police have sought to protect their autonomy and limit outside intrusions by seeking to narrow their accountability and establish it on their own terms.[47] In defining their mission as professional law enforcement and in seeing their main (or only) function as effective crime fighting, they have implicitly defined the dimensions of their accountability. Committing themselves to professionalism, they have agreed to be accountable for the qualifications of their officers, the training they provide, and the skill officers show in the field. Embracing the goal of crime control and offering a broad crime-fighting service to the public, they have, at least partly, accepted responsibility for levels of crime, invited individual citizens to make claims on them, and made themselves accountable for the rapidity and comprehensiveness of their responses to calls for service. To the extent that the police perform well in training their officers, fighting crime, and responding to calls, of course, their credibility, autonomy, and legitimacy increase. They may even be able to use successful performance in these domains as proof against criticism and intrusions when an inevitable mistake occurs (see the chapter on performance measurement).

Policing is one of the few occupations in which the individual first-line worker possesses substantial de facto power, through egregious misconduct, to "fire" his or her boss.

By seeking to define their accountability in this way, however, police ignore a central unresolved tension at the core of their relations with society (in all its multiplicity and complexity): the tension between crime fighting and professional crime fighting.

When citizens embrace the police as crime fighters, they focus on results and don't think of the means apart from the results. They like to see the bad guys behind bars—so they admire the toughness, courage, and technical skills the police use to capture dangerous criminals. They also tend to be impatient with legal rulings that "handcuff" the police, and they tend to regard civil suits against the police as the product of money-hungry lawyers and misguided agitators, not police misconduct. This perspective dominates the public view of policing. It dominates even more the police view of policing. In both cases, it is fed by Hollywood portraits of street cops who exalt ends over means.

At times, however, citizens see the police differently. When the police accidentally shoot an unarmed teenager, break into a person's home without a warrant, or are revealed to be corrupt, citizens begin to see the police as criminals. Instead of admiring the police capacity to lock up bad guys, citizens see the police as reckless abusers of the power that was entrusted to them. They demand a strict accounting.

To a degree, citizens' indignation is justified. Part of the ideal of police professionalism is that the police will use their powers in a disciplined, legal way. That has been part of the promise the police have made to society since the 1970s. This code of professionalism has been part of the unwritten social contract by which the police have sought and gained some degree of autonomy from political oversight.

From the police perspective, however, public indignation inevitably feels like betrayal. After all, up until the events that trigger the indignation, the police feel they are being encouraged to be tough. They think they have a deal with the public that they will be indulged a little in their efforts to control crime. That deal holds up only until the police make their first bad public mistake. Then a backlash occurs. In the backlash, individual officers are made scapegoats, careers are sacrificed, and department morale collapses.

The alternative to going through these cycles of limited and then broader accountability is for the police and the public to work harder at resolving the tension between effectiveness in crime fighting on the one hand and the disciplined, constitutional use of public authority by professional crime fighters on the other. After all, among the laws that it is most important to enforce are those regulating the police. A professional law enforcement agency accepts this regulation as an important goal, not just as a troubling constraint. It works to remind the public of the police's own interest in a disciplined police force, and it does so even, perhaps especially, at times when the citizens wish to indulge the police to ensure greater effectiveness in crime control. In short, professionalism calls on the police to stand for the values of fair and impartial law enforcement rather than ruthless crime fighting and vengeance.[48] That is a difficult thing to stand for if society is only too ready to accept less, but a broader sense of police mission—of the values that police should stand for in the community—is the key first step in giving police accountability a firmer foundation.

Structuring accountability relationships

The second step in firmly grounding police accountability is being clear about exactly how the police will structure their continuing relationships with those to whom they are accountable—local elected and appointed officials, the public in general, the citizens who call for assistance, and the criminal justice system. Partly because the police have sought to insulate themselves from improper political interference, these relationships are fragile, shifting, and episodic.

There are a variety of reporting relationships between the police chief and an elected or appointed executive. In some cities, for example, the chief reports directly to the city manager or mayor. In others the reporting relationship is through a public safety director, assistant city manager, or commissioner. In all cases the police are linked to the political authority largely through budget submissions and annual reports (see also the chapter on the governmental setting). The principal statistical measures used in those reports to evaluate police needs and accomplishments are statistics on crime rates, clearance rates, and response times (see a later section of this chapter, and see the chapter on performance measurement).[49]

Through media coverage of their activities, the police are also held directly accountable to the public. Media coverage, however, tends to focus principally on police performance in solving notorious cases or dealing with instances of officer misconduct. Rarely do the media focus on broader issues of police performance, such as the allocation of resources or policy on how calls for service are prioritized for response.[50]

In an important sense, police are also accountable to the citizens who call them for assistance. To begin with, the speed of their response to these calls traditionally has been one of the key measures of police performance (see the chapter on performance measurement). Furthermore, what they do at the scene of the call is primarily determined by whether or not a law has been violated and by the citizen's willingness to file charges.[51] And it is the concrete experience of the citizen's encounter with the police—and rumors in the neighborhood about the encounter—that provides the basis for the broad public view of the police department.

Finally, police are held accountable to the courts and other elements of the criminal justice system. Prosecutors can decide to process police cases or to reject them.[52] They can comment to the media and to other professional associations about police performance. Judges may hold the police accountable for their actions through evidentiary rulings in criminal cases and through decisions in civil liability cases.[53]

A review of the current structure of accountability reveals two important characteristics. The first is that the structure involves either very broad, overall patterns of police conduct or very specific incidents. Budgets, annual reports, and professional gossip about the police all tend to be about the overall performance of the department. Newspaper stories and civil suits focus on individual incidents. Such incidents may be seen as indicative of broader features of police performance, and that may be what gives them power, but the essential focus is on the individual incident. And the extent to which incidents are representative is often discussed but rarely analyzed. Thus, the specific incident often assumes great importance—without necessarily being an indicator of larger patterns.

The second characteristic of the current structure of accountability is that the most powerful pressures on the police are those associated with the individual incidents. The pressures on the police to perform well on average and across the board are, in general, quite weak. Political authority does not demand this. Oversight of the police budget imposes some financial discipline but does not lead to demands for gains in productivity or for innovations in policing. As for citizen demands for overall improvements in policing, they are quite rare. When they are made, typically they come from either established watchdog groups (crime commissions and other "good-government" groups) or neighborhood-based grass-roots organizations (see the chapter on crime prevention). As a result, most departments are organized to avoid individual mistakes and to handle single incidents well rather than to sustain broad improvements or initiate experiments in better ways of policing.

Over the years alternative mechanisms of accountability have been proposed and implemented with the idea of giving citizens or community groups more of a voice in calling for across-the-board improvements. Civilian review boards represent one commonly proposed mechanism for improving police accountability, but they are handicapped by their narrow focus on incidents of police misconduct and by the resulting police hostility toward them.[54] Some communities have created police commissions of various forms. Some of these have been temporary, and some permanent; some have been established by law, others by more informal means; some exist for limited purposes, such as appointing a chief, whereas others have broader, more continuing powers and responsibilities—at least on paper. The influence of these commissions over police operations depends to a large degree on their responsibilities, the stature of their members, their history, their specific written powers, and the support offered at any particular moment by the elected and appointed leadership of the municipality.

An important innovation in the structure of accountability is the growing tendency of the police to work with community groups (see the chapter on crime prevention). Sometimes the police create these groups as a way of dealing with neighborhood crime problems. At other times they meet regularly with existing groups. Community groups see and are concerned about problems that neither local officials nor individual citizens see as clearly. These groups also bring different capacities for acting in support of the police than are available at city- or county-wide or individual levels.

Some observers worry that attempting to improve accountability by encouraging police responsiveness to the concerns of groups at the neighborhood level will create problems. They fear the police may lose some of their autonomy and become subject to the parochial interests and needs of some elements of the community at the expense of others. One early police advocate of community involvement cautioned about the risks of "a blind pilgrimage to the temples of community control."[55] Of particular concern to some is the possibility that wealthy and well-organized communities will be able to demand more service from the police than poor and disorganized ones.[56] Although legitimate, this concern should not separate police from neighborhood groups. After all, the skills police executives need in order to forge productive community partnerships include skills in promoting the professional development and integrity of their organization without yielding to local groups their responsibilities for managing the resources entrusted to police. Police are obligated to respond on the basis of need rather than political clout or ability to pay. And they are obligated to protect the rights of the minority as well as the safety of the majority.

Police organizations must work hard to cultivate a constituency by expressing and acting on a commitment to important values.

Strong mechanisms of external accountability—accountability to those who look at across-the-board performance, gains in productivity, and innovative policing, not just at isolated incidents—are a key to public support. Police organizations must work hard to cultivate a constituency by expressing and acting on a commitment to important values.

Strong external accountability is also an important instrument of internal police leadership. This strikes many as a paradox. It seems as if police leaders could be strong only if they were independent of outside accountability, if their legitimacy depended only on their own expertise and vision. Past reality, however, is that when the police were separated from politics, police leaders did not become independent. They simply became more dependent on the most powerful group that was still interested in and capable of influencing police operations, namely, police officers themselves.

Without external accountability, police executives have little leverage over their own organizations. Thus, one of the important ways police leaders can bolster their leadership is to create and keep vital their relationship of accountability with the broader public.[57] That is one of the important lessons that has been learned by those who sought to professionalize the police and eliminate corruption and who are now trying to steer the police toward adopting a strategy of community policing. Without public demands for less corruption or improved policing—demands stimulated through external accountability—police executives are powerless to lead.

Internal organization and control

Once departmental values (or goals) and appropriate external accountability relations have been established, police executives must turn to organizing, staffing, and controlling police operations. The reason for resolving broad questions of organizational strategy before addressing these technical aspects of management is that decisions about the technical matters must be made to serve the strategy. All too often, however, police managers tinker with organizational structure and personnel systems without being able to relate their decisions to the purposes of the organization (see the chapter on human resources).

All too often police managers tinker with organizational structure and personnel systems without being able to relate their decisions to the purposes of the organization.

Although a police executive must continually push for a vision of what ought to be, he or she must also focus on what the organization can realistically accomplish. What can be realistically accomplished depends on how the instruments of managerial influence—namely, organizing, staffing, and controlling—are used to shape the organization's operations and capabilities. This section focuses on how those instruments can be used to create police departments capable of pursuing the broad goals described above. This section also discusses—as an extension of operational capability—how a department's value to society is assessed.

Organizing

Organizing involves structuring roles and reporting relationships within an organization.[58] The structure thus created is not an end in itself, but a means to an end. It must be appropriate to the task of the organization and the available personnel and other resources. Basically, there are three ways of structuring the work of an organization, and the decision about which way or ways to choose requires an understanding of the distinctions among line, staff, and support functions. It also requires addressing the issue of number of levels and degree of centralization.

Functional, programmatic, and geographical organization Generally speaking, the work of an organization can be structured in three ways: by function, by product or program, and by geographical area.

1. In functional organization (the most common type), work is divided on the basis of the kind of work it is—for example, administration, patrol, or investigations.
2. In programmatic organization, work is organized on the basis of its products of programs—which, in the case of police departments, might be kinds of crime (juvenile delinquency, narcotics, robbery, sex crimes).
3. In geographical organization, the work is assigned by area—a Main Street Division, a Lakeside Division, and so on.

Most organizations are hybrids in that they use all three types of structural units. Consequently, in characterizing a given organizational structure as functional, programmatic, or geographical, one is usually describing the dominant logic in the organization, the logic that is used to structure the organization at the highest level. In this sense, most police departments are organized *functionally* rather than programmatically or geographically. The divisions at the top of the organization typically reflect the major police functions.[59] Most police departments, however, also have some units that are defined in nonfunctional terms. Special units are often created to deal with particular kinds of crimes, and generally patrol is subdivided into geographical units. The investigations unit—a functional division—may be subdivided into units that deal with particular kinds of crime or are defined by geographical area.

Structuring police departments functionally has some important strengths. It can enable officers to develop expertise in their functional domain. It also can prevent special interest groups organized around geographical areas or specific kinds of crimes from exercising undue influence over police operations. Indeed, the decision during the 1960s to shift from a geographical structure of precinct commands to a functional structure was an important device used to break the power of geographically organized political machines.

But the functional structure also has some important weaknesses. It can promote parochialism and competition within the organization. It can make coordination across functional lines difficult. It can create artificial boundaries between divisions (if, for example, no investigative work can be done by the patrol unit). It can encourage managers to think of themselves as technical experts rather than as people whose special skills lie in getting others to work together and develop their own technical skills. Most important, it can mean that the organization often frustrates and fails to garner the support of neighborhood groups because no one short of the chief of police can deal with a problem that requires a multifunctional response.

Line, staff, and support functions   Designing a suitable organizational structure for a police department also requires an understanding of the distinctions among line, staff, and support functions:

1. Line functions are those that work directly on achieving the department's objectives. The patrol division, the detective bureau, and the traffic division are all line functions.
2. Staff functions are those that assist top management in directing the organization and in accounting for the organization's activities. The budget unit, the planning and evaluation unit, and legal counsel are all staff functions.
3. Support functions are those that provide services to the entire organization and that cut across the functional, programmatic, and geographical lines. Examples include personnel, vehicle maintenance, and procurement activities.[60]

A frequent problem in police organizations is that support functions or staff functions are placed within a single line unit. It is not unusual, for example, to find the records section (a support function) reporting to the commander of investigations (a line function). This would make some sense if detectives were the primary contributors to and users of records. But they are not—and other units may find it more difficult than necessary to gain access to the information and may be more reluctant than they should be to contribute to it. Not having the records section as a separate unit serving all of the organization's line operations means that attempts to get other units to produce better information for the records section or to use the records in planning their activities, will be less successful than might otherwise be the case.

Number of levels and degree of centralization   Two other crucial issues that must be addressed in organizing a police department are the number of levels in the organization and the degree of centralization that is desirable. In the past, police departments have been organized like the military—with unified command authority, strict hierarchies, and many organizational levels. One important characteristic of the military structure is that any one manager or supervisor has a relatively narrow span of control—that is, he or she oversees relatively few subordinates. The aims of such organizational structures are essentially to (1) ensure effective discipline and control through very close supervision; (2) pinpoint accountability for command decisions; and (3) enable the department to form into operational units of varying size ranging from the individual officer to the entire organization.

The commitment to unified command, strict hierarchy, and many levels tends to produce centralized decision making.

The commitment to unified command, strict hierarchy, and many levels tends to produce centralized decision making—at least formal decision making—in police organizations. This is partly because of the symbolism of tight control and command. Symbolically, each officer embodies the will of the chief, whose directives about how officers should behave are laid down in the organization's manual of policies and procedures and enforced by the ranks of mid-level managers. The department behaves in a uniform and correct manner and thereby reassures citizens that the law is applied equally and properly in individual cases.

Centralized control tends to create very steep vertical organizations with many levels of middle managers. It requires that officers look to higher levels of the organization for authorization to act. And those at higher levels are required to take responsibility for the actions of subordinates. It is for this reason that, as suggested earlier, the police officer can "fire" his or her boss through misconduct. Because there are a great many middle managers who conceive of their jobs as controlling the conduct of subordinates, there is always someone of higher rank with whom lower-level officers may consult. Moreover, such consultation will absolve the subordinates of any blame if the action goes sour. These arrangements tend to push formal decision making to the top in police organizations.

In a decentralized organization, individuals have much greater freedom to make decisions about what work should be done to contribute to the overall objectives of the organization and about how it should be done.

The opposite of centralization—decentralization—is a concept often misunderstood in a police organization. For some, decentralization means having substations and ministations in which patrol officers and investigators work. The existence of such facilities is often a basis for describing the department as "decentralized." In this chapter, though, a decentralized organization is defined as one in which initiative, decisions, and responsibility rest at the lowest possible level. In a decentralized organization, individuals have much greater freedom to make decisions about what work should be done to contribute to the overall objectives of the organizations and about how it should be done.

Decentralization has essentially three advantages. First, it frees higher-level managers from having to spend all their time and intellectual energy on pressing operational matters. It enables them to concentrate on strategies that will improve the organization's capabilities to perform in the future. Second, it improves operational decisions because those decisions are more timely and are made by people who are closer to the facts of the situation. Third, by pushing responsibility and initiative downward in the organization, decentralization challenges more people to be creative and useful workers. That generally results in higher job satisfaction, as well as a greater opportunity for managers to spot talent in the organization. To be sure, challenging people in this way makes it possible to identify personnel who, at least currently, lack the judgment that would justify managers' entrusting them with the power of the state.

Centralization is currently the dominant way of structuring decision making in police organizations, but it has several drawbacks. The principal one is that the day-to-day work of the police does not lend itself to this structure. Police officers have a wide range of discretion in handling situations.[61] Police officers and investigators operating on the street confront many nonroutine situations. They must decide largely on their own whether to arrest and whether to use force. The situations they confront often develop so quickly that they cannot ask in advance for advice or approval. Some situations are so nearly unique that they are not covered by existing policies and procedures, and officers must handle them using a great deal of informal discretion. In reality, then, the quality of policing generally depends on the initiative, values, and discretion of the officers rather than on the completeness of the policies and procedures manual and the closeness with which officers are supervised. A centralized, hierarchical police organization tends to discourage initiative and discretion in officers rather than guiding and harnessing these qualities.

A second drawback of centralization is that it works against police aspirations for professional status. The essence of being a professional is that one can be trusted to exercise discretion for the benefit of society on the basis of one's accumulated expertise and commitment to the values that guide the profession. Professionals are not seen as requiring close supervision. As a result, the institutions in which they serve have very few organizational levels. Professionals are held accountable through peer evaluations of their performance rather than through close supervision and prior authorization for their actions.

A third disadvantage of centralization is simply that it tends to make rising through the ranks the most important means of getting ahead in the organization. This can be valuable if mid-level managers find useful ways to contribute to the performance of the organization. It can be disastrous if the managerial ranks simply provide a refuge for officers who wish to escape the rigors of operating as the work force of the organization and who find no way to make important contributions as managers.

One can imagine a department in which lieutenants become mid-level managers not simply by dutifully writing out the shift schedule and staffing the station house but by proposing tactical solutions to problems, devising innovative police operations, or working with community groups to identify their priorities. One can imagine sergeants assuming primary responsibility for training and developing officers and coaching them on how to improve their performance, rather than overseeing the officers' activities and replacing their subordinates' expertise with their own. But in today's police organizations, mid-level managers seldom take on these kinds of responsibilities. In fact, with or without a redefinition of the role of sergeants and lieutenants, some observers question whether police departments need as many mid-level managers as most of them now have.

Reducing the number of levels and replacing the traditional centralized structure with a more decentralized one would leave two important problems unresolved, however. First, the department would have to develop other career paths through the organization (other than up through rank structures) to maintain the commitment and motivation of officers during the course of their careers. Second, the department would have to find a way to assure citizens that officers remain under control and that their actions are guided by the public values now formalized in policies and procedures. The section below on staffing ends by suggesting a solution to the issue of career path, and the section on controlling ends by suggesting alternatives to close operational supervision as a way to maintain the accountability of officers.

Staffing

Staffing is a critically important and complex function of police management. Staffing responsibilities encompass a range of activities—human resource planning, recruitment, selection, training, development, evaluation, and promotion[62]— all of which are discussed at greater length in the chapters on human resources and performance measurement. Each aspect of the staffing process presents challenges and opportunities for the police manager.

Human resource planning The first step in the staffing process is human resource planning. It involves setting out the framework for how future personnel needs will be met. It requires managers to determine how many employees are needed, when, and with what skills and experience. A human resource plan does not determine the number of positions needed to achieve organizational goals. Rather, it is a way for managers to use the department's resource allocation plan plus knowledge of the department's turnover and projected growth rates to develop a replacement chart that guides recruitment efforts. The human resource plan can help managers solve the age-old problem departments have in reducing the time associated with filling vacant positions. In most communities it takes a minimum of two years to fill a position with an officer functioning reasonably well on the street. A well thought out human resource plan will help reduce the effect of this process because it will provide the basis for hiring and training cycles that allow departments to stay within their personnel budgets.

Recruitment and selection Recruitment and selection have been particularly difficult for police departments for several reasons. In the first place, in many departments the police leadership itself plays a minor role in recruitment and selection, with the bulk of the work and decisions in the hands of a city or county personnel department. Moreover, regardless of who has primary responsibility for recruitment and selection, it can be difficult to find suitable candidates. On average, police agencies screen about ten candidates for every one who is hired, and many police departments are finding it difficult to fill vacant positions. Although this ratio is often considered an indicator of stringent employment standards, it may also reflect poor recruiting practices; that is, it may indicate that the department is failing to identify the strongest possible candidates. Drug abuse, too, is part of the problem. Departments across the nation indicate that as many as three-quarters of their applicants have experimented with drugs,[63] and many of these applicants are rejected. Moreover, population projections for the 1990s point to a shrinking of the age group from which the police generally recruit.[64]

Recruitment and selection are further complicated by police desires to increase entry-level educational standards and to meet affirmative action goals. Progress has been made in both areas. A 1988 study, for example, indicates that the educational level of the police increased from an average of 12.4 years in 1967 to 14 years in 1988.[65] The study also indicates growth in the number of women and minorities in policing, although not at the upper levels of most police departments. In an effort to increase their educational requirements without negatively affecting recruiting goals, some departments have developed special programs to recruit in high schools, including offering part-time jobs and tuition for students to attend community colleges after graduation. The idea is to develop in young people an interest in policing and to channel that interest before the students leave high school or develop other occupational interests.

Training and development of operational personnel   After a department has hired new officers, it must train them to carry out their responsibilities (see the chapter on human resources). One of the greatest investments a police department makes in new officers is their entry-level training, which usually begins with from three to six months of classroom training and is followed by from one to three months of field training. By the time an individual has completed classroom and field training and a probationary period, the department has worked with that person for about two years.

The costs of this training process are very high, and departments have begun to seek alternatives that are less expensive but will not increase their liability for failure to train properly. Minnesota, for example, has an innovative plan requiring that an officer be certified by the state before being employed.[66] Certification requires, among other things, that applicants complete most of their police training in state-supported schools at their own expense. Although the police department must still orient new officers to its policies, procedures, and customs, the cost is much lower than it was before. In Florida, individuals may attend state-certified training academies on their own under sponsorship of a police department. This procedure enables applicants to increase their employability and also reduces the department's costs. These programs are still exceptions to the norm, but they show considerable promise as low-cost alternatives to more traditional police practices.

Following the probationary period, police departments must continue to provide employees with opportunities for training and development so they can hone their skills in their current job and prepare themselves for promotion. Formal in-service training is one way of doing that, and some states require a specific number of hours for individuals to maintain certification. This training is of critical importance to the department and the community. It should be conducted at least annually on the basis of an analysis of training needs. Some departments routinely conduct training needs assessments. These assessments use a variety of informational analyses and surveys of personnel. The analysis of training needs enables a department to structure its training program to address specific organizational needs. The analysis is also useful to executives when they must make decisions about sending employees to training programs outside the department.

Executive and management development   One area that has been neglected in many departments is the development of supervisory and managerial personnel. The reasons for this vary, but most police executives would point to the cost of formal programs and the limited number of programs that have a police focus. Nevertheless, police departments do have opportunities both on and off the job for developing personnel in supervisory and managerial positions.

On the job, personnel can be developed in at least four ways. Perhaps the most effective way is through coaching. Coaching is day-to-day support and encouragement of employees by the supervisor to help them learn and develop to the best of their abilities. Under supervision, aspiring managers deal with supervisory and management problems in a real-life setting. A police department that makes conscious use of coaching can make great strides in developing a cadre of competent supervisors and managers. This method requires careful evaluation of potential coaches, and personnel in need of development must be carefully matched with those most capable of providing it. If a formal coaching program is viewed in the same light as a field training program, it may require training for the coaches.

The second method of on-the-job development is job rotation. This involves regularly moving supervisory and managerial personnel into different types of assignments so they can learn about various aspects of the organization. The third method is to designate certain staff positions as training positions. Some departments use aides to the chief or senior commanders in this way. The fourth method is planned work activity. This involves assigning individuals to a task force, committee, or major project. For example, an individual could be given the responsibility of managing the department's effort to become nationally accredited.[67] Many individuals have been promoted as a result of that kind of experience, and, in some cases, the experience has served as a springboard to the position of police chief.

Off-the-job opportunities for supervisory and managerial development range from enrollment in graduate degree programs offered at a local college or university to attendance at nationally recognized law enforcement programs. The FBI sponsors a number of national programs—the National Academy, the Law Enforcement Executive Development Seminar, and the National Executive Institute. Other national programs are offered by the Southern Police Institute, the Southwestern Law Enforcement Institute, and Northwestern University. The Police Executive Research Forum has sponsored the Senior Management Institute for Police since 1981. This three-week program is conducted in conjunction with faculty from the John F. Kennedy School of Government at Harvard University. All these programs—and others noted in the chapter on external resources—make a contribution, but they cannot fully meet the national demand for high-quality supervisory and managerial training.

Police departments continue to struggle with basic decisions on what aspects of performance to measure, and how.

This has led to the development of programs at the state level. One of the best known is the California Command College. Officers must participate in a rigorous selection process to attend. The two-year course combines classroom and field work with independent research on some aspect of policing and the future. Other state-level programs are being developed around the country—notably in Ohio and Florida.

Evaluation An important aspect of the staff development process is the use of performance evaluation (see the chapters on human resources and performance measurement). Police departments continue to struggle with basic decisions on what aspects of performance to measure, and how. This problem exists at all levels of the policing hierarchy. At both lower and higher levels the current emphasis is on "bean counting." At the lower levels, this means emphasizing the number of arrests, tickets written, and calls answered. Usually there is little regard for whether the number of those activities has anything to do with solving the problems they represent. At higher levels of the organization, the bean counting continues as managers and mayors count reported crime, response time, arrests, and crime clearances. As discussed more fully in other chapters, this preoccupation with crime-related statistics ignores major aspects of the police workload. Efforts to resolve this dilemma have met with minimal success. Police supervisors and managers—together with mayors, appointed managers, elected councils, chambers of commerce, and the media— are part of the problem and, potentially, part of the solution. Bean counting has its place in policing, but the emphasis has shifted to developing and using other measures that more accurately reflect the effectiveness and importance of what police do at all levels of the organization.

Promotion   The final aspect of staffing to be addressed here is promotion (for elaboration, see the chapter on human resources). Promotional decisions are of critical importance to any organization, and police departments are no exception. Some changes have been made in the promotional processes police use, but standardized written tests and interviews continue to be the most common methods of developing lists of candidates. Although tests and interviews are useful in measuring a candidate's knowledge, they are limited when it comes to predicting how that knowledge will be applied on the job. Moreover, the standard approaches to developing the promotional lists generally do not consider past performance (unless the individual has made a serious mistake)—yet past performance is frequently the best predictor of future performance. Many departments are using assessment centers, which are specially developed simulations designed to evaluate performance in job-related situations. This method, too, has its limitations, but if properly used it allows a much more in-depth evaluation of a candidate's potential.

Besides the process by which police make promotional decisions, two fundamental issues need to receive much more consideration by the police. The first has to do with a system that essentially forces officers to seek promotion to enhance both their financial condition and their status. As the pressure to do more with less continues, it will be important for the police to develop ways for officers to remain on the street or in an investigative capacity without sacrificing their ability to increase their status and salary (see the sidebar on "master" police officers in the chapter on human resources).

Second is the issue of lateral entry. Few police departments consider candidates from outside for filling vacancies in the sworn supervisory and management ranks. Although there is great resistance to the concept of lateral entry and some inherent practical problems (for example, pensions, reduced motivation for lower-ranking officers to develop managerial skills), this lack of mobility limits the development of individual officers and the department as a whole. The best witnesses on this point are the relatively small number of police leaders who have had the opportunity during their careers to participate in an executive exchange program, in which a department loans one or more key managers to a department in another community for a period of weeks or months. Almost invariably, the participating managers describe this experience as one of the high points of their executive development. For the most part, the only way to be hired in a sworn position is to enter at the bottom or at the top. The result is that police departments often end up filling key positions with the best they have, not necessaraily with the best they can get. In large departments, it is often an open question whether leaders are even aware of the best they have for particular assignments. In some states the opportunity for lateral entry is greater because of statewide pension systems and training programs, but even in those states little lateral movement between police departments actually takes place.

Controlling

The third key managerial function that police managers must perform, after organizing and staffing, is controlling the resources and operations of the department and accounting to external authorities for the financial costs and results of their efforts. Financial accounting includes assessing the police value to the community. Finally, the resources the police are responsible for controlling are not only monies but also the power to compel.

The principal mechanisms for controlling the organization's financial resources are the budget and the cost accounting system. The budget sets out a planned use of expenditures for the organization and is approved annually by higher political authority. The cost accounting system measures the flow of expenditures through the organization and attributes them to particular activities. Police executives must address three major issues associated with financial control systems: (1) how to develop the budget; (2) how to use the budget to reflect not only operational expenditures but also key investments needed to improve the organization's future performance; and (3) how to measure organizational activities and accomplishments.

Developing the budget In most police departments, budgets are prepared by civilians in administrative support units. The principal line commanders of the organization are not directly involved. Often, even the chief executive is not significantly involved. To the extent that police managers are involved in the process, they focus their attention on staffing levels in the units for which they are responsible. This kind of budgeting system makes sense in an organization that thinks about its activities in terms of staffing up existing organizational units, but it does not make sense in an organization that is forward thinking and that identifies problems to be resolved.

To the extent that new projects propose solutions to problems that the police department's overseers consider important they may garner additional resources for the police.

In a department that focuses on identifying and solving problems for the community, managers must constantly be thinking about specific initiatives to be undertaken, as well as about filling existing posts and assignments. Ideas about what problems to address should be reflected in budgeting decisions. Proposed projects may become contenders for the organization's resources— or, to the extent that new projects propose solutions to problems that the police department's overseers consider important, they may garner additional resources for the police. In a problem-oriented department, then, the budgeting process will be more participatory and bottom-up than it is in a traditional department (see the chapters on the patrol function, criminal investigations, and local drug control).

Investing in organizational capability Although most local governments budget for new police facilities and other capital investments, they sometimes fail to recognize another kind of expenditure that is crucially important in organizations that are labor intensive rather than capital intensive and that are going through periods of innovation. These are investments in organizational capabilities. Such investments do not look like capital expenditures because they do not involve bricks and mortar or even very large amounts of money. They are investments, however, because they are expenditures whose value will be realized in the improved future performance of the organization. Such expenditures could include the specialized training required to reorient a department from one kind of policing to another, the redesign of computer-aided dispatching systems to give as much emphasis to maintaining beat integrity as to minimizing response times, and the documentation of experimental approaches to commonly encountered police problems, such as domestic disputes (see the chapter on research and planning).

Because budgeting procedures make these kinds of expenditures difficult to identify, managers and overseers cannot really track the investment as a police department improves its operational capabilities. There is no routine way to observe the way a police department operates, manage it, or plead for funds to change it (see the discussion of resource generation in the chapter on external resources). The traditional police department budget reinforces the false assumption not only that the most effective programmatic and technological ways of achieving goals are well known but also that they are already incorporated in police department operations.

Measuring results   Current budgeting and cost accounting systems are also relatively weak in measuring the results of the police department's operations and attributing costs correctly to the different results. Consequently, it is hard for police executives and their overseers to determine the true value of police efforts for the citizenry and to pinpoint the activities that were particularly valuable.

As noted earlier, police departments generally measure their results in terms of crime-related statistics and response times. Some of these measures are relevant to judging effectivness because they are related to the desired *outcomes* of public policing (for example, the measured levels of reported crime). Others are relevant to judging efficiency because they measure only the organization's *outputs* (for example, arrests and response rates). Some analysts, however, make a strong argument for relying only on outcome measures, such as reduced crime, to assess the value of police departments. They argue that it is these anticipated results that define the value of the department and that only the demonstration of such results can justify continued expenditures on police departments.[68]

From a managerial perspective, however, such outcome measures have some important disadvantages. It is possible, for example, that the value of a police department for the citizens of the community is not well represented by the impact of the police department on levels of crime. Other outcome

---

Experimental police district   The Madison, Wisconsin, police department created an experimental police district (EPD) as a field laboratory to test new models of leadership and service improvement similar to those being used in the private sector.

The department established four measures to evaluate expected outcomes: crime statistics, pre-implementation customer research, incident-based customer surveys, and attitudes of the forty members working in the district.

From 1987 to 1989 the EPD increased traffic enforcement (a strong neighborhood concern) by 88 percent, while enforcement in other city districts remained the same. The EPD experienced a significant decrease in home burglaries (28 percent) between 1986 and 1989, while burglaries in the rest of the city increased 15 percent.

Although violent crime increased 5 percent during these years, the overall rate for the city was 13 percent.

Information on quality of service is gathered by an incident-based customer survey and then returned to the officer for direct feedback (see the chapter on performance measurement). A comparison revealed that EPD citizen customers (including arrested persons) provided significantly higher ratings than those in other districts.

When officers compare their experience in the EPD with previous assignments through internal surveys, they consistently report higher job satisfaction levels, greater belief that leaders are making positive efforts to improve work systems, increased perception of crime solving effectiveness, and improved interaction and feedback with supervisors.

measures may be more relevant. For instance, it might be as important that the police reduce fear, reduce the amount of money invested in private security, help improve self-defense, and respond competently to the wide variety of social and medical emergencies that occur within the community. There are some who see the police as an important health-protecting agency, for example, because they are the ones who can do something to prevent the things that kill people at an early age—driving recklessly, using alcohol, taking drugs, and engaging in gang violence.[69]

Even if one has chosen proper outcome measures, there is an enormous problem in measuring the police contribution to the results. In the case of levels of crime, for example, not only are there technical problems in measuring these levels and their changes from year to year,[70] but it is also difficult to attribute changes in crime levels to the police because many other things affect crime. It is also expensive to collect the data and do the analyses that measure the impact of police agencies on criminal victimization. As a result, the measurements are not done often.

These observations suggest that outcome measurement alone cannot be the managerial answer to assessing the value of police operations. The measurement of the quantity and quality of outputs, such as clearances, arrest rates, and response times, has some important advantages. These outputs can be easily collected and therefore measured often. They can be measured for many subordinate units, and they can be directly attributed to the actions of particular managers in police departments. These features make output measures much more managerially valuable than outcome measures, for they can be tied directly to a system of managerial accountability and control.

Output measures have two key weaknesses, however. The first is that, like outcome measures, they do not directly measure the value of the police. They may be related to the ultimate purposes of the organization, but if so, they are connected to the value of policing through a theory about the overall purposes of the police and the most effective means for achieving those purposes. For example, clearances and arrests, followed by successful prosecutions, are important in crime fighting (an overall purpose) because we believe that crime can be effectively controlled by deterring and incapacitating criminal offenders (the most effective means). If that theory is correct, then measuring arrests and successful prosecutions is almost as good as measuring direct reductions in crime. If, however, that theory is wrong, or if its validity is a function of actions taken by others in the system, such as prosecutors, judges, and prison wardens, then it is by no means clear that arrests measure the value of the police.

As police executives have been rethinking the mission and operations of their departments, they have begun tinkering with the systems that measure the departments' efficiency and effectiveness.

The second weakness of output measures is far easier to repair. In most departments, the standard measures of organizational output are not closely audited. Clearance rates are notoriously unreliable, and even arrest data are suspect. As a result, it is hard for police executives or their overseers to rely on these data.

As police executives have been rethinking the mission and operations of their departments, they have begun tinkering with the systems that measure the departments' efficiency and effectiveness. Some executives have begun describing reported crimes in terms of time, location, precipitating causes, losses to victims, and the relationships between victims and witnesses, as well as using the legal definitions of crimes.[71] In this way police can see whether there are some kinds of crime they can affect more than other kinds. And because large amounts of crime go unreported, concerns about levels of fear and citizen perceptions of the quality of police service have led some executives to use annual community surveys to see how their organization is affecting actual victimization and fear. Some executives are also beginning to survey people who have called the police, to determine their level of satisfaction with the police response. These are all new ways to think about and measure the value of police departments, and they seem to be well received by the departments and the communities where they are used.

Accounting internally for the use of authority   Budgeting and cost accounting systems measure the organization's use of the financial resources contributed by the city. They do not, however, measure the care, efficiency, or effectiveness with which the police use the authority that is granted to them. Indeed, the systems employed to manage the police use of authority tend to be quite different from those employed to manage the department's uses of money. The most common device for controlling the use of authority is the establishment of internal policies and procedures. These are inculcated through recruit and in-service training, and adherence to them is overseen by the line commanders and by an internal affairs unit (see the chapter on fostering integrity). The internal affairs unit is typically set up to receive complaints or allegations of misconduct from sources inside and outside the department and to investigate whether the complaints are justified and whether they warrant criminal prosecution or internal disciplinary proceedings. In a few departments, the internal affairs unit engages in proactive efforts to identify instances of misconduct, on the premise that many citizens might be afraid to make an allegation against a police officer even if the allegation were warranted.

Many city and county administrations, having decided that internal control procedures neither adequately protect citizens from police misconduct nor provide sufficiently accurate information about the extent of police misconduct, have set up external agencies to oversee the police. Sometimes these take the form of civilian complaint review boards or a citizen advocate's office (see the chapter on the governmental setting; see also the section above on securing public support).

Perhaps the most powerful control over police abuse of authority, however, is the growing threat of civil liability. Citizens who are abused by the police may sue them.[72] Plaintiffs may even be able to get help in investigating alleged instances of police misconduct by calling on the FBI's Civil Rights Program, which was established to receive and review citizens' complaints. So far, with some exceptions, local governments have been required by the courts to assume the liability for the misconduct of their police officers. But the financial cost of such actions has been rising, and that has brought new pressures to minimize police misconduct. It has also brought pressures to increase the likelihood that police departments will receive the benefit of the doubt from judges and juries in close cases. (One means is by seeking and attaining accreditation for the department, which helps assure the court that the department has professional policies and procedures in place.)

The effort to account for and control the use of police authority is, in an important sense, still in its infancy. Traditionally, the police have not thought of their authority as a resource that it was their duty to husband—to use economically, efficiently, and fairly. They have, instead, assumed that it was theirs to employ as they saw fit. What a generation of police reform has taught is that legitimate authority is a very precious asset to a police department and that if the public is to trust the police use of that resource—and is therefore to make more of that resource available to the police—the police must be able to control and account for their use of that authority.

Leadership and the future

Much is changing inside and outside policing. As a result, theories about the proper organization and management of police departments are changing as well. Although change is inevitably accompanied by uncertainty and stress, police leaders are recognizing that it also presents opportunities.

As this chapter has shown, traditional assumptions about police organization and management have been questioned in the face of several forces: changes in the environment of policing, changes in managerial thought, and changes in our knowledge about the effectiveness of current approaches to policing. The result has been new ideas about the police mission and how to accomplish it—ideas that have implications for the way police departments are organized and managed.

Imaginative leadership is required to lead police organizations as they evolve in the years ahead, and the remainder of this book is devoted to developing that leadership capacity.

1 James Q. Wilson, *Bureaucracy* (New York: Basic Books, 1990).

2 John M. Bryson, *Strategic Planning for Public and Non-Profit Organizations* (San Francisco: Jossey-Bass, 1988).

3 Henry Mintzberg, *The Structure of Organizations: A Synthesis of the Research* (Englewood Cliffs, NJ: Prentice-Hall, 1979).

4 Bryson, *Strategic Planning*.

5 Robert N. Anthony and Regina E. Herzlinger, *Management Control in Nonprofit Organizations* (Homewood, IL: Irwin, 1975).

6 Lawrence W. Sherman, *Police Corruption: A Sociological Perspective* (New York: Anchor Books, 1974).

7 James Q. Wilson, *The Investigators: Managing FBI and Narcotic Agents* (New York: Basic, 1978), 163–166.

8 George L. Kelling, *Police and Communities: The Quiet Revolution*, Perspectives on Policing, no. 1 (Washington, DC: National Institute of Justice, 1988). See also Jerome Skolnick and David Bayley, *The New Blue Line: Police Innovation in Six American Cities* (New York: Free Press, 1986).

9 Paul E. Peterson, ed., *The New Urban Reality* (Washington, DC: Brookings, 1985).

10 Brian J. Reaves, "Police Departments in Large Cities, 1987," Bureau of Justice Statistics Special Report (Washington, DC: Bureau of Justice Statistics, 1989), 7.

11 Mark H. Moore and Robert Trojanowicz, *Policing and the Fear of Crime*, Perspectives on Policing, no. 3 (Washington, DC: National Institute of Justice, 1988).

12 James K. Stewart, "The Urban Strangler: How Crime Causes Poverty in the Inner City," *Policy Review* 37 (Summer 1986): 2–6.

13 Vera Institute of Justice, *Felony Arrests: Their Prosecution and Disposition in New York City's Courts*, rev. ed. (New York: Vera Institute and Longman, 1981).

14 Ezra F. Vogel, *Japan as Number One: Lessons for America* (Cambridge: Harvard University Press, 1979); and William G. Ouchi, *Theory Z: How American Businesses Can Meet the Japanese Challenge* (Reading, MA: Addison-Wesley, 1981).

15 Thomas J. Peters and Robert H. Waterman, Jr., *In Search of Excellence: Lessons from America's Best-Run Companies* (New York: Harper and Row, 1982).

16 David K. Clifford, Jr., and Richard E. Cavanagh, *The Winning Performance: How America's High Growth Midsize Companies Succeed* (New York: Bantam Books, 1985).

17 Ouchi, *Theory Z*. See also Harry P. Hatry and John M. Greiner, *Improving the Use of Quality Circles in Police Departments* (Washington, DC: National Institute of Justice, 1986).

18 Malcolm K. Sparrow, Mark H. Moore, and David M. Kennedy, *Beyond 911: The New Era of Policing* (New York: Basic Books, 1990).

19 George L. Kelling and Mark H. Moore, *The Evolving Strategy of Policing*, Perspectives on Policing, no. 4 (Washington, DC: National Institute of Justice, 1988).

20 Herman Goldstein, *Policing a Free Society* (Cambridge, MA: Ballinger, 1977).

21 Herman Goldstein, *Problem-Oriented Policing* (New York: McGraw-Hill, 1990).

22 Kenneth R. Andrews, *The Concept of Corporate Strategy* (Chicago: Irwin, 1980), 9.

23 Edward R. Freeman, *Strategic Management: A Stakeholder's Approach* (Marshall, MA: Pittman, 1984), 10.

24 Edith Stokey and Richard Zeckhauser, *A Primer on Policy Analysis* (New York: Norton, 1978). For applications in policing, see Edward H. Kaplan, "Evaluating the Effectiveness of One-Officer versus Two-Officer Patrol Units," *Journal of Criminal Justice* 7: 325–55.

25 Laura Irwin Langbein, *Discovering Whether Programs Work: A Guide to Statistical Methods for Program Evaluation* (Santa Monica, CA: Goodyear, 1980). For applications in policing, see Mary Ann Wycoff, "Evaluating the Crime-Effectiveness of Municipal Police," in *Managing Police Work*, ed. Jack R. Greene (Newbury Park, CA: Sage, 1982), 15–36; and Lawrence W. Sherman

and Richard A. Berk, "The Minneapolis Domestic Violence Experiment," *Police Foundation Reports* (Washington, DC: Police Foundation, 1984).

26 See William A. Geller and Michael Scott, *Deadly Force: What We Know* (Washington, DC: Police Executive Research Forum, 1990).

27 Stokey and Zeckhauser, *A Primer on Policy Analysis*. For applications in policing, see Kaplan, "Evaluating the Effectiveness of One-Officer versus Two-Officer Patrol Units."

28 David H. Bayley, "Community Policing: A Report from the Devil's Advocate," in *Community Policing: Rhetoric or Reality*, ed. Jack R. Greene and Stephen D. Mastrofski (New York: Praeger, 1988).

29 Egon Bittner, *The Functions of the Police in Modern Society* (Washington, DC: U.S. Government Printing Office, 1970).

30 Mark H. Moore, Robert Trojanowicz, and George L. Kelling, *Crime and Policing*, Perspectives on Policing, no. 2 (Washington, DC: National Institute of Justice, 1988).

31 Mary Ann Wycoff, Charles E. Brown, and Robert E. Peterson, *Birmingham Anti-Robbery Unit: Evaluation Report, Draft 3* (Washington, DC: Police Foundation, March 1980).

32 Mark H. Moore, "Invisible Offenses: A Challenge to Minimally Intrusive Law Enforcement," in *ABSCAM Ethics: Moral Issues and Deception in Law Enforcement*, ed. Gerald M. Caplan (Washington, DC: Police Foundation, 1983).

33 Mark H. Moore, "Controlling Criminogenic Commodities: Drugs, Guns and Alcohol," in *Crime and Public Policy*, ed. James Q. Wilson (San Francisco: ICS Press, 1983).

34 Lawrence W. Sherman, "Policing Communities: What Works?" in *Crime and Justice: A Review of Research*, ed. Albert J. Reiss, Jr., and Michael Tonry, vol. 8, *Communities and Crime* (Chicago: University of Chicago Press, 1986), 343–86.

35 John E. Eck and William Spelman, *Problem-Solving: Problem-Oriented Policing in Newport News* (Washington, DC: Police Executive Research Forum, 1987).

36 Lawrence W. Sherman et al., *Repeat Calls to the Police in Minneapolis* (Washington, DC: Crime Control Institute, 1987); and Eck and Spelman, *Solving Problems*.

37 Wesley Skogan, "Fear of Crime and Neighborhood Change," in *Crime and Justice*, ed. Reiss and Tonry, vol. 8, 210.

38 Anthony M. Pate, Mary Ann Wycoff, Wesley G. Skogan, Lawrence W. Sherman, *Reducing Fear of Crime in Houston and Newark: A Summary Report* (Washington, DC: Police Foundation, 1986).

39 George L. Kelling et al., *Kansas City Preventive Patrol Experiment: A Summary Report* (Washington, DC: Police Foundation, 1974).

40 Kansas City Police Department, *Response Time Analysis* (Kansas City, MO: Kansas City Police Department, 1977).

41 Peter W. Greenwood, Jan M. Chaiken, and Joan Petersilia, *The Criminal Investigation Process* (Lexington, MA: D. C. Heath, 1977).

42 William Spelman and Dale K. Brown, *Calling the Police* (Washington, DC: Police Executive Research Forum, 1982).

43 The growth of private security is documented in William C. Cunningham and Todd H. Taylor,

The Hallcrest Report: Private Security and Police in America (Portland, OR: Chancellor Press, 1985).

44 David M. Kennedy, "Neighborhood Policing in Los Angeles," Case No. C16-86-717.0 (Cambridge: Case Program of John F. Kennedy School of Government, Harvard University, 1986).

45 National Advisory Commission on Criminal Justice Standards and Goals, *Police Chief Executive* (Washington, DC: U.S. Government Printing Office, 1976).

46 A useful discussion of this topic is Diana Gordon, "Police Guidelines," Case Nos. C14-75-024 and -0245, (Cambridge: Case Program of John F. Kennedy School of Government, Harvard University, 1975). See also Patrick V. Murphy, "The Prospective Chief's Negotiation of Authority with the Mayor," in *Police Leadership in America: Crisis and Opportunity*, ed. William A. Geller (New York: Praeger, 1985); and Allen H. Andrews, Jr., "Structuring the Political Independence of the Police Chief," in ibid.

47 Mark H. Moore, "Police Leadership: The Impossible Dream," in *Impossible Jobs in Public Management*, ed. Irwin Hargrove and John C. Glidewell (Lawrence: University of Kansas Press, 1990).

48 Robert Wasserman and Mark H. Moore, "Values in Policing," Working paper series no. 88-05-15 (Cambridge: Program in Criminal Justice Policy and Management, John F. Kennedy School of Government, Harvard University, 1988).

49 Budgetary constraints seem to explain the dearth of victimization data at the community level in contrast to data generated for the nation as a whole. The high cost of victimization surveys and the tight budgetary constraints in many municipalities currently preclude the routine use of community-level victimization surveys for evaluating many police departments.

50 Eric J. Scott, *Calls for Service: Citizen Demand and Initial Police Response* (Washington, DC: National Institute of Justice, 1981); Jerome H. Skolnick and Candace McCoy, "Police Accountability and the Media," in *Police Leadership in America*, ed. Geller, 102–35.

51 Albert J. Reiss, Jr., *The Police and the Public* (New Haven: Yale University Press, 1971): and Donald J. Black, "The Social Organization of Arrest," *Stanford Law Review* 23 (1971).

52 John Kaplan, "The Prosecutorial Discretion—A Comment," *Northwestern Law Review*, 60 (1965): 174, 178–93; and INSLAW, Inc., *Arrest Convictability as a Measure of Police Performance*, summary report, 23 April 1981 (Washington, DC: INSLAW, 1981).

53 Steven R. Schlesinger, "Criminal Procedure in the Courtroom," in *Crime and Public Policy*, ed. Wilson 183–206.

54 See Wayne Kerstetter, "Who Disciplines the Police? Who Should?" in *Police Leadership in America*, ed. Geller.

55 Raymond Davis, "Organizing the Community for Improved Policing," in *Police Leadership in America*, ed. Geller, 88.

56 See Greene and Mastrofski, *Community Policing*. But see also Dennis P. Rosenbaum, "Community Crime Prevention: A Review and Synthesis of the Literature," *Justice Quarterly* 5, no. 3 (1988): 323–95.

57 Moore, "Police Leadership."

58 Mintzberg, *The Structure of Organizations*.

59 Michael T. Farmer, *Survey of Police Operational and Administrative Practices* (Washington, DC: Police Executive Research Forum, 1978).

60 Michael Barzelay and Babak J. Amajani, "Managing State Government Operations: Changing Visions of Staff Agencies," *Journal of Policy Analysis and Management* 9, no. 3 (Summer 1990).

61 James Q. Wilson, *Varieties of Police Behavior* (Cambridge: Harvard University Press, 1968); Albert J. Reiss, Jr., *The Police and the Public* (New Haven: Yale University Press, 1971), and J. Rubinstein, *City Police* (New York: Farrar, Straus and Giroux, 1973).

62 Steven Hays, *Public Personnel Administration: Problems and Prospects* (Englewood Cliffs, NJ: Prentice-Hall, 1983).

63 Patricia Davis, "Suspected Drug Use Thins Ranks of Police Applicants; Fairfax Rejects Two-Thirds of 1986 Group," *Washington Post*, 28 Sept. 1986, p. 1, col. 2.

64 "The New America: Social Trends," *International Business Week*, 25 Sept. 1989, 84.

65 David L. Carter, Allen D. Sapp, and Darrel W. Stephens, *The State of Police Education: Policy Direction for the 21st Century* (Washington, DC: Police Executive Research Forum, 1989).

66 Ibid., 110.

67 James A. F. Stoner, *Management* (Englewood Cliffs, NJ: Prentice-Hall, 1978), 514–515. For an example of the application of these principles in other contexts, see *Executive Mobility: Thomas Winslow and the Navy's Rotation Policy*, Case No. C15-88-834.0 (Cambridge: Case Program of John F. Kennedy School of Government, Harvard University, 1986).

68 See generally David Couper, *How to Rate Your Local Police* (Washington, DC: Police Executive Research Forum, 1983).

69 National Research Council, *Injury in America: A Continuing Public Health Problem* (Washington, DC: National Academy Press, 1985).

70 Craig D. Uchida, C. Bridgeforth, and Charles F. Wellford, *Law Enforcement Statistics: The State of the Art* (College Park, MD: Institute of Criminal Justice and Criminology, 1984).

71 Police Executive Research Forum, *Summary Report on the Crime Classification System for the City of Colorado Springs, CO* (Washington, DC: Police Executive Research Forum, n.d.); and Police Executive Research Forum, *Summary Report on the Crime Classification System for the City of Peoria, IL* (Washington, DC: Police Executive Research Forum, n.d.).

72 Michael Avery and David Rudovsky, *Police Misconduct—Law and Litigation*, 2d ed. (New York: Clark Boardman, 1981) is a continually updated legal reference work that summarizes development in civil liability suits against police agencies.

Part two: Basic police services

The patrol function

If Sir Robert Peel, August Vollmer, O. W. Wilson, and others could muse on the evolution of the police patrol function since their days, they would be struck at how much has changed and how much has remained the same. Substantial shifts in strategic thinking have occurred, and some remarkable technological tools have been added to the police officer's tool kit. At the same time, however, patrol officers have remained "master generalists" and are still expected to handle competently a mind-boggling mix of calls. In the shorthand parlance of police dispatching and report writing, within a week's tour of duty a single officer might be dispatched to calls involving "lost and recovered property," "woman screaming," "assist an invalid," "deranged or disoriented person," "family fight," "missing person," "bar-room brawl," "crowd control," "shots fired," "abandoned car," "drug dealing in the school yard," "animal bite," "traffic accident," "prowler," "barking dog," "suspicious person," "speeding motorist," "wires down," "chemical spill," "loud noise," "terrorist threat," "intrusion alarm," and so forth. This crazy quilt constitutes the fabric of police work.[1]

In addition to being varied, this master generalist's job is also exceptionally important. Patrol officers maintain closer contact with the public than any other section of the police department, and to a large extent the public's satisfaction with the police depends on how patrol officers handle these calls. Although an "assist an invalid" call is just another routine assignment for a patrol officer, it may be a critical emergency for the invalid.

Given the variety and importance of calls for service as well as the emphasis that television series and other police fiction put on violent crime, the layperson can be excused for thinking that patrol work is exciting. For most patrol officers, it is not. Violent crimes account for only about 1 percent of a municipal police department's dispatched workload.[2] As for the rest, the grueling routine of answering call after call, taking report after report, and randomly driving the streets eventually becomes mind-numbing.

Challenging, important, and hazardous though patrol work may be, the laborious routine prevents it from getting the prestige it deserves.

In certain high-crime neighborhoods, of course, the percentage of violent crime is considerably higher. And every patrol officer knows that, in a split second, the most inconsequential and routine activity can develop into a potentially hazardous situation. Patrol work (at least as traditionally practiced) therefore consists of long periods of boredom punctuated by moments of terror. Increasingly, though, police leaders are attempting to refocus patrol so that the long periods of boredom are replaced by long periods of productivity.

Challenging, important, and hazardous though patrol work may be, the laborious routine prevents it from getting the prestige it deserves. In some departments, patrol is considered a "second-class assignment" to which officers who have "screwed up" in more specialized activities are returned. The forefathers of modern policing would be pleased, however, to see police executives increasingly trying to upgrade the prestige of patrol work. Yet despite these efforts, much more needs to be done to provide tangible career inducements for the best and brightest within policing to gravitate to patrol work.

Historically, many police executives, particularly in large departments, devoted little attention to regular patrol operations, instead directing their interests and energies toward administrative functions and the work of specialized units. Indeed, one wonders whether a good many police administrators, guided by the conventional wisdom of the day, might not have seen patrol as a resource pool from which officers could be drawn to staff an almost endless line of specialized details and units (tactical units, pawnshop details, crime prevention units, "report cars," abandoned auto units, print cars, school truancy units, and others). Yet these specialist functions address only minute fractions of the police workload and often deal with isolated incidents that are widely scattered in time and location. Moreover, research conducted during the early 1970s in the Kansas City (Missouri) police department indicates that police problems at the street level are affected far more by small gains in the overall performance of a patrol force than by quantum improvements in the efforts of smaller, specialized units.

One way to strengthen and redefine the roles of patrol officers (or any employees) is with departmental evaluation procedures (see the chapter on performance measurement). Police leaders nationwide are struggling to find creative ways of enhancing conventional evaluation and incentive structures. The problem, as they see it, is that daily activity logs emphasize such things as the number of tickets issued, the number of felony and misdemeanor arrests made, the number of calls handled, the number of reports taken, and the number of miles driven during a particular tour of day—in other words, "bean counting." Traditionally, after all, police administrators—responding partly to their elected and appointed superiors, chambers of commerce, the media, and others in the community—sought to gauge the effectiveness of their agencies solely by reported crime, arrest, and clearance rates. But it is increasingly apparent to police officials nationwide that the public's definition of crime problems—or police business—is broader than was traditionally recognized. Rather than "crime stats" based on Part I and Part II Uniform Crime Reports data, it is the broad mix of general service, emergency incidents, and crime and disorder problems that provides citizens with primary reference points in assessing how well the police are doing. And conspicuously absent from the evaluation systems of many departments is any mention of meaningful involvement with citizens in addressing neighborhood problems and concerns.

Today, police administrators share a general perception that they must move beyond bean counting and beyond the traditional preoccupation with internal issues and controls, such as police directives, record systems, and officer adherence to "military etiquette."

Today, police administrators share a general perception that they must move beyond bean counting, however much some of it can contribute to sound administrative decisions, and beyond the traditional preoccupation with internal issues and controls, such as policy directives, record systems, and officer adherence to "military etiquette." Internal issues cannot be ignored, but the police must devote primary attention to questions that any service industry needs to address: "consumer" satisfaction, the effectiveness of service, the likely emergence of new problems and the concomitant demands for service, and so forth. But few departments collect the data needed to identify effective ways to handle tough disorder and service calls, much less reward officers for implementing these ways. Still fewer departments regularly survey their customers, or reward officers for satisfying the customers.

The public's appetite for more effective policing is voracious. And many police administrators will recognize that this hunger provides a golden opportunity for constructively changing the orientation and strategic focus of their organizations. But restructuring field operations to deliver service more effectively does not come easily. Traditional assumptions and mind-sets about patrol operations must be modified; some must even be discarded. An organizational environment (or culture) must be created that encourages increased interaction with the public so that officers can gain first-hand knowledge of citizens' concerns about neighborhood problems, their perceptions of crime, and their fear of crime. All of this must be done in the pressure-cooker environment created by the nation's drug problem.

Examination of the patrol function in relation to citizen needs and expectations reveals the enormous complexity of properly managing patrol resources. A premise of this chapter, in fact, is that running an effective patrol operation is probably the most difficult managerial challenge in any police department, particularly in highly populated urban areas where police are dispatched to assist citizens of many different income brackets, races, and cultures. The needs, wants, and attitudes of such a populace are broad. The conditions of criminal violence that police encounter in a city vary as well. Some beats are "sleepy hollows"; others, beset by drug violence, may be virtual "free-fire zones." Yet the same patrol force must be prepared to serve the needs of all persons and all neighborhoods professionally, legally, and productively.

Moreover, patrol officers typically are first responders to emergency situations. This means that, despite care taken by communications personnel to alert officers to the circumstances they are about to encounter, patrol officers often face undefined and unpredictable situations. And although emergency response to potentially volatile incidents is a very small portion of the typical patrol force's workload, if such matters are handled without professional acumen, they can take on an organizational and community importance that far outstrips their numerical portion of the workload.

Effective management of patrol operations requires not only the involvement of top talent in the department but also continuing attention and support from the agency's chief executive. As these officials guide U.S. policing into the next century, they must recognize that they are standing at a critical crossroads. On the one hand, the Kansas City research mentioned earlier and other studies conducted during the past two decades, much of it initiated by practitioners, have provided powerful evidence that a number of traditional, basic patrol methods are largely ineffective. On the other hand, in policing, as elsewhere, there is frequently a long time lag between realizing that conventional wisdom is defective and taking concrete steps to translate new insights into new operational modes. The time lag is due partly to the inherent discomfort of relinquishing the familiar and partly to a reluctance to risk imposing on the community police methods that may be even less effective than those currently being used. It is another premise of this chapter that enough is now known about the weaknesses of several of the traditional patrol methods for responsible police administration to attempt innovation. It is a further premise that most U.S. police departments continue to perform patrol in the traditional manner—a manner that they know or ought to know is ineffective and wasteful.

The rest of this chapter considers a number of historical assumptions that continue to guide patrol administrators in most departments most of the time and reports research findings that have raised questions about many of these assumptions. It shows how departments have begun to break from tradition in developing new and more effective approaches to patrol and outlines the principles of effective patrol management and the "infrastructure" needed to support patrol operations.

Traditional assumptions

Patrol traditionally has been performed by officers assigned to specific geographical areas for the purpose of maintaining a mobile, usually visible, police presence. One reason for developing patrol was pure convenience: patrol gave officers something to do while they were waiting for the next call for service. At the same time, however, police administrators hoped that uniformed police would detect and thwart crimes in progress, which, in turn, would deter others from perpetrating offenses.

Despite nagging questions about the efficacy of uniformed patrols in preventing crime, the strategy of random preventive patrol continues to guide patrol operations in most police departments.

In the United States, patrol officers were originally on foot or on horseback. Shortly before the turn of this century, they became more mobile. As early as 1897, bicycles were used in Detroit. The automobile was first introduced in municipal policing in 1910 and soon gained in popularity, supplanting bicycles and, in some cases, horses. By the late 1920s the increased use of radio-equipped patrol cars combined with the widespread availability of the telephone to put a new weapon in the patrol arsenal: rapid response to calls for service. In 1929, the enthusiasm about fast police response was reflected in the following excerpt from an address to the International Association of Chiefs of Police:

Murderers have been caught at the scene of the crime before they had a chance to dispose of their weapons. . . . Burglars have been captured while still piling up their loot in homes. Bewildered auto thieves have gasped as the police cruiser roared alongside of them a few minutes after they had stolen a car. . . . [If] time permitted, I would . . . relate to you the most spectacular series of criminal apprehensions in the history of our profession.[3]

Today, few police managers remain this enthusiastic. But despite nagging questions about the efficacy of uniformed patrols in preventing crime,[4] the strategy of random preventive patrol continues to guide patrol operations in most police departments. Beginning in the early 1970s, however, a few police administrators and a handful of researchers began to reassess these assumptions about random preventive patrol and began searching for ways to test their validity. What they discovered was startling. Random preventive patrol was found to be a high-cost, low-payoff strategy in terms of intercepting crimes in progress and deterring criminals; and rapid response to calls had little effect on police ability to catch criminals.

Interception

When police witness a crime in progress, the offender(s) are very likely to be arrested. Unfortunately, the potential for patrol intervention in crimes in progress is extremely limited. Evidence suggests that two-thirds of all index crimes—and this includes the vast majority of homicides, rapes, and aggravated assaults—are committed indoors, where they are not visible to patrol personnel.[5] Of the remaining one-third of index crimes, which could be viewed from patrol beats, most are visible only for a short time. The average street robbery, for example, is visible only for sixty to ninety seconds.[6] And most burglars enter through a rear door or window, which is not generally visible from patrol cars, or through an unlocked front door, so that detection is all but impossible.

Not surprisingly, patrol officers in fact do not intercept many crimes in progress. In the mid-1960s, a study found that a Los Angeles patrol officer could expect to pass a robbery in progress—if he or she detected it as such—only once every fourteen years.[7] More recent studies conducted in Syracuse, San Diego, and Boston found that patrol officers could expect to intercept fewer than 1 percent of street crimes.[8]

Further evidence indicates that patrol officers themselves discover, usually after occurrence, only 5 to 6 percent of crime and noncrime incidents reported to their departments.[9] Efforts in the early 1970s to develop a seriousness index for crime showed that the more serious the crime in terms of victim trauma and economic loss, the less likely it was to be visible to patrolling officers.[10] Therefore, the few crimes that patrolling officers do discover are likely to be the least serious types of incidents, and many of them will probably be reported to the police anyway. Finally, in congested urban environments with numerous police vehicles present, the limited reliable evidence suggests that criminal events are most likely to be found by a patrol unit other than the one assigned to that area and that discovery is largely the result of a citizen complaint or patrol response to an unrelated call, rather than a direct result of random patrol.[11] This finding adds credence to the popular cliche: "Random patrol produces random results."

Deterrence

The sight of continually roving patrol cars was intended to create an illusion of police omnipresence. It was assumed that the sight of patrol cars would heighten citizens' sense of security and that the cars' presence, like a "human scarecrow," would deter would-be offenders. This illusion of police omnipresence was a much-touted advantage when the patrol car was introduced. In 1933, Vollmer wrote:

Districts of many square miles . . . are now covered by the roving patrol car; fast, efficient, stealthy . . . just as likely to be within 60 feet as 3 miles of the crook plying his trade—the very enigma of this specialized fellow who is coming to realize now that a few moments may bring [patrol cars] down about him like a swarm of bees—this lightning-swift "angel of death." [12]

In 1972, in research referred to earlier, the Kansas City police department provided a dramatic empirical challenge to the conventional wisdom about the deterrent effects of random patrol. In an internally generated effort to appraise time-hardened but untested standard operating procedures, that department tested the effects of three levels of marked patrol coverage in fifteen of its highest crime beats. The fifteen beats were randomly divided into three groups: proactive, reactive, and control. Officers assigned to proactive beats were expected to perform aggressive patrol work by making increased "car checks" and "ped checks" (that is, stopping and questioning drivers and occupants of cars, and pedestrians, who exhibited suspicious behavior). Officers assigned to reactive beats were not permitted to enter their beats unless officially dispatched or in hot pursuit of a fleeing suspect. They were, however, expected to enhance patrol in the proactive beats by entering those areas to engage in routine patrol. In the proactive areas, the proactive and reactive officers together generated approximately three times the normal level of police visibility. Finally, officers assigned to the control beats were expected to conduct business as usual: to patrol randomly through their beats unless interrupted by a dispatch.

After almost one year of maintaining this configuration, both researchers and practitioners were surprised to find no difference among the three sets of beats in levels of reported crime, victimization rates, and traffic accidents. Neither were there differences in citizens' perceptions of patrol levels, their reported fear of crime, or their satisfaction with the department. Tripling random patrols or eliminating them entirely appeared to have no discernible effect.[13]

Some questioned the validity of the Kansas City preventive patrol experiment on the grounds that the department had been unable to maintain pristine experimental conditions at all times during the study. Others challenged the experimental design itself, arguing, for example, that the disparity among the three types of areas was not large enough. That is, the way to deter criminals, it was argued, was to increase patrol levels by a factor of ten or twenty—in effect, putting a cop on almost every corner.

In 1977, the Nashville police department tested this hypothesis by increasing patrols to thirty times their previous levels in the downtown area. This "saturation patrol" did, in fact, reduce crime slightly—but only at night. During the daylight hours, crime levels remained the same.[14] After six weeks, the Nashville police department went back to business as usual. A thirtyfold increase in patrol levels was simply too expensive to maintain on a regular basis. Random preventive patrol thus appears to be ineffective in deterring criminality except at costs that far exceed benefits.

Psychologists have found that deterrence depends primarily on the certainty and swiftness of punishment.

Although these findings may be disconcerting, they should not be all that surprising. Psychologists have found that deterrence depends primarily on the certainty and swiftness of punishment. The "punishment" of a patrol arrest is anything but certain (not to mention the fact that court-imposed penalties after any arrest are not likely to be swift or certain). Given the data on the rarity of police interception of crimes in progress, an index crime offender's risk of arrest by random patrol units is only around 1 percent. Even when the police are notified of the on-going criminal activity, offenders are caught either on-scene or in flight in less than 4 percent of reported crimes. Thus, a criminal's risk of arrest by random preventive patrol is only around 5 percent. Stated conversely, 95 percent of the time an individual will not be arrested by randomly patrolling police during or immediately after the commission of an offense.

Random preventive patrol thus appears to produce random and minimal results and to be a waste of valuable police resources. The research results on the effectiveness of random patrol and citizen satisfaction with it becomes more intuitively acceptable when one thinks of the dramatic differences in officers' approaches to their beats. Under traditional patrol operations, there are no organizationally defined objectives for dealing with varied and often recurring problems in the distinct patrol beats. Officers are generally responsible for answering calls for service, returning to service as quickly as possible to handle the next call, and using their individual initiative to patrol their beats—but a candid review of even the small group of officers who relieve one another within a single patrol area will normally reveal that they differ extensively in how they define and understand area problems, in what they see as objectives and priorities among the problems and locations that should receive attention, and in the tactics they use. (The tactics are not only highly individualized; at times, they may also be inconsistent or wastefully duplicative.)

Rapid response

With the introduction of the radio patrol car, police response time began to emerge as a major measure of police effectiveness. To reduce response times, police departments began to invest substantial sums of money to bolster patrol resources. They also directed their officers to dispose of calls quickly so they could get "back in service" and be available for the next dispatch. In addition, many agencies lobbied for 9–1–1 telecommunications systems and spent considerable amounts of money to install computer-aided dispatching (CAD) systems (see the chapter on information management). A few departments went so far as to install automated vehicle location (AVL) systems.

Although it is not unreasonable to assume that rapid police response will produce more on-scene arrests, more witnesses, and increased citizen satisfaction, a more comprehensive examination of the issue of response time reveals that the police constitute only one side of the response time equation. The technologies and tactics mentioned above may, in fact, reduce police response time, but their effectiveness is limited by two factors on the other side of the equation, both of which appear to be common to all police departments.

First, fewer than 20 percent of dispatched calls for service involve crime. The vast majority of calls for service entail minor traffic accidents, disorders, and disputes among friends and families, none of which constitutes crime.[15] (It should be added, however, that police presence in volatile disputes reduces the probability that crime will occur—at least until the police depart.)

Second, at the time crime calls are placed, few of them are emergencies. Examination of the response issue throughout the country disclosed that approximately 75 percent of index crimes are "cold" when reported, that is, they are discovered by a citizen sometime after the perpetrator has left the scene.[16] This figure includes the overwhelming majority of burglaries, larcenies, and motor vehicle thefts. In the remaining 25 percent of index crimes, a citizen saw, heard, or became involved at some point during the commission of the offense—but one-half of those victims and witnesses did not notify the police until at least five minutes after first observing the crime. It is now known that the time taken to report an incident greatly determines the effect that police response time will have in apprehending offenders and in locating witnesses. Fast police response could reasonably be expected to affect on-scene criminal apprehensions in only 10 to 15 percent of reported crimes—those in which the police are called quickly. But, because criminals are often able to avoid capture no matter how quickly police respond, less than 4 percent of the reported crimes were found to result in on-scene criminal apprehensions that could be attributed to fast police response.[17] Thus, in the overwhelming majority of calls for service, citizens' inability (and occasional unwillingness) to report crimes quickly undercuts the benefits of rapid police response.[18]

The time taken to report an incident greatly determines the effect that police response time will have in apprehending offenders and in locating witnesses.

To police, citizen satisfaction with police response time has generally been a volatile issue. But the studies of response time found that citizen satisfaction with police response time was associated with neither dispatch nor travel times. Rather, citizen satisfaction with response time was dependent on whether citizens perceived response time to be faster or slower than what the dispatcher had led them to expect. For example, if a dispatcher told the victim of a cold burglary to expect a car "right away," the victim became angry if the police did not arrive within fifteen minutes. But if the dispatcher told a caller to expect a car within thirty minutes, perhaps explaining that all cars were currently busy, the caller was rarely dissatisfied if the car came within this conveyed estimate. Even long delays infrequently caused dissatisfaction, so long as the call was not an emergency and the victim knew what to expect.[19]

The studies' findings that only a small number of crimes are discovered in progress and that citizens take an inordinate amount of time to report such crimes have a major but unpopular implication: an infusion of additional resources to reduce response times would have negligible effect in increasing on-scene arrests or identifying helpful witnesses. However unwelcome the news, the truth apparently is that if police departments continue to invest more money to reduce response times, most of these expenditures will be wasted.

The historical emphasis on across-the-board rapid response has tended to make many police departments reactive and incident-driven. Officers are encouraged to resolve the immediate situation and return to service as quickly as possible for the next call. Although it is now known that a very small percentage of locations (approximately 10 percent) continually account for about 60 percent of a department's call-for-service workload, officers are not routinely encouraged to identify, understand, or help resolve the underlying difficulties that give rise to repeat calls at the same location or with the same actors.[20] Even when repetitive offenses involving the same site or participants are documented, the criminal investigation that may follow often continues to address discrete incidents (see the chapter on criminal investigation), and the cycle of incident-call-response continues.

New directions

The 1970s brought accelerated change to policing. Among the most visible and dramatic stimulants of the change were the previous decade's protest demonstrations and riots. The change was then fueled by a plethora of research findings (some of which have been cited) that began to question traditional assumptions underlying the management of both patrol and investigative operations. In addition, political figures—with the backing of police leaders—declared a "war on crime in the streets of America," and a search was on for more effective methods of combatting crime.

By the mid-1970s, the findings and implications of the Kansas City studies of preventive patrol and response time were stimulating further research. The preventive patrol experiment had disclosed that more than 60 percent of patrol officers' time was uncommitted (that is, the officer was "in service" and thus available to be dispatched). Researchers then began to examine the prospects for structuring this uncommitted patrol time to direct it into more productive use. In 1974 the federal Law Enforcement Assistance Administration's Patrol Emphasis Program emphasized that to structure uncommitted patrol time for directed patrol operations, information was needed; and that crime analysis procedures were important in producing that information. The Patrol Emphasis Program expanded and evolved into the Integrated Criminal Apprehension Program (ICAP) and the Managing Patrol Operations (MPO) program. Together, these programs involved more than fifty medium- to large-sized cities by 1982. These initiatives sought to improve field operations by having patrol managers rethink and restructure the patrol function, even if that meant discarding traditional assumptions.

The Kansas City response time study had a comparable effect. The finding prompted a reexamination of dispatch operations, and the reexamination revealed that formal procedures for discriminating between emergency and non-emergency incoming calls were lacking. During the mid-1970s, several departments involved with ICAP and MPO began experimenting with methods of managing incoming calls for service more effectively. Research involving the Birmingham (Alabama) police department and the Police Executive Research Forum drew these different techniques into a comprehensive model called *differential police response*. The model included call prioritization codes with built-in queue delays for low-priority calls. It also included alternative ways to handle some types of calls that did not require a mobile response by a sworn police officer. For example, some types of reports could be taken over the telephone or by having a citizen come to a police station; and when a mobile response was necessary, in some cases it could be made by a civilian "community service officer." The model was eventually made operational for empirical validation in three cities during the early 1980s (see subsection below on "Dispatch operations") and was found to be an effective tool for streamlining dispatch operations and freeing patrol officers' time for other activities.[21]

A number of other patrol initiatives and evaluative research efforts were undertaken during the 1970s. Several police departments, including those in Rochester (New York), Cincinnati and Dayton (Ohio), and Holyoke (Massachusetts) explored the merits of team policing (see the chapter on research). The San Diego police department sought to determine the effect of field interrogations on the crime rate. It also studied possible links between officer injuries and performance, on the one hand, and size of officer unit (whether one-officer or two), on the other hand. In the early 1970s, San Diego patrol officers also began to conduct regular citizen surveys, and found that citizens could help them identify and understand recurring problems on their beats.

In 1975, Wilmington (Delaware) split its patrol force into two parts: "basic" officers continued to answer calls, while "structured" officers implemented directed patrol activities. This split force proved more efficient, although most patrol officers preferred to conduct both types of activities. In 1974, New Haven sought to test the benefits of using crime analysis information for structuring directed deterrent patrols. Sparked by the Rand Corporation's assessment of criminal investigations (see the chapter on criminal investigations), many police departments began to restructure their operations to give patrol officers a greater role in preliminary investigations and to make detective operations more focused and accountable.

Experiments revealed a lot about police operations, particularly about patrol, but much of the literature seemed to report what didn't work rather than what did.

The experiments revealed a lot about police operations, particularly about patrol, but much of the literature seemed to report what didn't work rather than what did. This pattern of findings, coupled with the economic conditions of the 1970s (recession, inflation, fuel shortages, and various tax-limitation measures, such as "Proposition 13" in California), provided support for local officials who, in grappling with tough cutback decisions, sought to chop police budgets. And in many communities it became exceedingly difficult for chiefs of police to defend requests for more officers and new or additional equipment. There was no reason to believe that more money for the police department would result in better service to the public. In 1979, in the midst of widespread concern about how to do more with less, Herman Goldstein published a seminal article on what he called *problem-oriented policing*.[22] Reacting to what he perceived as an excessive concentration by police administrators on internal issues to the exclusion of external matters, Goldstein challenged police executives to shift their attention to the end products of policing—namely, how patrol officers were addressing the persistent crime and crime-related problems they encountered while performing routine patrol duties. Pointing out that there was little evidence that the traditional methods were enabling police to achieve their legitimate, longstanding goals, Goldstein argued that unquestioning adherence to the traditional methods was irresponsible.

Goldstein's observations, which gave voice to the simmering doubts of many police about conventional approaches, fostered a new approach to managing field operations. Before the 1970s, patrol generally had been reactive: officers primarily responded to incidents after they occurred. During the 1970s, patrol managers had been encouraged to become more *tactically* adept in developing and implementing proactive anticrime activities, such as directed patrol plans. Now Goldstein was recommending that police managers go a step further and develop more powerful *strategic* responses to deal with crime and noncrime police problems.

As patrol managers and police analysts in police departments, universities, and other research institutions began to think about what Goldstein was advocating, belief in the value of incident-oriented policing began to give ground. Although practices did not change overnight, serious interest arose in new patrol methods that would not merely document harm caused by crime and express sympathy to crime victims but would also attempt to attack the causes of criminal victimization, fear, and the community decay that contributes to both. There was no question that police would always need to be ready, willing, and able to respond reactively (and professionally) to calls for service, but the seeds were planted for a new, more comprehensive strategy for modern patrol operations.

This strategy, as it has been taking shape in the 1980s and 1990s, has many different names. Some practitioners and researchers call it *problem-oriented policing*; others call it *community-oriented* or *neighborhood-oriented policing*, *coproduction* of public safety, or some other term. (The term used in this chapter is strategic problem solving.) The proponents of each term and other observers of the police field find genuine and important differences among the sets of prescriptions attached to the different labels. But most people agree that the similarities are more important than the differences, for the similarities as a group contrast fundamentally with the strategic foundation underlying most traditional police work in America.

Basic to this emerging orientation is the importance of having the police think carefully about their mission and how to fulfill it successfully. In identifying, analyzing, and modifying conditions that produce crime and crime-related difficulties, the police may often find that a special bond between them and the public will prove to be very useful. Part of what is so appealing about Goldstein's notion of problem-oriented policing, therefore, is that this strategy gets right to the heart of policing: effective public service. It requires that when patrol officers are not either responding to emergency calls or engaged in directed patrol activities, they get to know the citizens who work and live in the areas they are responsible for policing. It requires that patrol officers, after establishing rapport with citizens, work with them to identify local problems and the contributing conditions. It requires, further, that officers work with citizens to seek mutually acceptable ways of reducing or eliminating problems. Thus, the relationship between the police and the public is reciprocal. Problem solving depends both on the resources the officer can muster to deal with problems and on the help citizens can give to patrol officers in alleviating the problems.

Officers and disabled children
Developmentally disabled children in Irvine, California, learn how police officers can help them—right from the officers themselves. Each month, police officers serve as aides in classrooms with developmentally disabled children.

During the day, the officers share information about their jobs, uniforms, and cars with the children. They also conduct mock field interviews with students to show them how to answer questions that are routinely asked.

As a result of the program, officers are more aware of the problems and behaviors of developmentally disabled children, and the children have gained confidence in police officers as community helpers.

Source: Cited in *The Guide to Management Improvement Projects in Local Government* (Washington, DC: International City Management Association, 1987).

The process described above—adding directed patrol to random patrol and emergency call handling and then supplementing all of these with problem-solving strategies—has not been occurring in all places in similar ways or with similar timetables. The localism of U.S. policing ensures a diversity of policies, practices, and standards that is both a blessing and a curse. This localism leaves police well equipped to tailor solutions to the idiosyncratic needs and opportunities of particular neighborhoods; it also makes coordination in dealing with regional and national problems—and with the rapid proliferation of better methods—exceedingly difficult.

The localism of U.S. policing ensures a diversity of policies, practices, and standards that is both a blessing and a curse.

The strategic developments occupying the attention of many police leaders not only point to a new direction for patrol operations and for patrol management and supervision, but they also suggest fundamental changes in the "infrastructure" of patrol. That is, as patrol strategies change, the support services for patrol operations will likewise need to evolve. Departments that expand their strategic outlook on the workload of police will need to enhance their crime (or problem) analysis support and their conceptions of the proper working relationships among police officers, between officers and supervisors, and between department personnel and the many individuals and groups that make up the external environment. The remaining sections of this chapter focus on the multiple functions that a modern patrol operation must perform simultaneously; the role of senior patrol management and first-line supervisors in guiding these functions; and the support services needed to maintain and enhance the quality of patrol.

Patrol operations

In a democracy the police and the community are vitally interdependent. The community looks to the police to maintain the basic order so necessary for true freedom. Even in this most basic police mission, the police depend upon the citizenry to call in incidents and emergencies, to provide information necessary for investigations, and to follow through with prosecution. A foundation of positive, collaborative working arrangements (not just public relations programs) between police and the community is essential if a community is to have confidence in and give support to its police department. Active outreach to and systematic engagement of the community provide the police with a better flow of information and a more accurate understanding of problems, concerns, and expectations in the various neighborhoods. Continual interaction can also serve as a catalyst in mobilizing neighborhoods to protect themselves better and to identify other resources and organizations that can assist the police in problem-solving efforts. Greatest responsibility for systematically developing and maintaining that dialogue and rapport lies with patrol officers—the police whose contact with the community is most direct and continuing. Developing dialogue and rapport is an objective that transcends each of the patrol functions discussed below.

To be effective, modern patrol officers must perform in three major spheres of activity—often simultaneously. There is no inherent priority among those functions. First, they must handle calls for service. When the service involves a genuine emergency, the call must be handled when the demand is received. Second, patrol officers must participate in tactical responses to apprehend perpetrators or to displace or disrupt problem patterns. These tactics must be undertaken when the chances of success are greatest. Third, patrol officers must engage in strategic problem-solving efforts with the community. These must occur when neighborhood residents, workers, community agencies, and other players are available to meet and work with police personnel—and when the officers themselves are not swamped by calls requiring immediate response. How effectively a department adjusts and readjusts its emphasis and activities in light of this ever-shifting array of demands and opportunities largely determines the potential effectiveness of its overall patrol operation.

Calls for service

The public calls upon the police to handle a vast range of incidents. For example, callers may expect the police to stabilize an out-of-control situation, apprehend violators, recover lost property, and launch an investigation, or at least document an incident's occurrence. All too often, the traditional emphasis on rapid police arrival has generated a parallel pressure on officers to handle calls as quickly as possible and get "back in service" for the next incident. In many cases officers receive little guidance regarding the action they could or should take to best resolve a given situation, and they develop highly individualized styles, of varying effectiveness, for handling the incidents they confront. Without review and guidance, they have little way of knowing what adjustments the department's leadership would find desirable.

The police and mentally disabled persons In every community, police are sent on calls to handle persons suffering from mental disabilities. For most officers, the calls are unpleasant. The persons may be obnoxious, incoherent, unkempt, or seemingly dangerous. The usual tactics used in managing conflicts often fail and; worse, they may even exacerbate the problem. Dispositions are problematic: jails may turn the person away, and if mental health facilities exist, they may have odd hours or admissions policies.

Consequently, all too often these calls are mismanaged. Officers may displace the problem or handle it inappropriately. Clients and officers may be injured or killed. Because managing calls involving persons with mental disabilities is fraught with problems, police managers often ask, "Why, then, are we responsible for them?"

There are several reasons for police involvement. One is that, in accordance with the philosophy of community mental health, many mentally ill persons live in the community.

Conversely, the lack of adequate mental health resources makes police officers front-line mental health providers. A third is that police are available every hour of every day at no cost (over and above taxes) to the caller.

More important, however, police are involved because they have an obligation. The official mandate of the police encompasses dealing with mentally ill persons from the perspectives of law enforcement (response to law breaking or disturbance), civil concerns (initiation of civil commitment), and service provision (referral to mental health resources).

Although these obligations are reasonably clear, managing these calls is not easy. They present unfamiliar problems and are not amenable to traditional responses. They require the development of alternative solutions and assistance from other community service providers. Clearly, the police have a legitimate role in mental health calls, but the police are just one agency among several that provide

---

We now know that the call-for-service workload can be handled in ways that better meet the needs of the callers, of the patrol officers, and of the police organization. As is discussed later in this chapter, improved methods of handling calls break the call-for-service workload into discrete parts, defining more clearly what the department is trying to achieve in each part and then developing guidelines or procedures to achieve those ends more effectively.

As noted earlier, analyses of the call workload in various cities have established that a high incidence of calls (approximately 65 percent) emanate year after year from the same small percentage of locations (approximately 10 percent of a city's addresses). That information has direct implications for the problem-solving process discussed below and strongly suggests the need to develop guidance for officers regarding response to individual calls at those locations.

Research has also shown the usefulness of managerial attention and guidance for officers responding to calls in various categories: crimes after the fact, crimes in progress, domestic violence, nuisance incidents, and repetitive types of complaints.

Research in the late 1960s and mid-1970s clearly indicated that the single most important factor in determining the success of a criminal investigation was information gathered by patrol officers at the time of the initial report.[23] This finding cast doubt on long-standing practices wherein the patrol officer's job was defined merely as taking a report to be followed up later by a detective. This clerical role gave patrol officers little sense of accomplishment, and their reports gen-

---

community-based mental health services. Unfortunately, in many communities effective coordination among these agencies does not exist—and will not, unless an agency initiates it. A police or sheriff's department can be that agency.

Proposing that police form a network of agencies should not be construed as proposing to give the police a mandate to lead in reforming community-based mental health care. Rather, the police should improve the coordination of joint police-mental health responses to emergencies. Not only are improvements clearly in the best interest of the police; they also benefit mentally ill persons, social service agencies, and the entire community.

A coordinated approach will enhance the quality of care that mentally ill persons receive. It can eliminate inappropriate dispositions, such as time in jail, referral to the wrong type of health care agency, or, worse yet, no referral at all. A coordinated approach will also benefit social service agencies, as costly and finite resources are used judiciously.

Police will benefit from a network in several ways. Networks can save time by establishing clear procedures for handling a call and effecting a disposition. Networks can also increase officer safety by using mental health expertise for training and on-scene guidance. In addition, networks can increase officers' job satisfaction and improve community perceptions of a department's ability to handle difficult problems.

Police departments must also examine the extent to which they need to improve their training, policies, and procedures for handling mental health calls. An initiative in the area of mental health can show the community that the police are committed to solving difficult problems and may spur other community groups to help with the management of persons suffering from mental disabilities.

Source: Gerard R. Murphy, Assistant to the Chief, Baltimore County (Maryland) Police Department.

erally were superficial. Detectives received the full volume of crime reports, usually a day or so later, and frequently based follow-up decisions on the sketchy information supplied by patrol. In many instances, complainants received either no follow-up or only a pro forma call back, both of which left them hanging regarding the status of their cases.

After pioneering work by the Rochester police department, many departments expanded the role of patrol officers to permit and, indeed, require patrol personnel to complete a competent preliminary investigation, including a full and active search for witnesses and solvability factors (see the chapter on criminal investigations). Some departments now provide patrol officers with basic photographic and latent fingerprint equipment to facilitate preliminary investigations. Detective involvement at this first investigative stage assists rather than preempts patrol. Determinations about investigative follow-up are made after supervisory screening to determine the need for such follow-up, based on the presence or absence of solvability factors or on the seriousness of the crime involved. Further, detective caseloads are significantly reduced, and the smaller number of assigned cases enhances detective accountability because each detective has a more reasonable and more specific focus for follow-up.

Research clearly indicated that the single most important factor in determining the success of a criminal investigation was information gathered by patrol officers at the time of the initial report.

Patrol officers express greater satisfaction with their expanded role, and the quantity and quality of information flowing into the department for crime or problem analysis improves significantly. In some departments, this enhancement of the patrol officer's role has been taken further: officers are given authority and guidance to prepare their own arrests for prosecution and to carry out entirely at least certain types of investigations in their patrol areas (see the chapter on criminal investigations).[24]

Another area of call handling that requires managerial attention is the initial response of officers to incidents in progress. Because of a very real concern for officer and civilian safety during police response to "hot calls," management must continually reassess the adequacy of policy (for example, on use of force and on emergency response driving), equipment, officer training in "survival" and "violence-reduction" techniques, and intelligence about known hazards. In addition, better techniques for apprehending fleeing crime suspects need to be developed, given court rulings and public opinion on the use of lethal force against various types of suspects.[25] There is much room for improved strategy and tactics in this regard. All too frequently, police units responding to an incident gravitate to the immediate area of the incident, which is usually the one place where the fleeing felony suspect is guaranteed not to be. In one of its studies, the Kansas City police department experimented with a procedure that coupled elapsed reporting-time information from the caller with precalculated information about travel distances and speeds, to develop containment and intercept perimeters following robberies. Called Tactical Response Apprehension Procedure (TRAP), the model expanded the perimeters outward as time passed and gave priority to covering the primary travel routes to the neighborhoods where known robbers were most likely to reside and toward which, presumably, they were most likely to flee. Field testing suggested that such a disciplined response by patrol personnel could achieve higher interception and apprehension rates.[26] This entire area of interception response still awaits high-quality research and development.

Protection against communicable diseases Because patrol officers are frequently the first responders at the scene of accidents and other critical injuries, they need to be protected against diseases that can be communicated by contact with blood, saliva, and other body fluids.

An important step in providing this protection is a written policy outlining specific practices for departmental personnel. A set of procedures for preventing communicable disease and for transport and custody follows. (The policy also should include procedures for disinfection and cleanup after contact with body fluids and for notification of other officers of the possible contamination of departmental vehicles.)

A. Communicable Disease Prevention

1. In order to minimize potential exposure to communicable diseases, officers should assume that all persons are potential carriers of a communicable disease.

2. Disposable gloves shall be worn when handling any persons, clothing, or equipment with body fluids on them.

3. Masks, protective eyewear, and coveralls shall be worn where body fluids may be splashed on the officer.

4. Plastic mouthpieces or other authorized barrier/resuscitation devices shall be used whenever an officer performs CPR or mouth-to-mouth resuscitation.

5. All sharp instruments such as knives, scalpels and needles shall be handled with extraordinary care, and should be considered contaminated items.

   a. Leather gloves shall be worn when searching for or handling sharp instruments.

   b. Officers shall not place their hands in areas where sharp instruments might be hidden. An initial visual search of the area should be conducted, using a flashlight where necessary. The suspect may also be asked to remove such objects from his person.

   c. Needles shall not be recapped, bent, broken, removed from a disposable syringe or otherwise manipulated by hand.

   d. Needles shall be placed in a puncture-resistant container when being collected for evidentiary or disposal purposes.

6. Officers shall not smoke, eat, drink, or apply makeup around body fluid spills.

7. Any evidence contaminated with body fluids will be dried, double bagged in plastic bags, and marked to identify potential or known communicable disease contamination.

B. Transport and Custody

1. Where appropriate protective equipment is available, no officer shall refuse to arrest or otherwise physically handle any person who may have a communicable disease.

2. Officers shall not put their fingers in or near any person's mouth.

3. Individuals with body fluids on their persons shall be transported in separate vehicles from other individuals. The individual may be required to wear a coverall and disposable gloves if he is bleeding or otherwise emitting body fluids.

4. Officers have an obligation to notify relevant support personnel during a transfer of custody when the suspect has body fluids present on his

(continued on next page)

(continued from previous page)
person, or has stated that he has a communicable disease.

5. Suspects taken into custody with body fluids on their persons shall be directly placed in the designated holding area for processing. The holding area shall be posted with an "Isolated Area—Do Not Enter" sign.

6. Officers shall document on the appropriate arrest or incident form when a suspect taken into custody has body fluids on his person, or has stated that he has a communicable disease.

Source of sample procedures: "Models for Management," *The Police Chief* (November 1989): 73–74.

Another area of new insight concerning officer call-handling techniques is connected with domestic violence calls. Research, prompted by concern over both officer safety and effectiveness, has affirmed that officers trained in crisis intervention techniques are better at handling domestic situations, receive fewer subsequent emergency calls about the same problem, and earn higher expressions of satisfaction from the involved parties. Research in the Minneapolis and Duluth police departments has suggested that a policy of making arrests in domestic violence situations may curb subsequent assaults more effectively than do the more informal methods of dispute resolution historically used by officers.[27] Further research is needed to examine the generalizability of these findings to other jurisdictions and the value of arrest versus other options (for example, referral to counseling). Nevertheless, the domestic violence studies illustrate that research can improve critical areas of call handling.

All too frequently, police units responding to an incident gravitate to the immediate area of the incident, which is usually the one place where the fleeing felony suspect is guaranteed not to be.

The call-for-service workload also includes certain categories of nuisance incidents, such as noise complaints, which in many communities constitute a high percentage of calls received. Rarely have police departments examined such complaint categories to determine the most effective responses. But in some college communities, for instance, where noise complaints frequently concern parties at a small number of locations, police departments have found that notices placing the burden of resolution upon landlords are often more effective in reducing the problem than repetitive police visits. Creative alternative responses also need to be fashioned for such chronic noise complaints as those involving off-road vehicles, barking dogs, loud machinery, and so forth.

Even for unpatterned but repetitive types of complaints for which police ability to reduce the frequency of calls for service may be limited, departments can develop responses that are more satisfying to the calling public. For example, a well-researched handout that patrol officers give to victims of obscene or harassing phone calls might be more effective in letting the victims know what to do if they receive subsequent calls than reliance on individual officers' knowledge and their inclination to share it at the time of taking a report. Similarly, a fact sheet that gives basic information and guidance to the parents of a runaway, including the information that 95 percent of such juveniles return within a day or so, may alleviate some anxiety and give the caller the feeling that the police are both concerned and sympathetic. In the same vein, a considerable body of literature and training materials has been developed on the needs and rights of victims of various kinds of crimes.

Tactical patrol responses

Random preventive patrol was originally conceived as a way to make productive use of officers waiting for the next call for service. Although it succeeded in giving officers something to do (and thus served administrative and other purposes), random preventive patrol did not prove effective at deterring crime or intercepting criminals. As a result, since the mid-1970s police departments have increasingly been adopting a variety of directed patrol methods that they believe to be more effective in focusing the attention of officers on the times when, and locations where, crimes, disorders, or other problems are most frequent.[28]

Directed patrol tactics use accurate and timely information to predict where and when crimes are likely to be committed, thus helping to allocate uncommitted patrol resources rationally and effectively. They encourage patrol officers and their supervisors to develop activities tailored to the problem. This allows patrol to take action against criminals who are undeterred by random patrol. In addition, and not insignificantly, the development and implementation of such tactics require patrol supervisors to plan responses in collaboration with their officers. As officers participate in developing plans, morale and job satisfaction increase.

The heart of directed patrol programs is timely feedback of information to patrol officers concerning problems and perpetrators in the beat areas. Generally, that information is provided through crime analysis of reported incidents. The information may, however, also include intelligence received by members of other units concerning active or career criminals or gang crimes, and it may include information concerning specific persons wanted on warrants. (Information is discussed in detail later in this chapter.)

Research has shown that the more-frequent offenders are fairly mobile and commit several kinds of crimes as opportunity permits and that their patterns tend to change frequently.[29] But rapidly shifting patterns may not be readily visible to the beat officer caught up in the daily activity of patrol. If a department is to mount a potentially effective directed response against crime patterns, it must identify the problem and act rapidly. This requires that analysts obtain and analyze crime reports within twenty-four hours of reporting and promptly alert patrol managers to their findings. The information must then be melded expeditiously with the knowledge of the beat officers most familiar with the neighborhood, individuals, and circumstances involved so that a tactical response can be tailored to the particular problem.

A wide variety of directed patrol tactics have been employed in such responses. Perhaps the most rudimentary is to saturate an area with patrol officers. As noted earlier, however, saturation works only at exorbitant expense.

Aggressive patrol tactics, such as field and traffic stops, may be a more cost-effective use of uniformed officers. By stopping potential perpetrators, patrol officers can gather information and show these persons that they are being watched. There is some evidence that such tactics deter offenders because they know if they commit a crime in the area soon after they are stopped, they may be prime suspects. Field and traffic stops are likely to be most effective when they are focused on specific areas experiencing a crime pattern or on individuals known to be, or suspected of being, active criminals. To focus field and traffic stops, crime analysts in some jurisdictions circulate suspect and vehicle information and known offender information and photographs to patrol officers. Some jurisdictions, for example, have creatively coupled such tactics with officers on bicycles or late-night canine tracking exercises to successfully terminate prowler problems.

Aggressive patrol tactics must be approached with caution, however. In all cases, officers must have legal cause to make a stop; equally important, the cause must be made sufficiently clear to the suspect so that it does not arouse undue hostility. Field or traffic stops that are perceived as arbitrary harassment of members of a particular social class or racial or ethnic group will undermine a department's efforts to develop a more effective working relationship with the community.

Covert tactics can also be useful methods of directed patrol. When employed at or near the scene of a potential crime, covert tactics may increase the chances of apprehending an offender in the act. Such activities may range from straight-forward stakeout and plainclothes patrol with nontraditional vehicles (for example, bicycles) to complex decoy and surveillance operations requiring special training.

The stakeout is the simplest covert tactic. When reliable information has been received that a particular location—a residence, store, or other building—is going to be robbed or burglarized, plainclothes officers may set up in or near that location, ready to arrest the offender if the crime is committed. Stakeouts have also been useful for controlling streetcorner drug dealing: the police either arrest the drug sellers or seize the vehicles of buyers, thereby emphasizing "user accountability" (see the chapter on local drug control).

Field or traffic stops that are perceived as arbitrary harassment of members of a particular social class or racial or ethnic group will undermine a department's efforts to develop a more effective working relationship with the community.

Patrol can broaden its coverage with "electronic stakeouts"—the use of alarms or cameras hidden in apartment buildings or stores likely to be robbed or burglarized. (Use of alarms and cameras require the full cooperation of the owner of the business or building.) Police-owned portable alarm systems transmit signals to a mobile base receiver; they may be activated by the motion of bill clips in cash registers, foot pedals, acoustic sensors, pressure mats, and the like. If officers respond quickly when an alarm is triggered, they may arrive before the criminal has left the scene. Portable cameras, usually hidden in unobtrusive boxes, can also be triggered by the removal of marked "bait bills" from a cash register. The pictures they take are often remarkably good, allowing rapid identification of the perpetrator. Because portable alarms and cameras are easily moved and installed, they can be used flexibly, in response to shifts in crime patterns. When the equipment is properly installed and used, the false alarm rate is usually much lower than with commercial burglar alarms.

If a series of robberies, rapes, or assaults has a discernible pattern, patrol officers may be able to take advantage of the offender's habits by using decoy tactics. Decoy officers disguise themselves as typical victims in an attempt to attract an attack while other plainclothes officers watch. To be effective, decoys must be carefully planted at the times when, and places where, offenders are most likely to strike. They must take care to avoid any actions that might be construed as entrapment. Although decoys and stakeouts are most often used by specialized tactical units, many jurisdictions have obtained good results by using specially trained patrol officers for both kinds of details.

Finally, if reliable information is available that an individual offender is committing crimes very frequently, surveillance of the suspect may be indicated. Surveillance is often the first tactic used by specialized repeat-offender units, but most such units rely on surveillance less and less as they become more experienced. One reason is that criminals get very "tail conscious." So-called unmarked patrol cars are often easy to spot, and inexperienced officers often follow too closely. Finally, surveillance can be very expensive, because three or four unmarked patrols are generally needed to follow a suspect efficiently. It is probably best to use surveillance only if good information is available that a particular offender is going to commit a particular crime. In these cases, surveillance can be invaluable.

Some managers have successfully combined tactics in a single directed patrol operation. For example, a patrol squad may use intensified patrols in one neighborhood to drive offenders into an adjacent neighborhood, where a decoy or stakeout is waiting for them

Both for the safety of officers and for the effectiveness of their mission, it is imperative that the officers assigned to covert activities be shielded from all but the most urgent calls for service. Furthermore, many stakeout, decoy, and surveillance tactics are labor intensive and time-consuming (and therefore expensive). Accordingly, covert activities should generally be used only when the information on which they are based is very solid and specific.

Directed patrol may be of little help against a seemingly limitless supply of offenders or against recurring problems that are caused by conditions in the area.

Directed patrol tactics can deal effectively with short-term problems—generally those caused by one or a few particularly active offenders. Most of the tactics have the same objective: to arrest the offenders. Thus, directed patrols may be of little help against a seemingly limitless supply of offenders or against recurring problems (high-crime neighborhoods, frequent trouble-spots, and so on) that are caused by conditions in the area. Perhaps more important, directed patrol tactics typically are limited to what the police can do acting alone. Both theory and experience suggest that crime patterns arising from a wide variety of conditions (including the availability of criminal opportunities, a lack of community watchfulness, or the presence of particularly vulnerable victims) are best handled by cooperative efforts bringing together the police, the public, and other public and private organizations.

Strategic problem solving

Recognizing that directed patrol tactics have limited usefulness as long-term problem-solving techniques, a growing number of police departments have developed a more broadly based strategic model. This approach uses directed tactics when appropriate but also gets other agencies and the public into the act to deal collaboratively with problems that, left unattended, would call for recurring police attention. This collaboration between police and community aims partly to make the community more willing to report crime and cooperate in police investigations and any resultant prosecutions. But more ambitiously, it also aims to heighten crime prevention and control by strengthening the community's ability and willingness to protect itself. In the parlance of community organizers, problem-oriented policing hopes to contribute to the development of "competent communities" (see the chapter on crime prevention). These are communities in which a variety of formal and informal social controls (family, religious institutions, schools, social clubs, and so forth) collectively help to define and maintain socially acceptable behavior by community members. In communities with competent networks of informal social control, police enforcement activities are a last resort rather than the first and practically only way of addressing incivilities, criminal tendencies, and public fear about such problems.

To understand the kinds of recurring, long-standing problems that patrol is often called upon—or calls upon itself—to handle, consider the following examples:

1. An apartment complex is notorious throughout the city for its high burglary rates. One of every four residents is burglarized each year;

follow-up investigations—and occasional arrests—seem to do no good at all.

2.   Disorderly kids invade a peaceful residential neighborhood. Although they have committed no serious crimes, they are noisy and unpredictable; some acts of vandalism have been reported. The kids are black and the residents white—and the beat officers fear a racial incident.

3.   Robberies are up 50 percent citywide, mostly because of an 80 percent increase in convenience-store holdups. The robbers do not appear to favor any particular neighborhoods; neither do most of the crimes appear to be committed by the same offenders.

4.   The police department is inundated with calls from citizens angry about burned-out street lights, the absence of stop signs or traffic lights at dangerous intersections, potholes, building code violations, stray dogs, and similar concerns. Apparently the telephone numbers for the city agencies that handle these concerns are always busy.

Note first that these problems differ in important ways. Problems 1 and 3 deal with crimes; problems 2 and 4 do not. Problems 1 and 2 are confined to a single neighborhood, but problems 3 and 4 are citywide. Problems 1 and 2 have been defined as problems by the public, and the residents of these neighborhoods expect the police to handle them; the pattern of incidents in problem 3, in contrast, has been identified by the police department itself. No one believes that the conditions making up problem 4 are primarily a police concern, but citizens expect someone to do something about them and look on the police as a convenient agency with which to lodge the complaints.

Despite these differences, the four problems have a variety of common elements. They are recurring—that is, they consist of a group of incidents, not a single incident. The incidents in each group are similar in one or more ways: they all may involve the same type of call, the same kind of behavior, the same neighborhood, or the same type of offender or victim. This suggests that the incidents in each group may have a common cause. If such a precipitating cause can be found and removed, the problem may cease; recurrences will be prevented as long as the underlying cause is absent or controlled.

Many of the crime or crime-related incidents with which the police must deal are parts of recurring problems because they are associated with high-rate offenders, high-risk victims, and/or high-risk places.

As these four examples indicate, the problems encompassed by such phrases as "problem-oriented policing" typically are matters directly involving the public, rather than matters of strictly internal administrative concern. Thus, "problem" as used here means "a group of incidents occurring in the community that are related in one or more ways and that are of concern to the public and the police."[30] Admittedly, this definition is very general, but at least it provides a starting point for a discussion of problem solving.

Although problems that fit this definition often involve the patrol force, only rarely can patrol officers solve these problems acting alone. Instead, they must persuade others—other units inside the police department, other local government agencies, citizens, merchants, and universities—to assist them. The entire community will not be involved in every problem, of course; instead, the "community of interest" that becomes involved will depend upon the location, nature, and causes of the problem. Properly engaged, a broad base of potential "problem busters" can be expected to work with its local police on any given, mutually

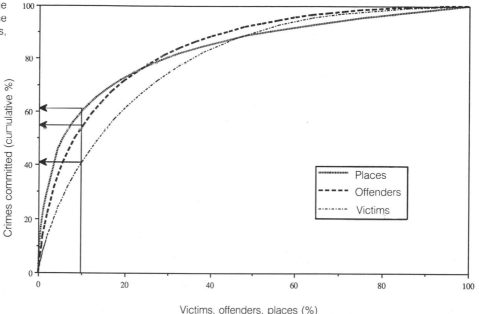

Figure 3–1 Percentage of crimes involving the same victims, offenders, or places.

identified problem, thereby increasing the scope of problem-solving efforts and the likelihood of success.

Many of the crime or crime-related incidents with which the police must deal are parts of recurring problems because they are associated with high-rate offenders, high-risk victims, and/or high-risk places. In conceptualizing crime problems and solutions, it is important to recognize that there are substantially different offending rates among criminals and substantially different victimization rates among people and locations. The most active 10 percent of offenders, for example, commit about 55 percent of the crimes (see Figure 3–1). By the same token, a relatively small number of particularly vulnerable people are disproportionately the victims of crimes and disorders. Examples include convenience-store proprietors and spouses of alcoholics. As shown in Figure 3–1, the most vulnerable 10 percent of victims are involved in about 40 percent of crimes. And more than 60 percent of crimes and disorders are committed at a few particularly dangerous locations—drug corners, biker bars, or public housing complexes, for example. If something can be done about these "ravenous wolves," "sitting ducks," and "dens of iniquity,"[31] crime and disorder can be dramatically reduced. The result will be greater public safety, a higher quality of community life, and reduced demand for the patrol force to respond to these incidents over and over again. "Doing something" means engaging in the process of problem solving—and the resources needed for successful problem solving need not be extensive.

Problem-solving process   Basically, problem solving is nothing but systematic thinking. People regularly solve problems by stopping to think about them and then planning solutions, and organizations rely on their employees to find ways of solving recurring problems in the population served. But police departments typically have not articulated the importance of having each member of the force take responsibility for creative problem solving; and departments have rarely been organized and managed to facilitate such activity. The problem-solving systems used by the police departments of Newport News (Virginia), New York City, San Diego, Tulsa, and other cities are exemplary in that they make the problem-solving priority and methodology

Policing public housing   Throughout the country, the neighborhoods most affected by drugs and violence are ones created by public housing complexes. Designed to provide shelter for a vulnerable population, these neighborhoods have become, instead, havens for those who prey on the vulnerable, intertwining their illegal acts with the day-to-day existence of the people who live there.

The complexity of the situation creates a multitude of problems for law enforcement. Some agencies would like to assault the lines and occupy the territory. Some would like to police from the perimeter and contain the problem within the confines of the public housing complex. Agencies that have experimented with the first approach have discovered that the problems return as soon as the occupation ends. Agencies that have experimented with the second have discovered that the perimeter cannot be maintained: eventually the drugs and violence spill out into the larger community.

The reason these two approaches are inadequate is directly connected to the relationship between the victimizer and the victim. The victim, a resident of public housing, is typically a single woman with children, no means of transportation, no telephone, little education, no support system, no exposure to the broader world, and no hope of getting out. The victimizer, an outsider and a man, offers the victim transportation to the grocery store or laundry facilities, provides companionship, and often provides, as

well, a few extra dollars for the use of her apartment to conduct his crack trade. Frequently, he gives her crack as part of the deal, adding another strand to the dependency that will have to be overcome. However, his expectations go beyond this simple exchange. Once the relationship is established, the niceties end. He charges $5 to $10 for a ride. For any reason, his temper may flare and violence may erupt. If she tries to lock him out, her door may be kicked in, windows broken out, or she may be physically assaulted. Her connection with the outside world is further diminished and controlled by the victimizer, as she becomes locked in by fear. If she informs the police and he is arrested, he will return and abuse her. And who will take her to the grocery store?

Agencies that fail to recognize the complexities of drug use and crime in public housing will never succeed in reducing the problem. They must recognize the needs of those in public housing and must advocate that those needs be met by the agencies, social or governmental, that are designed to meet them. Through the problem-solving process, the police are able to provide valuable information about the remedies appropriate to their particular neighborhoods. Indeed, this approach may be the only viable solution for the police and for the citizens who live in public housing.

Source: Major Carolyn M. Robison, Tulsa Police Department, Tulsa, Oklahoma.

explicit.[32] In these departments, the problem-solving process consists of four stages:

1. Scanning. As part of their daily routine, patrol officers look for recurring problems on their beats. Supervisors use street intelligence obtained from their officers and data obtained from crime analysis, operations analysis, and planning units to find patterns of crime and disorder that may not be immediately obvious.
2. Analysis. The supervisor then assigns the problem to an officer or team of officers, who collect information about the problem. By looking at the offenders, the victims, the social and physical environment of the incidents, and previous responses to the problem,

the officers get a better understanding of the scope, nature, and causes of the problem.

3. Response. The knowledge gained in the analysis stage is then used to develop and implement solutions. Officers seek the assistance of other police units, other public agencies, community groups, and anyone else who can help.

4. Assessment. Finally, officers and supervisors evaluate the effectiveness of their response. They may find they have solved the problem. If not, they may use the results to revise the response, collect more data, or even redefine the problem.

Although some problems can be solved within a few hours, more complex problems can be solved only after months or even years of work. Often the solutions implemented are outside the scope of what are regarded as traditional police responses. Some problems are never "solved" once and for all but, instead, are dealt with through changes in procedure or the development of new programs that operate indefinitely.

An illustration of problem solving: Newport News, Virginia The problem-solving process is illustrated by an example from Newport News, one of the first and most-studied departments to employ problem-oriented policing.[33]

Scanning Built as temporary housing for shipyard workers in 1942, the 450-unit New Briarfield apartment complex in Newport News remained in use during the postwar housing shortage and on into the 1980s. By 1984, the buildings were falling apart. Nearly 20 percent of the units were vacant, and most of these were uninhabitable. The burglary rate was exceptionally high—about 10 percent of the tenants reported a burglary each year, and many felt that most burglaries were never reported. When a department-wide task force was assembled to look for recurring problems in 1984, the consensus was that the New Briarfield apartment complex was the worst trouble-spot in the city.

This was not the first time New Briarfield had been identified as a problem. In 1981, the Newport News police department (NNPD) had persuaded the apartment manager to let it use, free of charge, one of the many vacant units as an office. Two officers were stationed there, and other patrol officers used it as an office. Officers familiar with New Briarfield's problems recommended crime prevention strategies (better locks, stronger doors, and so on), some of which were implemented. During the eighteen months the officers were there, burglary rates went down by 60 percent. But when the officers left late in 1982 to deal with other problems, the burglary rates increased to higher levels than ever before.

Analysis Certain that there was a way to solve the problem permanently, the NNPD task force assigned a detective named Tony Duke to study the problem. Duke began by analyzing data on reported crimes, looking for geographic patterns. He found that crime rates were much lower in adjacent low-income apartment complexes and in some of the better-kept streets within the New Briarfield complex. The burglaries committed throughout most of the New Briarfield complex had widely varied modi operandi, suggesting that many burglars were at work. Further, his study of arrest data showed that most of the burglars lived outside of the complex. Apparently neighborhood burglars found New Briarfield such easy pickings that they frequently turned attention to it.

Visits to the complex suggested one reason for the pattern: school-age youths from throughout the neighborhood hung out in New Briarfield during school hours. According to crime reports, most residents felt that the truant teenagers were responsible for the burglaries. Duke found evidence to support this belief when he realized that kids used the vacant units for drinking and drug use; once he even photographed some youths breaking into a recently vacated unit.

Recognizing that the residents might define the problems differently from the police, Duke secured permission from his supervisors for him and area patrol officers to survey one-third of the New Briarfield households in January 1985. The residents confirmed that burglary was a serious problem, but they were equally upset by the physical deterioration of the complex. New Briarfield had the lowest rents in the city and was filled with people who felt they had nowhere else to go.

Officer Duke then interviewed employees of other city agencies and found that the burglaries were indeed coupled with, and conceivably related to, the general deterioration of the complex. The fire department called New Briarfield a firetrap. Public Works worried about flooding: the complex had no storm sewers. The Department of Codes Compliance noted that standing water was rotting the floors. Cracks around doors and windows made it easier for burglars to force their way in. Vacant units, unfit to rent, sheltered burglars and drug addicts.

While making the rounds of the city agencies, Duke also learned that the owners of the complex were in default on a five-million-dollar loan and that the U.S. Department of Housing and Urban Development (HUD) was about to foreclose. Deciding the time was ripe for action, Duke wrote a report describing the crime problem, the tenants' discouragement, and the views of other city and federal agencies.

Response   The NNPD responded with a mixture of short- and long-term solutions. Given the complex's widespread deterioration and the excessive cost of maintenance, continuing to operate the complex seemed foolish. The police chief used Officer Duke's report to enlist other departments in a joint recommendation to the city manager: help the tenants find better housing, and demolish New Briarfield. All the city agencies involved in serving New Briarfield agreed, and the city manager approved. In June 1986, the manager proposed to HUD and the city council that New Briarfield be replaced with a new 220-unit complex, a middle school, and a small shopping center.

In the meantime, Officer Barry Haddix, responsible for patrolling the area during the day watch, had tried to improve physical conditions at the complex. Working with the apartment manager and city agencies, he arranged to have trash and discarded appliances removed, abandoned cars towed, potholes filled, and streets swept. The vacant apartments were boarded up—and boarded up again when juveniles and drug users tried to use them—and became secure for the first time in years. Haddix also worked with crime prevention officers to organize the tenants. In January 1986, the New Briarfield Community Association began persuading residents to take better care of the neighborhood and lobbying the apartment manager and city agencies to keep the complex properly maintained.

Eventually, HUD agreed to raze New Briarfield. Building by building, the tenants were moved to better low-income housing; and the vacated premises were leveled in preparation for new construction.

Assessment   Shortly after the NNPD began its cleanup campaign, the burglary rate began to drop. By mid-1986, burglaries were down 35 percent, and the rates continued to drop as more and more of the tenants were moved out to better subsidized housing nearby. Burglary rates in neighboring complexes did not increase, confirming Duke's view that most of the crimes had been committed by opportunistic juveniles. The NNPD's actions effectively controlled a runaway crime problem and improved the quality of life for area residents.

Basic principles   The Newport News experience suggests some basic principles of problem-oriented policing. First, the police need to rely heavily on others to define the problem. In this example, as in many others, scanning—or problem identification—need not be based on analysis of hard data. Successful scanning can be as simple as casual observation. Police, like other agencies, can usefully learn about problems from citizen complaints, informal discussions with people on the street, and referrals from other agencies. Even minor complaints can point to trouble-spots. Some problems are important because they pose serious risks to the safety and well-being of the public, but others may be important because, unsolved, they manifest themselves in ways that take a lot of police time.

Police, like other agencies, can usefully learn about problems from citizen complaints, informal discussions with people on the street, and referrals from other agencies.

Second, the officers working the problem need to be careful not to jump to conclusions. In this example, one obvious response would have been to stake out the complex with plainclothes officers, hoping to catch burglars in the act. But because so many juvenile burglars were active in the complex (and because plainclothes officers would have been highly conspicuous), this probably would have been futile as anything but a stop-gap measure. Similarly, high-intensity patrols might have scared the kids off—it had worked before— but would not solve the problem permanently and would be too expensive to maintain indefinitely. Instead, the assigned officer analyzed the problem thoroughly to define it clearly and find its causes. When it became apparent that most of the burglaries were committed by neighborhood kids who hung around abandoned units, it also became clear that something would have to be done about the deterioration and maintenance problems before any lasting headway could be made on the burglary problem.

Law enforcement—in the narrow sense of arrests and prosecutions—may be part of the police response but need not be.

Third, the department needs to deal with the precipitating causes, using whatever methods are available. Law enforcement—in the narrow sense of arrests and prosecutions—may be part of the police response but need not be. In this example, no one needed to threaten legal action to persuade the apartment manager to help clean the complex up or to convince other city agencies that there was no alternative to demolishing it. Except in criminal incidents, a patrol officers' formal powers are limited—but good results can be achieved by persuading others to act. Networks of need can be served through creative networks of authority, resources, and dedication.

This is especially true when, as in New Briarfield, reported crimes are only the tip of an iceberg. The assigned officer often will find that other local government agencies are "hidden allies," also concerned with recurring problems in a particular area or with a particular group. Sometimes, the officer will be pleasantly surprised to discover that another community institution is well on top of a particular problem and that the police role can be minimal. When necessary, problem-solving officers can be a catalyst, stimulating others to do what they know is right even though they have not gotten around to doing it. Yet, cooperation is a two-way street. Officers who hope to spark others to help with a worthy cause may be responsive when others make legitimate requests for police assistance on different worthy initiatives.

Finally, the department must monitor the problem to make sure it has been successfully addressed. At New Briarfield, boarding up the vacant units and cleaning up the complex reduced the burglary rate, and demolishing the complex naturally stopped the burglaries completely—without a premise to enter, burglary became a physical and legal impossibility. Continual monitoring of conditions in the new complex constructed in place of the old can ensure that history will not repeat itself.

Resources for problem solving   The NNPD spent hundreds of officer-hours on the New Briarfield problem, but few problem-solving efforts are this time-consuming. In Philadelphia, a noise problem at a neighborhood bar produced dozens of complaints each month and required dozens of patrol responses to the scene. Finally a patrol sergeant solved the problem by persuading the bar owner to move a juke box speaker to a different wall. In a Baltimore suburb, rowdy youths in a vacant lot intimidated residents of a middle-income neighborhood into not using a local park next to the lot; the Baltimore police drove the kids off by demolishing a shed they had constructed in the lot. In Pasadena (California), patrol officers closed down a drug market in a public housing project by persuading the city traffic engineer to paint the curbs red on the surrounding streets. When officers began giving tickets for parking in a "no stopping" zone, the dealers and their customers moved on. None of these efforts—or hundreds of similar ones that illustrate problem-solving ingenuity around the country—took more than a few hours, but they solved problems whose manifestations had consumed many hours of patrol time and would continue to do so if the problems were not attended to.[34] By looking for the source of the problem, developing creative solutions, and working with the public and other agencies to implement the solutions, these officers not only effectively served the public but also saved themselves and their departments many hours of continued response to repetitive incidents.

Patrol management and supervision

The challenge of running a patrol operation that seeks both to provide emergency service and to engage the full range of community resources in eradicating underlying causes of crime and other police-related problems is the most difficult and demanding managerial function in a police department. Arguably, it is the hardest management job in all of government service. The patrol resources of a problem-oriented department must be simultaneously focused on emergencies and the irreducible call-for-service workload, on directed patrol missions, and on longer-term problem-solving efforts. Activities with the community to foster quality interaction often require the same precision and efficiency as emergency calls. Tactical responses must be efficiently fitted into the mix of call processing and problem solving so that each takes place at the times when, and the locations where, it is most needed.

An effective patrol operation requires continual management of time and resources. Time must be looked at as a precious and perishable commodity. Senior management, surveying a range of organizational responsibilities, must ensure that time for purposeful problem solving is made available when the implementation of specific activities is most opportune, and must establish policy and procedures to shield officers from unnecessary interruptions of their work. Whenever possible, administratively required functions (in-service training, firearms qualification, vehicle and radio maintenance, and so forth) should be scheduled to minimally impede a patrol squad's work. As for patrol resources, mismanaging them is inevitably a very expensive error: on average, covering a single beat twenty-four hours per day, seven days per weeks, costs more than $300,000 a year.[35]

The requirements for an effective patrol operation present a major paradox for management and organization. For the system to function, it must have a solid administrative foundation. There must be an uncompromising insistence on compliance with rules for such matters as work schedules, uniform standards, and equipment use and care. After all, a cadre of individual police practitioners practicing their art on personal schedules and with idiosyncratic tactics would not prove very effective in crowd or riot control, traffic management, search warrant execution, hostage-barricade situations, or scores of other police responsibilities calling for operational precision and reliance on central authority. Similarly, because competent and timely information is important for department operations and management, high and consistent standards for report preparation must be implanted and maintained. The most effective way to enforce these standards and to perpetuate an agency's capacity to coordinate its members' activities in fighting crime and maintaining order is with a hierarchical organization.

The patrol resources of a problem-solving department must be simultaneously focused on emergencies and the irreducible call-for-service workload, on directed patrol missions, and on longer-term problem-solving efforts.

Within this organizational structure, however, the patrol manager must create an environment that encourages problem solving. Central features of this environment are incentives and guidance for officers to engage in free-ranging searches for effective, often nontraditional, solutions to problems. Free-ranging searches sometimes fail, however, and "permission to fail" (when motives were proper) is crucial. The need for creativity, as well as the need for officers' active involvement in both planning and implementing solutions to problems in their beats, requires broad use of participative planning. Arguably, such an environment flourishes best where the organizational structure is flat and emphasis is placed upon knowledge of the problems rather than on the authority of rank.

These contradictory structural requirements for an effective patrol operation require managers to be adept at using the full continuum of leadership styles. The patrol manager must be able to enforce the discipline necessary for ensuring a sound administrative base to the operation and for carrying out missions that do not permit participative decision making. He or she must be equally comfortable, however, sitting down with patrol officers to listen and assist them in creative, sometimes risky, problem solving. Although democratic exchanges are encouraged as part of the problem-solving routine, it must also be clearly understood that managers and supervisors will necessarily revert to rank authority and directives when an immediate and disciplined organizational response is required.

Although democratic exchanges are encouraged as part of the problem-solving routine, it must also be clearly understood that managers and supervisors will necessarily revert to rank authority and directives when an immediate and disciplined organizational response is required.

Like the mid-level manager, the first-line supervisor must balance the need for structure and authority against the need for creativity and discretion. In addition, the supervisor must also balance competing demands and facilitate patrol activities in the real-time environment of day-to-day operations. This supervisor must ensure that department-level concerns (special events, crime-pattern bulletins making particular operational demands, and so forth) are effectively integrated and addressed in his or her squad's planning and field activities. Working with higher-ups as needed, supervisors must ensure that other shifts and patrol sectors, other sections of the department, and other city agencies and community groups know what the supervisors' officers are up to.

The supervisor must thoroughly understand the squad's workload in order to make informed judgments on the number of patrol units needed to handle anticipated calls for service during each hour of the forthcoming tour and, conversely, on the number of units that can be freed—and when—for tactical and problem-solving activities. In the interest of conserving time and resources, supervisors must ensure, for example, that patrol units not needed at an incident leave the scene and that self-initiated officer activities remain focused on priority concerns. In exercising their authority, supervisors must not hesitate to override a dispatched communique for one of their officers that could be handled more effectively in other ways.

The effective supervisor not only monitors and guides officers' performance but also develops his or her squad as a team. What "teamwork" means in this context is that officers, sharing joint responsibility for the welfare of the patrol sector, assist one another in planning and implementing desired activities in the individual beats and neighborhoods that make it up. To be sure, individual accountability is maintained, but whenever possible performance appraisal should emphasize *group* or *unit* work and provide incentives for cooperation (see the chapters on performance measurement and criminal investigations).

Such teamwork and team appraisal enhance creativity and lead to more-effective solutions, greater flexibility, and better support for implementation.

Patrol deployment methods   Police administrators are continually plagued with the problem of managing a limited patrol force in the face of essentially unlimited demands. One part of the solution is effective resource allocation—determining how many patrol officers should be on the street for each time of the day, day of the week, and geographical area of the city. Although there are no universal standards, some staffing and deployment plans are likely to meet a jurisdiction's needs better than others. Developing an effective plan requires solid information and careful thought.

Parts of the problem are relatively easy. If the department's objective is to equalize the calls-for-service workload or minimize response time to emergency calls, then computerized dispatch records can be used to identify the volume and priority of calls for each time, day, and geographical area. To make the calculations easier, computer programs such as PCAM and PATROL/PLAN (for determining the number of units needed) and Hypercube and BEAT/PLAN (for determining beat boundaries) are now

available at reasonable cost for use on microcomputers. Once a deployment plan is developed, these programs can estimate how well it will perform and can suggest changes that will make the plan more effective.

In most jurisdictions, however, the patrol deployment problem is too complicated to let the computer do all the work. One reason is that the computer program is limited by the data put into it—and much of the data needed will be available only if the department's communications system is computerized. In addition, even the most sophisticated program provides only a very simplified model of the city. So when the computer estimates that a deployment plan will (for example) minimize response time, there is no guarantee it really will.

A more important problem is that easily measured objectives (such as minimizing response time or equalizing workload) compete with hard-to-measure but equally important objectives setting beat boundaries so that they are coterminous with natural neighborhood boundaries, for example,

As the department's sources of information increase the feedback to patrol officers on such matters as crime patterns and as officers become more involved with problem-solving activities, conflicts are more likely to arise over priorities and the scheduling of tasks. Again, the patrol supervisor plays the crucial role of balancing priorities and arbitrating the conflicts.

Support for patrol operations

The police experiments of the 1970s—in Kansas City, San Diego, Rochester, and elsewhere—were followed in the 1980s by further initiatives, with police again collaborating with researchers, in Madison (Wisconsin), Flint (Michigan), Newport News, Santa Ana (California), Minneapolis, and other communities. Combining the lessons learned in both decades, practitioners and researchers soon came to realize that effective management of patrol operations had to include support services or "infrastructure" that serves *at the same time* emergency call handling, directed tactical initiatives, and less conventional problem-solving efforts. An infrastructure that neglects the needs of any one of these patrol functions can lead to considerable inefficiencies and threaten effectiveness.

Infrastructure requirements to support effective management of police operations include pre-service and in-service training, performance evaluation, systems for fostering integrity, suitable equipment and facilities, and many other elements discussed elsewhere in this volume. Three crucial elements of the infrastructure of patrol that are directly related to day-to-day operations are discussed in this chapter: resource allocation, dispatch operations, and information support.

or equalizing the opportunities for strategic problem-solving and officer-initiated activities. Calls for service are only a part of the patrol officer's job, and it is unwise for this or any part to drive the whole deployment scheme.

Because of the complexities involved, patrol deployment is not primarily a technical problem. Because it involves balancing among competing objectives, getting the best solution will generally require the assistance and cooperation of command staff, mid-level managers, front-line supervisors, and patrol officers. Establishing an advisory board that includes representatives of the affected sections of the department is a good way to start.

The chief and the advisory board should grant principal responsibility for creating alternatives to an analyst or a small analysis team. The analyst's job is to work with the advisory board to "structure" the problem—formulate objectives, identify data sources, and establish data bases—and to create and analyze potential plans, perhaps with the assistance of a computer

program. Once alternative solutions are produced, they should be reviewed by the advisory board; one or two should be submitted to the chief (and, if appropriate, to officials outside the police department) for final approval. Finally, the advisory board and analysts should develop an implementation plan, including a schedule, provision for announcing and explaining the change to the personnel involved, and a monitoring procedure to review results of the change and make adjustments if necessary.

Although the time and effort required to create a sound deployment plan are substantial, so are the benefits. The planning process will provide patrol managers with a realistic picture of the demands placed on their personnel. It will probably identify significant weaknesses in current staffing patterns or beat configurations. It may suggest the need for changes in department policies, such as those regarding one- and two-officer units or response to non-emergency calls. Most important, it will help the patrol administrator provide better services while containing costs.

Resource allocation

The deployment of patrol personnel both geographically and during different blocks of time must be tailored to best match the diverse requirements encountered by a department. Departments where patrol operations are still primarily incident-driven require resource allocation formulas that, by now, are relatively familiar to most police administrators. Such formulas must take into account the number of calls by time of day and day of week and must deploy officers accordingly. Once this task is complete, adjustments will be required to ensure the safety of officers in handling incidents. These adjustments will depend largely on information that correctly forecasts the number of backup or secondary units needed.

The appropriate backup ratio can vary substantially by time of day. Generally, only about 15 percent of calls dispatched on the day shift (between 0700 and 1500 hours) will require backup. As darkness falls, however, it is not uncommon for departments to send secondary units for slightly more than half of the calls dispatched. Because violence and various types of disturbance calls are more likely during the evening and night shifts, officers mobilized as backup units during those shifts typically must stay considerably longer at the scene of an incident than backups dispatched during the day shift. These factors need to be included in allocation formulas, as do substantial swings in the volume of calls triggered by seasonal changes in weather.

Computer models can help departments determine the most effective deployment of personnel with respect to the call-for-service workload.

Computer models can help departments determine the most effective deployment of personnel with respect to the call-for-service workload.[36] Such proportional deployments have distinct advantages over equalized shifts, which are often maintained because of tradition or administrative convenience. Like any off-the-shelf software program, the alternative deployment configurations offered by computer simulation models must be tempered by a particular department's knowledge of the special problems and requirements of its own community. Distinct hazards and problems such as chronic traffic congestion, large-scale gatherings, and special events must also be factored into calculations, along with the desired response time for emergency and non-emergency calls.

In contrast to resource allocation under a random preventive patrol strategy, assignment and allocation of personnel for directed patrol or strategic problem-solving operations have become increasingly complex. Although the day shift generally accounts for one-third of the dispatches during a twenty-four–hour period, patrol managers may want to assign sufficient personnel so that no more than 25 percent of day-shift officers' time is committed to handling calls for service. Commanders may require that the remaining amount of time be devoted, for example, to conducting follow-up investigations, completing administrative chores, developing tactical plans for directed patrol operations, or engaging in neighborhood problem solving.

The allocation of personnel in a department with a commitment to problem solving will depend on many other factors besides the percentage of time committed to handling calls for service. These factors will include the availability of citizens to work with police on various activities (generally during afternoons, early evenings, and weekends); the days and times (usually evenings) when targeted crime and disorder problems are most vulnerable to intervention; and fluctuations in the emergency call workload. Unlike day-shift personnel, police on the midnight shifts (when there is little opportunity for community interaction and generally fewer targeted crime patterns) may have 75 percent of their time committed to calls for service. Methods used to allocate resources must recognize these differential call patterns and must incorporate "time cushions" to ensure that essential and desired work gets done.

Departments involved in directed patrol efforts and community problem solving will also need to come to grips with the issue of officer rotation. Officers who are expected to work with the public in identifying and then trying to solve problems must get to know their constituents. Fixed shifts enable officers to become more familiar with citizens and the types of crime, other problems, and resources for countermeasures peculiar to a particular shift. If officers are required to rotate too frequently, they tend to rotate away from problems and lose any sense of "ownership" or responsibility for dealing with the problems that occur on any one shift. In any event, regardless of the strategic approach being used by a police department, rotating shifts have come under considerable criticism by medical experts, who charge that such rotation patterns put needless physical and mental stress on officers.

Fixed shifts enable officers to become more familiar with citizens and the types of crime, other problems, and resources for countermeasures peculiar to a particular shift.

A department pursuing problem-oriented policing must also reconsider the spatial, or geographical, aspects of prior administrative and operational approaches. For instance, beat boundaries generally will need to be redrawn to respect natural neighborhood lines. A strong territorial sense is very useful for officers who must grapple with problems on a daily basis. Beat integrity helps advance officers' knowledge of their beats. This knowledge can include intelligence about possible or active suspects and can thus suggest various types of tactical and strategic initiatives. Beat integrity also helps advance the community's knowledge of its police officers and, accordingly, can facilitate police-citizen collaboration to address problems. As observed in the chapter on fostering integrity, traditional concerns about the possible corruptive influence of stable assignments must be considered. Some proponents of community policing believe that a close working relationship between police and citizens, guided by jointly articulated values, encourages the community to help ensure that its officers adhere to the highest professional standards. These are far from simple matters, but experiences to date suggest that, properly handled, beat integrity can indeed contribute to, or at least not undermine, officer integrity.

Dispatch operations

Management of dispatch operations directly affects the prospects for quality patrol operations and indirectly affects the success of criminal investigations (because investigative work largely depends on the value of preliminary investigations by patrol personnel).

Not surprisingly, therefore, efforts to improve patrol operations usually begin not in patrol, but in dispatch. If patrol managers are to stand any reasonable chance of managing their subordinates' time, they must first wrest control of their officers' time from the telephone. Historically, the preoccupation with rapid response has overshadowed a concern for identifying and addressing conditions that cause problems to occur and has tended to perpetuate a reactive mode of policing. In the reactive mode, patrol officers can be bounced around like billiard balls from one call to another without any organizationally sanctioned opportunity to reflect on conditions that generate the calls. As a result, the conditions are left to fester, and they generate more and more calls.

To help break this cycle, numerous police departments have adopted techniques to control the call-for-service workload. The eight techniques outlined below complement one another and have been applied in various combinations. All conserved valuable patrol resources when they were properly tailored to the requirements of particular jurisdictions.[37]

1. *Critically reexamining the call-for-service workload.* Every facet of the dispatch workload is examined to identify
   a. Low-priority services (e.g., escorts, mail runs) that may be substantially reduced or abolished altogether
   b. Services that might be better referred to other agencies of government or to community resources (e.g., heat complaints, neglect cases)
   c. Wasteful internal misuse of patrol officers as errand runners, or unproductive activities such as unnecessary report writing
   d. Services that might be handled by means other than dispatching a patrol officer.
2. *Implementing a strict dispatch policy that delineates the types of calls that will not be handled by patrol or that will be handled only in special circumstances.*
3. *Establishing a call prioritization policy* that delineates the categories of calls that will be answered immediately and the categories that may be delayed for specified amounts of time.
4. *Establishing a telephone reporting capability to handle certain categories of incidents* (e.g., auto theft, larceny from auto). In addition, an efficient response alternative for abating certain conditions, such as barking dogs or loud noise, is a "call back" procedure in which a call taker contacts the offending party via telephone with a warning of impending police action.
5. *Using civilian aides (patrol aides, community service officers, and so forth) to handle errand functions and to process low-priority calls* (e.g., minor accidents, routine reports on found property).
6. *Taking calls for follow-up appointments by assigned beat officers.* Rather than entering concerns about neighborhood problems and continuing conditions, such as abandoned vehicles and youth problems, into the regular dispatch system, community residents can be encouraged to call a separate number to request that a regularly assigned beat officer stop by to discuss the issue. A message is taken and relayed to the appropriate beat officer to follow up when convenient.
7. *Permitting field supervisors to delay or override a dispatch when they know that the assigned beat officer or a closer unit will be available shortly to handle that matter.*
8. *Establishing procedures whereby a patrol officer is shielded from interruption by calls for service.* A few jurisdictions employ a "split-force assignment" that normally protects a segment of officers from answering calls. Other jurisdictions have established policies whereby officers or supervisors can place a patrol unit out of service so that it can engage in some type of dedicated activity. Depending on the level of dedication specified, an officer in that unit is protected from all but extreme emergencies until the structured activity in which he or she is engaged has been completed.

In the early 1980s, the National Institute of Justice tested the effectiveness of these policies in three jurisdictions: Garden Grove (California), Greensboro (North Carolina), and Toledo (Ohio). By 1986, these three cities had demonstrated that 47 percent of all calls for service could be handled by a response mode other than immediate dispatch of sworn personnel. Further, they found that the overwhelming majority of callers freely accepted alternatives to the immediate dispatch of a patrol unit for non-emergency calls.[38] If the communication center is to play a productive role in the management of patrol, the call takers need to perform several tasks that will aid in controlling the call-for-service workload. Guided by screening procedures, they must accurately identify the nature and location of each call received. In doing so, the call taker must, as precisely as possible, identify the time elapsed since the incident and any extenuating circumstances (for example, injuries, a continuing threat to life or property, or the presence of an offender). After accurately categorizing the incident, the call taker must select the proper alternative for processing the call. If dispatch is to be delayed, the call taker must advise the caller of the expected time of response. The dispatchers are also crucial to effective patrol management in that they must select the appropriate unit to handle each call and, if processing is delayed, must monitor backlogs to ensure that calls are processed within specified time frames.[39]

Information support

Running an efficient patrol operation that continually services a broad array of incoming calls along with initiating directed patrol missions and various types of problem-solving activities requires an integrated system of information. That network must both support administrative agendas and facilitate tactical and strategic decision making. Such a comprehensive system must be able to produce the types of analysis needed for administrative reports, management assessments, short- and long-range planning projects, information requests from citizens and elected officials, and operations evaluations. Of paramount importance, the information system must be able to identify emergent and existing crime patterns and provide pertinent data to help officers identify and resolve problems at the beat and neighborhood levels.

For information to be useful, it must be readily accessible on a timely basis to both patrol officers and their managers.

As discussed in other chapters, for information to be useful, it must be readily accessible on a timely basis to both patrol officers and their managers. It must also cover the following categories: operations analysis, crime analysis, traffic analysis, and beat profiling.

Operations analysis Operations analysis must provide timely, accurate, and current statistical information about the call-for-service and dispatch workload of the department. Such data are essential for establishing and periodically reviewing the general allocation of patrol personnel. They are used to forecast anticipated call-for-service demands in a patrol sector by hour of the day and day of the week. Barring special events, inclement weather, and so forth, which must be factored into final decisions, call-for-service demands by day of the week and hour of the day show amazing stability from year to year. Armed with such information, the patrol supervisor can reasonably forecast the number of patrol units needed in a forthcoming time frame to handle calls for service. Conversely, he or she can decide how many units can be committed to other purposeful activities. This ability to statistically analyze high-volume data streams such as calls for service, traffic accidents, offense reports, and so forth for highly repetitive incidents and locations is also an effective means of identifying problems, behavior, and sites toward which problem-solving efforts should be directed. Similarly, the effectiveness of such problem-solving actions can be evaluated by relevant changes in the data streams, including reductions in reported incidents and in the call-for-service workload.[40]

Crime analysis   Most crime patterns appear as short-lived spurts of activity by a single offender or group of offenders. As the duration of these crime series is usually days or weeks, it is critical that a department maintain real-time analysis of crime reports with rapid feedback to allow patrol officers to be aware of and able to affect those patterns. Such analysis is distinct from administrative and statistical summaries. Instead, the crime analyst reviews offense reports on a daily basis to isolate any current or emerging pattern of criminal activity. Offense report information is promptly supplemented with relevant information on suspects and suspect vehicles from regularly maintained files of field interviews and known offenders. Crime analysis bulletins are immediately prepared and routed, providing patrol officers with a concise and accurate description of the crime pattern and location to which attention must be directed, as well as with the best available information on the suspects and vehicles believed to be involved. In addition to this real-time feedback of information about patterns, the crime analyst must fulfill a vital catalytic role by pooling and linking crime information known by officers in various parts of the department. The knowledge of the analyst and the data in his or her files must be readily accessible to any officer involved in investigative and problem-solving activities.[41]

Traffic analysis   Traffic analysis provides a similar on-going information base on motor vehicle accidents so that traffic enforcement can be directed to the proper times and locations. It also supports deeper analysis of the traffic-related problems being researched by patrol officers (see the chapter on traffic services).

Beat profiling   Beat profiling is a systematic means by which patrol officers capture and record critical information on the neighborhoods that make up the individual beats. Information is incorporated into a preformatted framework on the beats' workload, special problems, and resources. Assembling such information can significantly increase an officer's knowledge and understanding of his or her beat.[42] Such a system provides a means by which officers working the same beat on different tours can share critical information about their patrol area. Similarly, a beat profile helps newly assigned officers learn more quickly about a beat.

As departments increasingly look outside themselves to better identify and understand the community's perception of police problems, they face a growing need to enhance their analytic capabilities. The dimensions or substance of such problems as fear, conflict, and disorder are not reflected in the data routinely captured by police agencies. Competent analysis of such problem situations may require police departments to confer with other government agencies and community organizations to identify the data and information that those entities have about those issues. Such inquiry may also identify shared concerns and resources that may be instrumental in eventually effecting a solution. Departments have likewise found surveys of residents to be a useful way to better understand community perception of neighborhood problems and of citizens' relationship with the police. Where such surveys have been undertaken directly by police officers, the act of inquiring itself resulted in a more positive attitude among residents, who came to realize that the police were genuinely concerned about them and their problems.[43]

Although the modern view of patrol sees individual police officers as carrying out effective problem solving, it is neither fair nor realistic to assume that individual officers will have the skills or the ability to extract and analyze data in the department's information system. Neither is it realistic to assume that patrol officers will have ready knowledge of the information or resources that may exist in other departments of government or will know how to access them. For problem solving to become most effective and systematic, departments must develop an internal capability to help patrol officers access and analyze relevant data in the department and in outside agencies and organizations. Similarly, developing an internal capacity to conduct surveys and perform more sophisticated types of analysis or evaluation when needed, or obtaining outside help toward that end, may prove beneficial.

Conclusion

A police organization that includes tactical and strategic problem-solving approaches can significantly energize its patrol force. Around the country, officers doing such work report higher levels of job satisfaction, partly because the community recognizes and expresses appreciation for the department that is striving harder (and "smarter") to come to grips with the community's problems. The officers' satisfaction also stems from the fact that, with their jobs enriched and enlarged, they are more consistently encouraged by superiors to be intelligent and resourceful professionals.

The decision to move toward problem-oriented and related forms of policing and, more important, to sustain them has profound implications for both a department and its chief executive. The concepts underlying problem-oriented policing emphasize the central importance of patrol in accomplishing the police mission. They envision a patrol force highly attuned to problem conditions in various neighborhoods and ready, willing, and able to respond to those changing conditions quickly, creatively, and collaboratively. These expectations challenge the best and brightest talent in the police organization.

The police executive dedicated to improving patrol must take clear and consistent actions that demonstrate—both internally and externally—that patrol is the core function in the department. Specialization should be justified only if it provides a helpful component of the infrastructure of patrol. Specialization that depletes resources and reduces the flexibility of the basic patrol function must be curbed, if not eliminated. Training at all levels must be revamped to support the broadened role of the patrol officer. Performance evaluation procedures must be restructured to recognize and reinforce such attributes as knowledge of the officer's patrol area and creativity and leadership in mounting solutions to problems in that area. Perhaps even more necessary—and difficult—to the police field as a whole during the next decade will be for police executives to show effectiveness and creativity in modifying systems of promotion and compensation to acknowledge the complexity of the patrol function; to recognize patrol's central importance to the police mission; and to encourage experienced, talented officers to remain in direct public service roles within the patrol operation.

1 The diversity of patrol work is not a uniquely U.S. phenomenon. After studying police agencies throughout the world, David Bayley concluded that in all police forces, patrolling is both the most numerous and the most diverse assignment and the one involving the greatest number of encounters with the public (*Patterns of Policing: A Comparative International Analysis* [New Brunswick, NJ: Rutgers University Press, 1985], 114).

2 Eric J. Scott, *Calls for Service: Citizen Demand and Initial Police Response* (Washington, DC: U.S. Government Printing Office, 1981).

3 William P. Rutledge, "The Radio in Police Work" (Paper presented at the annual convention of the International Association of Chiefs of Police, Chicago, 1929).

4 The validity of the assumption that a uniformed police presence would deter crime was ques-

tioned even before Sir Robert Peel ushered in modern policing, as described in Chapter 1. Some scholars attribute the emergence of detectives in Europe in the late nineteenth century to the recognized failure of uniformed patrols to prevent crime: "Police patrol did not remove the need or motivation for crime, and the ingenuity and stealth of many criminals allowed them to commit crimes despite police patrols. Unsolved crimes led to public indignation. Crimes in an apparent series were particularly demonstrative of the impotence of police and revealed the need for diligent inquiry by persons with special skills" (Paul B. Weston and Kenneth M. Wells, *Criminal Investigations— Basic Perspective* [Englewood Cliffs, NJ: Prentice-Hall, 1979], 3).

5 Wesley G. Skogan and George E. Antunes, "Information, Apprehension, and Deterrence: Exploring the Limits of Police Productivity," *Journal of Criminal Justice* 7 (1979): 217–42; and Arthur L. Stinchcombe, "Institutions of Privacy in the Determination of Police Practices," *American Journal of Sociology* 69 (1963): 150–60.

6 Adrianne Weir, "The Robbery Event," in *The Prevention and Control of Robbery*, ed. Floyd Feeney and Adrianne Weir, vol. 1 (Davis: University of California Center on Administration of Criminal Justice, 1973); and Warner A. Eliot, J. R. Strock, and A. E. Witter, *Early Warning Robbery Reduction Projects: An Assessment of Performance* (McLean, VA: MITRE Corporation, 1975).

7 Herbert H. Isaacs, "A Study of Communications, Crimes and Arrests in a Metropolitan Police Department," in *Science and Technology Task Force Report*, President's Commission on Law Enforcement and the Administration of Justice (Washington, DC: U.S. Government Printing Office, 1967), app. B.

8 J. Elliott, *Interception Patrol: An Examination of the Theory of Random Patrol as a Municipal Police Tactic* (Springfield, IL: Charles C. Thomas, 1973); Edward H. Kaplan, "Evaluating the Effectiveness of One-Officer versus Two-Officer Patrol Units," *Journal of Criminal Justice* 7 (1979): 325–55; and William Spelman, Michael Oshima, and George L. Kelling, "On the Competitive Nature of Ferreting Out Crime," final report to the Florence V. Burden Foundation (Cambridge: Program on Criminal Justice Police and Management, John F. Kennedy School of Government, Harvard University, 1987).

9 Elliott, *Interception Patrol*; Albert J. Reiss, Jr., *The Police and the Public* (New Haven: Yale University Press, 1971); and Tony Pate, Robert A. Bowers, and Ron Parks, *Three Approaches to Criminal Apprehension in Kansas City: An Evaluation Report* (Washington, DC: Police Foundation, 1976).

10 Nelson B. Heller and J. Thomas McEwen, "Applications of Crime Seriousness Information in a Police Department," *Journal of Crime and Delinquency* 12 (1975): 44–50.

11 Reiss, *The Police and the Public*.

12 August Vollmer, "Police Progress in the Past Twenty-Five Years," *Journal of Criminal Law and Criminology* (1933): 161–75.

13 George L. Kelling, Tony Pate, Duane Dieckman, and Charles E. Brown, *The Kansas City Preventive Patrol Experiment: A Technical Report* (Washington, DC: Police Foundation, 1974).

14 John F. Schnelle, Robert E. Kirchner, Jr., Joe D. Casey, Paul H. Uselton, Jr., and M. Patrick McNess, "Patrol Evaluation Research: A Multiple-Baseline Analysis of Saturation Police Patrolling during Day and Night Hours," *Journal of Applied Behavior Analysis* 10 (1977): 33–40.

15 Scott, *Calls for Service*.

16 Kansas City Police Department, *Response Time Analysis* (Washington, DC: U.S. Government Printing Office, 1980), vol. 2, *Analysis*; William Spelman and Dale K. Brown, *Calling the Police: Citizen Reporting of Serious Crime* (Washington, DC: U.S. Government Printing Office, 1984).

17 Kansas City Police Department, *Response Time Analysis*, vol. 2; and Spelman and Brown, *Calling the Police*.

18 Citizen reporting delays were found to be primarily associated with apathy, skepticism about the usefulness of calling, and voluntary actions taken before the citizens decided to call the police. Such voluntary actions often included telephoning other persons, observing the situation to see what happened, investigating the scene themselves, and contacting their employer, a supervisor, or a security guard for advice.

19 Kansas City Police Department, *Response Time Analysis*, vol. 2; and Tony Pate, A. Ferrara, R. Bowers, and J. Lorence, *Police Response Time: Its Determinants and Effects* (Washington, DC: Police Foundation, 1976).

20 Glenn L. Pierce, Susan Spaar, and LeBaron R. Briggs, *The Character of Police Work: Strategic and Tactical Implications* (Boston: Center for Applied Social Research, Northeastern University, 1986); and Lawrence W. Sherman, Patrick R. Gartin, and Michael E. Buerger, "Hot Spots of Predatory Crime: Routine Activities and the Criminology of Place," *Criminology* 27 (1989): 27–55.

21 Michael T. Farmer, ed., *Differential Police Response Strategies* (Washington, DC: Police Executive Research Forum, 1981); and J. Thomas McEwen, Edward F. Connors III, and Marcia I. Cohen, *Evaluation of the Differential Police Response Field Test* (Washington, DC: U.S. Government Printing Office, 1986).

22 Herman Goldstein, "Improving Policing: A Problem-Oriented Approach," *Crime and Delinquency* 25 (1979): 236–58. Goldstein's latest book, *Problem-Oriented Policing* (New York: McGraw-Hill, 1990), expands the concept and discusses its implementation during the 1980s.

23 Bernard Greenberg, Carola V. Elliott, Lois P. Kraft, and H. Steven Procter, *Felony Investigation Decision Model: An Analysis of Investigative Elements of Information* (Menlo Park, CA: Stanford Research Institute, 1975); and Peter W. Greenwood, Jan Chaiken, Joan Petersilia, and Linda Prusoff, *The Criminal Investigation Process* (Santa Monica: Rand Corporation, 1975), vol. 3, *Observations and Analysis*.

24 Peter B. Block and James Bell, *Managing Investigations: The Rochester System* (Washington, DC: Police Foundation, 1976); Ilene Greenberg and Robert Wasserman, *Managing Criminal Investigations* (Washington, DC: National Institute of Law Enforcement and Criminal Justice, 1979); and Timothy N. Oettmeier, *An Evaluation of the Houston Police Department's D.A.R.T. Program* (Houston: Houston Police Department, 1985).

25 William A. Geller and Michael Scott, "Deadly

Force: What We Know," in *Thinking About Police: Contemporary Readings*, ed. Carl Klockars (New York: McGraw-Hill, 1990).

26 Kansas City Police Department, *Response Time Analysis: Executive Summary* (Washington, DC: U.S. Government Printing Office, 1980), 26–27.

27 Jack B. Pearce and John R. Snortum, "Police Effectiveness in Handling Disturbance Calls: An Evaluation of Crisis Intervention Training," *Criminal Justice and Behavior* 10 (March 1983): 71–92; and Lawrence W. Sherman and Richard A. Berk, "The Specific Deterrent Effects of Arrests for Domestic Default," *American Sociological Review* 49 (1984): 261–72.

28 For a general description, see William G. Gay, Theodore H. Schell, and Stephen Schack, *Routine Patrol*, vol. 1 of *Improving Patrol Productivity*, (Washington, DC: U.S. Government Printing Office, 1977).

29 Jan M. Chaiken and Marcia R. Chaiken, *Varieties of Criminal Behavior* (Santa Monica: Rand Corporation, 1982); and William M. Rhodes and Catherine Conly, "Crime and Mobility: An Empirical Study," in *Environmental Criminology*, ed. P. J. Brantingham and P. L. Brantingham (Beverly Hills, CA: Sage, 1981).

30 John E. Eck and William Spelman, *Problem-Solving: Problem-Oriented Policing in Newport News* (Washington, DC: Police Executive Research Forum, 1987), 42.

31 William Spelman and John E. Eck, "The Police and Delivery of Local Government Services: A Problem-Oriented Approach," in *Police Practice in the '90s: Key Management Issues*, ed. James J. Fyfe (Washington DC : International City Management Association, 1989), 58. See also Deborah L. Weisel, *Tackling Drug Problems in Public Housing: A Guide for Police* (Washington, DC: Police Executive Research Forum, 1990).

32 See, for example, New York City Police Department, *The Community Patrol Officer Program: Problem Solving Guide* (New York: New York City Police Department, 1988).

33 For more detail, see Eck and Spelman, *Problem-Solving*, 66–72.

34 The Police Executive Research Forum now publishes a journal, *Problem Solving Quarterly*, containing illustrations and advice for police problem solvers.

35 Bureau of Justice Statistics, U.S. Department of Justice, *Justice Expenditure and Employment, 1985* (Washington, DC, 1987); and National Associ-

ation of Criminal Justice Planners, "Survey of Selected Jurisdictions," Unpublished manuscript (1982).

36 For a solid reference on patrol deployment analysis techniques, see Margaret J. Levine and J. Thomas McEwen, *Patrol Deployment* (Washington, DC: National Institute of Justice, U.S. Department of Justice, 1985).

37 McEwen, Connors, and Cohen, *Evaluation of the Differential Police Response Field Test*.

38 Ibid.

39 Ibid; and Richard G. Grossie, Thomas J. Sweeney, Eugene A. Buzzi, Timothy D. Crowe, James Evans, and William D. Wallace, *The Role of Communications in Managing Patrol Operations* (Washington, DC: Law Enforcement Assistance Administration, U.S. Department of Justice, August 1978).

40 For further background on the concept and techniques of operations analysis, see Law Enforcement Assistance Administration, U.S. Department of Justice, ed., *Review of Patrol Operations Analysis: Selected Readings from ICAP Cities* (Washington, DC, June 1978); and Richard G. Grassie and John A. Hollister, *A Preliminary Guideline Manual for Patrol Operations Analysis* (Washington, DC: Law Enforcement Assistance Administration, U.S. Department of Justice, June 1977).

41 For further background on the concepts and techniques of crime analysis, see William H. Bieck, "Crime Analysis," in *Encyclopedia of Police Science*, ed. William G. Bailey (New York: Garland Publishing, 1989); G. Hobart Reiner, Thomas J. Sweeney, Raymond V. Waymire, Fred A. Newton, Richard G. Grassie, Suzanne M. White, and William D. Wallace, *Integrated Criminal Apprehension Program Crime Analysis Operations Manual* (Washington, DC: Law Enforcement Assistance Administration, U.S. Department of Justice, 1977); and Robert Austin, Gary Cooper, Don Gagnon, John Hodges, Kai Martensen, and Michael O'Neal, *Police Crime Analysis Unit Handbook* (Washington, DC: National Institute of Law Enforcement and Criminal Justice, U.S. Department of Justice, 1973).

42 John E. Boydstun and Michael E. Sherry, *San Diego Community Profile: Final Report* (Washington, DC: Police Foundation, 1975).

43 Philip B. Taft, Jr., *Fighting Fear: The Baltimore County C.O.P.E. Project* (Washington, DC: Police Executive Research Forum, 1986); and Eck and Spelman, *Problem-Solving*.

4 Crime prevention, fear reduction, and the community

A slow but fundamental change—a "quiet revolution"[1]—is occurring in the values and philosophies of police management. One manifestation of this change is a new understanding, supported by research, of how to control and prevent crime. At the core of this new understanding is a deep appreciation of the importance of nonpolice resources in fighting the war on crime, and especially an appreciation of the role of the community as a partner of the police in fostering public safety. Criminal justice scholars and administrators have come to recognize that one of the biggest mistakes in "modern" policing was to place total responsibility and accountability for public safety on the shoulders of law enforcement agencies.

This chapter focuses on the joint production—sometimes called "coproduction"—of public safety by the police and the community. "Producing" or fostering public safety involves controlling and preventing crime, maintaining public order, and—increasingly important—attempting to influence public fears, perceptions, and concerns about crime. How police departments elect to pursue these objectives (that is, what programs, strategies, and policies they develop and promote) depends to a large extent on their understanding of the causes of crime-related problems and their beliefs about the effectiveness of alternative approaches.

The long-held assumption that preventive patrols, rapid response, and follow-up investigations would significantly reduce the level of crime in the community was based on a limited understanding of what causes crime. Research findings, however, indicate that crime rates are heavily influenced by social forces in the community and that community-based actions must play a central role in any program to prevent crime.[2] Jane Jacobs effectively summarizes this orientation:

The first thing to understand is that public peace . . . is not kept primarily by the police, necessary as police are. It is kept primarily by an intricate, almost unconscious network of voluntary controls and standards among the people themselves, and enforced by the people themselves.[3]

Successful crime prevention depends more on the community than on the police. In contrast to the traditional view that citizens supplement the police, this perspective can be extended to suggest that the police supplement the citizens.

Thus, successful crime prevention depends more on the community than on the police. In contrast to the traditional view that citizens supplement the police, this perspective can be extended to suggest that the police supplement the citizens. However, because the resources for preventing crime reside with the police, they have a disproportionate responsibility to develop a working partnership with the community to promote public safety. Hence, police administrators should give priority attention to the question of how their employees can serve as catalysts and resources for community anticrime initiatives.

The problem of crime control is related to the problem of the public's fear of crime. There, too, police response should be grounded in a solid understanding of the contributing causes: what factors contribute to citizens' perceptions of crime and of their own risk of being victimized? Traditional preventive patrols, rapid response to calls, and efforts to identify and apprehend offenders are not sufficient to reduce citizens' fears because, as numerous research studies have shown, fear of crime is not simply an objective response to one's risk of being victimized but is, rather, determined by a host of other personal, social, and environmental factors.[4] Thus, police need to respond to these facts in seeking to develop creative new programs designed specifically to reduce fear.

Experienced administrators who are taking innovative steps in law enforcement know that the era of believing that more police officers and quicker response times will solve the problems of crime and fear is coming to a close, and the era of increasing police-community contact is being ushered in. How this quiet revolution translates into practical, publicly acceptable, cost-effective programs and policies is not entirely clear—nor are such matters usually clear in the midst of a revolution. Indeed, this issue may be the biggest challenge facing police executives.

The police have an important role in helping communities become independent, self-regulating neighborhoods.

This chapter offers guidance by describing a variety of crime prevention practices, fear reduction practices, and police-community approaches that have been employed in different cities. The approaches deal with individual self-protection; collective action; environmental design; the media and public education; school-based initiatives; business-based initiatives; and successful planning and implementation of community crime control programs. Throughout, the chapter suggests that police managers take a second look at community crime prevention—this time as a primary police function rather than as a secondary or auxiliary activity. It also suggests that police have an important role in helping communities become independent, self-regulating neighborhoods. Central to the notions of community crime prevention and community policing should be the pursuit of "community competence" or "perceived efficacy"[5]—building the skills and confidence of local residents and community organizations so they can successfully address major problems and deal with local institutions to effect change in their neighborhoods.

The proliferation of possible problems and strategies for the cooperative production of public safety raises questions about where police resources should be invested. Certain approaches can claim greater validation by rigorous research than others but, generally speaking, reliable research is too sparse to provide any strong guidance at this time. Obviously, at this juncture, as always, the thoughtful "seat-of-the-pants" assessments of experienced police and community leaders are of some value, pending more powerful and informative formal evaluations. One thing, though, is quite clear—there are as many definitions of "crime prevention" as there are program advocates. Furthermore, the popularity of specific programs changes with the winds of Washington politics and consequent federal funding priorities. So long as the reader understands these basic facts, what follows may not appear so fragmented—or, at least, the fragmentation can be seen as a necessary reflection of the current state of the art.[6]

The changing face of crime prevention

The meaning of "crime prevention" to law enforcement agencies has changed over the years. In the late 1960s and early 1970s, crime prevention was a public relations vehicle for police administrators to use in improving the public's image of the police. The term "community relations" was used interchangeably with "crime prevention,"[7] and a particular officer or unit of officers was assigned the task of promoting the police department at community and civic meetings, as well as responding to concerns about police misconduct or the failure to contain crime. A major purpose of these activities was to explain that the police were doing everything possible to prevent crime, catch criminals, and improve relations with minority communities (for example, reducing police brutality and hiring more minorities on the police force). During the early 1970s, when public recognition of "crime victims" as a group was on the rise, police began to encourage citizens to take action to protect themselves and their homes. By the early 1980s, many police departments were ready to promote collective (that is, group) anticrime activity—so long as the participating citizens did not go beyond their prescribed function of being the "eyes and ears" of the police. Neighborhood Watch, for example, was widely endorsed, but police managers took a much more cautious approach to citizen patrols. Patrols were too similar to what the police do, and they also represented the potential for vigilantism (despite little evidence of actual vigilantism).

Police support for citizen participation in crime prevention appeared to be a step in the direction of recognizing that police officers could not prevent crime by themselves and that collective citizen action might play an important role in helping the police. Although many police chiefs no doubt saw the preventive value of citizen involvement, often Neighborhood Watch and related programs were initiated for public relations purposes. These programs became extremely popular in many communities during the early 1980s, and police executives were quick to recognize their marketability.

Thus, police crime prevention in the United States has evolved from public relations to minority relations to the promotion of citizen participation in personal and household protection, and finally to the support of limited collective citizen action, namely, block or other localized meetings to discuss how citizens can watch for and report suspicious behavior to the police. In most of these efforts, citizens continue to be cast in a supplemental rather than a central role in the war on crime and drugs. As this chapter will show, a few police agencies are taking a further step—exploring the idea of meeting with citizen groups to jointly identify neighborhood problems, develop appropriate solutions, and implement programmatic responses.

The following sections briefly synopsize the progress that has occurred in crime prevention and describe programs and evaluation data (when these are available). Many other chapters in this volume chronicle progress in policing in areas other than community crime prevention, although the guiding philosophy behind them is the inherent value of greater police-citizen collaboration. Every police agency will need to pursue its own course based on the characteristics of the community it serves, the nature and severity of the problems it faces, the resources available for public safety, and the ingenuity of the police and the community in marshaling these resources constructively.

Theoretical foundations

Virtually all social programs are based on some theory, however primitive or unwritten, about social behavior; programs for preventing crime and reducing fear of crime are no exception. Essentially, two basic strategic models underlie efforts to prevent crime and reduce fear in the community: the *opportunity reduction* model and the *informal social control* model.[8]

The opportunity reduction model suggests that crime can be prevented by the removal or reduction of opportunities for criminal activity in specific situations, and that fear can be reduced by decreases in the level of crime in the community—decreases that will lower people's actual and perceived risk of being victimized (in other words, when crime decreases, people will feel safer). The primary ways of preventing or reducing opportunities for criminal activity are to remove potential offenders' access to the areas, objects, or persons needing protection (for example, by putting locks on doors, and fences around buildings) or to change the physical or social environment (or both) to increase the likelihood that offenders will be detected and apprehended (for example, by using human or electronic surveillance). Other opportunity reduction strategies to prevent or reduce crime include removing the target itself, removing the means of committing the crime, and reducing the payoff.[9] Opportunity reduction strategies to reduce the fear of crime range from high-visibility police patrols to stronger deadbolt locks. In other words, they are designed to reduce crime.

The informal social control model suggests that crime is caused by the decline of "community" and by the failure of traditional agents of social control (family, religious institutions, schools, ethnic groups, and others) to regulate behavior. Informal social control involves the use of rewards and punishments (such as verbal reprimands, warnings, social ostracism, or expulsion from clubs and community activities) by community members to encourage conformity with local customs and norms. This model also suggests that fear of crime is not always a simple response to the amount of local crime.

According to this model, the primary means of preventing crime is to foster a sense of "community." The prevailing belief is that this can be accomplished by organizing local residents, defining local problems, training citizens in how to deal with local institutions and government agencies, and encouraging more frequent positive social interaction among community members. Supposedly, this increased social contact sets in motion the social processes needed to strengthen informal social controls, which should lead to increased feelings of efficacy and competence, increased public surveillance of local problems, and a greater willingness to intervene in criminal and emergency situations.[10] Fear is decreased because, when communities are competent at self-regulation, they are able to control crime and other forms of deviance that cause fear. In addition (and this idea is of more recent vintage), when fear is viewed as not always a simple response to the amount of local crime, strategies should be designed and implemented to reduce fear directly, whether or not they also reduce crime.

In the meantime—which, admittedly, could be a long, long time—the absence of strong informal social controls in many communities forces us to rely relatively more often on formal mechanisms of social control, as reflected in the criminal code and the enforcement activities of the police. The key question here is not whether communities in the United States need police, but how much they need them to do certain tasks when the citizenry is beginning to shoulder more of its rightful obligations of citizenship.

Community-focused strategies, because of their diversity, are not easily incorporated into a single conceptual framework. Nevertheless, the two-dimensional framework that follows is a simple way of introducing the major approaches to community anticrime programming. First, the police-community partnership must decide on the primary target group: potential victims or potential offenders. In other words, whose behavior is the intervention seeking to influence directly? If the target is potential victims, the focus is on encouraging neighborhood residents to participate in programs to protect themselves, their property, or their neighborhood. These actions, in turn, are expected to influence the behavior of potential offenders, but the initial focus is on community residents. If the target is potential offenders, the programs and strategies will be designed to alter their desire or motivation to engage in criminal acts. (Thus, the distinction made here is similar to the one between primary and secondary prevention, with the offender-focused strategies serving a primary prevention function of altering the motivation to commit crime, and the victim-focused strategies serving a secondary prevention function of strengthening citizen resistance to the existing threat of victimization.)[11]

Second, the police-community partnership must select the primary target setting, that is, the setting in which the intervention is implemented. Activities can be developed and implemented in target neighborhoods, schools, businesses, or components of the criminal justice system.

Although this framework offers some sense of the range of possibilities (e.g., focusing on victims in schools or the criminal justice system, focusing on potential offenders in neighborhoods or the criminal justice system), it tells very little about the nature of the intervention. To plan, implement, and evaluate a specific strategy, the police and the community need to answer additional questions:

1. *Who has primary responsibility for executing the intervention?* Individual citizens or groups of residents? Individual police officers or select groups of police officers? Other city agencies? The mass media?
2. *What is the primary method of intervention?* The printed media? The electronic media? Informal door-to-door contacts? Group meetings? Formal presentations? High-visibility patrols on foot or by vehicle?
3. *What type of change is expected?* Change in social behavior? Change in the physical environment?

The strategies described in the remaining pages illustrate how police executives and community leaders have begun to answer these questions.

Cooperative strategies aimed at individual self-protection

Police involvement in crime prevention has been dominated by efforts to encourage residents individually to take measures to protect themselves, their own homes, and their property (in other words, the primary target group has been potential victims, and the primary setting has been the community, not the criminal justice system). Crime prevention officers across the country have distributed hundreds of thousands of pamphlets and brochures and have given thousands of presentations warning the public as individuals to take precautionary actions or else run the risk of becoming another crime statistic.[12] The list of recommendations is virtually endless, including such popular prescriptions as "Don't go out alone at night" and "Don't carry lots of cash or wear visible jewelry." Essentially, citizens have been instructed in methods of avoiding being victimized and methods of managing their risk of victimization—through resistance and self-defense activities—when this risk is unavoidable. In addition, victim services provide a special means of reaching individuals.

Risk avoidance

Crime is not a random event that is equally likely to occur to any person at any place at any time. To the contrary, the National Crime Survey has shown that a person's routine daily activities are an important predictor of his or her chances of victimization.[13] Thus, if police or community organizations can persuade citizens to alter their daily activities to avoid high-risk situations, then these same individuals should be less likely to suffer criminal victimization. The success of these efforts to change people's routine activities has yet to be carefully documented. However, many citizens do take precautionary action to avoid victimization, regardless of whether the action is motivated by targeted crime prevention appeals or simply by a general sense of vulnerability to crime. The most common action is some type of behavioral restriction to avoid risk, such as staying at home at night, avoiding certain areas or streets perceived as dangerous, and avoiding certain types of people perceived as dangerous.

Although citizens should be encouraged to use common sense and take reasonable precautions to avoid becoming crime victims, too much encouragement can be counterproductive. The reasons are essentially twofold. First, avoidance behavior is a double-edged sword; it may reduce a person's chances of victimization for a certain period, but if all the people in a neighborhood hide behind locked doors, they will lose their ability to prevent crime in the streets, and the level of criminality may increase in the long run. In effect, the streets will be turned over to the criminally minded. In fact, leading crime prevention experts are trying to encourage collective, public minded actions rather than individual, private-minded precautions as a strategy for building a sense of community. Second, too much self-protective action may serve as an excessive reminder that one lives in a dangerous environment and, consequently, may contribute to an increase in fear of crime.

Resistance and self-defense activities

The risk of victimization cannot be avoided entirely. Given this reality, the police and the community share the responsibility for educating the public—especially those who feel vulnerable—in methods of responding when faced with a possible offender. The first and most difficult question is whether resistance by the potential victim is a good idea. Over the years, police policy has typically discouraged citizens—especially women and older people—from resisting when confronted by an offender, arguing that the price of resistance (possible serious injury or death) is too high. However, this conventional wisdom has been challenged by women's groups and by studies on the effects of resistance. For example, research on sexual assault suggests that forceful strategies, such as screaming, yelling, and offering physical resistance, are often more effective in preventing rape than nonforceful strategies, such as pleading, crying, reasoning, and appealing to morality.[14] However, at least two qualifiers should be noted: (1) physical resistance is more likely to result in injury to the victim than either nonphysical resistance or nonresistance; and (2) nonphysical resistance (such as screaming) is nearly as effective as physical resistance in preventing the completion of rape. Thus, if policy decisions are necessary, our knowledge to date indicates that nonphysical resistance is the option most likely to reduce the chance of completion and the chance of harm to the victim. However, every crime situation is unique, and a woman must therefore apply this knowledge to the circumstances in which she finds herself (for example, if the offender has a knife or gun, nonforceful strategies are usually the most prudent course of action).

Leading crime prevention experts are trying to encourage collective, public-minded actions rather than individual, private-minded precautions as a strategy for building a sense of community.

Given that fear of crime is especially high among those who feel physically unable to defend themselves, the issue of self-defense training should be addressed by those who are planning crime prevention programs. Although the local police should not be expected to offer self-defense classes, they should take responsibility for telling the public what is known (and what remains unknown) about various self-defense strategies. Regardless of its preventive effects, there is some evidence that self-defense training may increase feelings of self-confidence and lower fear of crime. Similarly, other research suggests that people who participate in the WhistleStop program (i.e., who carry a whistle that they are to blow when observing criminal situations) may be more willing to go out at night, which, in turn, may make them less fearful.[15]

One dangerous trend in self-defense that law enforcement and community leaders must respond to is the "domestic arms buildup." In many urban areas, citizens who feel vulnerable to crime purchase handguns for self-protection. Personal ownership of firearms is a complex issue that has been the subject of considerable debate and some research.[16] The research to date does not clearly indicate whether the increase in firearms ownership has served to boost or to reduce levels of crime, but a number of researchers cite indirect evidence that handguns have contributed to the level of violence in the United States. Furthermore, there is little evidence that owning a gun reduces one's chances of victimization or lowers one's fear of crime. And there is some evidence that possession of a weapon actually increases one's chances of injury when one is confronting a criminal. In addition, statistics on gun-related accidents and guns stolen from legitimate owners should be considered when one is making decisions about practices and policies.

Handguns may be the most important law enforcement issue of the 1990s, and every community needs to decide what course of action is most appropriate, given local standards and values. If a community is not prepared for a total ban on handguns, it has two options: strong, enforceable restrictions on gun ownership, or comprehensive gun safety programs. The month-long Handgun Safety Campaign conducted in Charlotte, North Carolina, in 1987 is an example of how business, community, and civic leaders can come together to educate the public about the risks and responsibilities of handgun ownership, including storage, maintenance, training, handling and use, and legal requirements.[17]

Victim services

Additional opportunities for preventing crime and reducing fear of crime emerge when the physical, emotional, legal, economic, and security needs of crime victims are being responded to. A national victim rights movement became fully operational in the early 1980s, strongly supported by the president's 1982 Task Force on Victims of Crime and by federal legislation passed in 1982 and 1984. As a result, victim services have become institutionalized in state and local agencies, but gaps in service remain surprisingly large. In particular, law enforcement agencies have been slow in responding to the needs of crime victims. The vast majority of victim service programs are located in the office of the prosecutor or in community crisis centers rather than in police departments. But although crisis intervention experts have been critical of the police for their insensitivity to victims at crime scenes, in a number of cities police and civilians have teamed up to provide crisis and follow-up services. National police training programs have been initiated by the International Association of Chiefs of Police (IACP), the National Organization of Black Law Enforcement Executives (NOBLE), and the National Sheriffs' Association's Victim Assistance Program (NSAVAP). Moreover, a growing number of state legislatures have enacted "victims' bills of rights" to protect victims and guarantee that they receive a certain level of services.

Many victim service programs in police departments offer little more than information and assistance about court appearances, but others offer a full range of services, beginning with crisis intervention, to all victims who need it. Often these programs are assigned to special units staffed by civilians with special training. An alternative is to train all responding officers to help ensure that all victims of serious crime get at least some immediate service. Currently, it is often difficult to get responding officers to call in victim service specialists in a timely and appropriate manner. Training all responding officers, however, is not a one-time exercise. We have learned that a heightened sensitivity to victims among police officers who receive special training tends to dissipate within a

Victim-witness and youth outreach programs Victim service programs are traditionally located outside of police departments, but the times are changing, thanks to a few model programs and the recognition that early intervention is important for crisis victims.

In 1976 the Evanston, Illinois, police department received a grant from the Illinois Law Enforcement Commission to establish the Victim-Witness Advocacy Unit. The goals of this program are (1) to provide comprehensive social services to crime victims and witnesses, assist with problems resulting from victimization, and support victims and witnesses through the criminal justice system; and (2) to provide assistance to those who come into contact with the police in non-crime-related situations and who could benefit from social service intervention.

The program handled 1,857 cases in 1989. It served victims of homicide, criminal sexual assault, domestic violence, battery, home invasion, robbery, child abuse or neglect, burglary, and other crimes, as well as persons needing assistance for reasons unrelated to crime (for example, mental illness, confusion or other problems related to aging, homelessness, disputes with a neighbor, death notification, or juvenile and family problems).

Program services include the following:

Crisis intervention: In-person crisis intervention is provided to clients in need of emergency assistance seven days a week, twenty-four hours a day.

Counseling: Clients are helped to deal with their emotional responses to victimization.

Court advocacy: The program helps victims and witnesses at each stage of the criminal justice process by keeping them aware of their court dates; providing transportation to court; having someone appear in court with victims and advocate victims' rights; interceding with employers so that victims may appear in court without being docked time; and providing interpreters for victims when necessary.

Referral: Victims are referred to the appropriate social service agencies to meet their needs, and eligible victims are assisted in filing for monetary reimbursement under the Illinois Victims Compensation Act.

Emergency funding: The bureau has funds to help victims with emergency aid (i.e., shelter, food, health care) when appropriate.

Education/crime prevention: The bureau helps educate the police and community groups about prevention of sexual assault, domestic violence, and other crimes.

The Evanston program also has a youth outreach component that provides supervision, counseling, and psychological services to youths under the age of seventeen with social, behavioral, and/or family difficulties and who come in contact with the police department. Referrals are also accepted from youths themselves, parents, school personnel, and other social service agencies. The intent of the program is to divert youths from the criminal justice system and child welfare system.

The victim-witness and youth outreach programs are staffed with civilian employees: a director; four out-reach workers, and one part-time psychologist. They are part of the Division of Youth and Victim Services, which is responsible to the department's deputy chief of investigations.

few months after the officers return to the field; thus, refresher training is important.[18]

Finally, victim services can be linked to crime prevention services through such programs as home security surveys and Neighborhood Watch. Although many people express only a minimal interest in crime prevention, the experience of victimization can change this attitude rather quickly. Crime prevention practitioners can verify the perhaps common-sense proposition that persons who have been recently victimized are especially willing to listen to crime prevention recommendations. Advice about how to improve home security or personal security may help restore a recent victim's sense of control over his or her environment, but it can also be damaging if it is not presented properly. For example, blaming the victim for not exercising caution in the first place is not a helpful approach. Nevertheless, assigning such blame is a common reaction among police officers and neighbors. (As is discussed below, too much talk about crime at community meetings may contribute to an increase rather than a decrease in fear of crime.)

Collective approaches to crime prevention

Crime prevention theory and policy—although not necessarily law enforcement practice—have evolved to the point of recognizing that encouragement of individual, private-minded strategies may be dysfunctional in the long run if it causes community residents to think only about their own protection, to minimize social interaction, and to leave the streets to the troublemakers. Hiding behind a fortress of locks, peepholes, and alarm systems does little to create a sense of community or reduce the opportunities for crime in the streets. In fact, it may encourage street crime and disorder by reducing the number of "eyes and ears" in public places, thus reducing any given offender's risk of being detected and apprehended.

In the late 1970s, this change in thinking produced a change in national and local policy. Since then, greater emphasis has been placed on citizen participation in collective strategies designed to prevent crime in specific target areas where residents, business owners, or the businesses' clientele share an interest in public safety (areas such as a neighborhood, street, block, shopping mall, or apartment building). Hence, numerous public-minded, collective strategies developed in the 1980s. The police played a critical role in initiating many of these collective strategies and deserve substantial credit for the growing popularity of crime prevention in most U.S. cities. Nevertheless, the possibilities for cooperating in public safety are far from fully realized.

Watch programs

Citizen surveillance and crime reporting programs have emerged as the backbone of collective crime prevention practice. Neighborhood Watch (or Block Watch) is the prototype for many similar programs, including Apartment Watch, Business Watch, Employee Watch, and others. Essentially, these programs encourage people to be on the lookout—whether they are at home, at work, commuting, or engaged in other activities—for suspicious or criminal behavior and to report such behavior to the police immediately. What is significant about Watch programs is the use of meetings to encourage surveillance and reporting. Moreover, community or block meetings can be a vehicle for initiating a wide variety of preventive actions other than surveillance and reporting. In fact, using community anticrime meetings simply to encourage better citizen crime reporting is to grossly underutilize this resource. These gatherings can be used to identify and define local crime-related problems and to develop tailored solutions, including teaching participants about precautionary measures that people can take for self-protection or property protection. The potential for program planning in this regard is great.

However, Watch-type programs have been around long enough for some of the problems of this approach, as it is typically practiced, to be emerging. First, few citizens participate in group crime prevention activities, and it is difficult to sustain their participation. Police departments take pride in reporting how many Block Watches they have organized, but the important question is how many of these programs are still active. Second, for reasons that will be explained later, Watch programs are most difficult to initiate and sustain in neighborhoods that have the greatest need for crime prevention. Third, because Watch programs are not active on every block and participation levels are generally low, criminals may simply move to other readily available opportunities. Finally (and this set of potential problems has been given little attention to date), group meetings can have unexpected negative effects on the perceptions, fears, and attitudes of group participants. For example, it is now known that, after exposure to community anticrime meetings, residents can become significantly more fearful of crime and less optimistic about the future of their neighborhood.[19] To date, neither police officials nor researchers know the extent of this problem or the social factors that might contribute to it, but it may have something to do with the tendency among group participants to talk about local crime incidents without setting them in a proper frame of reference or proposing any course of action perceived as efficacious.

These limitations on Watch programs are by no means fatal. Some of them can be addressed with better planning and leadership from the police and the community.

Individual citizens and community groups are the major source of information about neighborhood problems and frequently can serve as the vehicles for program implementation.

Research indicates that community crime prevention programs are more likely to reduce crime and fear when the police are partners with the citizens rather than sole sponsors of a given initiative.[20] Perhaps the police, if properly trained, can serve as a source of reassurance (as well as a co-organizer) at community meetings. Clearly, individual citizens and community groups are the major source of information about neighborhood problems (see the chapters on the patrol function and criminal investigations) and frequently can serve as the vehicles for program implementation.

In recent years a great deal has been learned about how to sustain citizen participation in anticrime activities: "Successful maintenance requires a continuous group structure, strong leadership, links to outside resources, a full agenda (including social activities and noncrime issues), decentralized planning, and extensive activities to communicate with and reward participants."[21] Single-issue Watch programs that are organized by the police with little follow-up meet almost none of these survival criteria (perhaps they do have links to outside resources), and therefore are likely to be short-lived.

It must be recognized, however, that in most heterogeneous, high-crime neighborhoods, Watch strategies per se are of limited use. The desire to watch over a neighbor's property is very weak in areas where social bonds between neighbors are weak. Moreover, watching out for "suspicious persons" is a meaningless request in neighborhoods where nearly everyone is a stranger and behavior that may look suspicious to one person may be the norm rather than the exception. More to the point, in high-crime neighborhoods the "problem" frequently is not the presence of outsiders or strangers but a collection of local conditions that contribute to the criminality of local residents. Consequently, knowledgeable community leaders have been known to reject prepackaged Watch-type programs in favor of strategies tailored to the particular circumstances—the circumstances that give rise to their own community's crime problem. (This point is discussed more fully later in this chapter.)

Citizen patrols

In communities that prefer a more active approach to surveillance, citizens may form groups to patrol specific areas where public safety is a concern. There are many types of patrols—building patrols, neighborhood patrols, public transportation patrols, public park patrols, campus patrols, and so forth. Often equipped with two-way radios, these patrol teams cover their beats on foot, on bicycles, or in motor vehicles, and immediately report suspicious activity to the police. Some groups, such as the much-debated Guardian Angels, are more aggressive and encourage patrol members to intervene in suspicious or criminal activity in progress.

Although law enforcement officials and public policy analysts have begun to study citizen patrols,[22] little is known about the nature and extent of this activity. The available information is, for many police, counterintuitive. That is, the research paints a different picture from the one the police often paint for the public. Police administrators, seeing themselves as responsible for maintaining law and order, sometimes express concern that citizen patrols could lead to "vigilantism" and "hate violence." Certainly the media and, increasingly, the criminal justice system have devoted attention to fringe fanatics (for example, neo-Nazis, "skinheads," and KKK extensions) who express hatred toward particular ethnic, racial, or religious groups. Yet the great majority of anticrime citizen groups are relatively harmless and well-meaning. The majority of citizen patrols are made up of middle-class residents of middle-class neighborhoods who are interested in preventing residential crime and have no inclination to engage in vigilante behavior.

Police administrators—even those who are enthusiastic about Neighborhood Watch—have been slow to grant legitimacy to citizen patrols or citizen intervention in criminal situations. Although they have come to accept noninterventionist patrols (patrols that simply call the police), police executives have been reluctant to encourage any type of direct citizen action or arrest. The Guardian Angels illustrate this: many big-city chiefs have chosen not to recognize the Guardian Angels or support their efforts, despite their popularity with the general public and the positive way in which they were evaluated in a major study funded by the National Institute of Justice.[23] Police chiefs in large cities often feel that supporting aggressive citizen intervention in crime situations could make them and their departments liable for harm that might befall the accused. However, by ignoring the activities of groups like the Guardian Angels, police administrators increase the chances that such patrols will lead to problems of public safety (the possibility of vigilantism increases when citizens and police officials do not openly communicate). An alternative is to recognize their existence and encourage them in law-abiding conduct through training, monitoring, and communication.

Obviously, citizen intervention in criminal situations can have tragic consequences.[24] The question of how far citizens should go in "fighting back" has emerged as an important public policy issue and has received considerable media attention. At one extreme are those who think every citizen should be armed; at the other are those who think crime is a police problem and citizens have no business getting involved in it in any capacity. As might be expected, the latter group often proposes to solve a growing crime problem by increasing the number of police officers.

There are no easy answers to these issues, but the extreme positions are no longer acceptable in most U.S. communities, where the prevailing view is that public safety is compromised in a society armed with guns and where the idea of hiring more police is no longer feasible from the standpoint of either crime control theory or fiscal responsibility. Increasing the level of citizen involvement in the prevention and control of crime is helpful because criminally minded persons already know that police officers are few in number, and if criminals believe, in addition, that citizens on the street will watch a crime in progress without intervening, then citizens and police alike are in deep trouble.

Police must never forget that the public plays the most fundamental role in maintaining order. People must be encouraged to view citizenship as carrying both a right and a responsibility to help others in emergency situations, while at the same time using common sense about the bystander's own safety. For most citizens, there is a wide range of actions between doing nothing and physically harming the offender, and law enforcement agencies must work with community leaders to see that the public is educated about this range of alternative actions.

The question of how far citizens should go in "fighting back" has emerged as an important public policy issue and has received considerable media attention. At one extreme are those who think every citizen should be armed; at the other are those who think crime is a police problem and citizens have no business getting involved in it in any capacity.

Although citizen participation in anticrime activities is usually beneficial to persons in need and to the community as a whole, potential problems may arise and law enforcement should be aware of them. In terms of patrols, vigilante-like behavior, although rare, is more likely when patrol groups become bored with the absence of criminal activity and when they are recruited from youth factions within the local community.[25] In terms of both patrols and Watch programs, racist discussion and activity may develop. Police executives should be aware that the issues of crime, race, ethnicity, religion, and neighborhood transition can become confused and intertwined in the minds of fearful residents. Fear of strangers, newcomers (even those of the individual's same race or religion), and other ethnic or racial groups can easily be misconstrued as fear of crime. Police officers who participate in community meetings or interact with community residents in other ways can prevent or at least minimize this type of thinking by keeping the community's attention focused on legitimate crime prevention strategies. Surveys suggest that collective crime prevention activities are most frequent in middle-class neighborhoods that want to preserve the status quo. With this in mind, community organizers—be they police or private citizens—bear considerable responsibility for keeping the agenda of community meetings focused on crime-related problems and not on minorities moving into the area, real estate values, and other socially divisive issues—unless the skill level of the organizer is such that he or she can help neighbors constructively deal with, and reduce, tensions surrounding such issues. Similarly, the leader needs to achieve consensus that the color of a person's skin does not define him or her as a "suspicious person" who should be reported to the police.

The potential for community organizing activity to produce antisocial results raises the important issue of what role the police can and should play in this process. Clearly, the police must remain neutral in any matter that gives even the slightest appearance of exacerbating racial or ethnic conflict, but this warning does not preclude their participation in community organizing activities or their attempts to reduce such conflict. The possibilities for police involvement in

Bias crimes A bias crime is a threatened, attempted, or completed act by one or more persons against the person or property of another individual or group which constitutes an expression of hostility based on the victim's race, religion, nationality, ethnicity, or sexual orientation.

It is the duty of law enforcement personnel to respond quickly and responsibily to all reported incidents that are alleged to be bias crimes. The response must be based on established departmental policy and procedures.

Law enforcement chief executives must, therefore, establish a written policy that is disseminated to all personnel and to the community at large. The policy should include a definition of bias crime (based on relevant laws and city ordinances); state the department's opposition to bias crimes and its recognition that such crimes have a serious impact on the victim and on the community as a whole; and set forth clear and precise procedures for reporting, investigating, and following up on such incidents.

Once a policy has been developed, new recruits as well as veteran officers should be trained to implement it properly. Officers should also be provided with human relations training that covers intergroup relations and cultural awareness. The focus of the training should be on changing behavior rather than attitudes.

Every department should develop a reporting system for capturing information on bias crimes. An effective reporting system can be developed and implemented only after officers are trained to identify bias crimes.

Victims of these types of crimes may feel extremely tense and may even exhibit hostility toward the responding officer if the officer is of the same race or nationality as the perceived perpetrator. The police must make every effort to convince victims that the police are on their side. Minority leaders and organizations can play a key role in helping the police to gain cooperation from victims. In addition, many of the victims will need follow-up assistance; each department should therefore maintain a victim assistance referral list.

Bias crimes must be treated as serious so the community will understand that the police department will not tolerate such actions. Vigorously investigating and prosecuting such crimes will not only help make the particular victims feel "whole" again but may also help prevent future incidents.

Source: Elsie L. Scott, Deputy Commissioner of Training, New York City Police Department, and former Executive Director, National Organization of Black Law Enforcement Executives, Washington, DC.

organizing functions are illustrated in some of the programs described later in this chapter.

Neighborhood organizations

Crime prevention activities at the neighborhood level are primarily carried out by voluntary, grass-roots organizations. This is not to say that all such groups conduct crime prevention programs, however. There are many types of community organizations, and their agendas vary depending on the specific problems and needs expressed by their membership. Crime is often on their agendas, but it will be defined and responded to in many different ways. As earlier discussions have shown, small groups (representing a block or set of blocks) may play a central role in crime prevention, primarily through Block Watch programs. Although such groups are less likely than larger ones to have the multi-issue orientation that contributes to an organization's longevity, they have the potential to exercise greater influence over their members and their target service areas.

Many police agencies have not felt the need to learn about these local community organizations. Such groups are sometimes viewed as adversarial and critical of the police and, indeed, this perception is correct in some communities. However, these difficulties often stem from a failure to communicate and to initiate an open dialogue about important community issues. At the same time, local groups in many communities are openly and responsibly supportive of public safety programs mounted by the police and are eager for a closer working relationship with law enforcement. Police managers would be well-advised to learn as much as possible about these groups.

If and when the police have opportunities to work with churches, schools, families, businesses, city agencies, and community organizations, they should seek to define appropriate roles and encourage the development of effective and genuine partnerships.

Closely examined cooperative projects are beginning to reveal that police efforts to develop a true partnership with community associations will provide both groups with useful crime-related information that was previously unavailable to them and may reduce mutual misconceptions.[26] Above all, there is a need for police officers and administrators to see crime in its broader community context rather than as a series of discrete events involving isolated victims and offenders. Seasoned community organizers and street officers do not need research reports to know that abandoned buildings and autos, graffiti on walls, garbage on the street, prostitution, widespread drug abuse, and youths hanging out are factors that contribute to a cycle of neighborhood decline, including increases in serious crime, increases in fear of crime, and economic disinvestment. More important, there is a growing recognition that poverty, unemployment, poor educational systems, inadequate social services, and a host of family problems are among the central factors that contribute to these salient neighborhood conditions. Thus, in this context, the police can ill afford to let preconception and history limit their roles and responsibilities. If and when the police have opportunities to work with churches, schools, families, businesses, city agencies, and community organizations, they should seek to define appropriate roles and encourage the development of effective and genuine partnerships.

Boards, councils, and commissions

Another vehicle through which citizens participate in anticrime activities is service on various committees, commissions, boards, councils, and associations that seek to represent the interests of their constituents on crime-related issues. These groups are diverse, ranging in scope from local to international anticrime organizations. Examples of localized groups include the board of directors for a local community organization and the resident council in a public housing project. Examples of citywide groups include those representing business and other established sectors of the city (for example, crime commissions) and those representing a network of neighborhood organizations or communities across the city (for example, the Chicago Alliance for Neighborhood Safety and the Citizens' Committee for New York City). Examples of national groups include those representing certain types of crime prevention programs (for example, Crime Stoppers International) and those seeking to represent a broad coalition of interests (for example, the National Crime Prevention Council, the Crime Prevention Coalition, and the National Criminal Justice Association).

Locally, many communities have citizen boards to oversee police activities, to advise the police department on important policy issues, to review citizen complaints of police misconduct, or to provide other types of feedback to city administrators (see the chapter on the governmental setting). In contrast, fewer communities have been successful in using crime commissions and advisory boards in constructive, positive exchanges that could be considered "coproduction" or joint planning.

Social problems approach

Some criminal justice scholars argue that crime prevention is entering a new phase—that the limits of opportunity reduction strategies have been reached and that the possible benefits of a "social problems" approach to crime prevention are great. Based on the premise that crime is caused by social ills (for example, poverty and its many consequences, as well as the decline of institutions traditionally responsible for socialization), the social problems approach seeks, through programs, to attack the root causes of crime (for example, lack of job skills, unemployment, drug abuse) or, at least, tries to address some of the

---

Building competent communities
The ideas in "community policing," however that term is defined, all deal with the degree of closeness to neighborhood or broader community which is desirable for the police in carrying out their mission. An explicit statement by police that part of their mission is to further the development of a "competent community," a community that solves problems for itself and in which informal social controls play the major role in maintaining order and civility and in reducing crime and violence, will help define the desirable degree of closeness. Furthermore, police need to spell out their view of what a competent community is in enough detail so that the police themselves can measure progress toward it and so that others can adequately understand and share a common view of it.

What is a "competent community"?

The notion of "problem solving" has already been used as a defining characteristic. Other frequently used phrases are "self-regulating," "organized," "alert," "alive," "concerned," and "able to exert power on behalf of its interests."
  As a start, it is possible to list a few measurable, observable characteristics:

1. A high level of communication and interaction among residents, as evidenced by successful local newspapers or other media and by participation in community meetings or events.
2. A substantial number of local voluntary organizations with visible levels of membership and participation.
3. The emergence of some consensus about what is a desirable moral order, as evidenced in standards of permissible behavior or standards for maintaining private or public property.
4. The presence of a substantial number of identifiable local leaders with varying constituencies.
5. Evidence of success by local institutions and leaders in holding public officials accountable and in negotiating quality services for their area.

What needs to be stressed is that a competent community's success in achieving goals related to the police mission depends on its success in achieving goals in a seemingly unrelated variety of other areas.

Some obstacles stand in the way of expanding the police mission to include community development:

1. Attempts to define a desirable community are scattered and may be heavily ideological. A

immediate consequences of disadvantage. Typically, these programs focus on disadvantaged or high-risk youths, and the objectives are to engage them in positive activities (to keep them off the streets) and/or to provide them with specific skills and opportunities that will enhance their competence, self-respect, and likelihood of self-sufficiency. The Eisenhower Foundation's Neighborhood Anti-Crime Self-Help Program was an example of what can be accomplished in this area.[27] Youth activities can include programs emphasizing employment, athletics, drug abuse and pregnancy prevention, literacy, and many other matters of importance.

These social programs are based in the community and strive to change the local conditions that contribute to youth problems. Such efforts require comprehensive planning and follow-through. For example, offering job training skills to unemployed youths is of little help unless job opportunities are identified or created.

Any role the police can play in supporting legitimate youth-oriented programs is laudable. At a minimum, the police are an important source of referrals to social service agencies. In some communities, police officers volunteer to run after-school athletic programs for disadvantaged youths. In many locales, youth

---

consensus does not exist.

2. Action agendas to improve communities are as diverse and ideological as the various definitions.

3. Theoretical objections exist to having government intervene at all in natural local processes within a community. Even if these are overcome, the question remains: "Why should the police be the ones to do it?"

4. Any local intervention can be seen as taking sides in a way that is controversial or at least quasi-political. The police effort to maintain an image of fairness and impartiality may be damaged.

Are there reasons for doing it anyway? Yes, there are several:

1. Experienced police officials already have a gut sense of what a good community feels like. This is based on past experience and is already implicit in many police activities.

2. Police actions in any case have consequences for the development of communities. These actions can at least be consciously reviewed to see that no harm is being done to desirable processes. The distance between doing this and actually fostering those desirable processes is short.

3. If other points of view are being put forward, the police deserve an opportunity to put theirs forward. Doing so establishes a basis for cooperation, or at least negotiations, with local forces that police must rely on in carrying out large portions of their current mission.

4. The police are the unit of government that has most to gain from positive community developments and increased local cooperation. A "self regulating" community uses the police appropriately while freeing up police resources.

5. If the police are careful to avoid taking sides and careful in stating and acting on their goals for a community, they can stay above most local conflicts and assume the role of arbiter among competing forces in helping to build community solidarity.

If a consensus about the goal of building a "competent community" can be created within a police department and if a description of what such a community would look like can be fleshed out and communicated to others, then it becomes possible for police to ask the community for cooperation or parallel efforts on the basis of a shared view of the future.

Source: Peter Hunt, former Executive Director, Chicago Area Project, Chicago, Illinois.

officers are assigned during their duty hours to schools to perform a wide range of functions. Some departments encourage police officers (and expect supervisors and commanders) to serve on community boards and work with community groups on specific tasks related to youth. The possibilities are numerous, but each police department must decide for itself the type and amount of community activities that will be included in the officer's job description (or at least suggested to officers as worthwhile after-hours volunteer activities).

Helping troubled youths is an important contribution to society, but to maximize the chances of having a significant effect on crime, these programs must make every effort to (1) provide preventive services to the larger population of high-risk families (and not just to serious delinquents), including parents, and (2) take a systematic approach to understanding and correcting the local problems and conditions that are contributing to juvenile delinquency in a given neighborhood. These are neighborhood solutions, not simply individual solutions.

Community policing

Among the many developments in the rapidly evolving police field of the early 1990s are strategic approaches to policing that are variously called community policing or problem-oriented policing (see the chapters on evolution, the patrol function, criminal investigations, and local drug control). After decades of responding rapidly and reflexively to citizen complaints, police administrators are stopping to ask the basic question, What are we trying to accomplish? If the objective is to reduce crime and fear at the neighborhood and block level, then "business as usual" is simply inadequate. So long as police departments in urban areas rely primarily on the 9–1–1 system (see the chapter on information management), their capacity to engage in active preventive activities will be severely restricted.

Community policing and problem-oriented policing represent a change from past practices.[28] They represent a philosophy of policing more than a specific set of programs or activities. The central elements of this philosophy include

1. A broader definition of what constitutes legitimate police work
2. Emphasis on increasing the quantity and quality of interactions between the police and the citizenry
3. Greater attention to creative problem-solving and crime prevention strategies
4. Efforts to restructure police bureaucracies to provide more decentralized planning and service delivery.

At the core of this orientation is the recognition that joint police-community effort is the most fruitful approach to combatting crime and the fear of crime, given both the nature of crime and the limitations on police resources. Community policing promises to address a wide range of social and physical problems that contribute to neighborhood crime and fear of crime. Furthermore, it promises to mobilize numerous individuals and agencies in this effort.

Although demonstrations and evaluations of community and problem-oriented policing are still in their infancy, the early results are promising. Reductions in fear of crime and in victimization rates, increases in other quality-of-life indicators, and some valuable lessons in implementation have come about at several sites. A few of the key programs and activities to emerge in this area are described below to introduce some alternative ways of putting this philosophy of policing into operation.

Foot patrol Walking the beat has returned as a very popular form of community policing. This time around, however, more is expected from the officer on foot patrol. In addition to the traditional surveillance and arrest functions, this individual may be expected to take on any number of nontraditional functions, including attending community meetings, identifying community problems and needs, organizing citizen action, resolving neighborhood disputes, and/or making referrals to appropriate social service agencies. Just as Block Watch meetings are a vehicle for local residents to plan activities other than surveillance, foot patrols can be used by police administrators to initiate a host of anticrime activities. In fact, however, the basic function of foot patrol has been rather limited: according to a national survey of 143 police departments, the most common duties of the foot patrol officer are "to talk to the public, in particular with the merchants, to have high visibility, and to be concerned about relations between the police department and the citizens."[29] With this in mind, we can understand how foot patrol might reduce fear of crime. The basic assumption is that a highly visible presence of uniformed officers on foot will give residents and merchants a feeling of security, and, indeed, research generally supports this prediction. However, there is less evidence that foot patrols actually reduce the level of criminal activity in target areas.

Walking the beat has returned as a very popular form of community policing. This time around, however, much more is expected from the officer on foot patrol.

Among other resources available, the National Neighborhood Foot Patrol Center at Michigan State University provides specialized training and other expertise on foot patrol, and the Police Foundation and the Police Executive Research Forum have considerable expertise on community policing.

Neighborhood ministations and community centers   Another manifestation of community policing is the effort to decentralize the police service delivery system and bring police officers closer to the community they serve. One of the most ambitious programs, in Detroit, resulted in the development of fifty-two ministations in neighborhoods across the city. These small storefront operations were staffed by permanently assigned police officers relieved of responsibility for handling radio calls. Their primary job was community crime prevention: they assisted walk-in clients, offered crime prevention information at community meetings, patrolled the streets on foot and in cars, and provided

---

Mobile police precinct   In an effort to increase police visibility, the township of Middletown, New Jersey, put a precinct on wheels. The police van, formerly owned by Bell Labs, is equipped with sophisticated high-technology equipment and is worth approximately $215,000. Middletown purchased it for approximately $10,000.

Residents are notified through the news media when the van will be in their neighborhood. The mobile unit encourages citizens to voice their concerns about neighborhood problems such as crime and traffic flow, and it provides the police with a mobile command center for disasters, emergencies, and large public events. The precinct also serves as an information center, distributing crime prevention materials, surveys, and other information of interest to the community.

Source: Cited in *The Guide to Management Improvement Projects in Local Government* (Washington, DC: International City Management Association, 1987).

whatever police services were deemed most appropriate to the needs of local residents. Of course, the support of local volunteers was critical to keep such ministations running. Volunteers did everything from making coffee, sweeping, and cleaning to taking preliminary reports and issuing bike licenses. Those who were so inclined also received training in undertaking simple mediations, organizing ancillary services such as van pools or referrals, and performing other tasks of that sort. Officers in fact spent much time with volunteers—finding them and then training, supervising, and motivating them.[30]

In 1983 and 1984, storefront community centers were field tested as part of a fear reduction project in Houston and Newark, funded by the National Institute of Justice and carried out by the participating police departments and the Police Foundation.[31] The results were very promising. The introduction of the Houston center was associated with a reduction in local residents' fears of personal crime and perceptions of the amount of crime in the area. The effects of the Newark station could not be isolated from another program component (that is, door-to-door police-citizen contacts), but the overall strategy was successful at reducing fear and improving other perceptions as well.

Ministations can be used in numerous ways to close the physical and psychological distance between police officers and the communities they serve. In addition to housing standard police business, the facilities can be used for distributing newsletters, organizing and holding meetings, coordinating door-to-door activities, making referrals to other agencies, and so forth. The functions of any particular community station can and should be modified to meet the needs and concerns of the surrounding neighborhood.

Police organizing and outreach strategies   "Organizing" means different things to different people. For many police departments, organizing means getting local residents to attend a Block Watch meeting. For many community organizations, organizing means an ongoing process of empowering local residents, especially encouraging citizen participation in decisions that affect the quality of life in their neighborhood. As noted earlier, police departments sometimes start Block Watch programs without providing a structure or set of activities for sustaining citizen involvement. Experience indicates, however, that organizing is an ongoing process requiring continual attention. Thus, this is an area where police can learn from neighborhood groups with years of experience in community organizing. Moreover, many police departments have accumulated experience from Block Watch programs, but the police do not always use conventional organizing techniques. Handbooks have been prepared by civilian staff in Seattle, Minneapolis, and Chicago—cities with strong track records for mobilizing citizens in the fight against residential crime.[32]

"Organizing" means different things to different people. For many police departments, organizing means getting local residents to attend a Block Watch meeting. For many community organizations, organizing means an ongoing process of empowering local residents.

Whether community organizing is beyond the scope of police responsibility is much debated. Suffice it to say that a number of police departments have participated in successful demonstration programs involving community organizing activities. What made these activities unusual is that the initiatives went beyond the typical Block Watch objectives of surveillance and reporting, and focused on identifying and defining local problems and developing strategies to reduce the fear of crime.

A few examples are noteworthy. In Hartford, two community organizations and a police advisory committee were started in the Asylum Hill neighborhood to help plan and implement a comprehensive community crime prevention

"Don't Give a Thief a Merry Christmas" During the Christmas shopping season, the two major shopping centers In Albuquerque suffer many auto burglaries, larcenies, and robberies. Because local law enforcement and private security services are unable to curtail all of the criminal activity, the "Don't Give a Thief a Merry Christmas" program has become the "eyes" of the police in detecting criminal activity.

The program is coordinated by the police department and employs volunteer CB-radio owners to patrol the parking lot areas. The volunteer citizens take no enforcement action but report all criminal activity and other suspicious behavior to the police.

Because uniformed officers are assigned to the shopping centers during the holiday season, police have been able to respond Immediately to calls for service.

To reinforce the program, signs are placed in store windows and flyers are distributed reminding shoppers of ways to protect themselves and their belongings while they are shopping. As a result of this program, the occurrence of crimes in the shopping centers has substantially declined.

Source: Cited in *The Guide to Management Improvement Projects in Local Government* (Washington, DC: International City Management Association, 1987).

program. Input from the police and other city agencies, existing and new community organizations, business owners, academic experts, and staff at the National Institute of Justice led to changes in local policing, the physical environment, and citizen crime prevention practices. The Hartford program was associated initially with reductions in crime and later with reductions in fear of crime.

As part of its fear reduction project, the Houston police department started a community organization where none had existed in an attempt to create a sense of community among residents and bring together residents who could be counted on to work regularly with the police in identifying and solving neighborhood problems.[33] The process is worth noting: the Community Organizing Response Team (CORT) officers conducted a door-to-door survey of residents in the target area to seek their input in defining local problems and to locate persons who would be willing to host a small meeting of residents and police. After more than a dozen meetings, twelve people formed a neighborhood task force that met monthly with the district captain to discuss problems and develop solutions. A variety of programs emerged from this process (including a neighborhood clean-up campaign, "safe houses," a drug information seminar, property marking). Although fear of crime was not demonstrably influenced by the CORT initiatives, residents perceived that social disorders had declined and reported more positive evaluations of the police.

Other outreach strategies that stop short of community organizing can also be employed to initiate a fear reduction program and encourage citizen participation. Door-to-door contacts by police have been successful in gaining valuable information about local problems, improving public attitudes about the police, and apparently reducing fear of crime. The demonstration programs in Newark and Houston were partially modeled after the well-known Citizen Oriented Police Enforcement (COPE) teams in the Baltimore County police department. The fifteen-member COPE squads are deployed in areas where problems are reported, and their primary purpose is to reduce fear. In addition to maintaining high visibility, the COPE team tries to pinpoint the sources of fear in the community through police-citizen contacts. COPE officers use input from community residents and from patrol officers to develop action plans that are responsive to the fear-related problem.

Analysis and mapping of crime-related data The partnership between police and community begins with a planning process that identifies specific problems in specific neighborhoods. The analyzing and mapping of data on criminal activity and disorder help contribute to this objective. Today, many residents want to know more about crime in their neighborhood for crime prevention purposes, and in a growing number of cities the police and community organizations work together to distribute block-level crime statistics through regular newsletters.

Advancements in technology now allow computerized maps of neighborhood activity. The National Institute of Justice funded a test of mapping in a cooperative venture involving the Chicago police department, an alliance of community organizations, and two major universities.[34] Using personal computers with specially designed software, community groups were able to map data provided by daily police reports. These maps were then used by the community organizations, police patrols, and detectives to identify neighborhood "hot spots" where a pattern of criminal activity was observed. This geographically displayed information was useful for planning citizen crime prevention activities (such as Neighborhood Watch) and for initiating police enforcement activities. Moreover, this strategy holds considerable promise for mapping less-serious incivilities (not only the dramatic criminal incidents) that lower the quality of neighborhood life.

Many residents want to know more about crime in their neighborhood for crime prevention purposes, and in a growing number of cities the police and community organizations work together to distribute block-level crime statistics through regular newsletters.

To make this type of partnership possible, however, police departments (especially large ones) need to overcome their traditional concerns about the possible adverse effects of releasing crime-related data to citizens and community groups. Research suggests that releasing local crime statistics to the public will not increase the public's fear of crime so long as the statistics are accompanied by specific, feasible crime prevention recommendations.[35]

Crime prevention through environmental design

The physical environment can play a major role in determining the opportunities for crime and can be modified to prevent crime. It can influence crime in two ways—directly and indirectly. Directly, it can reduce access to property and can remove criminal opportunities; the standard way to do this is with security hardware. Indirectly, the physical environment can "reduce crime, fear, and related problems by influencing the social behavior and social perceptions of residents and/or potential offenders."[36] A more detailed picture of how the environment can affect opportunities for crime is provided by Oscar Newman's "defensible space" theory.[37] The results of research on that theory and on the principles behind "crime prevention through environmental design" (CPTED) have been mixed.[38] There is little doubt that the physical environment affects crime rates, but our ability to alter the "built" environment on a large scale and consequently to produce changes in social behavior (such as increases in "territoriality" and informal social control) has not been consistently demonstrated at levels that satisfy the proof requirements of rigorous empirical research. Certainly, part of the problem is the limited number of controlled evaluations with good measurement. But although the research evidence is mixed, there is renewed interest in these approaches.

This section introduces some CPTED strategies that have been tried—strategies ranging in focus from household security to architectural design to street lighting, street layout, and cameras and alarms.

Household target hardening

Protecting one's home from unlawful entry and one's property from theft have been at the heart of crime prevention in the United States for many years. Police have played a major role in educating local residents about the many crime prevention activities that can "harden" the possible targets of theft. Because a sizeable, well-known literature is available to police departments in this topic area, the range of activities will not be listed here, but a few general strategies deserve mention.

Conventional access control Research has supported the common-sense proposition that creating physical barriers to access (such as stronger locks, door bars, pins in windows, and fences) can be effective in reducing a homeowner's or renter's chances of victimization. Calls for collective citizen action to prevent crime are laudable, but there are few substitutes for a good set of deadbolt locks in the meantime, especially in neighborhoods where organizing is very difficult.

Calls for collective citizen action to prevent crime are laudable, but there are few substitutes for a good set of deadbolt locks in the meantime.

One of the problems with household protection is cost, and therefore security devices are not evenly distributed across all segments of the community. Perhaps the purchase and installation of deadbolt locks in low-income dwelling units could be placed on the public policy agenda of more local governments as a means of "redistributing" public safety.

Home security surveys Police departments have helped many residents by providing home security surveys. The security survey is a detailed inspection of the dwelling unit and the surrounding area to identify security deficiencies or risks and to make recommendations for improving security. There is some evidence that home security surveys can be useful in increasing residents' home protection behavior and lowering their risk of victimization. However, police and civilians must exercise caution in how they conduct these inspections lest they unwittingly increase the recipient's fear of crime and other concerns. Emphasizing vulnerabilities in a person's home with such comments as "no matter what you do, if a burglar wants to get in, he's going to get in" can be counterproductive.

Operation Identification The "Operation Identification" program has become familiar to virtually all police departments in the United States, and approximately 25 percent of all households have participated. Engraving or otherwise marking property with a unique identification number is intended to deter potential burglars and increase the odds of recovering stolen property. The National Sheriffs' Operation Identification Registry makes it possible for citizens and businesses across the country to register their property identification numbers in a nationwide computer file that is accessible to law enforcement agencies on a twenty-four–hour basis. If marked property is recovered, the identification number can be teletyped to the registry, a computer search can be conducted, and, if the owner is a subscriber to the registry, the property can be returned.

There is some evidence that residents who mark their property and post warning stickers are less likely to be victimized than residents who do not, but the program has been unable to make a difference in the rates of property recovery, apprehensions, or convictions. Perhaps the warning stickers on doors and windows are sufficient to deter a certain percentage of potential burglars, but this remains unknown. In any event, the Operation Identification program gives police another opportunity to get citizens involved in a relatively simple crime prevention program. Without an aggressive outreach program, however, those participating will remain a small minority of the total community.

Architectural design

Crime, it has been learned, is higher in places where the physical environment restricts the opportunity for human surveillance and lowers the risk of detection. A full discussion of design issues in urban planning is beyond the scope of this chapter, but police administrators should be educated about the crime prevention aspects of urban planning and should play a role in public decision making about the design of new buildings and surrounding areas. In public housing, for example, as the nation begins to move away from high-rise units and adopts more scattered-site housing plans, every effort should be made to create physical environments that are conducive to social interaction and that maximize feelings of safety and respect for property. Law enforcement can also continue to push for building codes that require adequate security hardware—and perhaps even software—to protect all dwellers.

Street lighting

The installation of street lights is often considered a useful anticrime measure. There is some evidence that better street lighting is associated with a reduction in fear of crime, but little evidence that it decreases crime itself.[39] Of course, having the public feel safer is an important outcome in its own right and may lead to other benefits (such as greater use of public and private facilities) that will affect crime rates in the long run.

Street lighting can be controversial. In a number of communities across the nation, public safety advocates (pushing for high-intensity lighting) have lost city hall battles to historic preservationists who wanted to retain antique low-intensity lights. Even where that happens, however, alley lighting is something that citizens and police can explore. And when a local government is unable to provide alley lights, individual citizens may be able to deal directly with the power company and pay for installation.

Street layout and traffic patterns

Research indicates that crime rates are higher in areas that are more easily accessible to criminals (that is, areas criminals can enter and escape from without detection) and that have a high volume of pedestrian traffic, especially stranger traffic. These observations (among others) have led researchers and urban planners to propose that residential streets be modified to change the patterns of social interaction and encourage more territorial behavior. The Hartford project, for example, involved closing several through streets and constructing culs-de-sac in an attempt to encourage more informal social control by the local residents. The project was apparently successful in lowering crime rates initially, but this trend was reversed when other social components of the program were relaxed. One conclusion to be drawn from this demonstration is that environmental changes do not have stand-alone effects and must be supported by continuing changes in the anticrime activities of police and citizens in the area.

The closing of residential streets is an idea that has spread to a number of other communities and appears to be motivated by thoughts of immediate self-protection rather than by long-term urban planning. In the Miami–Fort Lauderdale area, for example, sharp rises in crime and in fear of crime during the 1980s resulted in a wave of street closings. In at least a dozen areas, entire neighborhoods were sealed off from outsiders by bright orange barrels to block public roads.[40] On some streets checkpoints were established with gates and private guards who stop cars, question the occupants, and write down license plate numbers.

This phenomenon may spread to other communities if crime rates continue to climb and bring with them an increase in public fear. Although it raises serious questions of public access, this activity is unquestionably part of the growing privatization of security that is occurring in more-affluent communities across the nation. Some neighborhoods are becoming increasingly safe, but this development is likely to increase the risk that other neighborhoods (specifically, those that cannot afford the same level of security hardware and personnel) will become increasingly dangerous because of crime displacement. Public law enforcement should be aware of this problem (especially the privatization of public areas) and plan accordingly. Police should also be aware of the potential racial tension that can be created when either they or private guards stop and question nonwhite individuals who attempt to pass through largely white neighborhoods.

Cameras and alarms

Cameras and alarms also are widely used to increase the surveillance, detection, and documentation of criminal behavior. There have been few evaluations of the effectiveness of these crime prevention devices, but the available evidence is generally encouraging. In one community, the installation of alarms in school buildings and businesses was associated with decreases in burglaries; in another, the random installation of cameras in high-risk businesses was associated with an increase in arrest and clearance rates for robberies. Unfortunately, despite a booming business in the sale of residential alarms, it is not yet known whether they are effective for deterring or apprehending criminals.

Alarms and cameras appear to be a good idea for businesses, schools, and other institutions that need and can afford surveillance when people are not around. Whether the police should encourage continued expenditures on these devices by individual residents (given the sizeable costs and unknown benefits) is a decision that each department must make. Certainly, every department should encourage more research and, consistent with ethical research standards, should encourage the security industry to fund it (see the chapter on external resources).

Media and public education strategies

As this chapter has been suggesting, a fundamental problem for crime prevention is the issue of how best to encourage more citizen participation in anticrime activities. Many one-on-one and small-group methods have been tried by police and community volunteers; but to reach larger populations, crime prevention advocates have turned to the media.

On a small scale, newsletters are widely used to encourage and sustain citizen participation in crime prevention activities. Many active organizations (at the neighborhood, state, regional, and national levels) use newsletters to communicate with their members or target audiences. Even police departments in a few cities have become involved in publishing their own newsletter or a joint newsletter with local community organizations. The Evanston (Illinois) *ALERT* is a model newsletter, published as a cooperative venture between the Evanston police department and the citywide Residential Crime Prevention Committee.

Newsletters are an excellent vehicle for police managers to use in communicating with local residents on a regular basis about their values, goals, objectives, and plans for new coproduction activities.

On a larger scale, several national media campaigns have been employed. Two such strong initiatives are highlighted here: the "McGruff" campaign and Crime Stoppers.

"McGruff" national media campaign

In October 1979, a national media campaign was initiated to educate the U.S. public about its responsibility for preventing crime, a responsibility that included getting involved with local police and other citizens in a variety of anticrime activities. "McGruff," the animated crime dog, became the symbol for crime prevention in the 1980s, with his persistent call for the public to "take a bite out of crime." The McGruff campaign, managed by the National Crime Prevention Council, has remained strong. Public service ads for television, radio, and print are the backbone of the campaign, conducted by the nonprofit Advertising Council. McGruff has advised the public on a variety of special topics in crime prevention, including home security, Neighborhood Watch, child protection, and drug abuse.

The local effect of crime prevention messages undoubtedly depends on the level of adoption by local police departments, the media, and civic organizations.

Early evaluation data suggested that the McGruff campaign had reached a large majority of the public, had positively influenced their attitudes about crime prevention, and (but to a lesser extent) had had a positive effect on their crime prevention behavior. Leaving aside the research data, perhaps the most tangible gain from this campaign is the national network of organizations that has emerged to bring the McGruff messages home to local communities. The 118-member Crime Prevention Coalition, comprising state associations and programs, has played a major role in localizing the McGruff ads, developing working partnerships with local police departments, and encouraging local media to use the ads.[41] In addition, the National Crime Prevention Council has developed a massive array of crime prevention materials (kits, books, posters, topic bulletins, and a regular newsletter) to support the themes of the campaign and encourage local action. This is where law enforcement agencies become important. The local effect of crime prevention messages undoubtedly depends on the level of adoption by local police departments, the media, and civic organizations. In most jurisdictions, police managers should take the lead in developing relationships among these various groups and tailoring crime prevention messages to local concerns.

Crime Stoppers

Despite praise for instances of exemplary citizen involvement in the fight against crime, often the police are frustrated in their lonely pursuit of leads to solve serious crime. In many cases, the public does not come forth to report criminal activity (it is estimated that fewer than half of all felony crimes are reported to the police) or to help investigators solve crime (thus, less than one in five felony crimes are cleared by arrest—see the chapter on criminal investigations). Frustrated by the lack of citizen cooperation with law enforcement, a police officer in Albuquerque started a Crime Stoppers program in 1976. Essentially, the program offered both cash rewards of up to one thousand dollars (to overcome public apathy) and anonymity (to overcome fear of retaliation) to citizens willing to provide details that would lead to the arrest and/or indictment of felony suspects. What makes Crime Stoppers unique relative to other tipster programs is the central role of the mass media. Crime Stoppers is the modern version of a "WANTED" poster, with media outlets publicizing the details of unsolved crimes by producing a reenactment or description of the "Crime of the Week."

By 1989 there were more than seven hundred Crime Stoppers programs, linked by Crime Stoppers International. A national evaluation of these programs found that they are extremely popular among law enforcement agencies, media outlets, and community participants, although critics are concerned about the legal and social implications of a program that pays large rewards and offers anonymity to encourage citizen cooperation with police and prosecutors. (For example, will payment undermine the civic duty to report crime, or lead to biased testimony in court? Will anonymity encourage "snitching" about minor incidents, or submission of false reports?)

Law enforcement agencies have accepted primary responsibility for staffing and coordinating the daily operation of most Crime Stoppers programs. The authors of the national evaluation noted that the functions of law enforcement personnel include processing the crime information reported by anonymous callers, directing it to detectives for further investigation, selecting the "Crime of the Week," drafting press releases, keeping records and statistics on program performance, and serving as the liaison with the board of directors, the media, and the investigators.[42]

Like other crime prevention initiatives, Crime Stoppers is not a panacea, but this type of program can be a useful law enforcement tool for solving certain types of "dead-end" cases and for stimulating participation from certain segments of the population that otherwise might not be involved in the criminal justice system (for example, businesspersons who serve on the Crime Stoppers board of directors and callers who fear retaliation or are too apathetic to get deeply involved). Moreover, Crime Stoppers may affect the distribution and consumption of drugs because of the many informants involved who need the reward money and are willing to make an anonymous call against drug competitors or criminal acquaintances (see the chapter on drug control). More research is needed to confirm these hypotheses.

School-based prevention initiatives

The real hope for preventing criminal and antisocial behavior lies with the youth of America. But all too often, children are either the victims or the perpetrators of crime. Vandalism, shoplifting, drug abuse, alcohol abuse, child abuse, gang violence, teenage pregnancy, violence in the schools—the list is long, and the problems have serious implications for the future. In response to these problems, a number of educational programs have been started, many of them involving the police either directly or indirectly. The programs discussed here are related to the law and the criminal justice system, to crime prevention and safety, and to drug and alcohol abuse.

Law-related education

Law-related educational programs are designed to strengthen citizenship and leadership by teaching students about the laws that govern behavior, the students' own rights and responsibilities as citizens, and the operation of the criminal justice system. Emphasis is placed on critical thinking about issues of justice, authority, and responsibility. Some programs focus on reducing antisocial behavior by giving special attention to the development of analytic and decision-making skills in social settings. An evaluation of law-related education programs at seventy-five sites found that, as a result of such programs, high school students were more knowledgeable about the legal system, reported less of an inclination to resolve issues by resorting to violence, and depended less on delinquent peers.[43]

Law-related education can start much earlier than high school. At an early age, exposure to positive role models in law enforcement (for example, "Officer Friendly") can help shape children's images and attitudes about police. And many conflict resolution skills can be taught in the elementary grades (the Virginia TIPS program—Teaching Individuals Protective Strategies—is a good example of a comprehensive K through 12 approach). Police officers should be available to teachers as special resources who can visit the classroom to reinforce the lesson plans.

Crime prevention and safety programs

To protect children against crime both inside and outside the school walls, a variety of safety programs have been developed for elementary and high school students. Again, McGruff and the National Crime Prevention Council (NCPC) have taken the lead in educating youths about the dangers of crime and about methods of self-protection. The McGruff Elementary School Puppet Program has provided youngsters with information on many topics, including how to spot trouble from strangers, avoid being a victim, respond to child abuse, and respond to an emergency. By using "safe houses" or "McGruff houses," the neighborhood can be supportive by providing safe havens for children in trouble or needing assistance. The police can be supportive by participating in the McGruff program. Often police departments purchase a McGruff puppet or a McGruff character costume (in the latter case, Officer Friendly frequently plays the role of McGruff).

The McGruff program has been expanded to give considerable attention to drug and alcohol abuse (McGruff's Drug Prevention and Child Protection Program). More than fifty thousand classrooms are using the thirty-two–week program, which includes the McGruff puppet, teacher's guide, instruction booklet, and two audio cassette tapes.

At the high-school level, a two-week curriculum called "Teens, Crime, and the Community" allows students to learn what the consequences of crime are for teenage victims, how to avoid becoming a victim, and what role the students can play in community crime prevention. Developed by NCPC and the National Center for Citizen Education in the Law (and funded by the federal Office of Juvenile Justice and Delinquency Prevention), this curriculum has been pilot tested with nearly six thousand students in Dallas, Miami, New York City, Phoenix, and St. Louis as part of a larger program on law-related education. By mid-1987, the program had reached fifteen thousand teenagers in 156 schools in eleven cities.[44] Optional modules are available to encourage discussion of shoplifting, substance abuse, acquaintance rape, family violence, runaways, and drunk driving.

Drug and alcohol abuse prevention

In a national survey written up in 1989, chief law enforcement executives in the United States reported that two of their three top crime prevention priorities are reducing the supply of illegal drugs and reducing the demand for illegal drugs.[45] To date, most of the federal, state, and local expenditures to combat drugs have been directed at the supply rather than the demand side of the drug problem. Focal activities have included arresting users and dealers, seizing drugs, eradicating crops, and controlling foreign production. In contrast, little attention has been paid to preventing drug use by developing school curricula, organizing and training parents, involving community leaders, and enhancing public awareness about the adverse effects of drugs. The following paragraphs briefly describe some initiatives that attempt to address this imbalance (see also the chapter on local drug control). Without adequate funding and nationwide participation, however, these educational programs can be expected to have little effect on this massive set of problems.

Drug abuse prevention Examples of innovative programs to prevent drug abuse have been highlighted in manuals published by the International Association of Chiefs of Police and the Drug Enforcement Administration (DEA).[46] Clearly, the police must play a key role in community efforts to reduce the consumption and abuse of drugs. But experts in this field agree that what is needed is a comprehensive program that draws on all the resources of the community and attacks the problem from all sides. As experts on drugs, crime, and the requirements of the law, police executives must be involved and could be among the major facilitators.

At the federal level, in addition to the DEA manual, the Department of Education has promoted its Drug-Free School Challenge program in which it honors schools with exemplary drug prevention programs. The toughest work, however, must be carried out at the state and local levels. According to the IACP, by 1987, schools in 75 percent of the states were required to teach about substance abuse, and sixteen states had implemented statewide curricula. In addition to the popular McGruff program cited earlier, a host of antidrug programs have been developed, including Here's Looking at You, 2000; DARE; ME-OLOGY; Project Charlie; and Project Smart. At the state level, the Governor's Alliance Against Drugs in Massachusetts is widely considered the model program. Its strength lies in its coordination of a broad range of agencies and organizations across two hundred communities and in the variety of programs it offers, including public awareness campaigns, drug seminars, youth leadership programs, teen centers, and a statewide drug and alcohol hotline.

Clearly, the police must play a key role in community efforts to reduce the consumption and abuse of drugs. But experts in this field agree that what is needed is a comprehensive program that draws on all the resources of the community and attacks the problem from all sides.

Many of the school curricula referred to above provide an excellent opportunity for police officers to work with students and participate in drug education. In addition to McGruff, the Drug Abuse Resistance Education (DARE) program is designed so that law enforcement officers play the major role. Developed in 1983 by the Los Angeles Unified School District and the Los Angeles police department, this seventeen-week program for fifth- and sixth-graders is taught by specially trained uniformed police officers. DARE goes beyond mere warnings about the dangers of drugs to teach children how to resist both subtle and overt pressure from peers. The Greensboro, North Carolina, police department has demonstrated how the DARE program can be successfully implemented on a citywide basis, and the Illinois state police have shown how the program can be successfully implemented statewide. DARE has spread to some 398 communities in thirty-one states and has expanded to other age levels, as well. It is discussed further in the chapter on local drug control.

Alcohol abuse prevention   Although perhaps overshadowed in many communities by the drug problem, abuse of alcohol is a massive and costly problem, especially in terms of drunk drivers. The approach taken by society as a whole—spurred on by MADD (Mothers Against Drunk Driving) and other grass-roots organizations—has emphasized stricter enforcement of the laws and stiffer penalties for those convicted of driving under the influence. However, the limits of this approach may be reached all too soon, as the public realizes that the criminal justice system cannot afford to maintain "get tough" policies over an extended period of time.[47] Perhaps a more promising long-term strategy is to offer educational and preventive programs directed at young Americans. For example, the police can participate in the educational curricula identified earlier, which typically cover both drugs and alcohol.

Another possibility is for law enforcement agencies to encourage the alcohol industry to participate in "responsible drinking" programs and for the industry to provide educational materials to the community. As one example, Anheuser-Busch sponsors a number of programs with messages such as "know when to say when" and "use a nondrinking 'designated' driver," or with objectives such as getting taverns and restaurants to participate in taxi-ride programs, training bartenders and waitresses to recognize intoxication, and educating students about the dangers of drunk driving.

In the final analysis, fighting drugs and alcohol will require a multifaceted approach that recognizes the importance of partnership among many segments of the community, including parents, schools, social service agencies, busi-

---

Deterring underage drinking   Police are often frustrated by their inability to take action when they are called to residences where young people are gathered, alcoholic beverages are present, but only participants over age twenty-one are observed in possession of the alcohol.

In Portage, Michigan, the police department initiated a program designed to help deter teenage drinking. The day after a call, the police report is reviewed by a command officer, and a personalized form letter and accompanying pamphlet are sent to the homeowner or the renter of the premises.

The letter says that police went to the residence after receiving complaints from the neighborhood. It goes on to say: "Officers observed alcoholic beverages and persons under legal drinking age in your home. Although no violations were seen, it is our practice to inform homeowners, if they were not present, of circumstances which may suggest this type of activity."

The pamphlet, called "Parties and the Law," was prepared by the Kalamazoo Area Families in Action group to help parents and teens who are concerned about the illegal use and abuse of alcohol and drugs. It presents guidelines for hosting a party; information on curfew laws; guidelines for parents when their children attend a party; a brief overview of alcohol, drugs, and the law; and an explanation of parent/host civil liabilities.

The pamphlet points out, for example, that a person who furnishes alcohol may be liable for monetary damages if anyone suffers personal injury or property damage as a result of this action. Further, a person who serves alcohol to a minor may not be covered by his or her homeowner's liability insurance.

Source: Adapted from George E. Von Behren, "A Deterrent to Teenage 'Keggers'," *Michigan Municipal Review*, July 1990.

nesses, and the criminal justice system. The IACP has proposed a comprehensive two-pronged approach to reduce crime by reducing drug abuse: (1) establish a set of tasks for bringing together the players in the criminal justice system— police, prosecutors, judges, probation and parole officers, and jail and prison authorities; and (2) develop a plan for community action that brings together leaders of the community and the other key actors who share responsibility for defining and responding to the problem.[48] This model is discussed in more detail later.

Business crime prevention

The business community should have a strong interest in developing a partnership with local police to prevent crime in and around commercial establishments. Businesses need to protect their own assets and employees and create an environment that is attractive to customers. Furthermore, businesses are learning from the courts that they can be held liable for the safety of their customers. Businesses are also susceptible to white-collar crime.

Police departments with aggressive crime prevention programs have pursued a number of strategies to involve businesses. Security surveys of business establishments, crime prevention seminars on a variety of topics, and foot patrols in commercial areas have become common. In addition, police officers have sought to organize the business community with Business Crime Watch projects. Owners and employees in the area watch out for each other as in Neighborhood Watch. Participants meet regularly as a group and share information on crime and prevention tips, publish a newsletter, and display decals indicating their membership in Business Crime Watch. The business community often works with the police and courts to prosecute shoplifters aggressively.

In the future, as the severity and diversity of the problem of white-collar crime is more fully recognized, law enforcement agencies will also need to develop expertise in this area. At present, large businesses are often frustrated by police and prosecutors' lack of expertise in, and failure to give priority to, white-collar crime.[49] (See also the chapter on organized crime.)

The process of "doing" community crime prevention

Innovations in policing and crime control do not have a proud history. Although there have been a few success stories in the past several years (see the chapter on evolution), the bigger picture suggests that new crime control programs have had difficulty achieving their goals and objectives and are short-lived. Why is this? The answer given repeatedly by research and evaluation data is that, in community crime prevention, the major culprits are poor planning and weak implementation. Consequently, this chapter closes with observations from researchers and practitioners who have identified some basic ingredients necessary for planning and implementing a successful program.[50] Essentially, these ingredients can be viewed as stages in the process of program development, implementation, and evaluation (see also the chapter on research).

Defining the problem

Cooperative crime prevention programs should not be developed until the nature and extent of the target problems are reasonably well understood (recognizing that such problems may change over time). One of the major reasons that prepackaged programs do not work as often as expected is that, unless they are modified, they are not directly applicable to the particular problems and concerns of the community. Thus, one of the first steps is to define the problem, and this can be done with a variety of information-gathering strategies including, among others, surveys, key-person interviews, community meetings, public hearings, and analysis of police data.

It is also necessary to identify the persons and organizations who should be involved in the process of defining the problem and developing the program. To use the drug abuse example, the IACP has recommended the formation of a community task force that includes, but is not necessarily limited to, representatives of all political parties; local business, civic, and service groups (Rotary, Kiwanis, Lions, and others); parent groups; neighborhood organizations; the medical and mental health field; and the following occupational groups: pharmacists, religious leaders, school superintendents, treatment providers, social service administrators, and media managers.[51]

This group should serve as the planning vehicle, not as the only source of information. Formal surveys of the entire community or of specific target groups can be extremely informative for purposes of defining the problem, and often the results can be used as baseline data for evaluating the program. (In the drug abuse example, survey data might be collected on usage patterns among school-age children and on community priorities.) Several police departments have worked with local universities to seek community input in planning community crime prevention programs.

When defining the problem, planners must be careful to seek the input of all parties. Planning a cooperative initiative is, almost by definition, a political process in which differences in analyzing the problem and proposing solutions are inevitable. Not only is the inclusive approach politically astute, but it also offers a more complete picture of the nature and extent of the problem.

Developing the program

Once the problem has been clearly defined, the program components can be developed. The "problem definition" phase should help the planning team set priorities and identify the target group (for example, low-income areas, drug users under eighteen, crime victims, women, older citizens). The "program development" phase should focus on setting program goals, establishing objectives and strategies to achieve these goals, and then identifying the available resources to implement the program. As part of his process, planners must agree on the level of program intervention (for example, community, block, individual, school, or workplace) and the type of intervention (for example, Neighborhood Watch, school curriculum, media campaign, training programs). This effort should result in the development of an "action plan" that specifies what the group is planning to do and who will be responsible for doing it. An example is the Regional Drug Initiative in Portland, Oregon, which has been cited as an exemplary comprehensive antidrug program. It has a five-year action plan, which clearly establishes the program's goals, objectives, first-year priorities, implementation steps, and evaluation criteria.

There is evidence that comprehensive programs are more likely to affect crime problems than single-strategy interventions are.

Two points should be emphasized here. First, there is evidence that comprehensive programs are more likely to affect crime problems than single-strategy interventions are.[52] Second, given this fact, one of the primary objectives of the planning committee should be to identify the persons, agencies, and organizations that can carry out the various tasks identified in the action plan. Assessing current resources and current responses to the problem is an integral part of developing the program.

Implementing and maintaining the program

Once roles and responsibilities have been assigned, the program components can be implemented. Experience tells us that an implemented program rarely looks anything like the program that was described on paper. Most programs are implemented with less intensity, consistency, and resources than originally planned. Planners should be aware of this problem in advance and should make a special effort to monitor the implementation process and hold people accountable for their respective contributions.

In the field of community crime prevention, one of the largest problems is obtaining and sustaining adequate levels of citizen participation. Many strategies have been proposed to ensure the continuity of voluntary citizen action, including using existing organizations; providing technical assistance, good training, and strong leadership; encouraging input into the planning process; creating links to outside resources; maintaining an ongoing agenda; and, especially, trying to recognize and reward individual contributions.

Evaluating and giving feedback

Demonstrating the success of innovative coproduction programs will depend, to a large extent, on whether the processes and effects of these programs can be carefully documented through evaluation research. Without this documentation, police executives and their "coproducers" will be asking funding agencies and other interested parties to "trust me" when it comes to describing program success.

Evaluations can be useful at all stages of program development and implementation. They can help in determining the nature of the problem, the appropriate target population, and the nature of the intervention. They can be extremely helpful in documenting how the program was implemented and what resources were employed. Deviations from the original action plan can be noted, and feedback can be provided to program administrators so that modifications can be introduced if necessary. In addition, evaluations can answer the questions of whether the program was effective in meeting its goals and whether it was worth the cost.

Although evaluations are a good idea, the responsible public official needs to be careful in conducting evaluations, given the risk of wasting time and resources and creating or dashing false hopes on the base of a sloppy assessment. Several points are crucial. First, good evaluations require special skills; assistance should therefore be sought from professional researchers. Second, when an evaluation is being planned, everyone with an interest or stake in the results should have an opportunity to comment on the evaluation plans (for example, on the goals and objectives that will be used as the criteria for success). Third, the planning team should establish realistic goals for the program; otherwise they are inviting failure. Fourth, the measures and research design must be not only appropriate to the goals of the program but also methodologically sound. Finally, the major issues and problems in conducting evaluation in the crime prevention field, as described in the literature, should be thoroughly considered.[53] These include possible displacement rather than prevention of crime; overreliance on problematical police data rather than on survey data; overly narrow criteria for success; failure to select proper control groups; and an inability to examine program effects beyond the first year. None of these issues, however, should dissuade program advocates from thoughtfully seeking evaluations, as these will probably be preferable to complete ignorance about the costs and benefits of new programs. There are many types of evaluations serving many different purposes, and each, when coordinated with the best efforts of the police and community, can provide information that is useful for planning to make the environment safer for ourselves and future generations.

1   G. L. Kelling, *Police and Communities: The Quiet Revolution*, Perspectives on Policing, no. 1 (Washington, DC: National Institute of Justice, U.S. Department of Justice, 1988).

2   A. J. Reiss, Jr., "Why Are Communities Important in Understanding Crime?" in *Communities and Crime*, Crime and Justice Annual, ed. A. J. Reiss, Jr., and M. Tonry, vol. 8 (Chicago: University of Chicago Press, 1986); and D. P. Rosenbaum, "Community Crime Prevention: A Review and Synthesis of the Literature," *Justice Quarterly* 5 (1988): 323–95.

3   J. Jacobs, *The Death and Life of Great American Cities* (New York: Vintage, 1961), 31–32.

4   M. H. Moore and R. C. Trojanowicz, *Policing and the Fear of Crime*, Perspectives on Policing, no. 3 (Washington, DC: National Institute of Justice, 1988). For reviews of the research, see D. P. Rosenbaum and L. Heath, "The 'Psycho-Logic' of Fear Reduction and Crime Prevention Programs," in *Applied Social Psychology Annual*, ed. J. Edwards, E. Posavac, S. Tindale, F. Bryant, and L. Heath, vol. 9 (New York: Plenum, 1990); F. DuBow, E. McCabe, and G. Kaplan, *Reactions to Crime: A Critical Review of the Literature* (Washington, DC: National Institute of Justice, U. S. Department of Justice, 1979); and T.L. Baumer, "Research on Fear of Crime in the United States," *Victimology* 3 (1978): 254–64.

5   See P. Hunt, "Community Development: Should It Be Included as Part of the Police Mission?" Working paper, Harvard Executive Session on Policing (March 4, 1988); and D. P. Rosenbaum, D. A. Lewis, and J. A. Grant, "Neighborhood-Based Crime Prevention: Assessing the Efficacy of Community Organizing in Chicago," in *Community Crime Prevention: Does It Work?* ed. D. P. Rosenbaum (Beverly Hills, CA: Sage, 1986).

6   For further documentation on many programs cited in this chapter, see Rosenbaum, "Community Crime Prevention: A Review and Synthesis of the Literature."

7   A. J. Reiss, Jr., "Shaping and Serving the Community: The Role of the Police Chief Executive," in *Police Leadership in America: Crisis and Opportunity*, ed. W. A. Geller (New York: Praeger, 1985).

8   S. Greenberg, W. M. Rohe, and J. R. Williams, *Informal Citizen Action and Crime Prevention at the Neighborhood Level: Synthesis and Assessment of the Research* (Washington, DC: National Institute of Justice, U. S. Department of Justice, 1985); D. P. Rosenbaum, "The Theory and Research Behind Neighborhood Watch: Is It a Sound Fear and Crime Reduction Strategy?" *Crime and Delinquency* 33 (1987): 103–34; and Rosenbaum, "Community Crime Prevention: A Review and Synthesis of the Literature."

9   J. M. Hough, R. V. G. Clarke, and P. Mayhew, "Introduction," in *Designing Out Crime*, ed. R. G. V. Clarke and P. Mayhew (London: Her Majesty's Stationery Office, 1980).

10 Rosenbaum, Lewis, and Grant, "Neighborhood-Based Crime Prevention."

11 P. J. Lavrakas and S. F. Bennett, "Thinking about the Implementation of Citizen and Community Anti-Crime Measures," in *Communities and Crime Reduction*, ed. T. Hope and M. Shaw (London: Her Majesty's Stationery Office, 1988).

12 In addition to the publications by local law enforcement agencies, the National Crime Prevention Council provides information on all aspects of crime prevention. And although Americans have ignored some of this advice, most individuals have altered their behavior because of crime.

13 M. G. Maxfield, "Lifestyle and Routine Activity Theories of Crime: Empirical Studies of Victimization, Delinquency, and Offender Decision-Making," *Journal of Quantitative Criminology* 3 (1987): 275–82.

14 L. Furby and B. Fischoff, *Rape Self-Defense Strategies: A Review of Their Effectiveness*, technical report 86-3 (Eugene, OR: Eugene Research Institute, 1986).

15 On the effects of self-defense training, see E. S. Cohen, L. Kidder, and J. Harvey, "Crime Prevention vs. Victimization: The Psychology of Two Different Reactions," *Victimology* 3 (1978): 285–96. On WhistleStop, see D. E. Reed, *Whistle-Stop: A Community Alternative for Crime Prevention* (Ph.D. diss., Northwestern University, 1979).

16 See J. D. Wright, P. H. Rossi, and K. Daly, *Under the Gun: Weapons, Crime, and Violence in America* (New York: Aldine, 1983).

17 Among the useful educational materials is a brochure entitled *Handgun Safety Guidelines*, prepared by the Center to Prevent Handgun Violence and published by the Police Executive Research Forum.

18 D. P. Rosenbaum, "Coping With Victimization: The Effects of Police Intervention on Victims' Psychological Readjustment," *Crime and Delinquency* 33 (1987): 502–19.

19 Rosenbaum, Lewis, and Grant, "Neighborhood-Based Crime Prevention."

20 See R. K. Yin, "Community Crime Prevention: A Synthesis of Eleven Evaluations," in *Community Crime Prevention: Does It Work?* ed. Rosenbaum.

21 Rosenbaum, "Community Crime Prevention: A Review and Synthesis of the Literature," 377.

22 See J. Garofalo and M. McLeod, *Improving the Effectiveness and Utilization of Neighborhood Watch Programs*, draft final report to the National Institute of Justice (Albany: Hindelang Criminal Justice Research Center, State University of New York at Albany, 1986); S. Pennell, C. Curtis, and J. Henderson, *Guardian Angels: An Assessment of Citizen Responses to Crime*, vol. 2; technical report to the National Institute of Justice. (San Diego, CA: San Diego Association of Governments, 1985); A. M. Podolefsky and F. DuBow, *Strategies for Community Crime Prevention: Collective Responses to Crime in Urban America* (Springfield, IL: Charles C Thomas, 1981); and R. K. Yin, M. E. Vogel, J. M. Chaiken, and D. R. Both, *Patrolling the Neighborhood Beat: Residents and Residential Security* (Santa Monica, CA: Rand Corporation, 1976).

23 Pennell, Curtis, and Henderson, *Guardian Angels*.

24 W. E. Schmidt, "Rise in Chicago Transit Crime

Spotlights Witness's Dilemma," *New York Times*, 15 Oct. 1988, p. 1.

25 See Yin, Vogel, Chaiken, and Both, *Patrolling the Neighborhood Beat*.

26 M. Maltz, A. C. Gordon, and W. Friedman (forthcoming), *Mapping Crime in Its Community Context: A Study of Event Geography Analysis* (New York: Springer Verlag).

27 On the Eisenhower project, see S. Bennett and P. J. Lavrakas, *Evaluation of the Planning and Implementation of the Neighborhood Program*, final process report to the Eisenhower Foundation (Evanston, IL: Center for Urban Affairs and Policy Research, Northwestern University, 1988). For other scholars' support of the "social problems" approach, see E. Currie, "Two Visions of Community Crime Prevention," In *Communities and Crime Reduction*, ed. Hope and Shaw, 280–86; and L. A. Curtis, ed., *American Violence and Public Policy* (New Haven: Yale University Pres, 1985).

28 For reviews and experimental programs, see J. E. Eck and W. Spelman, *Problem-Solving: Problem-Oriented Policing in Newport News* (Washington, DC: Police Executive Research Forum, 1987); J. E. Eck and W. Spelman, "Who Ya Gonna Call? The Police as Problem Busters," *Crime and Delinquency* 33 (1987): 31–52; H. Goldstein, "Improving Policing: A Problem-Oriented Approach," *Crime and Delinquency* 25 (1979): 236–58; H. Goldstein, "Toward Community-Oriented Policing: Potential, Basic Requirements, and Threshold Questions," *Crime and Delinquency* 33 (1987): 6–30; Herman Goldstein, *Problem-Oriented Policing* (New York: McGraw-Hill, 1990); J. Greene and S. Mastrofski, eds., *Community Policing: Rhetoric or Reality* (New York: Praeger, 1988); C. Murphy and G. Muir, *Community Based Policing: A Review of the Critical Issues* (Ottawa: Ministry of the Solicitor General of Canada, 1984); A. M. Pate, M. A. Wycoff, W. G. Skogan, and L. Sherman, *Reducing Fear of Crime in Houston and Newark*, prepared for the National Institute of Justice, U. S. Department of Justice (Washington, DC: Police Foundation, 1986); Rosenbaum, "Community Crime Prevention: A Review and Synthesis of the Literature"; and J. H. Skolnick and D. H. Bayley, *The New Blue Line: Police Innovation in Six American Cities* (New York: Free Press, 1986).

29 R. C. Trojanowicz and H. A. Harden, *The Status of Contemporary Community Policing Programs* (East Lansing, MI: National Neighborhood Foot Patrol Center, School of Criminal Justice, Michigan State University, 1985). For further discussion of foot patrols as a community policing strategy, see also R. C. Trojanowicz, "Evaluating a Neighborhood Foot Patrol Program: The Flint Michigan, Project," in *Community Crime Prevention: Does It Work?* ed. Rosenbaum.

30 Skolnick and Bayley, *The New Blue Line*, 69.

31 Pate, Wycoff, Skogan, and Sherman, *Reducing Fear of Crime in Houston and Newark*.

32 For example, see Chicago Alliance for Neighborhood Safety, *Block Watch Organizing Handbook* (Chicago: Chicago Alliance for Neighborhood Safety, 1985); see also Seattle Police Department, *Citizen's Guide to Organizing a Block Watch* (Seattle: City of Seattle, n.d.).

33 Pate, Wycoff, Skogan, and Sherman, *Reducing Fear of Crime in Houston and Newark*, 8. For information about the Hartford program evaluation and results, see F. J. Fowler, Jr., and T. W. Mangione, "A Three-Pronged Effort to Reduce Crime and Fear of Crime: The Hartford Experiment," In *Community Crime Prevention: Does It Work?*, ed. Rosenbaum, 87–108.

34 Maltz, Gordon, and Friedman. *Mapping Crime in Its Community Context*. For information on the Evanston initiative, see P. J. Lavrakas, D. P. Rosenbaum, and F. Kaminski, "Transmitting Information About Crime and Crime Prevention: The Evanston Newsletter Quasi-Experiment," *Journal of Police Science and Administration* 2 (1983): 463–73.

35 Lavrakas, Rosenbaum, and Kaminski, "Transmitting Information About Crime and Crime Prevention"; P. J. Lavrakas, "Evaluating Police-Community Anti-Crime Newsletters: The Evanston, Houston, and Newark Field Studies," in *Community Crime Prevention: Does It Work?* ed. Rosenbaum.

36 Rosenbaum, "Community Crime Prevention: A Review and Synthesis of the Literature," 364.

37 O. Newman, *Defensible Space: Crime Prevention Through Environmental Design* (New York: Macmillan, 1972).

38 H. Rubenstein, C. Murray, T. Motoyama, and W. V. Rouse, *The Link Between Crime and the Built Environment: The Current State of Knowledge*, vol. 1 (Washington, DC: National Institute of Justice, U.S. Department of Justice, 1980); R. B. Taylor and S. Gottfredson, "Environmental Design, Crime, and Prevention: An Examination of Community Dynamics," in *Communities and Crime*, ed. A. J. Reiss, Jr., and M. Tonry, vol. 8 (Chicago: University of Chicago Press, 1986); and Rosenbaum, "Community Crime Prevention: A Review and Synthesis of the Literature."

39 J. M. Tien, V. F. O'Donnell, A. Barnett, and P. B. Mirchandani, *Street Lighting Projects: National Evaluation Program Phase 1 Report* (Washington, DC: U.S. Government Printing Office, 1979).

40 J. Schmalz, "Fearful and Angry Floridians Erect Street Barriers to Crime," *New York Times*, 6 Dec. 1988, p. 1.

41 J. F. O'Neil, "Crime Prevention Pays," *FBI Law Enforcement Bulletin* 57, no. 10 (1988): 13–17. Formal evaluation of the McGruff program appears in G. J. O'Keefe, "The McGruff National Media Campaign: Its Public Impact and Future Implications," in *Community Crime Prevention: Does It Work?* ed. Rosenbaum.

42 D. P. Rosenbaum, A. J. Lurigio, and P. J. Lavrakas, "Enhancing Citizen Participation and Solving Serious Crime: A National Evaluation of Crime Stoppers Programs," *Crime and Delinquency* 35 (1989): 401–20.

43 Office of Juvenile Justice and Delinquency Prevention, "Law-Related Education," *Juvenile Justice Technical Assistance Bulletin* (Washington, DC: Office of Juvenile Justice and Delinquency Prevention, U. S. Department of Justice, 1985).

44 National Crime Prevention Council, "Teens and Teachers Agree: 'Crime and the Community' Curriculum is Great!" *Catalyst* 7, no. 5 (1987): 1–2.

45 P. J. Lavrakas and D. P. Rosenbaum, *Crime Prevention Beliefs, Policies, and Practices of Chief Law Enforcment Executives: Results of a National*

Survey. Report prepared for the National Crime Prevention Council, Washington, DC, 1989.

46 International Association of Chiefs of Police, *Reducing Crime by Reducing Drug Abuse: A Manual for Police Chiefs and Sheriffs* (Washington, DC: International Association of Chiefs of Police, 1988); and Drug Enforcement Administration, *Demand Reduction Coordinator's Resource Guide* (Washington, DC: National Crime Prevention Council, 1988).

47 J. R. Gusfield, "The Control of Drinking-Driving in the United States: A Period of Transition?" in *Social Control of the Drinking Driver*, ed. M. D. Laurence, J. R. Snortum, and F. E. Zimring (Chicago: University of Chicago Press, 1988). Other articles in the same volume also contain helpful reviews of the research and policy analysis on alcohol abuse.

48 International Association of Chiefs of Police, *Reducing Crime by Reducing Drug Abuse*.

49 L. F. Mock and D. P. Rosenbaum, *A Study of Trade Secret Theft in High-Technology Industries* (Washington, DC: National Institute of Justice, 1988).

50 On the traditional problems with planning and implementation, see D. P. Rosenbaum, "The Theory and Research Behind Neighborhood Watch: Is It a Sound Fear and Crime Reduction Strategy?" *Crime and Delinquency* 33 (1987): 103–34; Rosenbaum, "Community Crime Prevention: A Review and Synthesis of the Literature";

Lavrakas and Bennett, "Thinking About the Implementation of Citizen and Community Anti-Crime Measures"; J. D. Fiens, *Partnerships for Neighborhood Crime Prevention* (Washington, DC: National Institute of Justice, U. S. Department of Justice, 1983); R. Linden, I. Barker, and D. Frisbie, *Working Together to Prevent Crime* (Ottawa: Solicitor General of Canada, 1984); M. McPherson and G. Silloway, *Program Models: Planning Community Crime Prevention Programs* (Minneapolis: Minnesota Crime Prevention Center, 1980); and Pate, Wycoff, Skogan, and Sherman, *Reducing Fear of Crime in Houston and Newark*.

51 International Association of Chiefs of Police, *Reducing Crime by Reducing Drug Abuse*, 38.

52 Rosenbaum, ed., *Community Crime Prevention: Does It Work?* and F. Heinzelmann, "Promoting Citizen Involvement in Crime Prevention and Control," in *Taking Care: Understanding and Encouraging Self-Protective Behavior*, ed. N. Weinstein (New York: Cambridge University Press, 1987).

53 See A. J. Lurigio and D. P. Rosenbaum, "Evaluation Research in Community Crime Prevention: A Critical Look at the Field," and R. K. Yin, "Community Crime Prevention: A Synthesis of Eleven Evaluations," both in *Community Crime Prevention: Does It Work?* ed. Rosenbaum; and Rosenbaum, "Community Crime Prevention: A Review and Synthesis of the Literature."

5 Criminal investigations

Investigating crime is an important function of modern, full-service police departments. In most medium to large police organizations in the United States, roughly 10 to 20 percent of sworn personnel are assigned to the criminal investigations section. Moreover, investigations involve many police personnel besides detectives. Patrol officers begin most investigations and, in some departments, they carry out the entire investigation of many crimes. (Although allocating complete investigative responsibility for certain crimes to patrol officers is more common in smaller departments, large ones do it as well. Some experts argue that the patrol force makes the greatest contribution to investigations even when they do not have the sole responsibility. They claim that without quality work at the start of an investigation, further efforts by detectives are not likely to solve the case.) Crime analysts, evidence technicians, records clerks, and many other individuals also make substantial contributions to investigations. Thus, any description of the management of investigations must be far beyond the management of detectives.

This chapter describes management principles for investigative work. Following a brief history of investigations, it summarizes the goals of criminal investigations and describes the steps in the investigative process. Next comes a summary of research indicating what is known—and unknown—about the effectiveness of case-oriented and offender-oriented investigative efforts. The rest of the chapter is devoted to management and organization of the investigative function, including performance measures and personnel issues.

Throughout this chapter the term *investigator* is used to mean any police employee who contributes to an investigation, whether a dectective, patrol officer, evidence technician, clerk, or other. The term *detective* is reserved for the sworn police officer assigned to a special unit whose primary function is investigating crimes or suspects. In the minds of the public, of course, investigations are most closely associated with detectives. This is due in part to the history of the detective role in modern policing.

A history of investigations

In Europe, detectives were originally employed to blend in with the populace and seek information as if they were ordinary citizens, not functionaries of the state. At that time, the detective's prime function was to identify opponents of the government—whether internal agitators and revolutionaries or external spies—and keep them from achieving their objectives. The minister of police under Napoleon, Joseph Fouché, created such a political force.[1] Much of the original resistance of the English to establishing a police force and then a detective branch was based on the fear of creating a similar force.[2] Despite these concerns, in the 1880s the London Metropolitan Police created the Special Irish Branch to control agitation for a separate Ireland.[3]

Another Napoleonic police official—a rival of Fouché's—engaged François Vidocq, a former convict, as an informer. Vidocq was later employed as a detective to track down ordinary criminals, and he eventually founded the Sûreté, the French detective police force. Vidocq created a system of files on known criminals, relying on a network of informants and on his operatives' intimate knowledge of the people he was employed to control.[4]

Preservation of the government (as under Napoleon) and the investigation of crimes both relied on similar procedures: the use of informants and the development of detailed knowledge about the political or criminal underworld. Detectives worked offenders, not cases.

In England, thief taking—as the identification, stalking, and arrest of criminals was called in the eighteenth and nineteenth centuries—was the responsibility of a variety of governmental officials and private citizens, all of whom collected bounties for catching offenders. By most accounts, these uncoordinated individuals and groups were almost totally ineffective at controlling criminality. One reason was that the bounty system gave law enforcers a strong incentive to take payoffs from major criminals for fabricating cases against minor offenders.[5]

One of the more effective of these groups was the Bow Street Runners, established in the early 1750s by Henry Fielding, a London magistrate (and the author of *Tom Jones* and other novels). Originally Fielding's investigators were mounted on horseback, wore standardized garb, and carried pistols, cutlasses, and handcuffs. After Henry Fielding's death in 1754, his brother John took over this police force. Like Vidocq, John Fielding systematized the investigation of criminals. He regularly published a newsletter to circulate information about the active criminals of the day, and he maintained a file of registered criminals. In 1782 John Fielding created a plainclothes detachment of investigators, who patrolled on foot, as part of the Bow Street Runners. These investigators also developed a profound knowledge of the London underworld and used informants to capture highwaymen, murderers, and thieves.[6]

In 1829, with the creation of the London Metropolitan Police, uniformed police forces began to be established throughout England and Wales, and the investigation of crimes fell to the constables. But their uniforms and policies kept them from blending in with the criminal underworld so, from the beginning, police administrators in most forces assigned a few constables to plainclothes detective work.[7] Then, thirteen years after its formation, the London Metropolitan Police created a detective branch to investigate crimes.[8] Again, informants and a knowledge of the criminal underworld gave these detectives the information they sought. In 1914, when the Royal Canadian Mounted Police established its first detective squad, the stated reason was that plainclothes constables would be able to penetrate the underworld, which uniformed constables could not.[9])

In the United States, nineteenth-century detectives also focused on suspects (when they were not carrying out missions from local political bosses). In 1886, Inspector Thomas Byrnes, chief of detectives of the New York City police, published a book describing the practices of 247 professional thieves.[10] As Arthur M. Schlesinger, Jr., notes in his introduction to the 1969 reprint of Byrnes's book, the inspector controlled criminals in New York through a combination of informants, treaties with criminals, and the application of torture to gain confessions (euphemistically called the "third degree").

During the late nineteenth and early twentieth centuries, the Pinkerton National Detective Agency also focused more on criminals than on crimes. Pinkerton operatives (as the business called their detectives) developed contacts with the criminal underworld, used informants extensively, and established detailed files on active criminals.[11]

This orientation toward offenders began to fade, at least in large cities, with the onset of the police reform era of the 1920s and 1930s. There is less information about police practices in smaller cities, but it is likely that, as these jurisdictions adopted reform practices, their orientation toward offenders faded also. In many large cities, the detective branch was a prime target of the reform police chiefs because it was virtually a power unto itself; its members often served the political bosses and sometimes accepted bribes from the criminals they were supposed to control. Further, allegations were made that detectives used the third degree.

But it was not only their powerful political allies and their corruption that made offender-oriented detectives hard for police administrators to control. Detectives could claim that much of their time was spent cultivating informants. This meant that they could spend a great deal of time in places where criminals were to be found—bars, brothels, pool halls, and other places that were out of their superiors' sight. Presumably, informants gave detectives many tips over sips of whiskey. Who knew where these tips could lead? Certainly not the detectives' supervisors. Thus, detectives generated their own work. Further, there was no way supervisors could judge their performance. If a superior questioned his performance, a detective could always make arrests for minor offenses.

So, as part of their department-wide reform efforts, police chiefs sought to change the focus of investigative work from offenders to cases. Under this approach to investigations, supervisors assigned detectives specific crimes, or cases, to investigate. Thus supervisors could more easily control the work of detectives. They could also measure detective performance statistically, through clearance rates. Control over workloads and the ability to measure performance, when combined with department-wide efforts to break the hold of political machines on the police force, helped supervisors control what detectives did.

These efforts to reform detective work took place over a long period and had varying effects. Court decisions reinforced administrative reform initiatives by forcing detectives to be more careful in how they went about collecting evidence and interviewing suspects. Though these changes had many positive effects, they also helped reduce detectives' knowledge of active criminals. And they changed the objectives of investigative work from controlling the activities of persistent offenders to solving crimes that had already been committed.

The investigations function has three goals: controlling criminals, pursuing justice, and addressing problems. These goals are not totally separable, nor are they necessarily harmonious.

Today, investigative work is usually case-oriented and fits well with the incident-driven nature of police work in general. (Some researchers and chiefs believe that this emphasis on incidents should be modified by increased concentration on solving community problems. For further discussion, see the chapter on the patrol function.)

Goals of criminal investigations

The investigations function has three goals: controlling criminals, pursuing justice, and addressing problems. These goals are not totally separable, nor are they necessarily harmonious. Pursuit of one goal may help achieve one or both of the other goals (for example, the capture and imprisonment of a serious offender may result in fewer crimes and in public feelings that the offender received the correct punishment). Or the three goals may be in conflict, as could happen if a victim's desire for retribution (an important part of justice) prevented the development of measures whose purpose was to prevent future occurrences of similar offenses. For example, if convicted burglars were offered the option of probation and mandatory drug treatment, that might help reduce property crimes, but victims might feel that such measures were too lenient.

Controlling criminals

Society has three basic mechanisms for controlling the behavior of those engaged in crime: deterrence, rehabilitation, and incapacitation. First, it can scare them into desisting from criminal behavior. In theory, deterrence can be achieved by making offenders believe that their chances of getting caught and severely punished are greater than the expected rewards of crime. Presumably, offenders who see other criminals being caught and punished implicitly calculate the costs and benefits of further criminal behavior. If the perceived costs are too high— still in theory—the offender makes the rational decision to stop offending. This is an indirect approach.

Second, criminals can be directly induced to stop committing crimes. Measures such as punishment, psychological counseling, job training, or drug treatment may alter the behavior of criminals. So even if criminals are undeterred by the punishment meted out to others, rehabilitation (or inducement to obey the law) may persuade them to abandon a life of crime.

Finally, active criminals can be caught and removed from free society by incarceration, which prevents them from preying on the public. If a few offenders commit most serious crime, then catching and imprisoning them could reduce crime substantially. In theory, even if persistent criminals cannot be deterred or rehabilitated, they can be incapacitated. In practice, this may be difficult to do.

These three mechanisms—deterrence, rehabilitation, and incapacitation— involve not only the police but the entire criminal justice system, and they have been the subject of a great deal of study. Research has shown that each mechanism has only limited abilities to control crime, though each can be effective under some circumstances. But for any of the three approaches to be effective, offenders have to be identified, caught, prosecuted, *and* convicted. In each of these activities, the investigations function plays a major role. Whereas the actions of other criminal justice agencies make substantial contributions to the prosecution and conviction of offenders, the information supplied by the police is essential at all stages of the criminal justice process.

Pursuing justice

An important function of the police is to help uphold community norms. That is, the police should help the community draw the line between acceptable and unacceptable behavior. As an arm of government, the police should enhance citizens' feelings that people who seriously misbehave will be punished.

If police continue investigations in order to show victims that the police care, even when investigators know there is little chance of solving these crimes, then the police are deceiving the public.

In addition, the police have a role in helping victims of crime seek justice against the perpetrators. In the United States a victim can take an offender to court only in a *civil* proceeding; the government has assumed individual citizens' rights to pursue justice in *criminal* proceedings. A victim of a burglary or a rape, for example, does not have the right to seek retribution against the offender in criminal courts; instead, the government assumes this right and seeks justice for the victim and for society. A victim could, individually, pursue a civil remedy, but most victims cannot afford the private investigators and attorneys needed to do so (and most common criminals have too few resources to make such an undertaking worthwhile). Thus, most victims must rely on the criminal justice system. So this system must demonstrate to victims that justice is being served.

Investigators help pursue justice by arresting offenders and providing evidence for their prosecution and conviction. Equally important, the process of investigating offenses, apart from the results, can affect victims' and society's perceptions of whether justice is served. Treating victims with sensitivity and showing a concern for their needs helps give victims a feeling that justice is being done. Conscientious investigation of serious crimes, even if the chances of a solution are small, can also contribute to a community's feeling that justice is being served. And strict adherence to the rules of due process can help assure all community members that the police treat people fairly and protect the innocent against false accusations.

But the police must be very careful here. If police continue investigations in order to show victims that the police care, even when investigators know there is little chance of solving these crimes, then the police are deceiving the public. Once an investigator has probed deeply enough into a case to be reasonably sure that the case is unlikely to be solved, then he or she should give the victim an honest appraisal of the situation and suspend the investigation. Similarly, to pretend that the investigation is proceeding when it is not will ultimately undermine citizens' faith in the integrity of the police. This topic is also discussed below.

Addressing problems

The final goal that is increasingly set for the investigative function is addressing the many and varied problems that the citizenry feels the police should resolve. Citizens' individual reports of crimes are usually investigated individually. However, crimes often are part of a larger pattern of incidents that is symptomatic of a set of troublesome circumstances for which the police may be held responsible. These circumstances may vary widely: a particularly vulnerable apartment building may be inviting to burglars; a gang of drug traffickers may assault and kill their competition; a serial rapist may prey on college students; a merchant may fill his clients' orders with items picked up during break-ins; prostitutes may rob their customers; a store manager may operate in a way that makes the store a target for thieves; people may assault their spouses or partners; a car repair business may defraud clients by claiming to use new parts, whereas it really uses second-hand parts; or any other set of circumstances may give rise to criminal behavior.

In fact, it has been argued that addressing troublesome circumstances, or problems, is *the* function of the police.[12] Criminality and injustice are two broad categories of problems the public calls upon the police to address. The reasons for addressing problems are to prevent future incidents, reduce the number or harmfulness of these incidents, and improve the way the police and other agencies handle these events.

Addressing problems is related to the goal of controlling criminals in that it aims to prevent future occurrences of crimes. It differs from the goal of controlling criminals in that, in the process of solving a problem, the police may do much more than simply control crime. Further, to address a problem, the police do not need to rely solely on the imposition of criminal sanctions.

Similarly, problem solving is like and unlike the goal of promoting justice. In problem solving, citizens should feel they have been treated equitably and appropriately under the circumstances. But problem solving is aimed at removing whatever creates unjust situations and is not simply an attempt to redress an existing grievance. For example, some women's groups have complained that assaults against females, especially by husbands and boyfriends, are not treated as seriously as other types of assaults. A problem-solving effort to address domestic violence would have to take this concern about justice into consideration in addition to trying to reduce violence. The problem-oriented approach to criminal investigations is examined again later in this chapter.

The investigative process

The ability of the investigations function to achieve the goals of controlling criminals, pursuing justice, and addressing problems depends on how investigations are organized.

Investigations are often described as a production line. This is a useful, though simplistic, model of the investigations process. Of course, police departments substantially vary in how they conduct investigations, and even within a single department investigators treat different types of crimes differently. So an overview of the investigative process can describe only the most basic and common elements of investigations. Still, such an overview offers a starting point for evaluating investigations and establishing improved investigative processes. The general overview presented in the following discussion uses a production-line model.

As shown in Figure 5–1, the process begins after the discovery of the crime, with notification of the police. Usually a victim or witness calls to report the crime. On occasion an officer may discover evidence of a crime before anyone calls. Alternatively, the police may initiate an investigation of a suspected active offender, without knowledge of a specific crime. Proactive investigations of this type are more common in connection with suspected drug and vice crimes. They are also used to apprehend repeat offenders. For reactive investigations, typically a patrol officer initiates the case after a citizen reports the crime.

Figure 5–1 An overview of the investigations process.

Stage	Police personnel	Official reports	Victim's role
Reporting crime to the police	Operators, dispatchers	Tape of initial communication	Reporting the crime
Initial investigation: determining basic facts of the case and arresting suspects, if present	Patrol officers (sometimes an evidence technician and detectives)	Crime reports (sometimes physical-evidence reports or arrest report)	Providing information
Case screening: deciding whether to continue with the investigation	Investigations supervisor (sometimes a patrol supervisor)	Note on crime report, or screening form (some agencies notify victims)	Sometimes notified about decisions
Follow-up investigation: pursuing leads developed earlier	Detective (sometimes a patrol officer for some crimes)	Supplemental report and perhaps an arrest report	Verifying information
Case preparation: presenting case to the prosecutor	Detective (sometimes a patrol officer)	Arrest report	No role (some agencies may notify victim of an arrest)
Prosecution: attempting to get a conviction	Patrol officers and detectives to present evidence in court	Prosecutor's reports, court records	Providing testimony, if the case goes to trial; otherwise, little role

Initial investigation

The quality of the initial investigation is critical to the success of the entire investigative process; and it usually takes place within hours, often minutes, of the report of the offense. The steps the officer takes during the initial investigation depend on department procedures, the nature of the crime, and the evidence available. If an obvious suspect is at or near the crime scene, the officer may make an arrest and collect available evidence. If the crime is very serious and the crime scene very complex and no obvious offender is present—an example of this type of crime scene is a multiple-victim homicide—the officer may only secure the crime scene and call in specialists: detectives, evidence technicians, and others. (An evidence technician typically is either a specially trained police officer or a civilian employee of the department. The technician can lift fingerprints, take photographs, and collect other physical evidence left by the offender and victim.)

In some police departments, a patrol officer only records the basic facts of the case and conducts no real initial investigation. In a few departments patrol officers conduct the entire investigation and send on to detectives only a few serious crimes—such as homicides, rapes, and forgeries. During the initial investigation, patrol officers may be able to request the assistance of evidence technicians. The patrol investigator usually completes the initial investigation by the end of his or her shift.

If done well, the initial investigation is as much an investigation as the work that follows it. That it is conducted by a patrol officer and not a detective does not in itself diminish its contribution.

At the end of this stage, the investigating officer completes a crime report. If the case is sent to a special investigation section and not handled by the patrol officer, the crime report forms the basis of any further investigation.

If done well, the initial investigation is as much an investigation as the work that follows it. That it is conducted by a patrol officer and not a detective does not in itself diminish its contribution. The thoroughness of the work is what matters, not the clothes or assignment of the investigator. If the investigation ends when this stage is completed, the case has been investigated. This point is critical for understanding the next stage: case screening.

Case screening

If the investigation is to be taken over by a detective, that will generally be done within twenty-four to forty-eight hours. In many departments a supervisor decides whether the case warrants further attention. The process of deciding whether to pursue the investigation beyond the initial stage is called case screening. Not every department formally screens cases, and even in those that do, only some types of crimes are screened. For example, supervisors may screen burglaries and thefts but assign all rapes and homicides. If a case has sufficient clues or is very serious, a supervisor generally assigns it to a detective, and it becomes part of his or her caseload.

The detective assigned to the case then determines whether there are any leads that he or she can follow up. If there are few leads and it is a property crime (such as larceny, fraud, or burglary), the entire follow-up investigation may consist of a phone call to the victim. This call may only verify the facts in the crime report and assure the victim that the case is being pursued. After the call, the detective no longer investigates the case unless new evidence comes to his or her attention.

At this stage, it is important that investigators not deceive victims, even unintentionally. The victim's crime has been investigated, but the available leads may not be enough to solve the case. Under these circumstances, the police department should inform the victim of the real status of the investigation. This can be done either by letter or telephone. Some police departments employ civilians or use volunteers to make such calls. But under no circumstances should victims be led to believe that their case is being pursued when it is not.

Follow-up investigation

If there are leads—such as suspect names and descriptions, license plate numbers, or other pieces of information that suggest a specific suspect—the detective pursues them. This may involve finding and talking to the most obvious suspect. Or it may involve conducting a complex set of interviews and checking records (arrest records and automobile licenses, for example).

Most property crimes with no witnesses and only a few leads can be investigated relatively rapidly, but solutions are not often forthcoming. Crimes involving victim-suspect encounters or independent witnesses take longer to investigate and are more likely to result in an arrest.

The leads the detective pursues come from the initial investigation (which explains why the initial investigation is critical to the success of the entire investigative process). Though a detective can go over the same ground as the investigating patrol officer, witnesses and others who have knowledge about the case become harder to find as time goes on.

If a detective can develop enough evidence to provide probable cause for an arrest, he or she must still locate the suspect before an arrest warrant can be served. Sometimes locating a suspect may be more difficult than determining who the suspect is. Because of this and the press of new cases, unserved arrest warrants can stack up in a police department unless investigations managers have procedures to keep this from happening. Some departments have a special squad to serve old warrants on hard-to-find suspects. Others use tickler files to remind investigators to look for suspects in old cases.

Physical evidence

In agencies facing a large crime caseload, physical evidence (especially fingerprints) will be useful only after an investigator links a suspect to the crime. The most frequently collected form of physical evidence is fingerprints, and a large police department has thousands of them on file. Matching the prints found at the scene to the prints on file has traditionally been a very time-consuming and tedious process—a bit like trying to find an orange straw in a yellow haystack. Thus, most police departments cannot afford enough fingerprint examiners to attempt to link all prints found at crime scenes to unknown suspects. (See also the chapter on forensic sciences.)

The usefulness of fingerprints before any suspect is identified depends on two things: (1) the likelihood that the offender has prints on file (that is, the likelihood of a prior arrest in the jurisdiction); and (2) the investigator's ability to search the files rapidly. But traditionally, the more prints on file, the longer the search process. There are two ways of getting around this dilemma.

First, the files can be organized in ways that make searches more efficient. One method involves filing prints not by the name of a suspect, as is frequently done, but by attribute. For example, the files could be organized by finger, with subcategories of major points of comparison. Then, if a thumb print with a plain loop were found at a crime scene, the section of the print file containing thumb prints with plain loops would be analyzed. In this way, only the portion of the file holding attributes matching the prints found at the crime scene needs to be searched. Another method of improving efficiency by reorganizing print files is to create subfiles containing the prints of particular types of repeat criminals— for example, sex offenders or burglars. Again, the investigator can concentrate his or her search on this smaller file. This can decrease the search time and improve the chances of detecting an unknown offender. Maintaining many separate files, however, can be costly. Someone must keep them up-to-date and must cross-reference the entries. In the past the use of card files made this enterprise extremely time-consuming, but today, with computers, such file systems are much easier to maintain.

The second way of speeding up the search process is by automating it. With automated fingerprint identification system (AFIS) technology, cold searches (searches that begin without a suspect name) are more efficient. Use of this technology is increasing, but because of the high costs of these systems, only large departments can afford them, unless several smaller departments share the purchase and operational expenses. But even with AFIS, few departments can afford to cold-search all the prints that investigators recover at the scenes of property crimes. So investigators use AFIS primarily for very serious crimes. Nevertheless, with AFIS, cold searches can be used for many more crimes in which prints have been recovered than is possible without AFIS (see further discussion of AFIS in the chapter on information management).

After arrest

Once an arrest is made, the detective usually attempts to question the suspect. At this stage the objective is to develop a case strong enough for the prosecutor's office to take for prosecution. If the prosecutor's office decides to pursue the case, the case and the offender become the responsibility of the prosecutor and the courts, and the police role is limited to holding the evidence and testifying in court, if the case goes that far. For some complex or serious cases, however, the prosecutor may ask the police to collect additional information.

Usually, the prosecutor does not involve the police officers who contributed to the investigation in decisions about the case's processing or disposition. Indeed, unless the police and the prosecutor's officer have made special arrangements (see below), investigating officers are often not told what the final disposition of the case is. Nor do police records usually show the final disposition of cases in which an arrest was made. This makes it very difficult to assess investigative effectiveness after arrest.

Making arrests cannot, as a matter of policy, be an end in itself. For this reason investigative managers and prosecutors should establish joint policies about handling cases. As discussed later in this chapter, these policies should cover the information requirements for cases sent to the prosecutor's office, feedback on case disposition, and handling of prosecutorial requests for additional investigative work.

Research on investigative effectiveness

Two decades of research on investigations contradict some of the conventional wisdom about the roles of detectives and patrol officers in the investigative process.[13] Research has focused on two investigative approaches: case-oriented investigation and offender-oriented investigation.

Case-oriented investigation

Research on criminal investigations suggests two competing hypotheses about investigative productivity. The first is that the efforts and skill of investigators are what determine success. This is the *effort-result hypothesis*. The second hypothesis is that chance events largely determine the results of investigations. This is the *circumstance-result hypothesis*.

To the extent that either of these hypotheses is valid, there are major implications for the management of case-oriented investigations. If the effort-result hypothesis is largely correct, then providing trained investigators with more time to develop and pursue leads will yield more arrests and prosecutions, everything else being equal. Alternatively, if the circumstance-result hypothesis is true, then the work of investigators is merely that of recording the facts that luck provides them with. Additional time to develop leads will not result in more arrests and prosecutions.

The effort-result hypothesis held sway until the mid-1970s. Then research findings began to suggest that investigative work was not effective at catching criminals because the evidence needed for making arrests was simply not available in most cases. Further, when evidence was discovered, it was usually found by patrol officers during their initial investigation.[14] The research therefore supported the circumstance-result hypothesis and the conclusion that, at least for property crimes, traditional detective work contributed little to investigations.

Such a view suggested that it would be futile to try to gain effectiveness by reforming the management of investigations and that investigating cases was inherently ineffective. And, in fact, Rand Corporation studies of investigations suggested that the way detectives were organized had little effect on results of investigations.[15] Improved management could cut costs, however, by improving the efficiency of investigators' work. (In other words, the bad news about these management improvements is that we still would not be doing anything particularly productive. The good news is that we would be saving a great deal of time.)

Other research contradicted this assertion. A study by the Police Foundation showed that the Rochester (New York) police department's shift to neighborhood team policing increased the rate of solving crimes.[16] Among the changes instituted in the Rochester police department that could have created this improvement were

1. Improving the quality of initial investigations by patrol officers
2. Using case screening extensively
3. Decentralizing detectives to neighborhood teams.

The combined weight of all the studies, coupled with the impulse to modify and improve rather than abandon traditional methods, gave rise to an approach that became known as *managing criminal investigations* (MCI).[17] MCI had a number of components, but the two that received widespread attention were

1. Upgrading patrol officers' roles in investigations to improve evidence gathering at the beginning of investigations
2. Using case screening to weed out cases that are unlikely to result in an arrest and to focus attention on those that could result in an arrest.

In other words, to improve the effectiveness of investigations, patrol involvement increased, and detectives worked on fewer cases.

Further research—using better data and improved analysis—revealed that neither the effort-result hypothesis nor the circumstance-result hypothesis was an adequate explanation for investigative effectiveness. A Police Executive Research Forum study revealed that, although quality initial investigations are critical to solving crimes, a follow-up investigation of the leads can improve the chances that an arrest will be made.[18] Of particular importance during a follow-up investigation are interviews with witnesses and informants in order to develop suspect names and links to other crimes. To some extent, these findings supported the effort-result hypothesis. Still, many crimes lack substantial leads and are unlikely to be solved through a case-oriented approach. So there was also evidence supporting the circumstance-result hypothesis. Several conclusions became evident:

1. The investigation of cases is a department-wide function; patrol officers, detectives, and other police department members are important contributors to the investigative process. This means that patrol officers (as well as detectives) need to be trained in investigative techniques.

2. Police managers need to pay attention to the identification of witnesses, especially during the initial investigation, by canvassing neighborhoods for witnesses.

The investigation of cases is a department-wide function; patrol officers, detectives, and other police department members are important contributors to the investigative process.

---

3. Investigators need to place greater emphasis on developing informants—information sources who are either criminals themselves or familiar with criminals.

4. Cases without substantial leads—particularly property crimes—should be screened out from the investigative process as soon as possible. The reasons for this decision should be explained to the victim. Continuing to invest police time in investigating these cases wastes police resources and raises false hopes.

Offender-oriented investigation

During the mid-1970s, research began to accumulate showing that a substantial proportion of serious crimes were committed by a relatively small number of people.[19] Though not a surprise to most police officers, the research had some profound implications that, for the most part, police officials had neither foreseen nor acted upon.

First, if the criminal justice system could remove a substantial number of repeat offenders from society, then crime could be reduced substantially. At first this hypothesis sounded plausible. Some analysts even estimated that crime could be reduced by more than 20 percent if repeat offenders were incapacitated at a higher rate and for longer durations.[20] More careful analysis showed that the gains from a comprehensive repeat offender incapacitation strategy (a strategy that would include the criminal justice decisions of police, prosecutors, judges, and corrections officials) would be more modest, reducing crime by 4 to 8 percent. One of the reasons for this modest effect was that prosecutors and courts were already showing little leniency toward repeat offenders once they had been caught and convicted.[21] Improving police and prosecutorial abilities to identify and catch repeat offenders without changing sentencing and correctional policies might decrease crime 2 to 4 percent.[22]

The second finding of the repeat offender research pertains to who the police catch. Some repeat offenders do not learn from their mistakes, so whereas they commit many crimes when they are not in jail, they are caught often. Yet the worse repeat offenders are more successful than other repeat offenders at eluding capture by the police.[23] Case-oriented investigations are ineffective at improving the arrest rate for the most prolific criminals. If repeat-offender research findings are true, then police investigators need to find new ways of detecting repeat offenders. One approach is to target offenders before an arrest by making extensive use of informants, surveillance, and criminal intelligence files. Two evaluations by the Police Foundation suggested that this type of investigation may be effective in helping to remove repeat offenders from society.[24] Interestingly, this approach is similar to the traditional investigative approaches that were widely used before the police reform efforts that began in the 1920s. Another approach is to target repeat offenders after they have been arrested to help ensure that they are convicted. There is little systematic evidence to show how effective this approach is.

Though promising in principle, the offender-oriented approach has not been studied enough to determine whether it is really more effective than case-oriented investigations at controlling crime.

Though promising in principle, the offender-oriented approach has not been studied enough to determine whether it is really more effective than case-oriented investigations at controlling crime. Unfortunately, it will be years before the research community is able to say with any degree of certainty which is more effective. At the present, offender-focused investigations are widely discussed but not widely used.

Implications for achieving goals

What does the research suggest about the effectiveness of current investigative practices in achieving the three goals described earlier—controlling criminals, pursuing justice, and addressing problems?

Effectiveness in controlling criminals   Case-oriented investigations seem to have a limited effect, at best, on crime. The research shows that, when this investigative approach is used, many crimes, especially property crimes in which the victim and the offender never meet, are unlikely to result in an arrest. Therefore, deterrence, rehabilitation, and incapacitation are seldom possible. There is a bit of evidence that focusing on repeat offenders could be more effective at controlling crime.

Much less is known about investigative effectiveness with regard to crimes of violence—assaults, robberies, rapes, and murders—because very little research into the investigation of these crimes has been conducted. These crimes involve encounters between a victim and an assailant. Therefore, information identifying the suspects is more likely and the chance of an arrest is greater. Still, the repeat-offender research suggests that those individuals who commit the most crimes will learn how to avoid detection.

Effectiveness in pursuing justice   The inability to make arrests in many cases also hinders the pursuit of justice as a criminal investigations goal. It is doubtful, however, that many people believe justice would be better served by not investigating cases. Some investigations are successful. Moreover, the process of conducting an investigation can enhance a victim's sense of justice. But victims—and the public—are often led to believe that the efforts being made on their behalf are more intense than they actually are. Under these circumstances, justice is not being served.

It is important to note that justice also requires the police to work to prevent innocent people from being accused of crimes. The success of these efforts to pursue justice, however, does not show up in arrest statistics, or shows up as an apparent problem, that is, as the *absence* of an arrest. Investigators do not get commendations or rewards for declining to arrest innocent people.

Effectiveness in addressing problems   Finally, as was said earlier, a third goal of the investigations function is to address problems. Case-oriented investigation does not address the problems that give rise to the cases. In fact, the development throughout this century of a case orientation has led to the virtual abandonment of a very rudimentary form of problem solving: focusing on offenders.

Still, many believe that having detectives address problems, in addition to cases, has great potential for improving effectiveness. In one department that has been studied intensively, a detective assigned to the homicide squad realized that half of the murders he investigated were the result of domestic violence and, in half of these, police officers had gone to the address on one or more occasions before the killing. So he decided to develop a department- and city-wide response to spousal abuse, with the objective of reducing murders. There is some evidence that his efforts did reduce the number of domestic killings.[25]

In another example of investigative problem solving, two detectives assigned to the robbery squad were stymied in their investigation of a series of hotel and motel robberies. Instead of just working the few leads available, the detectives conducted some basic research on the characteristics of the hotels that were robbed. They compared these hotels to others that had not been robbed and found some ways to prevent robberies. They then helped the hotel managers organize a regional motel crime watch to exchange infor- mation on crime prevention measures and crime-related issues. These efforts led to information on other crimes committed by the suspects, including several robberies of other types of businesses. In addition, the detectives were able to develop better suspect descriptions. When patrol officers arrested an offender fitting the suspect's description for a bank robbery, the robbery detectives were able to solve many business robberies in the city and in four neighboring jurisdictions. The detectives attributed their success to taking a problem-oriented approach to the investigation.[26]

Similar efforts in various locations to deal with fortified crack houses, convenience store robberies, and repeat sexual assaults[27] show that these kinds of investigative efforts can reduce problems. Problem solving is rarely employed as a routine part of investigations and hence has not been rigorously researched. Information about its effectiveness is found in anecdotal examples. In the face of considerable evidence that conventional methods do not work very well, however, police managers would be well advised to keep an open mind toward innovations that may hold promise for helping achieve the police mission.

Management and organization of the investigative function

History, practice, and research on the investigative function suggest a number of ways to improve its management and organization.

Managing the investigations process

The investigations process includes the initial investigation, screening, the follow- up investigation, the handling of physical evidence, and prosecution.

Initial investigation   As Figure 5–1 shows, case processing starts when a citizen reports a crime to the police and ends when the prosecutor has completed his or her work. The principal police officers involved are patrol officers and detectives, and they are backed up by evidence technicians, clerks, and com- munications employees. Therefore, the management of this function must cut across organizational unit boundaries. For this reason many departments adopt an organizational structure that places patrol officers and detectives under a single deputy chief for field operations. If patrol officers and detectives are separated into two units, each headed by its own deputy chief (as is also common), coordination and collaboration become more difficult.

Police telephone operators are usually the first people to gather information about crimes, so it is important that they be trained to help initiate an investigation. Though operators are often under some time constraints in handling calls, they should gather enough information for dispatchers to be able to send the appropriate investigators to the crime scene. Further, operators can advise callers on how to preserve the crime scene and what types of information the investigator will be seeking.

Patrol officers are typically the first investigators at a crime scene. They need to be trained to do more than merely record the fact that a crime took place. The more evidence they collect, the greater the likelihood that further investigation will be productive. Patrol supervisors need to be trained in how to manage the initial investigations by their officers. Ideally, at the completion of an initial investigation, the patrol or detective supervisor should know whether further investigative work is needed. If the initial investigation is perfunctory, a follow-up investigator will have to begin the investigation all over again.

For some very complex crimes (for example, burglaries in which alarm systems were defeated, rapes, child abuse, homicides), a specialist, usually a detective, has to be sent to the crime scene at the beginning of the investigation. Even in these cases, a patrol officer often gets there first, so he or she must receive some training in how to handle these cases.

Collection of physical evidence   As noted earlier, fingerprints are of little help unless at least one of three conditions exists:

1. A suspect is caught and the prints found at the scene can be compared with the arrestee's prints.
2. Fingerprint records are organized in such a manner that cold searches can be accomplished efficiently.
3. The police agency has access to an automated fingerprint identification system (AFIS).

The usefulness of other physical evidence depends even more on first identifying a suspect. For example, body fluids left by offenders at crime scenes (such as semen recovered during a rape investigation) may be matched to an offender using blood typing or, more recently, DNA matching—but before this can be done, the police must have a suspect. This means that investigations managers should aim to create systems that foster (1) the identification of suspects; (2) the collection of physical evidence at crime scenes; and (3) the ability to link the physical evidence to suspects. Gains can be achieved by improving any one of these. Such an improvement occurred with the development of DNA matching, which allows investigators to link body fluids found at crime scenes to suspects identified through other means in cases in which blood-type matching would not work (see the chapter on forensic sciences).

Despite the emphasis that investigative management texts place on collecting and processing physical evidence, many police departments do not have written policies governing this area. A survey of departments accredited by the end of 1987 found that before accreditation, 28 percent of these departments had no policy governing the responsibility of the persons who process crime scenes, and 33 percent had no policy addressing evidence collection in the field. In fact, the level of written directives for the collection and preservation of physical evidence was lower than that of directives in most other policy areas.[28] Developing written policies for this area, and for all parts of the investigative process, should be a high managerial priority.

Case screening   At the completion of an initial investigation of property crimes and of some personal crimes (depending on whether the volume of cases is so high that detectives cannot follow up all of them), the patrol supervisor or detective supervisor should determine whether there are enough leads to warrant further investigation. Most burglaries should be screened out at this stage, given what has been learned about their lack of helpful leads.[29] To pursue these cases further is a waste of time for patrol officers and for detectives who probably already have heavy workloads. Resistance to case screening— that is, resistance to formally declining to pursue certain leads—is often the result of equating investigations with detective work. But if the patrol officer has done a thorough initial investigation, then the agency has not shirked its responsibility.

At this point a police officer should politely inform the victim about the decision and the reasons for making it. The victim should also be told that if additional information appears, the case will be reopened. If told politely and honestly, most victims will understand.

The Commission on Accreditation for Law Enforcement Agencies has set a mandatory standard requiring case screening.[30] A variety of case-screening procedures are now in use by police departments. Some involve statistical prediction models based on past investigations, whereas others are based on investigators' experiences as revealed in interviews.[31]

Follow-up investigations   Police departments should consider having patrol officers conduct the follow-up investigations of some crimes instead of referring all cases to detectives for follow-up. Some of the conditions that favor assigning some cases to patrol officers are that

Many crimes are committed by persons who do not travel far from where they live.

Uniformed officers are very familiar with the people living, working, and hanging out in their patrol area.

The techniques or skills needed to investigate many crimes are relatively easy to acquire, either with formal training or with experience.

If patrol officers are to handle the investigation of some crimes completely, then they should have ready access to support and clerical assistance. Patrol cars and squad rooms do not make good offices.

If patrol officers are to handle the investigation of some crimes completely, then they should have ready access to support and clerical assistance. Patrol cars and squad rooms do not make good offices.

It is typical (though not necessarily better) for a detective to take over the case after case screening. In larger departments, this often means that the case will be referred to a special unit in the investigations section. Investigations sections of medium and large police departments are often divided into units that specialize in particular types of crimes. A common distinction is between crimes against persons (homicides, rapes, and assaults) and crimes against property (larceny, fraud, and burglary). Although robberies have elements of both types of crimes (the attack is against a person, but the motive is often property), they are normally classed with crimes against persons.

There is no research indicating which type of organization of investigative units is most productive, but several criteria have traditionally been used—and seem sound—for determining whether a special unit is warranted:

The crimes that the unit investigates should have some obvious, definable characteristic that makes it possible for them to be separated from other crimes (for example, it probably does not make sense to create a special unit to investigate burglaries committed by drug addicts because an investigator rarely knows this information about a suspect until an investigation is well under way).

The procedures that members of the special unit will routinely engage in are radically different from those routinely practiced by other investigators (for example, a drug-homicide squad may spend considerable time developing intelligence information on rival drug trafficking groups).

To investigate these special crimes or engage in these special procedures, unit investigators should possess some uncommon and hard-to-obtain knowledge or skills that other investigators do not normally possess.

Other investigators, because of the press of their normal workloads, cannot carry out these procedures or be expected to acquire the knowledge or skills needed to achieve the results required.

In general, the burden of persuasion should rest on those advocating a new special unit. Each new unit decreases coordination among police department members and reduces the ability of police managers to allocate resources flexibly.

Prosecution   Though under the control of a separate public agency, the prosecution of cases is still, in part, a police responsibility. After all, it is the police investigation that has revealed the links between the suspect and the crime. Therefore, it is vital that investigative managers develop procedures with the prosecutor's office to expedite the effective and efficient handling of cases. These procedures should address a number of issues:

The evidence, for each type of offense, that the prosecutor needs for pursuing the case. Prosecutors have a great deal of discretion in determining which cases they will pursue, so they may very well ask for more than the minimum evidence required by law.

The point at which the prosecutor's office becomes involved in a case. For most cases this will be after an investigator has made an arrest and questioned the suspect. For a few complex or serious cases, the prosecutor may prefer to assign an assistant to the case early in the investigation.

The means for resolving conflicts between investigators and assistant prosecutors.

Feedback to investigators about the disposition of cases sent to the prosecutor. This should include an explanation of why certain cases were not prosecuted, how police could have made the prosecution of cases more efficient and effective, the findings, and the sentences handed down.

Performance measures for case-oriented investigations

Typically, with case orientation, police managers use clearance rates to evaluate the performance of a police department's investigative function, and especially its detectives. Clearance statistics, however, have been seriously challenged as a useful performance measure.[32] They purport to show what percentage of the crimes brought to police attention are "solved," but the definition of "solved" varies so much among police departments, and can be subject to so many interpretations, that clearance information is useless as a standard. Further, cases can be cleared without significantly contributing to the primary goals of investigations. For example, a burglar charged with a single offense tells the police about twelve other crimes he has committed. The investigator clears thirteen crimes, but unless the investigator uses this information to develop additional prosecutable cases against the offender, the burglar's chances of being convicted and receiving a long sentence do not change. Simply knowing who committed the crimes only moves the cases from the active file to the inactive file. This may be a useful administrative procedure, but because these confessions did nothing to contribute to investigative goals, these clearances are not a measure of effective performance. A combination of other measures of performance is far more useful—both to assess how well the investigative function is achieving its goals and to diagnose management problems and recommend changes in procedure.

The measures proposed below are appropriate for assessing the performance of the investigative unit. They have little utility for assessing the performance of individual investigators. There are three reasons for this. First, the more emphasis a manager puts on statistics as a measure of individual performance, the more police officers will seek to produce the numbers asked for; they can increase statistical performance measures without improving effectiveness. So a heavy emphasis on statistical performance measures for personnel appraisal will, in all likelihood, be counterproductive.[33] Second, research has shown that the biggest improvements in productivity come from management changes that are outside the day-to-day control of workers.[34] Third, many important investigative activities are not measurable. That is why a good supervisor must know his or her personnel, their strengths and weaknesses, and their workloads. Maximum performance may be negotiated by the supervisor and investigators, but watching statistics can yield only compliance with minimum performance requirements. (For additional discussion of performance measurement, see below; see also the chapter on performance measurement.)

The more emphasis a manager puts on statistics as a measure of individual performance, the more police officers will seek to produce the numbers asked for; they can increase statistical performance measures without improving effectiveness.

Among the unit-level investigative performance measures that police managers should consider are follow-up rate, suspect detection rate, arrest rate, prosecution rate, and victim service level. Other performance measures are also available, but they are not discussed here.[35]

Follow-up rate   The follow-up rate is the percentage of all cases reported to the police (those in which an on-scene arrest was not made) that are assigned for a follow-up investigation. It is an indicator of how much information patrol officers are obtaining during the initial investigation. For this to be used as a measure of performance, the screening procedure must be standardized and not subject to frequent changes. Decreases in the follow-up rate may show a need for additional training of patrol officers or for changes in the way initial investigations are conducted. Decreases (or increases) in the follow-up rate also may be due to a change in the way criminals and victims are behaving. For example, an increase in break-ins to apartments may decrease the follow-up rate if there are fewer witnesses to apartment break-ins than to burglaries of other dwellings. Note that the follow-up rate could also decrease if patrol officers became more successful in apprehending offenders. In this circumstance, the decline in the follow-up rate should be accompanied by an increase in the initial investigation arrest rate (see below).

Suspect detection rate   The suspect detection rate is the percentage of cases followed up in which a suspect was identified after the initial investigation, regardless of whether an arrest was made. Changes in this measure describe the effectiveness with which follow-up investigators use initial investigation leads. A decrease in this measure may indicate a need for revised investigative procedures or for improved training of follow-up investigators. It also may reflect a change in the nature of crime (for example, from individual offenders to gang activity). This measure is particularly susceptible to "fudging" because investigators can easily record the names of suspects, no matter how unlikely. It will be useful only if there is a standard definition of a "suspect identification" and if all investigators see more value in adhering to the definition than in stretching it.

Arrest rate The arrest rate is the ratio of cases in which a suspect was arrested to all cases assigned for follow-up work. It indicates how well the investigative function is performing at capturing offenders. This measure can be split into an *initial investigation arrest rate* and a *follow-up investigation arrest rate*. Arrest rates, too, can be manipulated: officers can either screen in only the easy cases or lower the standards for making an arrest. Note that when clearance rates are used, a suspect can be counted many times (once for each crime he or she admits to), but when an arrest rate is used, each suspect is counted only once.

Prosecution rate The prosecution rate is the percentage of arrest cases that the prosecutor accepts. An arrest without a prosecution is far less useful in helping to control crime or further justice than an arrest resulting in a prosecution. Further, the prosecution rate is an independent rating of police investigative performance. In this regard it sets a high standard for performance. Note, however, that changes in the standards the prosecutor uses to accept cases can affect this measure, including changes due to factors largely beyond the prosecutor's direct control, such as overcrowding in prisons and jails. Further, the standard set by the prosecutor will be far higher than the standard needed to make an arrest: the prosecutor requires enough evidence to show guilt beyond a reasonable doubt, whereas an arrest requires only probable cause.

Victim service level Case-oriented investigation may be an inefficient method of controlling criminality, but it does help in the pursuit of justice. In this regard, it is important that investigations managers determine how well investigations are serving the needs of victims. Do victims feel that the police are handling their cases well? Do victims feel that they have been treated fairly by the police? And do they feel that justice was sought in their cases? The only way to answer these and related questions is to ask victims. Periodically—every six or twelve months—a random sample of victims who reported crimes should be selected and sent a questionnaire. This survey should be brief so as not to inconvenience the victims or make analysis too laborious.[36] Comparisons of survey results over time should show investigators and managers the extent to which victims feel the police are handling their cases well. These surveys should not be used to judge individual performance level. Because the surveys are anonymous and brief, it would be unfair to attribute a single victim's dissatisfaction with services to the work of a particular investigator. On average, however, the survey results should provide a reasonable performance measure for the investigations unit. If surveys consistently show that victims are dissatisfied, then changes in training, administration, or policies may be required.

Applying performance measures Police managers should use these measures as a set instead of singly, and they should select measures that cover the major stages in the investigations process. Each measure in itself has major limitations. Moreover, trends in a single measure can be misleading. But a comparison of trends across several measures may reveal developments that police managers will want to address. For example, if the arrest rate is decreasing, a manager will be uncertain as to the reasons. Trends in the follow-up rate and the suspect detection rate may hold clues. The manager may find that the suspect detection rate is declining and the follow-up rate is stable—which could mean that follow-up investigators are having a harder time converting leads into suspect identification and arrests. If, at the same time, the victim service level is declining, the manager may decide, quite sensibly, to focus attention first on the quality of police-citizen encounters. If, in contrast, the follow-up rate is declining and citizen service levels are constant, the manager may want to determine why patrol officers are having difficulty gathering information during the initial investigation.

Fluctuations in these measures, even used as a set, can be used only as *indicators* of improvements or declines in effectiveness. These statistics cannot substitute for a detailed understanding of the nonquantifiable aspects of investigations. A manager should do much more than watch the numbers. He or she should observe the investigators and discuss their work with them. Further, the supervisor should discuss trends in the statistics with his or her investigators and get their insights. If the measures help investigators find ways of improving their techniques and procedures, or help them show the department that additional resources or policy changes are needed, then investigators are more likely to use the measures to improve the investigative process and ensure that they are valid.

Offender-oriented investigations

There are two reasons (both discussed earlier) to incorporate an offender-oriented approach into a case-oriented investigations process. First, as research has shown, a case-oriented approach is not very effective at solving crimes. Second, some repeat offenders are more capable of eluding the police than their less criminally active colleagues. Investigating cases, therefore, has little effect on the worst criminals. But if the police pay special attention to the criminals who commit a disproportionate number of crimes, investigators may be able to catch them sooner than would otherwise be possible. If this approach is to work, prosecutors, courts, jails, and prisons must all be willing and able to help incapacitate these repeat offenders. If there is no prison space or if parole officials release such offenders prematurely, then much of the potential crime-reduction effect of repeat offender strategies will be lost.

There are a number of ways to take an offender-oriented approach to investigations, from creating proactive surveillance units to developing information systems serving all police officers.

There are a number of ways to take an offender-oriented approach to investigations, from creating proactive surveillance units to developing information systems serving all police officers. This section looks at three approaches to addressing the problem of repeat offenders.

Proactive surveillance units   Proactive surveillance units target a few very active criminals and then attempt to make cases against them. They either collect evidence linking suspected repeat offenders to reported crimes or attempt to catch offenders in the act of committing a crime. These units are very labor-intensive per arrest and make extensive use of covert investigative techniques such as stakeouts and informants.

When these types of investigations target offenders before they can be linked to a crime, and when they require the use of covert tactics, they risk violating the rights of individuals and investigating people not engaged in criminal activity—especially if informants are used to identify active offenders. Studies of proactive repeat offender operations show that informants are very important for identifying active repeat offenders.[37] But informants, having their own incentives for providing information (revenge, money, better treatment by the police or prosecutor), are often unconcerned about the truthfulness of their accusations. Without tight controls on informants, therefore, targeting that is based on informant information alone can lead investigators to pursue relatively minor offenders or innocent citizens.[38]

To prevent the abuse of civil liberties, such units must develop detailed written policies and procedures, and managers must strictly enforce these procedures. Topics that such policies and procedures should cover include the following:

Methods of recruiting informants (the policy should state that coercion will not be used)

Use of signed work agreements between the informant and the police or prosecutor

Permissible and impermissible types of promises and agreements with informants

Prohibitions against criminal activity by informants (the policy should state that such activity will result in arrest and prosecution)

The operational procedures that an informant must undertake—regular meetings with control investigator, circumstances for carrying recording devices, and methods of handling "buy money" and evidence

Conditions for use of informant testimony in court

Financial procedures to be followed in paying informants.

Policies and procedures should also be developed for verifying informant information. Three questions should be asked about the information and the informant. First, how did the informant come to know this information, and was the informant in a position to gain truthful information about the potential target? Second, does the informant have a history of providing truthful information? Third, can the informant's information be verified by an independent source? Positive answers to these questions (especially the first and third) should be required before anyone is selected as a target on the basis of an informant's tip. The reliability of the informant should be assessed on the basis of his or her previous activities for the police. And investigators should always obtain independent confirmation of the information.

Policies also need to be developed that govern when an investigator should intervene in the planned commission of a crime by a suspect under surveillance. Following repeat offenders, or watching their likely victims, will put investigators in an ethical dilemma. Once a crime has been committed, a strong case can be made against the offender. But letting a crime take place puts the victim at risk, and the police should not knowingly put the lives and property of uninformed citizens in jeopardy. Further, investigators should have contingency plans for protecting citizens from offenders who are under close police surveillance.

The definition of a "target" for such a unit needs to be carefully articulated. Here, the investigations manager faces another dilemma. If the criteria for defining an individual as a repeat offender are too broad, the target list will be unmanageable; a large proportion of those on the list may not be repeat offenders; the unit will be less effective (because some of the individuals pursued are not major causes of crime); and the unit will have a greater chance of violating the rights of individuals who are not engaged in current criminal behavior. Even with strict targeting criteria, the repeat offender list may be too long to be useful, and the unit may need to limit its efforts to the worst of the worst offenders. The other horn of this dilemma is that if the targeting criteria are too stringent, the risk of being accused of targeting innocent people is reduced, but, at the same time, many true repeat offenders will not become targets.

Post-arrest targeting   Another approach to repeat offenders is to target them once they have been arrested. Though this does not increase the chances of apprehending these offenders, it does help ensure that they receive long sentences.

After arrest, investigators thoroughly check the suspect's criminal record. If that record reveals that he or she fits the definition of a repeat offender, the police and the prosecutor give the arrestee special attention. They conduct a post-arrest investigation to be extra sure that they can prove the suspect is guilty and deserves a very long sentence. A special unit may have this responsibility, or post-arrest targeting and investigations can be conducted by suitably trained regular investigators.

Like proactive targeting, post-arrest targeting requires that police and prosecutors pay careful attention to the criteria for selecting their targets. And investigations managers face the same dilemmas with regard to strict versus lax targeting criteria. Before establishing a post-arrest approach, police managers should show that the likely targets are not already being given special attention.

Criminal intelligence sections   A third approach to high-rate offenders is to develop a criminal intelligence section whose function is to identify repeat offenders, provide descriptions and photographs of them, and develop information on their behaviors and hangouts. The intelligence section gives information on repeat offenders to detectives and patrol officers. Investigators can use this information in two ways: to focus attention on a list of likely suspects, and to keep track of repeat offenders operating in communities. Monitoring the activities of career criminals in the community can help prevent crimes and develop additional intelligence.

Useful sources of information for such monitoring are state corrections agencies and probation officials. They can provide information on high-rate offenders who are about to be placed on probation or parole. By working with these officials, police investigators can control repeat offenders who violate probation and parole agreements.

Once again, police departments must develop stringent policies and procedures that carefully define the characteristics of offenders who can be targets for this type of intelligence gathering.

Performance measures for offender-oriented activities

Because efforts to detect, monitor, arrest, and prosecute repeat offenders have the objective of removing active criminals from society, performance measures should reveal whether this is being accomplished. As with case-oriented investigations, there are measures that, collectively, can help a police manager determine the effectiveness of offender-oriented investigations. Like the measures described above for investigating cases, these measures should be used to assess the performance of the unit, not individual officers. Each measure has major limitations and, like all performance measures, can be manipulated to create an impression of good performance. Yet thoughtful interpretation of these measures in light of other, nonquantifiable information can help police managers identify and correct investigative problems.

Arrest rate   The arrest rate is the ratio of those arrested from the target list to those targeted for investigation. If the target list really contains the most active criminals known to the police, then one measure of effectiveness is the rate at which they are being apprehended. Again, unless consistent probable-cause standards are used, investigators can increase the number of arrests almost at will and undermine the utility of this measure.

Average seriousness   Offenders monitored, arrested, prosecuted, convicted, and sentenced under targeting programs should be more active than offenders who are not targeted for repeat offender investigations. The average rate at which targeted offenders commit crimes (as measured by prior arrests or convictions) compared with the average offending rate of all offenders known to the police is an indicator of whether repeat offender investigations are focusing on the most active criminals. These averages should be calculated for targeted offenders, arrestees, defendants, and convicts. Averages can be easily distorted by a few extreme cases. It is possible, for example, for all but a few repeat offenders targeted by a unit to be no more active than one-time or occasional offenders. But the few that are more active inflate the average activity rate. Using a median instead of a mean to calculate this measure will help.[39] Repeat offenders who are good at eluding detection and capture will have arrest and conviction records that make them appear to be less active. If these offenders are major targets, average seriousness will not be a good measure of performance, for obvious reasons.

Prosecution rate   The prosecution rate is the rate at which arrestees are accepted by the prosecutor's office for prosecution. As is true with case-oriented measures, acceptance by the prosecutor's office is an independent assessment of the quality of investigations, but it can be distorted by changes in prosecutorial policies.

Conviction rate   Unless repeat offenders are convicted, it is impossible to keep them from committing more crimes. The ratio of arrests resulting in convictions to all arrests is another indicator of how successful the repeat-offender investigations are in removing serious criminals from the street. Because so many factors outside of police control have an effect on convictions, managers should be careful intrepreting these figures. Still, conviction rates, when combined with other information, may suggest improvements that can be made in police procedures.

Average sentence   The longer the sentence, the longer the offender can be kept from committing crimes in the free community. So the average length of sentence received by convicted repeat offenders is a measure of crime control ability. Even more than the conviction rate, this measure is subject to many factors beyond police control. However, it may be useful to watch these statistics in order to monitor the performance of other parts of the criminal justice system.

Investigative problem solving and performance measures

Repeat offending is a problem, but it is only one of many types of problems investigators can address.[40] Case-oriented and repeat-offender–oriented investigators need to address a variety of problems that give rise to the cases and offenders they investigate. For example, an investigator of repeat burglars may find that a clause in a particular state law makes it easy for criminals to sell certain types of stolen property. In such a situation, the investigator should address this problem by focusing attention on a legislative remedy. Though it may not result in any arrests, such problem solving may prevent a large number of crimes. Preventing crimes, in turn, has the benefit of reducing investigative caseloads.

Investigators assigned to geographical areas of a city should identify and analyze crime problems endemic to their areas. Local knowledge will prove crucial when investigators work with other parts of the police department, other organizations, and local citizens to resolve these problems.

Case-oriented and repeat-offender–oriented investigators need to address a variety of problems that give rise to the cases and offenders they investigate.

Police managers can use several problem-solving performance measures to assess unit effectiveness but should bear in mind that no single measure tells the whole story.

Problems identified   The number of problems identified by investigators is a useful performance indicator. Changes in this measure may reflect fluctuations in investigators' attention to problem solving, and these fluctuations may be caused by factors outside investigators' control, such as changes in work schedule, caseloads, and overtime allowances. Because an infinite number of problems can be identified, however, this measure can always be inflated. Obviously, some problems are more serious than others, and seriousness must be considered.

Information sources used   Careful analysis sometimes shows that superficially similar problems are actually quite different. For this reason, investigators should tap a variety of information sources and not rely only on their own experience and police information. As a result, the diversity of information sources used is an indicator of the quality of a problem-solving effort. The types of information sources used will depend, to some extent, on the types of problems addressed. So it is possible for investigators to conduct competent problem-solving efforts even though they have tapped only a narrow range of information sources. If pressed, investigators can artificially inflate the number and diversity of their information sources by talking to many people about problems, knowing full well that most have little to contribute.

Degree of collaboration with others   Most problems require the collaborative efforts of a variety of police units, other organizations, and members of the public. So the degree of collaboration promoted by the investigator is also a measure of the quality of the problem-solving effort. Again, the number of others involved depends on the nature and scope of the problem. Some problems may not require a great deal of collaboration with others. Further, investigators can doctor this measure by talking to everyone imaginable about a problem and recording every contact. Therefore, some guidelines on what is meant by collaboration are useful.

Success of solutions   Ultimately, managers must assess the effectiveness of problem-solving efforts by their effect on problems. Managers should examine five goals of problem-solving efforts: (1) elimination of the problem (this is seldom possible), (2) reduction of the number of crimes resulting from the problem, (3) reduction in the level of harm from these crimes, (4) improved handling of the problem, and (5) referral of the problem to another agency with greater capability for handling it. The success of a problem-solving effort in achieving these five alternative goals is the best indicator of problem-solving quality. But these measures, too, can be manipulated to show artificially high levels of performance. The definition of success for each problem can be set low or changed to show apparent success. Comparison groups or time periods can be sought that make the problem-solving efforts look better than they really are. To avoid a misleading performance appraisal, managers and investigators must see the advantage in rigorously and honestly evaluating problem definition, goal setting, and corrective efforts.

Once again, these measures are best used as a set. The reason for a reduction in the number of problems being solved, for example, may be either a decrease in the quality of analysis or the limited number of other organizations involved in planning and implementing solutions. Without multiple performance measures, it is difficult to determine the source of the trouble.

Investigative personnel issues

This chapter has described the investigative function as spanning organizational unit boundaries. In this respect, investigative personnel issues do not differ from the personnel issues of the police department as a whole: rank and assignments; workloads; and specialization versus integration. The conflicts between specialization and integration, however, are particularly important for investigative managers.

Rank and assignments

Detectives and patrol officers with similar tenure in the department should receive the same status and rank. There is no good reason for assuming that detectives are somehow superior or that only high-ranking officers are capable of investigating serious crimes. To condone such distinctions invites divisive intraorganizational rivalry and wastes money.

Some specialization is required in the investigation of crimes and criminals. But when circumstances justify specialization, the specialists should be trained for the activities they perform.

More and more often, police departments are requiring newly promoted officers to rotate to a new assignment. Ideally, this practice allows new managers to learn about all functions of the department and become less parochial in their outlook. Nevertheless, such rotation can place officers who have only patrol experience in charge of detectives or can require detectives to move to some other unit. The two possible negative consequences are obvious: new detective managers may have little experience in detective work, and detectives who want to remain in their unit may not seek promotion. Though these can be problems, it is more important that police organizations operate as single entities and not as separate units collected under a single chief. Hence, rotation policies make good sense, as long as they are supplemented with proper in-service training.

Investigative workloads

If investigations are to be effective, investigators must have enough time to do their work well. If they are to be efficient, investigators must not have more time than they need to do their work well. How many detectives does a police department need to be effective and efficient? What is the maximum workload detectives can handle effectively?

Unfortunately, there are no universal answers to these questions. Comparisons of the percentage of departmental personnel that is assigned to detective units, for example, are useless for answering questions like these. Even if police departments of a given size in a particular region have similar percentages of sworn strength allocated to detective units, there is no assurance that the percentage allocated makes sense. Just as there are copycat crimes, there is copycat management. And though a police manager may take some comfort in knowing that his or her agency has no worse a misallocation of investigators than other similar organizations, this is little consolation. Therefore, each investigative unit within each department should address independently the question of how many investigators it needs to operate efficiently and effectively.

Managers need to develop measures of workload for their units. They can then compare workload changes with changes in unit effectiveness measures. After a manager has made these comparisons for a number of months, he or she should be able to determine the range of workloads that yields the most effective performance.

Periodically, a police department should determine the average amount of time it takes to process cases, investigate repeat offenders, and resolve problems. These average times can be multiplied by the number of cases, criminals, and problems handled during a time period to arrive at a measure of effort expended. One can then calculate a crude measure of workload by dividing this number by the number of hours worked during the time period (including overtime). When developing such workload measures, managers should consider four factors.

First, processing cases, investigating repeat offenders, and solving problems are not equivalent activities. One case does not equal one repeat offender or one problem. And even within a single category of work—say, case processing—there is a great deal of variation. The work involved in investigating the sexual molestation of a twelve-year-old boy is not directly comparable to the work involved in investigating an armed holdup of a convenience store, for example. Addressing the problem of burglaries in an apartment building may be very different from addressing the problem of thefts of construction material from building sites. Therefore, managers and investigators may need to develop several measures of workload.

Second, the concepts of caseload and workload—although often confused with each other—are very different. A burglary detective may have a very high caseload but a moderate workload. This can occur when many cases are assigned to a detective, but they do not have enough leads to merit follow-up. In this example, the caseload is larger than the workload. Case screening helps ensure that only cases with good leads are being assigned. If screening is used sensibly, caseloads may be a reasonable reflection of case-processing workloads.

Third, as with any performance measures, investigators have a strong interest in the types of workload measures being used. They also are the primary source of useful information about workloads. Thus for many of the same reasons that performance measures should be jointly determined by managers and investigators, the establishment of workload measures should also be a collaborative effort. A manager may find it useful to create a group of investigators whose assignment is to draft workload measures. After other investigators and supervisors review and comment on the draft measures, and the chain of command approves them, they could be used to determine future staffing levels.

Finally, workload measures can be only gross approximations of reality. At best, they can provide only a ballpark estimate. Therefore, managers must use judgment in interpreting these numbers. There is no substitute for managers' personal familiarity with the work patterns of investigators. But it is far better to have a ballpark estimate of workload based on reasonable calculations and know the weaknesses in the numbers than to have no measures of workload.

Decentralization of detectives

Some contributors to the investigative process are almost always decentralized. Patrol officers, for example, have small geographical areas in which they conduct investigations. Other contributors will almost always be centralized. For example, a crime lab will most likely serve the entire city or county because creating a duplicate lab in each precinct is too expensive. For many types of investigators, therefore, little needs to be said about decentralization.

Decentralizing detectives, however, requires a bit more of a discussion. There is some evidence, though far from definitive, that for detectives who investigate property crimes, decentralizing them to geographical areas (precincts, districts, divisions, and so forth) improves performance.[41] Further, there have been no rigorous studies showing the virtues of centralization. So little can be said on this matter on the basis of scientific knowledge. There are some practical considerations, however.

Because investigations depend largely on the information provided by citizens, decentralization may facilitate investigations by improving contacts with the public. In and of itself, decentralization probably will not help much. But if combined with a move to a problem-oriented approach and a department-wide emphasis on close police-community contacts, decentralization of case-processing detectives may be effective.[42] Decentralization may also be effective if it is coupled with an increased emphasis on developing detailed knowledge of the criminals operating in specific communities.

But there are three caveats. First, if the workload in a particular geographical area is too light, the increase in effectiveness may be too costly. Furthermore, splitting up the detectives into smaller geographically based sub-units will mean some loss in flexibility. This potential decrease in efficiency may be greatest in small to medium-sized departments—but these are the departments with less need to decentralize.

Second, some crimes require special skills and knowledge to investigate, but they occur relatively infrequently. Therefore, only a small number of detectives will be assigned to these cases (rape investigations are one example), and centralization of specialists may be the preferred approach.

Finally, if the criminals being investigated are highly mobile or operate across several area boundaries, centralization may be preferable. For example, detectives who investigate juvenile crimes may be decentralized because juveniles tend to operate over a small territory close to their homes. Bank robbers, in contrast, are more likely to operate over a large portion of the city, so specialists in this type of crime should be centralized.

In large cities, decentralization of most detectives makes more sense than the alternative. A few crimes may be investigated by central detective units. But there are enough crimes to keep each area's locally assigned detectives productively occupied; most crimes do not require esoteric skills for their investigation; and most offenders operate within a relatively local area. Thus, decentralization should be the rule, not the exception.

Conclusion

Investigations need to help achieve three goals: controlling criminals, pursuing justice, and addressing problems. Most police departments use a case-oriented approach to investigations, handling crimes on an incident-by-incident basis. After a crime is reported, it is investigated, screened, and followed up as appropriate, with the ultimate goal of presenting the prosecutor with enough evidence to convict the offender.

An accumulation of research, however, suggests that, to achieve its goals, traditional case-oriented investigation needs to be supplemented by programs designed to apprehend and prosecute repeat offenders, as most serious crimes are committed by a relatively small number of people. Research is also beginning to suggest that police can have an effect on crime by focusing on problems and other situations in the community that foster crime.

This chapter has provided information to help the police manager improve the organization of the investigations function, measure its performance, and assign personnel most efficiently and effectively. It also has urged managers to recognize the implications of research into repeat-offender and problem-solving approaches and to keep an open mind about incorporating these approaches into departmental operations.

1 Niels Forssell, *Fouché. The Man Napoleon Feared* (New York: AMS Press, 1970).

2 T. A. Critchley, *A History of Police in England and Wales* (London: Constable, 1979).

3 Bernard Porter, *The Origins of the Vigilant State: The London Metropolitan Police Special Branch before the First World War* (London: Weidenfeld and Nicolson, 1987).

4 Philip John Stead, *Vidocq: A Biography* (New York: Roy Publishers, n.d.).

5 Donald Rumbelow, *I Spy Blue: The Police and Crime in the City of London from Elizabeth I to Victoria* (London: Macmillan, 1971); and P. D. James and T. A. Critchley, *The Maul and the Pear Tree: The Ratcliff Highway Murders 1811* (New York: The Mysterious Press, 1971).

6 Edwin T. Woodhall, *Secrets of Scotland Yard* (London: The Bodley Head, 1936); and Dick Hobbs, *Doing Business: Entrepreneurship, the Working Class, and Detectives in the East End of London* (Oxford: Clarendon Press, 1988).

7 Critchley, *A History of Police in England and Wales*.

8 Belton Cobb, *The First Detectives and the Early Career of Richard Mayne, Commissioner of Police* (London: Faber and Faber, 1957).

9 Nora Kelly and William Kelly, *The Royal Canadian Mounted Police: A Century of History 1873–1973* (Edmonton: Hurtig, 1973).

10 Thomas Byrnes, *Rogues Gallery: 247 Professional Criminals of 19th-Century America* (New York: Chelsea House, 1969), a reprint of *Professional Criminals of America* (1886).

11 Frank Moran, *"The Eye That Never Sleeps": A History of the Pinkerton National Detective Agency* (Bloomington: Indiana University Press, 1982).

12 Herman Goldstein, "Improving Policing: A Problem-Oriented Approach," *Crime and Delinquency* 25, no. 2 (April 1979); and Herman Goldstein, *Problem-Oriented Policing* (New York: McGraw-Hill, 1990).

13 The vast majority of this research was on burglary and robbery investigations. Investigations of purely personal crimes, such as homicide and rape, were seldom studied. Neither were fraud investigations. Generalizing from research on burglary and robbery investigations to other types of investigations must be done with caution. Still, burglaries make up the largest component of investigative caseloads in most departments, and much of the logic behind the recommendations stemming from this research seems to apply to the investigations of personal crimes and frauds.

14 Peter Greenwood, *An Analysis of the Apprehension Activities of the New York City Police Department* (New York: Rand Institute, 1970); Peter Greenwood, Joan Petersilia, and Jan Chaiken, *The Investigation Process* (Lexington, MA: Lexington Books, 1977); and Bernard Greenberg, Carola V. Elliott, Lois P. Kraft, and H. Stephen Procter, *Felony Investigation Decision Model—An Analysis of Investigative Elements of Information* (Menlo Park, CA: Standford Research Institute, 1973).

15 Greenwood, Petersilia, and Chaiken, *The Investigation Process* (a revised and slightly more comprehensive version of a work originally published by the Rand Corporation).

16 Peter B. Bloch and James Bell, *Managing Investigations: The Rochester System* (Washington, DC: Police Foundation, 1976); and Peter B. Bloch and Cyrus Ulberg, *Auditing Clearance Rates* (Washington, DC: Police Foundation, 1974).

17 Ilene Greenberg and Robert Wasserman, *Managing Criminal Investigations* (Washington, DC: Law Enforcement Assistance Administration, U.S. Department of Justice, 1979).

18 John E. Eck, *Solving Crimes: The Investigation of Burglary and Robbery* (Washington, DC: Police Executive Research Forum, 1983).

19 Marvin E. Wolfgang, Robert M. Figlio, and Thorsten Sellin, *Delinquency in a Birth Cohort* (Chicago: University of Chicago Press, 1972); Jan Chaiken and Marcia Chaiken, *Varieties of Criminal Behavior* (Santa Monica, CA: Rand Corporation, 1982); and Alfred Blumstein, Jacqueline Cohen, Jeffrey Roth, and Christy Visher, eds., *Criminal Careers and "Career Criminals,"* vol. 1 (Washington, DC: National Academy Press, 1986).

20 Peter W. Greenwood with Allan Abrahamse, *Selective Incapacitation* (Santa Monica, CA: RAND Corporation, 1982).

21 Eleanor Chelimsky and Judith Dahmann, *Career Criminal Program National Evaluation: Final Report* (Washington, DC: U.S. Government Printing Office, 1981); and William Spelman, *The Incapacitation Benefits of Selective Criminal Justice Policies* (Ph.D. diss., Harvard University, 1988).

22 Spelman, *The Incapacitation Benefits of Selective Criminal Justice Policies*.

23 Ibid.

24 Tony Pate, Robert A. Bowers, and Ron Parks, *Three Approaches to Criminal Apprehension in Kansas City: An Evaluation Report* (Washington, DC: Police Foundation, 1976); Susan E. Martin and Lawrence W. Sherman, *Catching Career Criminals: The Washington, D.C. Repeat Offender Project*, Police Foundation Reports 3 (Washington, DC: Police Foundation, 1986); and Susan E. Martin, "Policing Career Criminals: An Examination of an Innovative Crime Control Policy," *Journal of Criminal Law and Criminology*, 77, no. 4 (Winter 1986)—an expanded version of a Police Foundation study.

25 John E. Eck and William Spelman, *Problem-Solving: Problem-Oriented Policing in Newport News* (Washington, DC: Police Executive Research Forum, 1987); and Edriene L. Johnson, *Annual Report on Problem Solving: An Evaluation of Problem-Oriented Policing in the Newport News Police Department* (Newport News, VA: Newport News Police Department, 1988). Hom-

icides, though all too common, are statistically rare. Domestic homicides are even rarer. Therefore, it is very difficult to be certain whether the decrease in domestic killings in Newport News was a chance event or was due in large measure to the new spouse abuse program. One thing is clear, however: domestic killings did decrease after the program was created.

26 Diane Hill, "The Analysis Model: An Investigative Tool," *Problem Solving Quarterly* 1, no. 4 (Fall 1988).

27 See Lee P. Brown, "Strategies for Dealing with Crack Houses," *FBI Law Enforcement Bulletin* 57, no. 6 (June 1988); Wayland Clifton, Jr., *Convenience Store Robberies in Gainesville, Florida: An Intervention Strategy by the Gainesville Police Department* (Gainesville, FL: Gainesville Police Department, n.d.); and Herman Goldstein and Charles E. Susmilch, *Experimenting with the Problem-Oriented Approach to Improving Police Service: A Report and Some Reflections on Two Case Studies* (Madison: Law School, University of Wisconsin, 1982).

28 Gerald L. Williams, *Law Enforcement Accreditation: An Effort to Professionalize American Law Enforcement* (Ph.D. diss., University of Colorado at Denver, 1988).

29 John E. Eck, *Managing Case Assignments: The Burglary Investigation Decision Model Replication* (Washington, DC: Police Executive Research Forum, 1979).

30 Commission on Accreditation for Law Enforcement Agencies, Inc., *Standards for Law Enforcement Agencies: The Standards Manual of the Law Enforcement Agency Accreditation Program* (Fairfax, VA: CALEA, 1983).

31 Eck, *Solving Crimes: The Investigation of Burglary and Robbery*.

32 The authors of this chapter would go further, asserting that clearance statistics are virtually meaningless and that departments should stop using them.

33 For excellent discussions of the effects of performance statistics on officer behavior, see Jerome H. Skolnick, *Justice without Trial: Law Enforcement in a Democratic Society* (New York: John Wiley and Sons, 1975), 168–81; Michael K. Brown, *Working the Street: Police Discretion and the Dilemmas of Reform* (New York: Russell Sage Foundation, 1988), 123–24, and William B. Sanders, *Detective Work: A Study of Criminal Investigations* (New York: The Free Press, 1977), 82–84.

34 W. Edward Deming, *Out of the Crisis* (Cam-

bridge: Center for Advanced Engineering Study, Massachusetts Institute of Technology, 1986).

35 For an extensive battery of such measures, see Eck, *Solving Crimes: The Investigation of Burglary and Robbery*.

36 For a description of how to design and administer a client satisfaction survey, see Michael J. Austin, *Evaluating Your Agency's Programs* (Newbury Park, CA: Sage Publications, 1982), 84–94. For a discussion of questionnaire design, see Floyd J. Fowler, Jr., *Survey Research Methods* (Newbury Park, CA: Sage Publications, 1984), chap. 6.

37 William G. Gay and Robert A. Bowers, *Targeting Law Enforcement Resources: The Career Criminal Focus* (Washington, DC: National Institute of Justice, 1985); and William Spelman et al., *Repeat Offender Programs for Law Enforcement: New Approaches to an Old Problem* (Washington, DC: Police Executive Research Forum, 1990). Much of the discussion in this chapter on proactive surveillance units is based on these two publications.

38 For a useful and balanced discussion of the benefits and problems of using informants and other covert tactics in police work, see Gary T. Marx, *Undercover: Police Surveillance in America* (Los Angeles: University of California Press, 1988).

39 For advice on how police personnel can effectively use statistical methods and other research techniques, see John E. Eck, *Using Research: A Primer for Law Enforcement Managers* (Washington, DC: Police Executive Research Forum, 1984).

40 For further discussion of problem-solving concepts and techniques, see Eck and Spelman, *Problem-Solving: Problem-Oriented Policing in Newport News*; Goldstein, *Problem-Oriented Policing*.

41 Peter B. Bloch and James Bell, *Managing Investigations: The Rochester System.* (Washington, DC: Police Foundation, 1976); and Alfred I. Schwartz and Sumner N. Clarren, *The Cincinnati Team Policing Experiment: A Summary Report* (Washington, DC: Police Foundation, 1977).

42 Goldstein, *Problem-Oriented Policing*; Timothy N. Oettmeier and William H. Bieck, *Integrating Investigative Operations Through Neighborhood Oriented Policing: Executive Session #2* (Houston: Houston Police Department, 1989); and Timothy Oettmeier and Lee P. Brown, "Developing a Neighborhood-Oriented Policing Style," in *Community Policing: Rhetoric or Reality*, ed. Jack R. Greene and Stephen D. Mastrofski (New York: Praeger, 1988).

6 Traffic services

When people talk about "the traffic problem," they are usually referring to long delays in their commute to work. For local governments, however, delays are just one facet of a complex transportation system that includes such diverse elements as pedestrians, motorcycles, street layout, air pollution, traffic signals, and roadway construction. The police, as one of several "control mechanisms" in the transportation system, have a dual role. First, through their day-to-day operational responsibilities, they help traffic move safely and expeditiously by monitoring and directing traffic flow and enforcing state and local laws and ordinances. Second, they play an important role in the processes of planning, designing, and rehabilitating the transportation system.

Because police are on the street at all times and are often the first to learn of a breakdown in the transportation system, they are in a unique position to provide operational information as well as to advise on overall system planning. For example, the police record and analyze information about drivers, vehicles, roadways, and traffic controls. Such data are used not only for police traffic services but also for the services performed by other agencies in the transportation system—the departments of public works and transportation engineering, the planning department, the zoning commission, the local traffic court, state highway and transportation departments, and licensing authorities. In their interaction with such agencies, the police play a key role in ensuring cooperation and standardization among agencies and jurisdictions.

Because police are on the street at all times and are often the first to learn of a breakdown in the transportation system, they are in a unique position to provide operational information as well as to advise on overall system planning.

Cooperation among jurisdictions and agencies has as its goal a comprehensive traffic management system—already a reality in some parts of the country. In the Los Angeles freeway system, which is one notable example, cooperation among planning groups and all levels of government has created a jointly supervised and monitored system. Although comprehensive management should be a long-term goal in all communities, it is particularly important in areas of rapid population growth and in older areas where transportation facilities are deteriorating. This chapter is written from the perspective that highway transportation management must be systematic, and the emphasis throughout is on connections between the two roles of the police—the operational role and the planning and coordinating role.[1]

The chapter first touches on the second role—the management responsibilities of the police and other agencies in transportation and engineering planning; it then describes the police department's operational functions in traffic services. Traffic law enforcement is covered in considerable detail, with emphasis on methods and on police responsibilities. The chapter then examines traffic accident investigation, alcohol- and drug-related traffic offenses, and other police traffic services.

Coordination of police and engineering functions

The police, both through their own observations and through citizen reports, become aware of inadequacies and deficiencies of traffic regulations, control devices, physical features of streets and highways, and special hazards—and make recommendations to transportation engineers for correcting and improving them. The police and the engineers rely on each other for information when executing their own responsibilities in managing the highway transportation system, but information cannot be exchanged without a specific and clearly defined working relationship. This requires that appropriate liaison roles be assigned in both departments and that lines of communication be sufficiently simple and direct so that messages do not get lost in the chain of command. Failure to act on a reported defect can create needless inconvenience or danger to the public as well as liability exposure for the local government.

In emergency situations such as traffic signal malfunctions, police obviously should notify appropriate authorities immediately, as well as prepare any needed follow-up report. Non-emergency reports and recommendations should be encouraged by minimizing the report preparation time for the officer—for example, by using a prepared list of common deficiencies so the officer need only check a box. To more fully motivate officers to be conscientious about this aspect of their responsibilities, a mechanism must be established for replies from the engineering department to show what action was taken or why no action was possible. Coordination of police and engineering functions requires careful planning, the training of police in proper procedures, and sound legal advice.

The titles, assignments, and size of engineering departments can vary, but such departments generally perform a number of standard functions, including surveys and studies, traffic control device installation, consultation on traffic regulations and ordinances, planning and design of streets, and the development of the master street plan. These functions—and their relation to police responsibilities—are outlined below. (All transportation engineering units are collectively referred to as transportation engineering departments or, simply, as engineers.)

Surveys and studies Engineering departments collect and analyze data on accident locations, traffic delays, speed, vehicle and pedestrian use, parking, traffic control devices, and the physical characteristics of the transportation

Figure 6–1 In the 1930s a relatively simple street system could handle auto traffic, and on-street parking was available and free. Police patrol was concerned largely with speeding and with parking violations.

system. Additional surveys may include studies classifying vehicles and streets, studies evaluating accidents, and inventories of the street system and its traffic-carrying capabilities. The police should know what surveys and studies exist, what ones are routinely done, and what special services are available to them on request.

Traffic control device installation Engineers recommend and plan the installation, operation, and timing of traffic control devices, including street lighting, traffic signs, pavement markings, and techniques for improving traffic flow (such as speed recommendations, turning restrictions, one-way streets, and pedestrian protection and control).[2] Cooperation with the police department is essential because the police are knowledgeable about problems of traffic operations and have direct responsibility for enforcing traffic regulations.

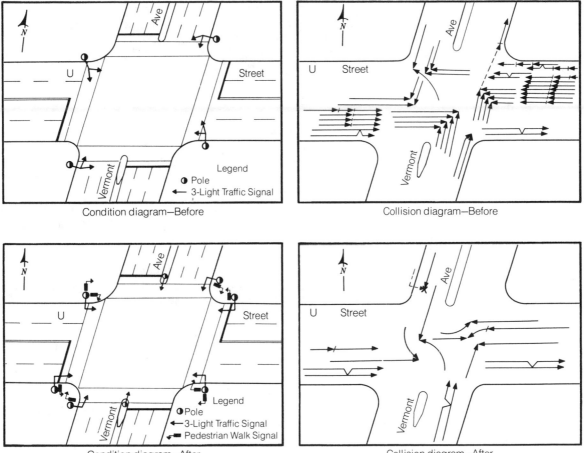

Condition diagram—Before

Collision diagram—Before

Condition diagram—After

Collision diagram—After

Figure 6–2 This figure illustrates how traffic engineering can make traffic regulation more effective. The "before" set of condition and collision diagrams for a busy intersection shows a situation that was hazardous to both motorists and pedestrians primarily because the signals were hard to see and the yellow interval clearance time was inadequate. The upper condition diagram shows the placement of all signals. The upper collision diagram shows the types of collisions and their relative locations at the intersection. A large majority of collisions were of the "rear-end" (two or more arrows in the same direction separated by a vertical line) and "right-angle" (two arrows meeting at a right angle) types. The "after" diagrams show how the situation was improved. The lower condition diagram shows how additional signals improved visibility. The lower collision diagram shows an almost complete elimination of rear-end and right-angle collisions.

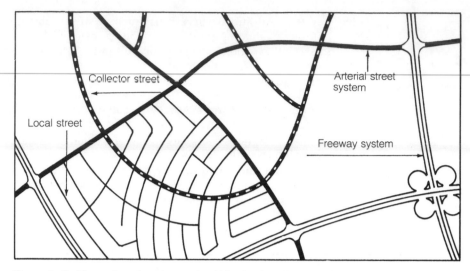

Figure 6–3   The police department should be involved in the planning and preliminary design stages of all roadway facilities. Among their objectives should be the inclusion of specific locations for police observation of traffic flow, safe locations for stopping violators, and access to various areas and across areas for both traffic services and crime prevention and suppression.

Traffic regulations and ordinances   Although responsibility for drafting and enacting traffic ordinances and codes usually rests with the local legislative body and legal department, both the engineering department and the police department are ordinarily consulted. In some areas of the country, the state has preempted authority for promulgating and revising traffic regulations. In either event, if traffic policy-making authorities do not consult police and traffic engineers before reaching decisions, steps should be taken promptly to correct this deficiency.

Planning and design of streets   Transportation engineering departments have the expertise to determine the effect of design features on traffic operations, but representatives of the police department should be involved in all traffic planning and design work.

The master street plan   A master street plan, including the classification of streets, contributes to effective traffic supervision. Engineers and police must review new developments, subdivision plans, and zoning changes that may affect traffic operations and street design. Police department review focuses on ensuring that the street plan facilitates traffic supervision, crime prevention, and emergency and driver services.

Objectives of police traffic services

The principal goal of police traffic services is to increase safety on the streets and highways, largely by enforcing traffic regulations.

The purpose of traffic regulations is to indicate to users of the transportation system what is expected of them, especially under conditions of unusual congestion or hazard.

Restrictions on operators of motor vehicles range from federal regulations to local ordinances. Under the Federal Highway Safety Act of 1966, the National Highway Traffic Safety Administration (NHTSA) of the U.S. Department of Transportation has issued eighteen program standards for the states to follow, including standards on police traffic services and traffic records. Every police administrator should be familiar with these standards, which describe basic programs and control the granting of federal monies.[3] State-imposed regulations include drivers' tests and vehicle registration requirements. Although local ordinances vary, the *Uniform Vehicle Code and Model Traffic Ordinance*, put out by the National Committee on Uniform Traffic Laws and Ordinances, is designed to help standardize them.[4]

To achieve the goal of increasing safety on streets and highways, police traffic services should be based on an enforcement model that not only deters people from violating the law but also encourages them to comply voluntarily. The perception that police enforce a regulation is often as important as the existence of the regulation itself. If it becomes publicly known that the police are not enforcing a specific regulation, that regulation ceases to influence the decisions made by motorists and others who affect traffic safety.

The principal goal of police traffic services is to increase safety on the streets and highways.

In addition to enforcement duties strictly related to safety, police often have obligations to enforce laws that produce revenue—such as parking ordinances. Whether this is an appropriate role for police is a matter of some controversy and is discussed below.

To enforce whichever traffic regulations a given jurisdiction deems appropriate, the police need support from several sectors of the community: the general public, the local government executive and governing body, the prosecutor's office and the court, and private organizations.

Public acceptance of enforcement priorities—as well as the informed support of the local government administrator and governing body—is needed to obtain the resources for an effective traffic services program. The police manager must be sensitive to the political considerations inherent in local government and must also ensure that elected and appointed officials understand police needs and objectives (see also the chapter on the governmental setting).

To enforce whichever traffic regulations a given jurisdiction deems appropriate, the police need support from the general public, the local government executive and governing body, the prosecutor's office and the court, and private organizations.

A close working relationship with the prosecutor's office and the court is essential. The police department should appoint a liaison who has responsibility for resolving problems in the relationship and for exploring new concepts and techniques to strengthen it. Although most judges understand the police role and are accustomed to "the system," it is best to notify the court at the outset when changes are implemented. For example, the police might demonstrate to judges (and prosecutors) how a radar speed-measuring device works or might take a judge on an aerial speed detail.

Given an opportunity, many civic organizations in the community can aid the police traffic services program. Such groups include local safety councils, chambers of commerce, business groups, and service clubs such as Rotary and Lions. Groups such as Mothers Against Drunk Driving (MADD) and Students Against Driving Drunk (SADD) focus on specific aspects of traffic safety. Efforts should also be made to gain the support of ethnic and religious organizations and of senior citizens. Police depend on public support, and these groups can provide valuable feedback on programs and policies (also see the chapter on crime prevention).

The news media are probably the most important nonofficial "organization" in a community. In dealing with the media, police must balance the rights of offenders and victims, on the one hand, with the public's right to know, on the

---

Decriminalization and administrative adjudication　Traditionally, traffic offenses have been classified as misdemeanors and tried in the criminal court system. Several states have experimented with alternative methods of processing and hearing traffic cases.

Of the several arguments for alternative methods, the most important is probably the overwhelming caseload in large metropolitan areas.
Another is that the 1972 Supreme Court decision in *Argersinger v. Hamilton*, 407 U.S. 25 (1972) requires that counsel be appointed for indigent persons in misdemeanor cases subject to a jail penalty—but the appointment of counsel for traffic defendants is beyond the resources of many jurisdictions. A third argument is that the right to a jury trial in some jurisdictions extends to every traffic offense, including parking violations. Holding a jury trial is expensive and time-consuming, and the large volume of cases combined with the limited resources available had led to the feeling that this right should be restricted in some manner.

Alternative approaches to hearing traffic cases often begin with the reclassification of most traffic offenses, which means that they are deemed noncriminal and called "infractions," "civil forfeitures," or something other than "crimes." States that have taken this approach usually have decriminalized all traffic offenses except DWI, vehicular homicide, hit-and-run, reckless driving, and driving on a revoked or suspended license.

The intent of decriminalization is to speed up the disposition of cases: decriminalization eliminates the need for a jury trial; reduces the burden of proof on the prosecution from "proof beyond a reasonable doubt" (the

required burden in criminal cases) to a lesser burden of a "preponderance of evidence" or "clear and convincing evidence"; and eliminates the need to appoint an attorney for indigent defendants (because normally decriminalization eliminates the possibility that a jail sentence will be imposed). At least twenty states have reclassified traffic offenses, although some of these states have continued to *hear* cases in the criminal court system. In others, such hearings are overseen by a hearing officer or referee under the supervision of a court.

New York City, Rochester, Buffalo, and Suffolk County (all in New York), the District of Columbia, and the state of Rhode Island have adopted another approach, which is called "administrative adjudication." In this approach, traffic case hearings are removed from the criminal court system entirely and held before a hearing officer of an administrative agency in the executive branch of government. In New York, this agency is the Department of Motor Vehicles.

In states that have decriminalized traffic offenses or that offer administrative adjudication, law enforcement officers generally appear and testify in fewer traffic cases, which saves police personnel time. Both procedures also offer the benefits of a streamlined hearing process and a speedier disposition of cases. But critics of decriminalization or administrative adjudication, while acknowledging that these approaches may improve the disposition of cases, question whether defendants' rights remain adequately protected. In an era of increased efforts to protect citizens from overuse of governmental powers, such concerns must be balanced against the benefits of expeditious determination of cases.

other. A policy of openness and honesty—within clearly defined boundaries—is most likely to prevent misunderstandings and render the press an ally. Indeed, the police rely on the cooperation of the media in publicizing new enforcement programs.

In the best of times, resources for police traffic services are limited. During times of economic downturn, funding for police traffic services may be among the first to be cut. Yet law enforcement agencies are being asked to place special emphasis on a variety of safety concerns that may require special equipment, additional personnel, and new expertise.

Outside funding can come both from the federal government and from the private sector. The most prominent outside source is Title 402 funds from NHTSA, which are available through the governor's highway safety office in each state.[5] The seven program areas determined to be most effective in reducing accidents, injuries, and fatalities have been given national priority for funding: occupant protection, alcohol and other drug countermeasures, police traffic services, emergency medical services, traffic records, pupil transportation, and motorcycle safety.[6]

Another source of federal funds is the Motor Carrier Safety Assistance Program (MCSAP) available through the Office of Motor Carrier Safety, Federal Highway Administration (FHWA). MCSAP was established by the Surface Transportation Act of 1982; its goal is to reduce commercial vehicle accidents by strict enforcement of the states' motor carrier laws. Each state has specified a lead agency through which funding can be obtained.

In the private sector, corporate and nonprofit organizations are an excellent source of funds, particularly in the area of public information materials. Insurance companies and organizations such as the American Automobile Association, MADD, and the Seat Belt Coalition have a vested interest in a variety of highway safety issues (see also the chapter on external resources).

Traffic law enforcement

The objectives of police traffic law enforcement are generally agreed to include the following:

Urging drivers to obey traffic laws, with presentations in schools; talks to civic groups; public service announcements on television, radio, and billboards; and help to agencies that are responsible for licensing drivers (for example, advice on criteria for restricting problem drivers).

Developing an enforcement program that encourages drivers to comply voluntarily and deters them from acting dangerously or illegally. Such a program would include, for example, techniques such as sobriety checkpoints that give drivers the impression that all violators will be detected and apprehended.

Developing new approaches to detecting and apprehending impaired drivers (for example, using drug recognition technicians).[7]

Enforcement action is the principal tool used by the police to reduce the number and severity of accidents. Although it is impossible to prove that increasing enforcement by some amount will decrease accidents by another amount, studies have shown that specific enforcement programs, especially when accompanied by public information and education, can reduce accident incidence.[8] Most police administrators agree that there is a relationship between enforcement and accidents and that a planned enforcement program, focusing on accident-producing violations, can reduce the number of accidents resulting from those violations.

If the police do not publicize both the need for traffic safety and their own traffic safety programs, the public will not understand why compliance with traffic laws is necessary. Many motorists believe that the reason for compliance is to avoid being stopped; they think traffic officers operate under a quota system in issuing citations. In fact, some police departments do measure and evaluate the work of individual officers on the basis of their work output on any given shift. However, this misses the objective of traffic services, which is to reduce congestion and the number and severity of accidents. Therefore, even if a police department does record the frequency of citations, in ensuring individual and departmental performance it should give real weight to the level of traffic problems in the community.

Foundations of traffic law enforcement

A wide variety of guides are available to help police design and evaluate enforcement programs. These guides can range from recommended policies to detailed and proven procedures, but they share a number of fundamental principles:[9]

Traffic law enforcement is not merely issuing traffic citations. Maintaining the visibility of police units and issuing oral and written warnings are all considered parts of enforcement.

Traffic law should be enforced at a substantial level. The quantity or visibility of enforcement should be sufficient to deter drivers from committing offenses.

The approach to enforcement is as important as the visibility of enforcement. Selective enforcement (the recommended approach) targets specific high-accident areas and accident-causing violations.

Every police officer, regardless of specific assignment—but only when properly equipped with warning equipment and when carrying proper identification—should take appropriate enforcement action when observing a traffic violation or nontraffic offense.

Traffic laws should be enforced to maintain safety on the highways, never to raise revenue. Certain revenue-producing laws are, however,

---

Accreditation standards for traffic services   The Commission on Accreditation for Law Enforcement Agencies, Inc., was formed in 1979 to create standards for the professionalization of law enforcement. The standards that relate to traffic services are an up-to-date presentation of what the professional community believes local police traffic services should entail.

The traffic operations section consists of six chapters of the standards manual, each addressing one of the major functional areas of traffic services: Traffic Administration, Traffic Law Enforcement, Traffic Accident Investigation, Traffic Direction and Control, Traffic Engineering, and Traffic Ancillary Services. In addition, other sections of the manual, such as

"Patrol," "Records," and "Evidence," are compatible with, and acceptable for, the delivery of traffic services.

Each of the eighty-eight traffic-related standards (there are more than nine hundred standards in all) consists of three parts: (1) a standard statement that places a clear-cut requirement or requirements on the department, (2) a commentary that explains or expands upon the standard, and (3) a description of levels of compliance for departments of various sizes, indicating whether a particular standard is mandatory, nonmandatory, or not applicable.

Source: Commission on Accreditation for Law Enforcement Agencies, *Standards for Law Enforcement Agencies* (Fairfax, VA, revised 1990).

legitimately enforced by police (for example, vehicle registration, parking ordinances, and single-trip permits—e.g., for oversized vehicles).

Within the bounds of flexibility allowed by justifiable selective enforcement policies, there should be one enforcement policy for all highway users, and this policy should be based on the violation that is committed and not on the violator committing it. For traffic law enforcement to be understood and accepted, it must be performed in a uniform manner.

Police officers should deal with offenders professionally and as courteously as the offenders themselves will allow. In "marketing" roadway safety to the public and to those caught violating traffic laws, police need to "sell" their product in a way that their customers will ultimately support.

Police departments should provide leadership in developing a public safety education program and should make every effort to educate community leaders about police responsibilities and roles.

Because the police cannot enforce traffic laws by themselves, they need the support of those who pass the laws and of the public at large. Police departments should provide leadership in developing a public safety education program and should make every effort to educate community leaders about police responsibilities and roles.

Police are committed to a policy of traffic patrol that is normally conducted by uniformed officers using easily identifiable vehicles, supplemented when necessary with "unmarked" vehicles. Concealment for purposes of traffic law enforcement is justifiable in situations in which violations cannot be controlled by the usual methods. Similarly, the use of devices such as mechanical, electronic, photographic, and chemical testing equipment is justifiable when it is required to enhance the lawful efforts of the police. The limits on the use of such equipment should be legality, scientific soundness, and demonstrable effect on the achievement of legitimate traffic safety objectives.[10]

Responsible supervisors will make allowances for the fact that sometimes individual officers have indeed taken the path of greatest public service in making non-enforcement decisions.

Although one of the goals of police traffic services is to apply traffic laws uniformly, the behavior of patrol personnel confronted with a specific traffic offense commonly shows variations. Traffic arrest data in a community, for example, might reveal that in most arrests for driving while impaired by alcohol, the driver's blood alcohol concentration was 0.18% or above—even though the state vehicle code sets 0.08 or 0.10% as the presumptive level of impairment. Traffic citations might indicate that some officers issue citations for speed violations only when speeds exceed the permitted limit by 20 miles per hour or more. Both of these findings could indicate either a problem with officer discretion or a need to train officers to recognize lower blood alcohol levels and to detect speeders at lower speeds.

In many situations when a police officer could enforce the law, he or she may conclude that it would be wiser not to do so. A good supervisory program will detect these instances and deal with them.[11] Responsible supervisors will make allowances for the fact that sometimes individual officers have indeed taken the path of greatest public service in making non-enforcement decisions; supervisors should not unthinkingly reprimand officers for non-enforcement without considering the possibility that the enforcement policy is overly rigid.

Departmental goals and objectives

Police administrators and all officers involved in traffic enforcement should collaborate on establishing departmental goals and objectives; such a collaborative effort is most likely to ensure that the plan will be acceptable both to the patrol officers and to management. Goals and objectives should be based on reliable traffic data identifying areas where a disproportionate number of accidents occur.

One issue in the organization of any police department involves the responsibilities assigned to the various sub-units. Most police departments have a patrol section, whereas others have both patrol and a traffic detail. In addition, as noted earlier, it is imperative that all uniformed officers driving marked cars be aware of the traffic enforcement programs and take action when they observe violations. If the department has no traffic unit, then objectives dealing specifically with traffic enforcement and traffic safety should be set for the patrol division. If the activity of personnel on patrol is not directed, the interest or energy level of each patrol officer is likely to dictate the kind and amount of traffic enforcement performed (see the chapter on the patrol function).

It is imperative that all uniformed officers driving marked cars be aware of the traffic enforcement programs and take action when they observe violations.

Because police officers may exercise wide discretion in enforcing traffic laws (for example, anything but a dead stop at a stop sign is a violation, but most police will not stop everyone who does not come to a dead stop), it is essential that police managers provide line supervisors and personnel with a uniform interpretation of traffic laws and clear enforcement guidelines. In addition, officers need special training in traffic law to be quick and certain in recognizing the violations that justify enforcement.

An effective approach to delivering police traffic services begins with realistic laws designed to prevent collisions and congestion; the laws must be enforced by police officers trained in vehicle traffic law, and must be administered and adjudicated by courts functioning according to modern standards for the administration of justice in traffic cases. The modern approach to reducing traffic accidents stresses prevention. Recognition of this principle, belated though it has been, has brought substantial results. It has encouraged authorities to give close attention to traffic laws and ordinances, many of which require extensive revision to be effective tools of prevention. It has also prompted police authorities to give proper attention to the qualifications and training of traffic officers.

Separation of traffic enforcement from general police functions

A number of arguments have been put forth in support of transferring responsibility for traffic law enforcement to some group or agency other than regular uniformed police officers. Supporters of such an approach believe that

Traffic supervision is primarily regulatory; as crimes go, most traffic violations are minor.

The volume of traffic offenses requires an inordinate amount of police time.

Traffic enforcement situations generate substantial hostility toward police.

The employment of full-authority, highly trained and paid police officers to enforce traffic laws is not an effective use of resources.

There have been a number of successful implementations using nonsworn personnel. For example, civilians are widely used as school crossing guards and enforcers of parking regulations. Some cities use civilians to record and investigate traffic accidents (although several local governments that adopted this approach later returned to full-authority police officers for accident investigation, primarily because of the civilians' limited enforcement powers).

There are a number of arguments against the use of civilians to provide police traffic services. First, traffic enforcement officers in high-crime areas are thought to act as a deterrent to general criminal behavior. Second, police departments must maintain a sufficient personnel pool to respond fully to the needs of their jurisdiction, and when full-authority police positions are traded for less than full-authority positions, a department's overall ability to respond may be diminished. Third, a substantial number of criminal activities are detected through routine traffic enforcement. Many departments with special traffic units provide their traffic officers with additional training in detecting and apprehending criminals and contraband.

No adequate proposal has been made as to how to distribute functional responsibilities between the police and any other agency—public or private—that handles public safety responsibilities. In the search for areas to civilianize, therefore, perhaps areas other than traffic safety should be considered first. For example, some jurisdictions have used civilian volunteers in burglary prevention education generally and in the inspection of premises for burglary vulnerabilities specifically. In any case, there is no question that civilianization of traffic services will continue to be an area of controversy and concern.

The selective enforcement principle

The realization that police cannot enforce all traffic laws (or all nontraffic laws) and cannot apprehend all violators legitimated the concept of selective enforcement. Selective traffic law enforcement is part of a planned allocation of police personnel and equipment and is guided by a study of the kinds of violators and road conditions that have been identified as contributing to accidents. Although selective enforcement is just one element in a traffic safety program (as noted earlier, enforcement strategies are not sufficient by themselves to fully address all traffic problems), selective enforcement is a valuable and tested mechanism for meeting particular needs.[12]

The proliferation of computers has been a tremendous boon to targeted enforcement efforts, enabling police to track behavior, locations, violations, types of drivers, and types of vehicles. Such data can be analyzed to identify the areas that have a disproportionately high frequency of accidents and to probe for causal factors. For example, if accident data indicate that a significant number of collisions in a particular area could be related to improper lane changing, officers could be instructed to target this violation for careful enforcement.

When analyzing accident data, it is important to make decisions from a sufficiently large data base. For example, identification of high-accident locations should be based on the analysis of several hundred accidents. In larger cities, this can be as little as one month's accident incidence; in smaller locales, it can be more than a year's. A change from fifteen accidents to ten at a location for similar time periods is positive but probably not statistically significant. In other words, the reduction is as likely to result from random chance as from any specific prevention program.

In the early days of traffic enforcement, when there were only 25 million licensed drivers in the nation, specialized traffic enforcement units were an adequate means to address problems targeted for selective enforcement. Today, with more than 160 million drivers, the solution of identified special traffic problems can be coordinated by a specialized traffic unit but requires the active participation of all uniformed police officers operating in the area of a selective enforcement target. Special enforcement units can enhance selective enforcement efforts, of course, when they are assigned to a relatively small area, such as a group of intersections, or to a single violation, such as driving while impaired (DWI).

Speed limit enforcement

Police officials view compliance with speed regulations as a means to a safer driving environment, although some motorists view speed enforcement as unnecessary regulation or an undeserved punishment. The majority of the public, however, recognizes that collisions at lower speeds tend to produce less severe personal injuries and less costly property damage than do those at higher speeds. Authorities agree that although speed in itself is not a major cause of accidents, speed enforcement in areas known to have high accident frequency will reduce the number and severity of accidents. At the local level, citations for speeding range from 10 percent of all traffic citations to over 70 percent.[13] There is no "right" percentage of speeding citations. The nature of the local roadway network, speed limits, congestion, permitted speed measurement techniques, and management policies all influence the number of speeding citations that can be written.

In areas with a high traffic volume and a large number of speed citations, it is possible that the speed limit is too low. In such a case, the police administrator should work with the traffic engineer to determine an appropriate adjustment. According to the most common rule of thumb, the speed limit should be set at that speed at or below which 85 percent of the traffic travels. It should be noted that although use of the 85th percentile is common, it does not necessarily reflect safety requirements. Certainly, raising the speed limit in a given area can increase voluntary obedience by drivers and reduce the need for enforcement; but parallel arguments could be made about decriminalizing a host of other harmful actions.

Speed limit enforcement has several objectives:

Maximizing safety by slowing those drivers whose speed endangers themselves and others.

Conserving energy by enforcing the current national maximum speed limit

Creating a safer environment for driving by narrowing the gap between the extremes—that is, by reducing the high and raising the low in vehicle speeds.

Police use a variety of instruments and techniques to control speed, including electronic devices, motorcycles, pacing a suspected violator, or following in a marked vehicle. Moving violations can, of course, be highly consequential to repeat violators. State licensing authorities and insurance companies make eligibility decisions on the basis of driving records or point systems that reflect citations received for hazardous moving violations. Consequently, the number of contested traffic cases is steadily increasing. The resulting scrutiny of police speed measurement techniques has led police to give increased attention to improving the accuracy of speed measurement, whether by patrol vehicle pacing or by use of an electronic instrument.

Photo-radar technology, which automatically takes a picture of the offending vehicle, is a relatively recent development in speed enforcement. Although this technology has been used in Europe for a number of years, in the United States the approach has met with a mixed response from both police officials and the public. Localities in the United States that have adopted this technology use a civil process to assess the penalty.

Traffic records and summaries

Police are expected to maintain records and compile summaries of their traffic activity. These records include accident reports, enforcement records (citations, arrests, court dispositions), roadway hazard reports, and activity reports. Traffic data are used to identify problems, demonstrate the effectiveness of solutions, and channel police resources. Traffic records and summaries are also used as the basis of agency requests for additional personnel. Cooperative efforts involving the police and engineers, educators, courts and prosecutors, licensing agencies, and nonofficial agencies can also benefit from the analysis of traffic data. Finally, the federal government uses accident reports to evaluate vehicle safety features and highway design.

Cooperative efforts involving the police and engineers, educators, courts and prosecutors, licensing agencies, and nonofficial agencies can benefit from the analysis of traffic data.

A number of reports are available to supplement local records; one is the Traffic Data Report prepared by the International Association of Chiefs of Police (IACP) under the auspices of NHTSA.[14] All traffic records and summaries should be made available to other departments with responsibilities in traffic management.

Civil lawsuits and traffic enforcement

A collision stemming from a violation of traffic laws can have one or both of two possible results: a moving violation citation and a civil negligence case for damages. Although police should keep separate the two purposes of investigating the accident and enforcing the traffic law, in fact police investigating the accident may tend to focus on whose "fault" the collision was, rather than on who violated the law.[15] But they should maintain the distinction between law enforcement and fault finding. Determining fault is the task of the court in a negligence lawsuit; and the investigating officer's duty is to record the facts so that the court can settle this issue objectively. Protecting the public interest by enforcing traffic laws is just as important as determining fault (see the section on accident investigation below).

Selection and training

An effective traffic unit must have the same standing as all other functions in a police department. Personnel should be selected for their interest and ability in the area of traffic safety—not on the basis of other criteria, such as temporary inability to perform other police functions.

Officers should receive sufficient training to be well grounded in both the requirements and the techniques of the job. The amount and level of training will depend on the officers' previous training and work exprience, but all training should combine classroom instruction with supervised active experience (see also the chapter on human resources). The following topics are suggested for inclusion in a training course:

Basic philosophy of police traffic services

Departmental goals and objectives in traffic safety and accident prevention

Policy, rules, and procedures that apply to police traffic services

Traffic laws and ordinances, including pertinent court interpretations and constraints

Techniques of patrol, traffic law enforcement, traffic direction, and accident investigation, including preparation of required reports

Specific procedures to be followed to ensure court acceptance of police findings (procedures such as breath test results and speed measurement)

Case preparation and court testimony

Officer-violator relations.

Determining fault is the task of the court in a negligence lawsuit; the investigating officer's duty is to record the facts so that the court can settle this issue objectively.

In addition, retraining, or in-service training, should be conducted regularly to reinforce the basics; introduce new concepts, approaches, or procedures; and help correct problems revealed through supervisory and command evaluation of the traffic program. Department administrators should ensure that all specialists and supervisory and command personnel receive advanced training.

Departments lacking the resources to carry out their own training should investigate traffic training courses offered through regional or area facilities. A number of traffic training institutes develop and present on-site training programs designed to meet the specific needs of a department or group of departments. Funds for such special training can sometimes be obtained through federal grants or grants from other agencies.

Traffic safety education

Although responsibility for educating a community about traffic safety should not rest solely with the police, experience has shown that police cooperation and participation in such education programs is necessary to their success. Many police departments, as part of their overall public relations program, designate a traffic safety officer or establish a traffic safety education unit whose task it is to visit schools and present information on traffic safety. The current trend is to expand these efforts beyond the schools to include civic groups and other organizations.

Traffic safety education should be conducted in three forms: (1) education of school groups; (2) continuing education to improve driving and pedestrian practices; and (3) remedial education to correct specific individual problems. In the first phase, police cooperate with school personnel and help them identify problem areas in communicating police objectives to the students (these include pedestrian and bicycle issues for younger students, and driver and passenger safety for those in high school). Police contribute to continuing education—the second phase—by supporting communitywide programs conducted by a local safety council or traffic safety association (programs such as the defensive driving

High-speed pursuits Attempts to control high-speed pursuits are often limited to narrow written directives; yet the most effective approach is more comprehensive.

The accompanying diagram reflects the deliberations of a committee of Houston patrol officers on the operational issues involved in high-speed pursuits. The department's responsibilities are divided into pre-pursuit, pursuit, and post-pursuit phases.

An early step is a public information campaign designed to inform citizens of police traffic stop procedures. Potential drivers should be taught as part of their driver education training that the only rational response to an officer signalling you to pull over is to do so. Another critical element is well-developed tactical training for officers.

In the actual pursuit, the foremost responsibility of the police administrator is clear and definitive policy guidance to patrol officers. Policy should cover the many associated issues of a pursuit situation (property damage, injuries, and deaths); urge that the seriousness of the offense be balanced against the danger of any pursuit; make it clear that a personal challenge to an officer should never enter into the decision to continue a pursuit; and allow for discontinuation of the pursuit regardless of the offense involved.

After a pursuit, it is vital that the officers involved receive some type of constructive feedback because this turns each pursuit situation into a vivid learning experience. The usefulness of the feedback process lies in the hope that it will help alter the organizational culture from "Chase them until the wheels fall off" to "Why risk your life to chase some traffic violator?"

Source: Adapted from James O'Keefe, "High-Speed Pursuits in Houston," *The Police Chief* (July 1989), 32–40.

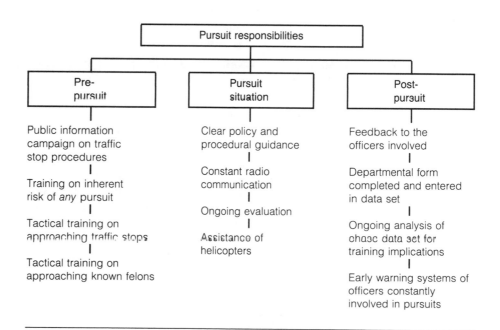

course developed by the National Safety Council). Police participation in the third phase emerges from the police responsibility to maintain records indicating which drivers need improvement and to transmit such information to the appropriate authority. (After a driver is found guilty of violating a traffic law, ordinance or state law frequently permits attendance at a driver improvement school as an alternative sentence).

Traffic accident investigation and reporting

Because data from police reports on traffic accidents are the prime source of information for accident prevention programs, police must understand the significance of traffic accident investigation and the uses of data obtained through it. Complete and reliable accident data allow the police and engineers to develop and evaluate effective countermeasures. Accident data are also necessary for planning, implementing, and evaluating selective enforcement programs.

Levels of investigation

One expert has noted that "laws relating to traffic accident investigations are brief and vague. In general they provide neither guidance nor constraints to the investigator or administrator."[16] The distinction between reporting and investigating a traffic accident is not defined adequately by law, professional associations, or a uniform operational standard. In practice, the investigation may be carried as far as the officer's interest and ability dictate. There is, however, a valuable distinction between reporting and investigating: generally, accident "reporting" requires simply the completion of a standard form that asks the "who, what, when, and where" of an accident. Only factual information is required, and most people could complete such a form with little training. Accident "investigation" implies a more thorough examination of participants and the scene of the accident and can include taking detailed measurements and photographs, examining vehicle systems for proper functioning, estimating speeds and precise vehicle locations at the time the accident occurred, and attempting to reconstruct the accident sequence. The greatest amount of attention is given to the "why."

Many police departments designate a traffic safety officer or establish a traffic safety education unit.

Confusion arises from the fact that what is usually referred to as "accident investigation" is, in reality, accident reporting. The risk in confusing accident reporting with accident investigation is that information vital to the objectives of the police department and to the needs of the involved parties may be lost. Properly conducted accident investigation requires clear policies and procedures for officers. Most state laws require only that an accident involving injury, death, or property damage greater than a specified level be reported to the police (who, in turn, forward a copy of their report to the state authority). Almost all states also prescribe a standard traffic accident report form; most state laws are similar and are based on the Uniform Vehicle Code.[17]

Police objectives

Officers assigned to a traffic accident have two general types of duties: (1) protecting persons and property at the accident scene and (2) recording the facts of the accident. The primary objective of officers at an accident scene is to keep the accident from getting worse. This involves noninvestigative tasks such as

Providing emergency care to the injured

Extinguishing fires or removing victims from fire danger

Summoning assistance, including additional police officers (accident investigation specialists, supervisors), emergency medical service personnel, fire fighters, and tow trucks

Physically protecting the accident scene with police vehicles, cones, and flares

Manually directing and controlling traffic around the accident scene

Recognizing and making arrangements to contain hazardous materials spills and exposures.

The need for and duration of these tasks depends on the circumstances of the accident, but the police department should set policy to establish responsibility for conducting and assigning them. In addition, agreements with adjoining and overlapping jurisdictions for additional personnel may be needed.

The primary objective of officers at an accident scene is to keep the accident from getting worse.

After ensuring that necessary noninvestigative tasks are being handled, the police officer's objective is to gather facts about the accident. This, too, entails several tasks, including

Obtaining and recording information that could be obliterated or lost because of traffic, weather conditions, persons leaving the scene, or the clearing of debris

Obtaining data about the roadway, vehicles, persons involved, and results of the collision so as to permit the data to be tabulated according to standard classifications

Taking enforcement action (citation, arrest) when the attending officer believes the evidence is sufficient to support such action and the circumstances do not require an alternative approach (as when there is a violator needing prompt medical attention)

Undertaking in-depth investigation to gather additional data that may be required for criminal or civil litigation or for special research studies of the highway transportation system.

Guidelines and resources for accident investigations

In theory, the police investigate every reported traffic accident in their jurisdiction. In reality, however, the presence of police at an accident scene, the extent of services provided, the amount of information recorded, and the time spent vary greatly from department to department—and perhaps from officer to officer and incident to incident. In most departments, the amount of police involvement and level of information gathering depend mainly on the seriousness of injuries or damage resulting from the accident. Every motor vehicle accident does not justify the dispatching of highly trained investigative personnel, although officers should be assigned to as many traffic accidents reported to the department as is consistent with agency "differential response" dispatching policies (see the chapter on the patrol function).

Few departments have established administrative guidelines delineating the extent of emergency services or investigation to be performed. Individual officers directed to the scene generally decide how much and what kind of information is useful or may be wanted—although they are influenced in such decisions by common practice in the department. Such variation makes it difficult not only to define exactly what "investigate" means but also to determine when an "investigation" is complete (see also the chapter on criminal investigations).

Several widely accepted references are available to help police departments establish policies and procedures for accident investigation. NHTSA's series of traffic safety programs for state and local governments includes a standard on accident investigation and reporting.[18] The IACP, which has developed model guidelines for various aspects of police services that can be adapted for local use, has created six policies and twenty-eight detailed procedures relating to the accident investigation process.[19]

Another set of guidelines for accident investigation has been developed by the Commission on Accreditation for Law Enforcement Agencies (CALEA). One section of the accreditation manual is concerned with police traffic services, and one chapter in the section covers accident investigation. The standards developed by CALEA require that departments have written directives governing all aspects of the investigative process, including both the scene-control and the fact-finding tasks.[20]

There are also two traditional guides for the police officer at an accident scene. The first is the state (or other standardized) accident report form, supplemented as necessary by temporary data-collection forms used to obtain the specialized

---

Hazardous materials and motor carriers Truck safety has always been something of a problem, but two developments have contributed to worsening it. The first is deregulation, which encouraged independent carriers to proliferate. The second is the increasing nationwide use of hazardous chemical compounds. New compounds are developed daily and are transported nationwide by all modes of transportation, including trucks. Hazardous materials can be anything from a plastic jug of muriatic acid (used in swimming pools) to a full truckload of rocket fuel. With the U.S. economy and way of life depending on these millions of shipments, it is likely that the problem will only increase.

Some large metropolitan police forces, very much aware of the threat posed by transportation of hazardous materials, have received federal funding through the Motor Carrier Safety Assistance Program. The funds can be used to supplement current programs for enforcing hazardous materials transport regulations or to plan and establish such programs. Although the storing, manufacture, and use of hazardous materials are often governed by fire regulations and agencies other than the police, this does not reduce the hazard of transport, nor does it relieve the police of responsibility during transport. Again, a working partnership with all the agencies involved is the key to success.

Hazardous materials shipments must be identified by a system of placards and markings. Information about shipments is available from the U.S. Department of Transportation, other federal agencies concerned with hazardous materials, and local fire departments.

Many approaches have been used to provide personnel for enforcing hazardous materials transport regulations. All traffic service officers and police officers should have sufficient training to recognize when a hazard exists. Each local government also needs a specialized unit with the expertise to deal with hazardous materials incidents—whether in the police department, the fire department, or some other agency.

information required for traffic accident research. The second is the discretionary authority of a supervisor or prosecutor to require that additional information be obtained—in other words, that evidence be collected to support a criminal charge.

A standard for police supervisors on when to send trained accident investigators might include guidelines such as the following:

1. A trained investigator is needed when one of the following circumstances exists: (1) a person is dead at the scene or appears likely to die as a result of the collision; (b) at least one person is seriously, although probably not fatally, injured; (c) an injury occurs in a public or commercial passenger-carrying vehicle; (d) a government-owned vehicle is involved; (e) more than one vehicle with three axles is involved and there is also a disabling injury; (f) there is destructive damage to major structures, such as a bridge collapse, fire, high-tension wires grounded, and so forth; (g) hazardous materials are involved; or (h) any other circumstance exists which may result in extensive litigation or cannot be explained by an untrained investigator.

2. A trained investigator is not needed when the accident involves no disabled person, traffic is not blocked, no hazardous materials are involved, or no assistance is needed to clear the scene of the accident.

The materials being transported are only one part of the problem: the other parts are the trucks and the drivers themselves. Some police departments use industry-staffed self-inspections conducted by trained personnel and periodically audited by the police. Given the number of motor carriers on the road, this seems to be a viable alternative to the police trying to inspect every rig on the highway; this approach is also in keeping with motor carrier rules that mandate inspection by the owner or operator before use.

The Commercial Vehicle Safety Alliance (CVSA) is a new group that is attempting to standardize many of the regulations under which motor carriers operate. CVSA, which exists in most states, has developed a twelve-point vehicle safety inspection protocol and has made progress toward standardizing and updating the out-of-service criteria.

Information on CVSA and funding for CVSA activities are available through a state's lead agency under the Motor Carrier Safety Assistance Program. Traditionally, about 90 percent of motor carrier inspection time is spent inspecting equipment, but 90 percent of motor carrier accidents are caused by the drivers. The notion that drivers need to be the focus of safety efforts is just now taking hold and will eventually affect the licensing of commercial drivers.

The Classified Driver's License (CDL) program, pursuant to Title XII of the Commercial Motor Vehicle Safety Act of 1986 (49 USCS), requires that drivers' licenses be classified and that drivers be tested in the type of vehicle they are licensed to drive. The regulations under which states will implement this program are now in place, but few implementation programs are actually in operation.

Another aspect of efforts to improve driver safety is the commercial drivers' license information system, which will allow states, carriers, and insurance companies access to drivers' license records nationwide. This access will make it easier to deny licenses to problem drivers and to prevent the issue of duplicate licenses from arising.

A report would be completed for all such collisions known to the police.

In cases that require a trained investigator, he or she would take photographs, perform tire and lamp examinations, measure vehicle movement and final position, and obtain any other information that might be useful for later reconstruction of the sequence of events. It should also be noted that different levels of training in accident investigation are available to the police, and investigators should be assigned to accidents on the basis of skill level.

When personnel are not available and a number of accidents are reported and awaiting service, policy and procedures are needed that will allocate police resources according to set priorities as well as meet public expectations of some form of service. When police cannot respond to the scene, alternative reporting procedures must be identified.

Alcohol- and drug-related traffic offenses

Driving under the influence of alcohol or drugs (DUI), or driving while impaired (DWI), is a major cause of serious traffic accidents. Vocal national groups such as Mothers Against Drunk Driving (MADD) and Remove Intoxicated Drivers (RID) have joined the DWI control system, helped to create a change in public policy and awareness, and supported stronger DWI laws as well as stricter enforcement of the laws now in place.

Considerable research has been undertaken to find effective countermeasures to reduce DWI incidents. Federally funded research has attempted to discover what factors influence police arrest decisions, what driving cues are likely to be exhibited by intoxicated drivers, how public information and education should be combined with enforcement, what enforcement strategies are best, and what field sobriety tests are most effective.[21]

The commitment of police management to a high level of enforcement against DWI offenses is essential to improved efforts. Departments must provide clear direction to patrol personnel through various forms of administrative guidance, such as policy statements and written procedures, so that enforcement of DWI-related laws continues to receive the attention it deserves. Policy and procedures, however, can do little more than remove some potential impediments to enforcement. Police managers, supervisors, and patrol personnel must understand what is expected of them and must possess the knowledge, skill, and desire necessary for meeting these expectations.

One element common to nearly all countermeasure programs is increased police enforcement of DWI laws, either through increased attention by patrol

---

Drunk driving doesn't pay   To recover public service costs associated with individuals who drive under the influence, Portage, Michigan, bills those involved in traffic accidents.

Police, fire, and ambulance charges are billed to individuals responsible for accidents. The average bill is $90.

The cost recovery program was started in September 1989, and by January 1991 it had billed $24,000 and collected $9,000.

In some cases, such as when the individual is incarcerated, the fee is dismissed, since collection is unlikely. The city hopes that the program will reduce the number of drunk driving related accidents.

Source: Cited in *The Guide to Management Improvement Projects in Local Government* (Washington, DC: International City Management Association, 1990).

and traffic officers or through the use of dedicated DWI task forces or patrol units. Such specialized units have been found effective in increasing both overall DWI enforcement levels and public awareness of such enforcement.

Public awareness is important because research indicates that deterring potential DWI violators can have a greater long-term safety effect than arresting limited numbers of actual violators.[22] Because studies have shown that a DWI violator has an arrest risk of between 1 in 500 and 1 in 2,000 for each DWI trip, even a substantial increase in the number of arrests will not significantly reduce the number of violations—unless the fear of arrest and ensuing consequences is enough to discourage people from driving while impaired.[23] Thus, no matter what type of enforcement program a department implements, it is essential that the enforcement efforts be publicized.

Legislative changes in many states have also played an important role in aiding DWI enforcement efforts. Many of these changes follow the guidelines suggested by the Presidential Commission on Drunk Driving.[24] Among the changes recommended by the commission that most states have adopted are the standardization of a 0.10% blood alcohol content (BAC) as the maximum for creating a presumption of impairment; a twenty-one–year–old minimum drinking age; the establishment of *per se* laws (laws that make a BAC above a certain level an offense in its own right without the officer's having to show impairment or intoxication); mandatory sentencing requirements; and immediate suspension of driver licenses. The commission also encouraged the availability of community alcohol and drug rehabilitation programs for DWI violators. Such programs can be used both to screen violators after conviction and before sentencing and to constitute part of the sentence or other sanction. The objective of the rehabilitation programs should be to modify attitudes and behavior with the hope of eliminating the violator's recidivism.

Factors influencing officers

Detecting and arresting DWI violators is a key component in general deterrence. Four main factors have been identified as affecting an officer's decision to arrest:[25]

1. Written administrative guidance describing the department's expectations about the detection and arrest of DWI violations, as well as efforts by supervisors to ensure that guidelines are being followed
2. Specific enforcement plans as to patrol locations and schedules, procedures for the processing of those cited, use of specialized units,

---

"Bar exam" may save lives   The village of Schaumburg, Illinois, took a step to reduce alcohol-related deaths on area roadways. It was the first community in Illinois to require that all bartenders be trained in alcohol awareness.

The village formed a partnership with local colleges to provide bartenders with a special program. The program consists of twelve hours of class instruction on topics such as the psychological effects of alcohol on the average drinker and how to recognize a problem drinker. Bartenders in the program are also drilled on when and how to successfully stop serving a potential problem customer.

During the first four and half years of the program, more than seven hundred bartenders completed the course.

Source: Cited in *The Guide to Management Improvement Projects in Local Government* (Washington, DC: International City Management Association, 1987).

---

and use of investigative techniques and equipment to aid the officer's arrest/no arrest decision
3. Training to develop skill in detecting borderline suspects, belief in the reasonableness of established impairment levels (BAC for alcohol violators), and awareness of the amount of alcohol and amount and type of narcotics that must be ingested to produce impairment
4. Active communication between police and judicial personnel on such issues as the scheduling of court dates, admissibility of evidence, plea bargaining, and the needs and problems of each agency.

New detection techniques

There has been a great deal of research and development concerning new detection techniques and training in the area of DWI. The most significant of these is the set of roadside sobriety tests developed by NHTSA.[26] The three recommended tests—walk and turn, one-leg stand, and horizontal gaze nystagmus (nystagmus is an involuntary jerking or twitching of the eye as it moves from side to side that becomes exaggerated as BAC levels increase)—have been shown to be almost 90 percent accurate in identifying persons with a BAC above 0.10 percent. In addition, NHTSA has developed a training program to help officers detect individuals driving under the influence of drugs or drug and alcohol combinations.

Although the roadside testing battery has been valuable in helping officers confirm suspected instances of DWI, other developments have helped with the initial detection. One of these is the "DWI Detection Guide," which describes the twenty driving behaviors (for example, making wide-radius turns, straddling lane markers) that DWI drivers are most likely to exhibit.[27] Other detection techniques or opportunities for detection include preliminary breath testers (PBTs), passive alcohol sensors, and sobriety checkpoints. Although sobriety checkpoints have been found to be very effective in increasing public awareness of DWI and local enforcement efforts, before setting them up the police must thoroughly check local laws and must carefully plan the entire checkpoint operation. Specific policies and procedures must be developed and adhered to in order to strike the required balance between citizens' liberty and public safety.

The magnitude of the problem of drug-impaired drivers has never been fully assessed, partly because of the lack of adequate techniques. However, an objective, physical observation system has been developed that a trained person known as a Drug Recognition Technician (DRT) can use. Research conducted at the University of Southern California and Johns Hopkins University has shown that a DRT can, in over 90% of cases, determine if an individual is under the influence of drugs and, in 94% of those cases, can accurately classify the drugs into seven categories. The Los Angeles police department, which was the first to apply the DRT approach, estimates that as many as 30% of those arrested for DWI have also ingested a drug other than alcohol.[28]

NHTSA, along with the IACP and various other agencies, has created pilot sites nationwide to train DRTs. Once trained, these experts go on to train additional officers in their own geographical area. Criteria have been designed for certification of instructors and new DRTs and for recertification of those already practicing. A drawback of the DRT approach is that a certain level of experience is necessary for someone to become a DRT and then to progress to the level of instructor. Thus, the approach will take time to be implemented nationally.

Federal drug control legislation now provides millions of dollars for training and equipment under the DRT program nationwide.

Other police traffic services

Other traffic services that police departments are often called upon to provide are generally not as time-consuming as the activities described earlier in this chapter. Some of these other services occur infrequently and are difficult to plan for, but others occur frequently and can require substantial staff resources.

Traffic direction and control Traffic direction and control (TD&C) can be broadly thought of as facilitating the safe and efficient movement of vehicular traffic in hazardous conditions or special circumstances.[29] Most TD&C assignments result from unexpected events such as traffic accidents, fires, and other civil or natural disturbances. The magnitude of the events can vary greatly, and administrative guidance is required to deal with them. Some agencies provide TD&C regularly at locations such as downtown intersections, factory gates, and sports arenas. For these regular arrangements, many departments use civilians or auxiliaries and have the owners of the private facility contract for TD&C personnel on an overtime basis.

Parking control Municipal police are often required to supervise street parking regulations. The purpose of parking control is to provide adequate road space for the movement of traffic and to ensure equitable use of curb space when on-street parking is permitted. The use of a trained, uniformed police officer to enforce time and place restrictions on curb lane parking is questionable, particularly when the enforcement of regulations is primarily a revenue operation rather than an effort to ensure the regular turnover of curb parking spaces. The use of civilian employees for this function should be considered. If civilians are used, a job classification that distinguishes this work from tasks performed by uniformed officers must be established.

Abandoned vehicles Motor vehicles abandoned on the public way are a growing problem in many communities. At a minimum, police should initiate the legal process for the removal of such vehicles. In some communities, police may be required to perform the entire removal process, including final disposition of vehicles not claimed by registered owners.

Bicycle traffic Spurred on by such diverse factors as interest in personal fitness, automobile commuting costs, concerns about air quality, and traffic and parking congestion, the bicycle has become a significant factor in the transportation system. Numerous communities have many miles of bicycle

---

Parking posses In Flint, Michigan, special "parking posses" are enforcing handicapped parking regulations. Volunteers recruited by the Mayor's Office on Aging and Handicapped receive eighteen hours of training by the police department's Traffic Enforcement Section.

Although they are civilians, the volunteers are empowered to ticket vehicles improperly parked in handicapped parking spaces.

The volunteer program is credited with significantly improving the city's enforcement of the handicapped parking regulations. In the program's first two years, participants issued 2,000 $100 tickets. Program manuals are available to other jurisdictions.

Source: Cited in *The Guide to Management Improvement Projects in Local Government* (Washington, DC: International City Management Association, 1988).

paths. Some of these paths are recreational, but those that parallel motor vehicle traffic lanes call for enforcement policies for both bicyclists and motorists who encroach on each other's designated space. Personal safety is perhaps the most serious problem: the National Safety Council estimates that each year there are at least fifty thousand bicycle/motor vehicle accidents and one-thousand fatalities nationwide. There is significant evidence to suggest that many of these accidents are not being officially reported. It is believed that as many as ten bicycle accidents may occur for every one that is reported.[30]

Accident statistics alone provide a sound argument in favor of local police departments acting to improve bicycle rider safety. Little has been written about police supervision of nonmotorized transportation, and innovative concepts and procedures are needed.

Traffic ancillary services In addition to the planning, enforcement, and accident-related activities already described, the police are called on to provide other service-oriented functions. These tasks most often take the form of direct assistance to the driving public.[31] In providing assistance to stranded motorists, the officer most often plays a role defined by the resources (and needs) of the community. Many communities limit the police role to having an officer call for a mechanic (or other provider). The police officer may provide limited traffic control—or may take no further action. Departments that are able to organize their resources in such a way as to permit patrol officers to assist motorists directly (changing a flat tire and so forth) often find that the public appreciation thus generated amply justifies this use of personnel.

Local police administrators and state officials must have clear understandings about jurisdiction and the responsibility for specific functions.

Disabled vehicles on controlled access routes that go through a city are a growing problem for police. Drivers of such vehicles often expect the local police to provide them with a number of services. Local police administrators and state officials must have clear understandings about jurisdiction and the responsibility for specific functions such as accident investigation and disabled vehicle assists. Such agreements must be communicated fully and clearly to all command, supervisory, and operational personnel. If the local police administrator accepts full responsibility for police traffic services on freeways, the extent or level of that service (for example, whether merely communicating the need for assistance or actually transporting the motorist to a point where assistance is available) must be decided. In many jurisdictions, local automobile clubs help the police provide disabled-vehicle services.

Conclusion

The loss of life and property from traffic accidents far exceeds that from all criminal categories combined. Given the seriousness of this aspect of police services, a police organization should ensure that traffic safety receives appropriate prominence within the department. Active involvement of the chief executive and management improves the quality of the traffic safety program and affects the attitude of officers throughout the department.

Traffic supervision and traffic law enforcement alone do not provide safe and efficient highway transportation. Traffic safety requires, in addition, a realistic and balanced program of sound traffic laws, highway automotive and traffic engineering, driver licensing and driver improvement policies, and consistent and fair prosecutors and traffic courts. Driver education before and during a driver's career is also important, as are the analysis and use of traffic and accident data. Coordination of these efforts by all participating agencies creates public understanding of, and support for, the traffic safety program. When such coordination is not possible, the police, through a carefully designed and continuing program of traffic services, must pick up the slack and direct their energies toward the most serious problems. This is only a stopgap measure, but it is a community's most effective control over losses of life and property from vehicle collisions, pending the development of a balanced and coordinated program.

Traffic safety requires a realistic and balanced program of sound traffic laws, highway automotive and traffic engineering, driver licensing and driver improvement policies, and consistent and fair prosecutors and traffic courts.

The National Safety Council and other independent sources have demonstrated that comprehensive programs for preventing and controlling accidents—programs in which the police play an important role—significantly reduce the number and severity of motor vehicle accidents. The organizational arrangements and degree of commitment to traffic safety programs vary from one community to another. This chapter has provided a framework within which all communities can try not only to maintain and improve police traffic services but also to mesh those services most productively with engineering, planning, and other crucial local government activities.

1   In this chapter, the term *highway* refers to all roadways used by vehicles in urban, suburban, and rural areas.

2   Recommendations in all these areas should conform to the guidelines in U.S. Department of Transportation, *Manual on Uniform Traffic Control Devices for Streets and Highways* (Washington, DC: Federal Highway Administration, 1988).

3   U.S. National Highway Traffic Safety Administration, *Highway Safety Program Standards*, "Standard 7: Police Traffic Services," 1968.

4   National Committee on Uniform Traffic Laws and Ordinances, *Uniform Vehicle Code and Model Traffic Ordinance*, rev. ed. (Evanston, IL: National Committee on Uniform Traffic Laws and Ordinances, 1987).

5   For more information on this office, contact the National Association of State Governors' Highway Safety Representatives, 444 North Capitol Street (Suite 530), Washington, DC 20001, telephone (202) 624–5877.

6   In most instances, considerable long-term planning is needed for 402 funding. To be included in the state's highway safety plan, proposals must be submitted to the governor's highway safety office well in advance of the beginning of the federal fiscal year—usually by about April 1. Funds for approved programs become available on or shortly after October 1 (the beginning of the federal fiscal year).

7   Daryl F. Gates and Thomas E. Page, "The Drug Recognition Expert Program: A National Update," *Police Chief* (July 1989): 41–44.

8   Two studies that have shown a specific, significant relationship between enforcement levels and accident frequency or severity are John H. Lacey et al., *Enforcement and Public Information Strategies for DWI General Deterrence*, DOT-HS-807-066 (Washington, DC: National Highway Traffic

Safety Administration, 1986), and Allan F. Williams et al., "Results of a Seat Belt Use Law Enforcement and Publicity Campaign in Elmira, New York," *Accident Prevention and Analysis* (August 1987): 243–49.

9   See, for example, National Advisory Commission on Criminal Justice Standards and Goals, *Police* (Washington, DC: U.S. Government Printing Office, 1973), Standard 9.6, 255–32.

10   International Association of Chiefs of Police, *Model Police Traffic Services (Procedures)* (Gaithersburg, MD: International Association of Chiefs of Police, 1976).

11   One study, Project STAR, introduced the term "situational enforcement" to describe the way in which a police officer deals with this condition. This concept is discussed in detail in California Commission on Peace Officers Standards and Training, *System and Training Analysis of Requirements for Criminal Justice Participants* (Sacramento: California Commission on Peace Officers Standards and Training, 1974).

12   In a federally funded study, the International Association of Chiefs of Police describes the principle of selective enforcement and advocates the use of police resources in accordance with that principle. See International Association of Chiefs of Police, *Selective Law Enforcement* (Gaithersburg, MD: International Association of Chiefs of Police, 1972).

13   *IACP Traffic Data Report*, DOT-HS-807-560 (Washington, DC: National Highway Traffic Safety Administration, 1990).

14   Ibid.

15   A more detailed discussion of this matter is found in Robert H. Reeder, *Civil versus Criminal Aspects of Traffic Accident Cases*, SN 2157 (Evanston, IL: Traffic Institute, Northwestern University, 1975).

16   J. Stannard Baker and Lynn M. Fricke, *The Traffic*

Accident Investigation Manual (Evanston, IL: Northwestern University Traffic Institute, 1986), 1:10–10.

17 National Committee on Uniform Traffic Laws and Ordinances, *Uniform Vehicle Code and Model Traffic Ordinance*.

18 U.S. National Highway Traffic Safety Administration, *Highway Safety Program Standards*, "Standard 18: Accident Investigation and Reporting," 1978.

19 International Association of Chiefs of Police, *Model Police Traffic Services (Policies)* (Gaithersburg, MD: International Association of Chiefs of Police, 1976); and IACP *Model Police Traffic Services (Procedures)*.

20 Commission on Accreditation for Law Enforcement Agencies, *Standards for Law Enforcement Agencies* (Fairfax, VA: Commission on Accreditation for Law Enforcement Agencies, revised 1989).

21 Information about these studies can be obtained from the governor's highway safety office or from a NHTSA regional office. See also Gates and Page, "The Drug Recognition Expert Program."

22 National Highway Traffic Safety Administration, *Alcohol and Highway Safety 1984: A Review of the State of Knowledge*, DOT-HS-806-569 (Washington, DC: National Highway Traffic Safety Administration, 1985).

23 Ibid.

24 Presidential Commission on Drunk Driving, *Final Report* (Washington, DC: Presidential Commission on Drunk Driving, 1983).

25 John Reynolds and Associates, *Factors Influencing State Police Officers' Arrest Rates for Alcohol Related Traffic Violations* (Lansing: Michigan State Police, 1983).

26 National Highway Traffic Safety Administration, *Improved Sobriety Testing Battery*, DOT-HS-806-512 (Washington, DC: National Highway Traffic Safety Administration, 1986).

27 Anacapa Sciences, *Guide for Detecting Drunk Drivers at Night* (Washington, DC: National Highway Traffic Safety Administration, 1982).

28 Gates and Page, "The Drug Recognition Expert Program."

29 Northwestern University Traffic Institute, *PTS Performance Measures* (Washington, DC: National Highway Traffic Safety Administration, 1991).

30 Seattle, Washington, Engineering Department, *Bikeway System Planning and Design Manual* (Seattle: Engineering Department, 1975).

31 Northwestern University Traffic Institute, *PTS Performance Measures*.

Part three: Special challenges

7 Local drug control

History has shown that public concern with drug abuse runs in cycles. Years of toleration are followed by mounting concern and then feverish activity, which is followed, in turn, by a slackening of interest and neglect, until renewed toleration sparks another peak in antidrug activity. At the turn of the century, opium, heroin, and cocaine were used nonmedicinally (to a degree that cannot be determined) without arousing much comment. For a variety of complex reasons, relative toleration was replaced by public antagonism to nonmedical drug use beginning in the second decade of the century.[1] Then, in the 1960s and early 1970s, consumption of marijuana, heroin, and other drugs increased. The public seemed unconcerned about the problems created by these two drugs, despite the continuing heavy consumption of marijuana and the stabilization of the number of heroin addicts at between 350,000 and 500,000 people. The police and others in both the criminal justice system and the medical professions, however, continued to have to deal with the consequences of heroin addiction. As for cocaine, in the late 1970s and early 1980s many people perceived it to be a relatively harmless, though expensive, recreational drug. But in the late 1980s, as the United States found itself in the midst of a cocaine epidemic, the public's concern about drug abuse once again was aroused.

The epidemic of cocaine and other drugs is creating problems that are overwhelming the capacity of the criminal justice system to cope with them. First, drugs and drug-related problems create many kinds of calls for police service. Criminals who are on drugs commit more crimes than criminals who are not using drugs.[2] Drugs, in particular crack cocaine, are becoming associated with increases in various forms of domestic violence. And the presence of street drug markets is associated with increased noise, traffic congestion, and other concerns that citizens expect the police to deal with.

Second, already overcrowded jails and prison facilities are strained even more as the number of drug crime arrests increases massively: between 1977 and 1988, the number of drug-related arrests per 100,000 people increased by 50 percent.[3] In the late 1980s, 74 percent of the state prison systems in the United States were under some form of court order to improve conditions and reduce crowding.[4] State prisons were occupied at from 107 percent to 123 percent of capacity, and 3 percent of state prisoners were being held in local jails because penitentiaries had no room for them. The federal system was no better. Its prisons were operating at 132 percent to 172 percent of capacity.[5]

Third, treatment facilities in many cities are inadequate. There are not enough spaces available, and facilities are geared toward treating abuse of alcohol and heroin, not cocaine. And whereas methadone maintenance is available for heroin, treatment for cocaine dependency merely consists of abstinence and counseling.

Furthermore, there are reports of schools, housing projects, and neighborhoods that are no longer under the control of teachers, residents, and local government but are terrorized by armed youths trafficking in cocaine and other drugs.

This chapter first surveys antidrug efforts at the national level. Then it goes into detail on the three local strategic options for controlling drug use. The chapter concludes with a discussion of performance measures for evaluating local antidrug efforts.

National antidrug efforts

Both national and local efforts to control drug abuse can be divided into two types: supply reduction and demand reduction. On the national level, supply theory suggests that if the United States could stem the flow of drugs from foreign and, increasingly, domestic sources to local users, the problem could be reduced. Potential and recreational users would not be able to find suppliers, and seasoned users would have to give up their habits for lack of the substance.

Demand theory suggests that the drug problem can be reduced if people are persuaded that drugs are harmful to their health and general well-being. Potential and recreational users would seek other, presumably more healthy, ways to get their kicks, and habitual users would seek treatment and return to non-drug-dependent life styles.

Drug supply

A number of supply reduction strategies have been applied both internationally and nationally: control of source crops, control of chemicals used in drug production, prosecution of high-level traffickers, border control, and asset seizure and forfeiture.

Control of sources   One strategy involves working out agreements with drug-exporting countries to eradicate source crops and stem drug production and export, but such agreements have limited usefulness. In the 1970s the United States and Turkey signed an agreement that succeeded in cutting down the flow of heroin from that country—but the supply of heroin did not end. Instead, Mexican and Southeast Asian sources became dominant suppliers. Similarly, it is conceivable that if production of cocaine in Peru and Bolivia were stopped, production would soon begin in other countries. There may be other climates where the coca leaf can be grown. Furthermore, regardless of the number of alternative sources for a single drug, illicit substitute drugs are constantly developed and introduced to take the place of established ones.

Control of input chemicals   Restricting the sale of chemicals needed in the production of illicit drugs is another international and national strategy, and it, too, is of limited use. For example, because ether is used in the manufacture of cocaine, attempts have been made to cut the flow of ether from the United States and Europe to drug processing labs in South and Central America. Without these precursor chemicals, drug processing can become impossible. Attempts to cut off such chemical supplies are unlikely to make substantial inroads into the production of cocaine, however. There are multiple sources of the chemicals, and new sources can be established.

Attacks on upper-level drug traffickers   Complex international and national investigations have been undertaken to bring the highest-level drug traffickers to trial. The assumption is that removing "Mr. Big" paralyzes an entire drug production and trafficking network, thus reducing the supply of drugs entering the country. But attacking upper-level dealers has significant inherent limitations. Not only are these people difficult to capture but also, once they are caught and convicted, there is no reason to believe that the vacuum they leave will remain unfilled. There are many who are eager to step into their shoes.

Control of borders   The U.S. government has put a great many resources into sealing the nation's borders against smugglers. Large balloons, known as aerostats, equipped with radar that can peer miles into Mexico and detect approaching aircraft have been installed along the southwest border. And Congress has demanded greater participation from the military in using sophisticated surveillance and command and control aircraft and ships to detect traffickers in the Caribbean. Stepped-up enforcement at major points of entry and the distribution of drug courier profiles have been used to curtail drug smuggling. However, a large proportion of illegal drugs enters the United States by private aircraft, and studies by the Rand Corporation (for the U.S. Department of Defense) and by the U.S. General Accounting Office have both concluded that closer monitoring of these aircraft would have only a small effect on drug supplies.[6]

Asset seizure and forfeiture   Asset seizure by the federal government and the assets' forfeiture are designed to take profits from drug dealers and are likened to a 100 percent tax on drug traffickers' profits. Possibly, if the government can take all that traffickers have gained through illegitimate enterprise, dealers will switch to a business with a lower "tax rate"—one that is more socially acceptable. Of course, there is only a small likelihood that the full bite of the tax will be imposed,[7] and asset seizure and forfeiture are unlikely to become such a major threat to drug traffickers that they substantially curtail their illicit business—if only because they need to be caught first, and this is very difficult to do. Further, traffickers have become savvy in laundering their cash and then hiding their assets.

Effects of supply reduction efforts   This review suggests that substantial increases in the federal resources devoted to supply reduction *alone* are unlikely to have much effect on drug problems. If we take cocaine as an example and use the price and purity of the cocaine sold on the street to measure the collective effect of these efforts, we see that current strategies to affect supply have had little effect. Between 1985 and 1988, the retail purity of cocaine in the United States increased 27 percent, to 70 percent purity, while retail prices for a gram of cocaine fell by 32 percent, to about $70.[8] These estimates, of course, vary a great deal from city to city, but the trend clearly means that users could get much more for their money in 1988 than in 1985—and thus that the supplies available to users increased dramatically.

Nevertheless, national supply strategies are still useful. Drug availability almost surely would be higher if these strategies were not used. In addition, some of these strategies, like asset forfeiture, have been introduced only relatively recently at the state and local levels; with increased experience and better laws, officials at those levels may be able to use the strategies more effectively. Finally, there are many reasons besides supply reduction for using these strategies. Going after high-level dealers and seizing their assets, for example, enhances citizens' perceptions of justice—no one is above the law, and people should not be allowed to gain from illegal behavior—and, at a minimum, society repossesses some of the wealth diverted to the drug trade. Still, these tactics must be seen for what they are: important but limited tools in what is likely to be a long and protracted effort to manage drug problems.

Drug demand

The other national approach to reducing drug abuse involves strategies to reduce demand. Advocates of this approach argue that until people stop demanding drugs, little headway will be made in controlling drug abuse. This seems like a reasonable assumption, and a number of tactics are used to further this approach:

educating the public and teaching youths to "Just Say No," stigmatizing users, and providing rehabilitation services.

Surveys have suggested some positive developments in the use of drugs by youths. Every year since 1975, the National Institute on Drug Abuse (NIDA) has funded a national survey of representative high school seniors and young adults to determine developing trends in drug use. From 1975 through 1985, the proportion of seniors who had used cocaine in their lifetime increased from 9 percent to 17.3 percent. But from 1985 through 1988, the figures declined from 17.3 percent to 12.1 percent. Further, during the same period the proportion of seniors who had used cocaine in the preceding thirty days also declined, going from 5.8 percent to 3.4 percent.[9]

NIDA also funds periodic surveys of a representative sample of the U.S. population to detect drug use patterns (see the accompanying sidebar). These surveys show that *recreational use of cocaine by people of all age groups is declining*. From 1985 to 1988 the number of people twelve to seventeen years old using cocaine in the twelve months preceding the survey declined 27.5 percent; 25.8 percent fewer people ages eighteen to twenty-five years reported using cocaine in the previous year; and the number of people over twenty-five years of age using cocaine in the previous year declined 35.7 percent.[10] (The 1987 survey results suggested that 40 percent of the U.S. population has tried cocaine by age twenty-seven.[11])

Though recreational use of cocaine was beginning to decline, the news about people dependent on cocaine was not nearly so good. From 1984 through 1988 *the number of medical emergencies related to all forms of cocaine in the United States quadrupled, with the number of crack-related medical emergencies rising 2,800 percent, from 549 to 15,306.*[12] Thus, whereas casual cocaine use by the general population may be declining, use of cocaine, especially crack cocaine, by addicted users may be increasing.

In other words, public campaigns to reduce demand for drugs may work, but they do not work equally well for all parts of society. Messages that are persuasive to the middle class and the educated may have less effect on the poor and those who did not graduate from high school. Furthermore, casual users are more easily persuaded to give up drugs than steady users are.

Drug use in the United States　Of the population over age 12 in 1985, more than 15 percent had used marijuana or hashish in the year preceding the survey, and more than 6 percent had used cocaine in the previous year. Of those aged 18 to 25 in 1985, more than 16 percent had used cocaine in the previous year. Among this same age group, whites (28 percent) were twice as likely as blacks (13 percent) or Hispanics (15 percent) to report that they had used cocaine sometime during their life.

Frequent cocaine use (as opposed to casual use) is more likely to be associated with lower education and higher unemployment within each demographic group. People 18 to 25 years old without a high school diploma were more likely to report cocaine use in the preceding month than those with more education. Overall, as educational attainment rises, the frequency of cocaine use falls. In terms of employment, 14 percent of unemployed 18 to 25 year olds in 1985 reported using cocaine "frequently" compared with 8 percent for employed people in the same age group.

Source: National Institute on Drug Abuse, *National Household Survey on Drug Abuse: Main Findings 1985* (Rockville, MD: NIDA, 1988).

Though use of almost all illicit drugs seems to be slowly but steadily declining,[13] poor and less-educated people may be disproportionately represented among chronic users. And it is among these groups that drug abuse causes the most serious harm. For example, a study conducted in the District of Columbia found that more than 80 percent of the murders in 1988 were drug related, and most victims were killed in their own neighborhoods. The murder patterns and street drug markets were closely associated with low-income census tracts.[14]

Public campaigns to reduce demand for drugs may work, but they do not work equally well for all parts of society. Messages that are persuasive to the middle class and the educated may have less effect on the poor and those who did not graduate from high school. Furthermore, casual users are more easily persuaded to give up drugs than steady users are.

The rise in drug usage in impoverished neighborhoods may be linked to increased concentrations of unemployed men in major urban centers.[15] This view is supported by anecdotal observations from police antidrug activities. For example, the Tulsa police department found that poor urban black males were being arrested for drug offenses out of proportion to their numbers in the city's population, and the arrest trend for this group in Tulsa was increasing.[16] It seems likely that drug abuse will become increasingly concentrated in impoverished urban neighborhoods, even as the overall trend in drug abuse declines.

Local strategic options

The low effectiveness of national efforts puts increased emphasis on efforts by local police to control drug abuse. Local control of drug dealing and abuse requires a range of strategies:

1. Investigative strategies, targeted above the street level, are designed to disrupt networks of drug wholesalers, thereby increasing the risk and cost of the business of drug trafficking. Investigative strategies address the *supply* of drugs.
2. Education strategies are designed to keep children from turning to drugs as they mature. These strategies address the *demand* for drugs.
3. Patrol strategies are designed to reduce drug problems in small geographical neighborhoods, communities, and blocks. They affect the *market*, where supply and demand come together.

The three strategies are complementary and need to be coordinated to control drug use and trafficking. All three are essential in a comprehensive local police antidrug policy. The three strategies are summarized briefly below and then discussed in greater detail in subsequent sections.

In investigative strategies, an investigative unit attempts to remove dealers and to disable drug distribution networks. The investigative tactics involve collecting evidence (such as surveillance photographs, wiretap recordings, informant reports, and documented sales of drugs to undercover officers or informants) and using it to make arrests, prosecute offenders, and seize their assets. Sometimes the distribution networks sell drugs wholesale in a defined geographical area, in which case a successful investigation may rid an area (temporarily) of drugs. But the investigation's objective is primarily to remove specific dealers and shut down distribution networks, and only secondarily to control drug use.

Education strategies focus on members of the public who are at risk of becoming drug users, typically children and young adults. Though this at-risk population may be concentrated in a specific area, the objective is to affect the behavior of the people getting the education rather than to eradicate drug dealing in a particular locale.

Finally, patrol strategies are designed to control drug abuse and dealing in a defined geographical area: a neighborhood, the vicinity of a school, a shopping center, and so forth. Patrol officers are usually deployed geographically by beats, precincts, and districts. Consequently they focus on drug market problems that occur in these areas. Though their tactics may involve arresting dealers and educating the public, their objective is to control drug abuse and dealing in their assigned areas.

Investigative strategies

What has been called the drug distribution pipeline is, in reality, a network of many interconnected delivery systems. One supply network that provides drugs to a city or large metropolitan area may consist of many overlapping pipelines, representing dealers at different levels, who cooperate in shifting alliances. This description is particularly apt for the traffic in cocaine. Because cocaine is dominant among law enforcement problems, the discussion of investigative strategies will focus on traffic in that drug.

Drug distribution pipelines are complex because of the multiple dealers and multiple levels that hook together in convoluted supply arrangements. For the flow of drugs to be interrupted for any length of time, each dealing network must be dismantled.

One critical group of domestic traffickers are those who forge a link between importers at one end of the pipeline and street sellers at the other, constituting the intermediate segments of the pipeline. These traffickers, known as drug *wholesalers*,[17] buy from importers and sell to other dealers further along the distribution chain.[18] Wholesalers who buy at the top levels of distribution systems occasionally sell their drugs directly to retailers, but typically they sell to other wholesalers one or two links farther along the distribution pathway.

At first glance, such an extended distribution system—with from two to as many as five different wholesale levels—appears unusually cumbersome, especially when compared with legitimate industries, which usually get by with one intermediate level. The reason for the multiplicity of levels lies in the illicit nature of drug trafficking, with the ever-present threat of police intervention. To reduce the threat of arrest and incarceration, dealers try to sell to other dealers as high in the distribution chain as possible, where police tend to penetrate less frequently, rather than at or just above the retail level, where police and their informants often saturate drug markets.[19] Therefore, these multiple layers of wholesalers provide layers of protection from detection and arrest. They also add to the cost of drugs, as each wholesaler dilutes the drug's purity (adding filler to increase its bulk) and appropriately marks up the price of the adulterated drugs. Nevertheless, the layers—with the inefficiencies they produce—remain because they are one of the major defense mechanisms that dealers have against the perils in their business environment.

This discussion is not intended either to make wholesalers seem more important than retailers or to argue for targeting one level rather than another. Both wholesalers and retailers are tightly bound together by a common interest and form loose but enduring distribution networks. Because of their interdependence, retailers and each wholesale level operating in the jurisdiction should all be targeted for investigative attention. As the following discussion notes, it is possible simultaneously to pursue strategies aimed at both retail and various wholesale levels—and strategies aimed at the pipeline networks that loosely unite them.

Analyzing the trafficking situation

A balanced investigative strategy should begin with an analysis of the local drug trafficking situation. That entails identifying the organized networks of both wholesalers and retailers, as well as the solo wholesale dealers operating in the jurisdiction.

Federal enforcement attention has focused on high-level drug suppliers—the foreign sources of production and export, domestic importers, and the upper-level (first-tier) wholesalers they supply. In contrast, local police have tended to focus on visible street-level retailers rather than the more anonymous wholesalers who supply them.[20] One effect of this division of effort has been that wholesalers in the middle range often have remained relatively immune to detection and arrest.

A balanced investigative strategy should begin with an analysis of the local drug trafficking situation. That entails identifying the organized networks of both wholesalers and retailers, as well as the solo wholesale dealers operating in the jurisdiction.

As a response to the challenge of providing investigative coverage all along the drug pipeline, formal interagency cooperative arrangements have been developed. Federal drug task forces, started by the Bureau of Narcotics and Dangerous Drugs in 1970, were the first joint responses. They were formed primarily to fill the enforcement vacuum involving mid-level wholesalers whose mobility was such that investigators had to follow them from city to city. However, later developments—such as mushrooming drug production and the attendant dropping of wholesale prices—resulted in an addition of thousands to the ranks of wholesalers at all levels. These numbers severely strain the enforcement capacities of agencies at all levels of government and can quickly lead to substantial gaps in coverage of key dealing levels. Clearly, investigators need to find a way to allocate their resources and target traffickers according to objective criteria that take into account the harm they create, the various levels of dealers, and the various dealing styles.

Need for objective targeting criteria   The criterion typically used to determine the importance of a dealer is the *quantity* of drugs he or she supplies—or claims to be able to supply—at any one time. By this criterion, a wholesaler who deals kilos is a more highly prized target than one who deals ounces. But the explosive growth of cocaine traffic makes it difficult to justify a targeting mechanism that assigns weight only to dealing quantity. Cocaine wholesalers typically buy quantities from their suppliers on the basis of the amount each customer wants. The quantities can shift from day to day as the mix of customers, their respective needs, enforcement pressures, and supplier connections are all factored in.

Other criteria used to set enforcement priorities are leadership positions in distribution organizations, international connections, and involvement in violence.

Unfortunately, because of the dynamics of contemporary drug traffic, suspects are often targeted on the basis of informal and sometimes subjective criteria—mainly, what self-serving informants tell investigators. These criteria often lead investigators to pursue "targets of opportunity"—those dealers who practically select themselves for investigation because of their greed or stupidity. It goes without saying that hundreds of arrests of targets of opportunity do not make up a departmental strategy—at least not a rational one.

Although the removal of stupid, greedy, or just plain unlucky drug dealers from active dealing has some merit, the wholesalers whose styles are more cautious and conservative tend to stay in business.

Cautions about depending on informants   Before moving on to enforcement strategies that do not depend primarily on "targets of opportunity," it may be useful to examine the reasons that informant-based strategies are so ingrained.[21] To maximize their use of time and resources, investigators usually take the most direct paths available in their targeting of traffickers. Usually that means going where the most recent information happens to take them. Often, this means following up the intelligence that their informants feed them—and trying, with limited available resources, to cultivate new informants.

Furthermore, when police resources are limited and the police are pressured to produce many arrests quickly, the obvious result is a hastily crafted response. Its major characteristic is that cases develop from information that is relatively inexpensive to obtain—that is, information obtained from informants. Put simply, in this situation quantity becomes favored over quality, as limited resources lead investigators to use informants and make large numbers of easy arrests.

If an investigator blindly follows the direction in which his or her informant has pointed, the investigator risks being steered away from targets the informant wants to shield and toward those targets' competitors and enemies.

But the limitations of such an enforcement approach are profound. Informants point investigators toward targets, and if investigators are dependent on their informants for direction, informants influence the scope and often the outcomes of investigations. If an investigator blindly follows the direction in which his or her informant has pointed, the investigator risks being steered away from targets the informant wants to shield and toward those targets' competitors and enemies. The cumulative effects of such informant-based cases are unknown, but it is hard to believe that this investigative strategy has any real effect on drug traffic.[22] Investigative managers must be watchful that longer-term objectives and not the prejudices of individual informants govern the overall direction of drug investigations as well as the selection of individual cases.

Determination of harm and strategies of attack

After surveying the principal dealing levels and operating styles in the community, the manager should determine what aspects of the wholesaling network create the greatest harm in a given locale. Two aspects of harm need to be addressed: wholesalers' contribution to the spread of drugs, and their promotion of violence. Wholesalers who are attempting to expand their market are more harmful than wholesalers who are content with an existing market because the former can encourage drug abuse among people who are not users or can increase use among recreational users. Wholesalers who promote violence (either directly or indirectly) to protect or expand their markets are more harmful than those who do not.

Priorities need to be set on the basis of these criteria. Unless harm is explicitly taken into account when targeting decisions are made, drug investigators may inadvertently focus attention on less-harmful traffickers and thereby blunt the effectiveness of police efforts. By targeting the most harmful wholesalers, police can reduce the pernicious effects of drug abuse as much as possible.

After using an objective process for targeting the most harmful wholesalers for investigation, managers must then turn to the most appropriate strategy for apprehending them. A number of targeting mechanisms are available; some emphasize the trafficker's role or rank in a distribution organization, and others rely solely on the volume of drugs that a trafficker is known to handle or purports to be able to supply. The appropriateness of a strategy depends on such factors as the level of trafficking (near the street, in the mid-level range, or near importation) and the style of dealing (aggressive or careful).

A coherent investigative strategy must be based on an understanding of the behavior of the most harmful drug wholesalers operating in the locality and should identify opportunities and vulnerabilities among the trafficking population. If the department cannot exploit these leads alone, then another agency or task force might be able to do so. Wholesale levels that extend beyond the reach of a single department's resources should become the topic of an immediate meeting with regional drug squad personnel, state police narcotics commanders, and the local office of the Drug Enforcement Administration (DEA).

Finding and exploiting dealer weaknesses

To arrest wholesalers, the police seek to transform dealers' apparent strengths into weaknesses. The weaknesses come from two important factors: a surplus of wholesalers and an abundance of drugs. Both factors mean that wholesalers face highly competitive markets with limited opportunities to expand their customer base and with increased risks of detection if they expand too quickly. As has been said before, police managers need to understand the dynamics of drug markets to create opportunities for inflicting more than fleeting damage on trafficking operations.

Targeting aggressive wholesalers   In a highly competitive drug market, the search for new customers—whether retailers or other wholesalers—tends to be aggressive, often frantic. The glut of drugs on the market forces wholesale prices (and thus profit margins) down all along the distribution pipeline, but especially at the higher and middle levels, where profit margins are slimmer. To increase their profits, some aggressive wholesalers buy large quantities from high-level suppliers, dilute and mark up the drugs, then bypass one or more intermediate wholesale levels, and sell the drugs much lower in the distribution chain than they had before. Sometimes, such wholesalers become retailers. The reason for buying high and skipping intermediate wholesale levels is to share more fully in the steep markup that occurs at the lowest wholesale and street retail levels. That is where profit margins are greatest, so that is where an increasing number of wholesalers reposition themselves to serve customers.

But wholesalers who bypass intermediate levels take extraordinary risks, because it is at the lowest end of the chain that local police presence is greatest. Further, DEA and regional police task forces concentrate on the wholesale levels one or two notches above the street.

Such "bypass" behavior by wholesalers may seem irrational because it increases the dealers' chances of being caught. However, the dealers are no doubt aware of the lopsided ratio of their numbers to the complement of investigators trying to catch them and know that the probability of arrest is low. In addition, if a wholesaler is caught for selling drugs broken down into small quantities and the police mistake him or her for a street retailer, the penalty may turn out to be very light. Overcrowded jails and prisons make it difficult to justify large penalties for small dealers.

Drug dealers at all levels are aggressive, profit-motivated entrepreneurs, so dazzled by the allure of quick wealth that their brazen behavior self-selects them as enforcement targets. The question of whether police should consciously pass up such easy targets is difficult to address, for dealers who virtually invite arrest will end up being arrested. The point is that drug market forces and dealer operating styles join together as pressures that help shape the nature of the police response.

Very often, however, the strategies that make up the police response take shape without adequate reflection on alternative responses that might be more effective or on combinations of responses that parallel the dealing styles that operate in the locality. One example of a possible response to aggressive dealers is "buy-bust."

The "buy-bust" enforcement technique was developed and has become widely accepted as a response to the prevalence of stranger-to-stranger transactions in the drug underworld. In part, its popularity is due to the aggressive marketing behavior of wholesalers, which makes it much easier to introduce those dealers to undercover investigators or their informants. Buy-bust may appear to work effectively because it results in so many "open and shut" cases against wholesale dealers—and street retailers, as well. Cultivation of informants and undercover drug "buys" are made easier by the market conditions discussed earlier. Also, the payments to informants to "set up" buy-bust situations are relatively modest and usually within the capabilities of most departmental informant funds.

Drug dealers at all levels are aggressive, profit-motivated entrepreneurs, so dazzled by the allure of quick wealth that their brazen behavior self-selects them as enforcement targets. The question of whether police should consciously pass up such easy targets is difficult to address, for dealers who virtually invite arrest will end up being arrested.

The popularity of such tactics as buy-bust should not exempt them from critical examination. The first question should be whether a concern for quality cases has been compromised by the volume arrests encouraged by the buy-bust approach. Usually, buy-bust works best against relatively low-level solo dealers seeking to unload their drugs as quickly as possible. But hundreds, even thousands, of such arrests may simply scratch the surface of the dealers who prefer that mode and may leave more cautious and high-level wholesalers untouched. Even when a major trafficker is caught, lack of intelligence information and of follow-up investigative work may make it impossible for police to know that that is what their arrestee is.

The main point is that widespread use of one enforcement tactic alone runs the risk that large numbers of one type of dealer alone will be captured. By implication, this limited approach permits other types of dealers to avoid detection and arrest.

Targeting "sleepers" There are investigative strategies to detect and target other types of wholesalers besides the aggressive ones. Although such techniques may take more time and consume more investigative resources than buy-bust, it is important that departments try to incorporate them or work with interagency task forces to ensure that at least someone targets the more cautious and less-visible dealers. Otherwise, the mass removal of aggressive dealers through buy-bust operations ends up creating a vacuum into which more cautious dealers will move. A comprehensive strategy that spreads the risks of arrest and incarceration fairly evenly across all dealing styles should have the effect of encouraging current dealers to retire and discouraging new dealers from beginning.

Some investigators view cautious wholesalers as "survivors" whose turn at becoming a target will come sooner or later. Others call them "sleepers" and have developed strategies for smoking out these dealers through indirect means, such as intelligence collection and financial profiling, that are every bit as plodding and cautious as the evasive tactics the dealers themselves use. Investigations of these wholesalers start with the reconstruction of past drug deals and of past purchases of assets rather than with intelligence and undercover buys planned in advance by police. Documentation of the critical past events is usually facilitated either by an informant or, better still, by a co-conspirator who was captured in a buy-bust or other type of investigation.

The two principal investigative techniques for reconstructing past events are (1) use of the grand jury as an investigative tool (for example, granting immunity to associates and employees to get them to talk) and (2) financial investigations of the dealer's hidden illegal wealth or off-record ownership of businesses and business assets. Electronic surveillance and wiretaps are used against wholesalers and suppliers who communicate with each other by telephone to arrange shipments, provide for payment terms, or launder drug proceeds. These techniques appear to work well in situations where the dealers are fairly well established in the community, which means they are fairly stationary for long enough periods to establish their "offices."

Other innovative investigative techniques spring from local dealing conditions and the ingenuity of local and federal investigators in responding to those conditions (see the accompanying sidebar).

Recap   Whether targeting aggressive or risk-averse wholesalers, the principle is the same: identify the strengths of the wholesaler and turn them into weaknesses. In the case of aggressive wholesalers, the strength is the high

---

Innovative investigation techniques   Drug investigators have used a number of unusual techniques to accomplish their goals. Special "secret witness" funds have been created to compensate informants who provide information on high-level dealers. Such rewards tend to exceed the dollar amounts available from department resources to pay informants. For example, the "silent witness" funds in Phoenix and in Broward County, Florida, have been supported, respectively, by an involved business community and an aggressive forfeiture program that turned hundreds of thousands of dollars back into the drug enforcement budget. In those examples, alternative sources of informant payments enabled the departments to attract information on wholesalers who were operating at very high levels in the locality. Many of those dealers had not come to the attention of the department through the debriefing of regular department informants.

In Broward County, investigators built relationships with cooperating proprietors to target transient dealers, their couriers, and others whose unusual behavior in hotels, motels, and rental apartments called for police attention. In many cases, landlords passed information on to police about people who inquired about short-term apartment sublets for high cash payments—and with no questions asked.

In Baltimore, police targeted murder-for-hire activity, particularly that undertaken by hired assassins who worked for entrenched heroin wholesalers. Those dealers were anxious about the possibility of "unauthorized" young aggressive dealers moving into vacuums left when older, established wholesalers were convicted and imprisoned. Cases against low-level assassins led to the major dealers who had hired them and who had been difficult to apprehend on drug-related charges.

profits made through many sales. The volume of sales means that the wholesaler will screen clients less thoroughly and make sales faster. Undercover investigators and informants can, therefore, make cases against such wholesalers relatively easily, if the investigators know who they are going after.

In the case of sleepers, their strength is in separating themselves from street dealing by selling to a small number of known individuals. Against these wholesalers, building conspiracy cases makes the most sense. By targeting their associates and turning them into informants and by using electronic surveillance, wiretaps, and financial investigations, the police can bring cases against sleepers. But such cases can be made only if intelligence information is routinely mined to determine who is wholesaling, what market forces are at work, and what level of risk wholesalers are willing to take.

Education strategies

Though traditionally the police have focused on supply strategies through investigative techniques, police departments have increasingly developed programs for preventing drug abuse. School-based drug education programs are now widely used, but other prevention programs are also needed, especially community-based programs for youths.

School-based drug use prevention programs

The two best-known school-based antidrug education programs are DARE (Drug Abuse Resistance Education), developed by the Los Angeles police department and the Unified Los Angeles School District, and SPECDA (School Program to Educate and Control Drug Abuse), developed by the New York City police department and board of education.[23] Although both programs are in very large departments, elements of the programs can be adapted by departments of all sizes.

In both programs, police officers are sent to elementary schools to serve as full-time instructors. They teach a series of fifth- and sixth-grade classes that provide facts about drug abuse, show students how to resist offers of drugs, promote self-esteem, and convey decision-making skills. In both types of programs, the police work closely with the school system.

Use of police officers to teach antidrug classes seems to be particularly beneficial for elementary school children. However, as children grow into teenagers and increasingly question authority, police officers may not be the best promoters of antidrug messages in schools.

Evaluations of these programs indicate that they are successful. Students who have attended these classes are more likely to know about the harmful effects of drugs, to report that they will not use drugs, and to have higher self-esteem than students from the same grades who did not attend these classes. Further, a comparison of seventh-graders who attended DARE classes in the sixth grade with seventh-grade students who did not attend DARE classes shows that DARE students reported less use of drugs in the year following the course.[24]

Use of police officers to teach antidrug classes seems to be particularly beneficial for elementary school children. However, as children grow into teenagers and increasingly question authority, police officers may not be the best promoters of antidrug messages in schools. The attitudes that peers and others in the neighborhood have toward drugs will become increasingly important.[25]

Youth drug use prevention in the community

Many police argue that, to prevent the spread of drugs, it is vitally important to remove drug dealers who serve as role models for youths. In addition, some departments, such as the Tulsa police department, have attempted to introduce positive role models into drug-infested neighborhoods: either police officers themselves or local celebrities or other well-known citizens who can command respect by virtue of their personal authority, experiences, and achievements. The Metro-Dade (Florida) police department's Police Athletic League engages youths in time- and energy-consuming activities that keep them out of trouble. Not only police officers but also local celebrity volunteers are engaged to serve as role models and help spread an antidrug message.

Peers may be effective communicators because their audiences can readily identify with them. Particularly effective are peers who can talk about their personal problems with drugs and the mistakes they have made.[26]

But, as an Urban Institute report on inner-city adolescent drug use points out, "Exaggeration of the risks of drug use may undermine the credibility of both the message and the messenger; it may even reverse the intended effect."[27] In this regard, the report also points out that the credibility of antidrug messages can be enhanced if the relative risks of different drugs are discussed. If all drugs are portrayed as equally harmful, young people are less likely to perceive the message as being credible: "To the extent that experimentation with alcohol or marijuana—two mildly psychoactive drugs—is placed in the same category as PCP or crack—much more potent substances—credibility will be lost and the risks of using the more dangerous substances [will be] downgraded."[28]

Adult drug use prevention programs

Though a variety of programs exist to divert children and teenagers from drug abuse, methods for preventing drug abuse among adults have received relatively less attention. Drug use prevention messages and materials have been incorporated into Neighborhood Watch and other community programs,[29] but the effectiveness of presentations that describe to adults the harmful consequences of drugs and that display samples and pictures of drugs and drug paraphernalia is unknown. Though these programs may provide valuable and convincing information, they also may be directed at people who are unlikely to become involved in drug abuse in any case.

A mixture of educational and punitive approaches to drug use prevention is being applied in Maricopa County, Arizona, under the joint administration of the Maricopa County sheriff's department, the Phoenix police department, the county attorney's office, and other local, state, and federal law enforcement agencies. Under this program, television, bus, newspaper, and billboard advertisements warn casual drug users with the message "Do Drugs—Do Time!"[30] People found by police officers and sheriff's deputies to possess even small quantities of drugs are arrested and jailed for a short period. The prosecutor then gives defendants with no prior arrests a choice of enrolling in (and paying for) drug treatment and education or being prosecuted and facing the risk of going to jail. Though this program has received a great deal of attention, its effects have not yet been evaluated.

Patrol strategies

Antidrug patrol strategies can be divided into three groups according to the method of deploying patrol officers. One patrol strategy is to create a special patrol unit that can move in and out of areas rapidly. Another is to establish foot patrol units in densely populated areas with high concentrations of drug abuse. The third is to rely on the regular patrol force to control drugs on their beats.

Special patrol units

For antidrug efforts, special patrol units are composed of a group of officers who can be moved into an area quickly to carry out a tactical operation and who then leave. Each area they move into is usually small (a block or a housing project, for example), and they stay there for a short time (varying from a few hours to several weeks). Such units are usually enforcement oriented. The types of tactics they use include saturation patrolling, street sweeps, street-level "stings," and problem-solving tactics.

Saturation patrolling   Saturation patrolling involves the use of many officers to deter drug dealers from selling in open markets and drug buyers from making contacts with dealers. It is often augmented by increased identification contacts with people walking or driving through the area. These contacts can include field interrogations, parking enforcement, traffic enforcement, and trespass enforcement. Because the deployment of a large number of officers in an area is costly, only a few areas can be covered at any one time. Consequently, the concentration of officers in one area cannot be maintained for very long. And once patrol levels decrease to normal levels, drug dealing is likely to return unless other things have been done to prevent this (see "Problem-solving tactics" below).

Street sweeps   Like saturation patrolling, street sweeps involve the use of many officers in an area for a short period. But instead of trying to deter drug dealers and users, the objective is to arrest as many as possible. Consequently, street sweeps are launched as a surprise raid on an area and are of much shorter duration, lasting just long enough to identify and arrest the users and dealers, collect evidence, and remove the arrestees from the area.

As with all raids, careful planning is required to reduce the chances of injuring officers and citizens, arresting innocent people, and allowing offenders to escape. Moreover, if local jails are crowded, if the drug charges are relatively minor, or if prosecutors have not been included in the planning process, there is a good chance that most of the arrestees will be released within a few days, if not hours, of the sweep. Under these conditions, the dealers and users may return to the same area relatively quickly.

Street-level reverse buys ("stings")   In reverse buys, or "stings," undercover officers sell drugs (or drug look-alikes) to purchasers and then arrest the purchasers on a charge of attempted drug purchasing. The purpose of reverse buys is to deter users from making drug purchases in an area. A standard procedure is for one group of officers to conduct a street sweep and remove the dealers from a known drug location. Then a second group of officers, posing as drug dealers, replaces the real dealers. A third group—a surveillance team—provides nearby security and documents transactions on videotape. On the outer perimeter of the reverse buy, a fourth group—uniformed officers—waits to capture drug users after they have made a purchase. A fifth group of officers handles a field booking and prisoner-holding facility. After the purchase, the surveillance team informs the uniformed officers and gives them a description of the car and the drug purchaser. The uniformed officers stop the purchaser a safe distance from the dealing site, make an arrest, take the drugs for evidence, and (if state law allows) seize the car on the grounds that it was used to further a crime.

Reverse buys are dangerous (some authorities insist that because a car is a potential danger to officers, the buyer should be required to leave his or her car to buy the drug and should then be immediately arrested).[31] These operations are also labor intensive and complex and require a great deal of training and planning. Like sweeps, they have to be moved frequently.

Reverse buys are probably most effective when (1) users come from areas far from the reverse-buy site (so they do not notice the initial sweep and switch); (2) users communicate with each other after the operation (so word is spread that the police are arresting users); and (3) buyers have a limited ability to determine whether the police are posing as dealers once the operation has ended (so that they are discouraged from returning). To deter drug buyers as much as possible, police try to publicize the use of the reverse-buy tactic. If any of these conditions is not met, this type of operation will have little or no lasting effect on users and will be no more effective than a sweep.

Problem-solving tactics   Unlike the three tactics just described, which involve standard practices applied to diverse sets of circumstances, problem-solving tactics are tailored to the special needs of the drug problem the unit is addressing. Officers conduct a careful analysis of the drug problem to determine the factors that create it and to discover methods for handling it. On the basis of this analysis, a set of objectives is established and a set of tactics selected to achieve the objectives. The tactics may involve the enforcement measures mentioned above, but they may also involve public education, changes in environmental design, collaboration with other public agencies, and community organizing. Though not developed to deal exclusively with drug problems, the Baltimore County police department's COPE units are a good example of problem-solving units.[32] Because such a unit seeks to change underlying conditions that foster drug problems, the solutions it implements may be long lasting. However, if the solution requires regular patrol to carry on once the special patrol unit has moved to a new problem somewhere else, then regular beat officers will need to be involved in the problem solving from the beginning. Otherwise they are unlikely to take personal ownership of the solution or to carry out the plan fully.

Strengths and weaknesses of special patrol units   These four special patrol unit tactics can be used by regular patrol officers, as well. Because the first three tactics are very labor intensive—requiring many officers in a small area for the duration of the operation—their routine use by regular patrol units is difficult. Concentrating a substantial portion of the patrol force in one small area may be possible on occasion, but doing so day after day may create difficulties in delivering other police services. Further, if saturation patrols, sweeps, and reverse buys are to be used routinely, the officers using these tactics will need special training. Training a small dedicated unit is less expensive than training the entire patrol force. Regular patrol officers can routinely engage in problem solving, however, as is discussed in greater detail below and in the chapter on patrol.

Special antidrug patrol units, regardless of tactic, suffer a serious limitation: their effect on their target areas is often fleeting. Without a sustained commitment on the part of the police or a change in the conditions that gave rise to the drug problem in the area, the drug problem is likely to return to its former level.

Special antidrug patrol units, regardless of tactic, suffer a serious limitation: their effect on their target areas is often fleeting. Drug dealing can be suppressed for short periods, possibly even beyond the time of the tactical operation. (There is some evidence that the beneficial effects of these tactical operations may last for a period after the "crackdown" has stopped.)[33] But without a sustained commitment on the part of the police or a change in the conditions that gave rise to the drug problem in the area, the drug problem is likely to return to its former level. Of the four tactics discussed above, only problem solving makes an attempt to change the underlying conditions. Thus, special unit approaches should be used to augment ongoing foot patrol and routine antidrug operations by regular patrol officers. These two approaches can "hold" territory and create changes in underlying conditions, whereas special units (not using problem-solving tactics) cannot.

Foot patrol units

Deploying officers on foot in high-density residential and commercial areas provides a continuous police presence that special patrol units cannot provide. The relevant feature of foot patrol units is not that their officers walk instead of drive (in many departments, foot patrol officers have cars available) but that they are assigned to a very small geographical area and do not necessarily have to answer calls for service. Thus they can spend more time meeting the residents, business people, and others who frequent the area. Foot patrol officers can help organize communities to develop the competence to protect themselves from drug dealers. Such officers can also deliver crime prevention and antidrug training and develop information networks that may facilitate the reduction of drug dealing and abuse in their beats.

Though there is evidence that the public feels safer when foot patrol officers are deployed, the evidence about whether crime is suppressed when officers are deployed on foot to small geographical areas and are freed from handling calls is contradictory.[34] Anecdotal evidence suggests that this deployment strategy can indeed reduce drug problems, but the single rigorous evaluation of the impact of this strategy on drugs found that foot patrols had little effect either on citizens' perceptions of safety or on drug problems.[35]

Deployment of foot patrol officers may be particularly useful in reducing drug problems in public housing complexes, neighborhoods with many low-income apartments, and mixed commercial and residential neighborhoods.

However, when police managers give foot patrol officers problem-solving training and direct them to address problems on their beats, drug problems can sometimes be reduced dramatically (see the chapter on patrol for a more detailed description of problem solving). Officers of the Community Police Officer Program (CPOP) in New York City have demonstrated a great deal of success in eliminating street drug markets and other drug problems in this way.[36] Similarly, officers assigned to foot patrol in and around housing projects in Philadelphia, Tampa, and Tulsa have been able to make substantial inroads in drug problems by using problem-solving methods.[37]

The principal difficulty with foot patrol operations is that they are relatively expensive: one or two officers are dedicated to a small area that also receives the services of the routine patrol force that covers the wider community. This means that a police department will usually be able to afford to use foot patrol officers only in a small proportion of its beats. Further, once foot patrols are established, removing them is difficult. Even if foot patrols are no longer needed to suppress drug problems in an area, they are generally so popular with local residents and businesses that their redeployment to neighborhoods with greater problems creates major difficulties.[38]

Still, problem-solving foot patrols may be worth the costs in densely populated neighborhoods where public areas are plagued by drugs. Deployment of foot patrol officers may be particularly useful in reducing drug problems in public housing complexes, neighborhoods with many low-income apartments, and mixed commercial and residential neighborhoods. In addition, because foot patrol officers have greater opportunities than car-bound patrol personnel do to meet people on their beats, they may be especially useful in areas in which the residents are suspicious of the police. Locals who would be unwilling to report drug problems to an anonymous officer may be more willing to work with someone they have come to know.

Regular patrol strategies

To form special units and foot patrols, patrol officers are separated from regular patrol squads. Except in the gravest crises, special units and foot patrols do not have to handle emergency calls for service, and they report through a separate chain of command. But because special units and foot patrols are staffed by officers who are removed from regular patrol squads, fewer officers are left to handle calls, and regular patrol officers perceive that their workloads increase. Furthermore, because special unit officers and foot patrol officers are separate and their work is atypical (highly aggressive in the case of special units, highly community-focused in the case of foot patrol officers), they receive a great deal of attention inside and outside the police department. Both the perception of increased workloads and the attention given to the separate groups can create friction between the separate groups of officers and the regular patrol officers.[39] Yet collaboration among these various groups is essential, so the friction must be considered one of the costs of deploying officers in separate groups.

Another cost is that the ability of regular patrol to handle drug problems can be undermined if police managers remove officers from regular patrol to handle these problems as part of a special unit or a foot patrol unit. The fewer officers available, the more calls each officer will have to handle, decreasing the time available to address drug problems and making it appear that the only sensible approach is to create additional special units. This can create a downward spiral in patrol effectiveness, as patrol is stripped of even more officers and becomes even more tied to call handling. The only way to break this cycle is to add many more officers or to rethink the way patrol handles drug problems.

Regular patrol officers can attack the conditions that give rise to drug problems by identifying drug-related problems occurring on their beats.[40] These problems may include drug-dealing locations, drug-involved domestic disturbances, drug-related crime patterns, youths who are particularly vulnerable to drug abuse, disorder problems stemming from dealing and using, failures in the provision of other government services, and so forth.

Once drug-related problems are identified, officers should investigate the underlying circumstances. Such investigations will have to tap the expertise of other police officers, police records, local residents and businesses, offenders, other public agencies, and anyone else who can reveal information that may help form a response to the problem. Officers should determine why the problem is at one location instead of at some similar site. They should find out why particular groups of people (victims, offenders, others) are involved in the problem. They need to investigate how the physical environment and social context foster drug problems. And officers should document existing police and other efforts to deal with the problems and their symptoms.

After the problem is described, a number of remedial options should become apparent. Working with other members of the police department, other city agencies, and the public, officers develop ways of managing drug problems on their beats. The response to the problem may involve selectively applying tra-

A community approach to street-level narcotics enforcement The Des Moines police department enlisted the help of neighborhood groups to tackle the proliferation of street dealers and crack houses in the city. Residents of areas where drug dealers worked met with officers, provided information on possible criminal activities, and proposed countermeasures.

These efforts resulted in the publication of a community handbook providing resources to help citizens combat drug-related activity in their neighborhoods. The handbook contains the following:

1. Guidelines for citizen action: notifying the police of suspicious behavior, working with landlords and businesses, getting to know patrol officers, involving elected representatives

2. Model letters that citizens can send to owners of vehicles seen in the vicinity of known illegal activity

3. Instructions for posting "no trespassing" and "no loitering" signs and authorizing police to arrest anyone who disobeys them

4. Phone numbers of agencies that can provide "no parking" signs, trim trees and shrubbery that obscure visibility, improve street lighting, board up abandoned houses, and correct other deficiencies that may increase the opportunity for crime

5. Tips on organizing a neighborhood association, including suggested meeting agendas, group activities, and publicity ideas.

Source: Des Moines Police, *Drugs: A "Municipal Approach,"* produced jointly with the United Way of Central Iowa and local neighborhood associations, 1990.

ditional enforcement techniques (such as undercover investigations, buy-bust tactics, street sweeps, and other tactics discussed earlier), but it is also likely to require a broader approach. Traffickers may be identified with the assistance of a citizens' group whose members are trained to look for and report drug dealing in their neighborhood. Apartment managers can be encouraged to enforce lease provisions, thus forcing drug dealers out of the buildings. Social service agencies can be steered toward people in need. Departments responsible for such services as roads, sanitation, or code enforcement can be mobilized to redirect traffic patterns, clean up vacant lots, and tear down abandoned buildings used by drug dealers. In some circumstances, officers may be able to get others, including government agencies, private enterprises, or citizens' groups, to take over the response to the problem. In other cases, officers may have to stay involved for longer periods of time.

The final step in this problem-solving process is for officers to assess the effect of their responses to the drug problems. Officers should look for evidence that the harm created by the problems has been reduced. They should also look for displacement and other unintended consequences of their efforts.[41]

This process requires officers to have stable beats and shift schedules so they can learn about problems and have enough time to address them. Officers must be given the authority as well as the responsibility to address the problems on their beats. Special units that moved into an area, carried out an assignment, and then left should be available to provide support at the request of beat officers—but the beat officer who addresses a drug problem remains in place and thus is able to try to minimize the chances that the problem will return.

Some of the difficulties with this approach are obvious. It requires changing the nature of regular patrol work from handling calls to handling problems. This requires new training, new performance measures, and new supervisory practices. It also requires that police managers free up officers' time through differential police response strategies.[42]

Despite its challenges, a number of police chiefs and researchers believe that a problem-oriented approach to patrol drug enforcement has some distinct advantages over exclusive reliance on special units and foot patrols. First, the patrol force is not fragmented into separate groups that then need to be coordinated. Second, regular patrol officers remain in an area, so they can be a stabilizing influence long after special units will have departed. Third, regular officers can address problems over a larger area than foot patrol officers, so this strategy can be used throughout the jurisdiction.

Summary of patrol strategies

Patrol strategies against drugs are used principally for reducing drug problems in a discrete geographical area. Three types of strategies can be applied: special units, foot patrol, and regular patrol. Each has distinct strengths and weaknesses. A comprehensive antidrug strategy makes use of each of these approaches. All patrol officers are given the responsibility to solve drug problems in their beats. In small, densely populated areas with high levels of drug problems and a history of antagonism to police, regular patrol is implemented by foot patrol. Finally, special units are available to carry out short-term tactical responses (saturation patrols, street sweeps, and reverse buys) to assist regular and foot patrol officers.

Performance measures

If a neighborhood is plagued with robberies, one can assess the effectiveness of police interventions to suppress robberies in the neighborhood by looking at reported robbery statistics. If citizens report fewer robberies after the intervention, the police can reasonably conclude that their antirobbery efforts paid off.

But citizens do not consistently report the existence of drug dealing networks, private transactions among teens, drug medical emergencies, or small indoor drug sales operations. Only after a problem becomes blatant and obviously disruptive do citizens call the police to complain. And they call only if they believe that (1) the problem is relatively serious; (2) the police are interested and will do something; and (3) the police are trustworthy. Moreover, when citizens do call, they may be calling about noise, trash, traffic congestion, crimes, and a host of other conditions or incidents that are not obviously drug related. Because drug crimes are consensual and hidden, police cannot rely solely on citizen reporting as a reliable measure of drug dealing levels. Measuring the effectiveness of antidrug efforts, therefore, is extremely difficult.

Among the measures used to assess the effectiveness of these programs are arrest rates, amount of drugs seized or assets forfeited, and number of children exposed to antidrug programs. But these statistics do not in fact measure the *results* of antidrug programs. Instead, these numbers measure *activities*—and they can be easily manipulated to make antidrug efforts look successful. For example, changes in drug arrests do not necessarily show that drug abuse and dealing are increasing or decreasing; they may reveal changes in police efforts to control drugs. Creating a squad of officers to disrupt street drug markets very likely will increase the number of arrests, but this does not mean that the drug problem has increased or decreased. Similarly, measuring the amount of drugs seized (either in dollars or in weight) does not help police managers understand whether antidrug efforts are having an effect on the problem. It suggests only that the police may be better at finding and counting drugs (for example, instead of destroying small amounts of drugs found or seized without measuring them, police officers may record every bit of the seized substances, thereby increasing their performance statistics). Using assets forfeited as a performance measure focuses drug investigators' attention on traffickers with many assets that are easy to seize and acquire through forfeiture proceedings. Counting the number of elementary school students who received drug resistance training does not indicate whether these children are less likely to use drugs later in life.

Developing objectives

Instead of focusing on global measures of performance, managers of antidrug efforts should develop objectives for very specific problems and should determine how well antidrug efforts are doing at reducing these problems and meeting these objectives.

For patrol officers and supervisors—whether assigned to a special unit, foot patrols, or regular patrol shifts—such problems would be based on geography: dealing locations, drug-infested housing and apartment complexes, businesses that indirectly support drug trafficking, areas where users congregate and disturb others, drug-related neighborhood crime patterns, repeat call locations, and so forth. Instead of measuring performance by counting the number of drug arrests a patrol unit makes, a patrol manager might determine that the principal drug problem in his or her officers' area is—for example—a dealer selling out of an apartment. The objective of the patrol unit would be to stop the dealer's drug sales. The performance measure would be whether the dealer was still selling drugs at the end of the police operation.

Instead of focusing on global measures of performance, managers of antidrug efforts should develop objectives for very specific problems and should determine how well antidrug efforts are doing at reducing these problems and meeting these objectives.

For investigative units, problems would be defined as networks of drug dealers, wholesalers, and traffickers. Instead of counting the amount of drugs seized or assets forfeited, a drug investigation unit might use intelligence information to identify the most harmful networks based on a number of factors: volume of drugs dealt; drug type (for example, crack versus marijuana); drug purity; use of violence; vulnerability of customers (for example, new users versus established addicts); extent to which the networks support the activities of other traffickers (for example, by laundering money, specializing in transportation, corrupting officials, or providing enforcers); and other factors. The objective might be to substantially reduce the ability of the largest network to transport and wholesale drugs in the area. Related performance measures might include intelligence information showing that lower-level dealers can no longer obtain drugs from this source.

For drug education officers, problems would be defined as the conditions that put groups of individuals at high risk of becoming involved—or more deeply involved—in drug abuse. Instead of counting the number of children attending antidrug classes, a drug education unit might consult social agencies, medical authorities, schools, housing officials, and other police officials so they can focus on specific subpopulations with specific educational needs. Such groups may include elementary school children or pregnant women living in neighborhoods where drug abuse is rampant, teenage school drop-outs, and others. An objective might be to reduce the proportion of schoolchildren in a high-risk group who use drugs in subsequent years. The performance measure would be the proportion of these pupils who use drugs in later years compared with baseline estimates of drug use by children of similar age in previous years.

In each of these examples the police manager identifies a specific target problem, sets an objective that can be achieved, and establishes a measure of the unit's effectiveness in achieving that objective.

Developing measures of effectiveness

There is no single set of valid measures that can describe the success of local antidrug efforts. The measures selected to assess performance depend on the nature of the problems targeted and the objectives set for problem-solving efforts. For some problems, the measures may be very quantitative. For example, for assessing an effort directed at street robberies by crack addicts near a shopping area, an appropriate measure would be changes in the number of reported robberies at that locale. A drug education effort might be assessed by use of surveys of attendees to elicit self-reports of drug usage. Some survey techniques ensure reasonably candid responses.

For other problems, the appropriate measures may be qualitative. "Before" and "after" photos of a location could be used to demonstrate that drug dealers have left a street corner. The inability of informants to make drug purchases from members of a gang could indicate that the gang is being less aggressive in marketing its drugs in order to reduce its members' risk of apprehension. The disappearance of tablets of crack cocaine marked with a dealer's particular brand may indicate that the dealer's network has been substantially disrupted.

And for still other problems, impressionistic measures may be the best way of assessing results. For example, greater use of a park by children, parents, and the elderly may mean that the police were successful in ridding the area of the drug dealers and users who hung out there. Public opinion surveys addressing levels of fear of crime and perceptions of drug problems might also be useful in particular situations.

Information enabling the police to monitor drug problems can come from a number of sources. Local governments have access to a variety of data sets that can be used to analyze, evaluate, and forecast drug problems in the jurisdiction. With proper attention to security and privacy, the police—as well as local health, education, and other human-service agencies—can use this information to identify neighborhoods and subpopulations in need of assistance. Other useful information includes records relating to crime and other police matters, school disciplinary actions related to drugs, housing agency lease revocations based on drug offenses, drug-related automobile accidents, emergency medical calls, drug-related hospital admissions, medical examiners' findings, drug use treatment, employer drug test results, and other sources. At least three types of information are needed about the drug problems identified in all such records: (1) the nature of the drug involvement; (2) the geographical placement of the incident or subject; and (3) social, economic, and demographic characteristics of the subject or location. Exact addresses and some personal characteristics could be eliminated from a computerized data set to preserve confidentiality (see the chapter on information management). The police or some other government agency should collect, collate, and disseminate this kind of comprehensive information to help focus local government attention on the people and neighborhoods where antidrug efforts are most needed and to help develop drug abuse measures.

1   David F. Musto, *The American Disease. Origins of Narcotic Control* (New York: Oxford University Press, 1987). This is the single best source of information on the history of drug control in the United States.

2   Bernard Gropper, *Probing the Links between Drugs and Crime*, Research in Brief (Washington, DC: National Institute of Justice, 1985); and Jan Chaiken and Marcia Chaiken, "Drugs and Predatory Crime," in *Drugs and Crime*, ed. Michael Tonry and James Q. Wilson (Chicago: University of Chicago Press, 1990).

3   Federal Bureau of Investigation, *Crime in the United States* (Washington, DC: Federal Bureau of Investigation, published annually).

4   The National Prison Project, *Status Report: The Courts and Prisons—A Summary* (Washington, DC: The National Prison Project, 1989).

5   Bureau of Justice Statistics, *Prisoner in 1988* (Washington, DC: Bureau of Justice Statistics, 1989).

6   Peter Reuter, Gordon Crawford, and Jonathan Cave, *Sealing the Borders: The Effects of Increased Military Participation in Drug Interdiction* (Santa Monica, CA: Rand Corporation, 1988); and U.S. General Accounting Office, *Drug Smuggling:*

Capabilities for Interdicting Private Aircraft Are Limited and Costly (Washington, DC: U.S. General Accounting Office, 1989).

7   J. Michael Polich, Phyllis L. Erickson, Peter Reuter, and James P. Kahan, *Strategies for Controlling Adolescent Drug Use* (Santa Monica, CA: Rand Corporation, 1984).

8   National Narcotics Intelligence Consumers Committee, *The NNICC Report 1988: Supply of Illicit Drugs to the United States* (Washington, DC: National Narcotics Intelligence Consumers Committee, 1989).

9   Lloyd D. Johnston, Patrick M. O'Malley, and Jerald G. Bachman, *Drug Use, Drinking, and Smoking: National Survey Results from High School, College, and Young Adult Populations: 1975–1988* (Rockville, MD: National Institute on Drug Abuse, 1989).

10 National Institute on Drug Abuse, *Overview of the 1988 National Household Survey on Drug Abuse*, NIDA Capsules (Rockville, MD: National Institute on Drug Abuse, August 1989).

11 Lloyd D. Johnston, Patrick M. O'Malley, and Jerald G. Bachman, *Illicit Drug Use, Smoking, and Drinking by America's High School Students, College Students, and Young Adults: 1975–1987* (Rockville, MD: National Institute on Drug Abuse, 1988).

12 National Institute on Drug Abuse, *Use and Consequences of Cocaine*, NIDA Capsules (Rockville, MD: National Institute on Drug Abuse, August 1989).

13 National Institute on Drug Abuse, *National Household Survey on Drug Abuse: Main Findings 1985* (Rockville, MD: National Institute on Drug Abuse, 1988); and Johnston, O'Malley, and Bachman, *Illicit Drug Use, Smoking, and Drinking by America's High School Students, College Students, and Young Adults: 1975–1987*.

14 Office of Criminal Justice Plans and Analysis, *Homicide in the District of Columbia* (Washington, DC: Office of Criminal Justice Plans and Analysis, 1989).

15 Gerald David Jaynes and Robin M. Williams, Jr., *A Common Destiny: Blacks and American Society* (Washington, DC: National Academy Press, 1989).

16 Tulsa Police Department, *Problem-Oriented Approach to Drug Enforcement: Drug Problem Inventory* (Tulsa, OK: Tulsa Police Department, 1989).

17 The information on drug wholesalers was developed as part of a study funded by the National Institute of Justice in 1987. Results will be reported in *Strategies for Incapacitating Narcotics Wholesalers* (Washington, DC: Police Executive Research Forum, forthcoming).

18 For a discussion of the roles of and differentiation among dealing levels of wholesalers, see Peter Reuter and John Haaga, *The Organization of Higher-Level Drug Markets: An Exploratory Study* (Santa Monica, CA: Rand Corporation, 1989); and Patricia Adler, *Wheeling and Dealing: An Ethnography of an Upper-Level Drug Smuggling Community* (New York: Columbia University Press, 1985).

19 For a discussion of the self-protective strategies of drug (primarily heroin) dealers, see Mark H. Moore, *Buy and Bust* (Lexington, MA: D. C. Heath and Company, 1977); and Peter Reuter and Mark Kleiman, "Risks and Prices: An Eco-

nomic Analysis of Drug Enforcement," in *Crime and Justice: An Annual Review of Research*, ed. Michael Tonry and Norval Morris (Chicago: University of Chicago Press, 1986).

20 Two studies address the differentiation of federal and nonfederal (state and local) enforcement strategies: U.S. Senate, Permanent Subcommittee on Investigations, *Interim Report: Federal Narcotics Enforcement* (Washington, DC: U.S. Government Printing Office, 1976); and Mark Kleiman, "Organized Crime and Drug Abuse Control," in *Major Issues in Organized Crime Control*, ed. Herbert Edelhertz (Washington, DC: National Institute of Justice, 1987).

21 For a discussion of the informant-based mode of drug enforcement, see Jay Williams, Lawrence Redlinger, and Peter Manning, *Police Narcotics Control: Patterns and Strategies* (Washington, DC: National Institute of Justice, 1979), especially chap. 5.

22 Although evaluative data are not available, a persuasive argument for the counterproductive nature of such strategies has been made by Jerome Skolnick in *Justice without Trial: Law Enforcement in a Democratic Society* (New York: John Wiley and Sons, 1967).

23 William DeJong, *Arresting the Demand for Drugs: Police and School Partnerships to Prevent Drug Abuse* (Washington, DC: National Institute of Justice, 1987). Much of the discussion of DARE and SPECDA that follows draws on this report. For a more critical appraisal of drug education strategies, see Gilbert J. Botvin, "Substance Abuse Prevention: Theory, Practice, and Effectiveness," in *Drugs and Crime*, ed. Tonry and Wilson.

24 DeJong, *Arresting the Demand for Drugs*.

25 Paul J. Brounstein, Harry P. Hatry, David M. Alschuler, and Louis H. Blair, *Patterns of Substance Use and Delinquency among Inner-City Adolescents* (Washington, DC: The Urban Institute, 1989).

26 Ibid.

27 Ibid., 186.

28 Ibid., 187.

29 More information on educating the public about drug abuse is available from the National Crime Prevention Council, 1700 M St., N.W., Suite 200, Washington, DC 20006.

30 Maricopa County Demand Reduction Program, *Do Drugs. Do Time. The Demand Reduction Program: Planning and Implementation* (Phoenix: Maricopa County Demand Reduction Program, 1989). More information on this program is available from the Community Demand Reduction Coordinator, Community Relations Bureau, Phoenix Police Department, 620 W. Washington St., Phoenix, AZ 85003.

31 Commander Steve Rothlein of the Metro-Dade police department's narcotics bureau has commented that "stopping drug purchasers once they have driven from the scene exposes officers and innocent citizens to unnecessary danger. A critical element in this type of operation is to establish a scenario where potential buyers are required to exit their vehicles in order to purchase narcotics from undercover officers posing as sellers. If this is not accomplished, buyers are driving 5,000-pound weapons that will be difficult to overcome when arrest teams move in. This will not only result in numerous police chases and consequential injuries, but violators may occasionally succeed

in escaping with the drugs. Our experience has been that an immediate arrest on the site following the purchase is the safest technique." More information on how to conduct street-level reverse buys is available from the Narcotics Bureau, Metro-Dade Police Department, 1320 N.W. 14th St., Miami, FL 33125.

32 Gary W. Cordner, "Fear of Crime and the Police: An Evaluation of a Fear-Reduction Strategy," *Journal of Police Science and Administration* 14, no. 3 (1986); Richard Kirk Higdon and Phillip G. Huber, *How to Fight Fear: The Citizen-Oriented Police Enforcement Program Package* (Washington, DC: Police Executive Research Forum, 1987); and Phillip B. Taft, Jr., *Fighting Fear: The Baltimore County C.O.P.E. Project* (Washington, DC: Police Executive Research Forum, 1986).

33 Lawrence W. Sherman, "Police Crackdowns: Initial and Residual Deterrences," in *Crime and Justice: A Review of Research*, ed. Michael Tonry and Norval Morris (Chicago: University of Chicago Press, 1990).

34 The claim that foot patrols suppress crime is supported by Robert Trojanowicz, *An Evaluation of the Neighborhood Foot Patrol Program in Flint, Michigan* (East Lansing: School of Criminal Justice, Michigan State University, n.d.). Contradictory evidence is provided by the Police Foundation, *The Newark Foot Patrol Experiment* (Washington, DC: Police Foundation, 1981).

35 Craig Uchida and Brian Forst, *Modern Policing and the Control of Illegal Drugs: Testing New Strategies in Two American Cities* (Washington, DC: Police Foundation, forthcoming).

36 New York City Police Department, *Community Patrol Officer Program: Problem-Solving Guide* (New York: New York City Police Department, 1988); and Vera Institute of Justice, *CPOP: Community Policing In Practice* (New York: Vera Institute of Justice, 1988).

37 Police Executive Research Forum, *Taking a Problem-Oriented Approach to Drugs: An Interim Report* (Washington, DC: Police Executive Research Forum, 1989); Deborah Lamm Weisel, "Playing the Home Field: A Problem-Oriented Approach to Drug Control," *American Journal of Police* (1990); and Deborah Lamm Weisel, *Tackling Drug Problems in Public Housing: A Guide for Police* (Washington, DC: Police Executive Research Forum, 1990).

38 Robert Trojanowicz, Marilyn Steele, and Susan Trojanowicz, *Community Policing: A Taxpayer's Perspective* (East Lansing, MI: National Neighborhood Foot Patrol Center, 1986); and A.R.A. Consultants, "Final Report on the Evaluation of the Toronto Mini-Station Pilot Project," no. 1985-2 (Ottawa, ON: Ministry of the Solicitor General of Canada, 1985).

39 For discussions of the friction between regular patrol officers and special units and foot patrol officers, see Taft, *Fighting Fear*; Trojanowicz, Steele, and Trojanowicz, *Community Policing*; and Robert C. Trojanowicz and Dennis W. Banas, *Job Satisfaction: A Comparison of Foot Patrol Versus Motor Patrol Officers* (East Lansing, MI: National Neighborhood Foot Patrol Center, 1985).

40 Herman Goldstein, *Problem-Oriented Policing* (New York: McGraw Hill, 1990); John E. Eck and William Spelman, *Problem-Solving: Problem-Oriented Policing in Newport News* (Washington, DC: Police Executive Research Forum, 1987); and Police Executive Research Forum, *Taking a Problem-Oriented Approach to Drugs*.

41 For more information on problem-solving methods and measures of the effectiveness of these methods, see Eck and Spelman, *Problem-Solving*; and Goldstein, *Problem-Oriented Policing*.

42 Michael T. Farmer, ed., *Differential Police Response Strategies* (Washington, DC: Police Executive Research Forum, 1981); and Thomas J. McEwen, Edward F. Connors III, and Marcia I. Cohen, *Evaluation of the Differential Police Reponse Field Test* (Washington, DC: U.S. Government Printing Office, 1984).

8 Organized crime

Organized crime adapts to survive, evolving in response to both the push of sanctions and the pull of opportunities. In addition, organized crime in the 1990s crosses jurisdictional and, increasingly, national boundaries. This places the local law enforcement administrator in a difficult position. One department alone cannot cope with most problems of organized crime, for when organized crime is prodded, it quickly moves beyond the department's boundaries and control. As a result, the police administrator must ask how much of the department's resources, time, personnel, and money should be allocated to controlling organized crime. How much in the way of the department's assets should be devoted to intelligence collection about organized crime, proactive intervention (that is, prevention), and, most important, interactive liaison with other agencies—regional, state, and federal?

After reading that paragraph, the police administrator might conclude that organized crime should be a relatively low priority on the budgetary and administrative agenda. This, however, would be a mistake. Just because a single department in a given jurisdiction cannot solve the problem of organized crime, this does not mean that a department does not have to recognize and understand the problem, deal with it as it occurs, or suffer the consequences in terms of crime, corruption, and violence. The local department and administrator remain in the front lines. Although they cannot solve the problem single-handedly, they are often the first to recognize and confront it. Detected early and dealt with swiftly by a department that uses good intelligence and proactive enforcement, organized crime can be shifted out of the jurisdiction and, with good liaison and interagency cooperation, prosecuted and neutralized.

This chapter examines the evolving nature of organized crime. It looks at the roots and organizational structure of both the more-familiar, more-studied organized crime groups and the so-called emerging nontraditional groups that are receiving increased attention. It also looks at the effects of organized crime on the community; organized crime and vice enforcement; and organized crime and white-collar offenses. The emphasis throughout is on techniques for identifying, rather than eradicating, the complex problem of organized crime. Thus, the police administrator working outside of an organized crime unit can remain alert to indicators of organized crime and can enlist the necessary assistance when they are detected. The final sections of the chapter discuss police intelligence gathering and tools for combatting organized crime, and these discussions introduce the array of countermeasures police may take. (Detailed discussion of those enforcement methods is, however, necessarily left to other treatments of organized crime and to the various specialized training programs presented by professional organizations around the nation.)

In describing the many faces of organized crime in the United States as the twenty-first century draws near, this chapter uses the term "traditional" to refer to the much-studied phenomenon of Italian-American organized crime—the "Cosa Nostra" or, as it is more commonly referred to, "La Cosa Nostra" (LCN). The term "nontraditional" is used to refer to organized crime groups thought of as "emerging" (Asian, Latin American, Jamaican, Russian, and so forth) even though many of these groups, such as the Chinese, are often older than the Italian-American groups and emerged in this country considerably earlier. But only recently have groups other than Cosa Nostra become highly visible within the United States. Thus, readers must recognize that the terms "traditional" and "nontraditional" are inherently inaccurate and misleading; but their use makes it easier for readers—who are already accustomed to these labels— to grasp similarities and differences among the several groups. This is but one of the many problems of definition facing law enforcement analysts and operational leaders in the area of organized crime. The concept of "organized crime" itself is enormously ambiguous and the source of much confusion.

The many definitions of "organized crime"

Each time concern intensifies over problems of "organized crime," the concern is expressed at first in a dedicated and sincere, but usually unsuccessful, attempt to arrive at a single definition. The definitions produced are usually based on the opinions of diverse experts (for example, police, lawyers, criminologists, political scientists, economists). Unfortunately, because interdisciplinary efforts rarely lead to agreement, the resulting definitions produce as much dissent as accord, and the term "organized crime" has become a buzzword in criminal justice with its own special meaning for each official who uses it.

Organized crime refers—at various times and in different contexts—to (1) a collection of criminals; (2) a type of organizational structure and hierarchy; (3) legal and illegal businesses; and (4) a variety of criminal acts that can build on each other in pyramidal fashion.

Depending on which expert is consulted, organized crime refers—at various times and in different contexts—to (1) a collection of criminals; (2) a type of organizational structure and hierarchy; (3) legal and illegal businesses; and (4) a variety of criminal acts that can build on each other in pyramidal fashion. A term that sometimes identifies people and at other times identifies organizations, businesses, or actions is not among the clearest. Furthermore, so comprehensive a term often encompasses activities and people that are not the subjects of consideration. Most professionals have simply stopped explaining what they mean when they use the term. Consequently, many officials—including, for example, police chiefs from two different departments—may talk past each other, using the same term but meaning different things.

This chapter does not propose a new, universally acceptable definition of organized crime. Rather, it accepts the reality that law enforcement professionals will continue to mean different things when they refer to organized crime. This chapter does provide an overview of the important topics likely to be on the minds of law enforcement experts when they talk about organized crime; the information will give generalist police managers a foundation for thoughtfully joining the conversation and, perhaps, bringing greater clarity to the discussion.

Often, it is easier to identify the attributes of organized crime than to define it (some indicators of organized crime are shown in Figure 8–1). The Federal Bureau of Investigation has listed important attributes in its definition of organized crime: those groups that have some type of organizational structure, engage in continuing criminal conspiracy, and have as a primary purpose the generation of profit. FBI managers are required under the bureau's Organized Crime National Strategy to ensure that only groups that have the requisite strategic characteristics with regard to structure, scope, and national impact become the focus of the FBI's organized crime efforts. Such requisites, and the attributes noted later in

The people	**Career criminals** with records and histories of offenses in the categories of providing illegal goods and services (e.g., gambling, loan-sharking)	and maintaining discipline and eliminating competition (e.g., by extortion, assault, homicide).
The organization	**Crime syndicate** hierarchical structure, including street soldiers, first-line supervisors, mid-level managers, and a top-level leader or boss.	**Entrance requirements** based on such factors as racial or ethnic background, prior criminal history, and commission of a significant crime (membership for life).
The enterprises	**Ongoing illegal businesses** to provide illegal goods (e.g., stolen food and clothing, precious metals) and services (e.g., gambling, loan-sharking, prostitution).	**Legitimate businesses** acquired through a pattern of illegal activity (e.g., default on illegal loan, extortion) or with the proceeds from an illegal business.
The acts	**Pyramid arrangement of crimes** to guarantee maximum return on investments or to disguise the commission of an earlier crime. **Continuous conspiracies** engaged in because of the ongoing nature of the illegal businesses and for the purpose of establishing, managing, maintaining, and protecting illegal enterprises from competition or official intervention. **Coercion and violence** committed to eliminate competition or to discipline employees or actual or potential witnesses in government proceedings.	**Corruption** of public officials in criminal justice and other agencies in order to neutralize their interference in the conduct of illegal businesses; to ensure that investments in legitimate businesses bring a maximum return; and to develop political influence as a service made available to others for a fee. **Monopolistic control** over an illegal good or service in a defined geographical area in order to maximize profits.

Figure 8–1 Indicators of the existence of organized crime.

this chapter, serve as useful criteria to guide resource allocation at the local level.

In looking for identifiers of organized crime—that is, for characteristics held in common by members of a group—law enforcement administrators have for decades focused on ethnicity as a key distinguishing variable. But although ethnicity is useful and descriptive, it is basically merely a labeling device. The true role of ethnicity, like culture, language, and kinship, is not to determine a group's characteristic behavior but to serve as a bonding mechanism unifying a group, enhancing trust, loyalty, and secrecy, and thus lessening the risks of exposure and penetration. More important to identifying and understanding organized crime are factors relating to the market niches these groups carve out for themselves and the enterprises they undertake in exploiting the opportunities available, regardless of the ethnicity or culture of the group under consideration. When understood, these structural variables can be used by the local law enforcement administrator to pinpoint the vulnerabilities of organized crime.

Phases of organized crime

Historically, organized crime evolves through three phases, or stages: the predatory phase, the parasitical phase, and the symbiotic phase.[1] This three-stage theory of the evolution of organized criminal groups highlights for the police administrator the ways in which organized crime interacts with the political and economic sectors of society, and it stresses political corruption as an essential component in the evolution of organized crime (see the chapter on fostering integrity).

Organized crime is rooted in the rational behavior of career criminals who seek to increase their probabilities of success in making money while minimizing attendant risks. They do this through acts of confederation, alliance, syndication, and organization. Historically, one key incubator of this kind of criminal behavior has been the neighborhood street gang, which has served both as a training ground for criminal skills and as a bonding mechanism holding members together in trust and mutual understanding. Other possible bonding mechanisms and incubators of organized crime are prison gangs, military combat groups, and groups engaging in high-risk work and recreational activities (for example, dock gangs and motorcycle gangs) when they are linked with crime, violence, and the resulting need to share secrets.[2]

For the local police administrator, the incubators of organized crime (for example, bonding mechanisms that produce alliances between criminals) are critically important. This is why local law enforcement officials should pay particular attention to youth gangs and other high-risk and risk-taking groups, such as local motorcycle gangs. The advantage for the police administrator of recognizing the signs of incipient criminal organization is that at this point the groups are usually confined to one jurisdiction, and the resources of a local police agency are still sufficient for managing them. The key, of course, is early detection and early intervention, which means that the administrator must have both solid linkages to the community and a first-class intelligence unit.

The predatory phase

In the predatory phase, the criminal group is basically a street gang, rooted in a specific "turf," or territory. Usually this is a physical territory—a neighborhood, block, or ethnic or cultural community. Occasionally, however, "turf" is occupational, as with the waterfront dock labor gangs of Sidney, Marseilles, Shanghai, Hong Kong, Naples, and New York City. In these cities, this critical high-risk occupational association has often been the incubator for organized criminal groups.[3]

Once established, dominance over turf gives a gang the ability to extort and prey upon both legal and illegal neighborhood businesses.

In the predatory phase, criminal activity is primarily defensive. Violence and the threat of violence are used to maintain dominance over the territory, to eliminate rivals and outsiders, and to create a local monopoly over the illicit use of force. Criminal acts in the predatory stage (for example, extortion) tend to be directed at achieving immediate rewards and satisfaction and not, as in later stages, at achieving secondary, longer-range power and political goals.

Once established, dominance over turf gives the gang the ability to extort and prey upon both legal and illegal neighborhood businesses. With dominance also comes recognition from territorial power brokers. The street gang now becomes an asset used by professional criminal entrepreneurs and by players in the legitimate business and political community. This asset is deployed as an extralegal force to carry out "depersonalized" violence and intimidation—killing and maiming for business reasons rather than for personal motives. Thus, for example, nineteenth- and early–twentieth-century youth street gangs were used by both professional criminals and political machines to maintain and expand their control over ethnic neighborhoods.[4] From the police administrator's point of view, it is during the predatory phase that emerging criminal organizations are the most manageable and, accordingly, can be controlled and neutralized. This requires both the skill to know what techniques to use and the skill to target police resources properly on groups whose harmful effects on the community are highly likely to escalate.

The parasitical phase

The second stage in the evolution of organized crime is the parasitical phase. In this stage, the predatory street gang has matured—in age, criminal skills, organizational leadership, and specialization of labor—and has melded its territorial base with the influence of local power brokers to provide the neighborhood with illicit goods and services. In the parasitical phase, the organized criminal group begins to develop a corruptive interaction with the legitimate power sectors in the political system.

Political corruption, which necessarily accompanies the ongoing provision of illicit goods and services, provides the essential glue binding together the legitimate sectors of the community with the underworld criminal organization.

For the parasitical phase to blossom fully, however, there must be some "window of opportunity" through which the predatory criminal gang can pass to become an organized crime group. Typically, changes in political power, shifts in regulatory rules, crises, wars, and economic or natural catastrophes have all served as "windows" to give the predatory criminal gangs increased legitimacy and parasitical interaction with the political system.[5] Most commonly, the "window" is created by a sharp shift in political or economic policies that creates the opportunity for a lucrative black market and the emergence of an illicit underground economy. (In the United States, Prohibition was just such a window. Street gang leaders, under the tutelage of older professional criminals, became the cadre of the bootlegging industry. Over time, the economies and efficiencies of intergroup cooperation were recognized, and with this there emerged criminal alliances, syndicates, and confederations. These budding organized crime groups, with the amassed capital of Prohibition profits, were now able to expand their corruptive activities from neighborhoods to whole cities and regions, penetrating the legitimate business sectors of the economy.) Political corruption, which necessarily accompanies the ongoing provision of illicit goods and services, provides the essential glue binding together the legitimate sectors of the community with the underworld criminal organization. It is in the parasitical stage that organized crime generally gets labeled as such by authorities, and it is this stage that is generally portrayed by the media and Hollywood. Its hallmark is ties of corruption between the criminal syndicate and the political system.

The predatory-stage street gang was dependent on individual politicians and the political system for protection and for permission to operate and maintain its control in the neighborhood. By the parasitical stage, organized crime has the money and power to make the politician dependent on the criminal organization for campaign funds and electoral support. Organized crime has the capital to buy protection from corrupt officials and to diversify and penetrate the business and economic sectors of society, thus acquiring further insulation and protection, along with tacit legitimacy.

For the police administrator, the parasitical phase offers special challenges. Although a chief can still mobilize resources to attempt to limit, control, and make organized crime manageable within one jurisdiction, achieving that goal is difficult, requiring significant managerial skills and involving substantial career risks. Frequently it means the chief must seek to mobilize the media to expose corruption, hoping that this exposure will mobilize the community to create and coordinate citizens' groups and blue-ribbon crime commissions that will reinforce law enforcement activities against organized crime. Fighting organized crime at the parasitical stage may also require seeking resources and assistance from law enforcement agencies outside the jurisdiction.

The symbiotic phase

The third stage in the evolution of organized criminal groups is the symbiotic phase, in which the parasitical relationship becomes mutual. The host, the legitimate political and economic system, becomes as dependent on the parasite, organized crime, as the criminal enterprise is on the host. In the United States, the symbiotic stage occurs only in certain criminal markets and businesses and in a few local jurisdictions. The symbiotic stage is, however, common in other countries. In Colombia, the Bahamas, Mexico, Peru, Japan, Italy, even the Soviet Union, organized crime maintains an ongoing, regularized interaction with elements of the legitimate political and economic system. In the symbiotic phase, organized crime's monopolistic control over certain sectors of the illegitimate and legitimate economies combines with the entrenched corruption it has promoted and with its ability to use threat, force, and violence. The result is that organized crime is an important player in the political system—a player that must be dealt with, even if it is not recognized formally or officially.

Indeed, at times the legitimate political system or the legitimate economy may become completely dependent for capital, for maintenance of order, or for the delivery of certain necessary goods and services upon the organized criminal element and its affiliates. For example, in Peru the unofficial exchange rate in Lima turns each day on the amount of U.S. drug dollars flown into the Alta Huallaga region by Colombian drug traffickers to buy coca. In New York City, the influence of traditional organized crime over the private carting industry, the wholesale meat, gasoline, and fish distribution systems, airport cargo freighting, and the ready-mix concrete and drywall construction industries has made the legitimate economy and political system dependent on enterprises influenced by organized crime to carry on the city's day-to-day business.[6] Although the Cosa Nostra has been dealt hard body blows by law enforcement, its continuing influence in the rackets, some trade union locals, and certain aspects of the entertainment industry make it a power to be recognized and addressed.

Once organized crime has evolved to the symbiotic stage, it is essentially beyond the control of local police agencies. Local police officials can still seek to intervene, but they do so only at great cost to their department and often to the community it serves. In the symbiotic stage, alternative, noninfiltrated, unmonopolized public services can be created only at great monetary and political cost. Symbiotic organized crime will yield, if at all, only to federal and multiagency interventions. Indeed, beyond a certain point in its symbiotic evolution, organized crime ceases to be principally a problem for the police or other guardians of public order and becomes a problem for public policy and regulatory administration, demanding political solutions.[7]

A "map" of organized crime in the United States

The three-stage theory helps the police administrator recognize that one of the most critical questions facing U.S. law enforcement policy makers is whether the drug crisis of the late 1980s and early 1990s provides a window of opportunity similar to that provided by Prohibition. More particularly, will drug trafficking provide opportunities for emerging nontraditional organized crime groups to establish the corruptive political ties necessary to allow them protection from, entrance to, and monopolization of certain sectors of the legitimate and illegitimate economics and political systems? If the answer to that question is "yes" or even "maybe," then new multinational approaches and police and intelligence organizations will have to be developed to deal with organized crime in the twenty-first century.

Because of the changes in technology—instant communications, electronic banking, air travel—that have made the planet a global village, the continued evolution of organized crime will probably require international law enforcement responses far beyond those at the command of the local police administrator. This does not mean that organized crime for the police to contend with at the local level is lacking or will be lacking; it simply means that greater emphasis on liaison and cooperation with other agencies will be essential. Taking the local perspective, let us now turn to identifying and describing current organized crime in the United States.

Because of the changes in technology that have made the planet a global village, the continued evolution of organized crime will probably require international law enforcement responses far beyond those at the command of the local police administrator.

Given the emerging emphasis on nontraditional organized crime groups, it is important for the police administrator to remember that organized crime in the United States follows no single organizational pattern. Moreover, not even the more traditional Italian-American organized crime groups follow a single organizational pattern. The early models of traditional organized crime, based on work primarily in the New York metropolitan area and focusing on the area's five Cosa Nostra families, were tightly structured.[8] Today it is known that the traditional groups in the rest of the country vary widely in their individual patterns of operation and cohesiveness, although all have similar hierarchical structures (running from boss to soldier—see Figure 8–2 later in this chapter). And in New York, the old five-family organizational model is also subject to question. Although there are still five LCN organized crime families that operate in New York City, there is a great deal of interfamily cooperation and a fluidity of association within and across families and criminal markets that did not exist when the earlier models were designed. For the law enforcement administrator, the important points about this evolution of traditional organized crime in the United States are that new loose alliances are occurring across jurisdictions and that an understanding of LCN activities depends more on models of criminal enterprises and criminal markets than on family models.

Although there is a great deal of fluidity and change in the structures of organized crime, the syndicate model, developed to help explain traditional organized crime, is a useful paradigm for the police administrator to keep in mind. (Market and enterprise models are used, below, to help explain nontraditional organized crime.) The term "syndicate" is used in the rest of this chapter to refer to all types of traditional organized crime, at whatever point on the organizational or evolutionary spectrum.

Structural aspects of traditional syndicates

The formation of an organized crime syndicate represents a refinement of the evolutionary process discussed above. As in legitimate enterprises, syndicate development depends on (1) conditions in the market in which a group anticipates operating; (2) the product or service provided; (3) the popular cultural or societal posture toward the product or service being offered; and (4) the barriers (law enforcement activity, criminal competition, the reliability of supply and demand, and so forth) to market entry and continued operation.[9] Although the organized crime syndicate model is but one model of organized crime enterprise, it is the classic one and a useful baseline against which to compare emerging groups.

A crime syndicate is a management apparatus that controls a diverse collection of legal and illegal enterprises. A larger syndicate typically operates as a board of directors led by an autocratic chairman, or boss. The holdings of some syndicates are small and very limited (for example, a numbers bank, a vending machine company, and perhaps a bar). The holdings of others may total in the hundreds. As the size and diversity of a syndicate's holdings increase, so do problems for police in controlling these activities. The starting point for police analysis should be to determine whether a crime syndicate exists in the community and, if so, what types of criminal activities it controls and supports. Next, in determining what countermeasures to take, the police need to understand the more prominent features of crime syndicates and the ways in which they are organized.

Ranks and responsibilities   The criminals who fill the rosters of crime syndicates are ranked according to the importance of their positions (see Figure 8–2). Each member either serves within the management structure or contributes to the operation of a particular enterprise. Several roles can be identified within this general structure. One important position in a syndicate is that of the "money mover." This person assists in the flow of cash from an illegal operation to a legitimate business front. Often this person lacks a criminal record, and this eases movement between the criminal and business worlds.

A second key syndicate role is the "corrupter," often a defense attorney or lobbyist who can operate freely in both the legitimate political system and the underworld. An attorney playing this role typically targets potential corruptees and passes bribe and corruption monies through "cutouts" while working to protect the group from exposure and minimize prosecutorial risks. One technique the attorney can employ to attempt to conceal conspiratorial conduct is assertion of the attorney-client privilege.[10]

A third potentially high-status syndicate role is that of "money maker." A low-level group member whose rackets or criminal genius brings in a lot of profits normally has status and contacts far above his or her formal rank in the organization.

Other important syndicate participants are the "enforcers"—members skilled in violence. They enforce discipline within the organization, collect debts from gambling and loan-sharking operations, and carry out extortionate threats and contract murders when called upon. Enforcers, if they are considered "stone killers" (people with a capacity for depersonalized violence), often have status in the syndicate that far exceeds their formal position.

Because the traditional organized crime syndicate engages in crime on a day-to-day basis, it is vital that the boss be protected from any connection with individual criminal acts. Therefore, most syndicates have someone in the position of "buffer" to the boss. This person conveys the orders of the boss without allowing any of the orders or acts to be traced back to their source.

Finally, there are nonmember associates who work in various criminal and expert capacities for organized criminal groups either on a regular or a contractual basis. It is estimated that, in the traditional syndicate model, there are seven to nine nonmember associates for every regular member of an organized crime group.

Figure 8–2   An organized crime family.

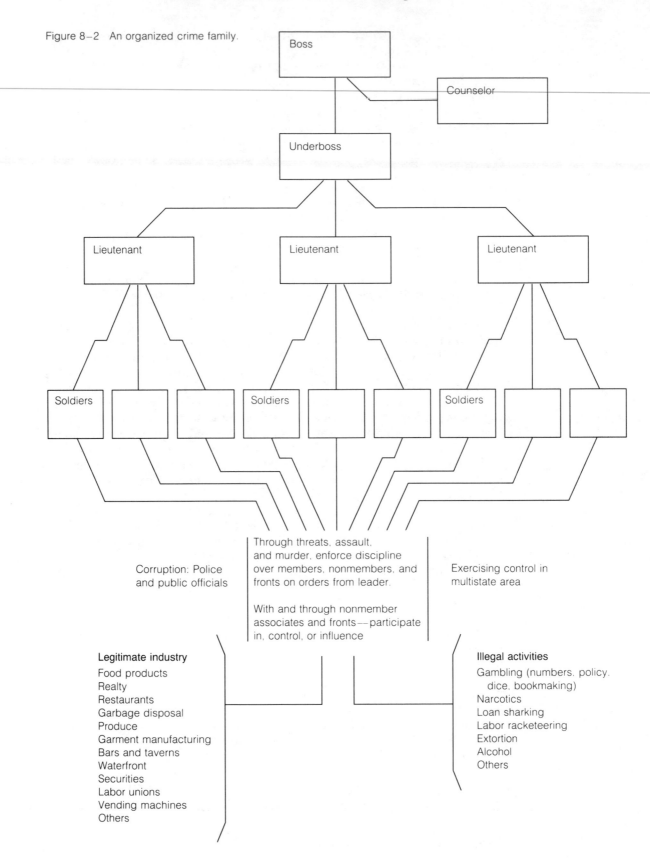

Through threats, assault,
and murder, enforce discipline
over members, nonmembers, and
fronts on orders from leader.

With and through nonmember
associates and fronts—participate
in, control, or influence

Corruption: Police
and public officials

Exercising control in
multistate area

Legitimate industry

Food products
Realty
Restaurants
Garbage disposal
Produce
Garment manufacturing
Bars and taverns
Waterfront
Securities
Labor unions
Vending machines
Others

Illegal activities

Gambling (numbers. policy.
   dice. bookmaking)
Narcotics
Loan sharking
Labor racketeering
Extortion
Alcohol
Others

As in any other organization, some members are aggressive and hard-working and upwardly mobile. Others seem content to remain at the lower levels, performing routine and often mundane tasks. In other words, there is a differentiation of responsibilities within a syndicate: some members spend their days running a numbers bank, others spend their days logging bets in a bank office, and still others devise illegal schemes for investing the money generated from the numbers bank in legitimate businesses.

Relationships between syndicates and enterprises   A crime syndicate, regardless of its size, has one or more of three types of relationships with individual criminal enterprises or rackets within its territory.

First is the syndicate-run operation, such as a numbers bank, where the syndicate's own employees and capital are used. Key members of the syndicate are usually installed in the top managerial positions of the operation, and lower-ranking members staff the offices.

The second arrangement is the syndicate franchise, whereby a distinct geographical area, such as a neighborhood or an entire city, is ceded to an independent operator for the purpose of running an illegal business. Here the syndicate attaches a price to the franchise, which operates like a tax on the business. The "tax" can be imposed by the syndicate's requiring the independent operator to subscribe to a syndicate-run operation such as a race wire or gambling layoff service. The fee for the use of the service adds up to a considerable sum over a period of time.

The third arrangement may be termed a joint venture. Unlike the syndicate-run or franchised arrangement, which is made between a powerful syndicate leader and an independent of lesser rank, a joint venture involves two criminal organizations of comparable size, wealth, power, and ability and readiness to employ violence. In such a situation a syndicate may enter into a joint venture with another syndicate. Here equals deal with equals, and both parties stand to make a considerable profit, given the many shortcuts that racketeers employ to maximize their profits. Such mutual arrangements promote friendship and stability and thus tend to decrease the chances that a rivalry over territory or over control of a new enterprise will lead to conflict and bloodshed.

Leadership styles   Whatever the organizational attributes of a given syndicate, the leaders choose their own styles of handling outside competition, internal disputes, and relationships with public officials.[11] Some leaders consciously choose a low profile that is consistent with the claim—usually traceable directly to them—that there is no organized crime in their community because no racketeers can be identified. Others seem to enjoy the public spotlight and the influence and prestige that go with a position noted for the cold, calculating exercise of power.

The personal style and visibility of a syndicate leader—and often of his lieutenants—are important determinants of whether there is a public perception that organized crime exists in the community.

The personal style and visibility of a syndicate leader—and often of his lieutenants—are important determinants of whether there is a public perception that organized crime exists in the community; in this way, they are a law enforcement problem. The police administrator who mounts an attack on organized crime without first convincing community leaders that the problem is real—sometimes by sharpening the syndicate's public profile—often faces a challenge that can range from mild static to unbending opposition. Means of heightening the citizenry's awareness of organized crime are discussed below in connection with the role of intelligence.

Emerging nontraditional organized crime

Organized crime is not peculiar to certain cultures or ethnic groups. It can be found in every society and culture. It existed in the Massachusetts Bay colony: organized prostitution and fencing rings were reported in the crime records of Suffolk County (Boston) in the 1680s.[12] It is rapidly expanding in the Soviet Union, as the cooperatives started under Perestroika have opened the door to massive extortion by Soviet organized crime.[13]

Organized crime is rooted in certain social niches, conditions of cultural strain, associational groups, and economic bottlenecks that create opportunities for organization and a lessening of risks among career criminals.[14] For operational purposes, however, the law enforcement community—including its literature— uses ethnic or nationality labels to designate various criminal organizations and groups. This is partly because blood, family, ethnicity, and nationality are important bonding mechanisms in organized crime groups, and partly because ethnicity and nationality often are easy law enforcement markers in the street. Moreover, many organized crime groups themselves use ethnic or nationality designations in naming their organizations and considering candidates for membership (as opposed to candidates for alliances, as in joint ventures). Thus, the self-adopted monikers of many organized crime groups alone point to an ethnic or national typology.

For these reasons and in conformity with standard categorizations of organized crime enterprises used by the FBI and other organizations, many of the emerging nontraditional groups cited here are listed by their ethnic or nationality identifiers.[15] This in no way implies that criminality is characteristic of any ethnic or national group. As the following sections show, in the long run market and enterprise models of criminal behavior provide greater explanatory power for understanding organized crime than these commonly used nationality labels— and than the classic syndicate model, although the police administrator who understands the typical syndicate organizational pattern and its enterprise formats has a useful point of departure for comparing the patterns presented by other groups in the spectrum of modern organized crime. (In addition to the emerging groups profiled below, many others dot the landscape of modern organized crime in the United States.)

Drug gangs Although drug gangs such as the "Crips" and the "Bloods" are often classified as organized crime, some observers question whether this is an accurate designation. The hierarchies in these groups often are weak and changing, and expressions of loyalty are based on symbols, dress, colors, language, codes, and fashions that almost anyone can choose to adopt. Initiation based on violence may build cohort and extortionate bonding but little else. Often, the Crips and the Bloods groups appear to resemble the perpetrators of chain-letter frauds and pyramid-type sales distributorships more than organized crime groups.

Commonly, in these groups a mid-level dealer gives an associate ten rocks of crack to sell, from which the associate can keep one to use or sell for himself. Assuming he sells it, over time the successful salesman can afford to buy ten rocks of his own and set up his own sales force in an adjoining territory. Whatever organizational structure exists is focused on the drug supplier and reflects an economic relationship; there is not necessarily an ongoing hierarchical structure based on the loyalty and respect that grow out of long-term bonding. Thus, the pattern of drug gang crime groups, at least at present, seems to resemble a free enterprise distributorship model more than a structured oligarchy, a confederated drug cartel, or an organized criminal group. Although some individuals within the Crips and the Bloods have diversified, moving their drug profits into legitimate businesses and front businesses, this diversification does not appear to be an organized effort. And although these groups are quite violent, the violence tends to be over sales spots, territories, or personal rivalries rather than intragroup violence directed at improving organizational discipline. Obviously the violence of these groups should command police attention. The point here is that law enforcement efforts to contain or neutralize them need to be informed by an understanding of their structural strengths and weaknesses.

These drug gangs do not appear to engage in traditional syndicate franchise operations (discussed earlier), where independent criminal entrepreneurs, bookmakers, chop shop owners, loan sharks, gamblers, and others are charged a fee for permission to operate at a particular location. In traditional syndicate groups, power and control flow from the center to the periphery, and tribute flows back to the bosses at the top. This does not appear to be the pattern with drug gangs. Research suggests there are other black-American organized crime groups that fit the syndicate model,[16] but the Crips and the Bloods are at a very different place in the spectrum of emerging organized crime.

Japanese organized crime groups   Japanese organized crime (the Boryokudan) is commonly known by the name "Yakuza."[17] In Japan it consists of some 2,300 groups with approximately 100,000 members. Some of the better-known groups are the Yamaguchi Gumi, Inagawa Kai, Sumiyoshi Rengo, Toa Huai Jigyo, Kumiai, and Nippon Kokusui Kai. Because in Japan organized crime has reached the symbiotic stage, there these groups maintain known organizational headquarters, wear distinctive lapel pins, publish newsletters, and at times hold televised news conferences to explain their positions. When operating in the United States, Japanese organized crime groups tend to focus their criminal enterprise activities on several rather narrow market niches. First, they focus on their compatriots, whether tourists, business executives, or corporations. A number of Japanese crime groups run tourist agencies and tours. These are then used to steer Japanese tourists to clubs, bars, restaurants, and other establishments under the control of Japanese crime groups. Such bars and restaurants may also be hangouts for Yakuza members outside Japan or "fronts" for gambling and prostitution. When used as fronts, these establishments serve a dual purpose—both generating income from the clientele and setting up Japanese tourists and business executives for blackmail and extortion at home or through their corporate ties.

The second niche in which the Yakuza operate is arms trafficking—primarily stolen handguns for export. Because possession of handguns is illegal in Japan, a handgun carries a black-market price there of $5,000 to $7,000.

Japanese crime groups invest their illicit proceeds and profits in U.S. real estate and business ventures for the lucrative returns available.

Vietnamese organized crime groups   Like the Japanese crime groups, Vietnamese groups tend to prey on their own nationals.[18] Unlike them, however, they tend to occupy a strong-arm and violent-crimes niche. Business extortion, via threats of violence, arson, bombings, and property destruction, is a common activity of Vietnamese groups. Another specialty is invasions of residential homes to steal gold, jewelry, and money (often gambling winnings). These crimes are frequently accompanied by the rape of any female residents present, an act that reduces the likelihood that the crime will be reported. Vietnamese crime groups generally have advance information about their victims and generally seek to carry out their crimes in communities other than the one where members of the particular crime group regularly live. The gold and gold jewelry stolen by Vietnamese gangs typically is quickly smelted by fences operating legitimate gold stores in the Vietnamese community. Other crimes often committed by Vietnamese groups include exploitation of fellow nationals through prostitution, gambling, loan-sharking, and rackets. Crimes targeted at those who wish to send goods and medicines to Vietnam are common. Making wide use of automobiles and juveniles, Vietnamese crime gangs roam from coast to coast engaging in these criminal activities. Because of tensions between refugee political groups, political factions use Vietnamese organized crime to carry out enforcement activities against their rivals. A few Vietnamese crime groups also appear to have close ties to Chinese organized crime and are engaged in Asian heroin drug trafficking.

Russian emigré gangs   Crime syndicates also operate within the rapidly growing Russian emigré communities in the United States. These groups, like many of the emergent nontraditional syndicates, see the United States as rich, ripe, and full of easy pickings. Stealing diamonds, gold, and furs, fencing stolen goods, and committing insurance fraud are among their specialties. Unlike the Japanese and Vietnamese groups, they tend to seek criminal alliances with traditional crime groups and operate both inside and outside their own ethnic community. Frequently, their immigration route is through Israel, where they sometimes interact with Israeli organized criminals, who tend to work the same criminal market niches in the United States as the Russian emigrés. In the future, Russian emigrés can be expected to form closer ties with organized crime in the Soviet Union. Moreover, the emigrés' role in exporting and selling stolen Russian religious art and gold should not be ignored.

Korean organized crime groups   Prostitution, massage parlors, and topless and nude bars appear to be the major specialities of Korean organized crime in the United States (according to one author, the Koreans control 75 percent of the prostitution in midtown Manhattan).[19] Korean crime groups often conduct these activities around major cities and in areas with large military bases. In this crime market niche, Korean crime groups appear to be forging ties with both outlaw motorcycle gangs and traditional LCN organizations, conducting much of that activity under franchise to these other syndicates. Within Korean communities, gangs tend to occupy two other niches: (1) extortion of Korean businesses, greengrocers, produce markets, and restaurants; and (2) control over illicit gambling and loan-sharking. Moreover, because there have long been ties between Japanese and Korean organized crime, Korean groups at times are used to mask, buffer, and protect Yakuza crime operations.

Chinese organized crime groups   Chinese organized crime groups are often closely linked to the legitimate business sectors in Chinese communities in the United States and are thus often buffered and protected by them. The Chinese groups are truly transnational in scope, movement, and operations. Long linked with Chinese self-help and benevolent associations, the triads and criminally influenced tongs have ties not only to the mainland, Hong Kong, and Taiwan but also to the many overseas areas in which the Chinese settled over time.[20] After the Vietnamese immigration to the United States in the early 1970s, it was discovered that many individuals with Vietnamese names were in fact overseas Chinese with Chinese crime group connections who had settled in Vietnam decades before. Thus, for the law enforcement administrator Chinese organized crime presents difficult and multinational problems. Heroin, black-market gold, and human trafficking, as well as the exploitation of new arrivals, are among the Chinese organized crime groups' specialties. The groups tend to be associated with street gangs of Chinese youths, who provide enforcement and violence. The Ghost Shadows, Flying Dragons, Wah Ching, United Bamboo, and Ping On are some major Chinese street gangs operating in the United States and Canada in support of various triad and tong factions within Chinese organized crime. These gangs are used in day-to-day operations to extort Chinese businesses, collect street taxes, protect gambling operations as "look-see boys," and carry out the riskier low-level aspects of enforcement and drug trafficking. Because these gangs tend to use military style semiautomatic weapons in their hit work, their activities often affect large numbers of bystanders. Experts expect that Chinese organized crime activities in the United States and Canada will continue to increase in the 1990s. The Chinese now control most of the heroin distribution in New York City, and Chinese influence in the heroin market and financial penetration of legitimate businesses is expected to continue.

Nigerian organized crime groups Nigerians have been employed as "mules" for the transport of Southwest Asian heroin entering the United States from Afghanistan and Pakistan via India. Their numbers in the United States are small. Where they do operate, they frequently pose as foreign exchange students and seek work with private security firms to gain access to businesses and their records. Among the Nigerians' specialties are "bust-out scams" (planned bankruptcies of large companies) and credit card frauds, as well as the exploitation of their compatriots and other West Coast African drug "mules" and street vendors. As they have become more established in the United States, the Nigerian groups have begun dealing—rather than working for other dealers—in Asian heroin.

Jamaican organized crime groups Much has been written about the Jamaican "posses." They specialize in drug dealing (cocaine, crack, and "Ganja"— marijuana) and arms trafficking. Known for their propensity for violence, the Jamaican gangs' calling card often is the use of automatic and semiautomatic military-style weapons in contract killings, coupled with random shooting to panic crowds at parties, picnics, and dances where these hits are carried out. The posses aggressively seek new areas of operation, which at times brings them into confrontations with drug gangs such as the Crips and the Bloods. They are not reluctant to settle into small towns and rural ghettos where there is a black community and a market niche for crack sales. Like outlaw motorcycle gangs, discussed below, they have expanded into a number of legitimate real estate and business holdings. Often such holdings include restaurants, music stores, discos, apartments, and import-export stores that tend to reflect elements of the posses' Caribbean heritage.

Latin American organized crime groups Cuban, Mexican, and Colombian organized crime groups that primarily engage in drug trafficking and money laundering are the best known of the Latin crime syndicates in the United States; Peruvians as well as Salvadorians and other Central Americans also operate criminally in the United States. Mexican syndicates control "black tar heroin" and marijuana distribution and increasingly operate as transporters and franchise wholesalers for Colombian drug cartels, of which there are some dozen, the best known being the Medellin Cartel. The Cali Cartel is active in both New York City and Los Angeles, while smaller cartels operate from the Colombian Atlantic Coast and from Leticia in the Colombian Amazon. For police administrators, the key features of the Colombian groups are that (1) they use a Colombian overseer in all the wholesale markets in which they operate; (2) they tend to use the same travel, car rental, and real estate agents over time; (3) they tend to maintain separate stash houses for drugs and for money; and (4) their area representatives keep meticulous records of every gram and dollar for which they are responsible. Colombian groups are known for their bloody retribution against their enemies, but this violence tends to be selective and targeted. Although entire families, including children and infants, as well as any witnesses may be brutally murdered, this is done to avoid retaliation and not wantonly or carelessly. Colombian syndicates generally require their representatives to maintain a low profile in the United States, whereas other Latino crime syndicate features stand out because of their flamboyant life styles. Women play an active role in Colombian organized crime syndicates, unlike in many other groups. Although they are well known as drug traffickers, Colombian organized crime groups also include many of the best counterfeiters in the world. They are also expert pickpockets, and organized gangs of young Colombian pickpockets roam the major cities of the United States each holiday season.

Outlaw motorcycle clubs　A majority of outlaw motorcycle clubs are still in the simple predatory phase. However, the "big four"—Hell's Angels, Outlaws, Pagans, and Bandidos—are well into the parasitical phase and, in a very few rural jurisdictions, may be moving into the symbiotic stage. The big four outlaw motorcycle organizations not only dominate the wholesale distribution of methamphetamines (crank, speed) but are also active in other drug trafficking (PCP, "angel dust," LSD, and so forth) and other crime markets. Chop shops, massage parlors, topless bars, prostitution, weapons trafficking, and contract violence are some of their typical crime market niches. They also have many legitimate holdings in business (for example, automotive junk yards, motorcycle sales, and catering) and real estate. Outlaw motorcycle groups at times choose not to cultivate the stereotypical biker image but instead lower their profile and blend into the community in which they operate.[21]

Other aspects of the traditional image of outlaw motorcycle groups are also being eroded. For example, the strong motorcycle gang rivalries, territorial inviolability, and long-term blood feuds have been replaced, in many parts of the United States, by agreements permitting operatives of one gang to travel unmolested through another gang's territory and even by operational cooperation. The law enforcement administrator should keep in mind that, for outlaw motorcycle gangs, "territory" is normally defined in terms of interstate highway corridors and the principal road networks extending from key "mother" chapters to outlying chapter headquarters. Thus, the gangs cross state and other jurisdictional lines. In a few cases, they cross national boundaries. Hell's Angels, for example, have sixty-seven chapters in thirteen countries on four continents. The headquarters in Oakland, California, contains a global communications facility.

In some rural states and outlying areas, the big four motorcycle gangs franchise small, independent biker gangs to "cook" and produce methamphetamines. In turn, the big four buy (at wholesale) and control distribution and retail sales of the drugs. Similar cooperative and collaborative arrangements also appear to be occurring where biker gangs own or control topless bars and massage parlors. Here they work with other motorcycle gangs and with other organized crime groups, especially Korean, to exploit the prostitution niche. They also work with LCN to provide enforcement, including contract violence. Thus, the organization and activities of outlaw motorcycle gangs are much looser and more fluid, characterized more by coalitions and confederations, than earlier models suggested.

One distinctive feature of illicit organized motorcycle riders is particularly important for law enforcement administrators, whether specialists in organized crime or generalists, to know about. They tend to be very interested in police organizations and often seek to infiltrate and carry out counterintelligence activities against law enforcement agencies. Frequently, they attempt this by having their female associates seek police employment or seek to gain corrupt access to public agencies and files through sexual favors. Like Colombian groups, outlaw motorcycle gangs make more use of women in their enterprise activities than do many other groups.

New Italian organized crime groups Although there are loose historical and family connections between many Italian-American, Sicilian, and mainland Italian crime syndicates, in the 1980s there was an influx of independent Sicilian and mainland Italian organized crime syndicates into the United States. One such Sicilian group was responsible for the "Pizza Connection" cases and was tied only loosely to the most traditional of New York's five Cosa Nostra families, the Bonnano organization.[22] Italian groups from Naples and Calabria also operate in the heroin—and, more recently, the cocaine—trafficking niche. The mainland groups tend to be linked to Canadian-Italian crime groups and to Venezuelan criminal organizations, whereas the Sicilians appear to have ties to Colombian and Peruvian drug traffickers through connections in Brazil.

Effects of organized crime on the community

Before a police administrator can convince others of the threat organized crime poses to the community, he or she must first clearly perceive the ways in which criminal enterprises undermine community welfare. The role of both traditional and nontraditional organized crime groups in narcotics trafficking and related violence is well known and has been noted already in this chapter. Police administrators hardly need convincing that illicit narcotics and associated violence represent threats to local communities. In other decades in U.S. history, however, police had considerably more difficulty persuading the public that syndicate crime is not "victimless" crime. The following two sections address "the pyramid effect" and "corruption" and show how organized crime produces genuine harm to individual citizens and the community at large.

The pyramid effect

The best illustration of the sometimes-hidden harmful effects of organized crime is the way in which the operation of an illegal enterprise forces its managers to commit other crimes. The objective of these other crimes is to ensure maximum profit from the original enterprise, to disguise and protect it from competition and from law enforcement, and to parlay the profits from that enterprise into investments in still other legal and illegal businesses. The growth or accumulation of crimes has a "pyramid effect"—one of the indicators of the existence of organized crime discussed earlier in this chapter.

The crime pyramid begins with a large-grossing illegal enterprise such as a numbers bank. To run the bank, its managers and employees must violate state lottery and perhaps other gambling laws, as well as state conspiracy laws, federal wagering tax laws, and probably federal income tax laws. If interstate communications facilities are used to lay off heavy bets or if the bank's personnel travel interstate to and from work, federal antiracketeering laws are violated each day that the bank operates.

Some observers, though, may be hard-pressed to identify any real harm done by such gambling operations to society, the individual bettors who patronize the bank, or citizens who live in the neighborhood where the numbers bank operates. A closer look reveals that the profits from the numbers operation are invested in other lucrative businesses and ventures, including real estate and loan-sharking, and that these investments have costly effects for the law-abiding community. For example, if gambling profits are plowed into real estate ventures that do not produce the return projected for the original investment, without compunction the racketeers may arrange to have the property burned in arson-for-profit schemes to collect fraudulent insurance claims. Even more vivid examples of the victimization of citizens come from documented cases of loan-shark operations. Crime syndicates place enormous pressure on loan sharks to move money on the street and collect installment payments on time, so that the money can be reinvested. The pressures are so intense that loan sharks frequently resort to threats and violence to effect their collections. The result is that loan-shark customers live with a degree of fear and face a degree of coercion usually unknown in most democratic societies.

The corruption of public institutions

The perpetuation of illegal enterprises depends on public corruption—the medium in which organized crime syndicates flourish and grow. Unless organized crime corrupts public institutions to minimize its risks, it cannot continue to exist. Such corruption undermines the political system and citizens' faith in their institutions. When public servants are dishonest, especially those in the front lines of protecting the public—law enforcement, the judiciary, other agencies of the criminal justice system, and administrative regulatory agencies—all citizens suffer. When public servants are dishonest, their loyalty is transferred from a public agency to a private interest group or an individual making bribe payments. As bribe payments continue, the corrupt employee becomes enmeshed in a system of private rewards that are reinforced (see the chapter on fostering integrity).

The perpetuation of illegal enterprises depends on public corruption—the medium in which organized crime syndicates flourish and grow.

Organized criminal groups engage in a number of forms of corruption to minimize risk. They seek to find the personal vulnerabilities of public officials so that they can be suborned and controlled. They use campaign contributions; they also use direct and indirect bribery, such as gifts, loans that the receiving officials need not repay, and insider information on investments, real estate, and business deals. Various types of assistance in the officials' career advancement are also employed. The organized crime groups' goal is to "hook" the official so that they can manipulate and control him or her. Once controlled, the official may be used immediately to facilitate organized crime–controlled businesses, contracts, loans, non-enforcement of laws or administrative regulations, gaining or shredding information, altering files, and the like. Or the compromised official may be kept "on ice" for those special occasions when an important favor or piece of information is needed.

In getting the edge, or minimizing risk, organized crime now finds inside information more important than "the pad" or other forms of police corruption that used to be common in some locales. Today, according to some experts, organized criminal groups also find it more important to corrupt the judicial system (courts, affiliated corrections agencies, and so forth), regulatory administrators, politicians, managers of contracts, and private citizens in positions of fiduciary trust than to corrupt law enforcement officials.

Corruption of law enforcement officials by organized crime occurs most frequently when the police confront the street activities and proceeds of drug trafficking and much less frequently when organized criminals seek generally to control or manipulate individual patrol officers. When police corruption does occur, either directly or through exposure to organized criminal activity such as drug trafficking, the consequences can be serious for the community and for the officer's peers.

Similarly, if employees of licensing, regulatory, and other public agencies (such as health and zoning boards) take bribe payments, the enforcement of laws, ordinances, and codes designed to protect the life and property of the general public is jeopardized. It follows that when more and more public agencies are nullified by syndicate-induced corruption, the community finds itself less able to meet urban problems and crises of every type. However difficult it may be under normal conditions for a public official such as a police administrator to define and then uphold the common good, under conditions of corruption the task is virtually impossible.

Organized crime and vice control

Corruption of public institutions is an essential environmental condition for the operation of such syndicate-controlled vice enterprises as prostitution, pornography, and gambling. Traditionally, however, when most police administrators have spoken of vice control, they have had one objective in mind: to reduce the ability of vice operators to conduct their trade in plain view (that is, in direct or close contact with the general public). These administrators have concluded that suppressing and displacing vice—that is, forcing the prostitute and gambler to begin to operate secretly, using the telephone or a courier rather than street contacts—is preferable to reducing vice operations to an irreducible minimum. One reason for concluding this is that the cost of enforcing vice laws is high: the only way to enforce these laws is to turn away from other pressing demands on police time, diverting officers from other crime control and peacekeeping functions. A second reason is the public's ambivalence about enforcing vice laws. A third is that many police administrators are simply resigned to the existence of vice as a fact of life.

One of the strongest arguments for enforcing vice laws is that it helps to dry up the huge revenues that otherwise would flow to organized crime groups.

However, reducing the visibility of vice operators has several consequences that the administrator should bear in mind. Decreased visibility makes it difficult for the police (and not only for their critics) to determine how much vice activity there really is. Beyond that, failure to treat displaced but still-thriving vice with the same seriousness as flagrant vice has two other, more serious consequences.

First, vice operators who have gone underground still cause problems, albeit different kinds. One of these is exacerbated corruption. Administrators who believe that the vice problem has disappeared tend to lose interest in vice enforcement and often no longer require—and may even choke off the flow of—information on the extent of vice activities. By doing this, they are allowing (and even tacitly encouraging) corruption in vice enforcement.

Second, when the police relax their enforcement of vice laws, organized crime groups may establish or enlarge their foothold in the lucrative vice rackets. In fact, one of the strongest arguments for enforcing vice laws is that it helps to dry up the huge revenues that otherwise would flow to organized crime groups.

Organized crime and white-collar offenses

Organized crime finds and operates in those gray areas between the legal and the illegal, where laws are vague and enforcement difficult. White-collar crime—which contemporary analysts frequently call business crime—has not generally been the province of organized criminals, but it is an area where civil and criminal violations come together, and therefore gaps in enforcement often appear that organized criminals can exploit. Shortly after the beginning of the twentieth century, before there were savings and loans or credit unions from which the small businessman could seek capital, successful criminals found themselves engaging in money lending and, before long, owning the borrowers' businesses. Similarly, today loan-sharking and drug dealing often result in organized criminals' gaining control of legitimate business enterprises and acquiring opportunities to engage in activities normally thought of as white-collar crime.

Organized crime frequently is involved in stolen securities, penny stock scams, and fraudulent bankruptcies ("bust-outs") because legitimate businesspeople, through gambling, drug use, or extortionate usury, find themselves indebted to members of criminal groups. The history of organized crime's involvement in the garment industry in New York City follows this pattern, just as labor strife in the first decade of the twentieth century gave organized crime an entry into labor racketeering. Indeed, control over labor union locals and their pension funds provided organized criminals with an entry into banking.[23] Law enforcement administrators need to stay sensitive to these linkages and not pigeonhole organized crime intelligence in police agency units focusing separately, and in isolation, on vice, drugs, and white-collar crime. Often, these illicit activities blend together. Some examples help illustrate the point.

Bankruptcy bust-out   A "bankruptcy bust-out" begins when organized criminals gain access to a legitimate retail business, often through gambling and loan-sharking debt. Then they may work to expand the credit with suppliers over several months, build up inventory, and then, often just before the holiday season, use that goodwill to place massive orders of new merchandise, sell it for cash at or below cost, loot the business, and leave the legitimate owner, suppliers, and creditors holding the debts. Sometimes a bust-out is orchestrated with a single step—the culprits simply buy increased inventory on the basis of the businessowner's credit rating and then gut the firm as just described. In both cases, the suppliers are victimized, the legitimate owner ruined, employees jobless, and the organized criminals often positioned beyond the reach of criminal investigations.

Securities theft and fraud   Organized criminal groups not only arrange for employees in their debt or under their control to "hand over" securities, but they also steal from the employees outright in burglaries and thefts. These securities are often used as collateral for bank loans. Pension funds in mob-controlled union locals have also been used in this manner. Through this process, loan officers and bank officials can be suborned and corrupted. The losses eventually fall on the bank's investors and insurance carriers and, through increased bank costs and insurance premiums, on the general public.

Money laundering   Whereas organized criminals may once have buried their money in the backyard or the trunk of an automobile, today they seek to launder, reuse, and continually profit from it. The myriad forms of money laundering would require another chapter to describe. But stated simply, money laundering is the process of taking illegally gotten, untaxable income and moving it through one or more accounts or false fronts so that it can return as legitimate business profits or as a loan to oneself that can be declared legitimate income (see Figure 8–3). Frequently the money moves through several jurisdictions in this process, and local law enforcement is likely to be aware of only parts of the journey.

What the local government can do is document what is happening in the community and pool its intelligence with that of other jurisdictions. The intelligence will help to answer several questions: Where is investment coming from? What large financial inputs into the community are occurring? What examples of obvious financial mismanagement are occurring?

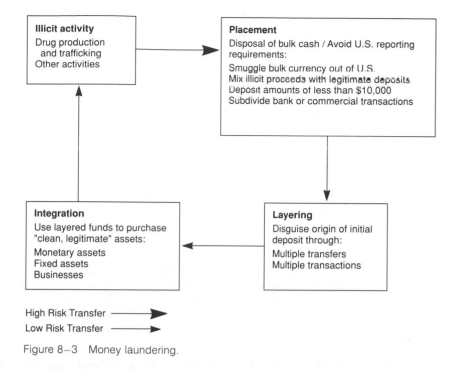

Figure 8–3   Money laundering.

Organized criminals traditionally like cash businesses; vending is a classic example. They also like businesses whose cash flow is difficult to track—pornography outlets, massage parlors, game rooms, restaurants, mobile canteens, legal gambling outlets (bingo, poker, Las Vegas nights), and the like. Shopping centers and small malls are popular legitimate investments as well. To the police official, knowing what is going on in the community, not just in law enforcement but in the banking and business sectors, can be a key proactive tool with respect to money laundering.

Labor racketeering   Labor racketeering is increasingly a blend of strong-arm and white-collar extortionate crime whose purpose is to access pension funds, obtain kickbacks, extort contracts, provide ghost jobs and income, or seek criminal monopolies over markets and industries. At the turn of the century in New York City, labor racketeering occurred in the ice and coal industries; today it is found in wholesale gasoline and heating oil distribution; airport cargo handling; drywall construction; sand, gravel, and cement; and the new immigrant sweat shops in the garment industry.[24] Other examples are solid waste carting, landfills, chemical and medical waste disposal, and other vital distribution systems.

In 1985 the federal government found that a number of labor union locals had been infiltrated by organized crime,[25] and a number of federal initiatives were undertaken to oust organized crime from these unions. Law enforcement administrators who have any unions in their jurisdictions should observe them carefully and watch that the locals are democratically run, do not use strong-arm methods, and are not subject to corruption or other forms of influence by organized crime.

Use of "front men"   Organized criminal control and ownership of legitimate business enterprises is usually masked and buffered by "front men" with no criminal records. False documentation is frequently used to obtain and renew licenses of various kinds. Liquor licenses are typical. When organized crime figures control bars, nightclubs, or retail outlets, their ownership is "off the books." A "beard"—or front owner—is listed as the owner of record. Thus, the application forms and other records are falsified. If they were not, uncorrupted regulatory agencies and their agents would refuse to grant or would revoke operating authority because of the ineligibility of the real owners. To assist such agencies, it is useful for states and cities to have business name laws requiring the true owners to be listed by name, address, date of birth, and social security number. This not only gives police better information about particular corporations, but it also provides an additional basis for enforcement against the criminal enterprise if the enterprise fails to comply with registration regulations.

Organized crime is moving more and more into white-collar-type crimes and rackets, as well as controlling legitimate business holdings acquired through the profits of crime.

Increasingly police officers must handle pens and computers as skillfully as they handle weapons. Documents, invoices, tax and bank records, and correspondence make up the paper trail that the effective organized crime investigator must follow. This is particularly so when drug money laundering is involved and when law enforcement authorities seek to use asset forfeiture to curtail organized crime activity (see the chapter on local drug control). Organized crime is moving more and more into white-collar-type crimes and rackets, as well as controlling legitimate business holdings acquired through the profits of crime. Criminals have an edge over legitimate businesspeople because of their willingness to use violence, intimidation, and corruption to gain their ends. Thus, local police departments must have—in-house or through interagency cooperation—broad-based skills in accounting and financial investigation, records and document search, and criminal intelligence.

The role of intelligence

A police department that maintains an effective intelligence program should be able to answer all of the following questions on organized crime:

Does it exist in this community and, if so, how extensive is it?

Who controls it?

Are leadership positions changing, and are new groups entering?

What illegal enterprises and legitimate businesses does organized crime control or have an interest in?

What section of the population is most directly victimized—drug addicts, loan-shark borrowers, businesspeople in certain industries, and so forth?

What is the extent of public corruption?

Answering these questions involves a five-step process in which raw information is developed into a finished intelligence product. The first step is the collection of raw information, and this is best done via an orderly collection plan. Such a plan could be developed out of the above questions, but it would be preferable to build it around some hypothesis about organized criminal intrusion into the local market (for example, a hypothesis about the role of loan-sharking in local sports-bet gambling). After information from all sources is collected and collated, the second step is to organize the information into specific categories, such as criminal networks, modi operandi, neighborhood territories, and the like. This lays the foundation for the third step—examination of overall trends and searches for offense patterns. Fourth, the analyst interprets the data to assess their immediate tactical and longer-term strategic usefulness. Finally, a summary of this assessment of problems and proposals for countermeasures is transmitted to law enforcement administrators for evaluation and action.

The kind of information collected and evaluated in this manner covers a broad range of subjects, including most of the following: the nature of organized criminal activity and degree of organization and monopolization; the kinds and degrees of violence, threat, and corruption; recruitment and career patterns among local organized criminals and groups; and the competitive or complementary nature of criminal networks in the community. Finally, it is also useful to profile the habits, personality, intellect, and other personal qualities of local criminal leaders and their cohorts.

E. Drexel Godfrey and Don R. Harris note that

the intelligence process is sometimes physical but always intellectual. Good intelligence analysts are highly skilled and unique professionals. Operational personnel must be educated to the key importance of intelligence in organized crime control. This requires a strong managerial commitment and the development of a skilled cadre. But once the intelligence concept is fully integrated into operations, the payoff in proactive and preventive crime control will be quickly seen.[26]

Gathering, analyzing, and acting upon information about criminal activity has always been an essential and legitimate police function. However, intelligence is a special class of information because it is cultivated either to identify crimes that otherwise would not be identified (because of their hidden nature) or to predict offenses that are likely to occur at a prearranged future time (for example, hijacking).

Intelligence information may be usefully conceptualized as either strategic or tactical information. In the context of organized crime, strategic intelligence identifies patterns and trends concerning the organized leadership structure, legal and illegal enterprises, and destinations of illegal profits. Tactical intelligence in its most useful form provides the police with information with which to make a criminal case. Therefore, to take the example of gambling, good strategic intelligence should identify the leaders and managers of a syndicate, their legal and illegal enterprises (such as a numbers bank and its office and layoff structure), and where gambling profits are invested. Good tactical intelligence should give the police probable cause to raid the numbers bank, each of its offices, and the layoff center and should develop evidence so that conspiracy cases can be built against the higher echelons in the syndicate.

Police often make the mistake of investing little time in strategic intelligence and spending most of their time gathering tactical intelligence. As a result, they conduct raid after raid and, in this way, try to drive illegal operations out of business. However, a good strategic picture can enable police to target the key managers and layoff people in the operation and move much higher in the operation's structure.

All too often, a lopsided investment in tactical intelligence serves primarily to generate large numbers of arrests and give the appearance that police are effectively attacking organized crime (see the chapter on performance measurement). Such efforts may result merely in forcing racketeers to shuffle numbers writers and lower level office locations around. As in most enterprises, low-level employees and storefront offices can be replaced with relative ease. The most honest and industrious police efforts aimed at street-level targets, unguided by accurate strategic information, barely make a dent in syndicate operations.

No discussion of the use of intelligence in controlling organized crime would be complete without some words of caution. In the beginning of the intelligence process, much information is developed about people whose associations with organized crime figures may be coincidental and unrelated to criminal acts. Care in safeguarding the reputations of these citizens is an essential aspect of any intelligence operation. Public concern over the indiscriminate collection and distribution of information is mounting. In some cases, this reaction is understandable; whether this general concern is exaggerated or not, the collection of information on the activities and associations of citizens is a serious issue. Police administrators who take precautionary steps to ensure the fairness and integrity of their intelligence effort can avoid demands that they abandon it.

The basic safeguards include collection only of information that is justified by reasonably suspected criminal conduct; development of standards for data that are to be included in the system; collation and analysis in a secure environment; purging of information or leads that are unfounded or out-of-date; and dissemination only to criminal justice agencies with a clear need to receive the information.[27] Although these safeguards typically are not difficult for a single department to adopt and follow, they become complicated in regional and other multijurisdictional intelligence-sharing arrangements. For this reason, a formal compact that sets forth explicit criteria and due process safeguards should precede the implementation of any intelligence-sharing arrangements.[28]

Because the intelligence process demands a major commitment of time and personnel, police must invest considerable effort before any useful information is developed. Frequently, therefore, the productivity of an intelligence program is called into question—not only by civil libertarians but also by police administrators themselves. As a result, many police administrators do not feel justified in supporting an intelligence effort in their department.

Departments that do have intelligence units complain that after a long time has been spent reducing raw intelligence to a few quality kernels of information, city officials or prosecutors remain uninterested in combating organized crime. There is no better way to destroy the morale of police intelligence personnel than to have them spend months developing good information only to see their product grow stale. Because this is not a rare occurrence, the police administrator should take care that proper emphasis is placed both on collecting the appropriate types of information and on improving the quality and usefulness of information.

Tools for combatting organized crime

Tremendous strides have been made in developing and honing the tools for combatting organized crime. Most of this effort has been at the federal level, but a good deal has been moving down to the state and local levels as well. This section briefly identifies for generalist police managers some of the principal resources and tools being used to combat organized crime today. These and similar law enforcement approaches merit detailed study by organized crime specialists in police departments and are the subject of many professional training programs.

The single most important tool in countering organized crime is a good intelligence unit.

The single most important tool in countering organized crime has already been discussed. It is a good intelligence unit, supported by files detailing over time the collection and analysis of intelligence. The second key tool is court-authorized wiretapping and electronic surveillance under Title III of the Omnibus Crime Control and Safe Streets Act of 1968. A number of states have adopted similar statutes, but their limitations—and thus their usefulness—vary. Wiretapping and electronic surveillance are vital tools, and the local law enforcement administrator can be assisted by a workable statute in his or her jurisdiction.

A third key tool is an immunity statute. The grant of immunity, when tied to wiretap or electronic surveillance information, has helped break the code of silence in organized crime. A fourth tool, at the federal level, is the witness security (or witness protection) program, which has helped to increase the effectiveness of the immunity statute. At the state level, other useful tools for helping to combat entrenched and corruptive organized crime are statewide or investigative grand juries, interagency task forces, and blue-ribbon citizens' crime commissions.

Informal interagency cooperation through entities such as the Law Enforcement Intelligence Unit (LEIU) that act as a clearinghouse for the exchange of law enforcement information, are also useful. Regional Information Sharing Systems (RISS) are helpful in providing a computerized investigative data base and some products of investigative analysis, such as toll call analysis and link charting (charting the connections in a social network), as well as technical assistance and referrals for local departments needing technical assistance. RISS is particularly useful when multijurisdictional drug trafficking enterprises are involved. Federal strike forces have also been vital in the successful prosecution of organized crime.[29] At the local level, joint interagency task forces, targeting specific criminal organizations or enterprises, can serve a similar function.

Interagency cooperation is a key to success in virtually all countermeasures against criminal enterprises.

Sometimes it is not the scope of the criminal enterprise but the nature of the intended victim that demands interagency cooperation. For example, there is evidence that organized crime groups are interested in exploiting Native American lands and developing enterprises on those lands. Native Americans are targeted by urban crime groups who see them as rural and thus as less sophisticated. In particular, various forms of legalized gambling and acquisition of sites for solid and toxic waste disposal are of interest to organized crime in Native American communities. Local law enforcement awareness and cooperation with the federal Bureau of Indian Affairs, tribal police, and other pertinent law enforcement authorities can help to reduce the organized crime threat to Native Americans.

Interagency cooperation is a key to success in virtually all countermeasures against criminal enterprises. Because criminal syndicates are multijurisdictional and increasingly transnational, cooperation and liaison among law enforcement agencies is essential. LEIU helps promote this, as do RISS and the learning and networking that can come from interagency task forces. Asset forfeiture laws, which permit participating law enforcement agencies to share both the equipment owned by criminal syndicates (planes, boats, cars, communications equipment, and so forth) and the proceeds of criminal endeavors, also have helped to cement cooperative ties and interagency liaison. Good tools and cooperative endeavors are critical to assisting local law enforcement in its front-line role of detecting and defeating organized crime.

Conclusion

This chapter has presented an overview of the evolution of organized crime and the spectrum of syndicate groups that constitute traditional and nontraditional organized crime. By describing the organizational elements of typical criminal enterprises, it has also suggested points of vulnerability that merit the attention of organized crime units in police departments. To identify the particular vulnerabilities of organized criminal operations in any given locale, law enforcement agencies must collect intelligence, analyze it, and safeguard its quality. Finally, for this intelligence to be used in meaningful countermeasures, carefully structured interagency cooperation and liaison are crucial. Without such joint action, efforts to strike at organized crime may do little more than displace it—to another block, another town, or another nation on this rapidly shrinking planet.

This chapter incorporates some material from the second edition's chapter on organized crime, and the author wishes to express his indebtedness to Charles Rogovin, who wrote that chapter, and to Clifford Karchmer, for his background research.

1　For more on the three-stage theory of the evolution of organized crime, see Peter A. Lupsha, "Organized Crime: Rational Choice, Not Ethnic Group Behavior—A Macro Perspective," *Law Enforcement Intelligence Analysis Digest* 3, no. 2 (Winter 1988): 1–8; and Edwin H. Stier and Peter R. Richards, "Strategic Decision Making in Organized Crime Control," in *Major Issues in Organized Crime Control: Symposium Proceedings*, ed. H. Edelhertz (Washington, DC: National Institute of Justice, 1987), 65–80.

2　The Nuestra Familia, Mexican Mafia, and Consolidated Crip Organization are important California prison gangs. Leslie "Ike" Atkinson and William H. Jackson, U.S. Army sergeants, ran a drug trafficking organization that moved heroin in body bags from Vietnam. The "Westies," an Irish dockworkers' group in New York City, did assassinations for LCN.

3　Seymour Martin Lipset, in *Political Man* (Garden City, NY: Doubleday, 1960), notes that high-risk occupational categories (mining, logging, fishing, etc.) also serve as political bonding mechanisms and incubators for political organizational movements such as the IWW.

4　These points are also made by Virgil W. Peterson, *The Mob: 200 Years of Organized Crime in New York* (Ottawa, IL: Green Hill Publishers, 1983); and Herbert Asbury, *The Gangs of New York* (New York: Knopf, 1928; New York: Capricorn Books, 1970).

5　Henner Hess, *Mafia and Mafiosi: The Structure of Power* (Lexington, MA: Lexington Books, 1973), and Normal Lewis, *The Honored Society* (New York: G. P. Putnam, 1964), see the emergence of the Sicilian Mafia as rooted in the weakness of the state, political change, and particular economic and social conditions.

6　Special federal strike forces and task forces have broken some of organized crime's stranglehold over these industries. But in many sectors organized crime–controlled enterprises, union locals, and trade associations remain an extortionate force in the marketplace. For one example, see New York State Organized Crime Task Force, *Interim Report on Corruption and Racketeering in the New York City Construction Industry* (Ithaca, NY: Institute for Labor Relations Press, Cornell University, 1988).

7　See Peter Reuter, *Racketeering in Legitimate Industries: A Study in the Economics of Intimidation* (Santa Monica, CA: Rand Corporation, 1987).

8　See Donald R. Cressey, *Theft of the Nation* (New York: Harper and Row, 1969); and Ralph Salerno and John Tompkins, *The Crime Confederation* (Garden City, NY: Doubleday, 1969).

9　The author is grateful to Robert J. Kelly, president of the New York–based International Association for the Study of Organized Crime, for assisting with this analysis.

10　See U.S. Government, "Mob Connected Lawyer," in President's Commission on Organized Crime: The Impact: *Organized Crime Today* (Washington, DC: U.S. Government Printing Office, 1986), 221–81.

11　For an excellent description of traditional LCN leadership styles, see John Cummings and Ernest Volkman, *Goombata* (Boston: Little, Brown and Company, 1990).

12　See Peter A. Lupsha, "Organized Crime in the United States," in *Organized Crime: A Global Perspective*, ed. Robert Kelly (Totowa, NJ: Rowman and Littlefield, 1986), 40–41; and Howard Abadinsky, *Organized Crime*, 3d ed. (Chicago: Nelson Hall, 1990), 45–59.

13　"Organized Crime in the Soviet Union," *C. J. International* 5, no. 6 (Nov.–Dec. 1989): 1–5.

14　See Lupsha, "Organized Crime: Rational Choice, Not Ethnic Behavior," 1–21.

15　Other examples of the use of racial, ethnic, and nationality identifiers can be found in the final report of the President's Commission on Organized Crime, *The Impact: Organized Crime Today* (Washington, DC: U.S. Government Printing Office, 1986); "Asian Organized Crime," *FBI Law Enforcement Bulletin* (October 1989); Pennsylvania Crime Commission, *1989 Report of the Pennsylvania Crime Commission* (October 1989); and the 1985–89 annual reports to the California legislature, each entitled *Organized Crime in California* (Sacramento: Department of Justice, state of California).

16　See Frederick Martens, "Black Organized Crime" (Paper presented at the Fourth Annual Symposium on International Criminal Justice Issues, University of Illinois at Chicago, 11–15 Sept. 1989).

17　For a political-historical view of Japanese organized crime, see David E. Kaplan and Alec Dubro, *Yakuza* (New York: MacMillan, 1986).

18　For a law enforcement–oriented overview of Asian organized crime, see James R. Brady, *Dragons and Tigers* (Loomis, CA: Palmer Enterprises, 1988).

19　See President's Commission on Organized Crime, Record of Hearing III, *Organized Crime of Asian Origin*, 23–25 Oct. 1984, New York, NY (Washington, DC: U.S. Government Printing Office, 1984); and Ko-lin Chin, *Chinese Subculture and Criminality: Non-traditional Crime Groups in America* (New York: Greenwood Press, 1990).

20　For an overview of Chinese organized crime, see Royal Hong Kong Police, *Triad Societies in Hong Kong* (Hong Kong: Government Press, 1960); Fenton Bresler, *The Chinese Mafia* (New York: Stein and Day, 1980); and Gerald Posner, *Warlords of Crime: Chinese Secret Societies—The New Mafia* (New York: McGraw-Hill, 1988).

21　For a good summary of government reports and an overview of outlaw motorcycle groups, see Yves Lavigne, *Hell's Angels: Taking Care of Business* (Toronto: Denneau and Wayne, 1987).

22 See Ralph Blumenthal, *The Last Days of the Sicilians: At War with the Mafia* (New York: Times Books, 1988); and the President's Commission on Organized Crime, Hearing V, *Organized Crime and Heroin Trafficking* (Washington, DC: Government Printing Office, 1985), 131–85.

23 See J. Kwitny, *Vicious Circles: The Mafia in the Marketplace* (New York: Norton, 1979).

24 New York State Organized Crime Task Force, *Interim Report on Corruption and Racketeering*.

25 President's Commission on Organized Crime, *"The Edge": Organized Crime, Business, and Labor Unions* (Washington, DC: U.S. Government Printing Office, 1985).

26 See E. Drexel Godfrey and Don R. Harris, *Basic Elements of Intelligence* (Washington, DC: U.S. Government Printing Office, 1971), 73–91; Paul P. Andrews, Jr., and Marilyn B. Peterson, *Criminal Intelligence Analysis* (Loomis, CA: Palmer Enterprises, 1990); and Justin Dintino and Frederick T. Martens, *Police Intelligence Systems and Crime Control* (Springfield, IL: Charles Thomas, 1983).

27 See Godfrey and Harris, *Basic Elements of Intelligence*, appendix A, 107–14.

28 A good example of a statewide system that publishes its objectives, methods of collection, and safeguards is the one described in New Jersey Department of Law and Public Safety, *New Jersey State Police Intelligence Manual* (West Trenton, NJ: Department of Law and Public Safety, 1975). See also Herbert Edelhertz, ed., *Major Issues in Organized Crime Control* (Washington, DC: U.S. Government Printing Office, 1987), especially chap. 7 (Frederick Martens, "The Intelligence Function," 131–53); International Association of Law Enforcement Intelligence Analysts (IALEIA) and their journal; and the publications of the National Association of Attorneys General on organized crime control.

29 In January 1990 Attorney General Richard Thornburgh eliminated the strike forces, distributing their staff among the U.S. attorneys' offices, an act criticized by U.S. senators, strike force members, and academic experts. See *Organized Crime Digest* 10, no. 17 (13 Sept. 1989): 1–2; and "DOJ Now Merging Organized Crime Strike Forces into U.S. Attorneys' Offices," *Crime Control Digest* 24, no. 1 (8 Jan. 1990): 3–4.

Part four: Departmental infrastructure

9 Fostering integrity

Next to tyranny, corruption is the great disease of government.[1]

This chapter discusses two different but often confused—or at least imprecisely distinguished—topics: *corruption* and *noncorrupt misconduct*.[2] Although the meanings of these terms for police behavior will become clear in the course of the chapter, brief definitions are necessary at the outset. The term "corruption" is used in its traditional sense: an officer's misuse of police authority for personal gain. "Misconduct" means nonconformity with police obligations and encompasses corruption and a host of other misdeeds (for example, using excessive force; abusing medical leave; sleeping on duty; and violating a suspect's Fourth or Fifth Amendment rights during a street stop or a stationhouse interrogation).

The heading under which these two concepts are discussed here draws attention to the positive rather than the negative: "Fostering Integrity" challenges police managers to strive not only for the absence of corruption or other misconduct but also for the presence of something positive. That "something" is integrity, which, by definition, is an uncompromising adherence to a code of values. In policing, integrity means a personal commitment by each member of the department to do his or her best (whether under a supervisor's or outsider's scrutiny or totally unobserved) to further the department's goal of honorably and lawfully serving and protecting the public in a host of ways. A premise of this chapter is that police executives charged with controlling corruption or other misconduct must see themselves as part of an administrative system whose ultimate goal is to create an environment in which each officer is challenged and helped to do his or her "personal best" so that the public is well served and protected. Put another way, the goal is to contain corruption and misconduct in ways that simultaneously improve, or at least do not impair, the organization's capacity to control crime and meet community needs. This is a tall order.

Because several other chapters touch on useful techniques for identifying and responding to noncompliance with official obligations (obligations that are expressed in agency policies, rules, regulations, and procedures), this chapter focuses most heavily on corruption and methods of controlling it. Discussed first are traditional attitudes toward corruption, the forms corruption takes, the damage it does, and the conditions that foster it. Discussed next is a many-faceted strategy for fostering integrity. Then the chapter describes internal control systems that can help detect, correct, and avert a variety of noncorrupt police misdeeds. After a discussion of disciplinary procedures, the chapter concludes by addressing two special problems likely to occupy the police executive's "in" box for the balance of this century: testing personnel for drug abuse, and devising ways of containing corruptive influences and temptations to other forms of misconduct as police departments adopt, or enhance their use of, community or problem-oriented policing methods.

Bringing corruption out of the closet

Most police officials treat corruption as a subject to be avoided. The prevailing view is that the less said, the better. Political oversight, public debate, or media

The public trust　The American ideal of government as a public trust to be carried on by disinterested men represents not the actuality but a long step ahead in the evolution of man. . . . It is a very difficult ideal to attain, and I know of no man in America even in our time who has felt able to be completely loyal to it. . . .The campaign . . . on behalf of the idea of trust is no mere repairing of something perfect that has broken down, but the implanting of a new habit of acting in the ancient consciousness of man.

Source: Walter Lippmann, "A Theory about Corruption," in *Police Corruption: Readings in Comparative Analysis*, ed. Arnold J. Heidenheimer (New York: Holt, Rinehart and Winston, 1970), 296–97.

scrutiny of corrupt practices is deemed risky. Even in the relative privacy of professional journals and law enforcement conferences, there is scant discussion of corruption. Though most police officials recognize it to be a chronic problem, not all concede that it is a serious one, and this is so even in departments with an acknowledged history of police wrongdoing.

In many ways, this perspective is understandable. The public does not realize that even in the best-managed departments there is an irreducible amount of misconduct—that some rule breaking is an integral part of bureaucratic life. Nor does the public appreciate that it is the conscientious, well-administered police department that struggles hardest to limit corrupt practices and that is most likely to expose corruption. Nor does anyone find it easy to identify precisely how the presence of corruption impairs overall departmental performance.

Police wrongdoing often arouses in the public a special feeling of betrayal. Citizens expect officers to be trustworthy and dependable. They do not expect officers to collaborate with criminals any more than they expect doctors to spread disease. When citizens find that officers have betrayed their trust, the tendency is to blame the messenger—the chief of police who not only failed to prevent the misconduct but also made it known to the public. Thus, the chief's initiatives are not likely to earn praise from the city council or the editors of the local newspaper; paradoxically, they may tarnish his or her reputation and that of the department.

Even in the relative privacy of professional journals and law enforcement conferences, there is scant discussion of corruption.

In cities where police corruption is part of the urban landscape, it eventually gains acceptance; the public becomes indifferent to reports of most kinds of wrongdoing. Citizens, to the extent that they think about corruption at all, may consider it the price they have to pay for effective law enforcement—and not too high a price, at that. In Philadelphia, for example, an opinion survey taken in 1986 revealed that residents view the police favorably, even though most believe that police engage extensively in wide-ranging misbehavior. For example, one-half of the respondents think the police take bribes "often" (11 percent) or "sometimes" (38 percent). Only 12 percent think they never do.[3] The problem is not new. Lincoln Steffens, who happened to be talking about Philadelphia but could just as easily have been describing other large cities of the day, described its citizenry as "corrupt but content."

Although corruption probably touches every police department to some extent at some time, its scope varies greatly. A few departments may be so corrupt that their officers are committing burglaries and making drug deals. Other departments are basically honest. In some departments with significant corruption problems, high officials may be on the take, whereas in others they may be honest but negligent in preventing and detecting wrongdoing by subordinates. In a few departments, law-abiding officers may be willing to provide information about the criminal behavior of other officers; in most, though, a code of protective silence prevails.

The history of police corruption in the United States is largely a history of vice enforcement (enforcement of the laws against drug trafficking, gambling, and prostitution). Therefore, serious police corruption seems to be an urban phenomenon. However, there are big city departments without major corruption, and there are suburban and small-town departments that are notoriously dishonest.

As a whole, apart from police involvement in drug trafficking, there is probably less corruption today than in the past, even one generation ago. The improvement is due partly to heightened police awareness and willingness to take more aggressive internal action, but it is also a consequence of political changes that have reduced outside pressures on police officials. As machine politics has diminished and police personnel have come to be selected and retained in accord with merit rules, fewer officers are being hired, promoted, or given desirable assignments because of favoritism.

When citizens find that officers have betrayed their trust, the tendency is to blame the messenger—the chief of police who not only failed to prevent the misconduct but also made it known to the public.

Still, corruption remains a problem. In the 1980s, prosecution for corruption created front-page stories in New York (officers found to have extorted money from crack dealers), Boston (alleged payoffs from vice purveyors), Los Angeles (county sheriff's deputies charged with theft of seized drug money), Miami (officers accused of running drug distribution enterprise), Chicago (officers alleged to have participated in a drug ring), Philadelphia (high-ranking officials charged with involvement in illegal gambling, fourteen vice officers indicted), and Detroit (twenty officers charged with felonies ranging from assault and armed robbery to murder).

These prosecutions highlight not only the persistence of the problem but also the potentially close relationship between vice enforcement and corruption, particularly with respect to narcotics. Today, drug trafficking poses a unique and perhaps unprecedented challenge to police integrity. Not since Prohibition have officers been subjected to so many opportunities for easy money as they are in today's drug environment, which involves vast sums of money. A few departments have responded openly and aggressively. For example, in 1987 New York City police officials publicly identified drug use as their foremost corruption problem[4] and established a special twelve-person undercover squad to investigate drug use among officers. But most departments have taken a business-as-usual approach. Thus it is hard to estimate the extent to which the free line of cocaine has replaced the free cup of coffee,[5] but it is clear that officers find it harder to resist involvement in what, traditionally, they have condemned as "dirty" graft[6]— illegal drug commerce.

Both the situation created by narcotics and the long history of corruption have led many police administrators to despair of change and to conclude that little can be done. In the sense that major reforms cannot ordinarily produce results in the short term, they are correct. But the experience of many cities demonstrates that honest law enforcement is attainable. These cities boast police forces that are well managed, have a clear sense of mission, and are free of systemic corruption.

This chapter treats corruption as a problem that needs continuing and perhaps increased scrutiny. The opportunities to profit from drug traffic threaten not only to erode the substantial progress the police have achieved in the last several decades but also to inhibit further progress. Though reducing corruption will not, by itself, transform unresponsive, backward bureaucracies into robust, efficient agencies, it will make it possible for the chief to establish a forum where innovation and effectiveness can occur—and where integrity can flourish.

Faces of corruption

Although the term "police corruption" is often used in reference to all kinds of wrongful police activities, including brutality, racial discrimination, perjury, and general arbitrariness, as well as payoffs, here the term is used more particularly to mean misuse of police authority for personal gain. Defined this narrowly, the term nonetheless embraces a wide range of misconduct—from accepting large payoffs from gamblers and drug dealers in return for immunizing them against arrest to accepting the more common "gifts" of a bottle of liquor or a five-dollar bill in return for performing some small favor, such as permitting illegal parking.

Most corruption is passive in that it does not involve the pursuit of payoffs by police officers. The officer simply accepts what is offered without discussing its size (perhaps there is a tacit understanding as to what the violation is "worth"). Another kind of corruption, more serious but involving fewer officers, might be called negotiable graft. The officer and the criminal engage in a kind of bargaining. The police officer who apprehends a burglar negotiates a payoff rather than shaking the suspect down for all he or she has. (Sophisticated burglars carry "insurance" money for just such occasions.) A third kind of corruption is hard-nosed extortion, engaged in by a small percentage of officers. These officers are entrepreneurs; determined to make as much money as possible, they are unlikely to be deterred by any measures short of arrest.

Accepting bribes from vice dealers

Of the many forms corruption takes, none is more common, or more sinister in its implications, than accepting bribes from dealers in vice, especially drug dealers. The police may be vulnerable to overtures from vice dealers not only because of the money to be made but also as a consequence of public apathy toward vice enforcement (an apathy that is changing as regards drug crimes). The police are acutely aware of the ambiguous and conflicting public sentiments toward prostitution and gambling and, historically, toward drug enforcement. The social consensus that supports the apprehension of rape, murder, assault, and robbery suspects often does not exist when it comes to "morals" offenses. Large segments of the public are not bothered by vice if the commerce is kept within certain geographical boundaries or off the street. The absence of broad public support for vice enforcement makes taking a bribe from a dealer in vice seem less wrongful to an officer.

The typical vice transaction involves two willing parties, a buyer and a seller, both of whom want to insulate themselves from police surveillance. It is the seller, particularly the representative of an organized criminal enterprise, who is the more dependent on police protection and provides the greater opportunity for police corruption: to continually serve their customers, sellers must purchase protection from arrest (see the chapters on organized crime and local drug control).

Historically, the form of vice that was most linked to police corruption was gambling. Gambling rings can provide a steady source of income to police officers. A monthly payment may be made to a single officer, who divides it up among those who would otherwise threaten the enterprise. Sometimes high-ranking officers get the largest amounts; sometimes only vice officers receive a share, while patrol officers are excluded.

During the 1980s drug trafficking overtook gambling as the most lucrative opportunity for graft. The illicit drug business calls for large interlocking networks connecting growers in foreign countries with importers and with street distributors, and at each link in the chain, there are prospects for bribes. For example, a rural sheriff who directs the county's only two patrol cars away from the field where a small aircraft loaded with marijuana will be landing can earn a few thousand dollars for his or her efforts. Or narcotics officers making arrests can withhold part or all of the drugs and money seized. Or, as researchers Mark Moore and Mark Kleiman have written, "Informants and undercover operations—so essential to effective drug enforcement—inevitably draw police officers into close, potentially corrupting relationships with the offenders they are pledged to control."[7] A case in Miami is particularly illustrative. The 1986 indictment of seven city officers known as the River Cops, or the Enterprise, revealed that they started by stealing drugs from motorists they had stopped for traffic violations and eventually worked their way up to major drug thefts with the help of informants, who told them where loads of cocaine were stored.[8] Instead of arresting the dealers, they stole the drugs. Similarly, in New York City, officers in a remote precinct made use of informants and undercover operations to regularly steal or accept drugs and money from marijuana and crack dealers. Similar stories from scores of other cities can be told.

Large segments of the public are not bothered by vice if the commerce is kept within certain geographical boundaries or off the street. The absence of broad public support for vice enforcement makes taking a bribe from a dealer in vice seem less wrongful to an officer.

Although it is unusual for drug dealers to file complaints against arresting officers, such complaints are made, most often by residents of the neighborhood where the drugs are sold. In 1985, the largest percentage of formal complaints about police misbehavior in New York City concerned narcotics, and most of these alleged drug use or the protection of drug dealers by members of the force.

Police involvement in the drug traffic, one can speculate, is probably greater than news accounts indicate. The absence of reports of drug-related misconduct in a large urban department may suggest the presence of honest officers—but it may just as easily suggest a failure to investigate by police administrators.

One variant of informant-related vice corruption, often suspected but difficult to prove, does not involve bribery but is the *invention* by vice officers or detectives of a confidential informant. In departments where investigators are given great latitude, supervisors sometimes do not scrutinize assertions that information was acquired from an informant or do not verify that such a person actually exists. Thus, a narcotics investigator, tipped off by a friendly drug dealer who wants to stifle competition, can defraud the department by pretending that the information was purchased from a confidential informant. In 1988, one Boston police officer secured thirty-one warrants during a ten-month period on the basis of information allegedly received from an informant named John. In fact, John did not exist, but the officer received several thousand dollars in department funds to pay "John" for his tips. These lies came to light only when an officer serving one of the search warrants was shot and killed by the occupant of the place to be searched, and subsequent judicial proceedings revealed the fraud.[9]

Accepting petty bribery

In addition to vice, other activities provide opportunities for graft. A common situation is that of the motorist who is stopped for a moving traffic violation, such as speeding or ignoring a red light. Wishing to avoid spending a day in court, paying a fine and higher insurance premiums, or losing driving privileges, the motorist offers the traffic cop a few dollars. In some cities, such petty bribery is so routine that drivers fold money, along with their driver's license, in a plastic container before passing it to the traffic officer. The officer can remove the bill without alerting passersby that he or she is taking a bribe.

Similarly, the professional criminal, when arrested, may seek to avoid prosecution by making a payoff to the arresting officer. One professional safecracker, arrested numerous times over a forty-year period, claimed that he frequently avoided prosecution by paying the investigators. Sometimes veteran officers turned down his first offer, hoping that, as his court date approached, he would better the offer.

With an inexperienced suspect, the arresting officer may try a different approach, that of a helping friend. Purporting to do the arrestee a favor, the officer steers him or her to a bondsman or attorney, but the real motive is to earn a kickback. Sometimes the soliciting officer, knowing that the prosecutor will decline to file charges in this type of case as a matter of office policy, claims that part or all of the money is for the prosecutor. When the decision is made to decline prosecution, the suspect who paid the bribe to the bondsman or attorney assumes that the money was responsible.

Accepting small gratuities

"As the Statue of Liberty is the symbol of freedom in the United States, the [free] cup of coffee may be the symbol of compromise in policing."[10] This quotation identifies a category of behavior so frequent and so apparently innocent that many do not identify it as corruption. It is the free cup of coffee, the half-price meal, the discount "police price" on merchandise, the Christmas present, the weekly "sawbuck" from the jeweler for more frequent patrol, the reward from the insurance company for recovering stolen property. Though these benefits arrive without a formal request by the police officer—he or she does not have to put out a hand—the officer nonetheless expects them. In some departments they are so customary that police officers come to look on them openly as "perks" (perquisites)—something to which they have a right, like dental insurance or other employee benefits.

Nor do the citizens who hand out these small favors regard their behavior as wrong, even though they expect a return on their "investment"—either special service or the overlooking of certain illegal acts or conditions.

Many police administrators allow these practices to continue. Because there is no victim who will complain, they can safely ignore them; the "gifts" are not solicited, after all, but are volunteered. Though departmental rules may prohibit officers from accepting such benefits, these administrators see other problems as far more important. If the patrol officer is otherwise doing the job satisfactorily and if the businessperson does not offer the gift in too blatant a manner, administrators do not seek out violators.

Taking kickbacks and similar "rewards"

The officer accustomed to accepting small rewards may become greedier over time. Establishing "relationships" with businesses can provide additional opportunities for income. The officer who refers customers can receive a kickback. The police officer at the scene of an automobile collision can steer the motorist whose car is damaged to a particular garage and receive a reward from the tow truck operator. Although the towing fee itself may be of small consequence to the operator, especially if set by municipal regulation, repairing the damaged car can be lucrative. Similar working relationships are often established between police officers and those who provide services in times of crisis—undertakers, bondsmen, criminal lawyers, and doctors.

Other common occasions for kickbacks arise from enforcement of municipal ordinances, such as Sunday blue laws, or background investigations for the issuance of licenses. For example, in states where the state liquor control board relies on the police to conduct character investigations of applicants, those with disqualifying backgrounds may pay the investigating officer to omit unfavorable information from the report, and there may be something in it for the investigator's supervisor as well.

Stealing

Another form of corruption may be characterized as "opportunistic theft" in that it arises naturally out of the performance of an officer's routine duties. The officer called upon to assist drunk or injured citizens, for example, has the

---

Doughnut shop ethics There is a popular perception that police officers accept free coffee and meals from local restaurants, and sometimes it is true. Many administrators have been embarrassed by police accepting gratuities, yet find it very difficult to enforce rules against the practice. Several things can help.

First, the following basic ethics tests may provide guidance for behavior:

1. Test of common sense: Does the act make sense, or would anyone look somewhat askance at it?

2. Test of publicity: Would you be willing to see what you did highlighted on the front page of your local newspaper?

3. Test of one's best self: Will the act fit the concept of yourself at your best?

4. Test of one's most admired person: What would Mom, Dad, your minister/priest/rabbi do in this situation?

5. Test of hurting someone else: Will the act contribute to "internal pain" for someone?

6. Test of foresight: What is the long-term likely result?

Second, police officers need new techniques so that they can tactfully

and with dignity avoid gratuities and the accompanying embarrassment. Three basic steps are the following:

1. Vary your habits and places. Take breaks, eat meals, and fill out reports at different times and places. If you're regularly seen in uniform at the same coffee shop by the same people, even if your presence is completely justified, the perception may build that this is how you spend most of your working time.

2. Develop a set response, without fanfare, for avoiding the offer of free coffee. Know the price of coffee and, on your way out, leave that amount at the cash register, with or without a bill. No matter what the cashier might say, simply lay down the money, add a smile and a "thank you," and leave.

3. Develop set responses for declining free or half-priced food. For example, you might say, "No, I feel much better paying the same as everyone else. But thanks for being thoughtful." If the cashier gives you an argument, even a well-meant one, place the money on the counter and leave, with a simple "thank you."

Source: Adapted from Bruce L. Benson and Gilbert H. Skinner, "Doughnut Shop Ethics: There are Answers," *The Police Chief* (December 1988): 32–33.

opportunity to commit theft with little chance of discovery. Similarly, officers on routine night patrol of commercial establishments may find a store unlocked or broken into and may take advantage of this opportunity to loot the premises. So, too, officers who arrest narcotics dealers may decide on the spur of the moment to hold back a portion of seized drugs or funds for self-enrichment.

Taking bribes from other officers

The types of corruption discussed so far occur between citizens and police officers. Another significant arrangement is that between officers. Herman Goldstein, summarizing the results of investigations in several large cities, identifies a number of such practices: street officers may pay inside officers to falsify attendance records, influence the vacations and days off they receive, and report them on duty when they are not; they may also pay to get records unusually quickly, to be called at the beginning of a court session, and to be given passing grades in training programs.[11] The street officer may also make a payoff for being assigned to an area with opportunities for graft.

Internal payoffs provide a way in which the police on the street share illegal gains with those working inside, who have fewer opportunities for corruption. It is safe to generalize that wherever there is widespread corruption between police and citizens, there are likely to be payoffs between police officers as well.

The damage done by corruption

The damage caused by corruption extends beyond the crime of corruption itself. Corruption facilitates criminality and decreases law enforcement. It may also reduce public confidence in the police, inhibiting citizens from cooperating in crime prevention and control. Within the department, corruption makes it difficult for officials to run the department efficiently and fairly or to introduce needed changes; it stymies innovation. Beyond this, corruption undermines departmental morale and individual self-esteem.

Corruption may reduce public confidence in the police, inhibiting citizens from cooperating in crime prevention and control.

Facilitation of crime

When police protect gamblers or drug dealers, they are allowing gambling and drug dealing to proceed unchecked. They are also facilitating the violence and criminality that characteristically attend the gambling rackets and drug trade. And when the police themselves use or (as was the case in several cities in the mid-1980s) sell drugs, they are not only acting criminally but also taking time from their enforcement duties: making a dishonest buck may consume most of their energy. In fact, police corruption undermines departmental discipline in ways that seriously affect street performance. Police officers who spend their working hours pursuing payoffs have little time and less inclination to perform their assigned duties. Moreover, when honest officers learn that others are on the take, they may seek a transfer, thereby creating a vacancy for others willing to break the law—or, worse, they may decide to get their share, too.

Erosion of public confidence

Police corruption is generally assumed to undermine public confidence in the police. It promotes an uneasiness in the community. Police officers are most effective when the public believes that they are on the job and can be depended upon. When corruption is exposed or believed to exist, the public feels both betrayed and vulnerable, and support for the police erodes. Citizens may question why they should struggle to play by the rules when the authorities do not, and they may be more reluctant to provide information to the police about unsolved crimes or to appear as witnesses in criminal proceedings.

Interference with departmental efficiency and effectiveness

Some police officials do not think that corruption interferes with the sound management of the department, especially when the corruption is confined to vice enforcement. They argue that any patterns of corruption will not prevent the chief from implementing whatever organizational changes or experiments he or she feels are necessary. But research suggests that this is wishful or self-serving thinking. As John Kaplan has pointed out, corrupt police organizations are also organizationally rigid, and this rigidity limits innovation and prevents the promotion of officials who are not bound to the status quo.[12] Corrupt police officers attempt to subvert reorganizations or changes of assignment that threaten to curtail their profit making. They also oppose directives from the chief's office intended to promote more enlightened law enforcement—for example, a directive not to enforce Sunday blue laws except with supervisory approval—if such directives would limit their "opportunities."

A supervisor who solicits or accepts bribes cannot easily control misconduct by subordinates.

Problems are compounded when supervisory personnel are on the take. A supervisor who solicits or accepts bribes cannot easily control misconduct by subordinates. He or she lacks the moral authority to compel obedience or maintain satisfactory levels of either discipline or productivity. When sergeants, lieutenants, or captains get the bulk of the graft, patrol officers learn that as long as they don't rock the boat, they need not worry about discipline and can take their duties lightly. If they find a cozy spot for taking a nap or lingering over a cup of coffee, they will not be penalized. Without effective supervision, officers are likely to respond more slowly to calls for assistance, avoid assigned duties, sleep on the job, look for ways to earn extra money, and perform poorly in situations requiring discipline and organization.

Impairment of departmental morale

When the public believes that corruption exists within the department, the honest officers pay a heavy psychological price. Individual officers may have to go about their business knowing that many citizens consider them simply as crooks in uniform. And such innocent acts by an officer as purchasing a new television set or new car can lead suspicious neighbors to speculate, or perhaps even to make a remark to the officer's children, about where the money came from. People who see gamblers, pushers, or hookers in their neighborhoods may treat every cop as if he or she were on the take.

Furthermore, because corruption is a first cousin to favoritism and nepotism, many officers in departments where corruption has long existed will probably be convinced that the department is not fairly run. In this atmosphere, it is harder for them to take pride in their everyday achievements of preventing crime, apprehending criminals, and assisting persons in distress. Honest administrators may find it difficult to motivate or supervise officers who lack such pride.

In addition, when a scandal is uncovered, the department may respond—naively or cynically—by imposing new rules and regulations, as if the absence of prohibitions were what caused officers to go on the take in the first place. These new rules will justifiably arouse skepticism among the rank and file. Street officers will question the aptitude and intentions of officials, wondering whether the new rules are just an attempt to make the public believe that something is being done.

If corruption continues, anticorruption rules accumulate in an effort to cover every conceivable situation, becoming a large storehouse of "thou shalt nots." But, as Goldstein observes, "This emphasis upon negative guidance creates an atmosphere of distrust that is demoralizing to honest and well-intentioned officers."[13]

Conditions that breed corruption

In some cities, despite continual, determined efforts by police chiefs to eradicate corruption, it manages to survive. Conversely, in places where chiefs pay little attention to corruption, it is apparently absent. In other words, it would appear that there are conditions other than the chief's behavior that help determine the presence or absence of police corruption.

In cities where corruption has long existed, it is likely to be embedded in a larger political and social culture of accommodation, favoritism, and dishonesty, and to be broadly tolerated by the chief of police, top officials, the rank and file, and the union or police association. In these departments, police discretion to investigate or arrest is largely unsupervised, and the police are likely to perceive the prosecutors and judges as antagonists who are at best ineffective and at worst corrupt.

Lax community standards

It is a truism that police corruption arises in a context of shared values and expectations. To a substantial degree, police behavior simply mirrors the ethics of the larger community in which the police carry out their duties. Machine politics and policing do not mix, but they are not strange bedfellows. No police department can remain an island of integrity in a sea of corruption; governmental and societal corruption spill over into policing.

To a substantial degree, police behavior simply mirrors the ethics of the larger community in which the police carry out their duties.

The 1980s and early 1990s were notorious for revelations of wrongdoing by persons of far higher status than police officers; at the highest levels of visibility, these revelations touched even White House staff. Almost daily, the media reported the wrongdoing of corporation executives, investment bankers, securities dealers, ministers, congressmen, and officials of federal departments. The breadth and variety of white-collar criminality has been as impressive as it is disheartening.

Operating in this larger environment, it is not surprising that police become cynical about their work and feel that "nothing is on the level." When they meet citizens from every walk of life who are willing to pay them to overlook the law—the citizen who wants to avoid a traffic ticket, the entrepreneur who wants to get the jump on competitors, the criminal who wants to be free to carry on an illegal operation—some officers come to see themselves as "operating in a world where 'notes' are constantly floating about, and only the stupid, the naive, and the fainthearted are unwilling to allow some of them to stick to their fingers."[14]

Hesitation of the police chief

At the outset, we noted that many police chiefs hesitate to deal with corruption. "Personally honest police chiefs," it has been said with only slight exaggeration, "will go to extraordinary lengths—even to the point of making fools or suspects of themselves in public—in efforts to shield from exposure crooks and incompetents within the ranks."[15] They will minimize the scope of departmental wrongdoing (just as corrupt officials will assert its omnipresence), declaring that it involves only a few "bad apples," when in fact the barrel is rotten.

One reason for this attitude has already been cited: the fear that once corruption is exposed, the public will exaggerate its scope and thereby damage the chief's and the department's reputation. Beyond this, there is often the belief that the problem is intractable, that the work environment provides too much temptation for the average officer. Some well-meaning community leaders may even reinforce this view by speculating that corruption is inevitable or not that serious, or that any action taken will be futile.

Apart from these considerations, uprooting corruption may involve investigating long-time colleagues and friends. Police officers charged with corruption are frequently well-known to the police chief. They may be people with whom the chief has worked for many years. The chief will be inclined to look tolerantly upon their faults. Even in situations where the chief does not know those charged, he or she is likely to be forgiving. Having come up through the ranks, the chief may have been exposed to, or even participated in, similar wrongdoing.

The chief who accepts the view that corruption is here to stay is unlikely to give much thought to how to combat it internally. Consequently, the department's internal affairs function is probably lethargic, understaffed, undertrained, and lacking in status. It waits for complaints to be brought to its attention—a passive method of operation that gives corruption a holiday from enforcement, particularly if the majority of personnel assigned to corruption control are in internal affairs.

The chief who accepts the view that corruption is here to stay is unlikely to give much thought to how to combat it internally.

Some chiefs fail to hold precinct and division commanders accountable for corruption in their commands. They purport to rely on their internal affairs staff, thus encouraging commanders to pass the buck. In deeply corrupt departments, such abdication of responsibility is the ultimate failing of chiefs who, though honest themselves, act as if survival is their only goal. They may be aware of the fate of police leaders at other times or in other places who launched vigorous anticorruption drives but did not, for the most part, win a public following and may have been pushed out of office. Career professionals who are hired from another department to combat corruption often know, going into the job, that their stay will necessarily be short, perhaps only two or three years.

Although some reform chiefs have been successful—witness the successes in eradicating systemic corruption in New York City in the early 1970s—too often anticorruption efforts are not sufficiently focused or long-lasting and achieve only transitory results while unleashing "years of turmoil, bitterness, intrigue and misery" and producing only minimal change.[16] The pattern then is a "cycle of deviance, scandal, reform and repression, followed by scandal. [When] the sound and fury die away, it is all too often a case of returning sooner, or later, to business as usual."[17] But, as this chapter will show, when the department takes a multifaceted approach, including both a positive agenda and punishment of wrongdoing, this need not be the case.

Tolerance among the rank and file and the unions

For a variety of reasons, officers look to their fellow officers for support and understanding. A spirit of solidarity binds them and, at the same time, segregates them from the rest of society. Vis-à-vis the rest of society, officers may feel unappreciated, misunderstood, and even beleaguered. If they are assigned to patrol, it is difficult for them to develop and retain civilian friends because their working hours change continually and they rarely have weekends off. Over time, some officers even come to see those outside the police service (that is, all civilians) as unsympathetic, uninformed, perhaps hostile. As a result, they may develop an excessive tolerance for the misconduct of fellow officers.

In departments where corruption is rife, new officers may have to engage in illegal conduct to be accepted. Their first wrongful act is a kind of initiation. It admits them to the group and proves that they can be "trusted." Conversely, those who decline to "take" are suspect. They will be pressured, almost from the beginning of their service, to accept bribes, to be like the others. Though honest at the start, they frequently fall under the influence of senior colleagues who have lost faith in the value of police work. Of course, not all rookies succumb. But those who don't must pay a price for asserting their integrity, and the price depends on the amount of corruption around them.

In departments where corruption is rife, new officers may have to engage in illegal conduct to be accepted.

The corrupting of a rookie is ordinarily a gradual process. It begins with little things—offers of a free drink, a discounted meal, a "tip" for good service—which other officers on the shift encourage the rookie to accept. Padding overtime (for example, an excessive number of officers show up at a drunk driving arrest so all can get paid extra for a court appearance) is another common example. (Unions may be of little assistance in thwarting such practices because the practices serve officers' economic interests.)

More substantial "rewards" follow. The officer begins to do his or her "friends" favors in return, cutting corners on assigned duties in the process. The officer rationalizes this: no one is hurt; other officers do it. After all, that's the way the whole world is; everybody cheats. As time passes, rationalization becomes easier.

Eventually, most police officers come to realize that their entire career will be spent on patrol, where there will be no promotions and no substantial pay increases, yet they will be required to perform complex, ill-defined, sometimes contradictory, and often thankless tasks that, in a perfect world, would be performed by social workers, psychologists, physicians, and lawyers—persons who enjoy higher status and higher compensation. Some officers will then rationalize their illegal gains as part of what society owes them for doing its dirty work. (Elsewhere in this volume police departments are urged to develop career paths for officers within the patrol assignment. If this is done, the temptations may be reduced for some officers.) If officers have come to depend on such outside income—"taking" provides them and their family with things they could not otherwise have—they may be quite tenacious in holding on to it.

To justify receipt of such outside "income," officers make specious distinctions between "good" and "bad" (meaning "acceptable" and "unacceptable") bribes. They overpower their consciences, insisting that taking a bribe from a gambler or a prostitute is not wrong because the corrupter is providing services demanded by otherwise law-abiding citizens.

Even police officers who are themselves honest tolerate corruption. They keep silent about and pretend not to know what other officers—officers with whom they have to work and on whom they depend—are doing. If interviewed by an investigator from the internal affairs unit, they will go far to avoid telling the truth. Not only do they want to remain uninvolved, but they also believe that police officers should not snitch on fellow officers. Covering up is seen as standing up.

Once caught, the corrupt officer often has much the same attitude, refusing to implicate other police officers—not only from fear but also from loyalty—while insisting, paradoxically, that the conduct he or she is accused of is widespread and that officials are well aware of it. To inform is regarded as both weak and disloyal. In the imagined battle between the police and the rest of the world, a lie is an act of political bravery. To some officers, the most serious aspersion that can be cast upon another officer is that he or she breached the code of silence and provided information to internal affairs investigators—"the headhunters."

To some officers, the most serious aspersion that can be cast upon another officer is that he or she breached the code of silence and provided information to internal affairs investigators.

Police unions reinforce this code of silence by their willingness to help virtually any officer subjected to departmental charges and by their opposition to reforms that would make detection of wrongdoing easier.[18] Employee organizations can get caught up in the tension between their obligation to the membership as a whole and their responsibilities to individual members, and they usually side with the individual. Thus, individual officers who have been discharged for drug use will very likely be defended by union lawyers who are helping them regain their positions, even though the union leadership believes they are guilty and believes it is not in the interest of union members for drug-dependent individuals to remain on the force. (No officer in a crisis situation wants a partner who is unreliable or incapable of reacting effectively.) One reason that union leadership does not give greater weight to its self-interest in promoting honesty and competency on the force is probably that the membership values such efforts less than it values assistance to individuals in trouble.

Difficulties in controlling corruption are further exacerbated in places where supervisors and managers are members of the same union as the rank and file. Membership in the same bargaining unit blurs essential distinctions between management and labor and creates serious potential conflicts of interest for officials. It is only natural for a manager who receives a call from a union official on behalf of an officer suspected of wrongdoing to consider his or her own dependence on the union before responding. It is the union that will represent his or her interests at the bargaining table. When salary increases and other benefits are at stake, even the most high-minded officials may be inclined to call the close ones the way the union urges. More important, officials with an eye to promotion or a favorable assignment may feel that they are better off if the union is on their side, or at least not against them.

Unguided police discretion and incompetence

Corruption also grows when police administrators give insufficient guidance on the use of discretion or when officers are incompetent because of poor training.

Many police chiefs are reluctant to acknowledge that the members of their department exercise substantial discretion in enforcing the laws and providing various other public services. As Goldstein has observed:

To acknowledge the exercise of discretion belies the very image in which [the chief] takes such pride and which he strives so hard to achieve. This is the image of total objectivity—of impartiality—and of enforcement without fear or favor.[19]

But the reticence of some chiefs is more than just a matter of image. They see the exercise of discretion as illegitimate. The "law" forbids it.

Yet it is obvious that police officers do and must exercise discretion. In most communities, far more rule violations occur each day and far more noncriminal problems compete for police attention than the police can attend to. This means that officers must routinely choose whom to arrest, warn, counsel, let go, or assist in myriad ways. Often, officers must make these choices without the benefit of rules or other guidelines. And if formal rules exist at all, they may be vague, wrong, or obsolete.

Another aspect of discretion that requires continuous attention, particularly given the emphasis on drug enforcement in the late 1980s and early 1990s, is agency procedures for dealing with confidential informants. Failing to guide undercover operatives' discretion is extremely risky. Eliciting useful information from those in a position to have it—criminals—and doing so in legal ways is a most challenging enterprise. The problems are heightened when the department does not provide sufficient buy money or other incentives for informant cooperation. To provide themselves with the operational funds they think they need, some officers fall into skimming seized drugs or drug money for operational use. Although this skimming does not constitute corruption as defined here, it nonetheless creates a chink in the officer's armor of integrity and leaves him or her susceptible to corruptive influences.

Though many situations are so fact-specific that they defy rulemaking by police administrators, more guidance in the exercise of discretion could be given. When discretion is unguided by articulated departmental values or policy, street officers are not only hindered in performing their duties but are also unnecessarily exposed to temptation. In the wrong hands, the discretion to decide whom to arrest becomes a hunting license for personal gain: the corrupt officer employs lawful authority to threaten arrest unless a bribe is forthcoming.

When discretion is unguided by articulated departmental values or policy, street officers are not only hindered in performing their duties but are also unnecessarily exposed to temptation.

Guiding officer discretion to avert corruption means providing concrete skills and tactical suggestions—during pre-service and in-service training and during operational planning and debriefing sessions—that can help police officers satisfactorily accomplish the various police missions. Failure to prepare officers adequately for the challenges and assignments they are given—that is, failure to foster integrity rather than incompetence—can lead to officer corruption.

Lack of guidance can also lead to corruption by giving rise to situations in which an officer—particularly a recruit on undercover assignment—is tempted to lie. A recruit who has not been property prepared for an undercover assignment is likely to make mistakes and be reluctant to admit them.[20]

The officer who steps onto the slippery slope of lying to cover simple mistakes may well slide further into ever-greater misdeeds. Both the loss of self-esteem involved in knowing oneself to be a liar, and the power that other, less-honest officers acquire over an officer by threatening to expose the earlier infractions if he or she does not "go along," leave the officer vulnerable to tempting opportunities for corruption.

Lack of support from prosecutors and courts

Another barrier to integrity is the operation of the criminal justice system as a whole. The administration of criminal justice is divided among several units of government: police officers arrest but do not prosecute or convict; charging is the province of the prosecuting attorney, and convicting is the province of judges and juries. This division of labor is a source of misunderstanding and mutual antagonism. The police see their good faith efforts to enforce the law and to control crime thwarted by prosecutors who dismiss cases or reduce charges without apparent reason or adequate explanation. And even when the prosecutor does charge, many cases are dismissed by the judge for reasons that the police consider "technicalities" and "nitpicking." Or, when conviction results, a small fine or short sentence may be the only consequence of diligent police work. For the police officer on the street, the process can be both baffling and discouraging.

When police officers suspect that prosecutors and judges are corrupt, the suspicion may grow, weedlike, into a self-serving justification for an officer's own misconduct. One high-ranking FBI official described judicial corruption as a significant contributor to police corruption, noting that "where the judges are corrupt, police corruption has virtually always followed."[21] The president of Miami's Fraternal Order of Police concurs: "When you're on the line offering your life for $25,000 a year and you see these cocaine cowboys getting off on light sentences and getting off on probation, it becomes an opportunity for the employee who's a little weak-willed."[22] An officer may choose to take a payoff rather than make an arrest that, for all he or she knows, may put money in the pockets of the prosecutor or judge. In actuality, lenient sentences may not be the product of prosecutorial or judicial corruption but may stem from a host of other factors, such as jail overcrowding, the unavailability of treatment programs, the prosecutors' political vulnerability, or the facts of the particular case.

A strategy for fostering integrity

Responsibility for combating police corruption ultimately falls on the police chief. When corruption is systemic and long-standing, however, what the chief can accomplish may be slight. Deeply embedded corruption is the product of a culture—widely shared values and attitudes that are not easily altered. Few cities have been successful in replacing a culture of police corruption with one relatively free of corruption. But success stories do exist, and invariably they center on dedicated, patient, and skillful chiefs of police who took the initiative in installing control measures and motivating compliance and who, by their personal conduct, set an example.

A chief promoted from within a department that has a significant corruption problem faces a special challenge. Because his or her entire professional life has been bound up with the organization, the chief cannot attack corruption without rejecting his or her own past and the friendships and alliances made over the years. This is almost too much to expect. Consequently, the main hope for significant reform ordinarily lies with chiefs recruited from the outside.

Even a chief recruited from another department is handicapped, however. He or she will know little about the new department or the political life of the community. The department's particular style of policing, the quality of its personnel, the names of those who can be depended upon, the ways in which corrupt activities are carried on, all must be learned, gradually and sometimes painfully.

Whether promoted from within or appointed from without, the corruption-fighting chief should have a strategy. The main elements of such a strategy are speaking out, holding those in authority accountable, improving the use of discretion, promoting integrity through training, and enlisting outside help.

Speaking out

The chief's first move should be to make clear to the force that corruption will not be tolerated, that the only "honest buck" is the paycheck. This is not as easy as it sounds. The rank and file will be skeptical. Is the chief sincere? Is the chief determined? Street officers are experts at interpreting the tone and innuendo of official pronouncements. They can distinguish public relations posturing from the real thing and are likely to have heard far more of the former. They will not respond positively unless they believe that the chief means what he or she says.

The main hope for significant reform ordinarily lies with chiefs recruited from the outside.

In formulating this message, the chief must take care not to attack all personnel. An anticorruption program should not offend those who have maintained standards. The chief's statements condemning corrupt officers should offer comfort to the honest and dedicated ones, as well as counsel and support to dishonest officers who are still redeemable. Finally, in defending a moral ideal, the chief should not be perceived as expressing meanness, envy, or moral superiority.

To be credible, the chief must set an example. He or she should not take gifts, accept discounts, or dine at fancy restaurants on the house. Nor should he or she fix traffic tickets for friends or family or accept free admission to sporting or entertainment events. The manifest integrity of the chief is a precondition for cleaning up a corrupt department. Over time, the chief's example will influence others.

A second audience for the chief is the public. Here the message is that those who offer bribes as well as those who accept them are guilty of a crime and subject to arrest. This point, if made repeatedly by the chief in talks to business and civic organizations and through news conferences or other media appearances, and if backed up by arrests, will have an effect.

The manifest integrity of the chief is a precondition for cleaning up a corrupt department.

In dealing with the public, the chief should remember that anticorruption drives have short life spans—they are at center stage for one moment and virtually forgotten a year later—and should take steps to sustain the momentum. Because members of the public who support honest government are not usually organized for that purpose, the chief should try to focus citizen lobbying groups on the problem and create an organized constituency for change, one that will not only lobby city hall but also critique the chief's own performance.

In addition to conveying messages to the department and the public and seeing to it that citizens who offer bribes are arrested, the chief also needs to speak by taking internal action. In the past, most police departments thought of corruption as an individual rather than an institutional problem and limited their efforts to tracking down and punishing individual offenders. But, as this chapter has emphasized, endemic police corruption is not just a failure of character but is, in large part, a failure of leadership, command, organization, and policy. The chief must ask not only who is to blame but also what reforms are worth trying. A reform strategy will seek the revision or elimination of the many arrangements, practices, and traditions that provide a breeding ground for corruption within a department. It will reward officials who uncover corrupt activities and will provide commendations and improved prospects for promotion for those who reject bribes.

A useful aid to achieving this change is a detailed statement from the chief spelling out what constitutes acceptable ethical behavior for the force. By using examples of dilemmas an officer is likely to encounter on the street, the statement can give concrete meaning to its overriding message: no police officer may accept any gift of money, goods, or services for which a civilian would be expected to pay or which is offered because the intended recipient is a police officer.

Holding those in authority accountable

Goldstein has observed that "corruption thrives best in poorly run organizations where lines of authority are vague and supervision is minimal."[23] In other words, sometimes supervisory structures and procedures are too lax to discourage patrol officers from seizing ever-present opportunities for illegitimate gain.[24] Only when the chief makes every manager and supervisor answerable for the misconduct of his or her subordinates can a department with serious corruption be reformed. This means that the chief must be able to select key aides and command officials and must have substantial discretion in assigning and transferring them. If the chief inherits a management team whose competence, loyalty, or integrity is suspect, he or she will be frustrated in any attempts to conceive and execute reforms. A chief's best hope in such circumstances is to find imaginative ways to create new staff positions outside civil service constraints so that at least a few trusted and competent persons will be in charge. Making managers and supervisors answerable for the misconduct of their subordinates also means extending such accountability throughout the agency. Nobody can be permitted to pass the buck.

Only when the chief makes every manager and supervisor answerable for the misconduct of his or her subordinates can a department with serious corruption be reformed.

However, some wrongdoing will escape even the most competent supervisors. Police supervision, in general, is necessarily fragmented; most of the time the bulk of the department's personnel—those in patrol and detective work—operate independently and more or less in isolation. Moreover, each shift has a different supervisor, and substitute supervisors routinely fill in when the regulars are out sick, on vacation, or in court. In this context, supervisors cannot reasonably be held strictly accountable for everything their subordinates do—only for misconduct that could have been prevented by diligent supervision and counseling.

In many departments, accountability for controlling corruption has been reduced to a ritual. For example, the chief may call in the commanders one by one and ask them if they have had any problems with corruption. Each replies, "Not a bit of it in my command, chief." And there the matter ends. The chief should have asked: "What are your problems? How are you resolving them? How can I help?" These questions treat corruption as more endemic, requiring a considered response. They also present the chief as a source of assistance, not simply a judge of performance.

When corruption is known to exist, the chief must be brutally frank. The chief should tell the assistant and deputy chiefs: "If corruption is found in your command, you will be held responsible. I'll use whatever power I have to take your job away. I'll force your retirement, demote you, even dismiss you."

A chief should not stop there, however. It is not enough to call in his or her assistants, make a speech, record their new responsibilities, and forget it. Should corruption in the department be exposed to the public, a chief will never survive by blaming his or her subordinates. The chief must continue to monitor performance. That means regular communication, discussion, and oversight. Routine interviews with officials may be helpful. In large departments, questionnaires can be employed. In addition, inspection teams, both overt and covert, should be sent into the field periodically to determine compliance with policy, to detect evidence of corruption, and to see how the officers deal with situations that could lead to corruption.

The chief should also take a close look at those seeking promotion to the highest ranks. Knowledge of precisely how managerial performance can be evaluated is still in its infancy (see the chapter on performance measurement), but this much seems clear: exemplary personal behavior should not be enough to warrant promotion. Ideally, the manager should also have demonstrated the capacity and courage to expose corruption and to discipline corrupt subordinates.

If an excessive span of control exists, the chief may be able to strengthen accountability by increasing the number of first-line supervisors (the sergeants)—though an increase in the number of supervisors does not automatically mean an increase in the level of supervision. Every officer should be under a single sergeant for continuing evaluation, and the duty schedules of both the officer and his or her sergeant should coincide as much as possible.

Paradoxically, accountability has been particularly lacking within detective units, although investigative work is particularly rich in opportunities for corruption. In most departments, detectives work largely on their own, either as generalists or as specialists. First- and second-line supervisors operate more as fellow investigators than as supervisors. Lack of oversight thus provides the detective with special opportunities for wrongdoing. Directing investigations more closely, narrowing the discretion of individual detectives, and broadening the role of supervisors and managers will help greatly (see the chapter on criminal investigations).

Improving the use of discretion

Increased accountability should lead to the improved use of discretion, especially in the decision to arrest. The arrest decision can be a difficult one. Often the proper choice is unclear. Following the formal rules may be neither just, customary, nor appropriate.

When departmental policy and guidelines covering the use of discretion are vague or nonexistent, supervisors cannot hold their subordinates accountable. It is the responsibility of the chief to define and harness discretion in ways that reduce the opportunities for graft. The chief should stipulate enforcement priorities; make certain that discretionary decisions are coached and assessed by supervisors; and eliminate arrest quotas, formal or understood, particularly in gambling and narcotics enforcement. Police departments under pressure to curb gambling and drug abuse have traditionally tried to take the easy route by stressing the quantity of arrests instead of the effect of arrests on the incidence of vice (see the chapters on patrol, criminal investiations, and local drug control). In the course of fulfilling quotas, police officers find numerous opportunities to extort payoffs from small-change operators.

Beyond this, the chief should be candid about the limits of enforcement and not maintain publicly that the department always enforces every law, when every patrol officer knows that some laws are generally unenforced or enforced only under certain circumstances. The complexity of law enforcement imposes upon police leaders a duty to clarify agency values and goals and ensure that officers are aware of what is expected.

One area where clarification will improve discretion is that of departmental oversight of confidential informants. The procedures for conducting undercover

Supervision for quality assurance   Under the traditional style of policing, with a quasi-military environment and rigid sets of rules and regulations, inspection and control was a relatively easy function to perform. Regular inspections and audits were conducted to determine whether or not officers were complying with regulations. The more mechanically the individual adhered to the letter of the rules, the less there was any chance of getting in trouble. Displaying unusual creativity, going beyond minimal requirements of the job, or exercising individual judgment were at odds with the rule-compliance mode. It is easy to see, then, that community problem solving—with its emphasis on self-motivation and individual initiative—requires a new approach to the inspection function.

Nevertheless, the importance of that function—of maintaining the quality and integrity of the police force—is in no way minimized by new concepts of policing. Indeed, the greater freedom of action afforded the individual police officer places greater reliance on effective systems for monitoring, evaluating, and, when necessary, disciplining police conduct. If there is to be ongoing community satisfaction with and confidence in the police department, executives still must ensure that internal wrongdoing is prevented and that sufficient safeguards are established to preserve the integrity, efficiency, and effectiveness of the force.

Source: Edwin Meese III, "Community Policing and the Police Officer," (working paper, Harvard Executive Session on Policing, February 28, 1991).

---

investigations and using paid informants need to be made more specific, and existing procedures need to be audited more strictly.[25]

Another area where discretion could be improved is the enforcement of municipal ordinances. Municipal statute books are filled with laws that are vague, archaic, unenforceable, or useless—except to the crooked police officer who can threaten their enforcement to extort payoffs. Rather than continue to allow officers a free hand in their enforcement, supervisors and managers should have the benefit of clearly enunciated policies on enforcement so that discretion is narrowed and focused as much as possible.

Promoting integrity through training

One way to measure a police department's interest in promoting integrity is to examine its training curriculum. Although the quality of recruit training has improved steadily, many police departments fail to provide adequate guidance on the temptations of graft, fearing that such training may open rookies up to the wrong ideas. The training that does occur is often abstract and idealistic. It does not adequately prepare rookies to resist the constant temptations—offers of free meals, tickets, tips, and discounts. As a result, too many officers begin their careers innocent of the world they are entering and ignorant of their legal and ethical obligations.

In a department with a culture that supports corruption, rookies without proper training can be drawn into the prevailing web of accommodation so quickly and unobtrusively that they are involved before they know it. For this reason, training must emphasize more than legal obligations. Training that prepares recruits for the temptations to which they will be exposed and that identifies ways of avoiding and resisting these temptations will be the most effective. Training also can provide recruits with a sense of the price they will pay for misconduct—the adverse effect that "taking" has on character, self-image, self-esteem, and career opportunities.

A major component of recruit training is familiarization with the departmental policy manual, yet the manual of almost every police department contains provisions so unrealistic that no officer, however dedicated, can obey all of them all the time. The existence of so many prohibitions can have an effect opposite to that intended. Officers will come to view the rules as a public relations ploy, as pious pronouncements not to be taken seriously. If the manual makes it seem as if everyone is eligible for disciplinary action, the threat of punishment loses much of its significance; when discipline does occur, it therefore seems arbitrary and unfair. In addition, overregulation creates "a pervasive fear of punishment for honest mistakes and a belief that even the most minor transgressions must be hidden"[26]—and, as we have seen, lying to conceal an honest mistake is a condition that fosters corruption. Ideally, the manual should be a useful resource for guiding conduct. It should be concrete and practical, providing specific illustrations of the appropriate response in particular situations. For instruction to make a lasting impression, it must be realistic, not moralistic.

Even when police training is effective, its influence is likely to be modest if early field experience does not reinforce what was learned in recruit school. To ensure that departmental values are integrated with work practices, handpicked senior officers should be assigned the task of guiding recruits through their initial street experiences.

It is the responsibility of the chief to define and harness discretion in ways that reduce the opportunities for graft.

Enlisting outside help

The success of police chiefs determined to root out corruption depends in large part on their ability to enlist help from local officials, the media, and, in cases of aggravated corruption, from local and federal prosecutors.

Local officials　The police chief needs the support of the mayor or appointed manager and at least a majority of the elected council or board. Without such support, the chief is unlikely to achieve more than transient success. The mayor and council have both formal and informal influence over the department's financial and political support. In places with the council-manager form of government or with a full-time professional administrator reporting to the mayor, the chief administrator has valuable resources—personnel, equipment, and money, as well as information and a host of intangibles—that can help police chiefs contend with corruption. In addition, he or she has access to community leaders who can assist the chief of police in carrying out the needed reform.

It is important to understand that the kind of organizational changes that mayors, appointed managers, and elected councils can help initiate are extraordinarily diverse. They include better screening systems for prospective police employees, improved training programs, more effective internal investigations and inspections, and genuinely useful employee assistance programs. Employee assistance programs (discussed in the chapter on human resources) can help officers who have psychological, family, financial, and other problems to better manage their difficulties before job performance deteriorates substantially. If not managed appropriately, some of these problems can make an officer more susceptible to corruption.

The media　If media leaders believe that the chief is right in his or her efforts to eliminate corruption, they can be an invaluable source of support. Or, if they think the chief is exaggerating a problem or hunting for scapegoats, they can effectively cripple an anticorruption campaign. In a community where corruption has existed for years and is treated as a fact of life, for example, some newspaper editors may not be particularly troubled by corruption among the police, and their support will need to be artfully recruited by the chief.

Enlisting the help of the media is likely to involve more than simply overcoming apathy or skepticism. Like politicians and much of the public, media leaders may tolerate police corruption for self-serving reasons. In a community where vice is common, there may be a tacit understanding not to disturb the status quo because many people profit from it. Editors may avoid rocking the boat if they feel that the status quo is good for business and that the easy availability of liquor, sex, and gambling attracts tourists and conventions.

Even when the media are supportive, however, there are pitfalls the chief should try to avoid. When the chief consciously enlists the media to sustain an anticorruption campaign, the police force may be angered by what it sees as the chief's manipulativeness and may feel that the force has been unfairly branded. This may be especially true when the internal affairs unit uses questionable investigative methods or when discipline is seen as too harsh.

The local prosecutor and federal authorities   The local prosecuting attorney wields great power by virtue of his or her discretion to decide which cases will be prosecuted. A sophisticated anticorruption drive should involve the local prosecutor unless he or she is part of the problem. Although on close calls the prosecutor may drop charges of corruption for what appear to be technical reasons, he or she may be inclined to prosecute if the chief is adamant. In some situations, however, a prosecuting attorney may provide only minimal cooperation with police investigators or may actually impede a corruption investigation. As elected officials, prosecutors may fear that the prosecution of police officers will embarrass the political party or the mayor or will work against them should they run for reelection or higher office. Prosecutors may also be unwilling to risk alienating members of the police department on whose cooperation they heavily depend in other cases; or, as indicated, they may themselves be corrupt.

If the local prosecutor refuses to prosecute corrupt officers, the chief should not settle for pressing administrative charges as the exclusive alternative. Resort to the FBI, the Internal Revenue Service, or the United States Attorney is justifiable under these circumstances. Federal authorities, both police and prosecutorial, are far less likely to be influenced by local politics and may have substantial experience in developing and prosecuting corruption cases.

Internal inspections

Since the police chief bears ultimate responsibility for the department's level of integrity, he or she must find out how well subordinates are complying with their obligations as reflected in policies, rules, and procedures. One way for the chief to become informed about corruption and other misconduct as well as about positive achievements is through line and staff inspections. Both kinds of inspections seek answers to five questions: (1) Are the department's procedures and policies being properly implemented? (2) Are they adequate to attain the goals of the department? (3) Are the department's resources (for example, personnel) being fully and sensibly utilized? (4) Are the resources adequate to attain the department's goals? (5) Are there deficiencies in integrity, training, morale, or supervision?

Line inspections

Line inspections are daily or weekly audits conducted by the supervisory personnel who have direct command over the officers who are the subjects of the inspection. Such inspections can result in supportive coaching or other immediate corrective action because line inspectors ordinarily have sufficient authority over their subordinates. Line officials, rather than an internal affairs unit, can effectively investigate most noncorruption complaints. New supervisors should be trained in inspection techniques and should be taught to recognize that some matters are best handled in-house, without a formal investigation.

Line inspections can result in supportive coaching or other immediate corrective action because line inspectors ordinarily have sufficient authority over their subordinates.

Although the line inspection is an important quality control mechanism, it has inherent limitations. There is the risk that the line supervisor may, perhaps out of a desire to be well liked, be lax in his or her supervision. In some instances, the line official may personally lack either integrity or the training necessary for conducting the inspection. For these reasons, a second type of inspection—staff inspection—is an essential supplement to line inspection and, in some instances, may be a more effective control mechanism.

Staff inspections

Staff inspections occur outside the normal lines of authority and responsibility. Those conducting staff inspections are not responsible to the commander of the units being inspected, nor are they responsible for the performance of the personnel in those units. Thus, they may operate with greater objectivity. To be effective, however, they must be sensitive to the subtleties of the pressures and problems confronting the unit being inspected.

Staff inspections seek answers to the five questions previously listed, and they also have another objective: to help operating line units plan their line inspections. For example, the staff should work with line supervisors in designing line inspection techniques and procedures. In this way, staff can train supervisors in techniques for more effectively monitoring their officers (see also the chapter on performance measurement).

Staff inspections should be conducted under the chief's supervision. If the department is large enough to have a staff inspection unit, its commander should report to the chief. The commanding officer must enjoy the chief's complete confidence.

For major inspections (for example, patrol divisions) in a large department, the staff unit's commanding officer should appoint a team. Such a team could include a member of the planning and research unit, a lieutenant or sergeant assigned to the investigations division, a member of the youth and women's unit, and a records supervisor. The personal integrity of each member of the team should be impeccable, and he or she should be completely objective about the element under inspection.

Staff inspections should be conducted under the chief's supervision.

The unit to be inspected should be given at least one week's advance notice. Following notification, the staff unit's inspector and the assembled team should meet with the chief, who should inform the team of the procedures for the upcoming inspection. In addition, to encourage cooperation between the staff team and members of the unit under inspection, the team should meet with the commanding officers of the unit before the inspection. This does not mean that spontaneous inspections are to be avoided. A well-coordinated plan for surprise visits is a useful component of the staff unit's overall inspection procedures.

To minimize inconsistency among inspectors during a given inspection and to ensure that the inspection's objectives are met, each inspection should follow a predetermined checklist. For example, a patrol division inspection might include personnel matters (such as attrition, morale, integrity, and appearance) as well as operational matters (such as the use of automobiles and radio communication policy). A patrol division inspection may also include more basic questions, such as effectiveness in meeting community needs and in responding to calls for service.

After the field work is completed, the commanding staff officer should compile a written report containing the inspection's findings along with any recommendations for improvements. The report should address departmental deficiencies in training and policy guidance as well as unit performance problems. The report should be made available only to the chief of police and the commanders of the inspected unit.

At specified intervals of thirty, sixty, and ninety days after presentation of the report, the inspecting team should review the progress of the unit—and, if applicable, of the department—in implementing the report's recommendations. After the last follow-up inspection, a final report should be presented to the chief.

Internal affairs units

Many departments have established a separate, staff-level internal affairs unit (IAU) to investigate complaints of police misconduct and report to the chief.

Establishing an IAU

Whether a department should create a full-time internal affairs unit depends on its size. Though there is no set formula, the guidelines presented here may be helpful in determining whether to establish an IAU. Given the diversity of operations in police departments with four hundred or more employees, a full-time unit outside the operational chain of command can be justified. A police department of between seventy-five and four hundred employees may not need a full-time IAU; rather, the chief can provide for the function by assigning responsibility to an employee who performs related duties. In agencies with fewer than seventy-five employees, the chief can appoint a temporary committee or task force to conduct an internal affairs investigation, or, in the case of very small agencies, the chief might personally conduct the investigation.

Selecting personnel for the IAU

The department must decide whether to select IAU personnel on a voluntary or mandatory-assignment basis. Some feel that assigning an officer who lacks a genuine desire to serve in the IAU is unwise and unfair. Others contend that corrupt officers may volunteer for the IAU to pursue corrupt ends or simply to undermine investigations. Thus, if a voluntary approach is adopted, the department should verify the volunteers' integrity through extensive background checks.

An argument for mandatory assignment is that, because all upper-level managers should have experience in addressing the problems of corruption, assignment to the IAU should be an essential tour of duty in career development.

The sensitive nature of the IAU's duties means that the selection of personnel must be based on established criteria. Obviously, candidates should have impeccable integrity and a record of solid job performance. In addition, they should be proficient in investigative, interviewing, and interrogative techniques and should be familiar with the department's internal affairs procedures. Finally, they should know and understand the community's various social and ethnic populations.

Encouraging citizens to file complaints

Complaints provide the police chief with valuable information for evaluating employee performance, identifying areas of police misconduct, monitoring police relations with the public, and identifying the need for new or revised policies or improved training. For these reasons, citizens should be encouraged to report matters of misconduct to the police.

The department should make the public aware of how to file a complaint against the police. (This is particularly important when the public is skeptical of a department's handling of citizen complaints.) One way to publicize the procedure is to distribute printed brochures throughout the community and to the media. The department should make clear that, although it prefers complainants to come forward to help in an investigation, it will accept and, to the extent possible, investigate anonymous complaints—from both the citizenry and members of the force.

Most citizens making complaints expect responsive action to be taken by the department. The complaint should be recorded upon receipt. What happens thereafter is discussed below—but the department should conduct a personal interview with the complainant. And the citizen should always be advised of the outcome of the investigation and the disposition of the complaint by the department. For minor complaints, oral notice by the investigating officer may suffice; however, in cases where the complainant has taken the trouble to put the complaint in writing, a written response is preferable. Some departments respond in writing to all complaints.

Responding to citizens' complaints

Preferably, only allegations of serious misconduct—such as an officer's accepting a bribe or participating in a crime—should become the province of internal affairs. More routine complaints should be handled by the immediate line supervisor, unless the public is skeptical about the department's handling of citizen complaints. In that case, a highly visible process is desirable (it may even be advisable to encourage complaints, as mentioned above).

Line officials, rather than the internal affairs unit, can effectively investigate most noncorruption complaints, and many of these can be handled informally. Citizen complaints that result from minor discourtesies do not require a full-blown investigation. A polite and thoughtful meeting of department officials with the complainant and officer involved, followed by a brief report for the files, will ordinarily suffice.

Having line officials deal with the alleged misconduct of subordinates is not only efficient, but it can also enhance performance. Though IAU inquiries might lead to more thorough investigations, improved overall performance is most likely to result when supervisors are responsible for investigating and dealing with complaints against subordinates. Line officials should not be permitted to delegate the unpopular function of supervising and training.

However, unless the line supervisor's own actions are reviewed, there is a risk that he or she, as one who is in daily contact with subordinates, may ignore complaints or process them too leniently. One way to prevent this is to structure the system for handling citizen complaints in such a way that the disposition of every written complaint is subject to review at a staff level by the IAU. This process need not bog line officials down in lengthy written statements and formal reports; in minor cases, only brief written (perhaps even handwritten) reports of findings and action should be required. The IAU can review these reports, guaranteeing their integrity by occasional follow-up audits, including interviews with the complaining citizens. Annual statistics can be compiled showing the distribution of complaints by category among the various units and members of the department. Thus, units, individuals, or specific activities with a high number of complaints can then be identified and corrective action taken by the chief, in the form of either changes in policy or changes in the conduct of particular personnel, or both.

Assessing the advantages and disadvantages of an IAU

The IAU plays an important role in investigating police misconduct. In a large department the unit's investigators can devote all their time to internal affairs, making investigations more thorough. In addition, IAU personnel gain expertise in this specialized investigative work. Often, therefore, an IAU investigation may be more objective than one conducted by the accused officer's supervisor— although the IAU staff must be sure they understand the subtleties of the particular problems and the causal factors in each case. Finally, the existence of a diligent IAU demonstrates to the public as well as to police personnel that the agency is serious about pursuing allegations of police misconduct. Depending on an agency's public reputation for integrity, it may be necessary to bolster the IAU's credibility through establishment of an external monitoring body, like the ombudsman's office used in European countries.[27]

The existence of a diligent internal affairs unit demonstrates to the public as well as to police personnel that the agency is serious about pursuing allegations of police misconduct.

However, the IAU should not be seen as a panacea. It has a number of problems. For example, IAU personnel, however honest and dedicated, cannot realistically be expected always to investigate zealously the activities of fellow officers. Moreover, resistance to the IAU's investigations from police unions may undermine its effectiveness. At the same time, poorly trained or supervised internal affairs investigators can become headhunters, unfairly targeting and harassing agency personnel and destroying whatever credibility the IAU may ever have had among fair-minded members of the force.

Still, internal affairs unit need to be proactive. All too often, instead of initiating investigations into misconduct and seeking to uncover corruption, the IAU may simply wait for charges of corruption to seep into the unit. The IAU should be alert to symptoms of corruption and, even in the absence of complaints, should take active steps to assess whether it is present.

Furthermore, in departments where there is serious corruption, it is important that the IAU not focus on patrol officers. Including top officials among those covered by the investigation sends the message that the chief is serious. Catching a few "big fish" may be more effective in interrupting the network of corruption than landing many "small fry," especially when investigations are coupled with preventive measures.

Disciplinary procedures and penalties

Disciplinary procedures in most departments tend to be unnecessarily long and complicated. At times, it seems harder to discipline a police officer than to convict an accused murderer (for example, a single judge is deemed sufficient to try a homicide case, but police disciplinary charges usually are decided by a trial board composed of three officials). The proceedings may be prolonged by lawyers raising evidentiary points that police officials are ill-equipped to judge. And, although in most cases dismissal is unlikely, the accused officer nevertheless

Civilian oversight association   The International Association for Civilian Oversight of Law Enforcement (IACOLE) is a nonprofit organization of local, state/provincial, and federal government officials who are responsible for examining and commenting on citizen complaints of police conduct. Through conferences, publications, and consultant services, the organization provides basic and specialized information about civilian oversight.

An annual international conference and occasional regioinal meetings provide information for those who are contemplating or initiating civilian oversight agencies and for experienced practitioners who are seeking to increase their skills or knowledge.

Publications include a compendium of civilian oversight agencies and annotated bibliographies of publications about civilian oversight.

The organization also consults with elected and appointed officials, police departments, and community interest groups on the design or redesign of civilian review mechanisms.

Inquiries about IACOLE should be directed to 1204 Wesley Avenue, Evanston, Illinois 60202.

usually takes the possibility into account in fashioning a defense, which also tends to prolong the hearing.

To avoid these problems, some departments use formal trial board proceedings only for serious cases in which it is clear that the penalty for guilt is likely to be demotion or discharge from the service. In routine cases, charges are reviewed by a hearing officer whose power is limited to recommending a fine or other punishment less serious than dismissal. The hearing officer hears the testimony, evaluates any extenuating circumstances cited by the accused officer, and then sets a proposed penalty, which becomes final unless the accused officer appeals in writing to the chief. This system benefits the department because it avoids the expense of formal proceedings and the calling of numerous witnesses on minor matters. It also may benefit the officer, who can avoid the expense of hiring an attorney and knows that the maximum penalty will be a fine or brief suspension.

A few police departments have used members of the officer's peer group to inquire into charges. One way to do this is to place officers of the same rank as the accused on the internal panel examining the case. Another way is for a group of peers and supervisors to hold an informal discussion with the officer and not only assess the facts but also counsel the officer on future performance.

Some departments go beyond disciplinary hearings, especially in cases of repeated infraction, and use psychological interviews and tests to help uncover the causes of errant behavior. Such interviews and tests, either individually or in combination, are worth serious consideration because they give added insight into the causes of the officer's misconduct. Not infrequently, the causes may be some combination of departmental deficiency (in training, policies, procedures, and supervision) and the officer's own inadequate performance.

In most police disciplinary actions, determining guilt is easier than deciding on the appropriate penalty. The officer's guilt may be easier to establish because, in contrast to the criminal court's beyond-a-reasonable-doubt standard of proof, administrative decisions are normally based on a preponderance of the evidence. But determining an appropriate and useful penalty or taking other corrective action can be very difficult. In the internal disciplinary process, as in the criminal justice system, the punishment or other corrective measures are calculated according to the degree of misconduct, modified by the offender's prior record and by the extent to which systemic defects in the agency may have contributed to the misconduct. Some departments have established formal penalty schedules for officers considered culpable; except for minor offenses, however, such schedules are likely to be ineffective because the specifics of the incident and any prior offenses should not be the only considerations. It is always necessary to determine, as well, whether the violation was committed out of ignorance, carelessness, misunderstanding, or intention. In short, each case should be judged on its own merits, with the penalties varying depending on the circumstances. When appropriate, departmental managers need to have courage to accept the blame for having tolerated systemic defects that virtually compelled the officer in question to misbehave.

When punishment of an individual officer is warranted, a typical range of penalties, in order of increasing severity, includes

1. Letter of reprimand in the officer's personnel file
2. Disciplinary transfer from a preferred assignment
3. Forfeiture of vacation, or imposition of extra duty
4. Monetary fine, or suspension without pay
5. Demotion in rank, and loss of promotional opportunity
6. Dismissal from the department.

Filing a letter of reprimand, though a modest action, can serve as a warning to the officer involved and to others that certain conduct is viewed with disapproval. This action is useful for minor matters.

Transfer to a less-preferred assignment sends a clear message to the offender, but an officer should not be transferred to a position of responsibility if it appears that he or she will be unable to perform there satisfactorily. Moreover, transfer should not be used simply to shift a persistent disciplinary problem from one commander to another. Rather, it is justified when a fresh assignment may contribute to improved performance. Sometimes an officer who is given a chance to start over in a new environment will perform well. His or her problems may have been situational—a clash of personalities—and may not reflect any deep-seated personal or character problems. In any event, the transferred employee's new supervisor should be briefed on the employee's apparent strengths and weaknesses, in the hope of better equipping the new supervisor to elicit excellent work from the employee.

Loss of vacation time or the imposition of extra-duty work may be useful measures. They punish the officer in a way that does not cause his or her dependents financial hardship, while compensating the government for some of the costs of the officer's misconduct. A fine or suspension without pay may be mandated by the severity of the offense, however.

Demotion in rank is used occasionally, either by itself or in conjunction with another sanction, to penalize misconduct. Some police administrators argue that any individual whose conduct justifies demotion should simply be dismissed. There are, however, certain employees who perform satisfactorily as officers but who lack the qualities to justify promotion to supervisory positions. When an errant supervisor is demoted, though, an agency must be careful about the message it is sending as to the stature of first-line patrol or detective work. Police leaders nationwide are now considering innovative possibilities of recognizing the importance of such patrol and investigative work. It would be counterproductive to suggest, through disciplinary decisions, that those who remain in first-line positions are untalented or of questionable integrity.

Dismissal from the force is obviously the most severe administrative disposition. When dismissal is considered as a penalty, at least two issues must be addressed. The first relates to a new employee on probation and the second to an officer with many years of service who is nearing retirement.

In many police departments, any single act of misconduct by a probationary employee automatically terminates the appointment. Although such a policy undoubtedly makes new employees extremely careful during their probationary period, in most cases the policy is counterproductive for the department and too harsh for the individual. For a single act of misconduct (assuming the individual, rather than the procedures or supervision, is at fault), the probationary employee should be subject to whatever the ordinary punishment would be, except that as part of the punishment the probationary period should be extended. The individual's misbehavior should, of course, be taken into consideration at the end of the probationary period, when his or her total performance is judged and a decision is made on whether to grant a permanent appointment. This policy enables a department to avoid firing an otherwise satisfactory or even outstanding probationary employee for a single and perhaps unintended act of misconduct.

With respect to veteran employees who are soon to become eligible for their pensions, dismissal for misconduct can result in deprivation of substantial retirement benefits, often leaving the officer with no more than a refund of the amount he or she paid into the system, plus interest. For noncriminal misconduct, this is obviously a very heavy penalty. But when serious purposeful criminal conduct is involved, the loss of pension may be warranted.

In debating which penalty to apply in any given situation, police officials should consider the rationale underlying punishment. Properly administered, punishment should deter future misconduct, not only by the particular offender involved (special deterrence) but also by others on the force who are or might be tempted (general deterrence). Stringent penalties for the guilty make it clear to everyone that serious misconduct will not be tolerated. Excessively stringent penalties, however, undermine management's credibility. In cases when the officer involved has an exceptionally good prior record, the most effective approach may be to impose the maximum penalty and then formally reduce it so that the more moderate penalty is not viewed as departmental condoning of officer misconduct. This is akin to a court's meting out a severe suspended sentence, intended to acknowledge both the seriousness of the offense and extenuating circumstances, or the particular offender's special prospects for rehabilitation.

In debating which penalty to apply in any given situation, police officials should consider the rationale underlying punishment.

Acceptance of resignation is often a permissible alternative to disciplinary action. However, an officer's resignation under investigation typically should not end the agency's inquiry into alleged wrongdoing. Although such a resignation might justifiably alter the focus of a misconduct investigation, the department has an obligation to both the complainant and the general public to analyze breaches of the public trust by officers so that any needed preventive measures can be installed to avert future wrongdoing by other personnel.

Special considerations

As police practice has evolved, two areas of concern present special considerations relating to departmental integrity. One is the question of drug testing for police officers; the other is the emergence of community policing.

Testing for drug abuse on the force

A growing number of police departments are requiring officers to submit to urine tests for illegal drugs. The programs vary in coverage and procedures and are a highly controversial issue in police labor relations (see the chapter on human resources). Though employees have successfully challenged some testing programs on constitutional grounds, Supreme Court decisions have indicated that a carefully designed program can be upheld. A testing program may focus on a class of employees in the absence of reasonable suspicion or probable cause for believing that a particular individual is using a controlled substance (the question of whether such testing is desirable is discussed below).

Although concern for privacy should shape the testing program and define the procedures by which it is implemented, such concern should not forestall implementation. Special considerations argue strongly for establishing a drug testing program for employees who are armed and authorized to use deadly force in responding to a wide variety of emergency situations. Officers under the influence of drugs may use poor judgment in aiding citizens in need of medical treatment or in deciding whether, and how much, force is necessary to apprehend a fleeing felon or break up a neighborhood quarrel. They may also show poor judgment when driving and when involved in life-threatening situations.

Beyond these considerations, street officers using drugs are likely to be unprofessional in enforcing drug laws. They may exempt certain drug dealers from arrest in exchange for being given drugs for personal use, or they may withhold narcotics or money seized during the arrest of a drug dealer. If officers in the internal affairs unit are using drugs, the added danger exists that they may avoid investigating corruption in the narcotics squad.

Special considerations argue strongly for establishing a drug testing program for employees who are armed and authorized to use deadly force in responding to a wide variety of emergency situations.

The chief, in consultation with his or her legal advisors, should issue a directive making clear that illegal drug use will not be tolerated and that a program of testing will be initiated. Detailed procedural safeguards relating to such matters as advance notification, chain of custody, confidentiality of test results, and the right to appeal the findings should be put in writing. The department's disciplinary policies on drug use should be clearly stated; it will not do simply to take an existing policy on alcohol use and merely insert the phrase "and other drugs." Although arguments can be made that drug users on the force should receive counseling and treatment—many police unions, for example, take this position—the more appropriate remedy is termination.

Arguing that a department should test employees for drug abuse still leaves open the question of what type of testing program would be best.[28] Wholly random testing in the absence of individualized suspicion is unnecessary and—in departments with no documented history of drug abuse on the force—probably undesirable. Ordinarily, it will be adequate to test the following categories of individuals: (1) all applicants; (2) members of the vice, narcotics, and internal affairs units; (3) individuals taking routine physicals in connection with promotions or changes in assignment; and (4) individuals who are reasonably suspected of drug use on the basis of documented erratic behavior or deteriorating performance. If random testing is deemed necessary, then it should be mathematically random and not subject to arbitrary manipulation. Moreover, it is wise to involve the police union in developing the program. The union has a legitimate interest in shaping the testing program and may have a contractual right to negotiate its terms.

One of the many difficult questions that space does not permit addressing here is what level of prior drug abuse a department should tolerate in applicants for employment. A fact of U.S. life since the 1960s is that student experimentation with narcotics is widespread. Thus, many police departments hire applicants with records of minor drug use.

Community policing

During the 1980s, some departments adopted a new approach toward policing that has implications for corruption control. Variously known as community policing, problem-oriented policing, fear-reducing policing, or team policing, this approach reflects a set of professional values that sees citizens, not the police, as the first line of defense in the neighborhood. In this new approach, the police and the community collaborate in both defining and executing the police mission. The community is viewed not as a constituency to be placated (or a terrain to be pacified) but as an active, essential partner in fighting crime and fear.

The police work with citizens to help them identify and solve problems, such as spousal abuse, burglary, and auto theft. The establishment of operational priorities under the community policing or problem-oriented approach becomes a joint enterprise. Because different neighborhoods express different concerns and ambitions—and have different capacities to participate as partners for public safety—there is no single formula for providing police services. From a community policing perspective, it is sufficient that a process for establishing priorities and measuring success is ongoing.

These new strategic insights are discussed in numerous other chapters. What is important here is the implications of community policing and problem-oriented policing for fostering integrity and controlling corruption. Under community policing, police officers are deployed in nontraditional ways. Thus, supervision and control must be viewed from a nontraditional perspective.

Given the philosophy that strategies for crime control and prevention are shaped jointly by a community's residents and the local police, not by the top of the police hierarchy, it becomes obvious that the traditional method of deploying officers will not work. In some community policing experiments, therefore, the three-shift rotation is abandoned, as is heavy reliance on assistance from specialized units from headquarters (except for such infrequent crimes as homicide). Instead, a small geographical area is identified—perhaps no larger than ten square blocks—and a team of officers is established there. The head of the team functions as a kind of chief of police for this area—responsible for adhering to basic departmental values and policies but much more autonomous administratively than a precinct commander in a traditional arrangement would be. The team of officers is held accountable for everything of police interest around the clock. Moreover, police and local citizens decide jointly what is of police interest. To allow the team to have a permanent post where business can be transacted and residents can turn for assistance, a ministation may be created.

Given this responsibility for the well-being of a neighborhood or neighborhood segment, the team leader must necessarily have broad discretion in deciding how to assign personnel. He or she is permitted to decide how best to utilize available time and resources. The team leader cannot be tightly supervised from above and still be held accountable for results. Analogously, problem-oriented and community policing, unlike more traditional methods, puts a premium on the inventiveness, the talents, and the potential of individual police officers. In keeping with this regard for the ingenuity of line officers, these officers are given a great deal of autonomy and are to exercise it responsibly. Armed with supportive training, guiding values, and supervision, the community policing officer no more resembles the traditionally constrained patrol officer than the team supervisor—the "local chief of police"—resembles a traditional precinct commander.

A number of police leaders and scholars believe that community policing holds enormous promise for reducing crime and improving neighborhood life, even in disadvantaged neighborhoods where there may be little cohesiveness or public spirit. But it is also reasonable to ask whether the relaxation of conventional methods of supervision and control may not afford a team of officers unusual latitude for engaging in undetected wrongdoing. Community policing exposes officers to different opportunities—for success and for corruption. Many of the job frustrations that push police officers into corruption under traditional regimes may be absent; the available literature suggests that problem-solving officers have high levels of job satisfaction. But it also seems true that an officer who wished to take advantage of a community policing assignment to engage in corrupt practices might escape detection more easily than one performing in a conventional setting under conventional procedures. Proponents of community policing argue that the close working relationship between problem-solving officers and community members, rather than serving as an invitation to corruption, is a safeguard against it. But many are skeptical of so optimistic a claim.

Community policing exposes officers to different opportunities—for success and for corruption.

In any event, there seems to be a general consensus that the mechanisms for controlling corruption in this setting still require a great deal of thought.[29] The advocates of community policing may be underestimating the threat it poses to reasonably effective integrity controls. For example, one method of controlling corruption is to rotate officers routinely in their precinct assignments—so that they serve different residents at regular intervals—or to limit the term of officers involved in vice enforcement to two years: changing both location and function inhibits the development of "sweetheart" arrangements. Community policing proponents would respond, however, that such changes also take a high toll in officer effectiveness and efficiency. Just when officers master their assignment or become familiar with the community they are policing, it is time for reassignment. Routine rotation is inconsistent with the philosophy of community policing; but its abandonment calls for new methods of forestalling police corruption. Centralizing authority, limiting discretion, and reducing intimacy between police and citizens are the traditional ways of controlling corruption. The challenge for police administrators is to allow the team sufficient flexibility to be effective, while maintaining enough oversight to ensure integrity and correct any breaches of the public trust that may arise in the new style of policing.

Many of the departments engaged in the most ambitious experiments with problem-oriented and community-oriented policing do not have a history of systemic corruption. In departments with a history of corruption, not only must officers selected for community policing experiments be screened with care, but novel audit procedures to measure performance also need to be installed. The chief of police should be informed not only about the extent to which the police team is meeting its goals but also about whether the team is operating within legal and ethical bounds. The goal of most problem-oriented and community policing strategies is not to create isolated departmental programs or units providing satisfactory public service but, instead, to train all sworn and civilian personnel of the agency in problem-solving skills and to instill in them a community orientation. Accordingly, whatever effective techniques are developed to foster integrity among community policing personnel may eventually become the department's dominant methods of ensuring an honest and energetic day's work for a day's pay.

Conclusion

The conditions that promote corruption, inside or outside the police service, are familiar and not at all mysterious. They are deep-rooted in human institutions and makeup. Combatting such conditions means not only attacking conventions, practices, and traditions, but also resisting the enemy within, the voice that silences conscience.

Within policing, corruption in vice enforcement is a dark tradition, but a tradition nonetheless. Opportunities for profiting from illegal commerce are great, particularly in an environment of aggressive drug enforcement. Given the breadth of the temptations, police administrators should be vigilant.

Any dedicated chief of a department plagued by corruption will have moments of despondency. This is to be expected, but the conviction that nothing can be done is ordinarily not valid. The chief's best weapon against what has aptly been termed "the great disease of government" is not the installation of some particular regime—the methods, approaches, and organization recommended here—but the chief's own tenacity: the forcefulness of his or her character, example, and initiative.

The great disease of government is not only the dishonesty of government employees but also their indifference to the public interest. It has, therefore, been the objective of this chapter to discuss the control of corruption and misconduct in the context most useful to it: the fostering of an environment in which the police not only decline to lie, steal, and cheat but also continually strive, under proper guidance, to find better ways of serving and protecting the public.

1   J. Noonan, *Bribes* (New York: Macmillan, 1984), 700.

2   The two subjects were discussed in separate chapters in the second edition of *Local Government Police Management*: chap. 7 (corruptive influences) and chap. 14 (internal controls). The authors of this chapter acknowledge their indebtedness to the authors of the earlier chapters, who were indebted to *their* predecessors. This chapter also draws significantly on G. Caplan and J. Wilson, "Police Discipline," in *Police Personnel Administration*, ed. O. Glenn Stahl and Richard A. Staufenberger (Boston: Duxbury Press 1974); and Philadelphia Police Study Task Force, *Philadelphia and Its Police: Toward a New Partnership* (privately printed, 1987).

3   Philadelphia Police Study Task Force, *Philadelphia and Its Police*, appendix A.

4   New York City Mayor's Advisory Committee on Police Management And Personnel Policy (1987), 24.

5   John Dombrink, "The Touchables: Vice and Police Corruption in the 1980's," *Law & contemporary problems* 51 (1988): 201, 227–28.

6   New York City Commission to Investigate Allegations of Police Corruption and the City's Anti-Corruption Procedures, *The Knapp Commission Report on Police Corruption* (New York: George Braziller, 1972), 91–115.

7   Mark Moore and Mark Kleiman, *The Police and Drugs* (Washington, DC: National Institute of Justice, 1989), 2

8   *The New York Times*, 6 Oct. 1986, p. 1.

9   The tangled facts of this matter are recounted in *Commonwealth v. Lewin*, 542 N.E. 2d 275 (MA 1989).

10 International Association of Chiefs of Police, *Building Integrity and Reducing Drug Corruption in Police Departments* (Washington, DC: IACP, 1989), 82.

11 Herman Goldstein, *Police Corruption* (Washington, DC: The Police Foundation, 1975), 21.

12 Quoted in Dombrink, "The Touchables," 232.

13 Goldstein, *Police Corruption*, 12.

14 Jonathan Rubinstein, "The Dilemma of Vice Work," in *Police Corruption: A Sociological Perspective*, ed. Lawrence W. Sherman (Garden City, NY: Anchor Books, 1974), 189.

15 T. Barker and J. Roebuck, *An Empirical Typology of Police Corruption* (Springfield, IL: Charles C. Thomas, 1973), 13.

16 M. Punch, *Conduct Unbecoming* (1985), 200. Punch details the corruption-fighting efforts of Commissioner Patrick Murphy in New York City and Commissioner Robert Mark of Scotland Yard during the 1970s.

17 Ibid. Cf. L. W. Sherman, ed., *Police Corruption* (1974), 33.

18 See A. V. Bouza, "Police Unions: Paper Tigers or Roaring Lions," in *Police Leadership in America: Crisis and Opportunity*, ed. William Geller (New York: Praeger, 1985), 257–58.

19 Herman Goldstein, "Police Discretion: The Ideal versus the Real," in *Police in America*, ed. Jerome H. Skolnick and Thomas C. Gray (Boston: Little, Brown and Company, 1975), 101.

20 International Association of Chiefs of Police, *Building Integrity and Reducing Drug Corruption in Police Departments* (Arlington, VA: IACP and Bureau of Justice Assistance, U.S. Department of Justice, 1989), 58.

21 The official is quoted in E. Delattre, *Character and Cops* (Lanham, MD: University Press of America, 1989), 73.

22 The Miami union leader is quoted in Morris S. Thompson, "Miami Vice: Police Trafficking in Drugs," *Washington Post*, 7 Feb. 1988.

23 Herman Goldstein, *Policing a Free Society* (Cambridge, MA: Ballinger, 1977), 210.

24 R. Lundman, ed., *Police Behavior: A Sociological Perspective* (New York: Oxford University Press, 1980).

25 The IACP's 1989 report on controlling drug corruption offers useful suggestions for implementing workable guidelines for officer-informant interactions. See IACP, *Building Integrity*, 64–67.

26 L. Potts, *Responsible Police Administration: Issues and Approaches* (Tuscaloosa: University of Alabama Press, 1983), 83.

27 Such an external body, and its possibly considerable benefits to police departments and their service populations, is described in Wayne A. Kerstetter, "Who Disciplines the Police? Who Should?" in *Police Leadership in America*, ed. Geller.

28 For a detailed discussion of drug-testing programs in five urban police departments, see Barbara Manili, Edward Connors, Darrel Stephens, and John Stedman, *Police Drug Testing* (Washington, DC: National Institute of Justice, 1987).

29 In this connection, see George L. Kelling, Robert Wasserman, and Hubert Williams, *Police Accountability and Community Policing*, Perspectives on Policing (Washington, DC: National Institute of Justice, 1988).

10 Human resource management

People are the police department's most important and valuable resource. The quality of policing depends on the quality of the people doing policing, and the success of the organization depends on how well these people are selected, trained, evaluated, promoted, and supported. Although the human resource or personnel officer has the lead role in these functions, every police manager and supervisor shares the responsibility for recruiting, developing, and retaining high-quality individuals. In fact, a strong argument can be made that good police management is essentially good personnel management.

So basic is human resource management to the quality of policing that the subject is in fact treated throughout this volume. Human resources planning and organizational development, for example, are discussed in the chapter on organization and management. The reinforcement of departmental values through human resource practices is examined in the chapter on research, planning, and implementation. Performance appraisal is examined at length in the chapter on performance measurement. And training, staffing, and performance measures are touched on in the chapters on patrol, investigations, and other specific police service areas.

This chapter introduces the mid-level manager and police executive to some basic principles of human resource management and its complexities. It also examines important issues that must be addressed as part of this area of administration. After an overview of the human resource or personnel function, including some notes on equal employment opportunity, it discusses eight areas of concern: recruitment and selection, training, promotion, performance appraisal, productivity improvement, support programs, collective bargaining, and the use of civilian personnel. As the chapter will show, it is important to seek and achieve coordination among these various elements of human resource management in a department.

The growing importance of human resource management in police administration parallels the emergence of this aspect of public administration as a sophisticated part of the state and local government service network. There are several reasons for the renewed interest in this area. First, departments are under increasing pressure to become performance based. Over the past three decades, public expectations of the police have changed. In the 1960s, antiwar confrontations, civil rights activity, urban riots, and an explosion of violent crime focused attention on the quality of policing.[1] The turmoil of that period led to the President's Commission on Law Enforcement and Administration of Justice, which produced a report entitled *Task Force Report: The Police*.[2] It echoed the same concerns as the report of the Wickersham Commission in the 1930s—emphasizing the need to upgrade the quality of personnel in law enforcement through selection, education, and training.

Second, the passage of the federal Equal Employment Opportunity Act of 1972 created the basis for successful legal challenges to traditional hiring practices that allegedly favored white males. This legislation and subsequent court decisions made it mandatory for departments to review their personnel policies and practices to be certain they were free of intentional or unintentional bias.

A third factor that enhanced the importance of the human resource or personnel function was publicly sanctioned collective bargaining. Police "social" organizations have evolved into unions in major cities, and most urban police departments today work with well-organized employee groups that take an active interest in personnel policies. Labor relations is an important part of managing human resources.[3]

The fourth reason for the emergence of human resource management as an important function is the growth of civil liability for personnel-related actions. Settlements and jury awards centering on such matters as hiring, promotion, training, and retention speak to the growing importance of this area of administration. Police managers are acutely aware of issues relating to employment discrimination, affirmative action goals, inadequate training, negligent retention, and employee rights. The legal environment of human resource management is complex.

The quality of policing depends on the quality of the people doing policing and on how well these people are selected, trained, evaluated, promoted, and supported.

Taken together, these political, social, economic, and legal factors have increased the importance of human resource management as a major function. Despite the fact that the operations side of the organization (that is, patrol and investigations) has traditionally been the pathway to top leadership positions, the complexity of law enforcement organization now gives the "people manager" growing significance.

Overview of the human resource function

The basic framework for the overall human resource or personnel function in a local government is usually established in state statutes or local charters and ordinances. Organizational structures for personnel administration usually include an independent civil service commission, an executive personnel system, or some combination of them. Civil service commissions may have only advisory powers, or they may be responsible for direct administration of the personnel function. Moreover, the size and scope of local government personnel programs vary widely. Some local governments have personnel departments headed by full-time professionals, whereas others assign personnel functions to individuals who have other responsibilities. In some police departments, personnel functions are supervised by a police officer or a civilian administrative assistant. In most medium-sized and large cities and counties, authority in police personnel matters is shared by the chief and an independent central personnel department or agency.

No matter where the official "personnel" function is housed, supervisors, mid-managers, and police executives all play a key role in human resources. It is not a responsibility to be delegated to others, any more than police-community relations, for example, can be delegated to a community relations unit.

Human resource responsibilities

The personnel or human resource function or unit has the following responsibilities:

Developing policies and procedures for personnel matters, and ensuring that practices are consistent throughout the government or the department

Making recommendations and giving advice to top managers on personnel policies and procedures

Administering a performance evaluation system

Implementing a record management system for personnel data

Coordinating a recruitment system to identify qualified candidates

Maintaining a relevant classification system based on task analysis and civil service requirements

Overseeing the promotion system and/or a career development system

Representing the department in relations with other organizations and groups, such as employee organizations and the civil service commission

Identifying factors related to resignations

Providing support services to help employees deal with performance or personal problems

Managing the disciplinary and appeals system for formal administrative review.[4]

The resources available to perform these functions vary widely among departments. For this reason, police managers and supervisors should become familiar with their department's personnel system and its capabilities. This involves understanding the law establishing the system and becoming familiar with the written policies, rules, and regulations that govern the administration of the system. They must also be aware of state and federal law on labor relations, affirmative action, equal employment opportunity, and employee safety.

Equal employment opportunity and affirmative action

The areas of equal employment opportunity and affirmative action deserve special note in any discussion of human resource management. The U.S. Congress established the Equal Employment Opportunity Commission (EEOC) in 1964 and gave it the mandate to oversee implementation of Title VII of the Civil Rights Act of 1964. (In 1972 the jurisdiction of the EEOC was expanded to include public-sector employees.) Title VII made it illegal for public employers to discriminate against persons on the basis of race, sex, color, religion, or national origin. All criteria for hiring and promotion must be based on "bona fide occupational qualifications" (BFOQs). Through decisions on a case-by-case basis, the EEOC has determined what are and are not BFOQs. Similarly, all decisions relating to termination, compensation, or other employment practices must be based on objective, defensible standards and on documented performance. EEOC guidelines and legal matters involving administrative due process are central concerns in managing human resources in the public sector.

Affirmative action refers to actions taken to redress past or present policies or practices that have resulted in discrimination. Affirmative action is most prominent in the areas of recruitment (as discussed in the next section) and promotion. Court decisions frequently affect the interpretation of equal employment opportunity and affirmative action, and decisions occasionally appear to contradict one another. Consequently, police managers are advised to establish a reliable source of up-to-date legal information and advice to assist them in their management decisions and practices.

Recruitment and selection

The basic goal of recruitment is to attract qualified individuals to serve as police officers. *Qualified* denotes persons who possess, or can acquire through entry-

Recommendations for increasing representatives   Programs designed to make a police department more representative of the diversity of the community are best adapted to the particular characteristics of the department, the governmental jurisdiction, and the community itself. These programs will be useless, however, unless management makes a sincere and sustained effort to ensure that the department is an equal opportunity employer. The following steps are recommended:

All job announcements should state that the department is an "equal opportunity employer."

Responsibility for affirmative action efforts should be assigned to a particular individual with management rank and authority.

Specially trained recruitment task forces should be developed and put into operation.

Referral sources (educational institutions, military services, minority-related organizations) should be identified, and continual liaison with them maintained.

The department should provide recruitment counseling at neighborhood centers and to walk-ins, if possible.

The time period from recruitment to selection should be kept to a minimum.

All tests should be validated and based on job-related skills and abilities, as determined by periodic job analyses.

All police personnel should participate in in-service training programs that develop their understanding of the need for representation and that elicit their involvement in it.

---

level training, the required skills, knowledge, abilities, and job behaviors to perform the tasks and duties of a police officer. In the interests of equity and to improve the department's effectiveness and responsiveness to the community, the department must at the same time hire and promote qualified women and other individuals who represent the racial, ethnic, and cultural diversity of the service area.

Further, it is very important to note experts' predictions that service industries (for example, policing) will create most of the new jobs at the turn of the next century and that the work force will become increasingly older, more female, and more populated by racial and ethnic minorities (only 15 percent of the new entrants to the labor force between 1990 and 2003 will be white males).[5]

Prodded by legal challenges and impelled by their own commitment to diversity, many law enforcement agencies have made significant improvements in hiring and promoting minorities and women. Aggressive agencies committed to affirmative action plans have been most successful in becoming more representative of the communities they serve. As one law enforcement manager put it:

We recruit women and minority candidates because it is right. And we recruit women and minorities because it makes us a better, more effective Sheriff's Department. And that, after all is said and done, should be the goal of any good organization.[6]

Application and screening

Potential applicants may be identified through a variety of sources, including current department employees, walk-ins, write-ins, colleges and other educational institutions, employment services, and consultants and professional recruiters.

Departments may employ public service announcements, posters, celebrity endorsements, and other means of attracting candidates.

Persons who are interested in seeking police employment typically begin by submitting an application form, which provides basic information about the applicant's background, characteristics, and personal history.

Next the applicant usually takes a written test. Preparation and administration of tests is complicated because of legal requirements related to potentially discriminatory practices. The use of written tests has come under EEOC review, and any tests or other requirements that are used to screen individuals must be demonstrably job-related and predictive of future job performance.

The state of the art of written tests has been often challenged, but basically a test must be validated by a statistically complex process (see the section on "Legal and technical considerations" below). In other words, an employer must be able to show that the items on the test do in fact measure job-related skills, knowledge, abilities, and behavior. Validation of a test does not mean an end to any controversy surrounding the use of a written examination, and the potential for litigation has led to personnel actions in many cities.

Another screening step involves some process of physical testing, often a medical examination and agility or other screening. In the years before Title VII, these tests frequently emphasized push-ups, pull-ups, and other manifestations of physical strength. Under pressure of litigation, many of these tests have come to focus, instead, on physical fitness or physical agility, both of which are more job-related and less discriminatory, especially against women. The tests also focus less on abilities that can be taught on the job with proper training, such as scaling walls or dragging weights. A small percentage of departments simply stopped using physical tests as a screening device because of the threat of legal challenges. Whether or not a test of this nature is valid often depends on specific case-by-case controversies that erupt periodically because of particular challenges by individuals. Some departments may still continue to use screening activities that have been successfully challenged elsewhere, but they do so with great risk of incurring liability when a disgruntled job applicant becomes aware of the standards set elsewhere.

Candidates who survive the written and physical testing are then screened further. In this phase, departments may use some or all of the following procedures: polygraph tests, psychological tests, stress tests, and background investigations. Obviously, among the more critical elements of an applicant's background that can be verified after an application is submitted are the applicant's criminal record, military record, credit record, and driver's record, especially with respect to serious offenses that would disqualify the applicant. (By and large, the order in which steps should be taken depends on the relative costs of implementation. For example, the written test should be given first because it is relatively inexpensive and can narrow the pool substantially before the other, more expensive screening devices and procedures are used.) Personnel managers need to be aware of the research literature that evaluates the advantages and disadvantages of using these various instruments or procedures. This literature is rapidly developing, and current materials can best be found through public administration, personnel management, and law enforcement professional associations and labor law and employment discrimination periodicals.

The application and screening phases are both time-consuming and costly, especially because large numbers of applicants must be considered. To reduce both the time and the costs, some agencies have come together on a regional basis to establish eligibility pools by sharing some of the expenses for the initial phases of recruiting. Another approach is to use a registry managed by a private vendor. The job applicant rather than the potential employer is required to pay the vendor the cost of a standardized and certified screening process. The vendor establishes a list of certified candidates whom the individual agencies using the service may interview and screen further. The advantage of the registry approach is that it offers a standardized procedure for pre-employment testing and screening that benefits both the agency and the candidate, at no cost to the agency.[7] However, key liability matters concerning this form of privatization still need further exploration.

Standards and requirements

Figure 10–1 lists nineteen selection standards or requirements, organized into three categories, which are employed by law enforcement agencies. For each standard or requirement, the figure indicates the extent to which measurement problems exist—that is, the degree of complexity involved in measuring the desired quality or attribute.

This list provides the police executive with a frame of reference for comparing his or her department's standards/requirements with those used elsewhere. Use of any of these standards/requirements in any jurisdiction should be based upon pertinent state statute, state case law, county-wide case law, research evidence, state and federal employee selection guidelines, and applicable provisions found in the standards promulgated by the Commission on Accreditation for Law Enforcement Agencies (CALEA). (An excellent resource for much of the foregoing information is the publication entitled *Fire and Police Personnel Reporter*.)[8] Other considerations affecting use of a particular standard/requirement should include those unique to a jurisdiction (for example, swimming proficiency might be a standard if the recruit would be working on waterways); the trainability of the standard/requirement (for example, physical agility can be developed by training); and the size of the department (for example, in a large department there may be many applicants, in which case an appointing-authority interview process could be cost-prohibitive and logistically difficult).

Legal and technical considerations

The legal and technical literature in the area of personnel selection increasingly contains much that is relevant to police recruit selection.[9] From a legal stand-

Figure 10–1 Selection standards/requirements and associated problems

Biographic/demograhic	Measurement problems
U.S. citizenship	None
Driver's license	None
Age (minimum and maximum)	None
Residency (pre and post)	None
Registered voter	None
Veteran's preference	None
Education	None
Personality/character/ability	
Written examination	Many
Oral board interview	Many
Background investigation	Some
Psychological appraisal	Many
Polygraph examination	Many
Appointing authority interview	Many
Assessment center	Many
Physical/medical	
Height	None
Vision (acuity and color)	None
Swimming proficiency	None
Physical agility examination	Some
Medical examination (drugs)	Some

point, two matters—job relatedness/test validity and employment discrimination—capture the most attention. The paramount concerns are that a department must have clear and written standards/requirements and must employ hiring procedures that are related to on-the-job performance. These concerns are *especially important when a department hires a greater percentage of white males (in* proportion to their share of the applicants) than females of any race and a greater percentage of white males than ethnic minorities.

If a department has a selection standard or requirement that results in the rejection of a greater percentage of females than males (for example, a physical agility test), or a greater percentage of blacks than whites (for example, written examinations), the EEOC holds that an "adverse impact" has occurred. When there is an "adverse impact," that is, when the *rate* of selection is different for special classes such as minorities and women than for the most selected class of applicants, the validity of the test or screening instrument must be documented. (The rule of thumb is that adverse impact occurs when the selection *rate*, or percentage passing, of any special class of persons is less than 80 percent of the selection rate of the top scoring group.)

Test validation is a complicated process that involves analyzing tasks to show that the test items or test procedures are indeed job-related. Whether or not the department uses a test that has been officially validated, it is important that any screening devices be scrutinized periodically to be sure they meet the criterion of job-relatedness.

Management issues

Virtually all scholars and practitioners in personnel agree that there is no certain way to ensure that the highest-quality applicants are identified, properly reviewed, and selected. They do, however, agree that a systematic form of selection must precede other employment procedures such as a probationary period, if only because of the cost involved.

In addition, after reviewing hundreds of research studies and reported experiences, personnel experts appear to be moving toward the view that selection procedures are part of a larger system; that is, personnel selection is complex and is linked to job performance in ways we only dimly understand.[10] This view has found scientific support among the law enforcement researchers who have concluded that some of the best predictors of employee behavior are related to recruit training and probationary performance—factors that are not operative during early selection and screening.[11]

Recruitment and selection should be viewed not as a way to identify and eliminate "bad apples" but as a way to nurture responsible employees.

Furthermore, "selection" actually encompasses the entire process of recruitment, hiring, early training, and orientation. A department should carefully track and monitor a recruit's performance during the early probationary period to be sure he or she can meet performance expectations. The consequences, legally, economically, and interpersonally, of allowing a new recruit to function in the capacity of a police officer when he or she clearly cannot successfully discharge those responsibilities are far more pronounced and severe than those to be incurred by an early termination.

The importance of hiring decisions is further supported by recent developments in police civil liability. Attempts to hold police chiefs or supervisors accountable for the actions of subordinates have had wider success. In civil cases, police executives have been named as defendants in suits alleging that they negligently performed some ministerial duty or that some act of omission was the proximate cause of the claimed harm. Findings of vicarious liability have been based on negligent appointment, negligent retention, negligent assignment, negligent entrustment, lack of necessary training, failure to properly supervise, and failure to direct.[12]

Finally, the history of personnel selection research and practice, including police recruit selection, suggests that many critical characteristics are not measurable at the entry level; that the initial screening or selection process is not so much a science as an art; and that, just as predictions of dangerousness among offender populations are highly inaccurate, so, too, the profession's ability to make accurate predictions about future behavior and conduct among police recruits and employees is limited.[13]

Contemporary police recruit selection programs must continue to be guided by research (including thoughtfully conducted validation research), by pertinent case law, by relevant statutes, and by adherence to a variety of guidelines promulgated by the federal government and the profession of psychology.[14] Collectively, this body of knowledge points to the need for a systemic approach to the subject of police recruit selection. That is, policy makers must understand that recruitment and selection are closely linked with academy training, field training, and probationary status as parts of a whole in which those admitted find a pathway of career development. This process should be viewed not as a way to identify and eliminate "bad apples" but as a way to nurture responsible employees.[15] In reality, of course, departments occasionally come across "bad apples," and when this happens, it is important to end their association with the department at an early stage.

Training

Every police department offers some kind of training—recruit training, in-service training, and/or specialized training for particular assignments. Training may be provided within the department or by outside organizations such as training institutes, community colleges, consulting firms, regional academies, state-sponsored mobile training units, or other organizations.

Components of a training program

Whether the training is conducted inside or outside the department, the department must assess its needs, articulate its objectives, select or develop a training program, deliver the training, and evaluate its effectiveness.

Needs assessment   A training program must meet the needs of the organization as a whole, the individual trainees, and the community served by the department. What do officers need to know to perform the various tasks required of them? What special assignments require special training? Are there any perceived deficiencies in officers' performance that can be corrected by training?

Training needs can be identified with the help of a variety of resources.[16] People both within and outside the department may have relevant ideas. Surveys can be an effective tool for assessing training needs. Appointed and elected officials, community leaders, and other citizens can provide very useful information. Relevant data can also provide important perspectives. For example, analysis of internal affairs complaints, civil actions, and causes of accidents and injuries can provide very useful data to those planning the training component.

Articulation of objectives   Objectives of training are based on the needs assessment. What is the intended outcome of the training? What specific behavior

Managing diversity In order for the beat officer to fully assume the role of a community-oriented facilitator, he or she must be knowledgeable about the community—the residents, workers, business owners, and so on. Today, this knowledge demands a multicultural focus that transcends sex, race, nationality, and ethnicity. Each culture (as opposed to each "race") within a community has unique needs that require serious consideration and must be addressed if departments are to truly "serve and protect."

Like the community, the labor force is changing, with increasing representation of minorities and women. As the population and labor force change, police departments have no option but to change as well. Law enforcement has traditionally required conformity and maintained the status quo through command and control, both inside the department and as part of policing the community. The internal police culture must change to reflect the cultures that actually exist in the department and the community. No longer are police departments homogeneous entities unto themselves, composed of people who are similar in appearance, backgrounds, and goals, ready to impose values on the community. Instead, policing requires a different set of values and better communication inside and outside the department. It requires an understanding of the conditions that give rise to conflicts within and between various cultures, and an approach in which differences are celebrated rather than viewed as a cause of conflict. In short, policing in a multicultural society requires that today's police learn how to manage diversity.

The key to managing diversity and celebrating cultural differences is training and education. While it may not be possible to get people to change their attitudes, it is possible to create an environment that will encourage a positive change in behavior. In a police department, this environment can be created by changes in the performance appraisal and reward systems, reinforced by sound training. Police personnel must be trained to become aware of their own values and behaviors and to develop and refine the interpersonal skills of active listening, coaching, and providing feedback. Managers and those who deal with the community must become adept at helping people maximize their potential within the department and within the community served by the department.

Source: Robert Stewart, Major, Tallahassee, Florida, Police Department, and Gayle Fisher-Stewart, Captain, Washington, D.C., Metropolitan Police Department.

should the trainee be able to exhibit when he or she has completed the training? How will the behavior be measured?

Selection or development of a program Sometimes training objectives can be achieved by courses or classes offered by organizations outside the department. If outside resources are not available or do not meet the department's needs, the department may need to develop its own training program. In this case, the department probably needs a skilled training officer who can locate the resources required to develop a program. A good source of information for training officers is the American Society of Law Enforcement Trainers (ASLET), which holds national conferences, publishes training-related material in newsletters, and functions as a professional organization for directors of training.

Program delivery Training can be delivered through a number of vehicles—lectures, demonstrations, discussions, case studies, computerized instruction, role playing, simulations. Many training programs combine several of these.

"Conduct in the Community" seminar   To enhance the police department's understanding and awareness of its community cultures, Long Beach, California, developed a training course that focuses on contemporary law enforcement issues, customer service, and interpersonal skills.

"Conduct in the Community" began in January 1990 as a forty-hour training course for all police personnel. The course contains sessions on criminal law, civil liability, search and seizure, and traffic stops. The course also contains sections focusing on the different communities in the city. These groups include African-American, Hispanic, Asian, and gay communities. The final part of the course deals with proper customer-service skills.

During 1990, the department's 1,100 sworn and nonsworn personnel attended these classes. The course helped all of the department's employees gain a better understanding of the communities they serve and helped make the police department more sensitive to residents' needs.

It is essential that training be conducted in such a way as to be as meaningful as possible to adult participants.[17] In this regard, recruits can be the easiest group to train because a career is being established; the motivation to learn is high, and the relationship between training and career success is well documented. In-service training can be more of a challenge, because the value and significance of the training may be less apparent to the trainees. In either kind of training, it is essential to realize that people *learn by doing* much more effectively than by listening.

Another important consideration in program delivery is the circumstances under which training is conducted. Efforts should be made to provide physical facilities that are as pleasant as possible and to select trainers who are capable of imparting values and skills and creating rapport with trainees.

Evaluation   It is critical that training programs be evaluated to determine whether they have achieved their objectives or whether supervisors are able to ascertain their effectiveness. On-going surveys can help document training effectiveness. Management training must be evaluated in terms of its contribution to organizational development.

Types of training

One type of training program shown to have a major effect on customs and practices is apprenticeships in the field. Training administered by field training officers (FTOs) is virtually universal for recruits.[18] FTO programs must be well coordinated with the training academy's classroom instruction, and the officers performing as FTOs must also receive specialized training. A well-known FTO model program is the one developed in the San Jose (California) police department.[19] It emphasizes the importance of devoting resources to this critical function because, as research shows, the learning that takes place during this period influences the career behavior of the recruit.

Another kind of training commonly offered in police departments is supervisory training. One technique for supervisory training, which some private-sector organizations have used for well over ten years, is "interaction modeling."[20] It is a practical, nuts-and-bolts approach to addressing frequent or critical supervisory problems. Some of these problems include how to improve a subordinate's performance, work habits, attendance, or work attitudes; how to handle employee complaints or overcome resistance to change; how to set and review performance objectives; and generally how to deal with subordinates.

Hazards in FTO training   Field officer training (FTO) programs have many advantages, but certain cautions must be attended to when developing and implementing them:

Overemphasis on technical skills. It is not unusual for an FTO program to overemphasize technical skills inherent in policing in contrast to the "soft" or interpersonal skills, such as attitude toward police work, self-initiated activity, and relationship with citizens, minorities, and other police personnel. The technical skills are where improvement is easily achieved and clearly revealed.

More evaluation than training. The field training officer must perform the dual role of training and evaluation. Evaluation in such a context is easier, especially when the recruit is not quickly responding to the training. When more creative training and/or patience is required, there may be a tendency for the FTO to become more evaluation-oriented, even to build a case against the value of continued training for the recruit.

"Typing" of recruits. Although there is some benefit to referring selection/screening and academy performance information to FTOs upon entry of a recruit into the program, there may be a tendency to prejudge the recruit, resulting in a compromised field training effort. Undocumented negative information must not be allowed to influence the levels of energy and conscientiousness devoted to the training of recruits by FTOs.

Expecting too much too soon. There is often a tendency for FTOs and FTO program administrators to expect too much too fast from recruits. This tendency must be tempered with a respect for the complexity of police work.

Too young and/or inexperienced FTOs. The prerequisites for a good FTO include skill and knowledge, motivation, patience, maturity, and a desire to train new recruits. Unless they have had prior police and/or other developmental experiences, personnel selected to perform as FTOs with just a couple of years of field exposure are inappropriate and counterproductive.

Disliked vs. incompetent recruits. Occasionally a recruit is recommended for termination more out of dislike than lack of competence. It is incumbent on FTO program personnel to ensure that all recruits get a fair shake, are afforded the training opportunities that each deserves, and are evaluated accordingly.

A final caveat is that these potential pitfalls may have particularly severe consequences for minority and female recruits, because their assimilation into the police subculture is often more difficult than that of white male recruits.

Source: Based on Terry Eisenberg, "Six Potential Hazards in Developing and Implementing Programs for Field Training Officers," *The Police Chief*, July 1981, 50–51.

This approach employs a number of structured steps and focuses on what to do, how to do it, and why to do it. A program of this type draws on some of the outside sources and models for training and supervisory workshops.

Many departments also offer specialized training for officers who aspire to management positions. A technique used in both management and supervisory training (as well as in high-level recruitment and promotional decision making) is the assessment center.

A variety of quality police management training and education programs, as well as programs designed for the private sector, are available today. Many departments develop training plans based on a needs assessment and the resources available. Career development systems, although rare, are growing in importance.

Enriching the training curriculum The content of training programs must provide recruits with an ample understanding of the police task. It should provide information on the history of law enforcement, the role of police in modern society, and the need for discretion in law enforcement. Rather than preparing the officer to perform police work mechanically, it should help the officer to understand his or her community, the police role, and even the imperfections of the criminal justice system. In addition, the following specific skills—which have not necessarily been a part of traditional police training curricula—must be taught:

1. Communication skills: the ability to talk effectively with all types of citizens, from community leaders to ordinary residents, as well as the ability to learn effectively

2. Public speaking: the ability to articulate ideas and motivate others, as well as the art of leading meetings so as to draw out the thoughts and ideas of those participating

3. Social, economic, and demographic conditions of the community

4. Supporting agencies in the community: the existence of city or county departments, social agencies, and other resources which can be used for referral of citizens and support for officers in their work

5. Problem-solving techniques: how to identify and analyze problems as well as how to develop effective responses and solutions

6. Conflict resolution and negotiating skills: how to assist citizens in resolving disputes within the community, rather than resorting to violence or "self-help" or having to engage formal legal mechanisms

7. The ability to type: more and more police work will involve the use of computer keyboards, whether on mobile digital terminals in the police car or lap-top computers. Being able to type quickly and accurately will save a great deal of time during an officer's career

8. Multi-lingual skills: the ability of an officer to converse, or at least understand, the languages spoken in his or her patrol area, is not only a valuable attribute but may be necessary for the officer's safety.

Source: Edwin Meese III, "Community Policing and the Police Officer." (working paper, Harvard Executive Session on Policing, February 28, 1991).

Management considerations

To be effective, training must reflect departmental values, goals, programs, policies, and procedures. The units responsible for training and the personnel units associated with the training function must be part of the management process. For example, if the goals and content of training are to be relevant, the training director must be familiar with various functions and practices in internal affairs, staff inspections, or planning and research. At the same time, one cannot effectively train a target group (such as sergeants) without, at the very least, familiarizing the higher levels in the organization with the training goals and content for that target group. The importance of communication up and across the chain of command about training objectives and content applies not only to recruit training but also to in-service and specialized training. Given the complexity of law enforcement, training is a core management function that is implemented through the human resource unit. Too often, the training function is not part of the mainstream of departmental affairs and therefore is not central to the planning and development process.

Another aspect of managing the training function relates to the implementation of training programs, especially those devoted to in-service training. It is common for mid-level managers and supervisors to raise concerns about scheduling because operational programs and projects may be jeopardized when personnel are assigned to receive training. Training unit and personnel managers must be prepared to secure resources and to have a scheduling plan widely distributed. When scheduling is arranged, efforts should be made to fit in-service training into the regular workday; necessary overtime funds and funds for annual in-service training programs should also be budgeted. Training is too often viewed as a luxury, and is thus the target of budget-cutting initiatives.

Management cannot solve problems with training alone. Training, whether it is more, better, or different, is not a panacea. Typically, individual and organizational problems must be approached through a variety of problem-solving strategies, only one of which is training. Further, the departmental training unit manager should not be viewed as the sole provider of training programs or as the only person responsible for identifying the need for training in particular subjects. Training is an inherent part of supervision and management, and the training unit should be treated as an extremely valuable departmental resource and mechanism for coordination. That is, the function must involve a variety of different people on a daily and continuing basis.

Management cannot solve problems with training alone. Training, whether it is more, better, or different, is not a panacea.

Anthropologist Margaret Mead once remarked that "the world in which we are born is not the world in which we live, nor is it the world in which we will die." She was referring to the phenomenon of change and to human beings' unavoidable and constant exposure to change. Popular psychologist Leo Buscaglia once put the point this way: "If you don't like change, you're going to hate life." Continuous in-service training prepares officers for change and helps them adapt and function more effectively. The critical importance of providing law enforcement officers with in-service training on an on-going basis was best stated by Charles Saunders in 1970:

As in any skilled occupation, training must be a continuing process to maintain effective performance in law enforcement. Changes in the laws, in technology, and in the needs of the community make periodic retraining of all personnel essential. Old skills need sharpening with new techniques; specialized knowledge and skills must be taught for certain assignments or for promotion to higher responsibilities.[21]

Promotion

Every police department needs a system for determining which officers should be promoted to higher ranks and responsibilities.

Components of the system

Components of a promotional system fall into three categories: those relating to pre-test eligibility requirements, those that are part of the testing procedures themselves, and those linked to the post-test/appointment elements of the system.

Eligibility requirements　Time in grade, educational level, and nomination are three types of pre-test eligibility requirements. Typically, time in grade is required to be in the vicinity of two to three years. Ordinarily, except for recruits and chiefs, candidates are primarily from within the organization. Some departments, however, have recruited and hired sworn personnel at

---

The cost-effectiveness of training With the exception of very small departments, it can be argued that a city or county would get more from its police department by spending $25,000 annually on in-service training than it would by hiring one more police officer. For example, if in-service training can be expected to increase productivity and/or decrease liability by as little as 5 percent annually, a department with as few as 20 officers would break even by spending $25,000 on training. To the extent that the percentage is higher than 5 percent, and/or the number of officers is greater than 20, the city or county is ahead.

---

supervisory and mid-management levels from outside the department (a practice known as lateral entry).

Levels of formal education required for different ranks or classifications are still highly controversial. In practice, the higher the level in the organization, the more formal educational credentials count. However, aside from departments with career development systems, fewer than 10 percent of departments require college hours or degrees for promotion.

The requirement that applicants must be nominated by supervisors and/or managers in order to participate in a promotional process is extremely rare in law enforcement, although not unheard of (for example, the Lakewood, Colorado, Department of Public Safety has used it). This procedure, which is more common in the private sector, is often resisted because it may appear to introduce favoritism or political considerations into the promotion process.

Testing procedures The following testing procedures or measures are used to varying degrees in promotional processes: written tests (both multiple choice and essay), oral board interviews, simulation exercises, assessment centers, supervisory ratings (of both past performance and potential), psychological appraisals, peer ratings, objective measures of performance, training and experience evaluations, seniority, and veteran's preference. None of these procedures is a certain predictor of supervisory, managerial, or executive performance.

The written multiple-choice test is an extremely popular and frequently employed screening procedure. Its popularity will continue because it costs relatively little when large numbers of people are being evaluated and because it is presumed to be objective. Essay examinations have rarely been employed but are considered to be very useful, especially for small numbers of candidates. Oral board interviews have been a common selection mechanism for promotions for many years.

A major and relatively recent change, however, has been the application of the assessment center method to the oral board process. This method uses simulation exercises (for example, fact-finding, in-basket) and other activities as testing devices to look at performance on task-related projects (see sidebar). Assessment centers, when validated and well-administered, are a popular approach to promotional decision making. Because of time and cost, however, some departments turn to structured oral boards, which have the advantage of some assessment center features.

Supervisory ratings of both past performance and promotional potential continue to be plagued by operational problems. Personality conflicts and organizational politics are alleged to be difficulties with this procedure. However, the use of multiple (anonymous or attributed) supervisory ratings of potential can be explored as a possible way to overcome some of these concerns.

Assessment centers   An increasingly popular method of evaluating candidates for promotion is an assessment center. Assessment centers employ several different techniques, such as written and oral communication exercises, problem-solving sessions, interview simulations, group activities, project assignments, and "in basket" projects. The purpose is to simulate activities and problems commonly found in a management or supervisory role. Usually a panel of assessors or raters evaluates the participants on some kind of numerical rating scale for each exercise. These evaluations lead to an overall assessment of the candidate and his or her qualifications for a particular job.

Advocates of this method believe that it has a number of advantages over traditional tests and screening devices. Through simulations and other types of job-related exercises, a candidate's ability to organize, plan, explain, and manage can be more accurately assessed. Advocates also believe that this method more closely approximates the kinds of skills necessary to perform effectively in an organizational role because it uses many different exercises, thus tapping a large amount of information about on-the-job behavior

The use of an assessment panel— whose members are normally from an agency other than the department—is presumed to yield evaluations that are more objective and independent. It is common for the assessors to be trained and briefed as a group to ensure that they understand their role and that they focus on common indicators.

Much like other performance evaluation systems, the assessment center can provide information about the strengths and weaknesses of candidates and can contribute information for an overall personnel development program. In other words, the assessment center may not only involve the selection of individuals for promotion, but it may also provide personnel units with information about the kinds of training and experiences needed to strengthen their work force.

One of the major concerns voiced about the use of assessment centers is the cost. This form of evaluation takes longer to complete, and the travel and related costs of the assessment panel considerably heighten expenditures. In addition, the larger the number of candidates, the more costly it will be to run an assessment center. Despite the merits of this approach, cost must be one factor when a department decides whether or not to use this particular method.

There is some controversy about whether assessment centers perpetuate a "good-ole-boy" system. Independent empirical evidence of assessment centers is difficult to find because many of the people evaluating this technique have been its advocates. The fact that many civil service agencies approve of this procedure as "objective" is a point in its favor. However, many departments also complement assessment center ratings with written tests, either as part of the experience or as an addition to the center's score.

The quality of an assessment center depends a great deal on the quality of the raters or assessors. Although a number of self-styled consulting firms provide this kind of service, there is no guarantee of high quality. Careful choice is important, and a department should contact references before making a decision on an assessment team.

Psychological appraisals are rarely employed for promotion purposes. They are used most often for exempt positions (for example, chief of police) or for lateral entrants. Peer rating systems provide a very powerful, relevant, and unique perspective on the suitability of candidates for promotion and it has been suggested that they should be used much more frequently in promotional decision making.[22]

Objective, easily quantifiable measures of performance (for example, arrests, traffic citations) should be considered when supervisors conduct their performance evaluations but should not be the only factors taken into account (see also the chapter on performance measurement). Training and experience evaluations, which have been very popular in some states (such as Massachusetts), improve the process. If seniority or veteran's preference is to be used, its impact should not be significant. Multiple indicators of performance may increase the likelihood that pertinent information will be used in the promotional decision.

Post-test and appointment components Finally, post-test and appointment components of the promotional system often consist of a medical examination, an interview with the chief (or other appointing authority), and the use of a discretionary provision, such as the "Rule of 3" (by which the chief or other appointing authority makes the final selection for promotion among the top three qualified candidates). The interview with the chief is often a critical step in the promotional process because, depending on the chief's interviewing skills, it may be a means of assessing many unquantifiable or intangible factors.

In many department processes, relevant information (for example, internal affairs record, past performance evaluations) may not be included in the procedures leading to an "eligibility" list. A discretionary provision such as the Rule of 3 permits the appointing authority to exercise discretion in a fair and job-related manner while making promotional decisions.

Management considerations

Promotional procedures are one of the most emotionally laden and challenging aspects of human resource development and management. Complicating these issues are affirmative action concerns and the opportunity structure for promotion in the law enforcement agency (in fact, there is *not* much opportunity for promotion in law enforcement). It is essential to the well-being of a police department's public service and internal administration that promotional processes be carefully managed.

Departmental history and culture Among the factors that must be considered in the promotional process are the traditions of the particular jurisdiction. Custom and practice create expectations and nurture stability. Changes in custom and practice can create conflict and uncertainty, yet a promotional system should reflect the basic idea of fairness and not violate EEOC guidelines.

Promotional practices are typically formulated in organizations for supportable and justifiable reasons. When these practices are to be changed, the prevailing "supportable and justifiable reasons" must be thoroughly examined and the new procedures justified by persuasive and compelling arguments. For example, failure to provide those participating in a promotional process with adequate justification for replacing oral board interviews with assessment centers has contributed to less than desirable results in some departments. As is generally the case, the way a change is managed affects the likelihood of its being accepted.

Women in the police service   The proportion of women in municipal police departments serving populations over 50,000 in the United States increased from 4.2 percent in 1978 to almost 9 percent in 1986, according to a study published in 1990 by the Police Foundation. Departments with affirmative action programs, either voluntary or court ordered, had a higher proportion of women officers than did departments without such programs.

The study also found that female officers had performance evaluations as high as those of men, used slightly more sick leave than men, and were more likely than men to be assigned to administrative and community service units and less likely to be assigned to tactical or patrol support units. Although eligible women had begun to gain a proportionate share of promotions to mid-management positions, they still faced barriers to promotion.

Among the recommendations to departments were: adopt clear policies prohibiting sexual harassment; assign qualified women as academy instructors so they can serve as role models for female recruits and demonstrate to male recruits that women can be effective officers; encourage women to seek promotion by creating an open system based on merit; reconsider scheduling practices that may increase stresses on women with family responsibilities; and ensure that women's versions of uniforms and lead vests and guns with smaller handgrips are available.

Source: Susan Martin, *On the Move: The Status of Women in Policing* (Washington, D.C.: The Police Foundation, 1990).

Selection of components   Another critical consideration is the configuration of elements in a promotional process. Typically, at least two of the testing elements outlined above are included in a promotion procedure. These two elements are a written component (e.g., multiple-choice test) and an oral component (e.g., a review board or an assessment center). Other elements such as seniority, performance ratings, and an interview with the chief may be part of the process.

There are no hard and fast rules for determining what the elements should be, how many there should be, what weight should be assigned to each, or how each element should be used (for example, as a screening device or as a weighted component). There are, however, some guidelines that can be proposed. First, traditions within an organization must be taken into account and any changes must be orchestrated. Second, several components should be combined to form the basis for promotional decisions; no such decision should be based on one component alone. Finally, whatever is done should be consistent with the results of previously conducted task analyses and should comply with relevant federal regulations, state and local statutes, and case law.

Discretion in promotion decisions   An additional consideration, and perhaps the most significant one, is the personnel system within the promotional processes. For most municipal departments, this is the civil service or merit system. Civil service, whether state or local, provides a measure of job security when political changes occur. In recent years, however, critics have been pointing to the bureaucratic rigidity of civil service and loss of discretion in personnel decisions. What has been lost in some civil service/merit systems is the flexibility and discretion to consider and use information that is often considered "subjective" but may nonetheless be relevant. This information is commonly found in documented or undocumented evaluations but is often neither considered nor evident in the formal promotional system. To increase flexibility and discretion in civil service/merit systems, certain practices such as the Rule of 3 can be helpful.

Performance appraisal

Because performance appraisal is such a critical element in any human resource development and management system, it is covered in substantial detail in the chapter on performance measurement. Coverage here is limited to a discussion of key management considerations.[23]

Performance appraisals serve a number of administrative purposes: they are used in employee development, promotions, assignment and transfer decisions, merit pay programs, training needs identification, coaching and counseling activities, and demotions and dismissals. They also help employees understand their own strengths and weaknesses as a basis for improving their performance.[24]

Objectivity Evaluating employees is one of the most important tasks of a supervisor. Every supervisor makes day-to-day informal appraisals, but supervisors should undertake a more systematic approach annually or semiannually to provide the department with a written record of individual performance.

In some police departments, promotions, demotions, and even employee retention are based primarily on the evaluations made by supervisors. Such evaluations occur whether or not there is a formal performance appraisal system. Personnel decisions made from informal evaluations are difficult to defend. A formal system establishes written performance standards, objective assessment of performance, and systematic documentation procedures to support personnel actions.

Legal considerations Because performance evaluations are frequently the basis for employment decisions, both the courts and the EEOC consider performance appraisal systems to be a form of testing similar to the screening instruments used for applicants.

The Uniform Guidelines on Employee Selection Procedures published by the EEOC specifically state that performance indices must be focused on important or critical work behavior. The guidelines further state that these indices should be based on a thorough job analysis, which is an examination of the tasks involved in performing the job, the means used, the services produced, the qualifications needed by the employee, and the level of performance required. In short, a job analysis identifies the behaviors needed to perform a job successfully. In addition, the EEOC requires that the instructions provided to the raters (persons making the evaluation) must be specified in detail.[25]

Court decisions have led to specific guidelines associated with performance appraisal procedures. A review of the case law reveals the following nine key considerations for developing a performance appraisal system:

1. The purpose of the appraisal system (promotions, layoffs, transfers, and so forth) must be specified.
2. The basis for the system must be a systematic job analysis.
3. Behavioral systems usually fare better than trait systems (i.e., indicators that rely on the description of an activity are preferable to judgments about character or qualities).
4. There should be evidence that individuals who use the system agree on an employee's evaluation.
5. Appraisals should be made frequently (or should be based on several frequent informal evaluations).
6. Training should be available to persons doing the rating.

7. Specific appraisal instructions should be given to persons filling out rating forms.
8. There must be some mechanism allowing the person being evaluated to discuss the process with the evaluator.
9. When possible, some attempt should be made to validate the procedure.[26]

Developing the system   The first task is to determine the purpose of the appraisal system. As noted earlier, if the system is to be used as an integral part of a promotional selection procedure, the processes used in the appraisal system must meet the tests of reliability and validity. But, if the system is used primarily to improve performance and productivity, no such tests are necessary.

Assuming that the system is to serve this second purpose, the task of designing it is somewhat easier. An initial step is to draft a statement setting forth the mission and values of the department. The next step is to specify the organizational goals, objectives, and activities. Finally, each job must be described, its critical elements identified, and performance standards established (this is the job analysis described earlier). Performance standards are the yardsticks by which supervisors assess the quantity, quality, and resource consumption of critical activities. Resource consumption includes time and money expended.

A means of gathering performance data throughout the rating period must be developed. Critical activities must be counted for each employee to be evaluated. Descriptive statements of the quality of a sampling of the activities of each employee must be recorded. The evaluating supervisor should have observed the employee performing his or her duties. The evaluator should also have access to department activity reports that are individually based. The evaluating supervisor compiles data for each employee being evaluated, and reaches a conclusion about the individual's performance.

Providing feedback   A performance appraisal interview should follow the evaluation and should probably take place at least twice a year. For newly hired employees and marginal performers, more frequent sessions are generally necessary. Performance appraisal forms should be reviewed by more senior managers before they are shown to the employee. It is important that the senior manager analyze the range of ratings given, look for abnormal ratings, and evaluate the quality of the raters' evaluations.

Preparation for the appraisal interview requires a review of the employee's record, identification of his or her strengths and weaknesses, and anticipation of the likely issues of concern to the employee. The interview itself should consist of (1) giving feedback on performance by providing examples of good performance as well as of performance needing improvement, (2) discussing both strengths and weaknesses, (3) obtaining the employee's acknowledgment of the session (usually the employee is asked to sign the evaluation form or a copy), and (4) agreeing on standards of performance and setting objectives for future goals and evaluation.

Performance interviews should be viewed as an opportunity for the supervisor to accomplish several important personnel management purposes:

1. Reinforce positive performance
2. Discuss perceived weaknesses and plans to use training or coaching to improve performance
3. Improve supervisor effectiveness by identifying shortcomings in training, procedures, and policies
4. Identify underlying personal problems, such as family difficulties, emotional problems, and substance abuse.

Focusing the system A performance appraisal system that tries to achieve too many objectives will serve none adequately. A multipurpose system can be so difficult and costly to develop and administer and can become so complex that both managers and employees reject it. Supervisors spend more time on the process and become less aware of the purpose of the evaluation. Confidence in the accuracy and objectivity of the performance appraisal is diluted. The remedy is to keep the purpose of a performance appraisal system somewhat limited.

Performance appraisal systems can be used most effectively as a motivational tool to improve productivity. This becomes a concrete way for the department to articulate and make operational its philosophy or vision of policing. Performance appraisal can be a means of telling the officer which activities are important, how they should be performed, and how well the officer performs. What gets measured gets done. What gets counted counts. Feedback on accomplishments or the lack of them lets the officer know how much he or she has contributed to the organizational goals.

Performance appraisal becomes a concrete way for the department to articulate and make operational its philosophy or vision of policing.

It is safe to say that developing and administering any good performance appraisal system will require considerable effort. The effort expended in development will have much to do with the quality and legitimacy of the system. Performance appraisals must be viewed as an integral part of the entire process of human resource administration. Top management must ensure that performance appraisals are conducted throughout the department in a fair and consistent manner and are based upon valid assumptions. Appropriately used, performance rating systems will strengthen the organization.

Productivity improvement

The fiscal constraints experienced by many police departments in the 1980s and 1990s require police managers to develop skills in "cutback" or retrenchment management. Because personnel costs (salaries and benefits) account for at least 75 percent of the budget, police managers are often compelled to control expenditures by regulating the size of their work force. Increases or decreases are measured in terms of positions filled, not filled, and authorized. In recent years, the demands for police service have increased because of the growth of rapid response strategies, for example, 9–1–1 systems. This mix of pressures requires police chiefs to focus their attention on productivity improvement measures as a major way to increase organizational effectiveness.

Improvement in productivity means improvement in the efficiency and effectiveness of the department's operations. Efficiency is the ratio of the services provided to the resources expended. Effectiveness is a measure of the actual impact of the efforts of the department members. In short, efficiency is doing things right, and effectiveness is doing the right things. For several reasons, productivity improvement is not easy to achieve.

First, because of the lack of a profit motive in the public sector and the concomitant limitations on incentives to do assigned tasks more efficiently, many employees find little to motivate them to better their productivity.

Second, because political considerations may have a greater effect on the tenure of elected officials than do financial consequences, these officials may be tempted to focus on short-term results. Increased productivity results from long-term, consistent policies and practices.

New roles for mid-managers Given the importance of attempting to develop a system in which innovation and renewal are to be valued, mid-managers will need to expand their roles in ways that may not be entirely familiar, dominated as police organizations have been by the need to control officers rather than help them be creative in support of departmental missions. Two elements of the new role come readily to mind. First, managers must function as team builders. Building coalitions, managing task forces, establishing linkages between departments and other units of the organization, and building relationships with consumers of police services will require extensive team-building efforts.

Second, and perhaps more fundamental, mid-managers must *truly* be managers rather than overseers of personnel. The focus of overseers is control. Overseers know best, and their

purpose is to ensure that their instructions are followed. The task of true managers is, or ought to be, to develop personnel so that they are free to innovate and adapt on behalf of the values of the organization. Thus, the central mandate of managers is to make long-term investments in the people they lead. They must coach, lead, protect, inspire, understand mistakes, tolerate failure, and in general work to develop the insights and abilities of their people. To accomplish this mandate, mid-managers must be provided with access to the training that can teach them team-building and personnel development skills critical to their role.

Source: Adapted from George L. Kelling and Mary Ann Wycoff, "Implementing Community Policing: The Administrative Problem" (working paper, Harvard Executive Session on Policing, 9 February 1991).

Third, measures of officer effectiveness are not readily available. Process measures are abundant, but measures of outcomes or impact are difficult to pinpoint.

Fourth, the collective bargaining environment may complicate the process. Although unions are not per se opposed to improving productivity, they may be reluctant to support programs that could result in personnel reductions and a consequent loss in union membership.[27]

John M. Greiner groups the variety of productivity improvement strategies into five broad categories: (1) introduction of new or improved technology, (2) improvement of operational procedures, (3) revision of organizational structures, (4) enhancement of the skills of management and line employees, and (5) improvement of employee motivation.[28] Because so high a percentage of police department budgets is spent on personnel, productivity improvement is a key human resource management concern. Some popular motivational techniques used by police departments include merit pay, job enlargement and enrichment, employee participation, and productivity bargaining.

Merit pay Merit pay is based on the assumptions that material results will motivate employees to produce desired behavior and that achievement-oriented people expect to be compensated for their efforts. A merit pay plan provides latitude for differences in compensation based upon performance. Although merit pay has not been shown to stimulate improved productivity, pay-for-performance programs are common in local government.[29]

Merit pay programs are not always effective because not all employees are motivated by material incentives. Employees may value other job aspects more, such as the nature of the work itself. Administering merit pay programs can also be difficult because such programs require fair and effective performance evaluation systems.

Job enlargement and enrichment Job enlargement increases the number of tasks assigned to an employee. Jobs of patrol officers can be enlarged, for example, if the patrol officers are assigned to activities such as an integrated criminal apprehension program, team policing, or problem-oriented policing.[30]

Job enrichment differs from job enlargement in that in addition to providing for more diversity, it also gives the employee greater responsibility. Problem-oriented policing provides an example of job enrichment as well as job enlargement in policing. Such programs can lead to increased job satisfaction and productivity.

Employee participation Giving employees an opportunity to participate in decisions relating to their work is another way to improve productivity. One means of providing opportunity for participation is to use quality circles—groups of employees brought together to solve job-related problems. Although quality circles can be established at any level in an agency, the idea behind them is that if employees are allowed to influence job-related decisions, they will take a more personal interest in their work and will develop a sense of pride in their accomplishments. Increased involvement leads to increased productivity.[31]

Quality circles as a participatory approach to organizing work developed primarily in Japan and Sweden. Their application in U.S. police departments has been limited, and no rigorous evaluation studies have been completed. What is fairly certain is that this approach involves participatory management and requires a cooperative work environment and a high level of trust. It

---

Master Police Officer program The Newport News, Virginia, police department has an enhanced career development program through which qualified nonranking officers may be elevated to a new level. Known as the Master Police Officer (MPO) program, it allows officers with special technical and administrative skills to use and be paid for those skills.

Typically, MPO participants help prepare for roll call and shift training, fill in as supervisors in the absence of sergeants, and oversee operations at crime scenes. Besides providing technical expertise, they are expected to observe the activities of junior officers and provide input on performance evaluations. They are also expected to be leaders in implementing and applying problem-oriented policing principles.

Only officers at or near the top of the three-level salary structure are eligible for this program and then only if they have highly developed knowledge, skills, and abilities. They must be

expert in at least two specialty areas such as defensive tactics, firearms instruction, or breathalyzer operation, and they must have demonstrated expertise in problem solving within thirty-six months of their application for the MPO program.

Once qualified, candidates participate in a selection process that includes recommendations from supervisors and review of relevant written material by a selection committee, which may also interview supervisors or peers of the candidates. Final approval comes from the chief. Once selected, officers must maintain MPO standards to remain in the program.

First authorized in 1988 for up to ten officers, the program has expanded by approximately ten new slots per year as more officers become eligible and qualify.

Source: Jay A. Carey, Jr., Chief of Police, Newport News, Virginia, Police Department.

seems clear, therefore, that this approach would not be successful unless it were preceded by a substantial change in the culture of most police departments, which are centralized and highly structured (see the chapter on organization and management).

Quality circles require strong commitment from top management and trust among employees. The start-up cost, in terms of employee time, can be substantial. Management must also be willing to follow through and carry out the recommendations of the group, providing additional resources when necessary. For quality circles to flourish among employees, team management is essential.

Support programs

Police departments across the country have established employee assistance programs to help employees deal with problems related to stress, substance abuse, traumatic incidents, personal problems, and assorted emotional difficulties. For the most part, use of these programs is voluntary. However, many departments have also developed methods to identify problem employees and direct them into programs designed to provide help. A proactive policy may be appropriate because many police officers may be reluctant to seek this type of assistance. (Many private and public programs are covered by insurance.) Planning in this area is a component of risk management because civil liability concerns come into play.

Many departments have developed methods to identify problem employees and direct them into programs designed to provide help.

The problem employee

Police managers and supervisors devote a large portion of their time to dealing with marginal or unsatisfactory employees. The *problem employee* can be defined in a variety of ways, but for purposes of this discussion, a problem employee is someone who consistently fails to meet the employing organization's expectations or norms. A problem employee lacks the interest, motivation, aptitudes, ability, skills, or psychological capacity necessary to perform the job properly.

Problem employees are found in all police departments and throughout the work force. In many private organizations it is less difficult to terminate problem employees. In many police departments, however, it is extremely difficult, given civil service systems and other protections for employees. Modern police departments exist in an environment that affords many legal protections to police personnel. Some labor contracts include "just-cause" standards and require a step-by-step response to grievances, with final review by an arbitrator. A police officer's "bill of rights" has been adopted in many departments by administrative action, collective bargaining, or legislative mandate. Career service rules often provide the individual employee with protections that can be administratively burdensome or, at least, time-consuming.

The first-line supervisor is a key to managing the problem employee and has part of the responsibility for detecting and identifying subordinates' problems. A system to respond to such problems should be publicized and should make both voluntary and involuntary programs available.

Behavioral alert system

In addition to the first-line supervisor, a personnel unit or individual can be responsible for maintaining an early warning system to ensure timely attention

Marginal performance and liability Marginal performance by police officers presents an omnipresent threat of civil liability even in the best-managed departments. Civil action is a possibility in virtually every interaction between a citizen and an officer, but the risk is immeasurably greater with officers who have track records of misconduct. To avoid the liability risks inherent in police work, police managers should establish a system of protection with six basic components:

1. Clear, concise, constitutionally acceptable policies and procedures on foreseeable activities of officers

2. Relevant training for all officers on the policies and procedures relating to high-risk activities that are a part of their work

3. Quality supervision and enforcement of those policies and procedures

4. Consistent and progressive discipline for transgressions of these policies and procedures

5. Constant review and revision of these policies and procedures in light of citizen complaints, police research, court decisions, management audits, and inspections

6. Legal advice and support, including updates and training on court decisions and periodic retraining on all major legal issues.

Obviously, sound recruitment and selection procedures can help ensure that the department has good officers, but even with the best of efforts, some officers will become "problems" or "liability time bombs."

When these officers are kept on the force, the department and the chief can become liable for suits based on "negligent retention." When chiefs attempt to terminate or seriously discipline these officers, however, they may find their decisions overturned by a civil service commission. Here are some suggestions for a department if this happens:

1. Do not assume that the civil service commission that reinstated the officer therefore becomes entirely responsible for the officer's actions

2. Do not blame the civil service commission; rather, examine the quality of the department's presentations in the case.

3. Train first-line supervisors to evaluate performance objectively and require them to gather precise performance data on their subordinates. If high performance evaluations are on file for an officer, they undermine even solid claims for termination in the eyes of a civil service commission.

4. Try to persuade the civil service commission to make the officer's return to active duty conditional by requiring a special probationary period, successful completion of critical retraining, additional evaluations, or close supervision.

5. Even if the civil service commission does not set special conditions, require the officer to undertake retraining and undergo extra performance evaluations.

6. Explore the state's statutes on decertification of police officers. The civil service commission cannot reinstate an officer in a position for which he or she is not eligible by law.

7. Refer the marginal officer to the department's employee assistance program or to another source of help if he or she has personal problems that may be contributing to deficient performance.

8. Beware of assigning marginal officers to "desk" jobs that give them more attractive working schedules than those of high-performing officers. This sends the wrong message to others in the department.

Source: G. Patrick Gallagher, Director, Institute for Liability Management, Leesburg, Virginia (a division of Gallagher Bassett Services, Inc.).

to potential problems. This unit should have access to various performance indicators that police departments routinely keep. These would include productivity measures, accident and injury records, citizens' complaints, attendance reports, disciplinary histories, performance ratings, and reports of unusual incidents.

Arrest records, cases handled, traffic tickets, and other quantifiable data, when reviewed periodically, can be used to establish norms. Departures from these norms may indicate a need for supervisory intervention. Records of vehicle and other kinds of accidents and injuries can be significant in determining when follow-up attention is needed. People who are accident-prone may have undiagnosed medical, psychological, or substance-abuse problems. Records of absenteeism or tardiness can be important indicators of an individual's physical and mental capacity for the job.

Supervisor evaluations over time should be reviewed to ascertain if there are unexplained fluctuations in the employee's performance. Reports of aberrant, unusual, or unacceptable conduct should be reviewed to determine if some immediate or extraordinary follow-up is warranted. Such incidents may demand discipline, but they could also be symptoms of emotional difficulty or substance abuse.

A behavioral alert system should include the following reporting elements:

Any discharge of firearms, whether accidental or duty related[32]

Excessive use-of-force reports

Any motor vehicle damage

Any loss of equipment

Injured-on-duty reports

Use of sick leave in excess of five days, or a regular pattern of periodically using one or two sick-leave days

All complaints, including supervisory reprimands and other disciplinary action.[33]

If an evaluation indicates that an investigation should focus on an individual officer, then the officer's supervisory evaluations, awards, and commendations should also be reviewed.[34]

The individual or unit responsible for reviewing these various behavior indicators should create a file for any employee whose performance in specified areas falls outside department norms and should periodically review the contents of the file. Corrective intervention should be based upon the type of incident/indicator, overall performance, and previous department efforts to remedy the problem.

Correcting deficiencies

The range of responses to a problem employee should be tailored to the problem and can include any one or a combination of the following:

Counseling by a supervisor

Remedial training

Referral to an employee assistance program (EAP)

Mandatory medical examination

Early warning signals   In an effort to retain as many trained police officers as possible, Long Beach, California, developed a nondisciplinary, proactive system to identify problems officers might be experiencing. The Early Warning System (EWS) uses a computer to track individual incidents and identify those officers who may be candidates for future problems. Examples of EWS incidents are: reportable use-of-force incidents; officer-involved shootings; in-custody deaths, where the deceased was under direct control of an employee; K-9 bites; personnel complaints that are sustained or ongoing.

All incidents are entered into a computer, which produces a report based on certain criteria for the EWS coordinator. These reports are confidential and distributed only to the employee's bureau chief. The deputy chief of the employee decides when and if a panel is to be convened to discuss the incident with the employee. Recommendations from the panel may include retraining, counseling, or other appropriate action. A report is then directed to the assistant chief of police. Included is a summary of the incident, panel discussion and response, and any action taken, scheduled, or planned. Follow-ups to the actions are completed a minimum of every 90 days.

The employee's progress and any further remedial action are noted. This program is directly responsible for a sizeable decrease in both citizen complaints and use-of-force complaints.

Source: Cited in *The Guide to Management Improvement Projects in Local Government* (Washington, DC: International City Management Association, 1990).

Psychological examination

Urinalysis to detect substance abuse

Disciplinary action.

Counseling   The least intrusive method—counseling by a supervisor—should be attempted first. Effective supervisory couseling of a problem employee requires a certain degree of skill. Departments need to train supervisors to ensure that the counseling is competent.

Training   Although training should not be viewed as the solution to all performance shortcomings, it may be that an individual's performance is deficient because the individual never acquired the necessary job skills. Remedial training both communicates concern and provides the means to change. But reliance on training should not obscure other relevant solutions.

Referral to an employee assistance program   An employee assistance program (EAP) should be an integral part of any department's human resource management program. The EAP refers employees to sources of counseling or other help for psychological or marital problems, substance abuse, financial problems, or other personal difficulties. An effective EAP can salvage productive employees who otherwise would be effectively lost to the organization. The financial benefits would be significant, given training costs, replacement costs, and the invaluable experience and personal knowledge employees contribute to the organization. Even disregarding the financial elements, humane concern for employees and their families would dictate the availability of an EAP.

Medical and psychological examinations   Officers who show seriously erratic or unexplained behavior may need to undergo a medical or psychological review to determine fitness for duty. Such review can be perceived as threatening and career damaging. Many experts advise that any mandatory evaluation process be entirely confidential and separate from the EAP: (1) any real or perceived conflicts of interest can be avoided, and (2) the review becomes more credible and ceases to be threatening.[35]

Urinalysis   Excessive absenteeism, proneness to accidents, repeated disciplining, and unexplained aberrant behavior can all serve as the legal basis for "reasonable suspicion" of drug use requiring a urinalysis. Although abuse of illicit drugs by law enforcement personnel is much more emotionally charged than abuse of alcohol, alcohol is still the single most abused substance.

Disciplinary action   When specific rule infractions have been investigated and sustained, employee assistance responses should not be used in lieu of disciplinary action. But when the problem is performance deficiencies, disciplinary action should generally be a last resort, after counseling, admonishments, and training have failed to bring about the desired results. The various possible management responses to an identified problem employee are not mutually exclusive. Management's response can include any one or any combination of responses that fit the specific needs of the individual problem employee.

Providing employee assistance and psychological services

A department must decide whether it will have in-house psychological evaluation and employee assistance programs or will contract out for either or both of these programs. The primary considerations are cost-effectiveness, professional competence, and credibility.

The array of services and the skills available through established outside professional contractors may outweigh the benefits of hiring one professional to handle the full spectrum of personal problems experienced by employees of any organization. Depending upon the scope of services to be provided, the professional staff or contractor should be judged on the appropriateness of its licensing, credentials, experience, professional stature, accomplishments, and affiliations. If the decision is made to provide this service in-house, organizational skills and management experience will have to be considered in addition to cost.

Professionals employed to conduct mandatory psychological examinations should be licensed clinical psychologists. The reputations and credentials of these persons are important because decisions based on their professional recommendations may be challenged before an arbitrator or judge. An external service provider with an established reputation and professional credentials may be able to withstand qualifications challenges more easily than a professional employed by a department.

Psychologists and psychiatrists participating in mandatory evaluation programs must be cognizant of the legal and operational implications of their recommendations. Essentially management must limit the psychologist's discretion to recommendations that can be carried out without major job restructuring, that are administratively reasonable, and that do not increase an organization's exposure to liability. Therefore, administrative and legal considerations may preclude recommendations such as the following:

May continue working under constant supervision

May continue working under close supervision

May continue working in a low-stress environment

May continue working in a non-law-enforcement capacity

May continue working in an unarmed capacity

May continue working in an assignment with limited contact with the public.[36]

An important aspect of monitoring people who have performance problems is the appropriate follow-up to professional recommendations. Psychological recommendations will often require administrative or medical follow-up or participation in an employee assistance program. It is essential that responsibility for ensuring follow-up be placed with a central office or individual. Failure to ensure follow-up to professional recommendations places the department at risk and poorly serves the individual employees.

The person responsible for monitoring the follow-up will have to establish and maintain communications and working relationships with virtually every unit and office within the department, including other governmental agencies and outside contractors who are involved in the human resource function. Certain lines of communications and responsibilities will have to be formally mandated.

The employee assistance professional staff must have internal credibility and the confidence of both the managers and the employees who suffer personal problems. A needs assessment of service requirements should be undertaken periodically. This serves both to obtain information for use in program development and to provide information to members of the department on the services available.

In summary, to deal effectively with problem behavior it is necessary (especially in large departments) to establish a centralized function that monitors performance, provides feedback to management, triggers remedial activities, and ensures appropriate professional attention. In departments of any size, responsibility for corrective efforts should remain within the chain of command. Finally, any human resource management program must balance the department's responsibility against the rights and dignity of the individual officer.

Collective bargaining

Public-sector collective bargaining at the state and local level has come of age. As of 1990, all but eight states had enacted statutes controlling collective bargaining by government employees, and only one state prohibited collective bargaining between all government employee organizations and any government entity.

Even though public policy seems to encourage police unionization, it is not inevitable. Unions are often the product of poor management: management practices that antagonize employees may compel employees to seek increased control over the workplace through collective bargaining. Sound personnel management practices can contribute to a work environment that lessens the likelihood of employee organizations. Effective mechanisms for communicating concerns, consistent and fair treatment of employees, and participatory management are all measures that will make employees less likely to organize to protect themselves. However, proactive management is no guarantee against unionization.

The context of public-sector labor relations

The conventional wisdom and practice among police managers through the 1960s was that unionization in law enforcement should be resisted. This approach created enormous conflicts and contributed to instability and low morale in many departments. In the 1990s the prevailing attitude is that unions exist and must be accepted as part of the administrative environment. "Labor relations" is viewed as a skill necessary for effective management. The question is how to establish a working relationship with unions rather than how to eliminate them or resist them in counterproductive ways.

In the private sector, the power of a labor union derives from its ability to withhold its labor and cause the employer serious economic loss. A strike in the public sector, however, might not cause severe economic losses to the organization—it might actually produce some short-term economic benefits because of budget savings. But a public-sector strike, especially a police strike, can embroil the government in controversy, attract adverse media attention, embarrass elected officials and public managers, and, most of all, cause economic and other hardship in the community and loss of vital emergency services.

A legislative body at the state or local level usually enacts laws affecting civil service status, employment, pensions, prevailing wages, and fiscal appropriations, all of which are the traditional concerns of labor unions. And multiple agencies of the executive branch of government usually share the responsibilities for rule making, administration of personnel management systems, and fiscal management. Thus it is difficult for any one police manager, or even any one government agency acting in isolation, to function effectively in a collective bargaining environment. Such separations of power "may operate as constraints on the authority of the public employer."[37]

Bargaining unit and recognition

A bargaining unit consists of one or more employees whose jobs have sufficient commonality for them to constitute the unit represented in the collective bargaining process. Among the factors that can influence the determination of the appropriate unit are pertinent collective bargaining history, community interests, and similarity of employee duties.

Before a group can begin representing employees as a bargaining unit, management must recognize the group as the sole bargaining agent for the employees. The recognition follows a representation election, that is, an election to determine whether the employees want to be represented by a bargaining agent and which agent they prefer. Under the federal Wagner Act, a labor law passed in 1932, and statutory extensions of its provisons to the public sector, public employees have the right to seek an election in most states as well as the right to bargain collectively over wages, hours, and working conditions.

The negotiating process

Who negotiates? The answer to that question may seem obvious: negotiations are carried on between union leaders and top management. However, because of the shared responsibility in public-sector management, who "management" is can vary, depending on the issue and the groups involved.

This ambiguity makes the negotiating process in the public sector more complicated and can have adverse consequences on the ability to reach settlements. For example, a union may attempt to bypass the chief or the chief's representative at the negotiating table and go directly to another individual whom it perceives as the decision maker on a particularly important issue. A union may use this ambiguity to further its own interests and to justify political lobbying as a means of influencing the collective bargaining process. An added complication is that the absence of the appropriate decision maker at the negotiating table sometimes leads unions to charge employers with "bargaining in bad faith," when in fact preliminary agreements may have been set aside by an official or agency not sitting at the table. It is important, therefore, that negotiators feel secure in their position, have adequate power, and have direct access to the police chief, the chief executive officer of the city, and relevant political leaders.

The makeup of the negotiating team deserves close attention. Labor negotiations affect public management in many ways: personnel administration, career service, budgeting, and the operations of the department. Consequently, a management committee should be formed to participate in the negotiations.

A chief spokesperson or negotiator should be designated. He or she should have experience in labor negotiations—at least as much experience as the union's representatives have. The committee might also include key managers from city departments such as personnel and budget; from legal counsel; and from operational units of the police department, to provide information about the effect of various proposals on their areas of expertise.

The failure to include an experienced negotiator on the team can be a costly mistake for cities or counties negotiating a contract. If a department is entering negotiations for the first time, it should consider retaining a labor-relations consultant. A consultant offers a way to handle negotiations in the short term and helps a member of the management staff develop the capability to assume this responsibility in the future.

Preparing for negotiations

Adequate preparation is the key to success in the negotiation process. The members of the negotiating committee should be involved in the preparation. It should be recognized from the outset that their participation on the committee will take considerable effort and time, particularly during the negotiations of an initial contract.

When a subsequent contract is being negotiated, sources of potential issues can be identified: the existing collective bargaining agreement, past grievances in the unit, and arbitration decisions previously rendered. The management team should also identify issues of concern to management, determine union positions, and develop their own affirmative (that is, not reactive) positions.

Although the negotiating committee has primary responsibility for preparing for the bargaining, all members of management should be involved to some degree. Input from all levels is particularly important when a subsequent contract is being negotiated. Supervisors and mid-level managers should be asked for practical suggestions on what provisions of the current contract need revision, why they need it, and what the revisions could be.

Having identified the issues and researched the other side's concerns, the committee must establish management's position on each issue. It should ask three questions about each issue:

1.   What laws apply to the issue?
2.   What impact, if any, will the issue have on department operations?
3.   What will the issue cost?

The negotiating committee must gather the information necessary to answer these questions.

The scope of bargaining

The scope of bargaining refers to the subjects that can be negotiated. Most state collective bargaining statutes separate the subject matter into three categories: (1) subjects that are voluntary and may be negotiated if both parties agree; (2) subjects that are mandatory and must be negotiated; (3) subjects that are forbidden and cannot be negotiated. State laws generally exclude from bargaining the mission and functions of the agency, how the work is to be done, and the tools that will be used to do the work. Sometimes organizational structure, the selection of new employees and supervisors, standards of service, and overall budget allocations in an agency are also excluded.

Mandatory subjects usually include all matters directly affecting wages, hours, and terms and conditions of employment. State laws also usually include as mandatory subjects any matter about which the employer and the union have previously bargained and agreed in a previous negotiation. Voluntary topics include such issues as safety, union security, and productivity bargaining.

Productivity bargaining is a way to obtain the support of the union in productivity improvement efforts. In essence, the benefits of improved productivity are shared with a union's members. The benefits can take the form of additional pay, compensatory time, or improved working conditions. Productivity bargaining can also mean using an incentive to "buy out" the employees in order to change a particularly costly work rule or staffing requirement.

Researchers have pointed out several problems with productivity bargaining. Preexisting power relationships between the union and management may prevent gains through productivity bargaining. That is, a union that has been able to obtain restrictive work rules or large wage gains that are now obsolete may continue to fare well in productivity bargaining.[38]

The motivational effect of any change or wage gain can diminish with time. Once employees become accustomed to the new arrangement, they may take it for granted. Or compensation formulas developed in the bargaining process may produce less of an increase in pay in subsequent years as marginal improvements in productivity diminish. The result may be new demands by the collective bargaining unit, and the cycle begins again.

Police union objectives

The immediate objectives of police unions are recognition, union security, improvements in wages and benefits, improvements in job conditions, and clearly defined procedures in disciplinary matters.

Recognition is primary because it grants to the union the status and right to bargain with the employer. Union security encompasses such specifics as dues deduction from wages, union access to new employees, use of bulletin boards, and provisions for using "company time" to conduct union business. In the public sector, a common union-security arrangement consists of a contract provision that requires a non-union member of a bargaining unit to pay the union a sum equal to the prorated amount it takes to negotiate and administer the contract.[39]

Modifications in department policy and procedures that are perceived as inequitable or oppressive may be discussed in negotiations. Such job-condition issues as the role of seniority, layoff policies, scheduling practices, and uniform and equipment specifications are common matters of concern.

Depending on the history of discipline within a department, the administration of a disciplinary system is often a matter to be defined by contract negotiation. Clauses commonly found in police collective bargaining agreements include the right to appeal disciplinary actions through a grievance procedure that ends in review by a "neutral" arbitrator, and provisions declaring that no discipline can be administered except for "just cause."

Key contract clauses

Although all areas of the contract are important and deserve the close attention of the management committee, five very important matters of concern are (1) a management rights clause, (2) the definition of a grievance procedure and a procedure for handling disciplinary matters, (3) a no-strike provision, (4) a "zipper" clause (explained below), and (5) a maintenance-of-benefits clause. In some states the contents of these contractual provisions may be controlled by law, with negotiators having little discretion.

Management rights   Traditionally the police chief's prerogatives were limited by civil service regulations, administrative law, and political considerations. Once a contract is negotiated, however, a fourth set of conditions limits the chief's prerogatives.

The idea of "residual rights" governs the interpretation of most contracts. The collective bargaining agreement limits the right of the employer to establish working conditions *only* to the extent that such conditions of employment are covered by the agreement. The preexisting rights of the employer continue in all matters not covered by the agreement. In other words, if the agreement is silent about a matter, then the employer is free to make unilateral changes as long as such changes are not inconsistent with the provisions of the current agreement and are legal. Put still another way, "management owns the gray areas."

To reinforce the rights of the local government and limit the authority of an arbitrator in a grievance process, many representatives of management have a management rights clause. A committee of the National Executive Institute examined both the impact of collective bargaining on management's rights and the appropriate scope of those rights, and identified the following list of basic, critical management rights that the committee believed administrators had to have if they are to direct their departments effectively:

To plan, direct, and control all police operations and set departmental policy, goals, and objectives

To discipline and fire employees and establish disciplinary procedures

To determine work and performance standards

To determine staffing levels

To determine work schedules, tours of duty, and daily assignments

To determine transfer policies

To hire employees and determine selection criteria

To promote employees and determine promotional procedures

To determine standards of conduct of employees, both on and off duty

To educate and train employees and determine criteria and procedures

To contract or subcontract out for goods and services.[40]

Despite the committee's recommendation, most contracts involve many of these matters, which are therefore subject to negotiations. This list actually represents a starting point as a management representative enters a negotiation.

Grievance and disciplinary procedures   Grievance clauses generally contain provisions that define such things as what constitutes a grievance, steps in the grievance process, time limits for processing grievances, procedures for review by a "neutral" arbitrator, definitions of the power of the arbitrator, and other special considerations in a grievance process.

In collective bargaining, a basic principle of "just cause" is part of any disciplinary process. This standard is often written into contracts or read into them by arbitrators. Although the definition of "just cause" necessarily varies from case to case, arbitrators over the years have developed criteria and guidelines that they apply to the facts of a case. Though not bound by the awards or reasoning of other arbitrators, they do tend to heed precedents in evaluating subsequent cases.

Under the "just cause" principle, a disciplinary case at arbitration must be presented in two distinct parts. First, management must prove that the act in question was actually committed by the grievant and that it violated some rule or policy. Second, management must show that the discipline imposed was not arbitrary, capricious, unreasonable, or discriminatory and that certain basic notions of just cause were followed.

Guidelines for determining whether there is just cause for disciplining an employee include the following:

Did the department give the employee forewarning or foreknowledge of the possible or probable disciplinary consequences of the employee's conduct?

Was the department's rule or policy reasonably related to (1) the orderly, efficient, and safe operation of the agency and (2) the performance that the department might properly expect of the employee?

Did the department, before administering discipline to the employee, make an effort to discover whether the employee did in fact violate or disobey a rule or policy?

Was the department's investigation conducted fairly and objectively?

At the conclusion of the investigation, did the person deciding culpability have substantial and compelling evidence or proof that the employee was guilty as charged?

Has the department applied its rules, orders, and penalties to all employees evenhandedly and without discrimination or favoritism?

Was the degree of discipline administered by the department reasonably related to (1) the seriousness of the employee's proven offense and (2) the record of the employee in his or her service with the department?

No-strike clause   Private-sector contracts always contain a no-strike provision. Because no-strike provisions in state statutes do not prevent strikes, additional protection can be gained through a negotiated no-strike clause. It puts the union on record against striking and involves union leadership in enforcement of the clause. If properly drafted, it could also allow the department to seek monetary damages from the union in case of a wildcat strike.

Zipper clause   A zipper clause simply states that the written contract is the complete and full agreement between the two parties and that neither party is obligated to negotiate on other items during the term of the contract. Its purpose is to avoid continuing negotiations after the contract has been ratified. When coupled with a strong management rights clause, it can limit the influence of "past practices" in grievance arbitration.

Maintenance-of-benefits clause   If a specific benefit is important, it should be discussed during negotiations. If agreement is reached, it should be addressed by a specific section of the contract. That section is a maintenance-of-benefits provision, which is (broadly speaking) a "catchall" clause. If such a clause is included in the contract, it should identify the specific benefits that will be maintained and describe them in detail.

Strike contingency plans

Despite impasse-resolution measures, no-strike provisions, and state statutes, public employees sometimes strike or engage in some other form of "job action." Because of the potential for a work stoppage or slowdown under such circumstances, it is important that police departments develop contingency plans to respond to these situations.[41]

The basic components of a contingency plan include an operational plan, a security plan, a communications plan, legal and personnel policies, and post-strike procedures. The plan should identify essential services that must be provided and services that could be either extended only in emergencies or discontinued altogether. The operational plan should include provisions for establishing an emergency headquarters and its security and for obtaining necessary supplies and services during the strike. It also should include training sessions to prepare management employees for strike duties and arrangements to establish backup communications systems.

The goal of labor negotiations is to produce an agreement that (1) is perceived as fair, (2) meets the needs of both parties as much as possible, (3) is lasting, and (4) can be implemented. Neither the agreement nor the process of reaching it should damage the relationship between the parties. Mutual understanding and trust among the parties is the best way to protect both the public safety and department's resources in a responsible manner.

Civilian personnel

Historically, police departments have been staffed primarily by sworn personnel, but that situation is changing. Between 1970 and 1980, for example, the average percentage of civilian employees in a sample of medium and large police departments throughout the United States increased from 15 to 20 percent. For a group of thirty police departments serving populations of 250,000 or more, the average (that is, the mean) percentage of civilians was 21 percent, with a range of from 7 percent to 31 percent.[42] These data make it clear that the percentage of civilian employees in police departments has increased, that the percentage itself is substantial (that is, one in five, on the average), and that the extent to which departments use civilian personnel varies considerably. Especially interesting, in light of the substantial contribution and role of civilians in law enforcement affairs, is the relative inattention that civilians have received in regard to such human resource issues as recruitment, selection, training, supervision, and promotion.

How civilians are used   Civilians are being used in police departments in four major categories. With some positions, the categories overlap or are classified differently from one department to another.

First, civilians are used in a great variety of voluntary/nonpaid capacities. Included in this category are Neighborhood Watch, reserves, auxiliaries, Explorer Scouts, and school crossing guards. Occasionally, some modest compensation is involved. Second, civilians perform a variety of noncritical para-police functions. Examples of these positions include cadets, school resource officers (SROs), and community service officers (CSOs). The third and most common category is civilians functioning in full-time paid capacities who are designated as clerks, secretaries, dispatchers, evidence/crime-scene technicians, and parking enforcement personnel. Finally, a variety of highly specialized occupations/functions are sometimes performed by civilians. These include legal advisor/counsel, psychologist, communications, research and planning, personnel and training, budgeting, and data processing.

Management considerations   The conversion of a sworn position to a civilian position involves several considerations: impact on sworn officers in the department, cost, expertise, and legality.

Sworn officers in the department are likely to feel threatened when positions are civilianized, and this change requires thought and planning on the part of the chief. Certain sworn slots will be lost, certain career development opportunities for sworn personnel will be eliminated, and these losses must be considered and accommodated.

Cost considerations encourage civilianization at lower levels in the organization, where more highly paid sworn personnel can be replaced in routine positions as long as there is no loss in expertise and the position does not call for a legally "sworn" position. In a police department, the dispatcher/complaint taker function is frequently civilianized for this reason. In making such a decision, costs other than base salary must be assessed thoroughly: initial through top step salary, time to reach top step salary, benefits, training requirements, and anticipated turnover rate.

Because law enforcement agencies are becoming more complex, sophisticated, and information-driven, the necessary expertise may not be available from the traditional "pool" of sworn personnel. This need for expertise increases the likelihood that civilians will hold important policy-making and decision-making positions. It is no longer unusual to find civilians playing significant roles in planning, budgeting, and research (information-related positions). The implications of this trend have yet to be studied.

The legality issues are a product of civil service regulations that vary from department to department.

In any conversion to civilian positions, the chief must also plan carefully to ensure that the new civilian employees receive appropriate training and supervision and that they not only possess the necessary technical skills but also "fit in" with the department's traditions and personnel.

Conclusion

It is clear that human resource management is a critical area of police administration. It determines the quality of the department's performance and thus the quality of the services the department provides to the community. In addition, each of the subspecialties in the human resource management field is becoming very complex—so much so that the volume of professional publications is substantial. This chapter only touches the surface of the vast body of knowledge and expertise related to personnel administration in the law enforcement community. It provides the senior and mid-level police practitioner with a working knowledge of some key areas within the human resource management arena that need the attention of all police executives and some key issues that will challenge the talents of all police professionals well into the next century. These issues suggest that some of the most controversial activities of a police department are those that come under the purview of the personnel unit. Affirmative action, selection, performance evaluation, training, promotion, labor relations, civilianization—all are functions of personnel administration.

1   For a brief overview, see Herman Goldstein, "Progress in Policing," chap. 2 in *Problem-Oriented Policing* (New York: McGraw-Hill, 1990).

2   The President's Commission on Law Enforcement and Administration of Justice, *Task Force Report: The Police* (Washington, DC: U.S. Government Printing Office, 1967); see also National Advisory Commission on Criminal Justice Standards and Goals, *Police* (Washington, DC: U.S. Government Printing Office, 1973).

3   N. Joseph Cayer, *Managing Human Resources: An Introduction to Public Personnel Administration* (New York: St. Martin's Press, 1980).

4   Charles R. Swanson, Leonard Territo, and Robert W. Taylor, *Police Administration: Structures, Processes, and Behavior*, 2d ed. (New York: Macmillan, 1988), 186–87.

5   Hudson Institute, *Workforce 2000: Work and Workers for the 21st Century* (Washington, DC: U.S. Government Printing Office, 1987).

6   Sheriff Michael Hennessey, San Francisco, California, *Law Enforcement News* (2 Feb. 1989). See also Susan Martin, *On the Move: The Status of Women in Policing* (Washington, DC: Police Foundation, 1990).

7   Thomas Rotunda, "A New Tool for More Cost-Effective Hiring: The Municipal Registry," *Police Chief*, February 1990, p. 19.

8   Wayne W. Schmidt, ed., *Fire and Police Personnel Reporter* (Public Safety Personnel Research Institute, 1989).

9   For a good discussion, see Leonard Territo, et al., *The Police Personnel Selection Process* (Indianapolis: Bobbs-Merrill, 1977); and Richard D. Arvey, *Fairness in Selecting Employees* (Reading, MA: Addison-Wesley, 1979).

10   William F. Walsh and Edwin J. Donovan, *The*

Supervision of Police Personnel: A Performance Based Approach (Dubuque, IA: Kendall/Hunt, 1990).

11 Bernard Cohen and Jan Chaiken, *Police Background Characteristics and Performance* (New York: New York City Rand Institute, 1972).

12 Wayne W. Schmidt, "Recent Developments in Police Civil Liability," *Journal of Police Science and Administration* 4 (1976): 197–202.

13 Terry Eisenberg and James M. Murray, "Police Selection," in *Police Personnel Administration* (Washington, DC: Police Foundation, 1974).

14 Swanson, Territo, and Taylor, *Police Administration*, 185–252; Equal Employment Opportunity Commission, "Uniform Guidelines on Employee Selection Procedures," *Federal Register* (1978); and Society for Industrial and Organizational Psychology, *Principles for the Validation and Use of Personnel Selection Procedures* (1987).

15 Swanson, Territo, and Taylor, *Police Administration*, 205–207.

16 Allison Rossett, *Training Needs Assessment* (Englewood Cliffs, NJ: Educational Tech. Publications, 1987).

17 Malcolm Knowles, *The Adult Learner: A Neglected Species*, 3d ed. (Houston: Gulf Publishing Co., 1984).

18 Michael S. McCampbell, *Field Training for Police Officers: State of the Art* (Washington, DC: National Institute of Justice, 1986); W. Bopp and P. M. Whisenand, *Police Personnel Administration*, 2d ed. (Boston: Allyn and Bacon, 1980); and Terry Eisenberg, "Six Potential Hazards in Developing and Implementing Programs for Field Training Officers," *Police Chief* 48 (1981): 50–51.

19 San Jose Police Department, *Field Training and Evaluation Program* (San Jose, CA, 1977).

20 William Byham and James Robinson, "Interaction Modeling: A New Concept in Supervisory Training," *Training and Development Journal* (February 1976): 20–33.

21 Charles B. Saunders, Jr., *Upgrading the American Police* (Washington, DC: Brookings Institution, 1970), 133.

22 Terry Eisenberg, "An Examination of Assessment Center Results and Peer Ratings," *Police Chief* 47 (1980): 46–47.

23 For a concise discussion of performance appraisal systems, see Perry Moore, *Public Personnel Management: A Contingency Approach* (Lexington, MA: Heath and Company, 1985), 131–54.

24 P. R. Conley, "The Effects of Rater Outcome Expectancies on Actual Rater Behavior" (Ph.D. diss., University of Illinois at Chicago, 1988).

25 H. S. Field and W. H. Holley, "The Relationship of Performance Appraisal Characteristics to Verdicts in Selected Employment Discrimination Cases," *Academy of Management Journal* 2 (1981): 392–406.

26 W. F. Cascio and H. J. Bernardin, "Implications of Performance Appraisal Litigation for Personnel Decisions," *Personnel Psychology*, 34 (1981): 211–26.

27 See, for example, Ronald G. Ehrenberg, Daniel R. Sherman, and Joshua L. Schwarz, "Unions and Productivity in the Public Sector: A Study of Municipal Libraries," *Industrial & Labor Relations Review* 36 (January 1983): 199.

28 John M. Greiner, "Motivational Programs and Productivity Improvements in Times of Limited Resources," *Public Productivity Review*, (Fall 1986).

29 John M. Greiner, Harry P. Hatry, Margo P. Koss, Annie P. Millar, and James P. Woodward, *Productivity and Motivation: A Review of State and Local Government Initiatives* (Washington, DC: Urban Institute Press, 1981).

30 Goldstein, *Problem-Oriented Policing*.

31 Deborah D. Melancon, "Quality Circles: The Shape of Things to Come?" in *Police Management Today: Issues and Case Studies*, ed. James J. Fyfe (Washington, DC: International City Management Association, 1985). For a discussion of an ambitious experiment with quality circles, see David Couper, *Quality Policing: The Madison Experience* (Washington, DC: Police Executive Research Forum, 1991).

32 See William A. Geller and Michael S. Scott, *Deadly Force: What We Know—A Practitioner's Desk Reference on Police-Involved Shootings* (Washington, DC: Police Executive Research Forum, 1991).

33 International Association of Chiefs of Police, *Building Integrity and Reducing Drug Corruption in Police Departments* (Washington, DC: Bureau of Justice Assistance, 1989), 80.

34 Ibid., 79–81.

35 Eric Ostrov, Dennis Nowicki, and Joseph Beazley, "Mandatory Police Evaluations: The Chicago Model," *Police Chief* (February 1987).

36 Ibid., p. 195.

37 Arvid Anderson, "The Structure of Public Sector Bargaining," in *Public Workers and Public Unions*, ed. Sam Zagoria (Englewood Cliffs, NJ: Prentice-Hall, 1972), 43.

38 Raymond D. Horton, "Productivity and Productivity Bargaining: The Environmental Context," *Public Personnel Management*, 9 (1980).

39 In *Abood v. Detroit Board of Education*, the Supreme Court ruled that no public employee could be compelled to contribute toward the union's pursuit of its political and ideological objectives.

40 Richard Ayers and Paul Coble, *Meeting Law Enforcement's Responsibilities by Safeguarding Management's Rights* (Gaithersburg, MD: International Association of Chiefs of Police, 1987).

41 Samuel M. Sharkey, *Public Employee Strikes: Causes and Effects* (Washington, DC: Labor Management Relations Service, 1970), 5. See also William D. Gentel and Martha L. Handman, *Police Strikes: Causes and Prevention* (Gaithersburg, MD: IACP, 1979); Anthony V. Bouza, "Police Unions: Paper Tigers or Roaring Lions?" in *Police Leadership in America: Crisis and Opportunity*, ed. William A. Geller (New York: Praeger, 1985); Robert B. Kliesmet, "The Chief and the Union: May the Force Be with You," in *Police Leadership*, ed. Geller, and James B. Jacobs, "Police Unions: How They Look from the Academic Side," in *Police Leadership*, ed. Geller.

42 International City Management Association, *The Municipal Year Book* (Washington, DC: ICMA, 1988). See also Bruce L. Heininger and Janine Urbanek, "Civilianization of the American Police: 1970–1980," *Journal of Police Science and Administration* 11 (1983): 200–205.

11 Information management

Probably the single greatest technical limitation on the criminal justice system's ability to make decisions wisely and fairly is that people in the system often are required to decide issues without information.[1]

Information technology for law enforcement has come a long way since 1967, when those words were written. Police and other criminal justice managers now face a bewildering array of computers and telecommunications systems designed to improve their departments' performance by providing information and ways of communicating it. But the availability of this technology raises a host of managerial questions: What functions can be improved through the use of automated information and communications systems? How can a nontechnical manager make sound decisions about the adoption and use of this technology? How does this technology affect the organization, and how can disruptions be anticipated and minimized?

This chapter examines information and communications technology in police services in light of these questions. It begins with an overview of information management in the police department; examines common applications and promising innovations; and concludes by summarizing key management and policy issues. The reason the focus is on *computerized* information and communications systems is that standards for *manual* record-keeping systems have been well documented by O. W. Wilson and others.[2]

Information management in the police department

Police managers need information in order to do their jobs. They need information on crime patterns, responses to calls for service, vehicle locations, personnel, finances, and various aspects of departmental performance. They use this information to identify strengths and weaknesses in the department's patrol and response strategies, to support changes in policies and procedures, to identify and recognize outstanding performance by individuals or units, and to support budgetary requests. In addition to collecting and using various forms of information, the police have a special need to communicate it rapidly to and from citizens, units in the field, and police stations.

The information in a department can be managed in a variety of ways—from filing it manually to using complex computerized systems. In his classic *Police Records*, published in 1951, Wilson detailed the form, content, and management of police records systems and pointed out that these systems must allow information to be stored, retrieved, and analyzed. Since 1951, as a long line of innovations has made record keeping easier, manual record keeping and analysis have virtually become things of the past. Various telecommunications systems have also evolved rapidly. Computers are now a fact of life almost everywhere.

Police information technologies have changed the way departments do their jobs and the way police officers relate to citizens and the other government agencies they work with. Technology now permits departments to provide new services for victims, witnesses, and neighborhood groups; and it can support problem-oriented or community-oriented policing by increasing the department's ability to identify emerging problems. When computers and telecommunications technology were first introduced into police departments, however, they were designed primarily to help departments perform ongoing tasks with more speed and precision. For example, personnel records, financial data, shift schedules, and other administrative records became more accurate and accessible when they were computerized, and the workload of clerical and administrative staff became lighter. Before very long, though, information technology became a major part of the lives not only of support staff but also of patrol officers, detectives, even police chief executives.

In the early days, computerization was available primarily to large departments. Over time, decreases in costs and improvements in technology have made computers available to virtually every department.

Before very long, information technology became a major part of the lives not only of support staff but also of patrol officers, detectives, even police chief executives.

Significant steps in the evolution of police department computerization were the following:

1. The development of "on-line" or "real-time" computing, which allows new items of information to be processed instantly as they are entered into the computer system
2. The gradual movement of computer equipment and expertise from a central data processing department serving the local government to a unit within the police department itself, assisted by outside consultants and vendors
3. The rapid development and spread of personal computers (PCs), which gave individual employees access to word processing for personal communication, to spreadsheets for financial modeling and analysis, and to departmental data bases for information relevant to their professional responsibilities.

All these changes mean that police can no longer delegate technology to "the experts"; the stakes are too high and the issues too broad.

The applications of information management in police departments are discussed below in two categories: departmental applications, which serve single agencies, and cross-organizational applications, which connect several agencies. Each kind of application poses its own challenges, and each requires the chief to employ substantial skills in managing organizational learning and change.

Departmental applications

Police departments use computers primarily to improve command, control, and communications and to manage records and information.

Command, control, and communications

Command, control, and communications systems are designed to improve response time, officer safety, and the information available to officers in the field. Examples include 9–1–1 and computer-aided dispatching (CAD) systems, computerized mobile communications, and automatic vehicle monitors. (Of special concern is communication during periods of severe crisis or natural disaster.) Large departments have long used these systems, and smaller departments are beginning to adopt them. Some managers swear by them (better central control, faster responsiveness, better record keeping and accountability), while others swear at them (a diversion of attention from police problem solving and community contact).

Emergency 9–1–1 systems   In 1968, responding to the recommendations of the President's Commission on Law Enforcement and Administration of Justice, the American Telephone and Telegraph Company announced "9–1–1" as a nationwide emergency number. Since then, 9–1–1 systems have reduced response time, improved citizen access to police service, and improved police coordination across jurisdictional boundaries. At the same time, however, 9–1–1 has created unforeseen problems, including steep increases in service demand, larger-than-anticipated potential for abuse, loss of control over local system input procedures, and a new set of expectations for police.

By allowing faster response, 9–1–1 has clearly saved lives in medical emergencies, particularly heart attacks.[3] And by providing an easy-to-remember number, 9–1–1 has centralized and simplified the process of requesting assistance, thereby broadening citizen access to police. Studies have shown that in areas without 9–1–1 service, one-third or less of the public knew the seven-digit phone number for police and/or emergency services, even when the number had been well publicized. In contrast, in areas with 9–1–1, 90 percent of citizens knew the police/emergency number (that is, 9–1–1).[4]

9–1–1 has created unforeseen problems, including steep increases in service demand, larger-than-anticipated potential for abuse, and a new set of expectations for police.

A new generation of systems and approaches has helped departments get the most out of 9–1–1. Some departments have extended the basic 9–1–1 system with Enhanced 9–1–1 systems (E 9–1–1). One of E 9–1–1's features, automatic number identification (ANI), displays the telephone number of the caller for the person receiving the call. Another E 9–1–1 feature, automatic location identification (ALI), displays the address to which the telephone number of the incoming call is assigned. Because persons who call 9–1–1 are often distressed and unable to communicate their location, ANI and ALI can prevent potentially tragic delays in police or other emergency response.[5]

Other common options for E 9–1–1 include internal selective routing (ISR) and automatic registered name identification (ARNI). ISR allows a 9–1–1 call taker to route a call electronically to another agency (for example, fire, emergency medical services, or a neighboring police department); this can help overcome mismatches between telephone exchange boundaries (city, town, or county boundaries) and political or administrative boundaries. ARNI displays the name under which the caller's telephone is registered.[6]

As suggested earlier, however, the convenience of 9–1–1 has also produced unanticipated consequences. Citizens tend to use 9–1–1 to report a broad range of non-emergency problems.

Calls to 9–1–1 concern not only public safety problems like public disorder (for example, drunk and disorderly conduct) and incivilities (for example, barking dogs, abandoned cars), but also many nonpolice issues (street lights, road conditions) and frivolous questions (for example, "What time does the Red Sox game start?"). The Las Vegas metropolitan police department reported a 43 percent increase in citizen calls following the introduction of 9–1–1.[7] Nine-one–one thus generates extra demand for the police and draws them in to become service brokers for a wide variety of government and private service agencies. In addition, when 9–1–1 systems are implemented on a regional basis, they can result in some loss of control over local system input procedures. Loss of control can occur when regional E 9–1–1 communication boards are formed but do not include representatives from every police department within the region. In these cases it is important to ensure that the needs and priorities of all communities are incorporated into the procedures developed for the regional E 9–1–1/computer-aided dispatching system.

In the late 1970s, three innovations were introduced to manage the heightened service demands of the 9–1–1 system: (1) more-specific classification schemes for calls; (2) service delivery response alternatives; and (3) assignment of officers to specialized units.[8] Fully developed differential police response systems offer four alternatives for non-emergency requests: (1) delayed response; (2) telephone transcription of non-urgent complaint reports (such as property crimes no longer in progress); (3) the scheduling of responses for a time with low demand for police services; and (4) requests that callers mail in complaint reports or come to the station to fill out reports.[9] When carefully implemented, differential response systems improve police performance (by allowing officers to spend time on high-priority calls) and citizen satisfaction (by communicating exactly what the caller can expect in terms of a response).

Differential response systems take increased demand as a given. However, some cities are also trying to manage demand instead of merely responding to it. For example, Washington, D.C., publishes two numbers, one (9–1–1) for public safety and the other (8 DC-HELP) for all other government problems.

The use of an alternative government phone number is often combined with publicity campaigns to discourage 9–1–1 usage for non-emergencies. A number of these efforts have been successful in reducing the demand for 9–1–1 services. The Shreveport, Louisiana, police department, for example, found that by working closely with the city's media, it was able to educate the public about the city's new 9–1–1 system before that system was actually implemented. As a result, the demand for police services increased by less than 20 percent after introduction of the system.

One potential problem with public education campaigns to divert non-emergency public safety problems from 9–1–1, however, is that such efforts may create uncertainty about what constitutes a public safety problem or a true emergency. This may cause delays in reporting events that do in fact require a prompt response. Such problems can be minimized through careful public education and through properly configured communications technology. For example, internal selective routing technology can be expanded beyond the three major types of emergency services (that is, police, fire, and emergency medical) to include other municipal services (as in the case of 8 DC-HELP) to respond to calls that do not represent an emergency or a public safety problem. With this type of system, takers of non-emergency calls can easily transfer emergencies to the appropriate 9–1–1 operator.

Computer-aided dispatching Many 9–1–1 systems are parts of larger computer-aided dispatching (CAD) systems. CAD, developed in the 1970s, coordinates dispatching, patrol allocation, and record keeping.[10] CAD assigns service priorities on the basis of data entered by operators. This information is routed to a dispatcher's terminal, which then shows pending requests for service, patrol units available, and units already assigned. CAD systems can verify addresses and incident types, determine the police district where a call originates, check for a "dangerous" history, and track the status of requests. CAD improves response time and helps managers and officers improve patrol assignments and patrol plans. Dispatch is often the first police department function to be computerized.

When first introduced, CAD made it easier for supervisors to monitor a large fleet of patrol units. This promoted centralized administration and strengthened the response capabilities of departments. But the first generation of 9–1–1/CAD systems had limitations that may have restricted police thinking about service options in subtle but powerful ways. By today's standards, early CAD systems were supported by extremely limited computer technology. Generally speaking, early systems (many of which are still in service) had less computer processing capability than today's PCs. Given these limitations, first-generation CAD systems did little more than serve as on-line inventory systems to track citizen requests and available patrol units. This type of CAD was adequate to support rapid response and preventive patrol but was far too limited to support more complex and varied policing strategies, including proactive and community-oriented approaches. In addition, 9–1–1/CAD systems focused the attention of many departments on a measurable performance objective: response time. The 9–1–1/CAD technology may thus have created barriers to innovation (see the chapter on the patrol function).

"Second-generation" CAD systems are more flexible. They have "intelligent" decision support capabilities, that is, they can track calls for service, can help assign patrol units, and can maintain a patrol plan. They help sort out which calls need rapid response and which do not. Intelligent CAD can also provide high-speed interaction with "hot files"—outstanding warrants, prior domestic disturbances, incidents with firearms—and can alert dispatchers to delayed responses that may signal a field patrol unit in trouble. Finally, integrated 9–1–1/CAD may help support problem-oriented and community-oriented policing (see the section on service innovation).

Mobile communications Communications technology includes mobile digital terminals and cellular phones. These can lead to increased arrest rates, greater problem-solving capability, and improved officer safety.

During the 1980s, some cities began using mobile digital terminals (MDTs) so that dispatchers and field officers could communicate without audio transmission. MDTs originally sent only canned status messages (for example, ENROUTE, ON-SCENE, AVAILABLE). Newer systems provide complete communication, full keyboards, and high-resolution screens in addition to canned messages. They also provide for faster, more accurate data transmission than voice radio. In addition, because transmissions are more efficient than voice, the system reduces radio traffic and dispatchers' workloads. MDTs provide officers in the field with information about wanted persons, automobile licenses, outstanding warrants, and so forth.[11] They provide, as well, access to data bases such as the FBI's National Crime Information Center (NCIC) files, outstanding local warrants, automobile registration and driver's license data, state or local criminal history records, and CAD data.[12] Furthermore, by providing an "emergency" status key, they improve officer safety. The area-wide law enforcement radio terminal system (ALERTS) used by the Illinois Criminal Justice Information Authority (discussed in more detail in the section on regional networks) demonstrates the power of these systems and suggests that MDTs lead to increases in "hot file" inquiries from the field, warrant arrests, and vehicle recoveries.[13]

But MDTs also produce surprises. Because digital transmission is so efficient, departments sometimes expect radio utilization to decline, but it may not. Although officers make far more inquiries with MDTs, they may also use the radio for additional voice messages once the channels are less congested. Departments must also consider the effect on privacy rights if MDTs encourage mass data checks rather than selective use of criminal justice data bases.[14]

On another front, some departments are putting cellular phones in patrol units. These allow officers to call providers of a broad range of non-emergency services (for example, the department of elderly affairs, a local neighborhood crime prevention group, a youth worker). Officers can also call in crime reports and call ahead to citizens requesting assistance. In Dallas, where officers are able to call in reports via cellular phones while remaining on patrol,[15] reports on the use of cellular phones are quite favorable.

Departments can control potential abuse of cellular phones by keeping track of calls. In this way, departments can identify overuse of the phones for private purposes, for example, when repeated calls are made to an officer's home number.

Automatic vehicle monitors   Automatic vehicle monitor (AVM) or automatic vehicle location (AVL) systems provide up-to-the minute information on vehicle location and status. In theory they improve supervision and back-up unit response time, thus officer safety. In practice, however, AVM systems have had trouble in tracking patrol units, and some officers resent them as a threat to their autonomy. The phenomenon of "lost cars" may account for low levels of AVM usage. Improved tracking may make AVMs a better option in the future (see accompanying sidebar for one department's experience).

Communications during natural disasters   Experience with Hurricane Hugo in September 1989 and with the Loma Prieta earthquake in California in October 1989 revealed two facts about public safety communications systems. First, these systems are absolutely essential for an effective response to extreme crises and natural disasters. Second, current systems typically fail or become overloaded in such extreme circumstances. Hugo and Loma Prieta indicate that communications failures are likely, due to electric power outages, destruc-

---

An automatic vehicle location system   Bolingbrook, Illinois, was perhaps the first community in the nation to use a real-time, on-line automatic vehicle location (AVL) system as an integral part of its computer-aided dispatch (CAD) system. Its police department of sixty sworn and thirty-seven civilian personnel patrols an area of approximately twelve square miles.

The AVL system enhances officer safety, reduces the response time to critical calls, and provides more efficient management of limited resources. It is installed in on-board laptop computers in twenty-seven police department vehicles and five fire department vehicles, transmitting latitude and longitude data from each vehicle to a central processor in the Tactical Operations Center (TOC).

In the TOC, vehicle locations are graphically displayed as small car "icons" with unit numbers on a computer-generated map of Bolingbrook. The map is displayed on a thirty-seven–inch color video monitor in the TOC to help telecommunicators assign responding units. Positions are automatically updated as vehicle locations change. Updates appear simultaneously on the map displayed on each vehicle's laptop computer, as well.

The AVL system uses existing LORAN (long-range navigation) technology developed by the U.S. Coast Guard for use by aircraft and watercraft. A LORAN radio receiver in each vehicle calculates its position by analyzing the signal intervals from a chain of strategically placed Coast Guard transmitters. Bolingbrook's experience has proven the system accurate to within approximately one hundred feet.

The department reports that it encountered no personnel problems when implementing AVL. The system was implemented as an aid to the officer on the street, not for disciplinary purposes.

Source: Adapted from *MicroSoftware News* 7, no. 6 (June 1990): 3. *MicroSoftware News* is published by the International City Management Association.

tion of telephone transmission lines, destruction of communications centers, and the overloading of regional or local systems or both.

In Charleston County, South Carolina, reviews after Hurricane Hugo revealed that the hurricane had devastated normal communications. The communications bases of many public safety departments were destroyed; Southern Bell telephone exchanges were jammed with calls. With sporadic communications available from only a few public safety communications centers and with landline telephone systems completely overloaded, two-way communication became a high priority. In Charleston (both the city and the county), two-way emergency communications were partially reestablished during and after the hurricane through a five-channel radio communications system, with seventy-five portable and fifty mobile radios provided by their manufacturer.[16] Cellular phones, with high transmission clarity and capabilities for simultaneous conversation, also proved important in providing contact with emergency situations during and after. The experience of Charleston suggests that cellular systems (which work through interconnected "cells," each of which is able to handle hundreds of conversations) may be more effective than conventional phones during disasters.[17]

After the Loma Prieta earthquake, the city of San Jose developed the following recommendations for public safety communications systems during a natural disaster:

1. Public safety CAD systems should have an uninterrupted power supply and two central processing units.
2. A previously designated public information officer should be available for both police and fire to handle incoming information requests (often from the media).
3. A manual dispatching system should be developed and ready to use.
4. Regular training should be given to all communications personnel to ensure familiarity with emergency procedures.
5. Regular training for emergencies should be given to all communications supervisors (because experience shows that supervisors' ability to reassure communications personnel is an important factor in maintaining an effective communications capability).[18]

Management of records and information

New technology has changed how police departments gather, store, retrieve, and analyze data. These changes also bring managerial challenges, as managers try to keep track of time saved, make sure the information is stored in ways that make it convenient for people to use, and anticipate how others might use the new information.

Report writing is one area in which the new technology has been prominent. In 1979, St. Louis provided police investigators with a telephone-accessible dictation system for reports.[19] This reduced the time investigators spent on report writing by 53 percent, making 14 percent more time available for investigations. As a result, St. Louis automated other functions and extended computer-assisted reporting to officers on the beat. Patrol officers now phone a unit called CARE (computer-assisted report entry), where an operator enters the information and probes for left-out details. According to the department, writing reports used to take 20 percent of the officer's time but now takes a negligible amount. In addition, the quality of reports has improved and reports are easier for officers and command staff to search for and retrieve.[20] Filing such reports posed no legal problems: prosecutors and defense attorneys approved the CARE system in advance.

Fort Collins, Colorado, uses a similar system. Guided by protocols on form and content, police use cassette recorders to dictate reports; clerical staff later

---

Laptop computers The police department in Marianna, Arkansas, found that the use of laptop computers by officers in the field had the following advantages:

Officers can type offense reports on a laptop computer while on the scene. This eliminates the need for a typist and means that information in the report is not secondhand.

Officers can type arrest reports for traffic and other violations that do not require the officer's presence at the police station. This keeps the officer on the street longer.

Officers can even type offense reports while in the living room of a victim, something they cannot do with portable computers installed in a police car.

Officers can type memos and letters while in the police car, instead of going to the office.

Officers can use the laptop computer while in the police car to run checks on vehicle registrations or investigate a crime by searching the known factors of a suspect (race, height, weight, vehicle used).

Before introducing laptops, the department began training officers by gradually requiring them to type their reports. The department also selected a software package that made it possible to design a computerized report form that was very similar to the forms formerly used by officers and typists.

Source: Adapted from Mark Robert Birchler, "The Future of Law Enforcement: Laptop Computers," *City & Town*, the official publication of the Arkansas Municipal League, November 1987.

---

enter these into the computer. Fort Collins has also used mobile digital terminals in conjunction with a CAD system to reduce the number of "written" reports required from officers. On the basis of department guidelines, officers can make short notations on their MDTs in lieu of reports. The information is captured on the CAD system and is available when needed.[21]

Many departments have eliminated the clerical link by having officers enter their reports directly. In St. Petersburg, Florida, police use laptops at the scene of the incident. In a survey of 150 St. Petersburg officers, 90 percent of the respondents said they spent less time writing reports with computers; 94 percent said it was easier writing reports with computers.[22]

"Formatted data entry," or "fill-in-the-blank" format, saves time and helps ensure complete reporting. These reporting systems can take information used in more than one type of record (incidents, arrests, wanted persons) and put it where it belongs with only one data entry operation. Similar systems can use formatted screens to prompt police through appropriate sequences of reporting. The computer can also routinely check to see whether sections of the report are incomplete—taking only seconds to do what a supervisor would need hours for.

After computerizing record entry, departments often move to record management. Computerized record management saves time, provides more complete information, and allows instant updates and changes. Once information is computerized, it is rarely lost. As a further advantage, computers are available twenty-four hours a day, seven days a week.[23] Many departments, of course, may wish to automate record entry and record management systems as part of a larger integrated system.

Computerized systems produce a broad range of reports and specific items of information (for example, outstanding warrants, a known offender's modus operandi (MO), the history of criminal reports from an address). Typically they also produce FBI Uniform Crime Reports. Computers allow police to cross-reference

---

Hazardous locations on file Police officers often receive calls from locations that have a history of problems, but unless they are aware of the history, they may not take adequate precautions. The police department in Fort Worth, Texas, is developing a computer file that will contain a list of known hazardous locations. Police officers will be able to obtain information about a particular location before arriving on the scene and will be able to prepare themselves to respond to potential emergencies.

Source: Cited in *The Guide to Management Improvement Projects in Local Government* (Washington, DC: International City Management Association, 1987).

---

and index information (for example, crime, arrest, property records) so that data can be found quickly. Personnel can "browse" for relevant information on offenders or other subjects, and such "browsing" has become an important tactic for many investigations.[24] In addition, advanced systems allow users to make natural-language inquiries ("Does Joe Smith have any known associates?").

Computerized record management tends to make editing and auditing easier and, ultimately, leads to greater accuracy and completeness of information. For example, in 1982 states with automated criminal history systems were more likely to report arrests and dispositions to NCIC than states with paper systems.[25] A national survey of state criminal history systems found that automation was one of the most frequently cited reasons for improvements in the quality of criminal records.[26]

"Garbage in/garbage out" applies to both paper and computerized records, but the garbage flows much faster and looks better when records are automated.

Taking advantage of auditing and editing capabilities is extremely important. Without rigorous data quality assurance, computerized records are no more accurate than paper records. Inaccurate computerized records can be more harmful than paper records because they are more easily retrieved and manipulated and because they provide the appearance of precision. In other words, "garbage in/garbage out" applies to both paper and computerized records, but the garbage flows much faster and looks better when records are automated.

Information technology in a police department can support far more than call taking, dispatching, and record management. Today, tasks once done manually or by mainframes—such as report writing, financial analysis, personnel allocation, calendaring/scheduling, offender sketching, electronic filing, and memo writing—can be automated at modest cost and handled with desktop or laptop computers. Once captured, the data involved in these tasks (including pictures) can be transmitted via electronic mail systems (E-MAIL) over local area networks (LANS) or wide area networks (WANS). Computers are becoming the central nervous system of the police community. Properly implemented, computerization can not only improve both the effectiveness and efficiency of police personnel but also lead to subtle yet significant changes in communications and departmental performance.

Cross-organizational applications

While computers can improve information flow within departments, successful policing often depends on getting information from outside the department as well. One reason is that criminals do not respect jurisdictional borders, so police

A pilot E-mail system In early 1984 the Fort Collins, Colorado, police department was selected by the city as a pilot for an E-mail system. The objective was to reduce paper correspondence and speed communications. The system started with a limited number of users, primarily managers and supervisors. Within several months, it became apparent that others—primarily line officers—wanted access to the system. In late 1985, the system was opened to all police department employees, and E-mail became a part of ongoing operations.

Shift commanders complete "tour of duty" reports at the end of each shift, highlighting significant events that took place during the tour. These reports are sent electronically to all employees, who can see what took place while they were off duty.

The investigation division gives division supervisors a weekly report highlighting activity in significant cases for all relevant personnel. For example, detectives who need patrol assistance in locating suspects can provide all patrol officers with leads via E-mail.

Command staff can use the system to communicate changes in policy and procedure before hard copies are prepared.

The crime analyst can send timely data to all officers.

Finally, all members of the department can use the system to send routine notices, memos, and messages. The system has helped break down the communications barriers created by the traditional paramilitary structure of the department. Every employee in the organization has access to others at any level via E-mail.

Source: Bruce Glasscock, chief, Fort Collins Police Services Department.

need information from other police departments. Another reason is that problem solving—which many departments now emphasize—often requires data collected by agencies other than the police. Today, national and regional networks provide data ranging from criminal histories to lists of stolen securities. Successful networks depend on interagency cooperation and offer substantial benefits.

National networks

Before 1971, when the FBI implemented an on-line system called the National Crime Information Center (NCIC), police had to apply by mail for FBI information. Since then, the NCIC has grown to provide a broad range of data bases: missing persons, wanted persons, stolen and recovered guns, stolen securities, stolen and recovered motor vehicles, stolen license plates, stolen boats, and other stolen articles. Through NCIC, departments can retrieve a comprehensive picture of a suspect's criminal activity across state and local boundaries. In the future, NCIC will also include information for tracking the subjects of drug, murder, and kidnapping investigations.[27]

Whereas NCIC provides a common data source, the National Law Enforcement Telecommunications System (NLETS) provides local departments with a computer network enabling them to communicate directly with one another. NLETS allows agencies to exchange data on arrests, dispositions, and other subjects.

Systems also are being developed to promote the discussion of common problems and issues among police administrators across the country. Nationally, the Police Executive Research Forum has implemented an electronic bulletin board and conferencing system called "METAPOL" that permits law enforcement executives and their staffs to exchange information on police-related issues, projects, and programs. In addition, subscribing police departments can, if they desire, join on-going discussions involving law enforcement officials and academics. They can participate by reading "conversations" of others and by posing questions to be answered by anyone on the network who has useful information to volunteer.

Similarly, SEARCH Group Inc. in Sacramento, California, has introduced an electronic bulletin board/conferencing system (SEARCH-BBS) for criminal justice practitioners. Users can send and receive messages and join electronic conferences on topics of interest to police. Users may also access the Automated Index of Criminal Justice Information Systems.

Regional networks

The success of NCIC and NLETS depends on the technical capabilities of the systems and on interagency cooperation. The FBI made the original NCIC system "low tech" so that many departments could use it. And because the system supported functions already controlled by the FBI, cooperation did not pose much of a problem. With regional systems, however, sometimes cooperation can be difficult to secure. Differences between police departments in codes and protocols for reporting can make the best-intentioned efforts go awry. One solution would be to establish national standards for police communication protocols.[28] Another problem with cross-departmental information sharing may be cost—but, because criminals often travel across jurisdictional lines, such information-sharing systems add substantial value.

The Illinois ALERTS systems cited earlier represents a more immediate, if less comprehensive, approach. It provides mobile digital communication to Illinois police departments; uses automatic switching to put police in direct communication with regional and state "hot file" data; and permits all squad cars on the network to communicate with squad cars in their own and other departments, increasing dramatically the capability to exchange information. The Illinois Criminal Justice Information Authority has also developed the Police Information Management System (PIMS), with forty-eight participating agencies. PIMS maintains data on arrestees, incidents, locations, and the like for each participating department. On request, PIMS can provide a broad range of reports. The ability of PIMS to network police has provided important benefits to participating agencies.[29]

The Illinois State Police Division of Criminal Investigation has also developed the Law Enforcement Intelligence Network (I-LEIN), supporting 118 agencies. Participating departments submit paper forms to the central I-LEIN office, where analysts check for completeness; the information is then input into an electronic system. Through I-LEIN, departments share information that is difficult to obtain through normal police channels, including bits and pieces of information from detectives' notes.[30] Although the program has been in existence only since 1986, agencies report that I-LEIN provides useful assistance in criminal investigations.[31]

National policies may promote cross-departmental data sharing. The FBI's Uniform Crime Reporting program is now shifting away from aggregate statistics toward incident-based crime reports through the new National Incident-Based Reporting System (see accompanying sidebar). The availability of incident-based crime data with geographical identifiers (street address, census tract, and so forth) will make it easier for departments to do cross-jurisdictional strategic planning and to make cross-departmental tactical decisions.

Finally, the very ease of electronic communication is likely to promote growth in cross-departmental information sharing. In 1988, for example, the Fort Collins police department added the county sheriff, the university police chief, and the district attorney to the department's existing E-MAIL system (see sidebar earlier in this chapter), promoting more extensive communication among these administrators. Plans were under way to expand E-MAIL to additional county personnel, such as investigators in the sheriff's department and the district attorney's office. The latter group would be able to use the system to notify police officers about court appearances.

Innovative systems

The systems described thus far are reasonably widespread. Several innovations are not widespread but may have major effects during the next decade. These include expert systems, automated fingerprint identification systems, computer mapping, and resource allocation modeling.

Expert and knowledge-based systems

Expert and knowledge-based systems are part of a larger class of technology called artificial intelligence (AI). These systems simulate the decision-making processes of experts in a given field—the data they use and the way they arrive at their judgments. Expert systems have demonstrated their usefulness in medicine and science and are now turning up in criminal justice.[32] So far, most work has been conducted at the federal level and specifically on offender profiles.[33] The FBI's "Big Floyd," used in labor racketeering cases, has been the most prominent of these systems.[34]

At the local level, few expert systems are currently operational, but agencies are developing applications for crime solving, real-time decision making, and program planning and design.[35] The first expert system for local police focuses on residential burglaries, using the characteristics of the burglary and the behavior of the suspects to identify likely subjects. The system produces a list of suspects and their probability of being the offender, along with helpful messages (for example, "This is probably a domestic offense").[36]

The expert systems approach, unlike the approach that matches existing MOs, does not require a one-to-one matching of offender to crime characteristics. For example, the expert system classifies breaking and entering techniques by level of sophistication—a classification scheme developed from interviews with expert detectives and investigators; the system can then use this scheme to suggest probable offenders.

Expert systems offer particular promise in the near term in producing electronic procedures manuals. The advantage of an automated procedures manual is that employees would be able to obtain information related to legal or procedural problems when they needed it, instead of memorizing procedures in advance or struggling with the index of a printed manual, trying to guess under which term a particular problem might have been indexed, and then having to find the referenced text manually. The quality of police officers' actions would improve.[37]

Other areas for expert systems include automated social service directories and training systems. Automated social service directories can help police identify appropriate social service agencies for citizens with problems that fall outside the purview of police. Automated training systems can help officers develop problem-solving skills.[38]

Automated fingerprint identification systems

Automated fingerprint identification systems (AFIS) can scan fingerprints, document spatial relationships that characterize the prints, and store the result in a form the computer can search. AFIS also allows computers to do in a matter of minutes what, done manually, is a time-consuming and error-prone process:

(*continued on page 322*)

NIBRS and UCR   In 1989 the FBI began pretesting the National Incident-Based Reporting System, which was designed to eventually replace the Uniform Crime Reporting program. In 1991 three states began reporting crime data in the new format, and the FBI expected about half the states to be doing so by 1993. What follows is a description of the significant differences between the two systems.

Incident-based versus summary reporting. This is clearly the most noteworthy change from the UCR to NIBRS. Under the traditional UCR scheme, agencies total the number of occurrences of Part I (Index) offenses, as well as arrest data for Part I and Part II offenses, and submit aggregate counts in monthly summary reports either to the FBI or to a state UCR program. In the NIBRS format, agencies collect detailed information on individual crime incidents and arrests and submit separate reports using prescribed data elements and data values to describe each incident and arrest. There are 52 data elements used in NIBRS to describe the victims, offenders, arrestees and circumstances of crimes.

Expanded offense reporting. Where the summary-based UCR system collected totals on criminal incidents in eight Part I offense classifications, NIBRS seeks detailed reporting on a 22-category, 46-offense Group A list of criminal events. Bribery, counterfeiting and forgery, vandalism, drug offenses, embezzlement, extortion and blackmail, fraud, gambling offenses, kidnapping, pornography offenses, prostitution, nonforcible sex offenses, weapons law violations, and stolen property offenses have been added to the traditional Part I crimes to make up Group A, and many of the Part I offenses have been significantly expanded. For example, the forcible-rape heading under the UCR has now been expanded to include all forcible sexual offenses, including forcible sodomy, sexual assault with an object, and forcible fondling.

New offense definitions. Beyond the simple expansion of offense categories, NIBRS also entailed the revision of existing definitions of crimes listed in the Uniform Crime Reporting Handbook. For example, rape is defined in the UCR handbook as "The carnal knowledge of a female forcibly and against her will." Under NIBRS, the crime is defined as "The carnal knowledge of a person, forcibly and/or against that person's will; or, not forcibly or against the person's will where the victim is incapable of giving consent because of his/her temporary or permanent mental or physical incapacity."

Elimination of the hierarchy rule. Under the summary-based system, the so-called "hierarchy rule" dictated that if more than one crime was committed by the same person or group of persons and the time/space intervals separating the crimes were insignificant, then the crime highest in the Crime Index hierarchy is the only one reported. For example, if a burglar broke into a dwelling, raped a woman who lived there, and then, as the man of the house returned from work, killed him, only the murder would be reported to the summary-based UCR; the burglary and the rape would not be reported. Under the NIBRS format, the hierarchy rule is not used, and all crimes are reported as offenses within the same incident. It will still be possible, however, for data analysts to capture the primary offense in a hierarchical series of related crimes.

Greater specificity of data. Because NIBRS collects the details of individual criminal incidents, it allows considerably greater specificity in reporting and crime analysis. When the publication of NIBRS data hits full stride, breakdowns will be possible involving crimes against individuals, businesses, financial institutions, government, religious organizations, society/public, and other victim entities; crimes committed by or against residents versus nonresidents; and crimes involving various types of weapons and injuries. In addition, NIBRS will collect the specific values of stolen and recovered property, thus permitting more breakdowns of monetary value.

"Crimes against society." As most people familiar with the UCR are aware, the eight offenses are generally broken down into two broad categories: crimes against persons, and crimes against property. The addition of numerous offense categories in the creation of NIBRS has necessitated the addition of a new category, crimes against society, which will account for crimes such as drug offenses, gambling offenses, pornography, and prostitution. The FBI notes that such crimes are not technically crimes against persons, since they do not actually involve a "victim," nor are they crimes against property, since property is not the true object of the crimes.

Attempted versus completed crimes. Under the summary-based system, many attempted crimes are reported as though they were completed. The expanded collection of incident-based data by NIBRS will include the designation of each offense as either attempted or completed, further clarifying the crime picture. (As with the summary-based system, however, assault with intent to murder or attempted murder will still be reported as aggravated assault.)

Accounting for computer crimes. Computer crimes—those offenses directed at or perpetrated through the use of computers and related equipment have grown in frequency in recent years as the use of computers has increased. The developers of NIBRS have taken the position that computer crimes actually involve historical common-law offenses such as larceny, embezzlement or trespass. To avoid distortion of the UCR program's traditional time series relating to such crimes, it was decided not to create a new classification called "Computer Crime," into which such offenses would be grouped. However, NIBRS provides the capability to indicate whether a computer was the object of the crime or the means by which the offender perpetrated the crime, thus maintaining statistical continuity while offering a way of isolating criminal incidents that involve computer crime.

Correlation between data elements. The summary-based system allowed only limited opportunity for correlating data between offenses, property, victims, offenders and arrestees. Only in homicides, for example, could the age, sex, race and ethnicity of offenders be correlated with the age, sex, race and ethnicity of their victims. The incident-based data submitted to NIBRS will use both explicit and implicit linkages of data elements, providing the capability to generate reports that reflect a wide array of interrelationships among the collected data.

Magnetic tape submission of data. Agencies participating on a direct basis in NIBRS (i.e., submitting directly to the FBI rather than through a state UCR program) must provide the data on magnetic tapes. Previously, direct submissions using manual forms were possible under the summary-based program. (The FBI has been working on an approach that will allow agencies to submit NIBRS data on either magnetic tapes or computer diskettes.)

Source: Peter C. Dodenhoff, "Shades of Difference: NIBRS vs. the UCR," *Law Enforcement News*, John Jay College of Criminal Justice, New York (31 Jan. 1990).

(*continued from page 319*)
compare a new fingerprint with massive collections of prints on file and identify the new one.[39]

The greatly increased speed and accuracy of fingerprint processing allows departments to execute "cold searches" (that is, searches without suspects) of latent prints found at a scene.[40] AFIS systems also improve the criminal identification process, particularly in identifying suspects who supply police with aliases.[41]

One problem with AFIS is that systems from different vendors usually are incompatible and cannot share information. This should be less of a problem in the future, however, because the technology is moving toward a national standard for the computer entry of fingerprint data and images.[42]

Computer mapping

Many police departments have attempted to use pin maps to track and analyze patterns of incidents. Unlike statistical techniques, spatial analysis requires very little training. A broad range of individuals (for example, police officers, crime analysts, community residents, police administrators) have the pattern recognition abilities needed.

By the mid-1990s, manual pin maps will be nonexistent, and their automated counterparts will be a regular feature of many police departments. For example, in Fairfax County, Virginia, dispatchers currently have high-resolution terminals that display the areas surrounding calls for assistance. The call taker can zoom into or out from the location. The data displayed include streets, addresses, shopping centers, and industrial complexes. The system provides the call taker with a reference and enables him or her to elicit information from the caller for patrol units.[43]

A National Institute of Justice project that used a PC mapping system on crimes in a Chicago police district indicated that PC-based workstations with geographical display and analysis capabilities might soon become an important tool for crime analysts, patrol officers, and others. Both police and community groups felt the mapping made a significant contribution to crime prevention.[44]

As PCs become more powerful and more easily linked to other information systems, PC-based mapping at desktop workstations should become a valuable tool. Its benefits include on-line support for call taking and dispatching, for directed patrol activities, for neighborhood crime prevention groups, and for longer-term strategic planning. Desktop workstations will allow users to do, for example, the following:

Superimpose crimes and calls for service on computerized displays of city streets and on a wide range of other geographical information

Integrate maps with data bases such as field interrogation reports, known offender reports from community crime prevention groups, emergency medical data, and so forth

Instantly retrieve historical and geographical data at any level of aggregation (for example, a city block, a small neighborhood, a patrol sector, a police district) and calls for service data

Employ statistical models to predict incidents on the basis of historical calls for service.

The Syracuse police department, which has workstations that incorporate many of the above features, uses a system that operates on five networked PCs that download data from a countywide, fourteen-agency law enforcement data base on a mainframe computer.[45] The system can plot crime data by attributes such as day of week, time of day, type of crime, arrest made, and unsolved cases in an area, or by any combination of these attributes. The system can automatically create digitized displays of street maps showing where incidents occur and can interactively redraw these maps when new information is requested. Early use of the system appears to have helped the police apprehend repeat burglary offenders.

Resource allocation modeling

Computer models have been developed to help departments allocate resources geographically and over time.[46] In the past, however, these models have been limited by the extensive manual data preparation they require.[47] Perhaps for this reason many departments have encountered difficulty in adapting resource allocation systems to their needs.[48]

Now, however, 9–1–1/CAD and computerized record management can provide address-level data and reference it to standard geographical data bases. For example, as of 1990 the Census Bureau had updated geographical data bases for virtually every city and town in the United States (the topographically integrated geographic encoded referencing, or TIGER, files), These data bases contain identifiers for each census tract, block, street intersection, and street address within towns or cities. Programs can draw on these data to evaluate the current distribution of police resources and to project future needs. Analysts using computerized maps can redraw police districts or beats to facilitate community-based problem solving or to serve other purposes. Once the boundaries have been redrawn, allocation models can readily reestimate resource needs; going through the same procedure manually would simply take too much time.

Management and policy issues

As law enforcement computing becomes more pervasive and powerful, technology per se is less of an issue than are management and policy. The most important management and policy issues include systems planning and implementation, service innovation, organizational structure, security and privacy, and the politics of information as law enforcement agencies become capable of integrating vast quantities of heretofore fragmented data.[49]

Planning and implementation

Guiding a police department through the process of planning for and implementing new technology is one of the chief's most important and challenging responsibilities. Some basic management issues are outlined in the accompanying sidebar.

Planning is of paramount importance. If the department has not formalized a comprehensive technology plan in the last three to five years, it is time to do so. The same is true of individual departmental projects with computerized components. In the planning process, the chief needs to be aware of potential pitfalls, provide guidance on certain policy questions and decisions, and prepare to manage the disruptions that computerization will inevitably cause in the organization.

One major pitfall for the unwary chief is to believe that if a system succeeded in one department, it will succeed in another. Even well-known and widely used applications may not fit every community's particular needs. Another pitfall is not to recognize that personnel will need to be trained to implement a new system once it is introduced. Still another is not to plan for coordination among the systems that support various programs or units inside and outside the department.

The chief needs to be involved in a number of basic decisions about computerization in the department. In the very smallest departments, the first question may be whether to computerize any functions at all. Manual record-keeping systems, combined with telephone and radio technology, may serve a small department's needs, and the answer to the first question is no.

More likely, however, computerization will be a given, and the chief will need to be sure the department finds answers to such questions as these:

1. For what purposes does the department collect and store information? What information does the department need to carry out its mission and to support decisions relating to personnel, finances, scheduling, and policing strategies?
2. Where does the information come from? Who will input it into the

---

Managing police information technology   The declining cost and increasing sophistication of technology and the increasing administrative and service demands made on law enforcement have simultaneously pushed and pulled almost all police departments into computerization. Meanwhile, those departments that automated their record keeping years ago are replacing existing systems with newer models.

Assessment. The first step in any modernization project is to weigh the value of the new technology against the organizational and financial resources to be expended in getting it. New technology should never be used to make a department look progressive—or used as a smoke screen to cover internal problems. Implemented for the wrong reasons, computerized systems can create chaos.

Management must look at the department's mission, structure, and practices and consider how a new system will affect them. Certain applications will support a particular mission, while others will conflict with that mission. For example, a computer-aided dispatch (CAD) system will support the mission of a municipal police department receiving many 9-1-1 calls better than that of a highway patrol department, which receives fewer calls. However, a CAD system can interfere with proactive management if the dispatch function is overemphasized.

The structure and practices of a department will influence the use and effectiveness of a particular application. For example, departments with a rigid command structure will find systems that provide line personnel with detailed information of little value if those personnel are not allowed to act on the new information. On the other hand, departments striving to make greater use of line personnel can use systems that provide detailed, timely information to encourage the growth of sophisticated and independent employees.

Planning. A steering committee strengthens systems planning. Such a group creates a sense of organizational ownership and helps the planning staff responsible for the project assimilate the differing needs and points of view encountered within a large organization.

Steering committee members commonly represent several different groups. Foremost are user group representatives. Since most police applications are designed to assist line personnel, respected and informed members of the rank and file should be assigned to the systems planning group. If vendors or staff from an MIS department are to be involved in the project, members of these groups should also be included.

If a department permits, the chief executive and the command staff should sit on the steering committee. Technologi-

system? How will it be screened or checked? How will the data base be maintained or updated as new information becomes available?

3. What kind of communications links are needed among officers, mobile units, dispatchers, citizens, and so on?

4. Who will have access to information and communications systems? How will the system be secured to prevent inappropriate use?

5. What software and hardware does the department need to achieve its current goals and to maintain flexibility to meet its future needs? Do new components have to be compatible with existing systems? Does new software have to be tailored to the needs of the department, or will standard packages serve?

6. Based on practical and financial considerations, what components should the department purchase? What ones should it lease? What

---

cal modernization efforts need the active and continuous attention of the chief executive or the chief's designee to gain the internal support necessary to succeed. Command staff participation gives voice to the views of the major units affected by the system and emphasizes the commitment of the chief executive.

Regardless of whether the prospective system will be developed in-house, by an MIS department, or by a vendor, the steering committee has a significant role to play in design and implementation. Although there are many different methods of system design, it may be best to use what some experts refer to as a "modular" approach, for three reasons: First, a modular system is constructed from discrete but interactive modules that can be implemented sequentially. The organization can break its information needs into manageable pieces and address them one at a time.

Second, since design and implementation proceed in small steps, damage caused by unmet completion dates or unexpected difficulties can be contained more easily. Delays are less likely to make the system a target for outside critics or discourage internal supporters.

Finally, the modular approach allows a department to refine and modify a system to meet changing information needs and to incorporate new technology.

Performance standards. The planning staff must adopt a set of written performance standards, clearly outlining the design intent of the system and functional specifics. However, planners should not make these standards so strict that all flexibility is eliminated. Unanticipated difficulties and schedule delays will almost always occur. Inflexible standards cost the system internal and external support.

When a vendor is to provide all or part of the system, an RFP may flow directly from the agreed-upon performance standards. However, standards are equally important for systems developed in-house, by a governmental MIS department, or by staff within the police department itself. Performance standards serve as an outline for programmers and developers as they work. Later, during implementation, they help focus the efforts of administrators, trainers, and users.

Preparing the organization. Information systems can cause notable and often unanticipated changes in formal and informal organizational relationships. Preparation for these changes begins with the command staff and political leaders, whose task it is to formalize modernization. Technology development benefits the organization most when it is viewed as an evolutionary process. Department management and employees must accept that their information needs, mission, technology, strategies, etc., will continue to change

(continued on next page)

services should be provided by contractors rather than the department? What vendors and consultants should the department use?

Finally, the chief must attend to the personnel issues that accompany the implementation of technological change. Employees need to be persuaded to take advantage of the capabilities of new systems and need to be trained in using them. Moreover, if officers do not see a personal advantage in a change, implementation can be difficult. For example, patrol officers may resist filing computer-based reports that will be useful to detectives but not necessarily to the patrol officers themselves. In this kind of situation, there are two basic approaches to implementation. One relies on participation, the other on top-down leadership. The participatory approach may be effective when immediate implementation is not required and when resistance is not intense—and especially when participants agree that some sort of change is called for. A variation of this approach, in the example given above, is to enlarge the job of the patrol officer to include tasks for which the information is being collected (for example, if patrol officers as well as detectives have investigative responsibilities, patrol officers will see

---

(continued from previous page)
and evolve. Modifications and alterations to the information system will be necessary to continue supplying all units with consistently high-quality information. The department that maintains an ongoing technology effort will be better able to respond to changes.

Formalizing this "evolutionary" approach can be accomplished in a number of ways. Permanently assigning some members of the steering committee to a technology planning unit will allow them to focus their efforts on the design process. In addition, advanced training in information systems for some or all committee members will enhance their contribution and signal the commitment of the department to the process. Chiefs who prepare their own budgets can signal their commitment by requesting long-term funding for technology research and development.

Regardless of the size and scope of a project, developing internal support, or organizational ownership as it is sometimes called, is crucial to the success of a new system. Departments can begin building internal support during the earliest stages of the project. Involving representatives from user groups, seeking meaningful feedback from them on their information needs, and providing feedback to them on the progress of the design effort will strengthen the development process.

development process, but failure to follow words with actions will reduce internal support. Feedback on the system's capabilities and timetable should be accurate and should not encourage unreasonable expectations that will be difficult or impossible to meet.

During the design phase, the planning group should continue to identify and reduce organizational barriers to the effective use of the information the new system will provide.

Design and implementation. System designers must consider what information is desirable as an end product, since computers can store an infinite variety of data sets and can report that data in an infinite number of ways. They must avoid the tendency to continue processing the same data in the same way without carefully assessing the value of the information and considering alternative ways of using it.

Many police departments begin automation with an interrelational records management system (RMS) to record and retrieve information on crimes and services provided to the public. Most personnel use or work with data stored in an RMS, so internal support and employee ownership are easy to generate.

The applications that a police department will find useful depend on the

more value in filing reports). The top-down approach may require more persistence and political effort than many police managers are willing to devote, unless implementing the system is a high priority. For some changes, however, especially those that threaten the status quo, fast and forceful top-down implementation may be the only feasible approach.

Service innovation

Although technology will rarely be the motive behind innovation in services, it will often be a significant enabling factor. Indeed, as service delivery systems become more complex, information technology will become an increasingly necessary supporting element of innovative policies and programs. Community-oriented policing is a prime example of this (see also the chapters on the patrol function and crime prevention). Many departments struggle to maintain a 9–1–1 capability for emergencies while also developing strategies for chronic community problems; but future information technologies will support com-

---

agency; however, beneficial applications have several common characteristics:

First, since patrol officers are the primary service users, their needs should be put first.

Second, any applications adopted should provide the user with information within an appropriate time frame. For example, stolen auto lookouts are most useful to a stolen auto unit during the first 24 hours following a theft. After this, much of the value of the information is lost since car thieves usually either abandon the car or strip it. Each type of data has a different "half-life." To maintain credibility among users, an information system must provide data when they are of greatest value.

Third, information must be relevant. A list of the most dangerous intersections is of little use to a traffic enforcement officer if the officer is prohibited from leaving his or her assigned area.

Finally, for obvious reasons the information contained in the system must be accurate.

Failing to meet any of these criteria will hurt the credibility of the system, and without credibility even the most advanced system will sit virtually unused.

Given the state of current technology, users can expect almost any application to be easy to use. Pull-down menus, on-demand help functions, graphic representations of complex information, and other features can reduce the amount of technical knowledge necessary to effectively operate a system.

Even systems that provide high-quality information and offer advanced user assistance features cannot be used to best effect without training. Many departments make the mistake of throwing all their resources into development and acquisition, while ignoring training. Training deserves a generous commitment of time and funds.

At the very minimum officers should be able to use applications that relate directly to their normal duties. Users should also learn about the type of information contained in the system and the processing routines that are available. As applications become more sophisticated and employees more technically astute, the power of information technologies will be released by the ad hoc efforts of the ordinary officer or supervisor.

Source: Excerpted from P. Steven Pendleton, "Managing Police Information Technology," *MicroSoftware News* 7, no. 6 (June 1990): 4–7. *Micro-Software News* is published by the International City Management Association.

Information technology in support of innovative policies and programs
When CAD/9–1–1 systems and automated record systems are integrated with other sources of information, such as tour of duty reports, citizen crime prevention groups, local businesses, and other city agencies, they can help maintain a department's rapid response capability by reducing the inappropriate dispatch of units; support problem-oriented as well as other forms of proactive policing by significantly improving a department's ability to identify problems; support community-oriented policing by maintaining sector integrity plans and by creating blocks of patrol officer time for community- or problem-oriented policing; and support community-oriented policing by incorporating neighborhood-specific priorities into both dispatching decisions and overall resource allocation.

munity-oriented policing in several ways while at the same time maintaining a rapid response capability for true emergencies.

First, the technologies will support far more complex service delivery systems than have been possible so far. New technology can reduce the misclassification of 9–1–1 calls that diverts resources to incidents that do not require mobilization of all personnel in the area. Computer prompts could help call takers obtain information from 9–1–1 callers, for example.[50] Differential police response systems can use this information, along with other computerized data, to prioritize requests and route them as appropriate to police, fire, emergency medical, or social services.

CAD systems could also incorporate neighborhood priorities into call management and dispatching schemes. Priorities could be tailored to meet neighborhood needs as articulated by crime prevention groups, patrol officers, calls for police assistance, and other sources of information. Thus, the system could alert call takers to the fact that gangs on the corner of Washington and Vine are a major community nuisance and should receive high priority. If priorities changed (for example, a citywide emergency needed attention), operators could easily change the priority classifications. CAD systems could also alert call takers to the availability of officers. Thus, the call taker could ask if the caller would like to wait for the neighborhood officer to respond the next day or would prefer an on-duty officer within two hours. The system would indicate the availability of patrol officers in the next week and also the availability of non-emergency officers within a few hours. The system could alert both call takers and dispatchers to changes in priorities derived from police intelligence. Thus, the priority on suspicious persons calls could be raised in areas with high reported levels of drug dealing. On a call from a household with a history of domestic violence, incidents could be given a high priority even if the current request appeared routine.

Public safety cable TV program   Fort Collins, Colorado, disseminates safety information to the public through a cable television program. The show, written and produced by the city, features personal safety tips, crime prevention measures for home and business, general information about police services, and tips on frequent crimes committed and areas prone to traffic accidents. The show is hosted by two police officers. Shows are taped monthly and aired by the local cable company several times a month. Taping is done in the field. Approximately 60,000 citizens have the opportunity to see the program.

Source: Cited in *The Guide to Management Improvement Projects in Local Government* (Washington, DC: International City Management Association, 1990).

Spreading the word In Milford, Connecticut, the police department is using a telephone tape machine to warn citizens and businesses of crime. The machine automatically makes calls to local businesses and residents warning them of crime trends and offering crime prevention tips. For example, the machine has warned area pharmacies of a false prescription scam and tipped off banks to recent robbery trends. The machine can make up to 100 calls per hour, saving officers hours of time and freeing them for other duties. The machine keeps track of all calls and calls back numbers that were busy or unanswered.

Source: Cited in *The Guide to Management Improvement Projects in Local Government* (Washington, DC: International City Management Association, 1990).

In large jurisdictions where police serve communities with quite different needs, flexible or neighborhood priority systems can be important. These systems may also be valuable for regional 9–1–1/CAD systems.

Information technology can also support community-oriented policing by making data accessible and thus improving police departments' ability to identify problems. For example, the RECAP (repeat call address policing) program in Minneapolis shows how information can be used to identify chronic problems. The program uses information generated from the Minneapolis 9–1–1/CAD to identify addresses or larger geographical areas with repetitive requests for assistance. Each month, the high-volume repeat-call locations are selected by the RECAP team (which includes five police officers) for investigation. The RECAP team reports that the 9–1–1/CAD information not only helps identify problems but also serves as an incentive to encourage interagency and public cooperation. Because the police can provide details about problems to organizations with jurisdictional responsibility, failure to cooperate is more likely to be visible and to lead to criticism.

These examples are not meant to argue the case for community or problem-oriented policing but to suggest that in these and other policing innovations, information technology can be an important enabling factor.

The key issue for managing information technologies in law enforcement may well be the problem of experimentation in tightly controlled and resource-poor police organizations. For technology to be used creatively, senior managers must understand that efficient performance with a given technology (E 9 1 1, MDTs, electronic mapping) is not achievable without the uncertainties and possible mistakes of learning. Management controls should thus be relatively loose and supportive in the case of experimental computer projects. Later, after the organization has learned to use a particular application, stronger controls are appropriate. Moreover, it is important to note that people at the street level (for example, patrol officers, sergeants, 9–1–1 call takers, police dispatchers) will soon be making important decisions by interacting with computer-aided technologies. Thus, resources for intensive training in these technologies throughout the organization are an urgent priority.

Organizational structure

Information technology is transforming the manner in which society manages and organizes itself. In the private sector, research has documented that information technology is creating flatter organizational structures, promoting decentralized decision making, and, at the same time, enhancing centralized oversight and control.[51] In police departments, too, information technology can be expected to influence departmental organization and decision making. Information technology can support decentralized decision making by giving field personnel the information they need (such as computerized maps of crime, and real-time searches through field investigation reports). At the same time, the technology can also give central administrators comprehensive and timely information on how the organization is operating and how individual employees are performing.

Security and privacy

In 1976, the Supreme Court found in *Paul v. Davis* that arrest records do not qualify for protection under the constitutional right to privacy because they do not relate to private conduct. This decision meant that confidentiality standards concerning criminal histories are largely a matter of legislative choice.[52] State governments exercise primary authority over criminal history information, while agencies within the states collect or receive the information.

Police departments, however, collect much sensitive information that is not incorporated into state files—for example, information on domestic violence, on suspects in drug cases, on field investigations. Departments must be careful about how they manage the security and privacy of the sensitive information they collect. Issues include how to maintain the security of automated information; who should have access to information; how to ensure that the records are accurate; and how to avoid problems of mistaken identity.[53]

The politics of information

The expanded use of computing and telecommunications and the broadened conception of the police mission are rapidly making the police a repository of a wide range of information on community problems. On the one hand, this represents a potential for far better law enforcement and community service. On the other hand, it also represents a potential for abuse. For example, by using computerized map displays of crime patterns, banks and insurance providers could make "red lining" a science. Obviously, communities need to be able to identify crime patterns without forfeiting their rights to mortgage loans and insurance coverage.

More accessible information on crime could also create public apprehension. For example, more police departments are reporting domestic violence disputes as criminal complaints to keep track of a major public safety problem. However, a side effect may be an increase in the number of reported assaults (the category into which domestic violence disputes are put). The department could then be criticized as the bearer of bad news.

Finally, individuals who have access to information may be tempted to select and use only the data that support their personal or organizational purposes. As many managers have learned, it is possible to argue almost any position with the help of statistics. The temptation becomes particularly great at budget time, when each government department is trying to justify its own budget requests. It is the chief's responsibility to ensure that the information maintained by the department is used responsibly.

Conclusion

Law enforcement is a prototypical "information-intensive" public service. To date, applications of information technology have focused on rapid response and traditional forms of record keeping and control. This restricted focus has perhaps been necessary, partly because of technological limitations and partly because of beliefs about the proper scope of and tactics for achieving police objectives. The results have not always been positive, however, especially for those who believe that flexibility of response is needed for community- and problem-oriented policing.

Only now is technology emerging that is powerful and flexible enough for the new policing strategies. For technology to be effective, however, police managers must clearly understand that results are produced neither by technology alone nor by people alone but by the two working together. Managers need to understand the technology, understand the people, and bring the two together in productive new ways.

1 President's Commission on Law Enforcement and Administration of Justice, *The Challenge of Crime in a Free Society* (Washington, DC: U.S. Government Printing Office, 1967), 13.

2 O. W. Wilson, *Police Records: Their Installation and Use* (Chicago: Public Administration Service, 1951).

3 Ronald Roth et al., "Out of Hospital Cardiac Arrest: Factors Associated With Survival," *Annals of Emergency Medicine* (April 1984): 237–43.

4 Kent W. Colton, Margret Bradeau, and James Tien, *A National Assessment of Police Command, Control and Communication Systems* (Washington, DC: National Institute of Justice, 1983).

5 Richard Larson, "The Future of Police Emergency Response Systems," *NIJ Reports* (Washington, DC: National Institute of Justice, 1985), 4.

6 Ibid., 2–4.

7 John Moran and Karen Layne, "Enhanced 911/CAD: Interfacing New Technology to Fight Crime," *Police Chief* (August 1988): 25–29.

8 Raymond Sumrall, Jane Roberts, and Michael Farmer, *Differential Police Response Strategies Study* (Birmingham, AL: Birmingham Police Department; Washington, DC: Police Executive Research Forum, 1980).

9 Thomas J. McEwen, Edward F. Conners, and Marcia I. Cohen, *Evaluation of the Differential Police Response Field Test* (Alexandria, VA: Research Management Associates, Inc., 1984).

10 Colton, Bradeau, and Tien, *A National Assessment of Police Command, Control and Communication Systems.*

11 Susan M. Dowse, "On the Alert: In-Car Terminal Network to Speed Police Communication," *The Compiler* 8, no. 3 (Chicago: Illinois Criminal Justice Information Authority, Winter 1988): 1, 13.

12 David Roberts and Judith Ryder, *New Technologies in Criminal Justice: An Appraisal* (Sacramento, CA: Search Group Inc., 1987).

13 Cohen, Bradeau, and Tien, *A National Assessment of Police Command, Control and Communication Systems.*

14 Ibid.

15 Letter from Dallas Chief of Police Mack M. Vines to William Geller, 24 July 1989.

16 Karyn Greenstone, "Cellular Equipment Becomes Valuable Alternative During Emergencies," *APCO Bulletin* (February 1990): 48.

17 Danita L. Osborne, "Examining What Happened and Why It Happened Provides Valuable Lessons After Quake," *APCO Bulletin* (February 1990): 9–18.

18 Terry Bonneau, "Re-Establishment of Two-Way Communications Vital to Recovery after Hurricane Hugo," *APCO Bulletin* (February 1990): 54, 55, 77.

19 Norman C. Boehm, "Using Computers in Crime

Fighting, Training, and Administration: A Practical Approach," *Police Chief* (March 1983): 123–30.

20 John Herbers, "Tales of Ten Governments That Show What Innovation Is All About," *Governing* (October 1988): 29–40.

21 Bruce Glasscock, "Information Technology Applications in the Fort Collins Police Services Department" (Memorandum to Glenn Pierce, 23 Oct. 1989).

22 Brewer S. Stone, "The High-Tech Beat in St. Pete," *Police Chief* (May 1988): 22.

23 William Spelman, *Beyond Bean Counting: New Approaches for Managing Crime Data* (Washington, DC: Police Executive Research Forum, 1988).

24 James Danziger and Kenneth Kraemer, "Computerized Data-Based Systems and Productivity among Professional Workers: The Case of Detectives," *Public Administration Review* (January/February 1985): 196–209.

25 U.S. Office of Technology Assessment, *Criminal Justice, New Technologies, and the Constitution* (Washington, DC: U.S. Government Printing Office, 1988).

26 P. Woodard, *State Criminal History Record Repositories: An Overview* (Sacramento, CA: Search Group Inc., 1988).

27 Office of Technology Assessment, *Criminal Justice, New Technologies, and the Constitution.*

28 John Probert, "Police Telecommunications: The Influence of Computers on Law Enforcement," *Police Chief* (May 1986): 53–55.

29 Letter from J. David Coldren, executive director of the Illinois Criminal Justice Information Authority, to William Geller, 20 July 1989.

30 Maureen Hickey, "Intelligence Network Helps Put Pieces Together," *The Compiler* 9, no. 1 (Chicago: Illinois Criminal Justice Information Authority, Summer 1988): 3.

31 Ibid.

32 Armand Hernandez, "Is Law Enforcement Ready for the Artificial Intelligence Explosion?" *Police Chief* (May 1986): 50–52.

33 Joan Jacoby and Edward Ratledge, "Expert Systems in Criminal Justice" (Paper presented to the American Society of Criminology, Montreal, 1987).

34 Hank Gilman, "Detectives on Disks. Law Enforcers Use New Computer Software to Solve Crime," *The Wall Street Journal*, 11 Sept. 1987.

35 Jacoby and Ratledge, "Expert Systems in Criminal Justice."

36 Ibid., 5.

37 Hernandez, "Is Law Enforcement Ready for the Artificial Intelligence Explosion?"

38 Ibid.

39 Roberts and Ryder, *New Technologies in Criminal Justice*, 14.

40 Ibid.

41 Kevin Morison, "Technology Wave Breaking over

Criminal Justice," *The Compiler* 7, no. 3 (Chicago: Illinois Criminal Justice Information Authority, Fall 1986): 1, 12.

42 Roberts and Ryder, *New Technologies in Criminal Justice.*

43 Bill Brown, "Fairfax County Steps up to CAD: Public Safety Communications Advances with Computer Aided Dispatching," *Sentinel* (Fairfax County, VA: Fairfax County Police Association, Fall 1987).

44 Michael D. Maltz, A. C. Gorden, and W. Friedman, "Mapping Crime in Its Community Setting: Event Geography Analysis" (Report to Chicago Police Department and National Criminal Justice Reference Service, National Institute of Justice, Washington, DC, December 1989).

45 Laura Lang, "To Catch a Thief: High Tech Cops Using Crime Information Systems," *Government Technology* 2, no. 6 (October 1989): 20–22.

46 Peter Kolesar and Arthur J. Swersey, "The Deployment of Urban Emergency Units: A Survey," in *Delivery of Urban Services with a View towards Applications in Management Science and Operations Research*, ed. Arthur J. Swersey and Edward J. Ingall (New York: Elsevier North-Holland, 1986), 87–119.

47 Colton, Bradeau, and Tien, *A National Assessment of Police Command, Control and Communication Systems.*

48 Letter from Vines to Geller.

49 Gary T. Marx, *Undercover: Police Surveillance in America* (Berkeley: University of California Press, 1988).

50 Richard Larson, "The New Crime Stoppers," *Technology Review* 92, no. 8 (Cambridge: Massachusetts Institute of Technology, November/December 1989): 26–31.

51 Lynda M. Applegate, James I. Cash, Jr., and D. Quinn Mills, "Information Technology and Tomorrow's Manager," *Harvard Business Review* (November/December 1988): 128–36.

52 Bureau of Justice Statistics, U.S. Department of Justice, *Public Access to Criminal History Record Information*, NCJ-111458 (November 1988), Report prepared by SEARCH Group Inc.

53 For a discussion of these issues, see ibid.

12 Research, planning, and implementation

Planning and research activities are essential to effective agency management. Complex demands for services and declining public resources require that law enforcement agencies carefully research operational alternatives and plan future programs.[1]

This chapter covers three closely related topics that, together, greatly influence a police organization's ability to establish and maintain effective operations, adapt to environmental changes, and improve the delivery of police services to the community:

1. *Research*—the careful, systematic study of a subject
2. *Planning*—the process of bringing together expectations about the future and data from the past to guide decision making in the present
3. *Implementation*—the process of carrying out organizational plans and following through on decisions.

The world is changing at increasingly faster rates, and citizens are demanding ever-greater safety and protection—but government resources are failing to keep pace. In this situation, police have an enormous need to acquire strategically and tactically useful knowledge (that is, to do research); to put that knowledge to use in effective and efficient planning; and to reap the benefits of quality planning by ensuring that the department's plans are faithfully implemented. For the good of both the department and the community, modern police administrators must increasingly concern themselves with research, planning, and implementation.

Research

Contrary to conventional wisdom, research is one of the most practical components of police administration. Research is used to discover "what works" in policing, to test new technologies, to analyze community problems, and to address a host of other practical needs. But because many police administrators associate research with libraries, laboratories, and impractical theories, they may tend to think of it as a frill, a luxury without important consequences for real-world affairs. Consider the following situations:

A police department prepares to implement fear-reduction strategy. Questions arise about the causes of fear in the jurisdiction.

A police chief wonders whether patrol officers in the department are correctly allocated and deployed to equalize workload.

A police department's personnel selection criteria are challenged in court. The department is required to prove that the criteria are bona fide occupational qualifications.

During its annual budget review process, a police department seeks continued funding for a foot patrol project. The city council asks for evidence to support the department's claim that foot patrol has reduced crime and increased citizen satisfaction.

Several police chiefs want to pressure prosecutors and judges in their area to treat repeat offenders more severely. They need information on the numbers of repeat offenders and the numbers of crimes they commit.

A police chief feels strongly that police officers' pay and benefits must be increased to improve motivation and reduce turnover. The department may be offering lower pay and benefits than comparable agencies in its region.

In any of these situations, the way to generate the necessary information is to collect and analyze data. And a police practitioner who sets about carefully and systematically collecting and analyzing data to generate useful information is doing research, whether or not he or she uses the word.

Research is used to discover "what works" in policing, to test new technologies, to analyze community problems, and to address a host of other practical needs.

Police administrators need information if they are to prepare rational plans, make rational decisions, solve problems, and ensure efficient and effective operations. Thus, they need research—good research. Research can enable a police administrator to achieve productivity gains by working smarter, not merely by working harder. It also can help police departments influence political decisions about budgets, policies, and legislation.[2]

Police administrators need information if they are to prepare rational plans, make rational decisions, solve problems, and ensure efficient and effective operations.

In short, research is simply the careful, systematic study of a subject. It can be done in a library, in an office, in a laboratory, or in the field. It can be done by specialists called researchers, scientists, and analysts, or by generalists such as police managers. It can be very sophisticated and technical, or it can be relatively simple. And like anything else, research can be good or bad depending on the competence and dedication of those doing it. The remainder of this section on research outlines the various types, the process, the applications, and the major issues that may arise.

Types of research

There are three general types of research: archival, analytical, and experimental.[3] They are suitable for different kinds of circumstances, and may be used separately or in combination.

Archival research   Archival research involves searching for information that others have already compiled. The information may be in books, articles, reports, documents, files, or data bases. Locating the information may require browsing in the library, using indexes, conducting computerized bibliographic searches, or getting assistance from specialized reference librarians.

In several of the scenarios mentioned above, archival research would contribute valuable information. Data on police officers' salaries and benefits in a state or region might be regularly published by a government or service

Major sources of information

Professional associations and government agencies that can provide police departments with information useful for research and planning include the following:

Commission on Accreditation for Law
  Enforcement Agencies
4242B Chain Bridge Road
Fairfax, VA 22030
(703) 352–4225

International Association of Chiefs of
  Police
1110 N. Glebe Road (Suite 200)
Arlington, VA 22201
(703) 243–6500

National Criminal Justice Reference
  Service
U.S. Department of Justice
Box 6000
Rockville, MD 20850
(301) 251–5500

National Institute of Justice
U.S. Department of Justice
633 Indiana Avenue, N.W.
Washington, DC 20531
(202) 724–2949

National Organization of Black Law
  Enforcement Executives
908 Pennsylvania Avenue, S.E.
Washington, DC 20003
(202) 546–8811

National Sheriffs' Association
1450 Duke Street
Alexandria, VA 22314
(703) 836–7827

Police Executive Research Forum
2300 M Street, N.W. (Suite 910)
Washington, DC 20037
(202) 466–7820

Police Foundation
1001 22d Street, N.W. (Suite 200)
Washington, DC 20037
(202) 833–1460

---

organization, for example. Or other jurisdictions might have prepared reports on the causes of fear of crime, the effects of foot patrol, and the offending rates of career criminals. The information in those reports might be valuable to local decision makers.

An important variety of archival research for police administration is legal research. Questions of criminal and administrative law frequently arise that can be answered only by careful review of statutory and case law.

In any field, routine archival research is necessary for keeping abreast of developments. In police administration, mechanisms are needed that enable officials to continually glean information about relevant books, journals, bulletins, newsletters, court decisions, and other documents. Professional associations can help by notifying their members of new publications and developments, as can the National Criminal Justice Reference Service of the U.S. Department of Justice (see accompanying sidebar).

Analytical research   Analytical research involves collecting and analyzing data about a condition, problem, situation, or relationship. A police chief who surveys surrounding departments about their salaries and benefits is conducting analytical research, as is a department that surveys citizens on their fear of crime. Departments that collect and analyze data on calls for service, on the tasks performed by police officers, or on repeat offenders also engage in analytical research. Some of the most influential research in the police field has been analytical—for example, the Rand study of criminal investigations (discussed in the chapter on criminal investigations) and the PERF study of police response time (discussed in the chapter on the patrol function).[4]

Analytical research primarily permits us to describe conditions and measure the relationships between two or more factors. The Rand study described how detectives spent their time and identified the factors associated with successful investigations. The PERF study examined the relationship between police response time and arrest productivity and found that, largely because of citizens' delays in reporting crime, the relationship was much weaker than had been generally believed.

Experimental research   Although analytical research can describe a condition or identify a relationship between two variables, only experimental research can convincingly demonstrate cause and effect, that is, can demonstrate that altering one or more factors will cause some other factor or factors to change.[5] For example, although the Rand study showed that detectives spend a considerable amount of time on cases that have a low probability of being solved, it could not establish what would happen if detectives reallocated their time or if the number of detectives was reduced. Some observers inferred from the Rand study that such changes were desirable, but the study itself did not test such alternatives. Similarly, the PERF response time study suggested that police response to many reported crimes could be delayed without reducing police effectiveness but did not actually test the effects of such a change in policy.

In an experiment, the researcher tests a causal relationship by manipulating one factor while carefully controlling and/or measuring the other important factors in the situation. The factor manipulated, often termed the "treatment" factor, is the one the researcher suspects is the cause of certain effects. The purpose of the intentional manipulation is to see whether changes in the treatment factor cause changes in other factors (the "dependent" factors). To the extent that experimental conditions (such as random assignment of subjects to treatment and control groups) can be maintained, any observed changes in the experimental subjects (the ones receiving the "treatment") or in the dependent factors, or conditions, can be attributed to change in the treatment factor.

Designing experiments   A 1988 publication in the National Institute of Justice "Research in Action" series identified nine critical issues in experiment design. Many of these issues are equally important for non-experimental studies.

1. Choose an interesting problem—a policy question that people really care about or an existing procedure that clearly needs improvement.

2. Do some creative thinking to resolve legal and ethical issues that may arise.

3. Understand and confront the political risks an experiment may involve.

4. Choose a design and methods of investigation that are appropriate both to the questions to be answered and to the available data.

5. Adopt a team approach involving both researchers and practitioners, and keep them working in close cooperation.

6. Throughout the experiment, rigorously maintain the random assignment of persons, cases, or other units into treatment groups and control groups.

7. Put as much into your experiment as you want to get out of it.

8. Use an experiment to inform policy, not to make policy.

9. Insofar as possible, see that the experiment is replicated in a variety of settings before encouraging the widespread adoption of experimentally successful treatments.

Source: Adapted from Joel H. Garner and Christy A. Visher, "Policy Experiments Come of Age," *NIJ Reports* no. 211 (September/October 1988): 7–8.

Of course, in a *field experiment* (as opposed to a laboratory experiment), it can be difficult to maintain experimental conditions. Consequently, the findings from field experiments are often less conclusive than those from laboratory experiments. The best that researchers can do is control conditions as much as they can, monitor conditions to detect any uncontrolled developments that might contaminate the experiment, and, most important, replicate experiments in order to verify findings.

Some of the most important and most controversial police research has been of the field experiment variety, including the Kansas City preventive patrol study, the San Diego field interrogation study, and the Minneapolis domestic violence study.[6] In the Minneapolis study, for example, officers responding to domestic assault calls randomly chose, before arrival, which of three alternatives they would employ: separation, mediation, or arrest. Researchers then tracked subsequent calls to see which alternative was most effective in preventing repeat violence.

The research process

The process of conducting research involves five stages: (1) problem definition, (2) research design, (3) data collection, (4) data analysis, and (5) reporting.[7]

In the *problem definition* stage, the researcher must identify and clearly state the issue or topic to be studied and must assess current knowledge. In other words, the researcher must answer the questions "What is the problem?" and "What do we already know about it?" At the beginning of this stage the researcher often has only a vague conception of the problem; before going further, he or she must sharpen and clarify that conception.

In the second step—*research design*—the researcher decides whether the research will be archival, analytical, or experimental. The choice of design should be determined by the definition of the problem (what do we need to learn?) and by practical and ethical considerations (such as cost, time constraints, and research capabilities). In archival research, research design means deciding how many and which sources of information will be checked. In analytical research, research design may include deciding about sampling, constructing questionnaires, devising interview schedules, or determining coding schemes for data from observation or official records. In experimental studies, research design includes determining how to test hypotheses, how to assign subjects to treatment and control groups, and what conditions to measure in order to detect changes in the subjects and in their environment.

In the *data collection* and *data analysis* stages, the research is carried out and the results are analyzed. The researcher collects data by examining archival sources and official records, by administering surveys or interviewing subjects, or by observing and measuring behavior. In analyzing data, the researcher uses qualitative and quantitative techniques for summarizing information and discovering patterns and relationships. In the *reporting* stage, the reseacher communicates the results of the research either orally or in writing.

In referring to the validity of research results, research experts use four terms that are frequently misunderstood by those outside the research community. (These terms apply most directly to experimental research, but the concerns about validity that they represent are also applicable to archival and analytical studies.) These terms are (1) internal validity, (2) external validity, (3) construct validity, and (4) statistical conclusion validity.[8]

Internal validity is a function of whether the research design established sufficient control to ensure that the results obtained can be linked to the program or technique being studied (for example, in the domestic violence study, were the different outcomes caused by the different tactics employed and not by differences in the cases in which the different tactics were employed). *External validity* refers to the applicability of the findings to other times and places (for example, were the results of the preventive patrol study peculiar to Kansas City or generalizable to other jurisdictions). *Construct validity* pertains to the soundness of the research hypotheses and measures and the jurstifiability of conclusions drawn from findings (for cxamples, can the San Diego field interrogation study justifiably be interpreted as demonstrating that "aggressive patrol" deters street crimes). Finally, *statistical conclusion validity* refers to the appropriateness of the statistical tests used to evaluate hypotheses and measure the strength of relationships (for example, were the proper statistical tests used in the Newark foot patrol study[9] that led to the conclusion that foot patrol had a statistically significant effect on fear of crime).

Research applications

One of the more important research applications in police departments is to describe the current state of affairs. From time to time administrators may need to know the portion of their employees that are minority group members, the average response time to domestic disputes, or the number of false alarm calls, for example. Many police departments have management information systems that routinely provide data on some of these matters, but questions always arise that require additional research.

A second application of police department research is to describe the nature and scope of community problems for which the police have some responsibility and perhaps to provide some clues as to their causes. For example, police—or others on their behalf—may conduct research on crime problems, traffic accidents, fear levels, and activities of extremist groups.

Another application of police department research is to help the department avoid reinventing the wheel: research can provide information about the mistakes and successes of others. Often when a department is considering purchasing a new type of equipment or preparing a new policy statement to govern some aspect of police operations or administration it contacts other departments to discover the range of options in use and others' experience with those options.

Some police departments engage in operations research, an application that relies heavily on quantitative analysis and mathematical models, to make the department's processes and subsystems work as efficiently and effectively as possible. The most widespread application of operations research in police departments has been in the area of patrol allocation and deployment. Highly sophisticated methods have been developed to calculate staffing requirements and beat configurations in order to equalize workload among patrol units and minimize emergency response times.[10] Operations research techniques can also be used to set solvability factor levels for case screening decisions within programs for managing criminal investigations.[11]

Evaluation research examines the *value* of a standard practice or a new program; in police departments, this is the kind of research for which experimental methods are most applicable. By identifying the good and bad effects—the cost and benefits—of a practice or program, evaluation research helps police decision makers decide whether the practice or program should be continued, modified, or eliminated.

There was a tremendous explosion of evaluation research in the police field in the 1970s and 1980s. Progressive police administrators realized they needed the results of evaluation research to make informed decisions about whether to continue, modify, or eliminate many kinds of practices, programs, and policies.

One additional research application that bears mention is called research and development (R&D): research aimed at inventing or discovering new equipment, techniques, strategies, tactics, and other methods for use in policing. Whereas

What is "R&D" really? In many organizations the major unit that seeks to shape both internal and external environments is the research and development (R&D) unit. As used here, research means empirical investigation that describes and explains how things behave and change their behavior; development means the actual implementation of models that demonstrate whether an intervention works in a predictable way.

Police organizations essentially lack research and development units understood in this way. The research unit of most police organizations typically is responsible for providing a statistical description of the organization and its inputs and outputs. Rarely does it undertake research that might lead to development, and the department typically makes no provision for development. Police organizations rely primarily upon universities for research that has R&D potential and upon private industry for development.

One might contrast the R&D budget of American police departments and related organizations that support research and development, such as the National Institute of Justice, with the R&D budget of the U.S. Department of Defense. Defense expenditures for R&D are variously estimated at 10 to 15 percent of the total defense budget. By contrast, less than half of 1 percent of the police budget ordinarily is allocated to research and development, and nationally it is estimated to be less than 1 percent of all expenditures on policing. Compared with expert estimates of the size and nature of the R&D industry, police organizations fall at the bottom in percentage of the budget expended for R&D, comparable perhaps to the furniture industry.

Clearly, research and development is not a core technology of police organizations. Adaptive organizations generally rely upon research and development as a core technology either to solve problems that fall within the organization's mandate or to adapt the organization to its changing environment. As Goldstein has argued, a problem-oriented police would require minimally that research be a core technology. Perhaps even more importantly, the applied research of engineering sciences, including social engineering, must be part of that core technology. Yet more is required in a genuine R&D model. Implementation of research requires the development of models and their testing under field conditions. The implications of this for police organizations are that the organization must alter the interface with its environment as well as provide for research and development units within the organization.

Source: Albert J. Reiss, William Graham Sumner Professor of Sociology, Yale University, New Haven, Connecticut.

private companies often invest substantial resources in R&D to improve existing products and develop new ones, government service organizations such as police departments have not often given R&D a high priority. Part of the reason has been that, unlike private enterprise, the police have not had to compete for their consumers' attention. But this is changing. Private police now outnumber public police two to one, and segments of many communities are putting their financial resources into strengthening their private rather than their public security forces. Another reason for the past lack of police sophistication in R&D may be that, for decades, police officials assumed their strategies and tactics worked well. (If it ain't broke, don't create a unit to fix it.) But given that many traditional police practices have been shown to be ineffective,[12] the need for considerable R&D work—not just on hardware but on strategies of policing—would seem to be evident.

Major research issues

To understand research generally, one needs to understand certain distinctions: between applied and basic research, between quantitative and qualitative research, and between descriptive and inferential research. Issues also arise about whether research should be done in-house or by outside consultants and about the ethics of research procedures. Finally, all research has inherent limitations that need to be recognized.

Most of the research conducted by police departments is *applied research*, that is, research intended to produce information for a specific purpose, usually to solve a problem or inform a decision. The most successful applied research is conducted with implementation in mind, so that it produces information that is not only valid but also useful and usable.[13] This type of research can be distinguished from *basic research*, which is intended to advance a body of knowledge or test a theoretical proposition. Although few police departments would be expected to engage in basic research, they certainly might profit from its findings. For example, research in materials science might ultimately lead to improvements in police equipment; research in human behavior might lead to better criminological theories, which could be used to improve police crime control strategies; and research on community structures might produce information quite helpful in implementing community policing.

Some researchers and research consumers mistakenly believe that *quantitative research* is inherently better than *qualitative research*. In fact, both types are valuable, and either can be appropriate, depending on the nature of the topic being investigated and the kind of information desired. Quantitative research tends to be more useful for summarizing a large amount of information and for identifying patterns and generalizations, as when we attempt to describe the status of crime in America. Qualitative research, in contrast, provides richer and more detailed information about a focused topic, such as the effects of crime on individuals or families. Under the best of circumstances, a blending of quantitative and qualitative methods is desirable in order to gain the advantages of each. For example, qualitative work was very helpful to those interpreting the quantitative findings in Newark on the relationships among foot patrol, crime, and fear.[14]

For major research projects, it is probably most desirable to have a combination of inside and outside researchers, or at least close departmental liaison with outside researchers.

Another important distinction is that between *descriptive* and *inferential* research. Descriptive research simply describes a problem, a condition, or some set of conditions, whereas inferential research seeks to draw inferences that transcend the data collected, as when a researcher generalizes from a sample to an entire population. (To draw such inferences, one needs proper sampling, and one uses statistical tests based on probability theory.) Thus, for example, before deciding whether to implement a particular policy department- or city-wide, a police department may assess the policy question by using representative segments of the police force and the community.

A practical issue that confronts police administrators is whether to use in-house or outside research. Research conducted by department members might have certain advantages, including lower cost, better insight into real organizational problems and constraints, and more credibility within the department (depending on the reputations of the inside researchers). Outside research might be more objective, less constrained by organizational tradition, and—depending on the skills of the researchers—more authoritative. For major research projects, it is probably most desirable to have a combination of inside and outside researchers, or at least close departmental liaison with outside researchers (see the chapter on external resources). For more routine studies, most sizeable departments will want to have competent in-house research capability. Smaller departments may want to develop relationships with local colleges, if adequate research skills or resources are not available and cannot be developed within their own organizations.

Rigorous research is *not* the only source of useful information—experience, wisdom, and casual inquiry also produce information that can be valid.

Police research sometimes raises difficult ethical issues. For example, random assignment of subjects to control and experimental groups is necessary to protect internal validity—but random assignment may also have the effect of denying "innocent" people the possible benefits of a standard practice (as when preventive patrol was removed from five beats in Kansas City). Or random assignment could expose some people to a possibly harmful intervention (as when one-third of spousal assault suspects in Minneapolis were randomly selected for arrest). Such selective benefits and deprivations are, of course, standard practice in medical and other experimental research. Nevertheless, whenever researchers and policy makers are dealing with human subjects, they must weigh the benefits of new knowledge against the possible harmful effects to people subjected to experimental treatments and conditions. In the Kansas City and Minneapolis studies and in many others in police research, ethical questions have been diluted by the lack of evidence that any traditional practices effectively protect or endanger the public. Hence, researchers cannot be certain that they are differentially helping or harming the participants in the research project—at least, until the results are in.

Research findings should not be seen as mandating certain decisions and policies for police executives. The findings can provide useful and valid information, but the decision maker must also consider values, customs, politics, and a host of other factors.

Finally, it is important to recognize the fundamental and inherent limitations of research, especially as they apply to police decision making and policy making.[15] One is that rigorous research is *not* the only source of useful information—experience, wisdom, and casual inquiry also produce information that can be valid. Another is that research frequently complicates a situation rather than simplifying it: other problems may be uncovered, complex interrelationships may be discovered, and findings (if honestly expressed) are frequently tentative and inconclusive. Most important, research findings should not be seen as mandating certain decisions and policies for police executives. The findings can provide useful and valid information, but the decision maker must also consider values, customs, constraints, politics, and a host of other factors when he or she chooses the most appropriate course of action for the police department. Thus, good, careful research can often help police administrators understand their situations and the likely consequences of different alternatives, but it cannot relieve them of the responsibility for weighing costs and benefits and making tough decisions. At the same time, once the tough decisions have been made, competent research can add powerful support for the decisions both inside and outside the police department.

Planning

Planning is the process of bringing together expectations about the future and data from the past to guide decision making in the present. The most effective planning process enables an organization to be change-oriented, flexible, and adaptive so that it can overcome the problems it faces as it works toward accomplishing its goals. Planning provides managers with a guide for moving the organization from one condition to another on purpose, instead of allowing changes in the organization to occur haphazardly. Through planning, managers attempt to replicate past successes and avoid past mistakes by basing their decisions on the desired future direction plus an analysis of the past.

All law enforcement agencies do some planning. In 1973, the National Advisory Commission on Criminal Justice Standards and Goals recognized that "planning can be formal or informal, structured or haphazard, painstakingly thought out or completed on the spur of the moment; whatever its form, planning takes place in every police agency."[16] The Commission on Accreditation for Law Enforcement Agencies (CALEA) reiterates this view:

All law enforcement agencies perform certain planning functions, depending upon their size and mandate. Among these are . . . development of an agency plan and budget recommendations, liaison with other criminal justice planning agencies, and development of operational procedures and policy guidelines [as well as] forms control, grant management, strategic and operational planning . . . and information management.[17]

The need for law enforcement planning was recognized a generation ago by O. W. Wilson, who argued that "police objectives are achieved most effectively and efficiently through the efficient operation of three interrelated processes: viz., planning, doing, and controlling. Of these, planning is basic."[18]

There can be no doubt that the commitment of top police leadership to planning and to the process of bringing about change is essential.

If all law enforcement agencies plan and if planning is basic, how can a department "best" plan? Research on how "excellent" organizations plan shows that effective planning is critical in producing constructive change. Effective planning promotes organizational innovation that allows organizations to adapt to rapidly changing conditions. The approaches used by organizations that have most successfully linked planning with innovation have had three ingredients in common: (1) a commitment from the top to plan and to carry out change; (2) a team approach to planning and change; and (3) the consideration and implementation of a series of small changes rather than a large-scale major alteration.

There can be no doubt that the commitment of top police leadership to planning and to the process of bringing about change is essential. This commitment must begin with a willingness to set future directions, then continue with the development of a course of action, and finally end with steps implementing that course. Today, many police administrators have that willingness. They have come to realize that to cope with problems of drug-related crime, increased fear of crime, a growing subculture of violence, and employee apathy, they must use all available resources to shape both the future of their organizations and their external environments. Police leaders recognize that they must articulate a clear vision of the desired future and exploit every opportunity to achieve it. Such an articulation of goals and objectives, and of values, is critical to creating a successful organization and is discussed elsewhere in this volume (see especially the chapter on practical ideals). Planning is the process that is used to devise methods to move the organization toward that future state; and the commitment to the process of planning and bringing about change has been called "modeling innovation": "If an institution is to pick up the pace of innovation . . . senior managers must regularly act—and be seen acting—to welcome change, rather than be observed and heard fighting it."[19]

The second critical factor in successful planning is a team approach, and this, too, is not new to law enforcement. Wilson and Roy Clinton McLaren recognized the need for wide involvement when they wrote:

All units in the department that may be affected by a plan must be actively involved in its preparation. Participation in the development of a plan will stimulate interest in its operation and promote an understanding of its purpose and application. It is essential that those who are affected by plans should consider them practical and acceptable. Those who contribute to the development of plans usually find them workable and sound and give sympathetic support to their implementation. In addition, this participation will lead to further awareness on the part of operating personnel of the need to recognize or seek out areas where planning is needed, thus keeping the planning function alive at a level below that of the central planning unit.[20]

Extending the planning process to all parts of the organization helps counter bureaucratic tendencies toward excessive documentation, extensive procedures, and rigidity in organizational structure. In a law enforcement organization, a change will not have the desired effect unless, from the earliest stages onward, the planning process involves employees from all the affected units and levels.

The third factor in successful efforts to plan for innovation and change is keeping changes manageable. "Take seriously the smaller project. A constant stream of such small starts is a must."[21] Most police chiefs know that large-scale, comprehensive plans, written down in thick volumes, tend to become dust catchers on shelves.

This section surveys the four types of planning; illustrates the importance of planning by describing the linkage between planning and organizational values; and explains the four steps of the planning process.

Types of planning

Planning in a police department may be of several kinds, depending on its purpose. These are (1) reactive planning, (2) contingency planning, (3) operational efficiency planning, and (4) long-range, or strategic, planning.

Reactive planning   Almost all police departments engage at one time or another in reactive planning, that is, they develop a plan in response to a crisis or when forced to do so to implement a decision made by some other body. For example, because of a very few but highly publicized crimes in a downtown area, the local governing body may instruct a department to start a downtown foot patrol. Whether downtown foot patrol is the best response to the problem becomes irrelevant; the elected body has mandated it. All that is left for the police department to do is plan for implementation. Some agencies view any other approach to planning as an unaffordable luxury. Their leaders operate on a day-to-day basis, trying to react effectively to each new demand. Good reactive planning depends, therefore, less on the vision of the leader than on the adaptability of the organization.

Contingency planning   Contingency planning envisions the possibility that some "special incident" such as a riot, hostage situation, or major transportation disaster may occur and is based on the department's wish to be prepared when it does occur. Contingency plans often result from lessons learned by other departments that had to face similar events and found that their preparation had been inadequate. For example, riots in urban ghettos in the late

Good strategic planning   What is a good strategic plan? There is none. But there is a good strategic planning process. A good strategic planning process (1) gets everyone involved, (2) is not constrained by overall corporate "assumptions" (e.g., about the general economic picture), (3) is perpetually fresh, forcing the asking of new questions, (4) is not to be left to planners, and (5) requires lots of noodling time and vigorous debate.

As for the document per se, it (1) is succinct, (2) emphasizes the development of strategic skills, and (3)

is burned the day before it is to go to the printer—that is, it is a living document, not an icon. . . .

Flexibility is the necessary watchword. Sound thinking and debate about the future, marked by the asking of novel questions, foster flexibility of thought and action. Two-hundred-page plans do not.

Source: Tom Peters, *Thriving on Chaos: Handbook for a Management Revolution* (New York: Knopf, 1988), 510.

1960s led not only to improved training and equipment but also to changes in radio frequencies so that police departments working near each other could communicate to coordinate tactics. Departments skilled at contingency planning are now focusing on plans to deal with computer crimes.

Operational efficiency planning   In operational efficiency planning, current processes are reviewed, and recommendations for improvements are made. Examples of this type of planning are resource allocation studies, studies of investigative efficiency, and examinations of patrol procedures. This planning

Policy and values   A police department's policies and procedures should reflect and be consistent with the best values of the organization. In order to have a profound effect on the department and the community, these values should also be consistent with the chief's personal philosophy of policing.

Whether the values are widely disseminated or simply appear as a statement of philosophy in the policy manual doesn't really matter for purposes of policy development. What does matter is that the chief has an articulated philosophy of policing that is known to everyone in the department.

Ideally, a police department would articulate its values and beliefs and *then* develop its policies and procedures, but few departments enjoy this luxury. As a matter of fact, many chiefs inherit a manual that represents years of policies derived from the differing philosophies of its various

chiefs. A policy manual may be very sparse if the policy development process has consisted largely of responding to crises, new legislation, or court rulings. Such a manual does not address the universe of policies needed in an agency.

Consequently, following the articulation and dissemination of values, it is important for the department to review its policies and procedures in their entirety for consistency with these values statements and revise them as needed. Of course, if the policy manual is incomplete, gaps must be filled by new policies.

One way to guarantee consistency is to reorganize the manual to relate all policies and procedures to the values that underlie the department's philosophy of policing. For example, if a basic tenet is that human life is to be valued, this principle does not apply only to the deadly force policy. It applies to all other uses of force, including chokeholds and the use of

often consists of short-term, one-time projects, although the planning really should be conducted periodically to ensure that the department's resources continue to be used wisely as conditions change.

Long-range, or strategic, planning   Strategic planning requires the department to set goals at least five years into the future and devise steps that need to be taken to achieve those goals. However, police executives often protest that long-range (multiyear) planning is useless because their budgets are prepared and approved on an annual basis. Despite this reality, the department still needs to set long-range targets and directions. Those in charge of providing resources will be in a much better position to make intelligent decisions if they are presented with long-range plans that show the resources that must be committed to achieve goals. Just as important, the organization's own members will be better able to see where the organization is headed and how it intends to get there. Moreover, the primary importance of strategic planning may lie less in the guideposts established for marking the progress of the organization than in the process itself. This process can be illustrated in the linkage between planning and values, as discussed below.

An illustration: Planning and organizational values

The increased emphasis now placed on organizational values in policing demonstrates powerfully the need to plan. Many chiefs, working with representatives of the various levels in their organizations, have developed statements of the values they wish their organizations to be guided by. Few, however, have generated plans to ensure that these values become supported by action throughout the organization. Identifying values is relatively easy compared with implementing them. To move values from paper, whether in the front of a policies

---

batons. It applies to how prisoners are treated. And it certainly has implications for the nature of the department's pursuit policy.

Likewise, a values statement that the department is concerned about the welfare of its employees serves as an organizing principle for a comprehensive wellness policy that emphasizes health care prevention programs as opposed to a minimalistic policy that requires officers periodically to pass a physical examination.

Each policy and procedure should begin with a statement of purpose, followed by a concise policy statement and then a procedures section. (The relevant value can actually appear in each policy.) The procedures become the operative or concrete expression, the how-to, of the policy. The language used in writing procedures is critical, since it will communicate the essence of the policy and related value more than any other mechanism.

During the policy review process, the department should also look closely at its hiring, complaint handling, training, promotion, accountability, and other subsystems, for each of these can support and reinforce values and policy or have the opposite effect. The promulgation of policy to personnel is through training and through the publication of orders. The execution of policy is accomplished through supervision, inspection, and accountability systems.

In the hiring process, obviously the selection criteria must reflect departmental values, but so too must all documents used to communicate with the applicant, as well as all policies and procedures relating to treatment of applicants. The method of interaction with applicants provides a model for the way the department expects officers to interact with citizens.

(*continued on next page*)

and procedures manual or on a card carried by officers, into reality requires a vision of what the organization will be like, how it will act, and how it will be perceived by the public if it implements its values at all levels.

Planning for values implementation requires examining how the values are to be inculcated throughout the organization. A demonstrable top-management commitment to the values is a crucial element of any such plan. But that obviously is not sufficient. What would the organization be like if the values of those at the top were not shared by those at the lower levels? Ongoing intraorganizational conflict would be the likely result.

Planners need to assess what specific behaviors by organizational members support or undermine the stated values. This assessment requires that the values be defined in operational terms such that an observer can know whether any particular employee action is on target or off target.

Administrators must also examine how much the organization needs to change for its actions to reflect its preferred values. The culture of the organization may need to be changed—and given the power and durability of police culture, this may be no small task. For example, in one police corruption trial the defense attorney explained that his client's acceptance of bribes, regardless of whether it was right or wrong, was the common practice thirty years before when the officer started the job and that therefore the officer should not be held accountable (see also the chapter on fostering integrity).

The difficulty of changing police culture and values is increased by the absence in most departments of lateral-entry possibilities for supervisory or managerial personnel. Police departments bring members in and socialize them to their cultures as entry-level employees, and virtually no outsiders steeped in other

---

(*continued from previous page*)
Policies on handling citizen complaints and disciplining officers for improper behavior is a second subsystem that can determine the ultimate impact of values. A department that professes to be accountable to the community must carefully review its policies and procedures for handling citizens' complaints. In addition, the chief should ensure that the personnel interacting with citizens who wish to register a complaint are not only accessible but welcoming. A procedure in which the department informs the citizen periodically of the status of the complaint, the eventual outcome, and even the reasons for the outcome is compatible with this value. Furthermore, everyone in the department and the community must understand and believe that the disciplinary system is there to be used to work, and to hold officers accountable. It must be consistent, swift, and fair. The chief must take responsibility for the behavior of all departmental personnel.

Similarly, the training process must be reviewed in its entirety. All materials and instruction must be consistent with articulated values and must be up-to-date with the policy manual.
Supervisors and managers should be trained before officers and recruits, for too often recruits are the only ones to receive formal training in new policies and procedures. The chief should not assume that managers automatically accept a new policy or understand the need for its implementation.
Supervisors must understand not only the significance of a new policy for improved street operations but also sense the consistent support for the new policy among their superiors. If this significance is not transmitted through training—or, better yet, through the participation of these supervisors in the policy development process—then chances are the policy will fall by the wayside.

The promotion system functions in much the same way as the selection process in that knowledge, abilities,

organizational cultures may enter, except occasionally as the chief executive. Few other public or private organizations are as closed to lateral entry. Even the military, through Officer Candidate School and ROTC, brings people into the organization above the entry level. A few business organizations, such as IBM, do strive to maintain only internal mobility, but IBM also consciously works to develop all of its employees and to make them throughly aware of the organization, its history, its culture, and its values. How many police departments have explicit plans to develop and take full advantage of their employees' highest talents? Moreover, how many police officers could articulate the official values of their departments? But ask employees of IBM or Federal Express or world-class hotels what their companies stand for, and they most certainly will be able to tell you.

Planning requires attention to how the behavior of individual members of the organization can be brought in line with values. Ways must be devised of defining and constructively publicizing on-target and off-target behavior. Desired behavior must be described clearly and unambiguously. Systems must be designed to suppress inappropriate behavior and provide errant employees with whatever new knowledge, skills, or positive incentives they may need to conform to the conduct implied by departmental values. Not only officers must behave appropriately; administrators and managers must, too. In a police organization, management perks and privileges may well need to be examined to determine whether they support the values of the organization.

Finally, planners must establish a timetable for implementation, designing a phased, incremental approach that is both practically and politically reasonable. Planners must also think clearly about how management will know whether the desired changes are taking place; feedback and evaluative steps must be developed.

---

and skills needed to support departmental values can be incorporated into examinations and other selection mechanisms. The chief should review the content of all promotion examinations, as this instrument helps shape the behavior of future commanders.

The system of accountability and rewards also serves to reinforce behavior that is consistent with departmental values. Accountability procedures should be designed for every unit, and standards of performance should be known to each member. All standards should be carefully crafted to be consistent with values as well as policy. And the performance evaluation system should be tied to these standards.

Policy should be developed in consultation with individuals who will be affected. If a drug dog policy is being formulated, for example, the chief should consult canine handlers,

security officers at the airport, FBI agents, and legal counsel. Early investment in a policy by those who will be expected to implement it will do much to institutionalize values in the long run.

The most important role of the chief of police as an empowering leader is to manage the culture of the department. Values are the dominant factor in creating the culture of an organization. The wise chief will recognize that members of the department who understand the organizational culture and whose work environment rewards positive values will be more productive and satisfied than those whose organization is driven by negative rules with no accompanying rationale.

Source: Phyllis P. McDonald, Director, Office of Management and Budget, New York City Transit Police Department.

The planning process

The steps used to plan for a value-based department are the same as those in other planning efforts. Good planning is composed of a series of steps, ideally followed in sequence: (1) setting planning goals; (2) preparing for planning by organizing and staffing the planning function; (3) identifying the problem; and (4) identifying and analyzing alternative solutions.[22]

Setting planning goals   Normally, the first planning question is "What needs to be accomplished?" "What is the desired future state?" The obviousness of the answer may depend on the kind of planning being done. For reactive planning, the goal is usually already given, often by the elected body. For contingency planning and operational efficiency planning, there is frequently a specific goal that has been established—often by police executives—for the desired change. Long-range or strategic planning may have a more general goal that may not be as clear at the outset as the goals at other levels of planning.

To move values from paper into reality requires a vision of what the organization will be like, how it will act, and how it will be perceived by the public if it implements its values at all levels.

A *goal* is the ultimate intended outcome of a process the department begins. An *objective* is an intermediate result that provides a benchmark against which to measure progress toward the goal. It is not unusual in planning to have multiple goals, each the end product of a series of objectives. At each level of planning, there has to be an organizational assessment of competing goals and priorities and a determination of whether goals are clear and measurable enough for the department to know when they have been achieved.

An example of contingency-planning goal setting might involve plans to deal with a hostage situation. The goals of police handling of a hostage situation may be several: contain the situation; avoid taking lives if at all possible; capture the hostage taker; and achieve a release of the hostage, unharmed. Priorities among these goals may be guided by the department's value orientation. If preserving human life is a primary value, plans for dealing with a hostage situation will probably be different from the plans made if the primary value is (as it may often be in international terrorist incidents) to engage in no negotiations whatsoever with hostage takers lest the police thereby legitimize the hostage takers.

Preparing for planning   Successful planning requires that some ongoing planning assignments be made. Someone must do the planning, although who this is may vary depending on the level or subject of planning. If the task is to write a contingency plan specifying the operational procedures to use in hostage situations, individuals who will be close to those situations should be involved. In planning for the long range, senior management must be involved regardless of the subject manner. Even in a department large enough to have a permanent planning staff, the most successful planning efforts typically use a team approach, involving all of those who will be affected by the plan.

CALEA standards provide some guidance on organizing and staffing planning units. The standards urge that "a full-time and permanent planning office is necessary for larger law enforcement agencies in order to respond to the amount and complexity of required planning and research." Larger agencies should employ "at least one full-time planning and research staff member." Furthermore, there should be "no more than one person in the chain of command between the director of the planning and research unit and the agency's chief executive officer."[23]

The ideal permanent planning staff should be a mixture of sworn and civilian employees. Sworn officers provide the perspective of street experience, whereas civilians often contribute training in research methods and planning techniques. For a sworn officer, a planning assignment should be viewed as a vehicle for advancement, not a symbol of a stalled career. By working in the planning function, officers will see the organization from very different vantage points and come to understand better not only the interrelationships of units within the department but also the broader community and governmental context in which the department operates.

Identifying the problem   The first step in beginning to identify problems (defined in this case as the discrepancy between where the department is and where it wants to be, based on its stated values) is to assess the present situation. Describing the current state of affairs may involve scanning the environment, performing research, and otherwise gathering information. Typically, data should come from sources both inside and outside the department.

For a sworn officer, a planning assignment should be viewed as a vehicle for advancement, not a symbol of a stalled career.

Another aspect of describing the current situation is estimating what is politically acceptable. Considering political acceptability at an early stage can save much time and grief later.

In assessing the current situation, planners must also consider (among other things) the strengths and weaknesses of the organization, what it does well, what it does poorly, its positive aspects, and its negative aspects. The best plan for Department A may be worthless for Department B, given the two departments' widely varying in-house capacities and external environmental conditions.

Careful thought at the outset about what information sources are available is also a good idea: it can prevent much duplication of work already done elsewhere. Planning does not occur and planners do not exist in a vacuum. Reading about how similar planning problems have been addressed elsewhere and talking with someone who has already dealt with a similar situation are invaluable. Experienced fellow police executives can be located through many organizations, including the National Association of Police Planners, Association of Police Planning and Research Officers, Police Management Association, Police Executive Research Forum, International Association of Chiefs of Police, National Organization of Black Law Enforcement Executives, National Sheriffs' Association, Criminal Justice Statistics Association, National Institute of Justice, National Criminal Justice Reference Service, Bureau of Justice Assistance, Bureau of Justice Statistics, and ICMA (see the chapter on external resources).

After assessing the current situation, the planner must engage in forecasting—projecting current trends into the future and attempting to anticipate what problems might arise that would impede implementation of the plan. Although certain factors are predictable, such as major construction projects with traffic interruptions that may split beats, others are not easily predicted, and the planner must simply make a best guess about the future. Are there trends that might cause an increase in this type of problem? Are there social changes that might affect crime and criminal behavior? Is the economy getting better or worse? Are drugs causing problem behavior to increase? Is alcohol abuse rising?

The planning forecast also needs to assess the possible effect of technology. For example, technology has made it more likely that a bank robbery will be detected in progress, by police and by private security. Consequently, it is more likely that a robber will be trapped in the bank and will take hostages. Contingency plans have to be carefully constructed to deal with such a situation and to try to avoid it. The growth of private security forces may also affect plans for handling future bank robberies because the training and priorities of private security forces may differ from those of the police.

Identifying the problem entails not only comparing the status quo with departmental goals but also comparing present conditions with the future conditions that are anticipated if the department makes no particular effort to alter current trends. This comparison produces questions as to whether the problem is worth doing anything about and whether the department can take action that may have an effect on the problem. In other words: Why should we do anything? What are the consequences of continuing to "muddle through"? Can we demonstrate to our public why it is worth committing resources to address this problem?

Identifying and analyzing alternative solutions Once a problem is identified, alternative courses of action must be laid out for analysis. The planner should consider the extent to which the different courses of action are likely to produce the desired goal, the assumptions underlying each course of action, and the criteria for judging the strength of each course of action.[24] In other words, once the goals are set, different ways of reaching them—and the critical characteristics of each way—must be analyzed and assessed. For example, in contingency planning for response to a hostage situation, if a goal of having the team on-site in forty-five minutes is established, several options need to be considered: Perhaps team members should be required to live inside the city. Perhaps new standards need to be set for the number of team members who are on duty or on on-call status. Perhaps more officers need to be trained to respond to hostage crises. Perhaps schedules need to be revised so that team members' normal work tasks are covered if they are activated while on duty.

Three basic approaches to identifying alternatives are reviewing, searching, and designing.[25] In *reviewing*, the planner checks to see whether similar problems have been confronted in the organization before, and if so, what alternatives were considered and chosen. Because most police departments are notoriously deficient in documenting the organizational strategies and tactics used to address most police work, reviewing will normally depend on haphazard conversations with experienced department members. *Searching* involves

Metapol Metapol is a nationwide on-line telecommunications network that allows police executives and educators to communicate about operational, administrative, legislative, and related issues facing police agencies.

Using a personal computer and modem, Metapol users can query all other users, send private messages (messages that no one except the addressee can access), or participate in focused electronic "conferences."

Metapol participants include chiefs of police, police administrators, professors of police studies, federal law enforcement executives, PERF national and regional staff, and others. For further information about this information network, contact the Police Executive Research Forum, 2300 M Street N.W. (Suite 910), Washington, DC 20037, (202) 466–7820.

scanning the practices of other departments to locate alternatives that have been tried elsewhere. The planner can do this by searching published accounts, making mail and telephone inquiries, and using electronic bulletin board systems such as Metapol (see accompanying sidebar). *Designing* involves undertaking research and development, stimulating individual creativity and inventiveness, and engaging in brainstorming, all aimed at inventing new alternatives.

Generally, before attempting to design brand-new alternatives, planners look for alternatives first within their own organizations and then within other organizations. It is usually important, however, that planners identify and consider a wide variety of alternatives. The common tendency—mainly because of workload pressures—is to adopt the first reasonable alternative, but planners should resist doing that because it preempts the possibility that innovative and possibly more effective alternatives may emerge.

After identifying a range of alternatives, planners must estimate their consequences in order to make a rational choice among them. Four methods of estimating consequences are (1) informal estimation, (2) formal estimation, (3) models or simulations, and (4) limited implementation.[26] *Informal estimation* is completely subjective; the planner relies on the judgments of experts, experienced observers, or whoever else has an opinion to offer. In *formal estimation*, the planner attempts to be less subjective by making his or her assumptions and theories explicit, often within such processes as scenario writing and brainstorming. By using *models or simulations*, the planner reduces subjectivity even further by employing mathematical or mechanical devices patterned after real phenomena, such as patrol allocation models that can estimate the effects on response time of different staffing levels. Finally, with *limited implementation*, the planner can estimate the effects of alternatives through pilot tests and field experiments in which the alternatives are actually put into place, with careful monitoring, on a limited basis.

Once the "best" alternative has been identified, the planning process has, strictly speaking, been completed. However, successful organizational performance requires that the succeeding stage—implementation—receive every bit as much attention as that given to goal setting, problem identification, and the analysis of alternatives. Furthermore, as part of implementation, it is imperative that the organization monitor and evaluate plans and programs, both to keep them on track and to learn whether the alternatives selected are in fact having the desired effects (see the chapters on performance measurement and crime prevention).

Implementation

During the early part of World War I, Will Rogers told a story that began with an account of the terrible losses America was suffering at the hands of German submarines. The problem, he said, had prompted a host of armchair generals to suggest countermeasures, and Rogers himself had even gotten into the act. He had sent a letter to Washington advising the government to heat up the ocean to 110 degrees, which would force the submarines to surface and become vulnerable to attack. Someone from the War Department had responded, thanking Mr. Rogers for the advice but inquiring just how he proposed to get the ocean that hot. "Don't ask me," Rogers said he had retorted. "That's implementation. I'm in policy."

Having conducted research and developed plans, managers frequently underestimate the importance of the next stage: transforming plans into practice. Then, when the new policy or program is instituted and nothing happens, they tend to attribute the failure to bad ideas or poor planning. Sometimes, the cause is in fact bad ideas or poor planning. There is considerable evidence, however,

Setting priorities   Any police manager has multiple items on his or her agenda—and a general idea of the importance or priority of each one. To accomplish change most effectively, however, the manager frequently must forgo rational priority setting in favor of such strategic considerations as the local political climate, community support for the police, and timing.

A new chief in town, for example, may decide that he or she wants to introduce one-officer cars, stricter shooting policies, and affirmative action hiring. The rational planner would consider the appropriate order for dealing with those issues.

If deadly force comes first, it could polarize the community (since many local citizens approve of shooting suspects of minor crimes) and appear to be an attack on the police department.

The one-officer car reform can be justified by efficiency, but opponents can dramatize it as disdain for officer safety.

The affirmative action issue, although also potentially polarizing, may be the best issue to start with, especially if there are few minorities and women on the force and if there is local political support for having a more representative police department. This community support makes such a reform effort harder for potential opponents—such as the police union—to attack.

If a controversial shooting occurs while the chief is making these plans, however, it may be time to revise the schedule again.

Source: Lawrence W. Sherman, President, Crime Control Institute, Washington, D.C.; and Anthony V. Bouza, former Chief of Police, Minneapolis, Minnesota.

---

that the quality of *implementation* efforts may determine whether a plan succeeds or fails. Case studies indicate that when programs and other initiatives (values statements, new strategies, and so forth) are poorly implemented, they have little chance of becoming institutionalized regardless of their merit.

Administrators who have seen their planners do careful research and then analyze the situation, identify alternatives, and choose the optimal solution often *assume* that the plan will be implemented exactly as intended. (In part this assumption may be based on the paramilitary nature of police organizations and the administrator's simplistic understanding of how—even in the military— orders compare with ensuing operations.) Experience shows, however, that regardless of the official authority of superiors to mandate conduct by subordinates, "it is excruciatingly hard to implement [plans] in a way that pleases anyone at all, including the supposed beneficiaries or clients."[27] Rather, the process of implementation nearly always defines and reshapes a program (hence the need for plans to be flexible).[28]

Police administrators need to be aware that any new policy, strategy, or program affects at least some, if not all, members of the department. Employees may have to work harder, give up some of their discretion or authority, and adopt new or abandon old work methods. For some, power and status in the department may be reduced; for others, it may be enhanced. Members of the department who are affected by a new initiative can be expected to take an interest in its implementation. If these individuals are directly responsible for implementation, they can be expected to try to influence it so as to maximize the benefits and minimize the costs *for them*.

In short, organizational politics and individual self-interest influence the implementation of virtually any new policy, strategy, or program.[29] As indicated above,

Thoughts on "police policy"   There is a tendency for the uninitiated to equate having no *written* policy with simply having "no policy" on a given subject.

Eventually, however, they realize (sometimes through an adverse court decision) that *every practice* of the department about which management knows or should have known constitutes "policy," whether or not it is written, encouraged, discouraged, or simply ignored. (This last condition the courts describe as a policy of "deliberate indifference.")

Where there is no written policy or other guidance, the de facto policy is "let the officers play this one by ear." This, of course, readily lends itself to second-guessing by management in the light of knowledge acquired later. Another tendency is to fail to appreciate that some of the written policy affecting the police service is promulgated by elected policy makers—legislators and chief executives. This policy is embodied in federal and state constitutions and statutes and local charters and ordinances (as interpreted by courts), executive orders, rules and regulations of administrative agencies and local personnel or civil service commissions, labor contract provisions affecting management rights, and so on.

Thus, in any given situation, the question is not "Do we have a policy?" Rather, the question is "Have we given our people policy *direction* in this matter?"

Source: Daniel Guido, Commissioner, Suffolk County, New York, Police Department.

police administrators have discovered that it is critically important to carefully consider the environment and values—articulated and unarticulated—of the organization in which a new initiative will be implemented. The implementation process has been described as a system of pressures and counterpressures akin to political maneuvering in which constant negotiating goes on, with managers exercising considerable persuasion in their attempt to obtain desired results.[30] Implementation then becomes a very dynamic process involving a complicated series of regulations, compromises, and trade-offs.

This section discusses the implementation process; provides a comparative illustration; and emphasizes the need for feedback.

The implementation process

In one sense, implementation simply requires good, solid management. Once a new policy or program has been designed, attention must be directed toward (1) providing necessary resources (including money, personnel, and authority); (2) providing direction so that employees know what to do and why; and (3) providing control to ensure that directions are followed. In an organization that is poorly managed, however, even these obvious prerequisites for successful implementation may be neglected. As suggested earlier, many police chiefs are guilty of issuing general orders by posting them on a bulletin board or handing each employee a copy and then assuming that the orders are both understood and followed.

But because a new policy or program usually requires some kind of *change* in employee behavior, its successful implementation may require special attention and extra effort over and above management's ordinary concerns. One approach is to implement changes in small pieces, with decentralized decision making and implementation. According to one observer, "When well-managed major organizations make significant changes in strategy, the approaches they

The best-laid plans   Rational planning works well in what theorists call a "closed system," one into which outside events do not intrude. But that is not how police departments or police politics work. Despite the best-laid plans, critical incidents crop up at unexpected moments.

Even the most proactice police executive is forced by events to be reactive. Long-term organizational changes can proceed through committee and task force consultation, arbitration, and court cases. But they can be pushed off center stage at a moment's notice by a critical event in another area. When that happens, it can be a serious mistake to ignore the new event in favor of the long-term plan. In fact, reacting to the new event can be a brilliant counterstroke.

A flexible manager has multiple plans for implementation when different opportunities arise. An unexpected critical event can provide the right setting for acting on a priority that, for strategic reasons, has been kept on the back burner.

Source: Lawrence W. Sherman, President, Crime Control Institute, Washington, D.C.; and Anthony V. Bouza, former Chief of Police, Minneapolis, Minnesota.

---

use frequently bear little resemblance to the rational analytical systems so often described in the formal literature."[31] In well-managed major organizations, top executives often implement change by taking a series of small steps, each one building on its predecessors, until eventually the changes extend throughout an entire system within the organization. This approach may help smooth the process of implementation, although coordinating the different aspects of the change and ensuring that the entire organization is heading toward the same goal may be more difficult.

Another approach is to use the project management method of implementation. The Baltimore County police department, which has used the project management method for several years, includes the following steps in implementation:

Designation of a project manager responsible for implementation

Designation of a project team to work with the project manager

Preparation of an implementation plan with required activities and timetable

Formal notification about the project to all members of the department

Formal monitoring of the project and reporting to executive staff

Continued oversight until the project is either disbanded or fully institutionalized.[32]

This approach has the advantages of encouraging wide participation in implementation, fixing responsbility, and ensuring more than the momentary attention that implementation of new programs often receives.

A comparative illustration of implementation

This subsection illustrates the elements of sound implementation by comparing the introduction of two widely discussed innovations: team policing and the more recent community-oriented or problem-oriented policing.[33] Although these concepts are similar in overall objective, they differ sharply in the ways they have been integrated into departments. Both implementation efforts hold lessons relevant to all police department attempts to transfer good ideas from paper to operation.

Experimentation with team policing had its heyday in the 1970s. In cities across the country, police administrators sensed that traditional forms of policing were not responsive to increasing levels of crime. Technological advances in policing, including computer-aided dispatching, 9–1–1 systems, and rapid response to emergency calls, in concert with more comprehensive recruitment and training programs, had been major advances, but they had failed to provide the community with what it considered substantially better policing. Terms such as "productivity," "workload analysis," and "solvability factors" had become the buzzwords of the emerging management-oriented police administrator. But against this backdrop of internally perceived productivity, the community was still not satisfied.

Thus, the implementation of team policing was partly a response to a level of community dissatisfaction with managerial programs that had had little perceptible effect on crime. Team policing was visionary with respect to its dependence on community involvement and, in many ways, it emerged as an aberration in a predominantly management-oriented world. In Boston, the concept of team policing found its way into the city's public housing projects, which had been poorly and ineffectively policed for years. The police department revitalized and expanded an old concept: take a group of officers and permanently assign them to a neighborhood. Further, let these officers have steady schedules, the same supervisors, offices in the targeted area, and, most important, responsibility for the overall crime problem in the area. One of the most controversial aspects of the program, but also one most appealing to the officers, was that team officers were allowed to follow up and investigate crimes that took place in their jurisdiction. Officers could work in plain clothes or in uniform—it was up to their supervisors to decide which. The commanding officer of each housing development could allocate resources as necessary and would be held accountable for everything that happened there. The results were exactly what was hoped for: the community was delighted because it felt that, for the first time, it was getting professional police services; and the police assigned to the development were highly motivated and enthusiastic because they had more control over what they did and how they did it.

Given the high marks that team policing received from residents and street officers alike, not in Boston only, but generally, it may seem surprising that it encountered enormous resistance from senior police management. Much of this can be attributed to what George Kelling has described as a lack of documented successes and failures of team policing implementation. As he notes:

> Those who experimented with team policing were not aware that elements of team policing were simply incompatible with preventive patrol and rapid response to calls for service. As a result, implementation of team policing followed a discouraging pattern: it would be implemented, officers and citizens would like it, it would have an initial impact on crime, and then business as usual would overwhelm it.[34]

It is not difficult to see why team policing might have been difficult to implement. Most police organizations were captive to what was then a new professional model according to which the measures of increased productivity were more calls taken, shorter response time, less time on each call for service, and decreased reported crime. Team policing worked *against* these objectives. Team policing encouraged greater community interaction to solve crime, less emphasis on response time, more emphasis on solving each problem (this was an important precursor of problem-oriented policing), and substantial involvement in nontraditional policing methods. Quite often this translated into a higher degree of interaction with the community, which, in turn, led to a higher degree of confidence in the police and therefore more reporting of crimes by citizens. Higher

Figure 12–1 Key aspects of the strategies for implementing team policing vs. community-oriented policing.

Characteristic	Team policing	Community-oriented policing
Planning and training	Limited to start-up phases	Significant at all stages
Role of chief	Critical at initial stage	Involved at all stages
Statement of values	Implicit	Explicit
Involvement of middle managers	Unclear and undefined	Substantial—considerable ownership
Involvement of patrol division	Tangential	Total
Involvement of investigative division	Non-existent	Gradual
Measurement tools	Traditional	More responsive and creative

reported crime in team policing areas, with substantially longer time spent on each call, was in direct conflict with management-ordered goals. It was not surprising that although chief executives liked the overall reaction they received from community members about team policing, senior and middle managers were less than enthusiastic about, if not downright hostile to, team policing. Team policing ultimately lessened senior management's control and affected the attainment of quantitative goals for which, ironically, chief executives still held managers accountable.

As noted earlier, community-oriented policing has much in common with team policing, yet its implementation has been much more successful. Team policing was threatening to patrol and investigative divisions as well as to senior administrators. It represented decentralization and therefore a loss of control by certain administrators and other interested parties. Community-oriented policing, however, was not designed as a separate, decentralized program. Rather, in most communities, it is a patrol philosophy and strategy that pervades all patrol units. Therefore it does not suffer from the perception that team policing suffered from: that resources—including officers viewed by many as the "cream of the crop"—were being siphoned off from patrol. Further, because *all* of patrol is intended to be involved in community-oriented policing, there is substantial reason for the department to modify traditional measurements of outcome to meet the objectives of community-oriented policing (see the chapter on performance measurement).

Figure 12–1 illustrates some of the differences in the implementation of these two approaches.

Planning and training   With team policing, the significant attention focused on designing strategies and training officers was often confined to the *initial* stages. Community-oriented policing, in contrast, usually builds in *feedback loops* so that officers in the field who are experiencing problems can talk with planners and trainers, who, in turn, can keep in touch with the initiative as it takes shape in the field. The feedback loop is critical to the success of a program.

Role of the chief   Very often in policing, the chief is instrumental in helping to provide the necessary resources and direction to get a program off the ground. But the chief acting alone is not enough. When team policing experienced difficulties at the field level, the chief often was unable to protect the program from gradual erosion at the hands of senior commanders. Because community-oriented policing involves not only the chief but also senior and middle-level managers in planning, training, and implementation, it is not perceived solely as "the chief's plan."

There is no question that, in most departments, the public statements of a chief coupled with *actual resources he or she commits* to a program determine whether the chief is "serious about this one" or whether the program is simply "window dressing" to meet today's priorities. For programs to succeed, incremental support and actual resources must be built in at all points of the implementation process (such as the key steps used by the Baltimore County police department, noted above). In addition, because traditionalists will ignore, test, and challenge new programs, immediate responses by the department's chief executive at crucial junctures are critical in determining whether the program succeeds or fails.

Values By the end of the 1980s, law enforcement leaders attempting to implement community- and problem-oriented policing had begun to recognize the importance of formally stating what they stood for: the underlying philosophies and values of their departments. They had also begun to recognize that the effort to implement community policing involves more than just stating the department's values—it involves the monumental task of changing the basic culture of the organization.[35]

The experiment with team policing taught a great lesson. Perhaps the greatest challenge team policing faced was that the values implicit in it conflicted with the traditional orientation of the rest of the department. It was as though police administrators thought they could graft team policing onto the larger department without fundamentally shifting the overall philosophy of the organization. Like an organ transplant that does not take, team policing was rejected by a host for which it was ill-suited. Team policing taught that if police executives are to institutionalize significantly different strategies of policing, they need to modify an organization's entire way of thinking—the organization's fundamental culture.

Police executives now understand that changing the department's way of thinking is an incremental process that will take years. According to Malcolm Sparrow, one implements change by creating both "directed imbalance" and "experimental imbalance." Directed imbalance is achieved by changes made before a planned change in the organization:

Examples of such directed imbalance would be the movement of the most talented and promising personnel into newly defined jobs; making it clear that the route to promotion lies within such jobs; disbanding those squads that embody and add weight to the traditional values; recategorizing the crime statistics according to their effect on the community.[36]

Experimental imbalance refers to tolerating error and actually encouraging officers to experiment with innovative strategies—to be responsible risk-takers.[37] A chief or other senior manager who encourages subordinates to think for themselves and then cuts them off at the knees for making well-intentioned decisions or recommendations that stray from the "party line" plays a cruel joke on his or her personnel.

Involvement of middle managers If team policing had a major structural flaw, it was that mid-level management had no clearly understood role—and for that reason lacked "ownership" of the concept. As community-oriented policing continues to evolve and becomes more widespread, the task for administrators will be to carve out roles for mid-level and senior managers; otherwise, community-oriented policing might suffer the same fate as team policing.

Timing Any administrator who implements new programs faces intangible factors that have major consequences for implementation. Most significant is timing in relation to the internal and external climates for implementation. Perhaps team policing suffered because it was simply ahead of its time. In the long run, it did not have either the community support or the organizational support that were necessary to sustain it. Maybe better "marketing" could have created a demand that would have overcome the powerful pockets of opposition. Historians can debate this point. A second example of a good idea implemented at the wrong time occurred in the 1970s when the new police commissioner in Boston sought to reform the department. His plans were quickly sidetracked when court-ordered school busing was implemented, draining the department's resources.

It is not enough to have a good idea and a textbook plan.

Thus, it is not enough to have a good idea and a textbook plan—it is also critical to understand the history of the organization, the local government, and the community; the present internal and external environments; and the specific ways in which the new program or strategy fits with competing, resource-hungry priorities in both the department and the larger community. In addition, sometimes it takes people and organizations a long time to see the wisdom of innovative strategies and programs. In the case of team policing, many departments *at the time* simply did not give sufficient priority to the values underlying the strategy. But the passing of time—and all that that implies about changing personnel, climates, attitudes, and values—can make an idea more acceptable. This has been true, for example, in the case of implementing department policies dealing with such matters as domestic and

---

Seizing opportunities for reform   To accomplish organizational reform, the police manager needs a combination of will and skill. The basic recommendations that follow can help managers seize opportunities for change in their departments.

Set flexible priorities. Police managers should plan their reform agendas but be prepared to change plans quickly. Effective managers always juggle their plans, putting some on hold while pursuing others. Priorities may vary with the manager's personal interests, the recent political history of the department, or the kind of pressures being brought on the department. They may also vary with issues largely unrelated to the police, such as a municipal election. There are reform agendas that will improve police performance, agendas that will heal community conflicts, and agendas that will advance personal careers. These are not always the same.

In any given situation there are issues that police managers feel are most important to address; there are also issues they can most effectively address in the current context. Police managers may find that their ideal goals are strategically impossible; the effective manager will set difficult but potentially achievable priorities. This is not to advocate cowardice in setting priorities; it is merely to counsel against folly.

Assemble resources. In order to effect reform, the police manager should accumulate political and other resources to strengthen his or her credibility and persuasiveness. It is important to have as many allies as possible. How these resources are accumulated, and which ones are chosen, depend very much on the personal style of the players in question. Police chiefs, for example, often choose whether to build support in the community, in the department, or

racially motivated violence, deadly force, and pursuit driving. It may also be true of community-oriented policing. The 1980s saw a stronger ground swell of support from the community for more responsive policing, and many police organizations began to redefine their missions and values to accommodate the expectations of the community.

Monitoring and evaluation

The importance of feedback for implementation and for planning, noted above, cannot be overstated. Feedback is provided through *monitoring*, which involves observation of the activities, outputs, and outcomes of a project and the resources it utilizes. The purposes of monitoring are to determine (1) whether the new policy or program is implemented as intended and (2) whether the desired results are achieved.

Although some minor organizational changes may require only routine and informal monitoring, major new programs typically require formal monitoring systems. For example, when the Baltimore County police department implemented its Citizen-Oriented Police Enforcement (COPE) program in 1982, it also instituted a system of data collection and reports so that the project management team and command staff would know how COPE officers were using their time, what kinds of problems the COPE units were tackling, and whether fear of crime decreased in targeted neighborhoods.[38] This monitoring system was instrumental in revealing the shortcomings of COPE in its initial stages; awareness of the shortcomings helped its managers evolve toward a problem-oriented style of policing.[39]

Although monitoring can provide an abundance of useful information, it cannot answer one key question: what effects, if any, were *caused* by the new policy

---

with local elected officials. Because community coalitions shift, however, it is important to seek a broad base of support—from citizen leaders, media, prosecutors, state legislators, and others.

Seize opportunities. With priorities set and resources in line, a police manager should be ready for a wide range of opportunities for change. These opportunities can be defined as events that can throw the spotlight on police policy and provide a "case in point" justification for a reform proposal.

Ironically, opportunities often come disguised as crises, and managers must resist the instinctive impulse to think first of damage control. Managers interested in reform will embrace crises and make the most of them. Several generic kinds of events provide opportunities to capitalize on crises to achieve reform.

Dramatic crimes, for example, can provide an opportunity for making needed improvements in departmental procedures. In one department the death of an officer in a traffic stop led to the development of a training course on officer survival skills. Other crimes have been used to bolster requests for additional police officers and financial resources.

Detected and publicized police misconduct cases are similar. If several officers are caught stealing drugs for their own use from people they arrest, the chief may follow up by instituting a drug testing program that he or she had suspected was warranted. A case of lockup brutality may allow the chief to implement a program of undercover jail inspections. Deadly force incidents may provide a reason for revising departmental firearms policies. A dramatic death during a high-speed chase may provide an opening for a

(continued on next page)

(*continued from previous page*)
chief who supports better control of
these chases.

Local or nationwide studies of a police
department or policing in general can
provide support for the chief's reform
agenda. Even if a report is critical, the
chief may be able to use its
conclusions for the benefit of the
department.

Budget crises and fiscal restraints—
even layoffs—provide open windows
for questioning traditional practices and
making hard choices. As a matter of
fiscal necessity, for example, many
departments have reordered their
priorities, adopted various forms of call
screening, and started to refer some
kinds of calls to nonpolice
organizations. For a chief who has long
argued that the police cannot do
everything, dramatic news about city
tax shortfalls can set the stage for
posing either-or choices.

Negotiating a union contract may allow
management to review and revise
unfavorable terms of past agreements.

Create opportunities. No matter how
skillfully a police manager seizes
opportunities, major items on the
reform agenda may still be left
unaddressed. The times may be so
sensitive or so complex that no
naturally occurring event opens a
window for them. In these possibly rare
cases, some police reformers have
opened their own windows by initiating
publicity concerning police problems.
At least four major methods of
highlighting simmering problems can
be identified. Each has its own
dangers, of course, and should be
undertaken only after consultation with
the local government manager or
mayor.

In highly publicized situations, police at
various ranks have tried to create
public debate through leaks or whistle

or program? Ultimately, police administrators need to be able to answer such a question if they are serious about providing the best possible police service with the limited resources available.

Determining whether a particular program really caused its intended effects requires the use of *evaluation research*, discussed above in connection with research issues. Data must be collected and analyzed in such a way that police administrators know whether program outputs and outcomes can be attributed to the program itself rather than to chance or extraneous causes. In other words, careful research—preferably experimental—is needed. The results of such evaluation research provide feedback for implementation and also for planning, in the form of better knowledge on which to base future programs and decisions.

Conclusion

This discussion of evaluation research brings the chapter full circle, back to its beginning. Initial research, planning, implementation, monitoring, and evaluation research are the phases of the continuous evolution of an organization. These processes never really end, any more than the larger process of police administration ends. Rather, researching, planning, implementing, monitoring, and evaluating are constantly taking place within police organizations. Each phase interacts with all the others, leading to continued adjustments and refinements. Done well, these processes contribute substantially to improved police service and police ability to adapt to changing conditions. In today's fast-changing world, no police department can afford to shortchange these crucial components of police administration.

blowing, with attendant press coverage. More quietly, some top executives have sought to freshen their agencies by airing out some of their own dirty laundry in order to provoke the press into demanding reforms sought by the executives themselves. Another way to call attention to departmental problems is to launch an internal investigation or commission a study. Clear proof of misconduct provides a firm excuse for radical reforms, and investigations are often the best way to produce that proof. Studies can be used to make people remember an old problem or to demonstrate the existence of a new one.

Managers also have created opportunities for change by filing a lawsuit or appealing an administrative ruling. No matter how the courts eventually rule, the suit can serve to make a convincing argument to the general public.

Follow through. In all these seized and nurtured opportunities, reform depends on more than just a single press conference. Announcing a planned change or signing an executive order is not usually enough to make change happen. Without a concerted follow-up effort, many or most reforms may die. Perhaps the most vulnerable are those that involve routine police activity that is rarely reviewed. And it is in these areas that the chief needs to concentrate the most effort to integrate reforms into the department.

Source: Lawrence W. Sherman, President, Crime Control Institute, Washington, D.C.; and Anthony V. Bouza, former Chief of Police, Minneapolis, Minnesota.

1 Commission on Accreditation for Law Enforcement Agencies, *Standards for Law Enforcement Agencies* (Fairfax, VA: Commission on Accreditation for Law Enforcement Agencies, 1987), 14-1.

2 James K. Stewart, "Research and the Police Administrator: Working Smarter, Not Harder," in *Police Leadership in America: Crisis and Opportunity*, ed. William A. Geller (New York: Praeger, 1985), 371–82; and Jack R. Greene, Tim S. Bynum, and Gary W. Cordner, "Planning and the Play of Power: Resource Acquisition among Criminal Justice Agencies," *Journal of Criminal Justice* 14, no. 6 (1986): 529–44.

3 For a good primer on various research methods of value to police, see John E. Eck, *Using Research: A Primer for Law Enforcement Managers* (Washington, DC: Police Executive Research Forum, 1984).

4 Peter W. Greenwood and Joan Petersilia, *Summary and Policy Implications*, vol. 1 of *The Criminal Investigation Process* (Santa Monica, CA: Rand Corporation, 1975); and William Spelman and Dale K. Brown, *Calling the Police: Citizen Reporting of Serious Crime* (Washington, DC: Police Executive Research Forum, 1981).

5 James Q. Wilson, "Police Research and Experimentation," in *Progress in Policing: Essays on Change*, ed. Richard A. Staufenberger (Cambridge, MA: Ballinger, 1980), 129–52.

6 George L. Kelling, Tony Pate, Duane Dieckman, and Charles E. Brown, *The Kansas City Preventive Patrol Experiment: A Summary Report* (Washington, DC: Police Foundation, 1974); John E. Boydstun, *San Diego Field Interrogation: Final Report* (Washington, DC: Police Foundation, 1975); and Lawrence W. Sherman and Richard A. Berk, *Minneapolis Domestic Violence Experiment* (Washington, DC: Police Foundation, 1984).

7 Eck, *Using Research*.

8 Thomas D. Cook and Donald T. Campbell, *Quasi-Experimentation: Design and Analysis Issues for Field Settings* (Chicago: Rand-McNally, 1979).

9 Police Foundation, *The Newark Foot Patrol Experiment* (Washington, DC: Police Foundation, 1981).

10 See, for example, Integrated Criminal Apprehension Program, *Review of Patrol Operations Analysis: Selected Readings from ICAP Cities* (Washington, DC: U.S. Department of Justice, 1978); and Margaret J. Levine and J. Thomas McEwen, *Patrol Deployment* (Washington, DC: National Institute of Justice, 1985).

11 John E. Eck, *Managing Case Assignments: The Burglary Investigation Decision Model Replication* (Washington, DC: Police Executive Research Forum, 1979).

12 Mark H. Moore, Robert C. Trojanowicz, and George L. Kelling, *Crime and Policing*, Perspectives on Policing (Washington, DC: National Institute of Justice, June 1988); and Gary W. Cordner and Donna C. Hale, *What Works in Policing?* (Cincinnati: Anderson, 1991).

13 Milton D. Hakel, Melvin Sarcher, Michael Beer, and Joseph L. Moses, *Making It Happen: Designing Research with Implementation in Mind* (Beverly Hills, CA: Sage, 1982).

14 Police Foundation, *The Newark Foot Patrol Experiment*; see also James Q. Wilson and George L. Kelling, "The Police and Neighborhood Safety:

Broken Windows," *The Atlantic Monthly* (March 1982): 29–38; and James Q. Wilson and George L. Kelling, "Making Neighborhoods Safe," *The Atlantic Monthly* (February 1989): 46–52.

15 Gary W. Cordner, "Police Research and Police Policy: Some Propositions about the Production and Use of Knowledge," in *Police Leadership in America*, ed. Geller, 383–96.

16 National Advisory Commission on Criminal Justice Standards and Goals, *Police* (Washington, DC: U.S. Government Printing Office, 1973), 123.

17 Commission on Accreditation for Law Enforcement Agencies, *Standards for Law Enforcement Agencies*, 14-1, 14-2.

18 O. W. Wilson, *Police Planning*, 2d ed. (Springfield, IL: Charles C. Thomas, 1971), 3.

19 Tom Peters and Nancy Austin, *A Passion for Excellence* (New York: Warner Books, 1985), 517, 533.

20 O. W. Wilson and Roy Clinton McClaren, *Police Administration*, 3d ed. (New York: McGraw Hill, 1972), 151–52.

21 Peters and Austin, *A Passion for Excellence*, 516.

22 Law Enforcement Assistance Administration, *Course in Criminal Justice Planning* (Washington, DC: U.S. Government Printing Office, 1982), IG 2-10; see also Robert Cushman, *Criminal Justice Planning for Local Governments* (Washington, DC: Law Enforcement Assistance Administration, 1980); and John K. Hudzik and Gary W. Cordner, *Planning in Criminal Justice Organizations and Systems* (New York: Macmillan, 1983).

23 Commission on Accreditation for Law Enforcement Agencies, *Standards for Law Enforcement Agencies*, 14-1.

24 Law Enforcement Assistance Administration, *Course in Criminal Justice Planning*, IG 2-13.

25 Hudzik and Cordner, *Planning in Criminal Justice Organizations and Systems*, 184–89.

26 Ibid., 189–95.

27 Eugene Bardach, *The Implementation Game: What Happens after a Bill Becomes Law* (Cambridge: MIT Press, 1977), 3.

28 Charles E. Lindblom, *The Policy-Making Process*, 2d ed. (Englewood Cliffs, NJ: Prentice-Hall, 1980).

29 Aaron Wildavsky and Jeffrey L. Pressman,

Implementation (Berkeley: University of California Press, 1973).

30 Bardach, *The Implementation Game*.

31 James Brian Quinn, "Formulating Strategy One Step at a Time," *Journal of Business Strategy* 1, no. 3 (Winter 1981):42.

32 Baltimore County Police Department, "Project Management Case History," mimeographed, n.d.

33 As noted elsewhere in this volume, there is considerable discussion in the police policy community over the proper definitions and strategic implications of such concepts as problem- and community-oriented policing. There are genuine differences between the two concepts, but for the purposes of this chapter, the differences will be glossed over. For convenience, we will use the term *community-oriented policing* and draw primarily on the experiences of departments that have used that term to describe their innovations. The implementation strategies used by the proponents of problem-oriented policing may well be different in some important ways.

34 George L. Kelling, *Police and Communities: The Quiet Revolution*, Perspectives on Policing series (Washington, DC: National Institute of Justice, June 1988), 5.

35 Malcolm Sparrow, *Implementing Community Policing*, Perspectives on Policing series (Washington, DC: National Institute of Justice, November 1988), 2, 3.

36 Ibid., 3.

37 Tolerance for risk-taking and failure was encouraged by a number of management guides in the 1980s. See, for example, Thomas J. Peters and Robert H. Waterman, Jr., *In Search of Excellence: Lessons from America's Best-Run Companies* (New York: Harper & Row, 1982).

38 Richard K. Higdon and Philip G. Huber, *How to Fight Fear: The COPE Program Package* (Washington, DC: Police Executive Research Forum, 1986).

39 Gary W. Cordner, "A Problem-Oriented Approach to Community-Oriented Policing," in *Community Policing: Rhetoric or Reality*, ed. Jack R. Greene and Stephen D. Mastrofski (New York: Praeger, 1988), 135–52.

Personnel and agency performance measurement

An occupation that aspires to a high degree of professionalism and accountability, as contemporary policing does, must have a means of defining, measuring, and verifying its performance according to acceptable scientific standards. Performance measurement is in fact essential in contemporary police policy making and administration. And the capacity of U.S. police to use scientific methods to assess performance has never been greater. Those who have striven so hard to achieve this may be proud of the increasing sophistication of performance measurement—but a sense of humility about our capacity to measure what police employees and organizations accomplish is still necessary. Thus, this chapter devotes as much space to questioning the state of the art as to celebrating it.

Indeed, it is important to view performance measurement as both imperfect and imperfectible. This is so not only because scientific methods are imperfect ways of obtaining knowledge, but also because the most difficult questions about performance simply cannot be answered scientifically. They involve questions of value: what *ought* the police try to accomplish, and what limits *ought* to be placed on the means they employ?

Police managers need not be pessimistic about conducting useful performance measurement, but they should be skeptical of the ten-easy-steps, one-size-fits-all, and never-fail approaches sometimes offered by self-proclaimed experts in the field. Consequently, this chapter for the most part avoids a "how-to" or "cookbook" approach. Rather, it identifies issues that should be addressed by those who would measure performance, and it suggests some pitfalls and opportunities they will meet in pursuing this objective.

Definitions and background

In simple terms, performance measurement is the use of scientific methods of observation and assessment to learn how well something or someone is doing something desired—or is avoiding doing something not desired. This chapter deals with two objects of measurement: (1) the rank-and-file police officer and (2) the police organization, unit, or program. The term *performance appraisal* is used here to refer to the process of determining how well an employee has performed his or her job.[1] The term *performance measurement* is used to refer to the process of determining the extent to which a police organization, unit, or program accomplishes something of interest.

Standards for police performance appraisal have been formalized to a much greater extent than standards for police performance measurement. Technical and legal standards for performance appraisal have been promulgated by federal, state, and local legislation; professional groups; the U.S. Equal Employment Opportunity Commission; other federal agencies; and a host of court decisions.[2] Part of the reason for this proliferation of performance appraisal standards is concern lest personnel practices unfairly discriminate against employees because of race, religion, sex, or other factors irrelevant to job performance. Largely in response to this concern, an immense body of research findings has been published on a multitude of techniques for appraising employee performance. Much of this literature is directly relevant to police and has heavily influenced performance appraisal systems designed specifically for police.

By comparison, standards for measuring police *organization* or *agency* performance have received relatively little attention from the makers of laws and rules. The courts have been wary of establishing standards of performance— much less, standards of performance *measurement*—except when some constitutional issues arise. Civil suits against police departments also occasionally require that courts rule on the adequacy of a department's performance, but general standards have not emerged from these rulings. Material most pertinent to police has come from police-related professional associations, blue-ribbon commissions, researchers, and reformers.[3]

Although interest in developing systematic methods of police performance measurement can be traced to at least 1871, when U.S. police chiefs called for routine collection of crime statistics, a standardized nationwide system did not appear until the FBI began publishing the *Uniform Crime Reports* (UCR) almost sixty years later. The limitations of the UCR data have been thoroughly discussed over the years. Yet today, more than half a century after their inception, they still constitute the closest thing U.S. police have to a national framework for performance measurement. Ironically, in practice performance measurement may be more standardized among the nation's many local police departments than performance appraisal, but it is certainly less scrutinized.

Despite the differences between performance appraisal and performance measurement, certain fundamental questions need to be answered for both:

Why is performance being measured?

What should be measured?

How should we observe and measure?

How should we use the observations and measurements?

The balance of this chapter addresses these issues as they relate first to performance appraisal and then to performance measurement.

Performance appraisal

As the following sections show, individual performance is measured for a number of reasons relating to the promotion and development of police officers. The appraisal process begins with an analysis of the content of each job in the department and the knowledge, skills, and abilities required to perform it. On the basis of this information, performance is observed and rated by means of a number of techniques, and the resulting ratings are used to help accomplish the department's objectives.

Reasons for measuring individual performance

There are a number of reasons to appraise the performance of an organization's employees:

Administration: to help managers make decisions about promotion, demotion, reward, discipline, training needs, salary, job assignment, retention, and termination

Guidance and counseling: to help supervisors give feedback to subordinates and assist them in career planning and preparation, and to improve employee motivation

Research: to validate selection and screening tests and training evaluations and to assess the effectiveness of interventions designed to improve individual performance.[4]

The use to which a performance appraisal will be put should influence decisions about what is measured, how data are collected, who uses the information, and how it is disseminated. For example, appraisals that are to be used to support disciplinary actions require good documentation over an extended time period, whereas those that are to be used to develop a training program need to generate detailed information on job responsibilities.

The use to which a performance appraisal will be put should influence decisions about what is measured, how data are collected, who uses the information, and how it is disseminated.

The legal environment of the last three decades has encouraged public agencies to use performance appraisal to make administrative decisions about who gets rewarded or disciplined. Many agencies have therefore attempted to develop appraisal systems that serve a variety of administrative functions in addition to guidance, counseling, and research functions. The problem with all-purpose appraisals, though, is that a single system does not serve multiple functions equally well. Consequently it is generally suggested that performance appraisal systems be narrowly focused to maximize the accomplishment of a limited range of goals.

Administrators are often so constrained by personnel rules, labor contracts, and other restrictions on their opportunities to offer rewards and impose penalties that they may wish to refocus the department's performance appraisal system on helping employees improve.

It has also become increasingly popular to recommend performance appraisal not for promotion, salary determinations, and other administrative purposes but rather as a way to help employees do a better job. Realistically, the need to protect the department from lawsuits will continue to exert strong pressure for using performance appraisal to support administrative decisions; but administrators are often so constrained by personnel rules, labor contracts, and other restrictions on their opportunities to offer rewards and impose penalties that they may wish to refocus the department's performance appraisal system on helping employees improve. In evaluating the advantages and disadvantages of different performance appraisal systems, each department must assess its own situation.[5]

The job analysis

A central requirement of performance appraisal is a description of the job each employee is required to perform. This description is accomplished by means of a *job analysis*, which consists of describing and evaluating a job in terms of tasks performed, methods or tools used, services provided, and knowledge, skills, and abilities required to perform the tasks successfully. Court cases that question the validity and fairness of a performance appraisal system tend to focus on the job analysis that served as its basis, and the most frequently cited reason courts give for rejecting a performance appraisal system is a poor job analysis. The U.S. Supreme Court has made clear in a series of rulings that failure to conduct *any* job analysis will assuredly result in the rejection of a performance appraisal system, regardless of what subsequent validation studies may show.

The most important function of a job analysis is to provide an accurate accounting of the responsibilities of the job in question. The resulting *job description* must be comprehensive in terms of duties, responsibilities, working conditions, knowledge, skills, and abilities required for successful performance of the job, and it should indicate the relative importance of the various work behaviors so identified. Not surprisingly, the kinds of job descriptions routinely written by administrators to summarize the requirements of positions are generally insufficient to satisfy courts.

Courts have not set forth strict guidelines on how the job analysis must be conducted, but they have required that it be comprehensive and systematic, specify the *relative* importance of work behaviors, and be documented as to method.

Methods for conducting and validating a job analysis vary, but they are of three general kinds:

1. Task-based methods, including the creation of task inventories that specify the work that is done and the working conditions under which it is performed
2. Attribute-based methods, which include analysis of the physical and intellectual demands of the job and the aptitudes required to perform the work
3. Behavior-based methods, which focus on what an employee *does* on the job, including behavior in "critical incidents."

Some experts suggest that a job analysis should include all three in what is called a "functional job analysis."[6] The greater the variety of methods used, the greater the likelihood that the job analysis will be considered valid by a court.

Gathering information Whatever method is used, the job analyst needs to begin by gathering information. Most professional (outside) job analysts first draw upon their own knowledge of the job and the department's existing documentation and data. Observations of employees performing the job are sometimes used, but for police work their usefulness is quite limited. It is difficult to obtain through observation a representative sample of the work a job entails—particularly when the job is complex and the employee has considerable leeway in deciding what to do and how to do it. Even more important, most police work requires exercising discretion, and the mental work of decision making is not readily apparent from simple observation. Therefore, the job analyst usually relies heavily upon the accounts of those who actually have made those choices. Outside analysts often interview or survey those who perform the job in question, or their supervisors.

For a sound job analysis that will stand up in court, a representative sample of experienced employees and supervisors (subject-matter experts) must participate. They are asked varying kinds of questions. Sometimes they are asked their opinions about the knowledge and skills required for effective job performance. Sometimes they are asked to maintain a diary or log of their activities. Sometimes they are asked to list examples of key situations and behaviors or "critical incidents" that distinguish good from poor performance. Sometimes they are asked to complete questionnaires. And sometimes they are asked to "brainstorm" as a group, working and reworking task statements until they are satisfied.

Quantitative analysis In some cases the information gathered for job analyses is subjected to extensive statistical analysis. An example is the Indiana Police Task Analysis, prepared to help the Indiana Law Enforcement Training Board evaluate the basic training curriculum of the state's law enforcement academy.[7] The job analysts adminstered a survey to six hundred patrol officers and one hundred police supervisors. Patrol officers were asked how frequently they performed each of almost five hundred tasks (task frequency); supervisors were asked to indicate the consequences of performing each task inadequately (task criticality). Statistical analysis of the questionnaire identified "core tasks"—those performed at least once annually or those with an average "criticality rating" of "fairly serious" or higher. More than forty criminal justice professionals and educators then used these results in small workshops to assess the adequacy of the existing training curriculum. Such an analysis is costly and time-consuming and requires access to an assortment of outside experts, but it generates data that could be used in developing a department's performance appraisal system.

Qualitative analysis   Job analysis can also be accomplished by the use of qualitative techniques. Sidney Fine, a proponent of functional job analysis, suggests a multistep process that makes extensive use of in-house expertise and does not require sophisticated statistics.[8] The department may secure the services of an outside job analyst, who sees that the following steps are taken:

1. Preliminary orientation of the job analyst himself or herself and invitation of subject-matter experts to participate
2. Group interviews, in which experts are asked to list job outputs, knowledge, skills, and abilities required
3. Creation of an inventory of tasks based upon the previously generated list, continuing until the group is satisfied that 95 percent of the job is covered
4. Grouping and rank ordering (or weighting) of tasks
5. Identification of performance criteria by asking experts to indicate how they would distinguish levels of work quality for each group of tasks
6. Reliability check, in which the analyst sends the subject-matter experts an edited task inventory for each part of the job, with performance standards for each category, for final review, revision, and approval
7. Validity check, in which the revised inventories are sent to a separate sample of employees who are subject-matter experts for verification.

Documentation of this process is important if the analysis is to withstand court challenge. Courts have been particularly interested in knowing how experts were selected, what instructions and questions were presented to them, and to what extent they agreed among themselves.

The broader the base of participation in job analysis among those who know and perform the job in the department, the more likely it is that the people to be appraised will understand and accept the appraisal process (which is the ultimate objective of the job analysis).

The job analysis, whether quantitative or qualitative, requires a considerable amount of advance planning, coordination, and participation by members of the department. Completing questionnaires or participating in interviews to compile a task inventory for just one job can take a number of employees several hours, removing them from their regular work assignments for that period. Therefore, it is particularly important to secure the commitment of these employees, who often initially fail to appreciate the need to go through a detailed process simply to describe a job. From a practical standpoint, the broader the base of participation in job analysis among those who know and perform the job in the department, the more likely it is that the people to be appraised will understand and accept the appraisal process (which is the ultimate objective of the job analysis).

Most guidelines for conducting a job analysis for police performance appraisal suggest that those who participate in identifying and weighting job dimensions should come from within policing and, specifically, should have experience at the job in question. This has the obvious merit of enhancing the professional status of the police (an occupation is deemed professional partly to the extent that its own members make authoritative judgments about what constitutes good or bad, proper or improper practice). Nevertheless, an argument can be made for incorporating the perspective of nonpolice, perhaps in an advisory capacity in the early "brainstorming" stages. Egon Bittner suggests that consumers of police service have a legitimate role to play in establishing criteria for evaluating police;[9] this is one way of integrating their input into the department's performance appraisal system.

Observing and rating employee performance

Once the department has completed the job analysis, it must decide how data on employee performance will be collected and structured to rate employees. One important choice is whether the department will use "objective" or "subjective" measures of performance. Objective data are those that can be seen, counted, and compared among employees. Subjective data are based upon the impressions of the person assigned the task of evaluating one or more employees; by their nature, they are more likely than objective data to vary depending on who does the evaluation.

Objective measures Days absent, accidents, arrests, citations, clearances, merit awards, and complaints filed against the officer are typical objective measures of individual performance used by police departments. These measures have the advantage of ready availability and the appearance of being unbiased and "factual." Their principal drawback is that things that are easily counted in police work rarely address the most important performance dimensions revealed in a careful job analysis. Objective measures reveal only the extent to which a given activity is performed, not the adeptness with which it was accomplished or whether it was the best activity for the circumstances.

Arrest statistics are perhaps the most used and most abused of objective measures.

Arrest statistics are perhaps the most used and most abused of objective measures, and they illustrate the drawbacks. First, enormous weight is commonly given to number of arrests in appraising the work of police officers, yet making arrests is only a small part of what most police do. Counting arrests fails to address many of the order-maintenance and service-provision activities that occupy most of a police officer's time. Indeed, counting arrests even ignores a number of ways in which officers can help control crime, such as issuing warnings, counseling offenders, helping victims undertake crime prevention measures, and helping address neighborhood problems that breed crime.

Second, the number of arrests made by an officer tells nothing about the quality of those arrest decisions. Was the arrest lawful? Did it result in prosecution and conviction? Did it facilitate the discovery of useful evidence or intelligence? Did it reduce the risk of future crime and disorder? Was it accomplished with the minimum coercion necessary? Was it accomplished so as to evoke minimum hostility toward the police? Did it reduce community tension?

Third, departmental arrest statistics on individual officers fail to provide crucial information about the arrests that would enable evaluators to make meaningful comparisons among officers. Officers assigned to high-crime shifts or areas might be expected to have higher arrest rates than those assigned to "slower" shifts or areas. Officers assigned to areas where residents have a cooperative attitude toward police have an easier task than those assigned to areas where many residents are hostile, fearful, or distrustful. Given the arrest opportunities available, do the officer's decisions to arrest represent the most strategic use of his or her time? An arrest profile that is optimal for one shift or area may not be optimal for another.

Finally, the reliability and accuracy of supposedly objective arrest statistics is open to question in many departments. Because of informal norms and agreements among officers, the officer who makes the "collar" is not necessarily the one who gets credit for it. An officer who "needs some arrest stats" may plead or bargain with others to get credit for arrests in which he or she had little or no involvement. In addition, in many cases it is difficult for a conscientious supervisor to determine who should receive credit for an arrest: if one detective conducts an extensive investigation that produces evidence of the crime and identifies the suspect, but another detective actually locates and apprehends the suspect, who is to receive credit? Increasingly, police administrators are being urged to reward collaborative efforts by appraising not only individual officers but also teams of officers.

All too often, police departments focus on objective measures of individual performance in a way that the rank and file understandably disparages as "bean counting."

Another drawback of objective measures of individual performance is that, all too often, police departments focus on them in a way that the rank and file understandably disparages as "bean counting." At best this bean-counting focus promotes among the rank and file a minimalist standard of what Bittner calls "legal sufficiency": showing up for work, avoiding citizen complaints, avoiding charges of rule violation, and showing some level of activity.[10] Although all these things are of course desirable, they hardly constitute an adequate standard of good police work, and, used alone, they are likely to lead to a trivialization of performance appraisal, manipulation of the system, and reporting that produces undesirable policing and misleading data.

Efforts have been undertaken to improve objective measures of officer productivity. For example, research on criminal investigations shows that certain characteristics of a case strongly affect its "solvability." Departments can conduct their own solvability analyses or can rely on standardized solvability scoring systems to classify cases according to their ease of solvability at the point when an investigator is assigned the case. By establishing the department's case-solving expectations in this way, the department can evaluate individuals as being above or below standard.[11] However, the validity of this approach rests heavily upon the accuracy with which the solvability scoring system can predict the probability of success.

Some researchers have attempted to develop objective indicators that go beyond the quantity of officers' work and reflect work *quality*. Several studies have focused on the conviction rate as an indicator of the quality of arrests officers make. These studies assume that police officers have done a better job if their arrests result in convictions. Arrests that fail to produce convictions are presumed to reflect poorly on police performance. Although acknowledging that the conviction rate is not the sole indicator of arrest quality, proponents have argued that it can provide some useful information about how well the officer is doing.[12] Other research, however, suggests that conviction rates may not be valid measures of performance because, among other things, arrests serve a variety of other legitimate purposes besides obtaining a conviction.[13] Indeed, the criminal law requires a different standard for arrest (probable cause) than for conviction (reasonable doubt), so it may be inappropriate to judge an arrest that fails to produce a conviction as necessarily lower in quality than one that does. If the appropriate legal criterion for making an arrest is probable cause, *that* would seem to be the criterion to apply in performance appraisal.

In addition, many factors beyond the officer's control influence the legal outcome of arrests. These factors include the mix of criminal offenses available to the officer, varying prosccutorial standards, and the general orientation of victims, witnesses, judges, and jurors toward the department. Some analysts have attempted to take these and other factors outside the officers' control into account by statistical means.[14] Although this research has been useful in suggesting strategies that increase the probability of obtaining quality evidence and securing convictions, it is still an open question whether the conviction measure is reasonable for purposes of performance appraisal.

At this point, two things are clear about attempts to measure performance quality objectively: (1) objective measures are not highly valued by police officers, and (2) to be used effectively, they require that departments collect and analyze considerably more information about each case than just its outcome (so that the quality of work performed can be judged more realistically).

"Stats" on individual officers are best used as a supplement to subjective measures of performance.

Departments will undoubtedly continue to collect "stats" on individual officers, but these are best used as a supplement to subjective measures of performance and should never constitute the only basis for appraising an officer's work. As a supplement, they can help structure the performance reviewer's inquiry concerning a given officer. For example, when a narcotics officer makes arrests for narcotics offenses at a rate markedly lower than that of his or her colleagues, the evaluator might regard this as a signal to probe further. Further inquiry could reveal that the low-arrest officer is more meticulous about adhering to due process constraints on search and seizure than others on the squad. Ultimately, the rater must be sensitive to the possibility that abnormal arrest rates may reflect good, poor, or average work, depending upon the particulars of the circumstances.

Subjective measures   Because useful objective measures of employee performance are so difficult to create, most departments have developed some form of subjective rating. Researchers and administrators have given a great deal of attention to identifying the best rating format to use. Space does not allow a detailed discussion of the strengths and weaknesses of the many varieties of rating methods, but some general comments can be offered.

Trait ratings   Many departments have employed rating scales that focus on personal traits, such as honesty, appearance, loyalty, judgment, leadership ability, and diligence. However, courts have consistently found trait ratings wanting because of their vagueness, high degree of subjectivity, and susceptibility to the rater's biases. In contrast, courts have shown a preference for rating scales based on work-related behaviors.

Comparison methods   Many organizations rate employees by *ranking* them (listing all of them from highest to lowest in terms of performance) or by using *paired comparisons* (selecting the better performer in each possible combination of pairs). Although these methods are easy for raters to understand and use, they typically provide only summary information on performance and hinder comparisons between employees evaluated by different raters. Thus, ranking and paired comparison methods are particularly unsuitable for large departments with many raters and for any department in which measures are used for detailed assessment of performance or for employee counseling.[15]

Criterion-referenced ratings   Instead of comparing employees, a number of other rating methods use some external standard or criterion to judge the performance of a given employee. These are called "criterion-referenced" scales and are becoming increasingly common among police departments. Examples are graphic rating scales, mixed-standard scales, forced-choice rating scales, behaviorally anchored rating scales (BARS), behavior observation scales (BOS), management-by-objective (MBO) measures, and a variety of checklists.[16]

Police personnel texts often recommend the behavior-based scales. These scales attempt to identify very specific work behaviors and numerically indicate the quality of work each behavior represents. For example, a scale for the handling of cold property-crime calls might give a higher value to the officer who provides victims with crime prevention information than to the officer who only obtains information for the incident report.

Goal-setting procedures, such as MBO, attempt to measure performance in terms of the *results* of actions taken, using predefined goals and objectives. The relevant goals for a given employee are often the product of an agreement between the employee and his or her supervisor. For example, an officer assigned to patrol a neighborhood that is experiencing many burglaries might have his or her performance assessed according to how much the incidence of reported burglary was reduced in a given time period.

At first blush both behavior-based scales and goal-based scales seem very attractive for police use, but it is important to sound a note of caution concerning these two types of appraisals. The value of either of these rating mechanisms depends upon the ability of the chief and other managers to articulate reasonable objectives and describe how they are to be achieved. This information must be communicated to officers clearly and with reasonable specificity, and for the most important aspects of police work, reducing the information to simple, workable lists is quite difficult to do.[17]

The problem with using highly specific behaviors to establish points on a rating scale, as required by the BARS format, is that it is virtually impossible to rate the desirability of various police alternatives without extensively discussing the subtle particulars of each circumstance. Imagine, for example, trying to specify good, mediocre, and poor police actions in handling domestic disputes.[18] What may be just right for one situation may be the worst possible choice in another. This view of the importance of the particular circumstances is pervasive among officers, and failing to account for it in developing a rating format can lead officers to look on the performance appraisal process as a precise but irrelevant exercise that trivializes their work.

The problem with goal setting is that it risks being either unrealistic or trivial. Goal setting that focuses, for example, on reducing burglaries by X percent is unrealistic because a single police officer's effect on the crime rate is virtually impossible to measure. If a goal-setting approach is used, the goals set for an officer should be reliably and demonstrably attainable through the officer's own efforts, but—on the other hand—must not focus on trivial or peripheral aspects of police work.

Selecting a rating method   From a practical perspective, the key differences among scaling formats relate to the nature and extent of the resources required to develop and use each one. The graphic rating scale would appear to be least time-consuming; behavior-based scales take far more time to develop and use.

Textbooks on police personnel administration devote considerable attention to selecting and developing the best rating format for performance appraisal. Although performance appraisal researchers seem unwilling to dismiss this interest as "much ado about nothing," there appears to be a growing consensus that little is to be gained by worrying about which format produces the most accurate appraisal information.[19] Some researchers have suggested that until they learn more about the *processes* by which judgments and rating decisions are made, they will have little more to contribute to the advancement of rating formats.[20] Until then, practitioners are well advised to exercise their own ingenuity, using whatever format is most likely to get their raters to anchor appraisals in the recollection of observed events instead of "run[ning] through a batch of ratings like unthinking automatons."[21] It is not so much the psychometric or statistical elegance of the rating system that should be important to the police administrator; rather, it is how best to get raters and the officers whose performance is being appraised committed to the fundamental function of performance appraisal—the differentiating of employee performance, based upon specific and verifiable instances of work behavior, according to fair criteria.

Practitioners are well advised to exercise their own ingenuity, using whatever format is most likely to get their raters to anchor appraisals in the recollection of observed events.

Rating errors   Despite efforts by those who design rating forms to minimize inaccuracies by raters, a number of errors are difficult to eliminate because of human nature and organizational influences. These errors may be intentional or unintentional. Some of the more common ones are

Leniency: rating performance higher than warranted

Personal bias: giving more favorable ratings to individuals whom the rater personally likes

Central tendency: giving everyone average or middle-of-the-scale scores

Halo effect: giving someone the same score on all aspects of performance in spite of real differences among those aspects

Overweighting: giving more weight than warranted to one occurrence (often one that came near the end of the rating period).[22]

Administrators may attempt to reduce these errors not only by the selection of rating scale formats but also by the selection of *who* will do the rating, *how frequently* they will do it, and how they will be *trained* to do it.

Selecting raters   One of the most important decisions police administrators can make about performance appraisal is who will do the rating. Although departments routinely assign this responsibility to supervisors, there may be advantages to supplementing these appraisals with ones done by others who are often in a better position to observe important aspects of an officer's work. One potential source of additional rating information is the officer's peer group. Most patrol and detective work is conducted beyond the purview of the sergeant, who must rely heavily upon written and verbal second-hand accounts of officer performance. But squad and team members of the same rank usually have more frequent opportunities to observe one another in action. Often the sergeant relies upon their informal accounts in forming an impression of an officer's performance. In fact, peer assessment is a routine, informal feature of police life, affecting partner and job assignments as well as supervisors' impressions. Including peer assessment in the department's formal performance appraisal process simply acknowledges and standardizes the practice. Training in appraisal techniques can also reduce the distortive impact of grapevine rumors by emphasizing that peers should evaluate their colleagues only on the basis of directly observed performance.

Research suggests that peer appraisals are neither more nor less valid than supervisory appraisals, although they may be superior for predicting an officer's potential for promotion.[23] If peer appraisals are used to supplement supervisory appraisals, supervisors could be required to take peer appraisals into account and justify significant differences between their own and the peer ratings; or peer appraisals could be used solely for counseling and not for administrative purposes.

One potential source of additional rating information is the officer's peer group.

Other rater options are review by subordinates, self-appraisals, and review by external auditors, all of which are relatively rare in police organizations.[24] Of these options, self-appraisals are used successfully as part of the appraisal process by many nonpolice organizations. Allowing employees to detail their accomplishments as input for the supervisor to consider in making his or her appraisal allows them to make the best possible case for themselves and reduces the possibility that the supervisor may overlook something. Moreover, it can enhance employees' acceptance of the organization's appraisal system. In police departments, it can reduce the employee perception—which is all too frequently accurate—that the department, in seeking to root out the negative aspects of performance, ignores the positive.

An increasingly common practice is the routine surveying of members of the community served by a given officer as one basis for evaluating that officer.

An increasingly common practice in police performance appraisal is the routine surveying of members of the community served by a given officer as one basis for evaluating that officer. This has been used in some community-policing programs as a means to determine the extent to which officers are developing positive and productive relations with members of the community. The supervisor routinely conducts follow-up interviews with a small sample of citizens recently served by each of his or her subordinates.[25] There are, of course, problems of obtaining a representative sample, securing candid citizen assessments, and being able to spend the amount of time required. Further, this method fails to include those citizens who might have reason to expect police attention but have been intentionally or unintentionally denied it. Nonetheless, this technique draws upon an underused source of information about officer performance. Citizen input is otherwise obtained only in rare and usually atypical cases—when a complaint or commendation is filed.

In deciding who should be involved in the rating process, administrators should bear in mind that studies vary in their assessments of the comparative benefits of supervisor, peer, self, and client appraisals. One recommendation is to use multiple raters whenever possible because each type of rater brings a particular perspective to the rating process. Used carefully, multiple raters can produce more data for making administrative decisions, help identify markedly biased ratings, offer a more comprehensive set of performance observations, facilitate an assessment of rating reliability, and increase commitment to the performance appraisal system by broadening participation in it. Yet, using multiple raters has certain drawbacks: (1) averaging ratings from multiple sources eliminates the advantage of having different perspectives on the same employee and may distort the results; (2) when rater groups differ in their evaluations, it may be difficult to determine whether the reason is difference in perspective or error; (3) multiple rater systems may reduce raters' feelings of accountability for accurate ratings; (4) interpreting the results of multiple ratings for the employee during feedback sessions may be difficult; and (5) multiple raters may not improve the rating process enough to be cost-effective.[26]

Frequency   Other aspects of the rating process require careful attention if the appraisal system is to be effective. The frequency of appraisals should be determined by the purpose(s) to which they will be put and the capacity of raters to recall relevant observations about performance. In general, the shorter the rating period, the more accurate the rater's recall. Research has shown that if the rating period is more than six months, raters have severe problems remembering, and although the research is limited, experts suggest that shorter periods will enhance accuracy considerably. Accuracy can also be enhanced if the rater routinely documents performance information on each individual throughout the rating period. This can help counteract the tendency to recall only recent performance at the time of the employee's appraisal.[27]

Using the quality of appraisals written by supervisors in the evaluation of the *supervisor's* performance can help to emphasize the importance of this function.

Another consideration in setting the appraisal time interval is the employee's experience. Some departments provide for frequent (even weekly) appraisals and feedback for rookie officers undergoing field training.[28] Departments might also routinely require more frequent appraisals of employees who have been newly promoted or assigned to their positions.

Rater training   Another important consideration is the training that raters and people being rated are given regarding performance appraisal. Because many departments treat performance appraisal as a minor part of the supervisor's job, it is not surprising that a large number of supervisors lack interest in a task that many regard as difficult, stressful, irrelevant, and unrewarding. Using the quality of appraisals written by supervisors in the evaluation of the *supervisor's* performance can help to emphasize the importance of this function. Devoting adequate time to training raters can increase the accuracy with which the particular rating format selected is used and the accuracy of observations and recordings, and can reduce common rating errors. Research suggests that the effects of rater training tend to be short term, which means that refresher training may be necessary.[29] Training of those being rated is likewise essential. Failure to explain the appraisal system to those being appraised will likely result in a mistrust of the process and will limit the system's ability to serve as a guide or incentive to improve performance.

Using performance appraisals effectively

Obtaining good information on police employee performance is meeting only half of the challenge of performance appraisal. Using that information to accomplish organizational objectives is the rest. Two purposes of appraisals are to assist in decisions about assignments and promotions, and to provide feedback to employees. At the same time, the appraisal system must meet legal requirements.

Making personnel decisions   When the appraisal is used in decisions about promotions and job assignments, it is essential to ensure that only those aspects of the appraisal that are relevant to the anticipated position are taken into account. Police organizations sometimes fail to consider that job candidates from different units or functions (for example, patrol, investigation, or crime prevention) will have appraisals with markedly differing relevance for the position in question—for example, detective. Yet some departments insist upon giving the same weight to the appraisals of each candidate.

Some departments also undervalue the appraisal of past performance in favor of written tests or assessment center results. An agency that gives only 20 percent weighting to the appraisal of past performance and 80 percent for the written examination has virtually neutralized an important incentive for improving on-the-job performance. In such a department, an officer desiring promotion could easily overcome a mediocre work record with high test scores.

Of course, tests and assessment center results that have demonstrably strong correlations with measures of actual performance are valuable. Yet a number of studies have found that assessment center ratings are generally not significantly better than simple appraisals of past performance.[30] Whenever possible, departments should conduct methodologically sound evaluations that permit them to assign performance appraisal a weighting appropriate to its capacity to predict future performance in a higher rank.

Providing feedback to employees   Performance appraisal can do little to improve the performance of the employee or the department unless its results are effectively communicated to those being rated. Feedback allows employees to correct errors, satisfies their desire to know how well they are doing, helps develop a sense of competence, and reduces uncertainty about the accomplishment of goals. Feedback also allows the organization to communicate its performance standards and expectations and review progress toward those objectives. Yet, providing quality performance appraisal feedback can be difficult. Some departments fail to provide *any* feedback or do it so poorly that the entire performance appraisal process becomes counterproductive. Managers and supervisors are often uneasy about discussing their subordinates' performance, particularly if the evaluation has produced negative ratings. Employees, too, are often apprehensive about the feedback because the organization has failed to prepare them to understand how the system works and what specific criteria will be used for rating them.[31] The discussion below provides suggestions for avoiding these problems.

In general, employees place a high value on the confidentiality of appraisal results. Although results can be communicated privately in writing, this technique is unlikely to prove satisfactory, and a private interview should be routine. The person who wrote the appraisal is usually the best person to conduct the interview because he or she will be most capable of discussing its specifics.

Do's and don'ts of interviewing can be found in performance appraisal and police management texts.[32] In general, the rater should show that he or she considers the appraisal interview important. An overall climate that is supportive and constructive is essential. Specific feedback is preferable to general comments, and specific feedback is most effective when linked to specific goals of the person being appraised.

Presenting negative feedback in a constructive manner is one of the greatest challenges of the interview. Two pitfalls to be avoided are refraining from negative feedback when the appraisal indicates it is justified or, in contrast, peppering the person being appraised with a lengthy series of criticisms. The first approach subverts the purpose of the interview. The second generates a high level of hostility and defensiveness in the employee, who will then fail to respond to suggestions for improvement. Many texts encourage the "sandwich" approach of beginning and ending with praise and putting criticism in the middle, but research suggests that employees soon learn the pattern and focus their attention on the negative feedback anyway. Some experts suggest that conducting more frequent interviews reduces the number of negative comments needed per session.

Feedback allows employees to correct errors, satisfies their desire to know how well they are doing, helps develop a sense of competence, and reduces uncertainty about the accomplishment of goals.

The employee usually accepts criticism better if the rater has specific examples and a specific plan for correcting problems. The rater's tactfulness can be crucial. Inexperienced officers often deserve more negative feedback and may be less likely to challenge it, but brutal candor can obliterate their self-confidence. Experienced officers, especially those accustomed to good evaluations, are more inclined to reject criticism, creating a very different challenge for the rater. In both instances, however, the rater can present criticism more effectively by offering it as a joint problem requiring both the employee's *and* the department's efforts to correct. Further, employee satisfaction with the interview and willingness to respond to it positively have been linked to the extent to which the employee is invited to participate. Employees will be more likely to participate if they are given an opportunity to respond to the rater's comments, help set new goals, and make suggestions on how to improve their own future performance.

Formal sessions cannot substitute for the informal, day-to-day feedback each employee should be receiving.

Clearly, the communication of performance appraisal feedback requires a rater with a strong professional reputation and good communications skills. Administrators should remember that although the principal purpose of the interview is to review the employee's performance, it is also a significant occasion for the employee to appraise the rater, the performance appraisal system, and the department—appraisals that will all affect the employee's future performance and commitment to the organization.

A final caveat on feedback interviews. Conducting more effective interviews may be the single most important way for police departments to improve their performance appraisal systems, but it is important to remember that these formal sessions cannot substitute for the informal, day-to-day feedback each employee should be receiving.[33] The formal sessions should produce no major surprises; the sessions should grow out of the routine, informal feedback occurring daily between the rater and the employee.

Meeting legal standards Whatever goals a given department seeks to serve through its performance appraisal system, administrators must be concerned that the system be able to withstand the scrutiny of administrative agencies and courts responsible for ruling on grievances claiming unfair discrimination in personnel actions. Courts, regulatory agencies, and professional standard-setting bodies have devoted considerable attention to the fairness of hiring and promotion standards, written tests, and assessment center procedures. Because on-the-job performance appraisals are needed to validate these devices and because performance appraisals themselves are often part of the rationale for a personnel decision, they, too, are given careful legal scrutiny.

Reviews of regulatory guidelines and court cases have suggested a number of steps that can bolster performance appraisal systems against legal challenges:

Performance appraisal ratings should be job related and valid.

The job-related performance criteria that are to be rated should be derived from a thorough job analysis that appropriately represents all significant performance dimensions.

Performance appraisal ratings should be collected under formal standardized conditions.

Performance appraisal ratings should be examined for bias. Care should be taken—in developing measures, selecting raters, training, and conducting ongoing review—to eliminate bias regarding race, ethnicity, sex, religion, or national origin.

Organizations should avoid using supervisory ratings that are based on vague and unvalidated factors.

Performance appraisal raters must have personal knowledge of and reasonable contact with the job performance that is to be rated; otherwise they cannot make the appropriate observatons.[34]

Courts, regulatory agencies, and professional standard-setting bodies have devoted considerable attention to the fairness of hiring and promotion standards, written tests, and assessment center procedures.

The first factor listed above—validity and job relatedness—deserves some elaboration. Validity is a technical concept and can be demonstrated in a number of ways. The department can demonstrate that the performance measure or appraisal instrument in question has *criterion-related validity*, which means that it has been shown to predict future job performance. Parenthetically, the performance appraisal measure *itself* is used as an indicator of on-the-job performance to validate other personnel measures (for example, promotion examinations). Or the department can demonstrate that a performance appraisal measure has what expert witnesses in a court case will refer to as *construct validity*, meaning that it can be shown to measure the underlying concept (or "construct") it is believed to represent. Construct validity is difficult to demonstrate. Historically, agencies sought to demonstrate it to support the use of personality traits as performance predictors, but these are no longer favored as evaluative criteria. A third type of validity is *content validity*, and demonstrating the content validity of a performance appraisal measurement system is the most frequent approach to satisfying authorities that a performance appraisal system is acceptable. Content validity is achieved to the extent that the measures adequately represent the job's content. The objective is to demonstrate that all important aspects of the job are included, that irrelevant features are excluded, and that measures are appropriately weighted.[35]

In summary, then, performance appraisal helps police managers and supervisors determine how well officers are performing and gives officers feedback on their day-to-day work, training needs, and promotional opportunities. Implementing a sound appraisal system requires careful thought about why appraisal is being undertaken, what is being measured, how measurement should be accomplished, and how the resulting information should be used. A good system will help ensure that the department makes the best possible use of its human resources and meets the legal requirements for objective, nonbiased personnel decisions.

Performance measurement

An assumption that usually underlies the measurement of the performance of a police *organization* is that the whole is greater than the sum of its parts. Otherwise the organization's performance could be computed simply by summing the performance of all of its individual employees. Increasingly, however, police organizations are attempting to integrate the work of their individual employees and units so that the accomplishment of objectives is hard to link to particular individuals.

The fashion in departmental performance measurement has long been to focus on the accomplishment of broad social goals—such as crime deterrence—that are not readily observable simply by watching police as they go about their duties.

The fashion in departmental performance measurement has long been to focus on the accomplishment of broad social goals—such as crime deterrence—that are not readily observable simply by watching police as they go about their duties. Consequently, when one focuses on the *department's* performance, attention shifts from the perspective of an individual's performance to a broader perspective of organizational missions, activities, and social effects. As suggested below, this approach to performance measurement sometimes creates difficulties for police, but it remains a fact of organizational life.

Reasons for measuring departmental performance

Police departments measure their performance for some reasons that are frequently acknowledged and for others that are rarely acknowledged, at least in public.

The widely acknowledged and accepted reasons for doing performance measurement are of two types: (1) to establish the police capacity to accomplish a given objective and (2) to monitor the extent to which a given department or program is in fact accomplishing a given objective. In the first case, the capacity of police to achieve some desired objective by a given method is not assumed but is the reason for the inquiry. The Kansas City preventive patrol experiment is an example of performance measurement conducted for this purpose; it was designed to learn the extent to which preventive patrol affected crime and citizens' perceptions of police service (see the chapters on the patrol function and research). To accomplish this objective, evaluators had to measure not only crime and citizens' perceptions but also the aspects of preventive patrol that were thought to affect those outcomes. Further, the research had to be structured in such a way that the effects of other possible influences on these outcomes could be controlled or taken into account. In this case, the researchers used an experimental design.

When departments monitor their performance, the requirements are less demanding. A variety of inputs (e.g., personnel hours), outputs (e.g., arrests), and outcomes (e.g., crime rates) may be measured, but the purpose is not to demonstrate how much inputs affect outputs or how much outputs affect outcomes. The capacity of the department to influence those outputs and outcomes is *assumed*. Rather, periodic reports of crime rates, arrests and clearances, citations issued, accidents, and calls for service are typically intended to serve a monitoring function.

Monitoring is a way of using an accepted measure of police performance to keep the organization on track and to alert administrators if things start to go awry. Carefully conducted, monitoring may even help identify ways to improve performance; it can help pinpoint where problems are occurring. Monitoring also provides elected officials, the public, and others with information about how well the department is doing relative to expectations—enabling them to make informed judgments about giving or withholding support, calling for policy changes, and so on.

Monitoring is a way of using an accepted measure of police performance to keep the organization on track and to alert administrators if things start to go awry.

Sometimes performance measures are put to less salutary uses—when they are employed to support or to weaken a particular agenda rather than to provide objective information. Performance measures may be designed, selected, or manipulated in ways that bias the findings of an evaluation either to justify programs, units, or practices or to torpedo programs that are not wanted for reasons unrelated to what those measures indicate. Performance measures can be and have been used in a cynical "numbers game" that keeps disgruntled constituents at bay, painting a "don't worry, be happy" picture for the public—or, in contrast, to generate a climate of fear and dissatisfaction among complacent constituents. That is, performance measurement, like any tool of the police, is neither inherently good nor inherently bad; its merits depend entirely on how it is used. Accidental or intentional abuses of performance measurement are hardly limited to the police world, but that does not lessen the need for police to strive for better methods and greater commitment to the ideals of scientific inquiry. The following sections attempt to help police managers work toward these goals.

Determining what to measure

Performance measurement has two fundamental components—one normative (defining what police ought to try to accomplish) and the other empirical (defining what they can accomplish or have accomplished). These two components are implicit in every performance measure. For example, when police monitor the burglary rate in a community to see how well their citizen crime prevention program is doing, they have decided that the police *should* try to reduce burglaries and that they *can* in fact reduce them by educating citizens to help prevent crimes. Although neither decision seems very controversial, they reflect assumptions that police and others who care about police performance should carefully examine.

What ought the police try to accomplish? Measuring police performance requires an answer to the question, "What do we *want* police to accomplish?" Answering this question is not as easy as it seems, because U.S. police are expected to accomplish many different things. Moreover, these diverse objectives sometimes conflict—such as catching criminals and protecting constitutional rights.

Even when several goals appear to be in harmony, all cannot be pursued with equal vigor, given finite police resources. Choosing to "crack down on crack" may require easing up on the enforcement of drunk-driving offenses. The police mission is further complicated by the political reality that segments of the public and, indeed, factions within the local government vary in their preferences about what police objectives should be and what police priorities should be. A relatively high degree of consensus may be reflected in opinion surveys about what police should and should not try to do in general terms, but police administrators know that in day-to-day operations, different segments of the community will offer conflicting views of police priorities.

Even when there is widespread agreement about the importance of the police mission in a given area—say, reducing illicit drug trafficking—the process of identifying the particular criteria by which performance should be judged is tremendously complex. Performance criteria can be grouped into four broad categories: effectiveness, efficiency, equity, and accountability.[36]

Effectiveness concerns the extent to which an objective is achieved, regardless of cost or other factors. A measure of effectiveness might be the change in the quantity of illicit drugs in a jurisdiction over a given time period.

Efficiency addresses the relationship between the cost of a program and its effectiveness. The efficiency of a narcotics strike force is greater to the extent that its cost per unit of crime reduction is lower. For example, if strategy A produces a 20 percent reduction in drug trafficking at a cost of one million dollars and strategy B produces a 10 percent reduction at a cost of one hundred thousand dollars, strategy B—though only half as effective as strategy A—is five times as efficient because of its more favorable ratio of effectiveness to cost.

Diverse objectives sometimes conflict—such as catching criminals and protecting constitutional rights.

Equity (or fairness) concerns the distribution of benefits and costs among those in the police service population. Definitions of equity differ widely. One possible definition is parity of service. For example, has neighborhood A received the same quantity of protection against drug trafficking as neighborhood B? Another definition recognizes variable needs and would find equity when neighborhoods receive protection in proportion to their level of crime or disorder. Still another possible view of equity would consider private security and other legitimate self-help measures taken by neighborhoods to foster public safety and would provide only those public police services needed to complement these private-sector initiatives.

Accountability requires that police act within the constraints set by duly constituted authority—the constraints of laws, rules and regulations, and directives of the governmental bodies with policy-making and oversight authority over police. For example, for the narcotics task force, accountability means performing searches and seizures in conformance with current legal standards. And in making selective enforcement decisions and setting other enforcement priorities, the department's policy makers must be accountable to local government officials whose responsibilities include ensuring that police operations are legitimately responsive to public needs (see also the chapter on the governmental setting).

There are usually trade-offs among effectiveness, efficiency, equity, and accountability, so that to the extent a department pursues one, others suffer.

What can the police accomplish?   What we *want* police to accomplish has been a powerful determinant of how police performance has been defined and measured for the last half century. Concern for the empirical aspect of identifying and selecting performance measures has arisen more recently and requires answering the question, "What *can* the police accomplish?" Answering this question (preferably on the basis of sound research) represents the practical aspect of selecting performance measures, for it would be unwise and unfair to hold police accountable for objectives that are not within their capacity to achieve. This means that the selection of measures of performance (especially for purposes of monitoring) must be constantly informed by a dialogue between what we want from police and what research shows we can reasonably expect of them.

Past practices in selecting performance measures   Police performance measurement, especially for monitoring purposes, has mostly been the responsibility of those within policing. It has tended to reflect fluctuations in professional fashions regarding the police mission and priorities. For many years fluctuations in the rate of crimes known to police were used as indices of police effectiveness; more recently it has become popular to measure police effectiveness by focusing on victimization data and citizens' satisfaction with police service. Performance measurement is one of the means by which police reformers in the United States have advanced their vision of professionalism. But, as a consequence, police performance measures tend to reflect narrow professional interests. For example, performance has been measured mostly in terms of effectiveness and efficiency, with equity and accountability downplayed or ignored altogether. Specifically, crime control and, more recently, maintenance of order have dominated both the research and monitoring applications of performance measurement with little regard either for the distribution of costs and benefits or for the extent to which police remain within the law. To be sure, police departments have never been able to ignore questions of equity and lawfulness, but they have not generally used their performance measurement systems to help them attend to these concerns.

Concern about equity in the distribution of police service can arise from any sector of the community, but it is perhaps most frequently voiced by racial and ethnic minority groups and the poor, who often feel that the policing they receive is inferior in quality to that provided to other segments of the community. Many police administrators believe that routine dissemination of performance data showing who is getting what from the department will lead to unnecessary bickering among community groups and that this, in turn, will only increase external pressure on police to change the allocation of services. Although this may be so in some jurisdictions, in many others the distribution of police services is already an issue. Here the routine availability of such information to both the police and the public could lead either to more equitable policies or to a better community understanding of why services are distributed as they are.

Routine performance-monitoring reports rarely give much visibility to the most sensitive aspects of police accountability: police misconduct, corrupt practices, misuse of force, and violations of due process and civil rights. Even in departments that routinely report such information, these issues are often not given much prominence. Aside from the reluctance of any organization to publicize its problems, obtaining accurate indicators in these areas is very difficult. Nonetheless, departments do maintain records on these matters, and researchers have suggested some indirect indicators of the items that are most difficult to measure, such as corruption.[37] Police leaders and the public clearly believe that these features reflect on the department's quality, yet they often remain in the shadows of routine performance measurement.

Improving the development of performance measures   To reduce the tendency to use narrow, incomplete definitions of performance, police administrators and others involved in police performance measurement can explicitly inject (nonpartisan) politics into the process of identifying performance dimensions and weighting criteria. They can abandon the convenient fiction that performance measures are neutral and without political implication and, instead, can acknowledge that the selection of performance measures, however they are constructed, does frame thinking about what is important in policing and ultimately serves to set the policy agenda.

In any community significant external participation is needed in deciding what aspects of police work are worth measuring.

In any community significant external participation is needed in deciding what aspects of police work are worth measuring. In devising and revising performance monitoring systems, elected officials should be expected to exercise leadership, and diverse community groups should be given the opportunity to voice their views in this process before it is a "done deed." One way to do this might be with a local advisory task force that broadly represents interested constituencies in the jurisdiction. Police administrators who strive to broaden performance measurement so that it gives proper weight to equity and accountability may very well find that involving local government officials and the public in the process of assessing agency operations will pay considerable dividends.

A second way in which administrators and others can improve the selection of performance measures is to pay much more attention to what we know and do not know about the capacity of police to produce desired results.

Making use of research results   Police employ a variety of strategies to reduce crime (the most frequently measured goal): numerous patrol and deployment options, sundry investigative strategies, community crime prevention programs, computerization of files, scientific analysis of evidence, and so on. But although police often point with pride to these tactics and strategies as the "technical core" of their capacity to reduce crime, the scientific validation of these measures is quite modest and, some would say, so weak as to be marginal or virtually nonexistent.[38]

Policing in this regard is unlike medicine, a profession in which practitioners receive tremendous support from scientific research, which supplies a great deal of information on rigorously tested methods of prevention, diagnosis, and treatment; many of those methods have well-validated probabilities of success. By comparison, rigorous evaluation of police tactics and strategies began only in the 1970s and has not had the vast financial support given to the health sciences. Although police and police researchers are sometimes eager to claim that old strategies do not work and new ones do, the reality of contemporary police science and policy evaluation is that an understanding of the relationships between police initiatives and desired outcomes is still only rudimentary. Thus (as should be the case in an increasingly professional occupation), serious arguments are advanced both in favor of and against the usefulness of a host of police strategies and programs. For example, the Kansas City preventive patrol experiment challenged conventional wisdom about the value of random preventive patrol—and was itself subjected to serious scholarly criticism.[39] Moreover, in varying degrees, police have embraced a host of strategies that researchers are not yet able to validate as useful. For example, scientific proof is substantially lacking that crime can be controlled by community-policing strategies, criminal investigations, community crime prevention, and undercover operations.[40]

One of the areas explored in recent years is the capacity of order-maintenance—or peacekeeping—activities to contribute to crime control and community well-being, especially by reducing citizens' fear of crime and disorder. Although there is some empirical support for the notion that some police tactics can influence levels of fear, some commentators believe that this indicator of police accomplishment is itself of debatable value. They argue that reducing fear of crime and disorder has not been shown to lead to greater personal or community safety or to other benefits. Although one might suggest that a lessened sense of fear is, by itself, desirable, the question remains whether reducing fear in some situations may not also reduce a healthy motivation to take self-protective actions. Researchers have not established at what threshold and under what conditions fear of crime shifts from being functional to being dysfunctional. Until the complex relationships among fear, safety, and quality of life are adequately demonstrated, police administrators who use fear reduction as a criterion of police performance must understand the tenuousness of the conclusions they can responsibly draw from these measurements. At worst, fear reduction efforts make some people feel safer than they should.

In the absence of scientific validation of the vast majority of departmental performance measures, the fact remains that police administrators will necessarily have to decide whether and how to use the imperfect measures currently available.

Still, in the absence of scientific validation of the vast majority of departmental performance measures, the fact remains that police administrators are paid to exercise their best judgment on enormously complex topics, and they will necessarily have to decide whether and how to use the imperfect measures currently available while efforts are being made to grapple with these problems. The plea of this chapter is not for managers or communities to avoid performance measurement but for them to understand its limitations so that they are not misled when making important decisions.[41]

Additional rigorous research is needed to determine the police capacity to accomplish desired results.[42] The research community and those who give it financial support can and are making a significant contribution, although their scope has been narrow—focusing for the most part on crime control.

A tactical approach to performance measurement   Another step administrators can take is to curb their own appetite for the ambitious, unvalidated performance measures too often found in their periodic department reports—at least until these measures are supported by a substantial body of rigorous empirical research. Instead of the usual lengthy recitation of crime statistics, departments might select from a more modest menu of performance measures—ones that there is more reason to believe police work can influence. A perspective on police work that is anchored in the daily tasks undertaken by officers may prove most useful here.

The craft of patrol work focuses on how well police handle individual incidents. At least some of the consequences of police decisions in those incidents are much easier to observe than are the effects of police decisions on communitywide crime rates and fear of crime. Bittner has suggested that the essence of the police role is intervention in pressing situations, or emergencies.[43] The special capacity of the police to intervene in citizens' private affairs under these circumstances and to select from among a variety of more or less forceful, intrusive, and controlling actions focuses evaluation at a tactical level.

Scholarly field research on police-citizen interactions has tended to focus on aspects of police performance in handling uncooperative subjects or in dealing with other pressing situations. In these circumstances, certain elements of policing as a *craft* guide the selection of potential performance measures: economical use of force, ability to minimize injury to self and others, skill in persuasion and negotiation, knowledge of people and places, ability to judge people and situations quickly on the basis of scant information of unknown reliability, a capacity to develop informants, ablity to avoid unnecessary hostility but maximize fear and respect when really needed, and so on.[44] A limited amount of research attempting to validate tactics by using such performance measures has been conducted,[45] but a great deal more should be done. Although more research is needed on these matters, those who practice the craft of policing know enough already to begin to formulate some indicators of a job well done, which is indeed part of the task of performance *appraisal* and could provide a foundation for performance *measurement*.

In their tactical analysis of police performance, administrators should consider not only police tactics in potentially touchy incidents but also police behavior in a broader range of situations. For example, a large proportion of police-citizen interactions involve requests for assistance from generally cooperative citizens in non-emergency situations (for example, cold property-crime reports and requests for help in mobilizing other public service agencies). Police departments rarely attempt to evaluate their own performance in these routine situations, yet these incidents consume a substantial proportion of most departments' resources.

In the absence of a steady flow of plausible illustrations of quality policing, the public is prone to lose sight of the "small victories" won by police departments.

One important issue that needs attention is how far police should go in responding to these sorts of problems. Thoroughness is generally valued among professionals (partly because it may prevent recurrence of the problem and partly because it increases client satisfaction). But the desirability of thoroughness must be weighed against the need to distribute services equitably among a large number of service requesters and the need to use officer time to greatest strategic advantage. This is particularly important for departments that are moving toward a problem-solving orientation. Committing more resources to the strategic allocation of resources to solve specific problems usually requires being more selective about the calls for service the department chooses to answer with an immediate dispatch. Without a careful analysis of these non-emergency incidents, police will not have a good understanding of what is lost and gained by a given policy about how to respond to them.

For a number of reasons, attempting to build a performance measurement system around a department's patterns of tactical decisions may not be as easy as it seems. A department may not be able to collect detailed information on *all* incidents or circumstances its officers handle; so selecting a small, representative sample for intensive evaluation may be necessary. Other issues are more perplexing. How does one evaluate the nonincident—the overlooked offense? How does one compare the value of the officer-initiated public relations encounter to other encounters or activities the officer might have initiated instead (working traffic, staking out likely robbery sites, handling disorderly drunks)? Police officers make strategic as well as tactical choices, but knowledge of the consequences of tactical choices remains even more limited and requires scientific validation.

This tactical approach to performance measurement, however, overlooks the assumption that departmental performance is more than the sum of the separate accomplishments of its individual employees. Thus the tactical approach may be troubling to many administrators accustomed to viewing the police mission in terms of broader social impact—yet it does provide tangible measures linked to readily observable aspects of policing. In the long run, these tangible measures may better integrate the department's performance measurement with its performance appraisal system and meet with greater acceptance among those who actually do police work. Just as important, they may provide an effective format for regularly calling public and governmental attention to the many, often low-visibility, accomplishments of police. In the absence of a steady flow of plausible illustrations of quality policing, the public is prone to lose sight of the "small victories" won by police departments. Because these may be largely overlooked, the department's performance may be viewed inaccurately as *less* than the sum of its parts.

Collecting and analyzing performance data

Information is the principal tool of police work—and, for citizens who need advice, prosecutors who need evidence, insurance companies that need accident reports, and so on, information is also a significant product of police work. As a result, police departments over time have developed reasonably sophisticated information systems that support operations, personnel, and accounting (see the chapter on information management). Yet the information systems that support evaluation have been substantially neglected—with some notable exceptions (discussed in the chapter on research). This section highlights some of the major obstacles to effective data collection and analysis for purposes of performance measurement.

Police data: Famine in the land of plenty Police organizations are awash in information that might be used to assess their performance, but much of it is underused. This is often because of poor record systems planning.

Suppose the mayor wants to know what the department has done to deal with disorders in or near bars because the press has recently given this problem a lot of publicity. Somewhere in the department's record system is this information, but the department must first be able to identify all complaints of barroom-related disorder. The department might do this from calls-for-service records, but these usually provide little information about what police action was taken and why. A separate incident report file is maintained on complaints that responding officers considered to have some basis. This file must be searched to learn the specific nature of the incident; the number of people involved; the laws that were violated; the extent of injury, property damage, and public disturbance; the role of the establishment in trying to maintain and restore order; the complaints that resulted in citations, arrests, referrals; and so on. Yet another file may be maintained on departmental recommendations to revoke local licenses, but it may be difficult to match these recommendations with specific incidents. Typically, only some of this information is in a computer-readable format, and in any event, few departments have a program designed to extract all this information efficiently from computerized data sets. In such circumstances the department can produce the requested performance data only with great effort. Some advance planning and record file integration, however, would make the task much easier.

Sometimes departments err in the other direction, compiling reams of computer printouts on aspects of the department's performance that no one uses. By periodically reviewing performance reports and data files for their relevance and usefulness and modifying them to fit user needs, departments can help focus limited resources on things that matter most.

When departments attempt to evaluate new programs, they tend to collect data that indicate only the "bottom line" performance, which can rarely reveal why the programs succeeded or failed. If, for example, a department experiments with a new foot patrol program in a few residential neighborhoods, it may simply monitor indicators of desired outcomes (for example, victimization rates, fear of crime, resident satisfaction with police service) to see if they change in these neighborhoods after the program has been in operation for some time. However, if the department fails to monitor the *implementation* of the foot patrol program itself, it will be unable to say with confidence what it was that produced the failure or success. In this case the department might collect data on how and where footbeat officers spend their time, what kinds of encounters they initiate with citizens, how they handle various kinds of incidents, and what changes occur in their perceptions and knowledge of the neighborhood.

When departments attempt to evaluate new programs, they tend to collect data that indicate only the "bottom line" performance, which can rarely reveal why the programs succeeded or failed.

It is also a good idea, if possible, to monitor extraneous conditions that may influence the performance measures of interest. In the example of foot patrol, it would be a good idea to monitor the nature and amount of work performed by other police units in the neighborhoods of interest. Some research designs are better able to control for "outside influences" than others, yet most routine police evaluations cannot afford the time and resources necessary to conduct the more rigorous experimental and quasi-experimental designs.[46]

Performance data: Getting the right stuff   Performance data are available from a variety of sources inside and outside the department. They include incident reports, computer records, and community resources.

Incident-level data   Departments attempting to focus performance monitoring on the tactical aspects of police work very likely will find they need to devise better methods for detailing the tactics used by police officers. The incident report offers an already available format, although greater complexity and detail may be required to provide precoded categories summarizing actions taken by citizens and police.

An encouraging development for incident-based performance measurement is the FBI's National Incident-Based Reporting System (NIBRS), which is being incorporated into its UCR system (see also the chapter on information management). Participating departments will provide detailed data on individual crime and arrest incidents rather than just aggregated, summary data.[47] Such a data base will allow police departments to learn much more about how they and other departments are handling particular kinds of incidents.

The principal limitation of NIBRS is its exclusive focus on criminal offenses and arrests. It provides no data on the numerous incidents that are not alleged to involve criminal offenses, and it does not record the kinds of nonarrest alternatives that officers use far more frequently in addressing citizens' problems—both crime and noncrime. Nonetheless, participating departments will have an incident-based framework that they can expand locally to incorporate a broader range of incidents and police actions. This will be particularly important for departments that wish to undertake a comprehensive analysis of their problem-solving efforts.[48]

Computers   Rapid advances in computerized record systems and techniques for managing and analyzing data are revolutionizing the technological features of performance measurement. As discussed in the chapter on information management, microcomputers and software development make sophisticated systems available even to the smallest departments at reasonably low cost. As more and more aspects of the police information system are entered into computers, the potential for generating useful performance information expands. At the same time, computers may give a police executive false confidence in the results of performance measurement. No matter how sophisticated the system and no matter how captivating the graphics it generates, the output is no better than what *people* put into the system. As the cliche says, "Garbage in, garbage out."

To avoid putting "garbage" in, departments must focus on what it takes to train and motivate their personnel to provide accurate information. The training can be relatively straightforward and reinforced by supervision. Far more challenging is the motivational aspect.

First, police officers have to believe that accurate record keeping—especially for performance measurement purposes—is worthwhile. If those whose work will be documented are involved in redesigning the records system, their appreciation of and trust in the system will be enhanced. Perhaps more important, to the extent that street-level personnel who make the initial decisions about data entry see the benefits of accurate data for themselves and the organization, they will be committed to doing a good job. Routinely providing them feedback that summarizes and makes meaningful the data they collect will make an important contribution. One feature of problem-oriented policing is that officers doing the work on the street are intimately involved in all aspects of data collection for the purpose of solving problems and evaluating the results.[49]

The second point about motivation is that there must be a commitment *not* to misrepresent incidents and police actions. The temptation to misrepresent is particularly great under circumstances that may reflect poorly on the report writer, other officers, or the department. Indeed, learning how to "cover your ass" in written reports is unfortunately one of the basic parts of the traditional police socialization process.[50] Although it is very difficult for a department to reduce intentional distortions of the data for reasons of self-protection, departments may achieve some success by minimizing aspects of their disciplinary process that result in arbitrary, capricious, and overly severe sanctions (see the chapter on fostering integrity).

Multiple sources   Another way of improving confidence in evaluation results is to use measures of performance that are derived from different sources. Suppose, for example, that an administrator is interested in evaluating the capacity of patrol officers to develop positive community relations in an area where there is a history of tension. The administrator can survey the officers to get their perspective and self-reported practices, review files of complaints about police officers and service, and survey the area's residents or its leaders. Each of these methods provides a somewhat different picture, each with its own set of potential biases, but together they can provide a balanced portrayal of how well the department is doing in terms of community relations (see the chapter on research).

Cameras keep the record straight
By using electronic recording devices, the police department in Hazelwood, Missouri, is protecting itself from arrest-related lawsuits.

The city realized that the majority of complaints filed against police personnel centered around the booking process and usually came down to the complainant's word against the officer's. The department bought $20,000 worth of video equipment, including closed-circuit television cameras, video recorders and monitors, and two time/date generators.

The system provides twenty-four-hour surveillance of the police department parking lot, prisoner unloading zone, cell area, booking area, and passageways used to move prisoners from one area to another. Each cell area also has audio receivers connected to the master recorder system. The cameras record processing of prisoners until they are placed in the cell area or released.

Only the chief of police and administrative staff who have the chief's permission view the tapes.

Source: Cited in *The Guide to Management Improvement Projects in Local Government* (Washington, DC: International City Management Association, 1990).

Many police departments are making good use of external resources for data collection and analysis. Linking police data systems to those of courts, correctional facilities, and public health and traffic safety agencies can help police learn much more about the consequences of their actions and the conditions under which programs are undertaken. Local universities and research institutes can prove particularly useful when a department requires special data collection, such as public opinion surveys or in-person observations. Outside experts may be especially useful to smaller departments that do not have sufficient expertise and resources to design data collection instruments and collect data. It is important to remember, however, that to maximize the chances of producing useful data and analysis, the department should remain actively involved with the outside analysts. Although evaluation consultants may have excellent technical expertise, the organization's decision makers are usually in the best position to give the consultants guidance so that the evaluation ends up being as helpful as possible (see the chapter on external resources).

Although evaluation consultants may have excellent technical expertise, the organization's decision makers are usually in the best position to give the consultants guidance so that the evaluation ends up being as helpful as possible.

Obtaining data from sources entirely unconnected with the department can be particularly valuable because police departments, like all organizations, tend to structure their informaton gathering to fit their own assumptions about how things operate. For example, communications records are an important means for the department to monitor demands for service, yet the way citizens' calls for service are routed and the way information is recorded can distort or fail to record important, potentially useful information about the reasons, timing, and conditions under which people seek (or fail to seek) police assistance.[51] An occasional small, well-designed citizen survey might provide beneficial insights as a supplement (see Figure 13–1).

City of
Madison

Madison Police Department

Customer Survey

The City of Madison's Experimental Police District, located at 835 W. Badger Road, was established in January of 1988 to achieve a closer working relationship with Madison's near west and southside communities. An important aspect of this closer relationship involves increased interaction and feedback between the police officers providing services and citizens like yourself, our customers. Since you recently were a customer of the Experimental Police District, we ask that you provide us with some feedback on the quality of service you experienced. Please take a moment to complete this questionnaire and return it by mailing it to us in the enclosed postage paid envelope.

1. Please indicate the number of contacts you have had with the Madison Police Department over the past 12 months: _____ One   _____ Two   _____ Three or more

2. What was the nature of this last contact with the Madison Police:
   _____ I called to report a problem or incident.   _____ I was arrested or issued a citation.
   _____ I was the victim of a crime or offense.   _____ I was contacted about a problem or
   _____ I was a witness to a crime or incident.   disturbance.
   _____ I was involved in a motor vehicle accident.   _____ I was involved in another way with
   _____ I requested information from the   the Madison Police Department.
   Department.
   Please specify the nature of your contact:
   _____

3. Please check the statement below which best reflects your attitude toward the **"quality of service"** you experienced in this last contact with police officers from the Experimental Police District. *(Check only one)*
   _____ The **quality of service** I received was somewhat **"lower"** than I had expected.
   _____ The **quality of service** I received was **about** what I had expected.
   _____ The **quality of service** I received was somewhat **"higher"** than I had expected.

4. Using the scale below, please rate your last contact in the following areas of service:

	Excellent	Good	Fair	Poor	Very poor
a. Concern	_____	_____	_____	_____	_____
b. Helpfulness	_____	_____	_____	_____	_____
c. Knowledge	_____	_____	_____	_____	_____
d. Fairness	_____	_____	_____	_____	_____
e. Solving the problem	_____	_____	_____	_____	_____
f. Putting you at ease	_____	_____	_____	_____	_____
g. Professional conduct	_____	_____	_____	_____	_____
h. Response time	_____	_____	_____	_____	_____

5. How would you sugest that officers in the Experimental Police District might improve the quality of their services in the future? *(Attach additional pages if you'd like!)*

6. Would you please supply the following information about yourself?
   I am: _____ male   _____ female
   My race is: _____ white   _____ black   _____ Hispanic   _____ other
   My age is: _____ under 17   _____ 18–20   _____ 21–24   _____ 25–39   _____ over 40
   I earn: _____ under $5,000   _____ $5–19,000   _____ $20–34,000   _____ over $35,000

The men and women of the Experimental Police District
thank you for completing this questionnaire!

Figure 13–1   Customer survey, Madison, Wisconsin, police department.

Accreditation   One form of outside evaluation may be particularly appealing to many police administrators—the police agency accreditation process conducted by the Commission on Accreditation for Law Enforcement Agencies (CALEA).[52] Applicants for accreditation must meet a large number of standards regarding organizational structure, physical plant, policies, rules, and record-keeping functions. A department that undertakes the accreditation process spends many months reviewing its status and bringing its practices into compliance with the commission's standards. When department managers believe that the department has satisfied the requisite standards, a small team of specially selected and trained law enforcement professionals from departments outside the locale conduct a site review of several days to verify whether the department is in fact in compliance. The team does this by talking to

---

Accreditation of law enforcement agencies   The Commission on Accreditation for Law Enforcement Agencies, Inc., provides comprehensive standards that serve as points of reference by which a police agency can measure and improve its performance.

The development of standards and a process for achieving accreditation began in 1979 as a cooperative undertaking by four associations of law enforcement leaders: the International Association of Chiefs of Police, the National Organization of Black Law Enforcement Executives, the National Sheriffs' Association, and the Police Executive Research Forum. The program itself became operational in 1983.

A twenty-one-member body, the commission, guided the development and continues to have final authority for setting standards and policy for granting accreditation. The commission's members, appointed by unanimous consent of the four organizations, consist of eleven law enforcement practitioners and ten public- and private-sector leaders.

The underlying philosophy of the commission was, and still is, that participation in the program is voluntary; that standards are a positive statement of what, not how an agency fulfills its role and carries out its authority; that standards are to be evaluated and updated to reflect the state of the art; that accreditation requirements are based on the size

and responsibilities of the agency; and that the highest level of objectivity is maintained throughout the process.

Standards cover four major areas: (1) policies and procedures; (2) administration, including personnel-related questions such as recruitment, selection, and promotion; (3) operations, such as investigation, traffic, juvenile operations, public information, and community relations; and (4) support services, such as communications, records, and property management.

To become accredited, a department begins by filing an application. Next it completes a profile questionnaire to ascertain which standards apply to it. A self-assessment follows to make sure it meets the required standards. Then an on-site accreditation team visits the department and prepares a report for the commission, which decides whether to award accreditation or require further action.

Accreditation is for five years. During that time, a department offers annual reports verifying that it remains in compliance with the required standards. Before the five-year anniversary, a department that wishes to remain accredited again goes through the formal process, meeting more standards each time.

Source: Ken Medeiros, Executive Director, Commission on Accreditation for Law Enforcement Agencies, Inc., 4242B Chain Bridge Road, Fairfax, Virginia 22030.

department administrators and personnel, reviewing records, observing operations, talking to local public officials, and inviting input from members of
the community at a public hearing. The site team reports to the commissioners, who decide whether to grant the department accredited status or to
indicate that further work is needed. Before making this decision, the commission holds a hearing to review the site team report and to question members
of the team and representatives of the department.

Pursuing accreditation is a major undertaking that requires considerable
commitment of departmental energies. Departments that achieve accredited
status are justifiably proud of the accomplishment but may be tempted to
draw inferences that accreditation does not necessarily warrant. Accreditation
focuses on administrative matters, not on the accomplishment of ultimate
police objectives. For example, the commission's evaluation does not include
a direct assessment of the extent to which the department has controlled crime
or disorder. Nor does the commission systematically assess officers' performance in making arrests, handling domestic crises, or undertaking the host of
other police functions. But it does assess the extent to which the department
has complied with guidelines that the commission feels are associated with
good administrative practice. To the extent that these administrative practices
produce better performance on the street, a chief may claim (indirectly) that
his department is a high performer.

As yet, however, there has been very little rigorous scientific validation of
the effect of most of the commission's standards (separately or together) on
the kinds of things that citizens care about.[53] In fact, most of the standards
are purposefully flexible as to what the substance of department policy should
be, leaving that to the department to decide. (There are important exceptions,
however, such as the standard on police use of deadly force.) Most standards
require only that the department have an explicit policy on a given topic or
that its policies take certain factors into account. It is thus appropriate to
think of CALEA accreditation as signifying the attainment of certain administrative objectives but not as signifying anything one way or the other about
the quality of street-level policing.

Using performance measurement

Performance measures can serve their intended purpose only if they are *used*
in policy making, administration, and external assessments of the department.
Making effective use of performance measurement requires both administrative
and political acumen and is influenced by the political environment in which the
results of a performance study are reported. From the police administrator's
perspective, it is usually better for the department to receive a positive assessment
than a negative one, but not always. Negative results can be used to generate
momentum to change the organization. Moreover, even a negative assessment
is better than a scandal or a crisis: the police executive is generally able to
anticipate the timing and format of the release of performance information and
to use it constructively, whereas advance knowledge of a scandal or crisis is rare,
so such problems are less manageable as tools for departmental assessment. In
other words, the administrator who uncovers a problem is in a politically preferable position to the one who has it thrust upon him or her, for in the former
case the administrator appears to have some control and the intention to correct
the problem.

Police administrators are understandably jittery when outsiders are hired to
evaluate the department, because the outsiders may not provide sufficient briefing before releasing the results, and the chief may not have a chance to fully
absorb the findings and their significance. This is easily rectified in most cases

Community policing and law enforcement accreditation: emerging issues

Creative police practitioners throughout the country during the 1980s began to explore new ways of dealing with the overwhelming burden of crime, violence, and drugs. New strategies began to evolve which were distinguished by the fact that they pooled the collective resources of both public and private sectors for the purpose of reclaiming targeted neighborhoods. Increasingly, it became apparent that broad coalitions between the police department and the larger community were far more effective than traditional law enforcement, which has been dominated by more narrowly focused operational responses driven in large part reactively from citizens through 9–1–1.

This realization, in turn, caused many to reexamine—and sometimes to redefine—the role of the police in the areas of restoring and maintaining order. In the course of this reevaluation, time-honored traditions and practices have come under the magnifying glass of the evolving community policing and problem-oriented policing movements.

Basic questions are being asked: Is the semi-military model still the best way to organize and structure the organization in an emerging environment which emphasizes creative problem solving at the patrol officer level? Is professional and optimal police performance that demands the achievement of results best ensured by comprehensive written directive systems that define and constrain the latitude of employee actions as they perform their jobs? Is the flexible exercise of discretion by police officers appropriate given the responsibility of the police chief and other administrators to maintain control of the organization and to avert the police corruption and political influence-peddling that occurred much more often in bygone eras? How can the accountability of individual police officers delivering "tailored" services to neighborhoods and groups within neighborhoods be ensured? When the police service-delivery orientation changes from one focused primarily on means (quantitative) to one that gives primacy to results (qualitative), can adequate measures of effectiveness and efficiency be developed?

At about the same time this rethinking of traditional police roles and accountability structures was initiated, many police departments were actively pursuing national accreditation through the Commission on Accreditation for Law Enforcement Agencies. Proponents of this process hailed it as the long-awaited and much-needed means for the police to attain true "professional" status. By achieving compliance with nationally established and recognized standards, it was thought that police organizations could strive for and ultimately achieve a higher and more professional level of performance and service.

The question which arises now, however, is whether the neighborhood-oriented, creative problem-solving approach of community policing is on a collision course with the requirements of the accreditation program. The discussion is beginning to be focused on one particularly crucial issue of uniformity versus individuality. Once a problem has been identified in a

---

by asking that the department receive a detailed briefing on any study before it is made public.

Even when police executives have a good grasp of an evaluation and its implications, it is still disappointing if the target of what turns out to be a negative evaluation is a new program that was initiated with enthusiastic support from the chief. This, too, can be handled if, *from the very beginning of the program*, the chief has emphasized that it is an *experiment* and therefore needs careful evaluation to see if it should be modified, retained, or expanded. The important thing is to be hopeful or even enthusiastic without providing promises and

community policing or problem-oriented policing department, the challenge for the organization and the officers becomes one of customizing a strategy that has the best chance of resolving it. Thus, creativity, individuality, and the attainment of desired outcomes are prized and encouraged. Accreditation, on the other hand, is primarily process-oriented. Once the decision has been made to seek accreditation, the challenge becomes one of achieving compliance with an established national set of several hundred specific standards. Accordingly, uniformity and consistency—not only across neighborhoods but across cities—are prized and encouraged.

An argument can be made that accreditation and community based, problem-focused policing are complementary rather than contradictory. The point would be that accreditation provides policy and procedural boundaries within which creative problem-solving and tailored service delivery can occur and outside of which these initiatives would be extremely risky. Unrestricted discretion in agents of the government—even in pursuit of the highest goals—is inconsistent with U.S. constitutional democracy, and any appearance of such broad license will exacerbate the concerns expressed by the detractors of community policing. Accreditation advocates note, moreover, that nothing within the accreditation standards hamstrings the efforts of police agencies to be less restrictive, more problem-focused, and more creative.

Still, an increasing number of police executives are expressing doubts that it is possible to encourage and facilitate innovation, flexibility, and empowerment, from the top to the bottom of the police organization and from the top to the bottom of the community, while at the same time emphasizing conformance to predetermined, nationally uniform rules, regulations, policies, and procedures.

Proponents of community policing are beginning to ask whether the accreditation process, *as currently structured and defined*, is the best means in the future to achieve professional status in a way that helps the profession become and remain the best that it can be. Practitioners who believe that community policing and accreditation can coexist and indeed are interdependent ask whether accreditation provides a foundation that is needed for the proper development of the philosophy of community policing.

The time has come for placing the role of accreditation vis-à-vis community policing under the magnifying glass. The law of nature that all species must adapt to their changing environments to survive applies in full measure to such important man-made institutions as national accreditation.

Source: Elizabeth M. Watson, Chief, Houston Police Department; and Gerald L. Williams, Chief, Aurora, Colorado, Police Department, and Commissioner, Commission on Accreditation for Law Enforcement Agencies. The Houston and Aurora police departments have been active participants in the accreditation process and are both accredited departments.

guarantees. Premature endorsement of a program, policy, or practice—before it is evaluated—is both unwise management and unsound politics. Conversely, premature evaluation of an ambitious innovation (before it has had time to be fully implemented) is poor use of evaluation methodology and tends to make practitioners suspicious of research.

Improving performance in fact requires trial and error, and the more administrators, politicians, and evaluators acknowledge this, the more receptive the public is when results are less than hoped for. Sometimes results highlight correctible weaknesses, giving the department an opportunity to stress the value of the lessons learned from the experiment. It is also important to remember that most performance studies fail to produce uniformly positive or negative results. There is usually a mix, so the good news can soften the disappointment of objectives not accomplished. Sometimes this can be carried too far. There is a difference between giving performance results a balanced presentation and allowing "spin doctors" to present them in a way that makes things seem what they are not.

Performance measurement results can also be misused when they are positive. Perhaps the most frequent abuse occurs every time UCR results are reported and police administrators around the nation are asked for an interpretation of their local statistics. When reported crime has declined from the previous year, a number of chiefs suggest that their favorite program or policy was responsible, although in fact UCR crime rates may not reflect actual crime trends, and the report in no way controls for the multitude of factors that affect crime trends from year to year.

Premature endorsement of a program, policy, or practice—before it is evaluated—is both unwise management and unsound politics.

In addition to using performance measurement results for policy making and administration, police executives can share them with others outside the department to great advantage. Other police departments and researchers can benefit from seeing how measures were developed, data collected, and results analyzed. It is particularly important to disseminate and publicize results of interest to the public at large. Recipients of the information should be encouraged to offer reactions to the report, to improve not only performance but also performance *measurement*. In the case of elected and appointed officials with oversight responsibility for police, it pays to find out what interests them and to present the results of performance measurements in those areas in a concise, readily comprehensible form. Far too many routine police reports to these officials offer page after page of mind-numbing statistics in which the readers have no interest.

Conclusion

Measuring the performance of police employees and departments responds to our curiosity to know "how we're doin'." This chapter has suggested that individual performance appraisal and departmental performance measurement require the resolution of both political issues (what *ought* the police try to accomplish?) and empirical issues (what *can* they accomplish?), and that the answer to each should inform inquiry into the other. Performance appraisal and measurement are technical matters, but police managers must not lose sight of the fact that technical excellence is only one challenge, and perhaps not even the most important one, in this area. Performance appraisal and measurement should be undertaken to influence what police and others do. The development of social science methodology, computer capability, and sophisticated statistical techniques—and their increasing accessibility to police and researchers—may give the impression that objectivity and systematic scientific inquiry (as manifest in performance appraisal and measurement) are the dominant influence on police policy making and administration. Realistically, though, many other factors necessarily compete for influence in policy making and administration, and performance evaluation is rarely the determining factor in much high-level decision making. It is too often used selectively to justify only the course of action an executive wishes to take. The challenge connected with performance appraisal and measurement is thus not only to *do* them better but also to *use* them better. The significant advances made by police and researchers suggest that the prospects for substantially improving police performance appraisal and measurement in the final decade of the twentieth century are good.

1   This chapter excludes from consideration assessments that focus on contrived situations or instruments to elicit information on the skills and capabilities of employees—such as paper and pencil tests, interviews, and assessment center exercises. It considers only on-the-job behaviors that occur under actual work conditions, and the consequences of those behaviors.

2   Barry R. Nathan and Wayne F. Cascio, "Introduction: Technical and Legal Standards," in *Performance Assessment: Methods and Applications*, ed. Ronald A. Berk (Baltimore: Johns Hopkins University Press, 1986), 1–52. This source is drawn on throughout the chapter, particularly for discussions of court decisions on performance appraisal, and it is not separately cited in each instance.

3   American Bar Association, *The Urban Police Function*, Standards supplement (Chicago: American Bar Association, 1982), 1-249–66; American Justice Institute, *Tools and Guidelines for Measuring Police Effectiveness and Productivity* (Sacramento, CA: American Justice Institute, 1978); Commission on Accreditation for Law Enforcement Agencies, *Standards for Law Enforcement Agencies* (Fairfax, VA: Commission on Accreditation for Law Enforcement Agencies, 1983); David C. Couper, "How to Rate Your Local Police" (Washington, DC: Police Executive Research Forum, 1983); National Advisory Commission on Criminal Justice Standards and Goals, *Police* (Washington, DC: U.S. Government Printing Office, 1973); Gordon P. Whitaker, Stephen Mastrofski, Elinor Ostrom, Roger B. Parks, and Stephen L. Percy, *Basic Issues in Police Performance* (Washington, DC: U.S. Department of Justice, 1982); Gordon P. Whitaker et al., "Performance Measurement," in *The Encyclopedia of Police Science*, ed. William G. Bailey (New York: Garland Publishing, 1989), 384–88; O. W. Wilson, *Police Administration*, 2d ed. (New York: McGraw-Hill, 1963); and Samuel Walker, "Setting the Standards: The Efforts and Impact of Blue-Ribbon Commissions on the Police," in *Police Leadership in America: Crisis and Opportunity*, ed. William A. Geller (New York: Praeger, 1985).

4   Ronald A. Berk, "Preface," in *Performance Assessment*, ed. Berk, x; David L. DeVries, Ann M. Morrison, Sandra L. Shullman, and Michael L. Gerlach, *Performance Appraisal on the Line* (New York: John Wiley and Sons, 1981), 21–23; and Frank J. Landy and James L. Farr, *The Measurement of Work Performance* (New York: Academic Press, 1983), 3–4 and chaps. 6 and 7.

5   DeVries et al., *Performance Appraisal on the Line*, chap. 5.

6   Sidney A. Fine, "Job Analysis," in *Performance Assessment*, ed. Berk, 54–60.

7   Michael G. Maxfield, *Indiana Police Task Analysis* (Indianapolis: Center for Criminal Justice Research and Information, Indiana Criminal Justice Institute, 1989).

8   Fine, "Job Analysis," 66–69.

9   Egon Bittner, "Legality and Workmanship: Introduction to Control in the Police Organization," in *Control in the Police Organization*, ed. Maurice Punch (Cambridge: MIT Press, 1983), 1–8.

10 Ibid.

11 Bernard Cohen and Jan Chaiken, *Investigators Who Perform Well* (Washington, DC: U.S. Department of Justice, 1987), 32; and John E. Eck, *Solving Crimes: The Investigation of Burglary and Robbery* (Washington, DC: National Institute of Justice and Police Executive Research Forum, 1983).

12 Brian Forst, F. Leahy, J. Shirhall, H. Tyson, J. Bartolomeo, and E. Wish, *Arrest Convictability as a Measure of Police Performance* (Washington, DC: National Institute of Justice, 1982); Floyd Feeney, F. Dill, and A. Weir, *Arrests without Conviction: How Often They Occur and Why* (Washington, DC: National Institute of Justice, 1983); and Peter Greenwood, Jan M. Chaiken, and Joan Petersilia, *The Criminal Investigation Process* (Lexington, MA: D. C. Heath and Company, 1977).

13 Joan Petersilia, Allan Abrahamse, and James Q. Wilson, *Police Performance and Case Attrition* (Washington, DC: National Institute of Justice, 1987), 42; and Couper, "How to Rate Your Local Police," 6.

14 Forst et al., *Arrest Convictability*.

15 DeVries et al., *Performance Appraisal on the Line*, 45; Rick R. Jacobs, "Numerical Rating Scales," in *Performance Assessment*, ed. Berk, 88–97; and Landy and Farr, *The Measurement of Work Performance*, 73–76.

16 Walter C. Borman, "Behavior-based Rating Scales," in *Performance Assessment*, ed. Berk, 82–120; DeVries et al., *Performance Appraisal on the Line*, 38–59; Jacobs, "Numerical Rating Scales"; and Landy and Farr, *The Measurement of Work Performance*, chap. 3.

17 William Ker Muir, Jr., *Police: Streetcorner Politicians* (Chicago: University of Chicago Press, 1977); and David H. Bayley and Egon Bittner, "Learning the Skills of Policing," in *Critical Issues in Policing: Contemporary Readings*, ed. Roger G. Dunham and Geoffrey P. Alpert (Prospect Heights, IL: Waveland Press, 1989), 87–110.

18 The difficulty in using the BARS format in this and other types of situations is discussed in Paul M. Whisenand, *The Effective Police Manager* (Englewood Cliffs, NJ: Prentice-Hall, 1981), 213–25.

19 DeVries et al., *Performance Appraisal on the Line*, 56–59; and Frank J. Landy and James L. Farr, "Performance Rating," *Psychological Bulletin* 87, no. 1 (1980): 89.

20 Landy and Farr, *The Measurement of Work Performance*, 90; and Borman, "Behavior-based Rating Scales," 117.

21 Robert M. Guion, "Personnel Evaluation," in *Performance Assessment*, ed. Berk, 345–60.

22 DeVries et al., *Performance Appraisal on the Line*, 33–34; and N. F. Iannone, *Supervision of Police*

Personnel, 4th ed. (Englewood Cliffs, NJ: Prentice-Hall, 1987), 264–69.

23 Landy and Farr, *The Measurement of Work Performance*, 132; and James L. Farr and Frank J. Landy, "The Development and Use of Supervisory and Peer Scales," in *Police Selection and Evaluation: Issues and Techniques*, ed. Charles D. Spielberger (New York: Praeger, 1979), 73.

24 For a brief discussion of these options, see DeVries et al., *Performance Appraisal on the Line*, chap. 4; and Jacobs, "Numerical Rating Scales," 86.

25 David Weisburd, Jerome McElroy, and Patricia Hardyman, "Challenges to Supervision in Community Policing: Observations on a Pilot Project," *American Journal of Police* 7 (1988).

26 On the benefits and drawbacks of multiple raters, see DeVries et al., *Performance Appraisal on the Line*, 64–68; and C. E. Schneier, "Multiple Rater Groups and Performance Appraisal," *Public Personnel Management*, 6 (1977): 13–20.

27 Apparently "in-process documentation" can be carried too far, however. One expert reports the use of a daily diary system, on a trial basis, by police training officers to evaluate the performance of recruits. Raters were asked to record at the end of each day the best and worst thing each recruit had done during the day. The training officers found the amount of paperwork onerous, and one facetiously reported, "[T]he worst thing one recruit did all day was to kill an insect in the patrol car without asking permission, while the best thing he had done all day was to remove a dead insect from the patrol car on his own initiative!" (Guion, "Personnel Evaluation," 358).

28 Michael S. McCampbell, "Field Training for Police Officers: State of the Art" (Washington, DC: National Institute of Justice, 1986).

29 Landy and Farr, *The Measurement of Work Performance*, 145.

30 James H. McGinnis, "Validity in the Assessment Center," in *The Police Assessment Center*, ed. Harry W. More and Peter C. Unsinger (Springfield, IL: Charles C. Thomas, 1987), 105–11.

31 DeVries et al., *Performance Appraisal on the Line*, 71–72; and Landy and Farr, *The Measurement of Work Performance*, 171–73.

32 See, for example, Iannone, *Supervision of Police Personnel*, 142–45; the collection of readings in Section 7 of A. Dale Timpe, ed., *The Art and Science of Business Management: Performance* (New York: Facts on File, 1988), 293–365; and Roger J. Plachy, *Performance Management: Getting Results from Your Performance Planning and Appraisal System* (New York: American Management Association, 1988), chap. 7.

33 M. M. Greller and D. M. Herold, "Sources of Feedback: A Preliminary Investigation," *Organizational Behavior and Human Performance*, 13 (1975): 244–56.

34 DeVries et al., *Performance Appraisal on the Line*, 38; see also Wayne F. Cascio and H. John Bernardin, "Implications of Performance Appraisal Litigation for Personnel Decisions," *Personnel Psychology* 34 (1981): 211–26; Plachy, *Performance Management*, chap. 11.

35 DeVries et al., *Performance Appraisal on the Line*, 31–33; and Lawrence R. O'Leary, *The Selection and Promotion of the Successful Police Officer* (Springfield, IL: Charles C. Thomas, 1979), 18–22.

36 Whitaker et al., *Basic Issues in Police Performance*, chap. 9.

37 Richard H. Ward and Robert McCormack, *Managing Police Corruption: International Perspectives* (Chicago: Office of International Criminal Justice, The University of Illinois at Chicago, 1987), 33–76; Thomas Barker and David L. Carter, eds., *Police Deviance* (Cincinnati: Pilgrimage, 1986).

38 Carl B. Klockars, "The Rhetoric of Community Policing," in *Community Policing: Rhetoric or Reality*, ed. Jack R. Greene and Stephen D. Mastrofski (New York: Praeger, 1988), 239–58; and Peter K. Manning, *Police Work: The Social Organization of Policing* (Cambridge: MIT Press, 1977), 369–70. For a more positive assessment of the police capacity, see Lawrence W. Sherman, "Policing Communities: What Works?" in *Communities and Crime*, ed. Albert J. Reiss, Jr., and Michael Tonry (Chicago: University of Chicago Press, 1986), 343–86. See also the chapters in this volume on the patrol function, criminal investigations, local drug control, and crime prevention.

39 E. Davis and L. Knowles, "A Critique of the Report: An Evaluation of the Kansas City Preventive Patrol Experiment," *The Police Chief* 42 (1975); S. Fienberg, K. Larntz, and A. Reiss, "Redesigning the Kansas City Preventive Patrol Experiment," *Evaluation* 3 (1976): 124–31; and Richard C. Larson, "What Happened to Patrol Operations in Kansas City? A Review of the Kansas City Preventive Patrol Experiment," *Journal of Criminal Justice* 3 (1975).

40 On community policing, see the chapter in this volume on crime prevention; and Jack R. Greene and Ralph B. Taylor, "Community-Based Policing and Foot Patrol: Issues of Theory and Evaluation," in *Community Policing*, ed. Greene and Mastrofski, 195–223. On criminal investigation, see Eck, *Solving Crimes*, and this volume's chapter on criminal investigations. On community crime prevention, see the chapter on crime prevention and Dennis P. Rosenbaum, "Community Crime Prevention: A Review and Synthesis of the Literature," *Justice Quarterly* 5 (1988): 323–95. On undercover operations, see Gary T. Marx, *Undercover: Police Surveillance in America* (Berkeley: University of California Press, 1988). On police effectiveness in controlling crime, see generally Mike Hough, "Thinking about Effectiveness," *British Journal of Criminology* 27 (1987): 70–79; and Michael Chatterton, "Assessing Police Effectiveness—Future Prospects," *British Journal of Criminology* 27 (1987): 80–86.

41 For an argument in favor of developing such measures of order maintenance, see George L. Kelling, "Order Maintenance, the Quality of Urban Life, and Police: A Line of Argument," in *Police Leadership in America*, ed. Geller, 307. See also Mark H. Moore and Robert C. Trojanowicz, *Policing and the Fear of Crime*, Perspectives on Policing (Washington, DC: National Institute of Justice, 1988). For a critique of fear of crime as a performance indicator, see Stephen D. Mastrofski, "Community Policing As Reform: A Cautionary Tale," in *Community Policing*, ed. Greene and Mastrofski, 47–67.

42 A large number of well-written introductory books and manuals have been published on conducting research for the purpose of performance measurement and policy evaluation. Two useful general texts are Emil J. Posavac and Raymond G. Carey, *Program Evaluation: Methods and Case Studies*, 2d ed. (Englewood Cliffs, NJ: Prentice-Hall, 1985); and Peter H. Rossi and Howard E. Freeman,

Evaluation: A Systematic Approach, 4th ed. (Newbury Park, CA: Sage, 1989). A useful primer with examples focused on law enforcement management issues is John E. Eck, *Using Research: A Primer for Law Enforcement Managers* (Washington, DC: Police Executive Research Forum, 1984).

43 Egon Bittner, *The Functions of Police in Modern Society* (Washington, DC: U.S. Government Printing Office, 1970); and Hough, "Thinking about Effectiveness," 78.

44 See for example, Muir, *Police*; Richard E. Sykes and Edward E. Brent, "The Regulation of Interaction by Police: A Systems View of Taking Charge," *Criminology* (August 1980): 182–97; Richard E. Sykes and Edward E. Brent, *Policing: A Social Behaviorist Perspective* (New Brunswick, NJ: Rutgers University Press); Jonathan Rubinstein, *City Police* (New York: Farrar, Straus and Giroux, 1973); John Van Maanen, "Working the Street: A Developmental View of Police Behavior," in *The Potential for Reform of Criminal Justice*, ed. Herbert Jacob (Beverly Hills, CA: Sage, 1974), 83–130.

45 John P. McIver and Roger B. Parks, "Evaluating Police Performance: Identification of Effective and Ineffective Police Actions," in *Police at Work: Policy Issues and Analysis*, ed. Richard R. Bennett (Beverly Hills, CA: Sage, 1983), 21–44; David H. Bayley, "The Tactical Choices of Police Patrol Officers," *Journal of Criminal Justice* 14 (1986): 329–48; David H. Bayley and James Garofalo, "The Management of Violence by Police Patrol Officers," *Criminology* 27 (1989): 1–25; James J. Fyfe, "The Metro-Dade Police/Citizen Violence Reduction Project: A Summary of Findings and Implications," *FBI Law Enforcement Bulletin* 5, no. 5 (May 1989): 18–22; and William A. Geller, "Officer Restraint in the Use of Deadly Force: The Next Frontier in Police Shooting Research," *Journal of Police Science and Administration* 13 (1985): 153.

46 For a readable introduction to program evalua-

tion designs, see Posavac and Carey, *Program Evaluation*.

47 Federal Bureau of Investigation, "The Redesigned UCR Program" (Washington, DC: Federal Bureau of Investigation, 1988), 6. For detailed information on NIBRS, departments can obtain a three-volume set of documents on data collection guidelines, data submission specifications, and approaches to implementing an incident-based system by contacting the Uniform Crime Reporting Section of the FBI.

48 John E. Eck and William Spelman, *Problem-Solving: Problem-oriented Policing in Newport News* (Washington, DC: Police Executive Research Forum, 1987); and William Spelman, *Beyond Bean Counting: New Approaches for Managing Crime Data* (Washington, DC: Police Executive Research Forum, 1988).

49 Eck and Spelman, *Problem-Solving*, chap. 5.

50 John Van Maanen, "The Boss: First-Line Supervision in an American Police Agency," in *Control in the Police Organization*, ed. Punch, 275–317; Van Maanen, "Working the Street"; and Michael R. Chatterton, "Police Work and Assault Charges," in *Control in the Police Organization*, ed. Punch, 201.

51 Peter K. Manning, *Symbolic Communication: Signifying Calls and Police Response* (Cambridge: MIT Press, 1988).

52 For a discussion of agency accreditation, see Stephen D. Mastrofski, "Police Agency Accreditation: The Prospects of Reform," *American Journal of Police* 8 (1986): 45–81; and Cornelius J. Behan, "The Accreditation Process," in *Police Practice in the '90s: Key Management Issues*, ed. James J. Fyfe (Washington, DC: International City Management Association, 1989), 124–34.

53 For the most comprehensive empirical review of accreditation to date, see Gerald L. Williams, *Making the Grade: The Benefits of Law Enforcement Accreditation* (Washington, DC: Police Executive Research Forum, 1989).

14 Equipment and facilities

Like any professionals, police officers must have the equipment and facilities that will allow them to perform their job properly. The quantity and quality of equipment in a law enforcement agency affects employee job satisfaction, departmental liability, and quality of service to the community. And one of the most significant decisions a police executive will ever make is the decision to undertake a major facility construction or renovation.

In modern police service, the array of available equipment is vast. Departments must evaluate and test products to determine the weaponry, personal safety equipment, and vehicles that meet their individual needs for effectiveness, efficiency, and risk management. They must also manage property—the property they own and acquire and the property (and evidence) they seize. The equipment portion of this chapter focuses on weapons, other self-protection devices, property management, and vehicles. Other equally crucial tools for the modern police officer—communication devices, computers, and other information management equipment—are discussed in the chapter on information management.

The quantity and quality of equipment affects employee job satisfaction, department liability, and quality of service to the community.

Facility construction and renovation—the choices made in the course of the project and the ability to complete it as planned—severely test an administrator's managerial and interpersonal skills. More important, decisions made in the current fiscal year may significantly affect the organization over the next twenty-five to fifty years. The long-range strategic planning that shapes the police facility and the foresight and flexibility embodied in the plan will either limit future administrative and operational activities or provide the flexibility necessary for change. The facilities portion of this chapter does not answer every question about facilities construction and renovation, nor does it guide architects and planners. Rather, it sums up the primary issues and processes to be considered in most major facilities projects.

Armament

In recent years, few subjects have stimulated as much research and sparked as much controversy as police armament. The need to provide law enforcement officers with the weapons and safety equipment necessary to face an increasingly well-armed opponent in a street encounter has been a key issue faced by police administrators, city and county managers, elected officials, employee organizations, and others. The proliferating use by criminals of sophisticated weaponry—specifically assault weapons—has led to local and state legislation and even a presidential ban on imports. Thus, the issue of weaponry and the proper armament of law enforcement officers clearly is no longer solely the concern of police and sheriffs' departments.

At the same time that concern for more effective weaponry is increasing, public demand for alternatives to deadly force are also on the rise. The use of nonlethal weapons and nonlethal techniques of apprehension have become essential components of the law enforcement agency's policy and the individual officer's training. In determining the type of armament best suited to the police operation, therefore, law enforcement agencies must consider not only the threat to officer safety but also the nature and requirements of their individual communities. Arming officers is a tremendous responsibility as well as a potential liability.

The armament requirements of a police department include service weapons and ammunition; shotguns; special purpose weapons, munitions, and equipment; chemical munitions; nonlethal weapons; and soft body armor.

Service weapons

It has been observed that, for modern policing, the police officer's most important tool is often his or her verbal skills. Nevertheless, it is undeniable that a quality side arm, whether a revolver or a semiautomatic pistol, is another essential law enforcement tool. In fact, an officer's service weapon is one of the first recognizable symbols of his or her authority.

In recent years, few subjects have stimulated as much research and sparked as much controversy as police armament.

Officers must have confidence not only in the weapon but also in their ability to use it accurately. Thus, training is as important as—and, many believe, more important than—the type of weapon carried.[1] Proper and frequent training on whatever weaponry a department deems appropriate improves response, enhances officer survival, and reduces liability. Moreover, because officers encounter and confiscate a wide variety of weapons during field operations, they must be familiar with safe techniques for handling these weapons (officers must know, for example, how to render these weapons safe to avoid an accidental discharge).

The type of weapon carried is certainly a major consideration. One of the most important decisions a law enforcement officer may have to make involves the application of deadly force. His or her decision may affect the department, other officers, and possibly his or her own career. Most significantly, it may mean saving the life of an innocent party or fellow officer and taking the life of a suspect. It is the department's responsibility to provide the officer with the best weapon possible to ensure that, when the decision to apply deadly force is made, that decision can be carried out effectively. It is important to reiterate, however, that whatever type of weapon is issued to officers, effective use of it depends on sound policy (policy deemed credible by officers and the community alike), quality training, and practice.

In recent years the comparative values of semiautomatic pistols and traditional revolvers have been much debated. Choosing between the two requires research and testing, and many departments have spent considerable time and effort exploring to see which alternative best meets their needs.

Historically, officers in the field have carried revolvers. Revolvers can be placed into action quickly. They have no external safeties, and, with speed loaders, they can be reloaded relatively quickly. They accept a variety of ammunition. Quality revolvers have built-in safety mechanisms to prevent accidental firing in the event they are dropped. If a cartridge misfires, a squeeze of the trigger brings another round into the ready position.

But semiautomatic pistols also offer a number of advantages; and, at the same time, problems traditionally associated with semiautomatic pistols, such as jamming, have been virtually eliminated from the latest generation of weaponry. Thus, many departments have changed from revolvers.

The most frequent reason for changing to semiautomatics is increased fire power through greater ammunition capacity. For example, many semiautomatics hold fifteen or more rounds in a magazine, whereas the standard revolver holds six rounds. In addition, semiautomatic pistols can be reloaded quickly with less dexterity than is needed to reload a revolver. Semiautomatics can also be fired more rapidly than revolvers. And, depending upon the size of the frame, semi-automatics can be mandated as both an on-duty and an off-duty pistol, so that officers no longer carry an excessive variety of weapons.

One of the many issues that departments have considered in changing from revolvers to semiautomatics is cost. A semiautomatic often costs more than a revolver. To overcome the cost difference, some departments have phased in the conversion. Semiautomatics have been issued to special operations personnel and certain other units in the first year and, as budgets allow, to additional personnel in subsequent years.

Whatever type of weapon is issued to officers, effective use of it depends on sound policy (policy deemed credible by officers and the community alike), quality training, and practice.

In converting to a semiautomatic, a department must retrain personnel in the maintenance and use of the weapon. Training should be an essential element of the change and should be provided before or upon issue of the new weapons but, in any event, before any field use of the weapons is authorized. A comprehensive classroom and firing range conversion course requires sixteen hours or more of training per officer.

Other considerations besides cost and training include the following:

Grip circumference (on certain models, grip circumference is too large for small hands)

Quality of the ammunition magazine (a poorly manufactured or damaged magazine may cause the pistol to malfunction)

Physical configuration (some semiautomatics are historically designed for right-handed shooters)

Ease of use (some models require two hands to make the weapon ready for action; this would be a problem if the officer's hand were injured in a combat situation or if one hand were needed for some tactical maneuver).

In choosing the type of weapon and ammunition that officers will carry, the department should consider effectiveness, firepower, safety, and related factors. The FBI is currently experimenting with a 10-mm semiautomatic pistol that may well become the standard for law enforcement into the twenty-first century.

Whatever service weapon is chosen, pre-issue and ongoing service inspections and testing should be conducted. No new weapon should be issued until an armorer has tested and inspected it. And every department, regardless of size, should implement a program of regular weapon inspections. Armorers or range officers or both, along with field supervisors, should participate in these inspections. (Maintenance is discussed below in connection with ammunition.)

In selecting a service weapon for officers, a department may also consider special needs. As one example, many departments equip special operations officers with a side arm different from those carried by other officers (special-purpose weapons are addressed more fully below). This is done to meet the unique needs of the function. As another example, some departments have selected small-framed weapons, requiring officers to carry the same weapon both on duty and off duty and in plain clothes as well as in uniform.

Ammunition

Ammunition for revolvers and semiautomatic pistols is also a matter of discussion, debate, research, and testing. When choosing ammunition for service weapons, departments must consider myriad issues, including not only stopping power, reliability, accuracy, and liability but also public perception. Because contemporary strategies of policing depend on harnessing community members as full partners in the struggle against crime and disorder, any weapon or ammunition policy that causes serious disaffection within the community may erode a powerful line of defense against officer injuries and liability. The tactically useful information (for example, about whether a suspect whom police are seeking is armed, and with what type of weaponry) that cooperative citizens offer to police may do more to save officers' lives than an armory full of weapons.

Officers patrolling in rural communities may be provided with more powerful ammunition, such as a .357-caliber round, than their counterparts in high-density urban environments. In the rural areas, there is less chance that a round will overpenetrate into a nearby residence or strike an innocent onlooker or bystander. Uncontrolled shots and ricochets in an urban area may create accidental suffering and liability.

Any weapon or ammunition policy that causes serious disaffection within the community may erode a powerful line of defense against officer injuries and liability.

Essentially, in either kind of community, the penetration power needed is whatever will penetrate the human body and stop the opponent's action promptly. To meet this need, the standard ammunition of many law enforcement agencies historically has been the high-speed, semijacketed, hollow point round.

Many firearms experts agree that, in the interest of proficiency, the most powerful weapon and round are not necessarily the best for law enforcement. They point out that, as the caliber of the ammunition and service weapon increases, officer accuracy has a tendency to decrease. This has prevented many departments from moving toward larger-caliber weapons. The focus should be on obtaining the most accurate, best-handling weapon and round.

Like quality equipment and ongoing training, proper maintenance of both weapon and ammunition is essential.

Practice with actual service rounds is essential to familiarize officers with the characteristics of the ammunition in the weapon. Some departments train with wadcutters and other types of inexpensive training rounds. Although this may be practical for making officers familiar with their weapon, it is important for officers to experience firing the round they will have available on the street. Training with the "street round" allows officers to learn to adjust for accuracy, sound, recoil, and recovery time.

Like quality equipment and ongoing training, proper maintenance of both weapon and ammunition is essential. Effective maintenance reduces the potential for malfunction, reduces the department's liability, and enhances officers' confidence in the weaponry. Every department should have a program of regular inspections for all departmental weapons and ammunition—including off-duty equipment.

Each department, regardless of size, should also designate at least one person to handle the inspection, assignment, and maintenance of weaponry. Although additional personnel may be involved in these processes, such as field supervisors who play a key role in inspecting weapons during roll calls, the assignment of specific weapons coordinators to oversee all phases of weaponry will improve the department's efficiency, effectiveness, and dependability and may reduce liability.

The individual officer, too, bears significant responsibility for maintenance of weapons and ammunition, and written policy should affix this responsibility. But, as in any other aspect of police work, committing an obligation to writing obviously does not ensure compliance, so the department's procedures should reinforce the policy. And officers will be more attentive to their weapons if they believe the weapons provide the best possible performance in a crisis. Officers should therefore be made aware of the department's efforts to identify the best possible weapon.

Shotguns

The shotgun is one of the most versatile and potent weapons an officer has at his or her disposal. It provides firepower at both long distances and close range. Its primary purpose is to provide the field officer with an extra measure of support in a crisis encounter, particularly when he or she is dealing with armed or potentially armed people. Despite the consideration given to police use of automatic and assault-type weaponry, the shotgun remains the support weapon most used by police departments, second only to the side arm.

The issuing of shotguns to police officers has been advocated for many years. Almost two decades ago, the National Advisory Commission on Criminal Justice Standards and Goals stated: "Every police agency should insure that the officers of every automobile patrol unit are equipped with a shotgun and appropriate ammunition. An easily accessible shotgun receptacle that can be locked should be installed in every vehicle."[2]

The shotgun's greatest strength is also its greatest weakness. It offers reliable stopping power without requiring precise aim. Thus, it has the potential to harm innocent parties, such as onlookers or other officers. Before firing a shotgun, an officer must consider the type of round carried and its spread or dispersion over an area.

Traditionally, law enforcement agencies have used the pump action, twelve-gauge shotgun, which has been regarded as an effective, relatively inexpensive weapon with few maintenance problems. Mastering the traditional shotgun, like mastering any other weapon, requires quality training, and annual shotgun qualification has become a standard element of the firearms training and risk management programs of many departments. In particular, training and practice are needed to learn combat loading techniques and to become oriented toward automatically "pumping" a round in the chamber.

In recent years, some departments have switched to the gas-operated, self-loading, semiautomatic shotgun. This model ejects a spent cartridge after it is fired and automatically chambers a new one. It has a seven-round magazine (holding more rounds than the traditional weapon). Folding stocks and pistol grips are available to meet specific needs and provide ease in handling. These features meet the requirements of plainclothes officers, special operations officers, and others with specific needs for storage and concealment.

Shotguns accommodate a variety of ammunition, from buckshot to slugs. Standard "00 buckshot" has been the traditional round used, with officers carrying the "slug" round for use if it is needed. Departments should standardize and monitor the shotgun ammunition issued to field personnel.

Regular inspection of shotguns by both officers and supervisors is essential, particularly because many of these weapons are carried in vehicle shotgun racks, where they are subject to dirt, wear, and possible abuse. Carrying shotguns in vehicle trunks, a traditional practice in some departments, may place the officer at a disadvantage because the weapon is then less quickly accessible. If police vehicles are going to be equipped with shotguns, carrying the weapons in secure mechanisms attached to the front seat or dash is preferable to storing them in the trunk. As vehicles continue to downsize so that the trunk becomes the only choice, the distinction may become moot. Automatic trunk releases and careful positioning can lessen the disadvantage. Whenever they are not in use, shotguns should be safely stored and secured.

Every department should have a written policy and procedures governing the issuance, use, and care of shotguns and shotgun ammunition. Policy and procedures should also address the transferring of a shotgun from one officer to another between shifts, with the focus on handling, logging in, loading, and unloading.

Special-purpose weapons, munitions, and equipment

The special operations or quick-response function, traditionally called special weapons and tactics (SWAT), is an important component of many police departments, particularly large ones. Departments that, because of size or funding, are unable to maintain full-time special operations or quick-response teams generally have officers trained in these skills or have access to a nearby department's team. Officers given special operations responsibility must be prepared to respond to unusual or crisis situations—often ones requiring special weaponry, and often on short notice. Among such assignments are VIP escorts, executive and dignitary protection, barricaded subjects, hostage taking, undercover stakeouts, riot control, raids, high-priority crimes in progress, and special events (for example, parades, athletic contests, and public demonstrations). Each department should have written policy and procedures on the assignment and use of these teams.

Officers assigned to quick-response or SWAT teams, as well as patrol officers and those assigned to other specialty units who may be assigned automatic weapons, require special training. An important element of this training is learning when the use of special weaponry is appropriate. Today, weapons assigned to field officers and special operations teams range from fully automatic weapons to semiautomatic antisniper rifles. Special teams may also be issued gas guns designed to disperse a variety of chemicals. In addition, they may be issued a variety of nonlethal weapons (discussed below).

Given the high visibility of most SWAT situations, the public is likely to form lasting impressions of a police department's competence on the basis of its handling of these events.

In selecting special weaponry, a department must consider a variety of factors, including (among others) the nature of the jurisdiction (for example, urban, suburban, rural), penetration power, range, accuracy, and weight. Other considerations include high-capacity magazines, folding stocks and pistol grip configurations, recoil, sights, and ease of clearing if and when a weapon jams. As with other aspects of armament, the effective police department also gives careful consideration to the question of what legitimate arguments support the need for SWAT teams to have special, highly-destructive equipment. Given the high visibility of most SWAT situations, the public is likely to form lasting impressions of a police department's competence on the basis of its handling of these events.

Another area of tactical expertise is the ordnance or bomb disposal unit. As criminals and terrorists become more sophisticated in using explosives, so must police personnel. Regardless of the size of a department, officers should be trained to identify various explosive devices, secure an area, and summon a support unit from their own or another department for assistance. Both the military and state fire marshals' offices provide this training to police departments nationwide.

Ordnance disposal units require the latest in safety equipment. This equipment should include at least the following: a bomb disposal trailer with a receptacle to direct an explosion, rope, nonmagnetic tools, utility uniforms, bomb blankets or netting, armored shields, sand bags, and protective body armor for the unit members. To further protect unit personnel, many units utilize X-ray devices, sound-sensitive monitors, and even robots.

Chemical munitions

Special operations often demand the use of chemical munitions. The choice of the chemical to be used will most likely be dictated by the situation at hand and normally will be made by supervisors rather than individual officers. In all cases, the primary considerations should be accuracy, effectiveness, and safety.

Generally, there are three ways in which chemical munitions are deployed. They are (1) thrown by hand, (2) propelled from a shotgun or projectile launcher, or (3) dispersed from a helicopter. When a law enforcement agency purchases chemical munitions, it should seek those that are nonburning and nonexplosive, have no throw-back capability, and have a long shelf life.

Chemical munitions should be used only by officers who have received specific training in their deployment and effect. Officers assigned to deploy chemical munitions should be issued gas masks and other protective equipment—both for their own protection and for safe removal of hostages, suspects, and others from the area. Officers coming in contact with chemical munitions at a scene should be decontaminated afterward, observed for any signs of reaction to the chemical irritant, and checked by a physician if so warranted.

Individually assigned chemical agents, such as mace, were designed to provide a nonlethal and nontraumatic method of subduing violent persons. When first introduced, these hand-held agents were worn on the gun belt and were issued to almost every law enforcement officer. They were relied upon heavily in situations involving nonlethal force.

Today, fewer officers carry or rely on them. Only 50 percent of the almost three thousand police agencies surveyed by the International Association of Chiefs of Police (IACP) in 1987 authorized the carrying of chemical weapons.[3] A major concern when a chemical is sprayed has been the "backspray" or "overspray." The chemical can affect the officer as much as the suspect. In practice, many officers either carry containers in their police cruisers or wear them on their belts. Chemical agents do, in fact, have a debilitating effect on most suspects.

Nonlethal weapons

In many potentially hazardous situations, use of nonlethal force by law enforcement officers is a viable means of control, and in the proper circumstances nonlethal weapons represent a professionally desirable alternative to deadly force. From controlling combative people to restraining suspects, proper application of nonlethal force can prevent potentially explosive situations from getting out of hand, save lives, and reduce liability. Some definitional clarity is important here, however. Calling a weapon either nonlethal or less than lethal does not constitute an ironclad guarantee that it will never kill a subject on which it is used. Rather, a weapon should be considered nonlethal if, used as prescribed by its manufacturer, it is not intended to and rarely does cause death or serious bodily harm.[4]

Some departments are using electronic weapons, such as the stun gun and TASER. These are nonlethal weapons that can help control a violent person quickly—but they cause some bodily damage. A stun gun can leave burn marks, and a TASER shoots a dart that must sometimes be surgically removed.

Electronic weapons are not without other problems, nor are they without critics. Some electronic weapons have proven ineffective on large, aggressive subjects. Some have also proven ineffective on people under the influence of certain drugs. Furthermore, an officer using certain electronic weapons must make direct contact with the subject, which places that officer in a potentially hazardous situation. And the TASER—the electronic weapon that projects a dart—requires the officer to fire without any type of jerking motion, which may be very difficult. In addition, in some locales, public perceptions have presented enormous obstacles to the use of such contact weapons as stun guns. These obstacles stem partly from isolated cases of inept or abusive use of the weapon and partly from powerful, unshakable images from the past of police using cattle prods against demonstrators. Thus, questions of equipment effectiveness can become inextricably mixed with questions of police attitude and skill.

Proper application of nonlethal force can prevent potentially explosive situations from getting out of hand, save lives, and reduce liability.

Batons are nonlethal impact weapons that have a long-standing role in law enforcement. In recent years, these traditional weapons have undergone change. The straight twenty-four- to twenty-six-inch baton evolved from wood to plastic or fiberglass; and a baton that has a perpendicular protrusion to the main part of the device is now widely used. Officers are trained to use the batons to gain control of a suspect.

Of the 2,914 departments participating in the 1987 IACP survey referred to above, 75 percent authorized the use of nightsticks (batons); 89 percent authorized three-to six-cell flashlights as an impact weapon. Use of a flashlight for this purpose has its proponents and its critics. Proponents point out that the long, narrow flashlights serve a dual purpose, thus reducing the weight on the officer's utility belt; do not have the outward appearance of an aggressive weapon; are sturdy; can be handled easily; and have tactical uses other than serving as an impact weapon. Besides the obvious—illuminating dark areas—their beams can be used to momentarily blind or distract a potentially dangerous opponent. Critics of using flashlights as impact weapons note that the flashlights are heavy and serrated, causing excessive personal injury; do not allow for rapid, effective response or quick recovery; and are not endorsed by manufacturers as impact weapons.

Other nonlethal weapons being deployed in some departments for certain types of controlled encounters are nets, reaching and grabbing devices, and soft projectiles.

Regardless of the nature of the nonlethal equipment provided by the department, sound policy and procedures on the use and the reporting of nonlethal force are essential. For example, the policy of the Jacksonville, Florida, sheriff's office on the use of nonlethal force states: "In certain circumstances, an officer may find it necessary to use non-deadly force in the form of physical restraint, chemical agents, or the police baton. Force may be used only to a degree sufficient to overcome resistance, effect an arrest or to protect [the officer] from great personal injury."[5]

In short, nonlethal weapons provide effective alternatives in potentially dangerous situations in which use of deadly force is inappropriate. Nonlethal weapons are effective, though, only when used by qualified, trained officers and when supported by sound, detailed policy and procedures. Although a department's reporting and debriefing requirements for the use of nonlethal force may not be as rigorous as those for the use of force that is intended to cause death or great bodily harm, reporting and review are nontheless critical.

Regardless of the nature of the nonlethal equipment provided by the department, sound policy and procedures on the use and the reporting of nonlethal force are essential.

Many departments find it highly rewarding to thoroughly debrief officers involved in *noninjurious* uses of either deadly or nondeadly force, for they are facing much lower risks of discipline or civil liability and are therefore often willing to cooperate more fully in identifying aspects of departmental policy, training, and equipment that could be changed to provide better protection to officers and civilians alike in future encounters.[6]

Soft body armor

The use of soft body armor in the field has saved law enforcement officers not only from death by bullets and other types of weapons but also, occasionally, from injuries in motorcycle and automobile accidents. All sworn officers should be issued protective body armor. When selecting body armor, departments should consider protection, comfort, versatility, and concealability. The National Institute of Justice of the U.S. Department of Justice has developed national standards (after extensive testing) that departments will find useful when selecting soft body armor for purchase.

With the variety of soft body armor on the market, law enforcement agencies should be able to find products to meet their local or regional needs. Climate, for example, will influence the type of vest purchased. A moderate climate might dictate a light-weight T-shirt style of vest or the wearing of only the front panel with a back harness.

Selecting and issuing body armor are the first steps in providing protection to officers. The chief of police or sheriff must then determine whether wearing the armor is to be mandatory or optional. If policy mandates that officers wear body armor at all times while on duty, the department must conduct inspections and enforce the policy. This will take some creativity, for national and regional surveys have suggested that the majority of officers who have been issued soft body armor prefer not to wear it while on routine street duty. If wear is optional, policy should dictate that body armor be carried in the police vehicle (with specific guidelines) and be worn—over the uniform, if necessary—when the officer is approaching potentially hazardous situations. To do any less creates undue departmental liability and, more important, does a disservice to the department's officers.

Regardless of the policy on wearing the armor, body armor should be regularly inspected for fit, wear, and abuse. Like any piece of equipment, body armor has a useful life and begins to deteriorate after a certain period of time. No precise time frame can be given on when this deterioration occurs, because there are many different brands, and use and wear vary by individual and region. When either inspection or the manufacturer's guidelines identify the deterioration as excessive, the equipment should be replaced. When soft body armor has been through a traumatic incident and has demonstrably helped save an officer's life, most manufacturers are only too happy to replace the equipment free of charge.

Property

Law enforcement agencies are responsible for the custody, control, and care of three types of property: property that has been seized or taken into control as evidence; property that has been turned in to the department or has been recovered by officers; and property that the agency owns or has acquired. Managing property is a complex process, requiring careful monitoring and documentation. The effective management of property by a law enforcement agency is also a legal and fiscal necessity.

Evidence and recovered property

Evidence and recovered property are generally managed together, and most large law enforcement agencies have full-time property/evidence sections. Smaller and mid-sized departments often assign responsibility for the property/evidence function to an investigator or other officer in the department as a part-time or add-on function. Regardless of the size of the department, the handling of evidence (with attention to local legal requirements for chain of custody) and the control and return of property are critical functions.

Property/evidence personnel must cope with a wide variety of items. Recovered property ranges from small items such as jewelry and cameras to large items such as bicycles, complete stereo systems, and vehicles, and it may also include weapons and money.

Personnel must carefully document the receipt and storage of both recovered property and evidence. All law enforcement agencies, regardless of size, should maintain a master log and a cross-index system to record information about the recovered property and evidence. The master log should correspond to information recorded on a property/evidence form and on a property tag attached to the item(s). Detailed information recorded at the time the property or evidence is taken into custody will prove invaluable when the department wants to dispose of it at a later date. The information will also protect the department from false claims of damage, tampering, theft, and so forth.

At a minimum, information to be considered on a recovered property/evidence form should include

Date, time, and place of recovery

Incident report number (and other identifying case numbers that may aid in return or cross-referencing later)

Detailed description, including brand names, identifying marks, obvious damage, etc.

How and where recovered

How and where stored

Name and ID number of officer(s) submitting the property/evidence for secure storage

If money, the amount by denomination (a witness should give a second count and sign the property/evidence form)

If medication or narcotics, volume by weight or count, e.g., the number of capsules or pills (again, a witness should conduct a second measurement and sign the form, and any field testing conducted on the substance should be cited; special care must be taken with the documentation of seized narcotics, given the powerful temptations to corruption; for example, evidence room personnel need to be able to distinguish authoritatively between the change in weight that may occur after powdered narcotics are exposed to humidity and any change that is due to illicit handling; furthermore, the use of some portion of the narcotic for crime lab testing should not be confused with skimming)[7]

If evidence, all personnel handling the item(s), by date, as well as the name of the owner or criminal suspect involved.

The property tag attached to the item(s) should include the date, time of recovery, corresponding incident report number, brief description, and submitting officer's name and ID number.

Large and mid-sized departments have learned that the best way to maintain control of the massive amount of property and evidence they store is by using an automated system. The simplest of data-base or spread-sheet software can be used to establish a system. When an officer turns in an item for storage, it is logged into the computer. The item is described, and all of the necessary information relating to it is recorded. In the ideal environment, the information is cross-referenced against stolen-property information within the department's data bank. At a minimum, the computerized information provides greater accountability and more efficient recovery and property management.

In some departments, the item is labeled with a bar-code tab generated by the computer. When personnel take inventory, they use a light wand to read the bar-code, and the attached reader interprets the code. This method is quick, is more reliable than repeated manual entry of property numbers on a computer keyboard, and provides a convenient method of locating property.

A safe or vault system is necessary for items that require special protection, such as cash, jewelry, weapons, gold and other precious metals, dangerous drugs, and so forth. Special security containers separate from those used for money and jewelry should be purchased to store dangerous narcotics. When, as sometimes happens, the narcotics seizure is so massive as to require makeshift storage (for example, in a truck trailer), the storage container must be secured against theft, tampering, or credible accusations of mishandling. A separate storage or vaulting system should be included for handguns and shoulder weapons.

Refrigerated storage units are required for perishable items. Evidence such as blood samples or urine specimens require special handling and preservation before transport to the lab and storage in the refrigerated unit. (See the chapter on forensic sciences.)

Whatever system is selected for managing and storing recovered property and evidence, the department should be able to completely trace the history of each item.

The property storage area should be kept clean, orderly, and, if possible, climate controlled. Moreover, certain items, such as audio and video tape recordings of undercover operations or suspect interrogations, will need to be protected against powerful magnetic fields (generated by almost any motor), which can erase tapes and make crucial evidence worthless. Security of all property and evidence is vital, and access to it should be limited. An alarm system should be installed. Contemporary security designs feature video cameras and monitors so that personnel can observe the section at all times. If the property/evidence room is not staffed on a twenty-four–hour basis, a system should be established by which officers can secure evidence and property during "off" hours. Lockers have been used successfully for this purpose; however, control by a single authority or property/evidence unit is essential. The chain of custody must be safeguarded. No unauthorized persons should be allowed in the storage area.

The property/evidence room should be inspected regularly, whether the department uses a large multiroom facility or a small closet for storage. Inspections should be conducted by an individual or group appointed by the chief or sheriff for that purpose (see the chapter on fostering integrity). Inspections should include random checks of the records for comparison with property tags and a general review of the storage facility and process to ensure that damage is not occurring in the storeroom.

After final disposition of the case by the courts, evidence can be removed. The department should set criteria for the length of time property will be held. With respect to property, attempts have to be made to return it to its owner. If return of the property is not possible, the department must eventually dispose of it through auction, use it within the department, or dispose of it by other means allowed by local law.

Selling items at auction creates revenue for the department or jurisdiction and frees up space in the storage area. Many departments choose to have the sale handled by someone from outside the department: the government's auditor, a finance clerk, or an independent auction house. Careful records on property sales must be kept.

Whatever system is selected for managing and storing recovered property and evidence, the department should be able to completely trace the history of each item. Its records should include date of receipt; a complete description, including quantity and condition; the chain of events that occurred during storage (including removal to the crime lab or court); and final disposition.

Departmental property

Departmental property is everything the department owns or has acquired. It includes capital assets such as office furniture, computer and copying equipment, vehicles, radios, weaponry, and radar sets. It includes individual equipment such

---

Management of special-purpose supplies Clear policies are an important part of a department's property management system. Here is a sample policy statement governing supplies that help protect officers against communicable diseases.

1. Supervisors are responsible for continuously maintaining and storing in a convenient location an adequate amount of communicable disease control supplies for their unit.
2. Supervisors are responsible for dissemination of supplies for infectious disease control. Protective gloves, other first aid supplies and disinfecting materials will be made readily available at all times.
3. All departmental vehicles shall be continuously stocked with the following communicable disease control supplies:
   a. Clean coveralls in appropriate sizes
   b. Disposable gloves and leather gloves
   c. Puncture-resistant containers and sealable plastic bags
   d. Barrier resuscitation equipment, goggles and masks
   e. Liquid germicidal cleaner
   f. Disposable towelettes (70 percent isopropyl alcohol)
   g. Waterproof bandages
   h. Absorbent cleaning materials
   i. "Isolation Area—Do Not Enter" signs
4. Officers using supplies stored in police vehicles are responsible for their immediate replacement.
5. Officers are required to keep disposable gloves in their possession while on either motor or foot patrol.

Source: "IACP Model Communicable Disease Policy," *The Police Chief* (November 1989): 76.

as uniforms, side arms, batons, and identification cards and badges. (Although the individual employees who are issued property are generally responsible for its upkeep, the department bears overall responsibility for assignment and readiness of this equipment.) Departmental property also includes supplies for office work and specialized purposes. The special challenge of vehicle fleet management is discussed in the next section.

Every department should have an employee designated as property manager. Depending upon the size of the department, this may be a full-time assignment for an individual or group of people or a part-time specialty designation given to a patrol officer or commander in addition to other duties.

As with the handling of property and evidence, a bar-code system to label equipment and a light wand to scan the code provide an efficient method for maintaining inventory. If bar-code systems are not available, a computerized data base or spread sheet for maintaining property and equipment information will save considerable time, allow for efficient inspections, and reduce paperwork.

Ultimately, a weak system of property control takes its toll in the form of unnecessary expenditures, long delays in obtaining new equipment, and employee frustration.

Too often, law enforcement agencies take their capital and expendable assets for granted: inspections are minimal, maintenance is haphazard, and budgetary allotments to equipment maintenance are given low priority. Ultimately, a weak system of property control takes its toll in the form of unnecessary expenditures, long delays in obtaining new equipment, and employee frustration.

Effective property management is neither expensive nor excessively time-consuming. Benefits include knowing where assets are located and how they are being used, a reduction in capital expenditures, greater efficiency in replacing worn and disabled equipment, increased employee satisfaction, and a more professional public image for the department.

Fleet management

In many law enforcement agencies, vehicles represents the second largest expense item in the budget, led only by personnel costs (salaries, benefits, overtime, and so forth). And, along with uniformed officers, the fleet is the most visible representation of the department in the community.

Unless an officer is on foot patrol, the police vehicle serves as his or her daily workplace and provides shelter against the elements and secure transport for suspects. The vehicle must be comfortable, durable, and versatile. It should also have a professional appearance that both the officer and the public can take pride in. Most important, it must perform well—and must be well maintained, because it may be used at high speeds and in maneuvers that can expose the department to liability if the vehicle malfunctions.

Types of vehicles

In the past, law enforcement agencies used large, four-door vehicles with big-block engines, often given titles such as "interceptor" or "pursuit package." Today, a wide variety of vehicles are being used.

In developing a fleet program, departments must consider their unique vehicle needs. Relevant factors include terrain, climate, hours of performance (the number of consecutive shifts the vehicle will be used), special community needs, and, of course, the vehicle replacement budget. Standard specifications or design factors to be considered include leg and head room; cargo capacity of trunk; fuel economy; engine power; suspension; cornering and braking capability; maintenance history and costs; and ability to accommodate radio, computer terminal, and emergency equipment.

Patrol vehicles   Most vehicles in a typical law enforcement fleet are marked and are assigned to patrol. They often function for long periods of time in a variety of traffic conditions. They also sit at idle for extended periods.

Patrol vehicles require special equipment: emergency lights; a siren; when appropriate, a gun rack to store a shotgun safely; radio and, increasingly, computer communications equipment; and a protective screen to separate the driver from suspects. Other options available include push bumpers; automatic vehicle locators; miniature video cameras to document street stops; and cellular telephones. Although the installation of cellular phones in patrol vehicles may at first seem unnecessary, some departments may find this expenditure to be cost-effective. In any event, a number of departments have considered it sensible to put cellular phones in command staff and supervisors' vehicles.

Driver safety may dictate possible use of additional options. Some departments have purchased vehicles with air bags. Some have considered roll bars. Others are considering antilock brakes. If a department is serious about insisting on seat belt usage, the seat belt must be designed so that it is comfortable for an officer wearing a utility belt. Departments that buy seat belts designed for civilian use find that officers almost universally decline to buckle up.

Patrol vehicles no longer have to be full-sized, although the larger vehicles remain the popular choice of many departments. Mid-sized and smaller vehicles have been used successfully in urban and suburban departments. Rural and highway patrol agencies should consider cars that provide maximum stability at high speeds. Some departments have also placed four-wheel-drive vehicles in patrol.

Special operations vehicles   Special operations personnel require vehicles that can store and transport more equipment than a patrol officer generally carries. Special operations personnel carry a multitude of support gear, including rope, battering rams, additional lethal and nonlethal weaponry, gas masks, body armor, communications equipment, bullhorns, helmets and shields, and so forth.

A command-post vehicle is useful in departments facing the potential of a number of situations requiring large-scale response. Smaller departments within a single region may share a single command-post vehicle or rely on one maintained by a larger department or a state agency. The command post provides a nucleus for command personnel, communications, negotiators, public information officers, and so forth.

Traffic units often expose their vehicles to long periods of idling followed by sudden bursts of performance. Special attention must be given to monitoring traffic unit vehicles for potential problems resulting from this specialized use. Like the vehicles used by highway patrols, those used by traffic units should provide maximum stability at high speeds.

Administrative and investigations vehicles   Administrators' and investigators' cars generally take less wear and tear than the cars assigned to patrol and special operations. Generally unmarked, they idle less, run less, and work fewer consecutive shifts. Proper equipment and maintenance are nonetheless important.

Some departments have opted for compact cars for administrative and technical support units. And some departments have had great success in purchasing used fleet cars, primarily from large rental car companies, to assign to investigators and administrative and support functions. These vehicles, generally well maintained by the companies, are sold at relatively low mileage and cost far less than new cars. Still other departments have leased cars for administrative and support purposes.

Motorcycles   Law enforcement agencies use motorcycles for a variety of purposes. Some agencies maintain them for ceremonial purposes only (parades, funeral escorts, and so forth). Others use them in traffic enforcement and routine patrol. Still others use them for special events where large volumes of people gather, such as concerts, sports events, and holiday celebrations. Light-weight motorcycles (mopeds, small-engine cycles, and so forth) have also been used on bike paths and in business and downtown regions. Some departments still employ the three-wheeled motorcycle, primarily for urban area patrol. In considering the appropriate model, the fleet manager or departmental administrator should look for cycles that provide the officer with safety, maneuverability, and acceleration. In all cases, the motorcycle should be adequately equipped with emergency lights and radio communications. Many departments find that individual portable radios suffice for this purpose.

Along with uniformed officers, the fleet is the most visible representation of the department in the community.

Marine craft   Law enforcement agencies with responsibility for shoreline or harbor areas often maintain marine craft. The type of marine craft, whether speedboat, pontoon boat, or large cruiser, must meet the unique needs of the body of water to be patrolled. In recent years, some shore patrols have used hovercraft. These vehicles are extremely versatile, capable of traveling over mud, water, land, and ice.

The use of marine craft has increased in those areas in which shore patrol includes drug interdiction activity. Marine police have become an important element in the nation's drug enforcement efforts. The primary use of marine craft, however, is in recreational areas with a large volume of boat traffic. Marine craft enable police to offer rapid rescue to boaters, to carry essential first aid equipment, and to tow stalled boaters to safety.

Aircraft   Aircraft, both helicopters and fixed-wing, are now widely used in law enforcement. Purchase and maintenance of aircraft is a major expense, however.

Helicopters have a proven capacity to track vehicles and people, reach remote regions quickly, illuminate large areas, and provide general guidance to officers on the ground. In urban areas, helicopters enable officers to respond to a serious call quickly and efficiently and can provide them with a visual perspective not otherwise available. When state law enforcement agencies bear responsibility for emergency medical evacuation, helicopters are equipped with essential medical trauma and victim support devices in addition to traditional police service tools.

Departments responsible for large land masses have relied on fixed-wing aircraft with short-range takeoff and landing capability. In addition to general response and surveillance functions, these aircraft have been used for activities such as traffic enforcement in which radar is projected from the air.

Vans and multipurpose vehicles Vans and multipurpose vehicles are used increasedly by law enforcement agencies. These vehicles offer versatility, and their flexible interior configurations allow them to fulfill a variety of routine and special functions. For public safety agencies, in which officers provide both police and fire services, multipurpose vehicles offer considerable benefit. Among other things, they can be used to conduct surveillance, provide mobile communications, and transport prisoners. The interior design of prisoner transport vehicles must minimize the chance of prisoner injury during transport and the possibility of false allegations concerning such injuries.

Four-wheel-drive vehicles are no longer limited to mountainous areas or regions with unusual terrain but are used in urban, suburban, and rural departments. Canine and tactical units in many departments prefer them for their space, durability, and performance in rural territory. Their maneuverability in poor weather is a plus. In foul weather, they have been used to transport emergency medical personnel to hospitals and to render assistance in calls for service when a standard two-wheel-drive vehicle might find roads impassable.

Mounted patrol and special vehicles Law enforcement agencies face a number of unique situations that require alternative forms of transportation. Mounted patrols are popular in some jurisdictions. Mounted units are functional and serve as an excellent public relations tool. Horses provide officers with a good vantage point. They serve well in congested traffic areas and parks and during special events. To transport horses to and from areas where they are needed, a truck and horse trailer is necessary. Stables are also needed; and whereas some departments own and maintain their own, others rent or lease facilities from area horse farms or horse owners.

Golf carts—open or enclosed and heated—have been used successfully to patrol downtown areas, especially for parking enforcement. They provide the benefits of both mobile and foot patrol, allowing officers to move quickly from one place to another or slowly from one storefront to the next. Golf carts are relatively inexpensive and easy to maintain. They also present the department with another community relations tool because officers in golf carts are able to stop and speak with the public more easily than can officers in full-sized squad cars.

Bicycles have been used for patrol in parks, business districts, and high-density residential and recreational areas and on university campuses. They can maneuver through traffic easily, are quiet, and can be ridden in areas where there is pedestrian traffic. They can be transported in cars and cost very little to maintain. Like horses and golf carts, bicycles have proved to have community relations benefits in a number of police departments.

Departments with responsibility for beach patrol have used all-terrain vehicles with success. Four-wheeled vehicles are preferred to three-wheeled because the former have less tendency to tip.

Vehicle maintenance and management

As important as purchasing the proper types of vehicles to meet a department's needs is having an effective maintenance program. Policy should dictate that officers assigned to a vehicle bear responsibility for ensuring that certain operator maintenance is performed. This may include delivering the vehicle or giving notification—at the appropriate mileage level—for oil changes, tune-ups, and other routine services. Officers should be held accountable for ensuring the regular checking of oil, inflation of tires, light bars, transmission fluid, coolant level, windshield washer, headlights, siren, horn, and seat belts. Officers should also be required to check for body damage. Regular vehicle inspections, both announced and unannounced, should be held to ensure that proper care and maintenance are taking place.

After a vehicle is run for a specific number of hours, it should be routinely inspected by someone other than its drivers for brake wear, fluid levels, and other first-line maintenance problems.

In most departments officers do not take cars home except for certain command personnel expected to report to the scenes of crises around the clock. But to the extent possible, officers should be assigned to specific vehicles to enhance accountability. (Ideally, vehicles should not be run more than two shifts in succession, in order to allow daily downtime.) In take-home car programs, departments can demand greater accountability and can require officers to assume a larger role in ensuring adequate care and maintenance.

As important as purchasing the proper types of vehicles to meet a department's needs is having an effective maintenance program.

Some communities assign responsibility for police vehicle maintenance to the department of public works or another agency. In such cases, the maintenance and vehicle purchase program is often dictated by that agency, but policy decisions on such issues as specifications, purchasing, and maintenance of police vehicles often remain the prerogative of the chief.

Effective vehicle maintenance requires documentation. Data should be kept on officers assigned to vehicles, miles traveled, shifts assigned, problems identified, maintenance provided, and more. Preprogrammed vehicle maintenance computer software is available, but many departments have established good vehicle maintenance monitoring systems using simple general data-base programs.

Data logs, in which officers enter essential maintenance information, should be kept inside each vehicle. Every time the vehicle is used, entries should be made in the log. Vehicles should be taken out of service when serious maintenance or repairs are needed. Ultimately, data in the logs will provide the department with cost-per-mile information, allowing for the establishment of a standard to guide the department in removing vehicles from service and purchasing new vehicles.

Take-home car program   In 1987 the Oklahoma City police department began assigning marked patrol vehicles to officers to take home.

The program has made the police more visible in the community because officers use marked vehicles during their off-duty hours. It has also increased the ability of officers to respond to emergencies and take enforcement action while off duty, because a fully equipped vehicle is immediately available. Furthermore, officers keep their take-home cars in better condition than regular fleet vehicles.

The one drawback of the program is operating costs. Although take-home cars have lower per-mile operating costs than general fleet vehicles, the program required the department to purchase additional vehicles. For that reason, the program was phased in to reduce its impact in any one budget year.

Source: Douglas F. Schaeffer, "Could a Take-Home Car Program Benefit Your Community?" *IACP News* (August 1990): 2.

A vehicular life-cycle accounting system, whether computerized or manual, is essential for every law enforcement agency. Some fleet managers have implemented detailed data systems to track the service life of each vehicle. From an officer's daily log, gas invoices, and repair work orders, the vehicle's maintenance, special problems, abuse, and potential longevity are determined.

The appropriate time to remove a vehicle from service is a major issue for many departments. Although they recognize the need to pull a vehicle from service after a reasonable amount of mileage, they can do so only when the budget allows for sufficient vehicle replacements. Some departments adhere to precise mileage indicators, normally ranging from 60,000 to 75,000 miles. However, many law enforcement agencies continue to run vehicles far beyond 100,000 miles. Often, departments will assign higher-mileage vehicles to administrative and support functions and assign new and low-mileage cars to patrol.

Clean vehicles last longer and present a positive image to the public. Some departments maintain their own car-washing systems. Others contract with local vendors to provide the service.

Departments often seek ways to reduce fleet maintenance costs. Leasing provides one such way and allows the department to rotate unmarked cars to avoid identification. Some departments require officers to take their vehicle to oil change franchises, where an oil change, lubrication, and general inspection are done quickly and inexpensively with a minimum of officer and vehicle downtime.

The law enforcement fleet is a major investment within a community's budget, and the investment should be protected through careful maintenance. In addition, poorly maintained vehicles will have an adverse impact on employee attitude and community pride and may present the municipality with liability that could have been averted. In other words, effective vehicle maintenance benefits many: the individual officer or deputy, the department, and the community. Strict policies and good maintenance improve safety, save money, and reduce liability.

Facilities

Facilities needs vary from department to department. A small organization may require a self-contained facility, capable of meeting all needs. In contrast, a precinct building in a large city where patrol receives support from a number of specialty units and has access to headquarters may have to meet very select or special needs.

Many of the inadequacies of police facilities can be traced to lack of adequate planning and insufficient involvement by law enforcement practitioners.

Just as there are myriad concerns, there are relatively few standard solutions. But, by following a commonly used process, most departments can effectively meet their facilities planning needs. The process of designing and building a new facility, or planning the renovation of an existing one, follows the same types of steps as the process used in other areas of planning and decision making (see the chapter on research).

At the beginning it is important to realize that many of the inadequacies of police facilities can be traced to lack of adequate planning and insufficient involvement by law enforcement practitioners. Police administrators and commanders who spend hours laboring over plans for operational problems, traffic control, or special events sometimes find it very difficult to become involved in planning a police building. An architect or consultant is hired, the administrators provide a list of wants, and then everybody forgets the whole thing until the first set of drawings is produced. The plans are altered and altered again. Eventually a decision is reached and a set of plans is accepted. But the lack of departmental involvement probably results in a building that is unacceptable. The police department must therefore actively participate in planning the building.

Responsibility for the design of new or renovated facilities rests with the police department's chief. Although specific tasks may be delegated, control over these processes should remain with the chief's office.

Discussed in this section are planning the facilities; making decisions, both within the department and within the elected governing body; selecting and working with the architect; some of the major design considerations; furnishings; maintenance; and financing.

Planning the facilities

The process of evaluating the needs to be met by a new or renovated law enforcement facility entails basic strategic planning. This is a logical, step-by-step approach to analyzing needs and taking appropriate steps to meet those needs.

An essential first step in the planning process is to review the department's stated values, mission, and goals as well as to consider the physical factors that affect basic design decisions. At this stage, and before any other steps can take place, basic questions need to be answered. For example:

Is the department committed to a central facility or to decentralization into neighborhoods and communities within the jurisdiction?

Do city or county government officials require that the facility be located near other government buildings?

Is there an opportunity to share facility space with other government agencies, such as fire, emergency medical, and central communications, and are those agencies receptive to the possibility of sharing?

Will the police department be responsible for overnight detention of prisoners, or can that task be turned over to corrections agencies (see the chapter on lockup management)?

Do considerations of crime prevention or accessibility suggest locating the facility in a specific area?

Will the funding body allow the facility to be expandable?

What role will be played in the development of the facility (site selection and planning, architectural design, environmental impact assessment, selection of architectural and construction firms, and so forth) by other local law enforcement or public safety agencies and by line-level personnel from the department whose facilities are being developed?

The next step in the planning process is to assess the strengths and weaknesses of the existing facility and determine whether it should be replaced, extended, or renovated. This step is critical for understanding the needs and justifying them to funding bodies. Although this step seems basic, many departments, when faced with the prospect of a new facility, forget about the strengths of existing buildings and begin their design process from scratch. Some departments have built new facilities only to lament that their old building was preferable in many ways.

To gather information on the pros and cons of an existing facility, the department should develop a simple, logical matrix. Its format will vary from department to department, for there are no precise formulas meeting all situations; but both the internal and the external environment should be considered. Figures 14–1 and 14–2 together are an example of such a matrix. The example, of course, is in no way complete. It simply shows the types of internal and external factors to be considered and allows the user to assign each factor a weight (for example, from one to ten in ascending order of importance) and to note the factor's strengths and weaknesses).

A weighted total for each of the two sets of factors can be computed (assigning positive numbers to strengths and negative numbers to weaknesses to provide an overview of perceptions about the existing facility and its ability or inability to meet needs. This type of matrix is easily charted to provide visual support during presentations.

Some departments have built new facilities only to lament that their old building was preferable in many ways.

The third step in the strategic planning process for the development of a facility involves identifying special needs and circumstances by analyzing the real and perceived political and community relations opportunities and risks associated with developing a new facility. This analysis should cover, among other things, threats posed by certain locations, proximity to essential support services, location in a community where public support for the facility is strong, special concerns of the decision-making or elected body, and pressure from special interest groups.

In addition to involving employees, a department should also involve members of the community. Doing so will generate important ideas for consideration and

Figure 14–1 Internal factors to consider in evaluating an existing facility.

Factor	Weight (1 to 10)	Strengths	Weaknesses
Age of facility			
Structural soundness			
Mechanical systems			
Compliance with existing codes			
Is it aesthetically pleasing?			
Exterior			
Interior			
Is space adequate?			
Can space be expanded?			
Is the facility flexible so that layouts can be modified to accommodate change?			
Do design constraints restrict desirable communication channels between employees?			
Is adequate conference space available?			
Is the facility adaptable to new technology (e.g., PCs, LANs)?			
If a jail or lockup is included, does it meet current standards?			
Is overcrowding a problem?			
Is the work space for employees both functional and pleasing?			
Is security adequate?			
Are there separate circulation systems for the public, police, and prisoners?			
Is the design free of inherent safety hazards?			
Is there adequate storage space for evidence?			

Figure 14–2 External factors to consider in evaluating an existing facility.

Factor	Weight (1 to 10)	Strengths	Weaknesses
Does the facility project a realistic and desirable image of the organization and create an impression of ease and convenience?			
Does the facility match its surroundings?			
Can this facility support the organization's mission, structure, and growth for			
5 years?			
10 years?			
Does the facility have historic value?			
Is the facility accessible and inviting to the public, including people with handicaps?			
Is the facility near other justice system agencies (courts, jail, maintenance shop, etc.)?			
Does the facility provide adequate parking for employees and visitors?			

avert criticism later. Among those to be included in the facilities planning process are the chief's or sheriff's direct superior, elected officials, community leaders, and representatives of the neighborhood or business district in which the facility will be built.

The chief or sheriff needs to assess the external community and political environment in order to understand the internal and external public relations activities that will have to take place before space analysts, site planners, architects, and others perform logistical and technical work. The chief should answer questions such as the following: Does the plan for the facility meet the department's values, mission, and goals? Is the plan supported within the department? What are the most important issues to be addressed during the design and construction stages? Is funding adequate? How can additional support be generated, if needed? Does the facility plan realistically allow for departmental expansion or reallocation of resources (for example, decentralization) and projected community growth?

The initial phase of the planning process involves carefully reviewing the department's mission and goals, identifying specific facility needs, and assessing community sentiment.

In summary, the initial phase of the planning process—in which personnel within the organization should participate—involves carefully reviewing the department's mission and goals, identifying specific facility needs with reference to both the adequacy and the inadequacy of existing space, and assessing community sentiment in support of a police facility. In the initial phase the department systematically analyzes the scope and nature of facility-related problems and develops a strategy for garnering support and resources to deal with them. Through careful planning, both the organization and the governing authority reach the point at which important decisions must be made about the nature, location, and funding of a new facility.

Making decisions

Internal decisions A well-prepared, logical proposal citing facility needs is more likely to gain acceptance than one that simply states a problem and asks an elected body or another government agency for help and support. For this reason, the law enforcement organization must make a number of fundamental internal decisions. For example, if the department does not have a long-range plan (projecting three, five, or ten years into the future), it needs to develop one before requesting a new or renovated facility.

When a department makes internal decisions about needs, the following questions are among the more important ones it should ask:

What are the demographics of the jurisdiction and the surrounding area? Will these demographics change significantly in the future? If so, how might the changes affect site selection?

Where will the greatest demand for service be?

What are the major transportation corridors? What benefits or problems are there in locating a facility near these corridors?

Based on workload and political and fiscal projections and estimates, how many employees should the department anticipate over the coming three, five, and ten years?

What style of policing will the department employ? Will the department be decentralized, use storefronts, etc.?

How will technology affect the department? What space requirements are imposed on the department by high-technology information management systems such as local computer networks, individual computer work stations, mainframes, paperless record-keeping systems, and vehicle-based laptop and on-line digital terminals? Are changes to the department's current technology, such as new radio communications and automated fingerprint systems, viable? (See the chapters on information management, forensic sciences, criminal investigations, and the patrol function.)

Will consolidation, annexation, or regionalization of services affect facilities needs?

In considering future growth and allocation of resources, the department must gain access to a variety of projections. Population, housing, public works projects, and the like are generally projected for five to ten years, and at least some helpful data are readily available from local planning departments, private corporations, universities, and elsewhere (see the chapter on external resources). The department must carefully project its own functions—patrol, investigations, specialty units, community-based programs—to avoid completing a facility that is soon overcrowded, outdated, or inappropriately located.

By carefully projecting internal staffing needs, the department can begin shaping a precise although necessarily speculative model for a new or renovated facility.

External decisions The most critical point in any project comes when the governing body evaluates it against competing demands for capital resources. It is this process that culminates in a decision either to proceed and provide funds or to shelve the project. A good plan—one that is visionary, flexible, and well prepared—will prevail over less-attractive competing proposals. Simply to have a good idea is not enough when one is competing for scarce public-sector capital resources.

The process of approving a project differs from project to project, depending on local laws, funds availability, degree of support, and other variables. At this point in the project, however, *it is absolutely critical* not to set an expenditure limit or fixed funding allocation. A structure has not been designed, nor have bids been requested. To fix funding prematurely will most likely have one of two outcomes: the project may incur cost overruns, or it may have to be scaled back and will be inadequate when completed. Ideally, at this stage authorization and funds should be provided to hire an architect to proceed through site selection (if applicable) and preliminary design.

Development through site selection and preliminary design will result in schematic drawings, scale markups, and other deliverables, as well as project cost estimates based on site, materials, space, and market. Though costs may exceed earlier expectations, the opportunity for decision makers to view a schematic of the project while reviewing the goals of the organization will substantially enhance the probability of adequate funding.

Selecting the architect

An architect can help guide a police department through the process of planning, designing, and constructing a facility.[8] The use of an architect's services as early as possible in the planning process is recommended. For much of the design stage, involvement of a professional architect is a legal requirement.

Most architects, if not employed full-time by the jurisdiction, will be selected through competitive bidding. The police department should have representatives involved in the selection. The selection criteria should include, at a minimum, prior work in the design of government facilities in general and public safety buildings in particular. It is important to remember that very few architectural firms specialize in police facilities, so judgments will usually have to be based on other types of buildings. The selection considerations for an architect should also include commitment to on-site time and follow-up activity.

The American Institute of Architects suggests that basic data be solicited from competing firms and compared. The data should include

Date the firm was organized

Demonstrated knowledge of public safety, or a credible plan for gaining this knowledge

References from former clients and financial institutions

Number of technical staff members

Ability to undertake the project under consideration

A list of similar projects built in recent years

Project cost data from prior projects

Efficiency factors, such as cost per square foot, from prior projects

Unique solutions to problems and issues on prior projects

Consultants normally used for services not provided directly by the architect

Nature of follow-up work performed on prior projects.

Other steps a department should take in evaluating any consultant are discussed in the chapter on external resources.

A selection team or committee should review the responses and rank the architectural firms. An interview and background review process should follow. For the interview and presentation, large firms may use personnel who may not be assigned directly to the project, but the selection committee should require that the people who will be working directly with the department be present at interviews. Legal counsel must be involved in the selection process and in contractual negotiations with the vendor.

In addition, many architectural firms specialize in local or regional work. To ensure knowledge of local architectural style and historical site requirements, those firms should be considered. The use of a local firm also facilitates communication and hands-on involvement.

If funding allows, representatives of the law enforcement agency should visit facilities designed by the finalists in the competition. In any event, representatives of the cities and towns where those facilities are located should be contacted.

A fixed-fee agreement with the architect, rather than one that is open-ended or based on a percentage of construction costs, is preferable. A fixed-fee arrangement protects the department and the city in case the architect underestimates the difficulty or cost of the project.

Working with the architect

The client (both the governing authority and the police department) and the architect must agree, preferably in the written agreement, on the terms of their relationship. Generally, the client can expect the architect to guide the project through six phases:

1. Schematic design
2. Design development
3. Construction documents
4. Bidding
5. Administration of the construction contract
6. Postconstruction problem solving.[9]

The client can also expect all required professional services to be provided by or through the architect firm. These services would include engineering for mechanical, structural, and electrical design; landscape and interior design; and a host of other specialty services.

During the construction phase, the architect has an obligation to the client and should intervene with building contractors on behalf of the project coordinator and others to ensure that specifications are met and changes from the original plans are addressed. In a large project, changes are frequent and inevitable.

One of the prevalent misconceptions is that, once an architect is hired, the client's involvement diminishes to that of an observer.

The architect should expect the client to participate actively. One of the prevalent misconceptions in this process is that, once an architect is hired, the client's involvement diminishes to that of an observer. The opposite is true. The client's most important involvement is during the design (and, later, the construction) phase. The design phase is the part of the project when space and other needs are clarified and incorporated into the building design.

The vehicle for the client's participation in the design and construction phases is the project team. The project team may take several forms, depending upon organizational size and resources. In a small or mid-sized department, the chief may represent the organization and work closely with the architect and other professionals as the plans take shape. He or she must envision future operational and administrative needs and involve staff in the process. Larger departments may assign several personnel (often a combination of police employees and representatives of other government agencies) to the team on a full-time basis to ensure that schedules are maintained, input is provided, and information is exchanged. Any project team structure that brings the users and architect together harmoniously helps ensure that the facility supports the visions and expectations of the users.

One member of the team is the project coordinator, who represents the contracting police department or jurisdiction and has the following design and construction duties, among others:

Maintaining coordination with the architect

Serving as liaison between the architect and the department's or jurisdiction's legal counsel

Consulting with all major units and personnel on space needs

Coordinating work flow and communication needs

Briefing the chief and other local officials

Monitoring costs and expenditures

Administering project fund accounts

Bringing in police specialists, as needed, to address unique problems (e.g., forensic laboratory staff, communication specialists, evidence control officers, fleet coordinator)

Facilitating planning for interior design (colors, carpets, fabrics, etc.) and furniture

Monitoring construction

Coordinating the delivery of equipment and furnishings

Working to maintain police operations during construction, and coordinating the move into the new facility

Preparing and monitoring "punch lists" (the small jobs that still need to be finished after the project is substantially completed).

Through regular reports and briefings by the project coordinator, managers can remain abreast of the complex design process, which is foreign to most law enforcement executives. The coordinator should be given the mandate to involve many parts of the organization in the process, to probe, question, test, suggest, and generally ensure that the completed design meets the department's needs.

Design considerations

A well-designed structure that blends with its surroundings, meets functional needs, and is friendly and inviting when entered will have a lasting effect on the community's perception of the department and on the efficiency and satisfaction of employees. The importance of design has been extolled by law enforcement leaders and has been cited in the *Standards for Law Enforcement Agencies* published by the Commission on Accreditation for Law Enforcement Agencies.[10]

A well-designed structure that blends with its surroundings, meets functional needs, and is friendly and inviting when entered will have a lasting effect on the community's perception of the department and on the efficiency and satisfaction of employees.

Factors considered in the designing of modern police facilities have ranged from personal storage space for employees to sophisticated fitness centers to meeting rooms that community organizations can use. Gone are the stark, fortress-like buildings of the past, replaced by modern centers that take into account ergonomics, networked data systems, sophisticated law enforcement

Buildings and equipment The satisfactory performance of the varied duties included in a well-rounded police program is dependent on suitable buildings and equipment. Their adequacy and condition decisively influence the quality and efficiency of service as well as the morale of the force. Good police buildings and equipment create a favorable public impression, raise the prestige of the department, and aid substantially in creating public relations

Source: O. W. Wilson and Roy C. McLaren, *Police Administration*, 3d ed. (New York: McGraw-Hill, 1972), 541.

---

technology, responsiveness to the community, and the character of the organization.

Above all, modern facilities are designed to be flexible in order to accommodate future change. From walls that can be rearranged at minimal cost to electrical outlets that make possible a variety of computer and telecommunications configurations, facilities are being designed with the knowledge that change, brought on by technology, is inevitable. Innovations such as local area networks (LANs), individual computer workstations, facsimile transmissions, and other computer-based digital communication systems have caused dated design restrictions to be removed and have opened the doors to creativity in organizing space. This new flexibility not only affects the planning process; it also becomes part of the process. The process requires that departments look as far into the future as possible to determine what technologies will be utilized and to plan for them. Just a few of the considerations that might apply are wiring for future networks, workstation design to support automation, reduced paper-record storage areas, and space for equipment.

Facilities are also being designed to accommodate individual employee needs in ways that were neglected in the past. Most new and renovated buildings include training areas conducive to learning, separate locker and shower facilities for female employees, and private office areas where supervisors can meet with officers.

Finally, facilities can be designed to embody the character of the organization. Most chiefs would use adjectives such as open, fair, ethical, caring, service-oriented, and efficient to describe their organization—and one of the design goals is to convey that message with the facility.

The rest of this subsection discusses particular aspects of layout and physical design.

Networks and relationships The layout of a facility dramatically influences efficiency and even effectiveness by fostering or hindering interaction among people, units, and equipment. A good design considers patterns of movement in an office environment or among a group of workers and the people they serve. Who visits whom and for what purpose? Does the department's current network adequately support operations and administrative functions? Is it logically designed?

Most law enforcement agencies have interdependent groups such as investigations, patrol operations, technical support, records and information processing, radio communications, custodial services, and management. It is important to determine the nature, frequency, and importance of the interaction among the members of these groups when they are inside the physical plant.

Accessibility of the department to the public must also be assessed. For some departments, a small lobby area is sufficient. For others, a large walk-in center, public meeting rooms, and courtrooms have to be considered.

Security In most law enforcement facilities, from the main headquarters building to the lot where police vehicles are parked to the auto pounds where towed civilian vehicles are stored, security is a primary consideration. Besides being aesthetically pleasing and appearing open and inviting to employees and the public, a facility must also house prisoners, sensitive records, seized narcotics, valuable property, weapons, and costly equipment. Security precautions are essential.

Security is provided through both procedures and physical design. The foundation of a successful security effort is proper precautions taken by employees, as directed by policy and procedures, but physical design contributes to security through the building's layout, physical barriers, lighting, alarms, high-resolution video cameras, and so forth. Procedural and physical design security measures are complementary. Neither can provide adequate security without the other.

Security design is unique to each facility and each organization and is based on many considerations, including perceived threats and the organization's culture and history.

Decentralization For some departments, housing all operations and administrative functions in a central facility is inefficient. Geography, population, and the nature and frequency of calls for service are among the factors that influence a department's decision to decentralize (see the chapters on the patrol function, crime prevention, and criminal investigations). In addition, regardless of geographical boundaries or data on calls for service, some departments decentralize patrol operations in the interests of developing positive community relations and performing more effective crime control and other tasks within neighborhoods. Over the next several decades, the extent to which decentralized facility planning and construction become standard parts of capital budgets will depend largely on the continuing effectiveness of various problem- and community-oriented strategies that use decentralized operations as a cornerstone of their approach.

The long-range strategic planning that shapes the police facility and the foresight and flexibility embodied in the plan will either limit future administrative and operational activities or provide the flexibility necessary for change.

Building substations throughout a jurisdiction, however, may be neither practical nor cost-effective, so alternative methods of housing neighborhood police operations are often sought. The available options are many and varied. Leasing vacant commercial space is one way in which a department can meet its need for additional facilities, achieving high visibility and better localized service at minimal cost. Leasing commercial space on a short-term basis also allows the department maximum flexibility to accommodate to changing needs.

Another possibility is using other community-based facilities. When the St. Paul police department introduced team policing, it housed the program in a small school building that the school district no longer used, four small centers in existing commercial buildings, and a vacant fire station. Naturally, some alterations and remodeling were necessary at each location to accommodate the program.

One of the first alterations necessary whenever a community-based site is adapted is to ensure physical security. Another significant (yet often overlooked) consideration, if the aim of the department is to have beat officers make regular visits to the facility, is ease of parking. Many commercial sites do not offer ready access to parking spaces. Thus, sites that may meet all other criteria are often rejected. A third possible problem in adapting existing commercial space may be its layout. Office space, storage facilities, areas for conducting private interviews, and so forth generally are not configured suitably for law enforcement needs; and making the necessary alterations may not be cost-effective. However, most departments will find that by carefully screening possible sites and planning to economize on needed changes, they can meet their primary needs.

Shared space   Some departments have turned to sharing space with other agencies as a means of increasing visibility in neighborhoods, providing work space for beat officers, and avoiding costly construction of new facilities. For example, some departments have shared-space agreements with local fire departments. Officers are provided with work areas, telephone service, and an interview room in fire stations, and signs identifying the neighborhood police center are posted on the front of the fire station.

Other departments share space with public works agencies, social service centers, and local community colleges. When shared space arrangements are made with other government agencies, little, if any, extra cost is incurred.

Another way to reduce the cost of constructing new space is for one police department to allow others to share its facilities. For example, in areas where the state police, county sheriff, and local police have concurrent jurisdiction, one of the departments may offer the others work areas, access to phones, and interview rooms. Several law enforcement agencies in the same locale also may join together to build or lease facilities to be shared by all. Specific examples of such arrangements involve shared training facilities, central communications centers, firing ranges, and fleet maintenance shops.

Specialized units   The uniqueness of certain specialty functions in large police departments may warrant separate facilities. Such arrangements often involve stables, canine facilities, training centers, and aviation facilities.

Whether newly built or leased, space for specialized functions is often costly. Before starting a capital project for a specialized function, a department can gain much by consulting with agencies that have similar facilities. Architects and planners should be required to review comparable facilities of other agencies as part of their contract.

Furnishings

By the time a department needs to replace or renovate a facility, it generally also needs to replace furnishings (unless, through inadequate long-range planning, the department refurnished shortly before building or renovating). Furnishings are important to the overall effect of a finished facility. Although the architect and interior designer will be helpful, it is the users' needs that must dictate the nature of furnishings and the layout of equipment.

In selecting furnishings and equipment as in conducting other aspects of planning and design, employee input is important.

Current approaches to facility design allow either partitions or full-height walls to be moved relatively easily and inexpensively. Partitions may be ideal for the records section, communications, and general office areas, where absolute privacy is normally not needed. In areas where individual units or offices need to be completely separate from one another, use of full-height demountable partitions should be considered. These partitions offer all of the advantages of permanent walls and fully private rooms, as required by certain investigative, administrative, and support functions, along with the advantage of adaptability.

The selection of furniture, fabrics, paint colors, and window coverings, like the basic facility design, requires careful planning. Too often, government and law enforcement agency officials give low priority to furnishing a facility. In one case, a New England police department moved into a fully renovated, spacious building—a converted school—whose furnishings were from the old police building and the state's surplus warehouse. Few items matched, and few were in good condition. Although the renovation itself had been successful, the building quickly became a major focus of complaint among personnel, just as the old police building had been.

In selecting furnishings and equipment as in conducting other aspects of planning and design, employee input is important. Allowing employees actually to design part of the project by selecting furnishing options in cooperation with the designer creates a heightened sense of pride and ownership.

Maintenance

Maintenance needs in a new or renovated facility may be substantially different from those in an old building. In an older facility maintenance is often substandard, partly because of neglect and partly because of general apathy about the space. In a new or renovated facility, maintenance requirements and techniques will have to take into account such things as new carpeting, tile, fixtures, and so forth. The maintenance equipment and schedule used in the old building will almost always be unacceptable in the new or renovated facility. Working with architects and applying standard industry formulas, the department can precisely plan the facility's maintenance needs.

To reduce costs and enhance quality, some departments contract maintenance services to private companies. The costs and benefits must be weighed against security and overall responsiveness to departmental needs. Bonding, reliable background checks, and precise standards for performance may reduce the risks and potential adverse consequences of contracting to a private maintenance service.

Financing

Often the harsh realities of competing demands and scarce capital resources, rather than demonstrated need, become the final determinants in the decision process. Unless adequate funds are guaranteed at the outset, fall-back strategies should be built into the plan. These strategies include

Reducing the scope of the project

Phasing the project

Providing for later expansion

Deferring segments of the project.

Some of the financing dilemmas that are often encountered are the inability of the taxing authority to raise capital because bonding limits have been met, interest rates are high, or the electorate refuses to approve a funding referendum. Some cities are finding alternative funding strategies attractive, financing capital projects through public/private cooperative ventures. The principal mechanisms for forging partnerships are leasing variations. The most common of these are the lease-purchase, straight operating lease, and the sale-leaseback.

The lease-purchase is actually an installment purchase in which the lessee (government unit) makes to the lessor (developer) payments that are divided into principal and interest. Much as with a mortgage, the lessee becomes the owner of the property after an agreed-upon number of payments (the number agreed to in the lease agreement).

An operating lease basically allows the lessee to acquire a facility or property for a period of time, with the lessee paying all expenses, insurance, and taxes.

A sale-leaseback is an arrangement whereby an asset is simultaneously sold to, and leased back from, the buyer. Such an arrangement could include a provision for the buyer to renovate or remodel.

These and other complex financial arrangements require the participation of legal counsel and financial advisors. The success of such arrangements is largely dependent on the tax laws in place. Therefore, the viability of these options may change over time.

Conclusion

The process of bringing a construction or renovation project to fruition is substantially more complicated than most law enforcement administrators anticipate. It does, however, provide a rare opportunity to make a positive, lasting impact on a department. Through every phase of the facilities development and construction process, careful planning is the department's best defense against costly mistakes. Employee involvement is essential to success and to creating an atmosphere of "ownership" among the people who will work in the facility on a day-to-day basis. Close interaction with architects, officials in other government agencies, and the community are also prerequisites to success.

Through every phase of the facilities development and construction process, careful planning is the department's best defense against costly mistakes.

Horror stories in police facilities design and construction abound. However, more and more successes are being achieved as administrators recognize the importance of their role and commit their time and energy when needed in the capital improvement process. Facilities planning, design, and construction can be a "win-win" effort for the department and all those involved in the process.

Note: Credit and appreciation are due the architectural firm of Toltz, King, Duvall and Anderson of St. Paul, Minnesota, for the technical review of portions of this chapter.

1 See, for example, W. A. Geller and M. Scott, "Deadly Force: What We Know," in *Thinking about Police: Contemporary Readings*, ed. Carl Klockars, 2d ed. (New York: McGraw-Hill, 1990).

2 National Advisory Commission on Criminal Justice Standards and Goals, *Police* (Washington, DC: U.S. Government Printing Office, 1973), 520.

3 See Geller and Scott, "Deadly Force"; and Sherri Sweetman, *Report of the Attorney General's Conference on Less Than Lethal Weapons* (Washington, DC: National Institute of Justice, 1987).

4 International Association of Chiefs of Police, unpublished survey (Arlington, VA, 1987).

5 Office of the Sheriff, *General Orders Manual* (Jacksonville, FL, 3 May 1985).

6 See Geller and Scott, "Deadly Force"; and W. A. Geller, "Officer Restraint in the Use of Deadly Force: The Next Frontier in Police Shooting Research," *Journal of Police Science and Administration* 13 (1985): 153–71.

7 International Association of Chiefs of Police, *Building Integrity and Reducing Drug Corruption in Police Departments* (Arlington, VA: IACP and Bureau of Justice Assistance, U.S. Department of Justice, 1989).

8 For an architect's perspective on this process, see David R. Dibner, *You and Your Architect* (Washington, DC: American Institute of Architects, catalog number 4N802, rev. 1978), 2.

9 American Institute of Architects, *The Architect and Client*, Pamphlet 5 (Washington, DC: AIA, 1975), 3.

10 Commission on Accreditation for Law Enforcement Agencies, Inc., *Standards for Law Enforcement Agencies* (Fairfax, VA, 1987).

Part five: External linkages

15 The governmental setting

Police are an anomaly in a democratic society, as Herman Goldstein demonstrated in his groundbreaking book, *Policing a Free Society*.[1] Although governmental powers are deliberately limited in order to safeguard the liberties of citizens, police officers hold concentrated powers to intervene in citizens' daily lives. To safeguard life and property, laws give police officers the authority to stop and question anyone, to arrest those who the officer believes are breaking the law, and even to kill a person in defense of human life. Necessary as such powers are for the government to maintain order, their exercise must be carefully controlled if the government is to remain democratic. Although the time-honored phrase "enforcing the law" continues to apply to police work, a new phrase summarizes the police role in a democratic society: "enforcing freedom."[2]

To safeguard citizens against tyranny, the framers of the Constitution created both a federal system reserving authority to the states and a separation of powers at the national level. Some fifty years later the architects of police agencies again sought democratic safeguards by creating departments that were small, housed within a local government, and responsible to locally elected political leaders. Since that time, all suggestions tending toward a national police have been rebuffed by U.S. policy makers. Recently, many police leaders have voiced the desirability of broad public involvement in setting priorities for police departments: "Police policy is public policy. There are virtually no matters of a policy nature which do not impinge upon the public. The involvement of the client in policy formation is an important goal."[3]

This chapter, which has six major sections and a summary, begins with an examination of the local character of police departments, a development stemming directly from concerns about the danger of uncontrolled police powers (see also the chapter on the evolution of police service). The second section discusses the two central means for controlling the police: obedience to the law by individual officers and accountability of department heads to the citizens through the manner in which heads are selected, the involvement of political leaders in police policy making, and control over the tenure of department heads. The third section explains the supplemental external controls that have gained importance when the direct modes of accountability have been ineffective. The fourth section inquires into distinctions between political "holding to account" and political "interference." The fifth section identifies common problems of interagency coordination within the criminal justice system, and the sixth provides a brief overview of coordination with other government-funded service agencies that address the same societal problems as the police. The chapter as a whole addresses two central problems of democracy: how to maintain appropriate governmental controls on the police so that individual liberties are secure and how to direct resources to benefit the public.

Police service as a local function

Two aspects of the local character of police service are discussed in this section: the highly diverse police service industry and the multiple responsibilities of the police.

The police service industry

The police departments that provide direct police services to the public and the agencies that provide support services to police departments constitute the highly diverse U.S. police service industry. Departments range in size from one officer (in Coyle, Oklahoma) to 36,000 employees (in New York City). In 1989 almost 16,000 law enforcement agencies submitted crime statistics for inclusion in the FBI's Uniform Crime Reports (UCR). Of that total, 10,374 are municipal agencies and 5,376 are county agencies. Of the municipal agencies, 63 serve cities of 250,000-plus inhabitants, 126 serve cities of 100,000-plus, 338 serve cities of 50,000-plus, 714 serve cities of 25,000-plus, 1,176 serve cities of 10,000-plus, and 7,417 serve municipalities of under 10,000. Of the county agencies, typically headed by an elected sheriff, 1,683 serve suburban and 3,693 serve rural counties. In this chapter, for brevity, the term "police department" refers to all local agencies providing direct service, and "police chief" refers to heads of such agencies. In all states except Hawaii, a state police department provides direct services to the least-populated rural areas and along major highways. Altogether, these agencies reporting to the UCR serve an estimated 96 percent of the nation's population. In addition to the full-service departments of cities, townships, and counties, over a thousand agencies specialize in providing police service at particular sites, such as universities, military bases, public housing projects, and transportation systems.

All services provided by all police agencies in 1987 cost $29 billion out of total expenditures of $1.8 trillion by all levels of government. Altogether, governments spent $118 per capita for police protection, compared with $644 for elementary and secondary education, $298 for health and hospitals, $217 for highways, $72 for corrections, and $45 for fire protection.[4] Local governments spend three-fourths of the total outlay on police protection, as shown in Figure 15–1. Police protection accounts for only 0.3% of the federal budget, 1% of a typical state budget, 5% of a typical county budget, and 12% of a typical city budget. Because cities usually finance education out of a separate school budget, the police department is often the largest agency funded by the municipal budget. Suburbs have consistently spent less per capita than central cities on police services.[5] In fact, all cities under 75,000 in population spent an average of $79 per capita in 1987–88, but cities with more than 1 million inhabitants averaged $178 per resident.[6]

The complex patterns of U.S. police service become clear when one uses a service industry approach, first applied in 1975 by Indiana University researchers

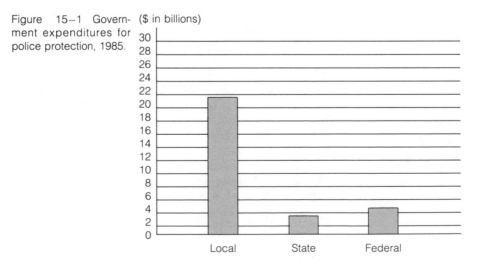

Figure 15–1 Government expenditures for police protection, 1985.

in studying eighty metropolitan areas.[7] The slow pace of structural change in policing makes their findings relevant to the 1990s. Not only did the research team describe which agencies provided which citizens with the three direct services of patrol, traffic safety, and criminal investigation, but they also examined which agencies provided other agencies with the four auxiliary services of patrol dispatching, adult pretrial detention, crime laboratory analysis, and entry-level training.

The researchers found that all three direct services were performed by more than 90 percent of municipal police departments in the size range of five to ten officers and by all municipal police departments with more than fifty officers. Whereas highway patrol agencies obviously specialize in traffic safety, and detectives from the prosecutor's office clearly specialize in criminal investigation, small municipal agencies concentrate on patrol services.

Agencies are more diverse in the provision of auxiliary police services. Dispatching for other police departments is provided by more than 60 percent of county departments and about 10 percent of municipal departments. Adult pretrial detention is usually provided by the county agencies that also provide patrol service, but not by municipal departments. Crime lab analysis is usually performed by state agencies. Entry-level training is usually provided by departments with more than 150 employees, but state agencies or regional academies tend to train the personnel of smaller departments. (Coordination among the many agencies that provide direct or auxiliary services is discussed in a later section.) In understanding the operations of any police department, one needs first to ascertain what type and size of jurisdiction it serves and what direct and auxiliary services it provides.

Multiple responsibilities of the police

A police department is a city's multipurpose agency for dealing with a wide variety of social disorders. The longer an organization has been in existence, the more functions it is likely to perform, because it picks up new functions in response to changing demands. This tendency to diversify is reinforced when an organization is open twenty-four hours a day and its services are free. Although during this century changes in technology, resources, and needs have permitted many police departments to drop some services, such as providing lodging for wayfarers, conducting a dog census, guarding polling places, and providing business and funeral escorts, usually changes have propelled departments to expand services. The automobile created the need for traffic safety; the increased use of illicit drugs created the need for drug enforcement; and broad societal changes required the police to increase their concern about familial violence, noise abatement, and missing children. The future will bring added responsibilities, possibly including control of hazardous materials and investigation of computer crimes.

The tendency to diversify is reinforced when an organization is open twenty-four hours a day and its services are free.

The International Association of Chiefs of Police (IACP) officially recognized the diversity of police responsibilities when its board of officers unanimously endorsed the Standards Relating to the Urban Police Function, developed by the American Bar Association in 1972. The standards recognize that the police, by design or default, have a broad range of responsibilities. It is worthwhile to itemize these eleven major responsibilities in order to help locate the police on the map of local service provision:

1. to identify criminal offenders and criminal activity and, where appropriate, to apprehend offenders and participate in subsequent court proceedings;

2. to reduce the opportunities for the commission of some crimes through preventive patrol and other measures;
3. to aid individuals who are in danger of physical harm;
4. to protect constitutional guarantees;
5. to facilitate the movement of people and vehicles;
6. to assist those who cannot care for themselves;
7. to resolve conflict;
8. to identify problems that are potentially serious law enforcement or governmental problems;
9. to create and maintain a feeling of security in the community;
10. to promote and preserve civil order; and
11. to provide other services on an emergency basis.[8]

For convenience these eleven responsibilities may be grouped into four broad functions: enforcing laws, maintaining order, protecting constitutional rights, and providing services. In endorsing the diverse list, both the bar association and the IACP made clear that these responsibilities are not fixed for all time. Rather, the standards explicitly call for each local government to develop overall direction for its own police department. A careful national study of police performance came to the same conclusion: local governments are the appropriate bodies to select the broad responsibilities of their own police.[9]

The commentary attached to the standards suggests that five factors explain the wide range of responsibilities given the police. First, police departments usually have broad legislative mandates. In defining police responsibility, state statutes typically employ sweeping phrases such as "to enforce the law" and "to maintain the peace," and the usually specific language of city charters contains enumerations without guidance as to priorities, such as "preserve the peace, detect and arrest offenders, disperse unlawful assemblages, protect the rights of persons, regulate traffic. . . ." Second, because the police have special authority to use force lawfully, citizens rely upon them in a wide range of potentially dangerous situations. Third, because of the investigative ability of the police, citizens call upon the police not only when crimes have been committed but also in myriad daily occurrences when something has gone awry. Fourth, the twenty-four–hour availability of the police gives citizens reason to turn to them when other governmental and private social services agencies are closed. Fifth, pressure for more service comes from neighborhoods, commercial interests, and citizens' groups, with the cumulative effect that police increase the scope of their services.

Whenever an agency has multiple responsibilities, policies are needed to set priorities among them.

As police departments entering the 1990s adopt a community problem-solving mode of work (see the chapters on the patrol function, criminal investigations, and local drug control), a sixth factor needs to be added to this list. Officers possessing rich knowledge of neighborhoods will be applying themselves to a broader range of social problems, even identifying problems not articulated by citizens.

Whenever an agency has multiple responsibilities, policies are needed to set priorities among them. The Commission on Accreditation for Law Enforcement Agencies (CALEA) has set policy formation as its first standard: "A written directive requires the formulation, annual updating, and distribution to all personnel of written goals and objectives for the agency and for each organizational component within the agency."[10]

Local governments and police departments cannot evade the need for decision making and priority setting by declaring that police merely enforce the law. In practice, it is impossible for a department to enforce 100 percent of the laws 100 percent of the time. (An approximation of 100 percent enforcement can take place if police union members put pressure on a city administration by greatly increasing their rate of issuing traffic tickets, but citizen outrage quickly brings pressure for a return to usual levels.) Formally and informally, police departments set priorities on where to invest their efforts. In a climate of fiscal constraint, local departments have greater need to set priorities in a formal manner. In addition, the growing interest in problem-oriented policing is encouraging rational deliberation about policy objectives and the means to attain them. All such transformations of informal practices into explicit policies help keep departments accountable to the public.

Direct governmental controls

The authority of police officers to use force creates a need for effective mechanisms to ensure accountability and control. From the progressive movement at the beginning of the century into the 1960s, the major advances in the quality of police service were directed by police administrators who fought political domination that tied an officer's rank in the department to his standing in the local party organization. O. W. Wilson, the foremost police administrator at mid-century, emphasized the advantages of professional police autonomy.[11]

Responsible police executives no longer advocate autonomy with respect to local government control. Instead, they recognize that the need for government officials to hold them responsible for the quality of the department's performance complements their own need to hold police officers accountable for *their* actions.

Law-abiding officers

Obedience to the law is probably the most fundamental principle for police officers in a free society. If it were not and the very individuals who enforce the law failed to obey it, the democratic system of holding government accountable to the people would be undermined.

The law begins with the federal and state constitutions and the courts' interpretations of them and extends to federal and state statutes and local ordinances. Given the law's complexity, enforcement power carries numerous opportunities for self-serving under-enforcement and over-enforcement, both of which can result in corruption, favoritism, and harassment.

The democratic system of holding government accountable to the people would be undermined if the very individuals who enforce the law failed to obey it.

Moreover, police work continually raises the fundamental question: to what extent do good ends justify evil means? All concerned with police policy must consider how far officers should go in using repugnant or dangerous means when morally good means are ineffective. What deceptions are justified in conducting undercover work?[12] Under what circumstances should an officer break a promise? Should officers make threats they know they have no authority to carry out?

A particularly difficult subset of questions concerns whether or not there are circumstances in which officers should ever break laws. In fact, there are occasions when some police officers yield to the temptation to break the law, and most of them are low-visibility events: making illegal wiretaps, lying on the witness stand, planting contraband. Although a few commentators find some circumstances that justify an officer's breaking the law,[13] others conclude that even against dangerous offenders, police officers should not use deceptive and morally repugnant means. Police officers must stop short of breaking the law:

Police simply cannot be allowed to use *any* means, under *any* circumstances, that are outside the law. Men and women who are police officers have absolutely no identity or power as police officers outside the law. . . . [I]f they operate outside the law, they become criminals just as everyone else and should be punished.[14]

The most effective controls on the behavior of any practitioner stem from self-restraint. Peers and colleagues are also powerful sources of norms. Hierarchical and administrative controls are less effective in police work than in more closely supervised occupations because police officers deliver a service that requires them to exercise judgment, work alone or in pairs, and usually work out of sight of their supervisors. The head of a police department promotes officers' self-restraint and responsible review through appropriate policies in recruiting, training, motivating, supervising, creating the organizational climate, and defining the department's mission. The police executive plays the central role in motivating members of the department to hold themselves accountable for the quality of their performance.

Ways of holding the police executive accountable

The crucial means by which citizens hold a police department accountable is their authority over the department head, whether that person be police chief, police commissioner, or sheriff. This section first examines the direct modes of controlling the department head—selection, policy directives, and termination—and then discusses many secondary means, including legislation, courts, and review agencies.

Election or appointment?   Local governments use three basic methods for selecting the head of the police department (the numbers given here are approximate, and their derivation is explained in the endnote):

1. Direct election of the police executive (this is the case in about 600 municipal departments and 2,825 county departments)
2. Election of the mayor, county executive, or county commissioners, who appoint the police executive (about 6,900 municipal and 50 county departments)
3. Election of the governing body, which appoints a manager, who appoints the police executive (about 2,600 municipal and 25 county departments).[15]

As these numbers show, the first alternative—direct election of law enforcement executives—is characteristic of county government. The second alternative is used under a mayor-council government. The mayor, as the chief executive, appoints the police executive. At the county level, the equivalent arrangement is for the elected county executive to appoint the police executive. Direct appointment of the police executive by elected officials also takes place in an uncommon form of local government: representative town meeting. The third alternative—council-manager government—is characteristic of cities with populations of between 10,000 and 100,000. Here the elected city council appoints a city manager who, in turn, appoints a police chief. Under some council-manager governments, the police chief reports also to a committee of the city council.

Each of these three basic structures for democratic accountability affects the degree to which the police executive must undertake political bargaining with local legislators. Elected sheriffs have the most direct involvement in politics. Not only must they gain the endorsement of the county party leaders in order

A city manager's view: The importance of partnership Law enforcement is an extraordinary function of government. The fact is that the police department's daily and hourly contact with the community's citizens is extensive, involving a number of different types of problems, many of which can have powerful and lifelong effects on the participants.

In many places in times past, police organizations have enjoyed special status compared with other local government functions, to the extent that in some cases they have not had a strong identity as being a part of the city or county organization. In recent years, however, the police function has become more and more the object of interest and concern by special groups and the community at large, and the "police department on a pedestal" phenomenon has diminished.

As a result of these changes, it has become increasingly important for [city] managers to develop partnerships with their chiefs much like the professional partnerships that have existed between managers and other key department heads. The police manager is ultimately responsible for minimizing the occurrence of crime and solving those crimes that are committed in the community. Like other department heads, the chief must organize the department's resources and manage those resources in meeting the overall objectives of the department.

Perhaps the first and most important element in the manager/chief partnership is mutual competency. Assuming that the manager is competent, he or she should make every effort to select a police chief who is a proven manager and a highly competent individual. Gone should be the days when police chiefs are selected by seniority, or by some other criterion not relating to competence. If managerial and leadership competence is the standard for selecting other key department heads, then the same should be true for the police chief. And the police chief must realize that the position of chief is a management position and that his or her role as a member of the management team is far greater than merely being a senior police officer.

After competence comes cooperation. Managers and chiefs must demonstrate to the department and the community that they are working cooperatively to provide the community with effective police services. A necessary part of this is that the manager must be willing to exercise involvement and oversight in the police operation, just as in other departments.

There must be open communication between the manager and police chief, and each must possess the very important personal quality of flexibility. Open communication and flexibility can lead to another key element—shared values. Shared values are very important, if not essential, in the making of a good partnership.

Ultimately, the test of any local government endeavor is effectiveness. That means that there is really only one basic standard by which the relationship between the manager and the chief can be judged, and that is whether the police service is meeting the needs of the community. It is of no value to have the manager and the chief feeling good about each other if the job isn't getting done.

Source: Bill Stuart, "Competence and Cooperation Are Necessary," *Public Management* (June 1988): 17–18.

to have support in running for office, but annually they must also negotiate with the county legislators on behalf of their budgets.

The police chief appointed by an elected executive reports to this executive on policy and budget and, in some cities, must also defend the departmental budget in testimony before the elected council. Mayors in mayor-council governments tend to be intimately acquainted with the history and idiosyncracies

Figure 15–2 Rating the police: questions to ask.

Leadership characteristics

What kind of a person is the chief?

What tone does the chief set for the agency?

Does the chief articulate the policies of the agency clearly and understandably?

Policy characteristics

Does the police agency have a clear sense of its objectives?

Are there written policies for operational practices?

Does the police agency select the best-qualified individuals to be police officers?

Does the police agency provide high-quality training for its officers?

Does the police agency reinforce the minimum requirement for a good police officer?

Does the police agency guide, train, and supervise police officers to exercise restraint in the use of force?

Is the police agency willing to investigate and discipline officers engaging in misconduct?

Organizational characteristics

Do police officers respect individual rights?

Does the police agency address crime and order problems by using all community resources?

Does the police agency cooperate and coordinate with neighboring law enforcement agencies and with other agencies in the criminal justice system?

Does the police agency communicate well with the public?

How does the police agency approach the media?

of their locality, and, because the mayor's reputation and future leadership are tied to the locality, he or she will tend to be responsive to local demands—both the pressures that are in keeping with the long-term interest of the city and those that reflect narrow special interests.

A police executive who reports to a city or county manager is initially likely to have more intimate knowledge of the community than the manager because the great majority of police chiefs have come up through the ranks of the departments they head, but city and county managers make their careers by serving a series of municipalities. Moreover, aiming to be nonpartisan, they typically begin each position with a strong command of administrative techniques but without a circle of local political allies.

A minimum expectation of city and county executives for the performance of their police chief is that the chief will work toward agreed-upon goals and prevent police scandals. If a scandal breaks, the chief is expected to take responsibility for the problem and for its solution. Reciprocally, a minimum expectation of police chiefs for the performance of their local government executive is that the executive will support the chief in conflicts with the police union. When local government officials appraise the performance of the police executive and the department, they could begin with the set of questions in Figure 15–2.

Involvement in police policy making   The only systematic, comparative examination of police policy formation took place in 1977 in the three metropolitan areas of Rochester, St. Louis, and Tampa–St. Petersburg.[16] Interviews with politically knowledgeable individuals enabled the researchers to identify three types of relationships between city executives and their police executives: political activism, joint decisions, and professional autonomy. The study concluded that close to half of the police executives made policy alone. (See Figure 15–3.)

Figure 15–3 Policy making in the Rochester, St. Louis, and Tampa-St. Petersburg metropolitan areas.

	No. responding	Size of jurisdiction[a]		
		Small	Medium	Large
Political activism	4	4	0	0
Joint decisions	9	3	2	4
Professional autonomy	11	1	7	3
Total	24	8	9	7

[a]The large departments serve the four central cities and three counties, and the seventeen small and medium departments serve suburbs.

Although professional autonomy was once an unquestioned goal of police leaders, now there is widespread recognition that police executives should collaborate closely with the head of their local government. The researchers' broadly defined category of "joint decisions" ranges from city executives giving a few broad suggestions to city executives deciding most details. The final category, which this study found in small suburbs, is political activism, where many individuals become involved in controlling and directing the police department. If the findings of this study hold true more broadly, a possible explanation for the political activism in small suburbs is that police responsibilities there may seem simple enough for local leaders to believe that expert knowledge is unnecessary. The National League of Cities and the U.S. Conference of Mayors hold an ongoing series of joint meetings between mayors and their police executives which help to debunk the myth that police work requires little expertise. Collaboration is facilitated when mayors grasp the fundamentals of police service and when police executives take a citywide perspective that recognizes the importance of other municipal services.

Appointment and dismissal of police executives   When selecting the police executive, the local government executive has the most opportunity to shape the policy direction of the department. Typically, this opportunity arises once every eight years, according to a 1982–83 study of two hundred departments with appointed heads.[17] Great variation in length of service exists among states, ranging from New York and New Jersey, which mandate civil service tenure for police chiefs, to the majority of states, where the formal arrangements stipulate that police chiefs serve at the pleasure of the mayors and city managers. Occasionally, a city executive abuses this power by dismissing an agency head without good cause. Frequently, however, despite formal authority to dismiss, a city executive lacks the political strength to require a chief who has union backing to heed policy directives or resign.

Fixed-term contracts have been suggested as an alternative to the present dichotomy between chiefs who can defy the city executive and those who can be removed without an accounting to the public. Opponents of fixed-term contracts point out that they impede a change of police leadership even in cases when a change may be urgently needed. Proponents argue that the need to pay a dismissed police chief for the time remaining in the contract will prompt the city leadership not to dismiss a chief without building a case for termination that the public can believe. The Police Executive Research Forum has suggested that a fixed-term contract should set the terms for early dismissal; require the city executive and the policy executive to meet annually to develop objectives; require the city executive to evaluate the police executive's performance annually; and authorize the police executive to voice his or her opinion on all issues of public safety.[18]

Supplemental external controls

The controls on a police department take many forms besides the formal reporting of the police executive to the city or county executive. This section of the chapter concerns eight types of institutions that have formal authority over some police functions:

1. Local legislative body
2. State lawmaking body
3. Federal lawmaking body
4. Civil service system
5. Police union
6. Judicial review
7. External review boards and citizen advocates
8. State and federal special investigative agencies.

As experienced executives know, these controls often conflict and overlap.

Only one of these power centers has a broad concern with local policy: the local legislative body. The involvement of state and federal lawmaking bodies is generally limited to passing criminal laws to be enforced, enacting legislation affecting personnel management, and providing funding. The civil service system has a narrow focus on personnel issues but a profound effect on the whole operation of the department. The police union has no direct policy role but does exert strong influence, directly on department management and indirectly via city government officials, the labor relations board, and other review agencies. The other institutional controls lie dormant until triggered by some event, usually a specific act of police malpractice. Judicial review, through both civil and criminal suits filed against the department, is seldom invoked in either state or federal courts. In some cities and counties, external review boards and citizen advocates supplement the police internal review. Special investigative agencies at state and federal levels are also a source of control over local police.

As a first step in sorting out the multiplicity of agencies that have formal authority to make policy for the police, one can distinguish between policies controlling police services delivered to the community and policies on personnel matters. The agencies that share authority to make these two types of policies are shown in Figures 15–4 and 15–5.

Figure 15–4 shows the central authority of the local legislative body, the local executive, and the police executive. The state legislature and Congress also exercise regular and self-initiated controls on police services, depicted by solid lines. Agencies that do not initiate directives but review practices formally brought to their attention, such as courts and a civil rights commission, are shown con-

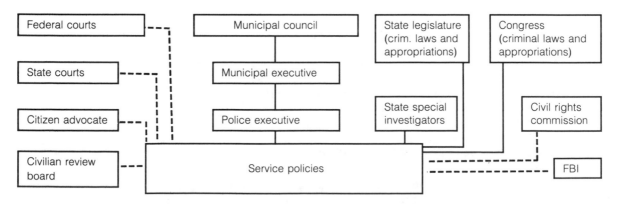

Figure 15–4 Agencies influencing police service policies.

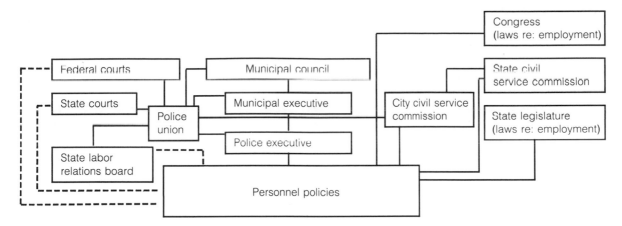

Figure 15–5 Agencies influencing police personnel policies.

nected to policies by dotted lines symbolizing their intermittent influence on a case-by-case basis. Figure 15–5 indicates strong, continual influences from the state and city civil service commissions and the police union; although the union has formal authority only to bargain collectively and to bring grievances, its informal powers may be much broader, depending on its leadership. The major difference between policy decisions on service and policy decisions on personnel is that the choices of the police chief and the municipal executive are more restricted in personnel matters.

The two figures show which agencies have formal authority over aspects of police policy, but cities and counties vary greatly in how that authority is exercised. In cities where the police executive has professional autonomy, the city executive does not give policy direction to the police executive and prevents others from doing so. However, even in a police department with substantial autonomy, the police executive's policy choices are guided by state and federal laws, civil service and labor relations board rulings, and court decisions. For police departments where joint policy making takes place between the city executive and the police executive, the city executive again buffers the department from the city council and, often, also mutes the influence of the union and

---

Mass media and police accountability Information, which is essential for governmental and public control of the police, is provided to a great extent by the mass media. Because the nature of police work makes shoddy service and illegal actions easier to hide than in most other local services, such as fire fighting, street repair, garbage collection, or property assessment, the media play a crucial role in informing the public and in shaping the way elected political leaders deal with the police agency.

To keep the police accountable to the public, it is essential that the department have an open policy for

communicating with the media. Although some information, such as names of suspects under investigation, must be withheld and policies must be guided by state law on freedom of information, if a departmental policy errs, it should be on the side of openness.

Most information conveyed by police departments to the media comes not from prepared news releases but from on-the-spot interviews on fast-breaking news stories. The policy that is most in accord with ensuring freedom of speech and that provides the most news to the public permits every officer to speak to the press.

of the civil service system. In cities characterized by political activism, the city executive fails to buffer the department, which receives directives from many quarters.

Local councils and boards

Democratic theory and practice vest the power of the purse in legislatures. However, governing bodies have difficulty controlling a police department through the budget, for three reasons. First, 90 percent of the typical police operating budget is for personnel.[19] In a budget contraction, only retrenchment of personnel provides large savings, but civil service rules and union contracts specify that layoffs will affect only the most junior personnel, regardless of the positions they fill. No matter how talented, the newest officers must be laid off, but no oldtimer can be required to retire. Neither can a budget expansion selectively hire specialists unless they are nonsworn, because police departments typically permit sworn personnel to enter only at the bottom.

Second, although two-thirds of larger cities now make use of program budgeting for some departments of municipal government,[20] program budgeting is difficult to use in police departments, given the way services are structured and delivered. Police work is not divided into separate, self-contained programs provided by separate units. All of the responsibilities listed in the 1972 ABA standards are, in whole or in part, the responsibility of the patrol division. Within patrol, all officers except the few who are assigned to a specialist unit share the diverse responsibilities, with variations depending upon the character of the neighborhood, the shift, and personal preference. For example, because the same patrol officers make preliminary investigations of burglaries and also maintain order through responding to disorderly conduct calls, both services are covered by the budget allocation for the patrol division. A budget change can commit more funds outside patrol to a burglary investigation squad if the department has one, but it cannot reallocate patrol effort to burglaries.

Collaboration between legislators and police executives can produce quick results.

Because of the generalist character of the patrol officer's work, the same personnel, using the same equipment, in fact carry out many different programs. Given the unmeasured contribution of the patrol division to different police programs, estimations of what programs cost in direct personnel, support personnel, or equipment are based on only the specialist units, which are the tip of the iceberg. In another example, funds budgeted for a youth services unit are only a small fraction of departmental effort expended on troublemaking youths through the patrol division. Further, if the council of a large city allocates funds for a new squad to deal with crimes motivated by racial and religious bigotry but patrol officers fail to give special attention to hate crimes, the new funding will have little effect. Internal managerial decisions, not external budget allocations, are required for changing most priorities in policing. An ironic twist is that program budgeting is most widely used in grant applications to federal and state agencies. Thus, explicit approval by the city executive and the city council is mandatory for programs that spend other governments' funds but is rarely required for the usual programs covered by municipal funds.

Third, annual budgets are often prepared under tight deadlines, and if communication is poor during budgeting, the governing body may make irrational line-item cuts without fully understanding their effect.

As elected representatives who are close to their constituents, council members are often approached by people who want their voices amplified in speaking to police policy makers. The result is often the common annoyance of both city council members and the police executive. Council members regard the issues they bring up as extremely urgent, but the police executive wants to maintain the principle that requests directly from citizens will be considered as important as those carried by council members. Alternatively, collaboration between legislators and police executives can produce quick results.

State government

Cities are creatures of the states, as is painfully obvious whenever a city verges on bankruptcy. Because states control the extent to which cities may levy taxes, they set important, but indirect, limits on police budgets. Among the direct influences exerted by states, the three most important derive from the powers to enact and repeal criminal laws, to establish personnel regulations, and to provide funding for specific police programs.

Criminal laws   An example of state legislation that caused nationwide changes in police policies is the removal of public intoxication from penal codes in the 1970s and 1980s, after it was recognized that jail terms do not solve social, psychological, and medical problems. In 1970 public intoxication was the charge placed for 25 percent of all criminal arrests by municipal police departments. The figure plunged to 15 percent in 1975 and continued downward to 11 percent in 1980 and 6 percent in 1988. Police departments actually changed their street practices. Police officers, squad sergeants, precinct captains, patrol commanders, and police executives all could have adapted to the repeal of public intoxication statutes by increasing their use of the broad and vague laws forbidding disorderly conduct in order to continue arresting intoxicated people. Instead, since the creation of detoxification centers and other alternatives, officers have made millions of decisions not to arrest. The combined rate of arrests for intoxication and related offenses—disorderly conduct, curfew violations, loitering, and vagrancy—fell from 1,893 per 100,000 population in 1970 to 845 in 1988.[21]

State standards and training organizations   All states set some standards for police qualification and certification, often through a state-level commission. In 1985 the highest number of hours as the state standard for entry-level training was 954 in Hawaii, and the lowest was 120 in Missouri.[22] A major effort in which police departments share a common interest with the state training agency is the establishment of a system of state funding similar to the one California established in 1959 for the Commission on Peace Officer Standards and Training (POST). The united efforts of California's police associations resulted in state legislation to levy a surcharge on criminal fines that goes into the Peace Officers' Training Fund. The $38.9 million in revenue for the fiscal year 1988–89 supports a wide variety of training across the state and reimburses departments for 40 percent of the salary of officers in training.

States are increasingly using their authority to set higher standards for police officers. Minnesota was the first state to require two years of college for new officers. Minimum state requirements for in-service training, however, are expanding slowly. A few states recognize the need for managerial education and require executive development programs; officers can meet the requirement by enrolling in university programs in business and public administration. Conversely, some states have established review procedures to bar from practice in any department officers who have shown themselves clearly unfit. The standards for decertification range from requiring a felony conviction (Texas) to requiring a demonstration of gross incompetence or an act that does intentional harm (Florida).

Personnel regulations The civil procedure codes of many states still include laws that police associations obtained decades ago when they lacked the power to engage in collective bargaining and sought favorable state legislation as an alternative way to protect their members. In New York State, for example, a law enacted in 1910 requires three platoons in every municipality except New York City and Syracuse and thus prevents management from creating a fourth platoon that would put extra officers on the street during high-activity evening hours.[23] Another example is some state civil service laws that mandate costly fringe benefits such as noncontributory pensions. Recently unions have persuaded some states to legislate a police officers' "bills of rights" that often provides extraordinary job protection. In a Rhode Island case an officer convicted of a felony could not be dismissed until he had spent three years exhausting judicial appeals and a special bill of rights hearing had confirmed his firing. Another officer in the same city who was found guilty of a drug misdemeanor could not be denied suspension with pay until he had made all appeals—lasting almost eighteen months.[24]

Funding Of all funds spent by local governments in 1987, $313 billion came from local taxes, $137 billion came from state aid, and $20 billion came from direct federal assistance.[25] The fact that one-third of local expenditures are supported by state and federal funding strongly affects police service. In an era of tight budgets, federal and state governments reduce their funding to localities, the level of government with the fewest sources of revenue to replace the funds that were cut. Moreover, states tend to earmark funds for specific police programs, and those programs may not fit local needs.

The President and Congress

The federal government signals the importance of problems through presidential addresses, the appointment of national commissions, and congressional legislation. The heyday of federal involvement began in the 1960s, when public concern about police issues grew so intense that between 1967 and 1973 five presidential commissions inquired into law and order and the criminal justice system. The 1967 Commission on Law Enforcement and Administration of Justice contracted for social science research and made prescient recommendations. The largest program funding in the history of U.S. policing came through the Law Enforcement Assistance Administration (LEAA) between 1968 and 1982.[26] Of the $8 billion spent by LEAA, the lion's share went to police departments because they were the quickest to devise ways of spending the funds. LEAA appears to have substantially promoted coordination among criminal justice agencies, the use of computers, and the increase in the education of personnel. The proportion of police officers with college degrees rose from 4 percent in 1970 to 9 percent in 1974 and to 23 percent in 1988.[27] A consequence of the upgrading efforts of the 1970s and 1980s has been to increase the unevenness in the police field, as some departments have adopted a sequence of new techniques and others have resisted change.

Federal criminal legislation affects police work both by increasing the body of laws to enforce and by providing new enforcement tools, such as asset forfeiture by those arrested for narcotics crimes (see the chapter on local drug control). To lobby at the federal level, the police management organizations and union associations have created the Law Enforcement Coordinating Committee. Its first issues have been officer safety and gun control.

Passage of the Equal Employment Opportunity Act of 1972 led to changes in the composition of police departments to make them more representative of the demographic diversity of the nation. In some departments direct court orders promoted the hiring of women and minority group members. Women increased as a proportion of sworn officers from 1% in 1971 to 7% in 1987. In 1987, in large cities and suburban counties, 11% of the officers were women, but in cities of less than 50,000, only 5% were.[28] Also in 1987, nationally 9% of all local police officers were black and 5% were Hispanic, whereas in the largest cities the comparable figures were 13% and 8%, respectively.[29]

Federal criminal legislation affects police work both by increasing the body of laws to enforce and by providing new enforcement tools.

Civil service systems

During the heyday of political machines and before the emergence of public employee unions, independent civil service commissions had a unique role in ensuring procedural fairness. Today in municipal and county government the power to make personnel decisions is usually fragmented. The only national study of the effect of civil service systems on municipal police management begins by noting that more than two-thirds of U.S. cities have civil service commissions. The researchers concluded from intensive study of forty-two representative cities that authority over personnel is divided in a remarkable number of ways, that the police executive is intermittently involved, and that the illogic of the systems "defeats efforts to determine or fix accountability for the personnel program."[30] In general, the study found that civil service commissions are weak under mayor-council government but strong under council-manager government. A forceful mayor or city manager who works with a personnel department rather than with an independent civil service commission can help department heads consolidate power over personnel decisions. As long ago as 1970 the National Civil Service League, which had helped draft the initial Civil Service Act of 1883, recommended abolishing independent civil service commissions in order to increase the authority executives had over personnel decisions.[31]

Although the selection of employees is crucial, police executives across the nation have limited authority in this regard.

In a city with a civil service commission, the commission defines job categories, establishes position classifications, and creates lists of candidates from which the chief must make all appointments or promotions. The great dependence of a police executive on the local civil service commission is shown in Figure 15–6. Although the selection of employees is crucial, police executives across the nation have limited authority in this regard. The police chief's ability to reward excellent work with a promotion is usually very restricted by civil service rules. Nowhere is police pay entirely within the control of the police executive. Police executives must use great creativity to make sound personnel decisions within the constraints of civil service systems.

Unions

Police unions seldom initiate change but often use government institutions to delay or overturn police management decisions. After 1963, when the federal government permitted its employees to engage in collective bargaining, states

Figure 15–6   Authority over personnel matters in cities with a civil service commission (CSC).

Question: Who has authority to—	
Create positions?	City Civil Service Commission (CSC) defines each job category; police executive creates the table of organization.
Set position qualifications?	State and city CSC for officers; city CSC for nonsworn personnel.
Select new members?	City CSC creates a list; the police executive picks from among the top three.
Terminate members?	Police executive, with the concurrence of the city CSC.
Promote members?	City CSC creates a list; the police executive picks from among the top three.
Set pay scales?	Unions and city executive, approved by the city council.
Tie pay to performance?	No one.

began to follow suit. By 1989, through state legislation, local law, case decision, or attorney general's opinion, forty-two states permitted collective bargaining.[32]

Police contracts are negotiated by the city executive and ratified by the city council. Both have bargained away management rights in lieu of raising salaries in times of fiscal constraint. Clauses that most hamper sound management are provisions specifying staffing levels, creating a short workweek, requiring positions to be assigned by seniority, prohibiting the termination of existing practices (often called maintenance-of-standards clauses), and narrowly restricting disciplinary procedures.[33]

Unions protect members against harsh and incompetent management through a two-step process: contract language to define proper working conditions and then a grievance procedure to force management to abide by the contract. If a state has established an employee review board, the board ultimately decides the merits of grievances.

Here it is important to emphasize that public-sector bargaining is political bargaining and that, in seeking to alter management decisions, the union may take direct political action, possibly supporting candidates and even electing police officers to city council. To make new policy, unions must persuade city and state legislatures to enact legislation; but to challenge management decisions, they simply appeal to employee review boards, civil service agencies, and the courts.

Judicial review

A number of cities have made improvements in their departments following adverse findings in liability cases. The number of federal lawsuits for violations of civil rights increased greatly after the Supreme Court's 1978 decision in *Monell v. Department of Social Services* that municipal governments are liable for the malpractice of their employees.[34] A Police Foundation study found that the major grounds for lawsuits in ninety-nine large jurisdictions were the use of force, high-speed pursuits, and abuse of constitutional rights during arrests and searches.[35] A local jurisdiction must ensure that officers are qualified in their knowledge of policies and in their use of handguns, batons, Kel lights, and any other weapons or potential weapons. Courts have held cities and counties negligent for the malpractice of individual officers through their failure to provide appropriate initial and refresher training in the use of weapons. Small departments, primarily in New England and New Jersey, have risked lawsuits by giving provisional employment to individuals who have not received the basic training required for regular officers. If these provisional employees do not abide by standard operating procedures, they place the jurisdiction in a very precarious position.

Jurisdictions are also being confronted with liability suits in which the plaintiff's expert witnesses challenge the jurisdiction's standard operating procedures by referring to the standards of the Commission on Accreditation for Law Enforcement Agencies (CALEA). The other side of the coin is that jurisdictions are increasingly able to defend against civil suits by demonstrating their compliance with the CALEA standards. A jurisdiction's best defense is to adopt a sound liability management program in which the department systematically examines and strengthens its policy, training, supervision, discipline, reviews, and legal support.[36] Despite the increase in litigation, only the largest departments employ their own attorneys. Others rely upon the municipal attorney for legal advice.

Courts have held cities and counties negligent for the malpractice of individual officers through their failure to provide appropriate initial and refresher training in the use of weapons.

External review boards and citizen advocates

When citizens regard police malpractice as flagrant and police investigation of charges against officers as self-serving, they consider establishing a civilian review board. The detection and reduction of police malpractice is a complex problem (see the chapter on fostering integrity). The basic arguments against establishing an external board are that the powers of police executives are already too fragmented and that boards may disregard due process. The central arguments

---

Using a legal advisor   Some departments employ a legal advisor to serve as a liaison with the prosecutor's office, to provide legal advice to the chief and other officers, and to serve as a training resource.

As liaison to the prosecutor's office, the legal advisor has the responsibility to communicate the department's needs and priorities to the district attorney's office and vice versa.

As a legal resource, the legal advisor counsels members of the department on points of criminal law and procedure before, during, and after police action is taken. For example, he or she should be capable of providing advice concerning appropriate criminal charges upon arrest, identification procedures, special treatment of juvenile offenders, and applications for search warrants. The legal advisor should also be able to provide written legal opinions to help the chief establish new policies and procedures, assess risks, or evaluate new patrol or investigative

tactics. He or she should alert the department to any policies or practices that may need to be changed for legal reasons.

As a training resource, the legal advisor should oversee preparation of training materials on constitutional and criminal law and procedure. He or she can also make presentations on request or identify potential guest lecturers.

Because the average police chief in the United States presides over the equivalent of a multi-million-dollar corporation, it is imperative that the chief demand and get legal advice of a quality commensurate with his or her department's importance. This is all the more crucial given the capacity of police-citizen contacts to generate very significant liability claims.

Source: Dean M. Esserman, Counsel to the Chief, New York City Transit Police Department.

in favor are that the powers of police make any malpractice serious and that in most occupations practitioners tend to do little about the malpractice of their colleagues. External review boards may be seen in terms of three categories that describe their powers: (1) those that *monitor*, reviewing police actions after the fact; (2) those that provide *input*, allowing citizen participation when the complaint is received and investigated; and (3) those that perform a fresh *review*, providing citizen views at all stages, including adjudication and punishment.[37] The International Association for Civilian Oversight of Law Enforcement, founded in 1985, had grown to forty members by 1990, including oversight organizations in New York, Chicago, Detroit, Miami, and New Orleans (see sidebar on page 264).

State and federal special investigations

Each level of government is expected to correct its own shortcomings, but when blatant injustices and crimes recur, decision makers at higher levels of government can set in motion special investigations. The state attorney general can investigate a police department. Most urban states have an investigative unit within the state police which looks into corruption and other abuses in local government. Some states create a special investigative commission or a special prosecutor's office. Usually, a policy decision in the governor's office is required for initiating state-level investigation of a local police agency.

Federal agencies become involved when personnel in local police departments appear to be flagrantly and repeatedly violating federal law. Federal prosecutors can initiate investigations. For example, the Department of Justice created a civil rights division within its southern district to investigate possible civil rights violations in the use by Houston police officers of deadly force—incidents that received national attention in 1977. On rare occasions the U.S. Civil Rights Commission investigates departments and holds hearings to inquire into citizen abuse. In the process of investigating organized crime, the FBI has uncovered local police corruption. Federal investigation of a local police department is almost always based on allegations that malpractice has been long-standing, flagrant, and notorious.

Holding the police accountable versus interfering

One of the tenets of the police reform movement between 1900 and the mid-1960s was that police executives demanded, and political leaders solemnly promised, independence from "political interference." Although most citizens take it for granted that police departments operate independently of machine politics and small-town favoritism, democratic politics cannot possibly be taken out of policing. Police services are invariably subjects of political decisions, and police executives are always political decision makers in the sense of allocating taxpayers' dollars to provide services. The police executive's concern over the legitimacy of police operations in the eyes of the citizenry inevitably involves the police in politics.

Police executives are always political decision makers in the sense of allocating taxpayers' dollars to provide services.

Whenever police policies are framed and implemented, power is exercised over the actions of police department members. In any particular instance, this power can be exercised solely from within the department or can be exercised by governmental agencies outside the department. Given the multiple responsibilities of the police, it is obvious that mayors, city managers, and city councils

A city manager's view: The chief-manager relationship There are five basic elements to a good chief-manager relationship. First is a commitment to professionalism. Certainly no other area of municipal activity more deserves that commitment than law enforcement. An understanding between a chief and a manager that professional management and professional law enforcement represent a mutual commitment is basic to a good relationship.

Second is the acknowledgment that the chief of police runs the police department. The assurance of being able to run the police operation is basic to the confidence the chief has in local government management.

Third is the mutual acknowledgment that just as the chief runs the department, the city manager deals with the city council. The insulation of the chief from the political environment of the council is important. There are other reasons for this basic commitment, however. They include the recognition of the manager's principal responsibil-

ity as spokesperson for the municipal organization.

Fourth is a commitment to accessibility by both the chief and the manager. They should recognize the importance of keeping each other adequately informed, particularly on items that may be controversial or that might interest the city council.

Fifth is a mutually agreed-upon set of performance objectives. Annual objectives are mutually negotiated and form the basis for a work program that is reviewed periodically by the manager. The work program provides the chief and the manager with an opportunity not only to set specific objectives and chart progress toward them but also to discuss departmental and organizational issues periodically and to communicate from a broader perspective than that reflected in the normal day-to-day problems and issues.

Source: Adapted from W. H. Carstarphen, "Responsive Police/Management Functions in Greensboro," *Public Management* (June 1988): 19–21.

are exercising political power in a reasonable manner when setting priorities among those responsibilities. In the following discussion, using external power irresponsibly is called "interfering," whereas using external power appropriately and responsibly is termed "holding the police accountable." Four criteria may be used to help one judge whether or not a specific policy is a responsible exercise of power: legality, efficiency, effectiveness, and fairness.[38] The criteria should be applied so as to give the benefit of the doubt to the external agency that is directing the police. However, if a particular directive clearly fails to meet any of the criteria, it should be considered an act of political interference.

Legality

The essential condition for democratic control of police power is that police officers obey the law in the face of both internal temptations and external commands. Any directive by a local government executive for police officers to take illegal actions or to protect illegal activities constitutes political interference. An example would be a mayor's order that any intoxicated derelicts in the town park be arrested despite state laws that had decriminalized public intoxication. In some localities the preferences of the political leaders and community members may be at variance with the law. In one logging town, for example, local residents wanted a house of prostitution to operate undisturbed because it deflected the attentions of loggers from other young women in the town. In practice, almost all directives to police departments meet the criterion of legality; and a grossly illegal directive, such as one ordering protection for a fencing operation, is easily recognized for what it is, if it becomes known. If a directive falls in the gray area between what is obviously legal and what is clearly illegal, it is properly the subject of public debate.

Efficiency

Efficiency is a measurement that compares the inputs and outputs of a program against those of another program, against a standard, or over time. In record keeping, vehicle maintenance, and the like, where efficiency can be fairly accurately measured, police executives and government executives demand it. The term "efficiency" conveys precision, but in policing precision is largely illusory because measuring both inputs and outputs is difficult to do (see also the chapter on performance measurement). The criterion of efficiency means that a directive that clearly decreases the efficiency of a police service constitutes interference. For example, the prosecutor and city council members in a city of 50,000 insisted that the police department assign detectives to the midnight tour, as the previous chief had. Six years earlier, however, the current police executive had established a well-functioning system to recall detectives as needed to work midnights, with patrol officers assuming more initial investigative tasks. The investigative results under the new system were as good as those under the old, but the cost was only the occasional overtime for the detectives recalled. The alternative of creating a detective position on midnights would cost a full salary and fringe because a police officer would need to be promoted to detective and a new officer hired to fill the slot vacated by the promotion. The city manager joined the police executive to rebuff this attempt at interference.

Issues of efficiency often arise at budget time. When the legislative body cuts line items in a budget, the action may undermine efficiency, as when a city council eliminated the purchase of six new patrol cars while simultaneously cutting the repair service account and the vehicle parts account. The department head is in the best position to evaluate how specific cuts affect efficiency.

Because police statistics primarily concern crime, their use as performance measures slights the importance of service activities that are not tied directly to crime control objectives.

An example of a responsible demand for efficiency occurred in a city of 50,000 where, one year, the city council refused to raise taxes. The city manager warned the public safety commissioner that an 8.6 percent cut appeared necessary in the police and fire budgets. A cut of that size would have required the layoff of 16 of the 130 police officers. The commissioner proposed work sharing as an alternative, with all members of the department reduced from a 40-hour week to a 36½-hour week and with pay cut proportionately. Two months later, when such drastic measures proved unnecessary, he developed a plan to save 25 percent annually on the cost of police and fire communications systems by merging them into a single operational unit. The unit was staffed by a mix of police and nonsworn personnel who, in the second year of operation, undertook cross-training to perform both sets of communications and dispatching activities. This is holding the police executive accountable: the city manager demanded a dollar figure in budget cuts but permitted the department head to make the hard decisions.

In police departments the concept of efficiency has been indiscriminately applied to such statistics as response time, reported crime rates, traffic accident rates, arrest rates, and crime clearances. However, measures of response time merely count inputs without regard to the outputs: a quick average response time does not indicate how often police officers arrived at a dispute before anyone was hurt. Moreover, measures of reported crimes ignore many influences on crime which are beyond the control of the police: a community's housing, education, population mobility, economics, transportation system, and the like. Because police statistics primarily concern crime, their use as performance measures slights the importance of service activities that are not tied directly to crime control objectives. Any use of statistics to measure the quantity and quality of direct service should be developed jointly by the department and the government executive.

Effectiveness

Techniques are effective if they accomplish the stated goals, but criteria of effectiveness are difficult to apply when goals are multiple and conflicting. A line between holding the police department accountable and interfering may be drawn between directives that define the problem and those that require some specific steps as the solution. This distinction between problems and solutions is blurred in practice because the very way in which a problem is formulated limits the choice of solutions. In general, demands making the department accountable are phrased, "Do something!" Interference is usually phrased, "Do this!" Although it is possible that a local government executive may have the police expertise to choose effective measures, it is also possible that specific orders from outside the department will fit so poorly with what the department is already doing as to be ineffective.

Some cases of interference are fairly clear-cut. If a mayor demands that the department develop and implement a program to reduce drunk driving, that is holding the department accountable. However, if the mayor insists that the department solve the drunk driving problem by mounting road blocks, that is interfering.

The difference between holding accountable and interfering is illustrated by the case of an urban department serving 250,000 whose chief was required to cut his budget by 10 percent but was prevented from cutting two marginal programs: a downtown unit on motor scooters and a newly created air unit. The chief considered neither program to be as effective in reducing crime as radio car patrol, but the city manager, mayor, and council saw both programs as attractive and highly visible forms of police service. In this situation, the direct order to preserve the two programs falls under the definition of interference, according to the criterion discussed here. In contrast, if the city officials had set as a priority the maintenance of citizen awareness of police presence, they would have been holding the chief accountable for achieving the objective regardless of whether he preserved the questionable programs at the expense of patrol or found another means to achieve the same end.

A simple example of holding the police executive accountable occurred in a city preparing to open a shopping mall adjacent to a low-income area. The city manager set for the police executive a priority of addressing the problem of shoppers' sense of safety. The police executive developed and implemented a plan for training mall security guards and coordinating their work with that of the police.

The question of holding to account versus interfering becomes particularly sensitive in personnel questions. Most police executives maintain that every appointment, promotion, assignment, or termination decision taken against their judgment is political interference. Recall that Figure 15–5 shows the several outside agencies that influence decisions on personnel. Recall also that personnel decisions may be made for reasons other than effectiveness—for example, to make the department more representative of the demographic makeup of the community. Even if an outside decision has the immediate result of using per-

Criterion	Application
Single universal standard	All neighborhoods receive the same density of patrol coverage.
Demand criterion	All neighborhoods where residents and businesses ask for more patrol coverage receive it.
Need criterion	Neighborhoods that have more serious problems of crime and order receive more patrol coverage.

Figure 15–7
Application of alternative criteria of fairness to geographical allocation of patrol.

sonnel more effectively, department members will perceive that outsiders are determining rewards and punishments and will be more likely to go to outsiders next time to get a favorable decision. Some assistance on procedures for staffing is provided by CALEA standard 16.1.6, which requires departments to develop an annual workload plan as the basis of their personnel allocations. Such documentation of staffing needs provides a sound starting point for making responsible personnel decisions.

Fairness

Fairness, the last criterion discussed here, has fundamental importance in policing. Everyone can agree that fairness has been achieved when similar situations are treated similarly. However, the world is full of situations in which people have honest disagreements about whether two situations are similar and about what ways of treating different situations are fair. When situations are dissimilar, there are at least three different standards of fairness that could be applied: a single universal standard; a standard reflecting demand; and a standard reflecting need. Figure 15–7 shows how the three standards can be applied to define a fair distribution of service.

The local government executive and the police executive need to commit themselves clearly to fairness in their service allocation decisions.

In the competitiveness of local politics, neighborhoods and interest groups tend to promote their own pet projects without paying particular attention to any standard of communitywide fairness. The local government executive and the police executive need to commit themselves clearly to fairness in their service allocation decisions. In a small midwestern town, the city council was surprised to learn that two merchants accounted for 80 percent of the police department's bank escorts, although most merchants did not request the service. The police chief was able to persuade the two merchants to engage private armed guards. Thus, the basis of equity in this service moved from meeting all demands, with a potentially skyrocketing total demand, to providing roughly the same small amount of service to all. In terms of the broad responsibilities of patrol, the change made more patrol time available to all, including those without the resources to hire private security. Promoting fairness and the perception of fairness is one of the most important ongoing responsibilities of police executives and of municipal and county executives.

Coordination with other criminal justice agencies

As gatekeepers for the criminal justice system, local police have substantial effect on the workload of prosecutors and probation officers, the demand for more judges, the overcrowding of prisons, and the need for parole officers. The convenient phrase "the criminal justice system" disguises the fact that each criminal justice agency has its own philosophy, constituencies, priorities, and resources. Although coordination is essential, it is difficult for at least three reasons: (1) agencies work in overlapping territorial jurisdictions, (2) they report to different levels of government, and (3) their practice of never exchanging personnel fosters insular views.

A good way to understand the extent of coordination among local police and other criminal justice agencies in any geographical area is to use the service industry approach described earlier in this chapter. Which agencies, housed at which level of government, deliver the direct police services of patrol, traffic safety, and criminal investigation? Which criminal justice agencies provide prosecutorial and defense services? Which agencies provide the judges and which the probation services? Which other agencies provide the detention services, the secure corrections facilities, the community-based corrections programs, and the parole programs? Which agencies provide any of these services to youths? Which agencies provide the whole criminal justice system with computer-based information? The answers to these questions will quickly highlight the involvement of various levels of government and the presence of duplication.

The convenient phrase "the criminal justice system" disguises the fact that each criminal justice agency has its own philosophy, constituencies, priorities, and resources.

Interagency coordination was introduced on a national scale by LEAA.[39] The LEAA-funded programs that required interdepartmental cooperation usually were in new areas, such as sting programs and strike forces, and thus did not threaten traditional working arrangements. Similar state planning requirements are found in the 1984 Safe Streets Act and in the 1988 Omnibus Drug Initiative Act. In many localities planners from various criminal justice agencies hold periodic meetings. These interagency committees can help mayors and managers assess the effects of various programs. Although such joint bodies do not review agency budgets, they have conducted staff research to identify the fiscal effects of new programs on relevant agencies.

When the police department or another agency gains a new head, the agency heads should meet. Subsequent working contacts at middle management can handle many of the agenda items that, for the sake of brevity, are described here as responsibilities of the chief. Decisions on which coordination problems require the personal attention of the chief and which should be delegated depend upon the complexity of the problem and the size of the department.

The prosecutor

Coordination between the police department and the prosecutor's office is essential to the effective functioning of both agencies. Routine meetings between the police chief and the prosecutor are desirable.[40] Because new police programs have the potential for influencing the prosecutor's workload, the chief should bring them to the prosecutor's attention well in advance of implementation. For instance, some police departments in major cities have made street sweeps of drug users only to find that the prosecutor did not have the staff to meet the "speedy trial" standard and that laboratory resources were not available to assess the evidence. Some of the issues that the chief and prosecutor should discuss are

Policies and procedures in bringing criminal charges

Police acceptance of the prosecutor's needs for well-prepared witnesses and carefully gathered physical evidence

Routine, systematic prosecutorial feedback to police agencies on the quality of case preparation and testimony and on case outcomes

Prosecutorial assistance available to the police on an "on-call" basis for major cases

Prosecutorial assistance in training officers to take depositions, obtain search warrants, present testimony, and interpret recent case decisions

Appropriate expansion of programs to release arrestees on their own recognizance.

In some jurisdictions police and prosecutors have developed joint programs. Collaboration in investigating and prosecuting career criminals takes place throughout Dade County, Florida, and between the city of Aurora, Colorado, and surrounding counties. Teams on computer crimes are active in Alameda and Santa Clara counties, California, and in Maricopa County, Arizona. Elsewhere jurisdictions have worked together to develop procedures for asset seizure and forfeiture and to create various joint federal and local drug task forces. In 1988, Illinois created a six-county multijurisdictional prosecutors' network in the Chicago area to focus on drug enforcement. Network personnel also hold routine quarterly meetings with representatives of law enforcement agencies and forensic laboratories in the metropolitan area.

Repeat offender and career criminal programs are a major focus of the Bureau of Justice Assistance of the U.S. Department of Justice under the terms of the Justice Assistance Act of 1984. Technical assistance is provided through model program materials, training, and consulting services that stress the need for police and prosecutor collaboration aimed at the serious habitual offender.

A fundamental problem remains: neither the police department nor the prosecutor's office takes responsibility for the large number of cases that do not survive the prosecutor's initial screening. Police executives tend to attach importance to the proportion of crimes cleared by arrest; prosecutors tend to measure their success by the percentage of convictions among the cases they decide to prosecute. Part of the gap between the number of arrests and the number of prosecutions is caused by the fact that police officers frequently have sound reasons to make arrests in cases that should not be prosecuted. For example, an officer may arrest a combatant on a disorderly conduct charge to prevent a fight from resuming the minute the officer leaves the scene. However, among cases in which police have grounds to believe that a serious crime has been committed, no one takes responsibility for the cases that the prosecutor chooses to drop.

The courts

Inter-agency planning does not come naturally to courts because they place priority on safeguarding their independence. Indeed, it is important to set any expectations for cooperation with the courts within the context of the constitutional separation of powers. Police, prosecutors, and detention and corrections officials operate within the executive branches of local, state, and federal governments. By contrast, judges, court administrators, and, in most states, probation officers serve within the judicial branch of government.

The police executive should establish an open line of communication with the administrative judge, or at least with the court administrator, instead of communicating only when there is a "hot issue." They can hold ongoing discussions about

The quality of officers' testimony and demeanor

The scheduling of cases to reduce unnecessary officer overtime

The scheduling of judicial personnel to accommodate anticipated mass arrest proceedings

Implementation of police programs, such as arrest and prosecution of spouse abusers, repeat offender programs, and narcotics sting operations, that augment judicial workload by increasing the number of continuances and trials.

Detention centers

Usually police departments are responsible for the custody of an arrestee until arraignment, when custody passes to the sheriff or corrections department (see the chapter on arrestee and lockup management). Crowding of detention centers and jails that hold prisoners before trial has been exacerbated by a number of trends.[41] First, the cohort at the end of the baby-boom population bulge is now in its late twenties. Although by 1990 the members of this group had passed beyond the crime-prone age, individuals who did begin criminal careers tend to have a history of arrests, which will influence judges to give them long sentences for new offenses. Second, because of pressure from victims' rights groups, police are now making custody arrests of offenders who previously were left in the community, such as drunk drivers, spouse batterers, and parents delinquent in support payments. Third, any increase in the prosecutor's workload prolongs the waiting period before trial, which greatly exacerbates the crowding in detention centers. Fourth, all persons convicted of misdemeanors serve their time in a jail, which also houses pretrial defendants. Increasing the sentences for people convicted of misdemeanors therefore increases the crowding in jails. Fifth, the crowding of state prisons pushes inmates into jails.[42] In this crisis police departments can enter into mutually beneficial collaboration with the incarcerating agency in the following areas:

Expediting booking procedures

Providing notification about dangerous or suicidal arrestees

Transporting prisoners to and from court

Guarding prisoners in the hospital

Developing alternative sentences, including work release, community service, and restitution.

The state department of corrections

Because the police and corrections are at opposite ends of the criminal justice system and usually are located at different levels of government, little coordination typically takes place between a police chief and the director of corrections. Subjects of common interest for discussion include

The corrections department automatically notifying the police upon an inmate's release from custody

Corrections providing information on inmates placed in halfway houses, work release programs, and local school programs

Police providing feedback to the corrections department on arrests of individuals in community-based programs

Police assisting probation and prosecution to send promptly to the reception center information such as the presentence investigation, community impact statement on dangerous offenders, and standard criminal history records.

Probation and parole agencies

Because most inmates eventually return to the community, police have a critical need to maintain close contact with the agencies that provide community supervision. Police need to be cognizant of the general location and numbers of people who are in the community under supervision of the justice system. The police executive should discuss issues of common concern with the regional heads of probation, parole, and community corrections facilities. Detectives and supervising parole agents share responsibility for removing from the street individuals who are committing crimes and violating their conditions of parole. The probation department can help the police identify habitual offenders who do not receive jail terms, and parole officers can give police early warning of the release of habitual offenders. Parole and probation agents should follow through on technical revocation hearings for individuals who are continuing to commit crimes.

The juvenile authority

The fact that youth authorities are usually state agencies should not deter the chief of police from sitting down with the regional or state director of the youth authority to discuss common problems. In 1988, youths under age eighteen accounted for 22% of the nation's robbery arrests, 33% of the burglary arrests, and 39% of the motor vehicle theft arrests.[43] Research teams have established that the most violent juvenile offenders tend to continue criminal careers into adulthood.[44] The more quickly police can provide solid evidence to juvenile authorities, the more quickly these youths can be placed in appropriate corrective programs. The other issues a police executive may want to discuss with juvenile authorities include

Separating youths from adults in local lockups

Separating status offenders from juvenile delinquents

Identifying repeat offenders, apprehending them, and placing them in a secure facility

Sensitively and thoroughly handling child abuse cases

Ensuring that police conduct quality investigations

Improving police training on working with youths.

State criminal justice information systems

Almost all full-time police departments have twenty-four–hour access to state computerized criminal justice information systems, known as CJIS, which are linked, in turn, to the National Crime Information Center (NCIC) operated by the FBI (see the chapter on information management). Police departments, as the major sources of data and the major users, should have a voice in designing policies and procedures ensuring that records are complete, accurate, and secure. Because of the sensitivity of criminal history and investigative records, all state and local jurisdiction information systems should be audited to ensure high quality and integrity of information. Intergovernmental cooperation on the flow of information is essential. In Maryland, for example, local police departments participating in repeat offender programs wanted quick notification on release of inmates. Representatives of local police departments and the director of Maryland's CJIS agreed that CJIS would automatically notify each jurisdiction of the release of repeat offenders who came from or were released into the jurisdiction.

Models for coordination

Police isolation and parochialism are giving way to teamwork in specific areas where the effectiveness of coordination becomes clear. In the development of 9–1–1 emergency communications centers, the telephone company has required localities to provide a central communications point with a single number for the three emergency services: police, fire, and emergency medical service. A police department that is moving away from deployment of field resources dictated by calls for service should be working with communications managers to adopt the technical systems that exploit the advantages of a 9–1–1 system, differential police response, automatic vehicle locators, and other techniques that make up a modern command and control function (see the chapter on information management).

As police departments review their operations looking for appropriate strategic partnerships, support and auxiliary services offer many opportunities. Several departments in an area can begin by exchanging investigative information and developing consolidated files. In the 1930s the city of Raleigh and Wake County (North Carolina) created a single bureau of identification, which now performs all crime scene investigations for all law enforcement units within the county. In the Denver area joint recruiting was developed when departments were experiencing shortfalls because candidates passed the entrance examinations of several neighboring police departments, were placed on each department's eligibility list, and then accepted the first job offered. In 1981 the Denver regional criminal justice council sponsored a regional recruiting center. As of 1987, the sixteen departments that had joined were experiencing a more regular flow of qualified candidates and were providing recruits with an easier choice among departments.

Consolidation of city and suburban police departments into a single large department occurs on the rare occasions when metropolitan governmental functions as a whole are consolidated, as in Indianapolis or in Jacksonville (Florida). In some instances, suburban jurisdictions keep most of their municipal functions but contract for police services with the county sheriff or police department. In 1954 Lakewood, California, became the nation's first municipality to contract for police services when it executed an agreement with the Los Angeles County sheriff's department. Thirty years later, when the sheriff's office was planning to upgrade its Lakewood substation by building a new facility elsewhere in the county, Lakewood invested a million dollars in renovating the agency building and entered into a twenty-year agreement to contract for service and lease the building from the county. The San Diego County sheriff's department, one of the nation's largest, provides full service to four hundred thousand inhabitants in unincorporated areas and to three hundred thousand who live in nine municipalities that contract for service.

Consolidation of police and fire departments has elicited interest as an efficient way of using the working hours that fire fighters do not spend at fires.[45] The simplest step is consolidating the two dispatching operations by cross-training the personnel. More extensive modes create a single department in which some or all of the personnel are cross-trained as police officers and fire fighters and thereafter called public safety officers. Michigan and Florida lead in number of consolidations, each having more than fifty jurisdictions with consolidated public safety departments. When Sunnyvale, California, incorporated in 1950, it formed a consolidated public safety department and now serves a population of 110,000. Winston-Salem has operated a merged department since 1970. Some departments add a third set of skills—emergency medical training—and in the Midwest some departments combine police and emergency medical training.

The advantages of public safety consolidation compared with separate police and fire departments are an increased patrol presence and a quicker response time to fires and to police calls. Proponents claim that if the new department is well managed and conservatively staffed and if not all members are cross-trained and given incentive pay, consolidation reduces total expenditures by between 5 and 20 percent.[46] Opposition to consolidation is usually strong from the fire fighters' union.

The reason to exercise caution in any plan to combine police service and fire fighting is that these services have very different patterns of work and require different skills, and personnel suited by ability and temperament to one of these services may not be suited to the other.

Coordination with other government-funded agencies

Police departments serve clients who are also served by social service agencies, hospital emergency rooms, mental health programs, alcohol detoxification centers, drug rehabilitation programs, shelters for the homeless, and dispute resolution centers. These various government and private agencies are not considered part of a system in the way that criminal justice agencies are; thus, coordination with them is more difficult. Although this section explicitly calls for the head of the police agency to meet directly with counterparts in other agencies, many subsequent committee meetings of agency personnel will be required to make coordination work.

Social service agencies A potentially fruitful approach to interagency cooperation is to identify families who have multiple problems and are being served by multiple agencies. If each agency sees only a fragment of the family's situation, counterproductive efforts, duplication, and gaps in service are likely. To assist troubled families, the relevant agencies should collaborate. These may include police, schools, the child protection agency, welfare, vocational rehabilitation, health and mental health, recreation, probation, and parole. A police executive should establish working relationships with the heads of each of these agencies.

A potentially fruitful approach to interagency cooperation is to identify families who have multiple problems and are being served by multiple agencies.

Police departments that adopt problem-oriented policing therefore need to collaborate frequently with other agencies to address the concerns of a neighborhood. Yet other agency heads can regard an active police role as meddling, as the following example from the Baltimore County Citizen Oriented Police Enforcement (COPE) program shows. The county executive received a number of complaints from department heads that their planned schedules were interrupted by police officers demanding instant pothole repair, graffiti removal, shrub thinning, and the like. He arranged for the police chief to give a presentation to department heads on the COPE program, emphasizing that the requests for service came from citizens who feared for their safety and were waiting to see how government reacted to their concerns. Even after this top-level meeting, resistance lingered. Sometimes it is one thing to talk about coordination among units of local government, and quite another to carry it out.

Hospital emergency rooms The police chief should initially meet with hospital administrators to ensure hospital cooperation in handling a variety of situations. Their discussion will probably cover the following topics:

Interagency cooperation In Multnomah County, Oregon, the department of public safety has taken the lead in serving residents of a large public housing complex through a team approach that coordinates the efforts of agencies as diverse as the visiting nurse service and the schools.

The value of coordination changes from desirable to essential if a police department begins to adopt a problem-oriented mode of policing, because officers increasingly identify ways in which efforts of other agencies could effectively address components of neighborhood problems.

Allowing police access, when medically appropriate, to accident victims, crime victims, witnesses, and defendants

Providing appropriate space for police to guard or interview patients

Reporting cases of drug overdose, shootings, and child abuse to police

When legally permissible, notifying agencies whose personnel handled an emergency patient who tests HIV positive

Adopting a mutually agreeable policy for release of information to the mass media.

Mental health, detoxification, and drug treatment programs The police department is often the agency that identifies people in crisis.[47] Mental health professionals can help train officers to apply medical and legal criteria for making referrals and arrests. As police officers well know, the need for crisis mental health services rarely arises during normal business hours. The police chief should initiate meetings with the heads of health and mental health agencies on such issues as

Officer training and education

Emergency handling of situations involving individuals who are mentally disturbed, intoxicated, under the influence of drugs, or engaging in bizarre behavior

Referrals outside of business hours

Reporting with due regard for confidentiality

Notification concerning, and handling of, escapes.

Shelters for the homeless The number of homeless people in the United States increases each time a count is taken. Some of the key concerns that a police executive needs to address with the agencies that run shelters are

Policy regarding sleeping in public places

Responsibility for transportation

Services provided, including counseling and help locating housing and employment

Requests for police assistance.

Dispute resolution centers The overcrowded criminal courts, the long delays in civil proceedings, and the lack of adequate administrative hearings have demonstrated a need for less-formal means to resolve disputes. Police officers are usually a major source of referral to dispute resolution centers. The police executive should meet with the head of the dispute resolution center to identify common concerns.

Summary

Tension will always exist between the autonomy required for effective police performance and the external control necessary to safeguard the liberties of citizens. The fundamental U.S. solution to this dilemma has been to create a police department within each unit of municipal government and to establish the position of elected sheriff within most counties. The smallness and multiplicity of the police departments makes less threatening the possibility that officers could fail to be law-abiding. In the late twentieth century, the U.S. police service industry is composed of over sixteen thousand agencies providing primary services, including order maintenance, criminal investigation and apprehension, traffic safety, emergency assistance, conflict resolution, and other direct services to citizens. Auxiliary services such as patrol dispatching, adult pretrial detention, crime laboratory analysis, and entry-level training are supplied to the primary providers by an array of municipal, county, and state agencies.

Local governments paid $21 billion for police services in 1985, compared with $3.6 billion by states and $4 billion by the federal government. In the 1990s states will probably increase their provision of auxiliary and support services, ranging from the essential setting of standards for appointment as a police officer to the ancillary funding of laboratories that test for DNA identification. Cities and counties will continue to be the levels of government primarily responsible for direct police service. Because local government has the poorest tax base, most police departments are unlikely to receive the amount of funding that police executives deem adequate. A fundamental choice that police executives and governing bodies must make is whether to keep present personnel levels while inflation erodes real earnings or to preside over a shrinkage in the number of officers in order to raise salary levels.

Because unrestricted police power destroys freedom and democracy, multiple governmental controls have been developed to make police officers accountable for their actions.

Effective police performance requires coordination with other agencies of the criminal justice system, beginning with the prosecutor's office. The quality of consultation and coordination has improved over the years since the 1960s when federal funding first supported joint efforts. Coordination with a large array of government-funded service agencies is also essential, but unlike the criminal justice system, these agencies do not have a collective name, nor do their staff members have a sense of belonging to a common system. To enhance coordination with all of these agencies, the head of the police department should meet with the head of each agency to lay the groundwork for staff cooperation. The great expansion of computerized data systems will improve interagency communication, but coordination will remain difficult because the various agencies report to different levels of government.

Because unrestrained police power is inconsistent with freedom and democracy, multiple governmental controls have been developed to make police officers accountable for their actions. The fundamental controls on the actions of every police officer are the U.S. Constitution, state consitutions, state and federal laws, and municipal ordinances. The elected or appointed executive to whom the police chief reports is the key individual outside the department who is responsible for making the department accountable to the public. In addition, the local governing body often has a committee that oversees the police. The controls exerted intermittently by courts and investigative agencies are appropriate as safeguards because of the great potential for the abuse of police power.

However, the oversight actions of courts and investigative agencies usually are neither consistent nor effective. Too much external control is particularly obvious in personnel matters, where civil service rules have produced narrow procedures for attracting new department members and, together with union contracts, have set severe restrictions on dismissing any incompetent or dangerous officer.

Police leadership has traditionally discouraged elected and appointed officials from exerting policy control, but teamwork between the local government executive and the police executive is now a recognized goal. By taking responsibility for educating political leaders and city managers in the complexities of police work, police leaders will help develop fruitful collaboration. A shared view of the perplexing societal problems that police address, such as use of illegal drugs, is essential to the development and implementation of realistic policies. As policing moves into the 1990s, increased police accountability to the public will enhance the quality of life in the community.

1 Herman Goldstein, *Policing a Free Society* (Cambridge, MA: Ballinger, 1977).

2 Cornelius J. Behan, Remarks at the Baltimore County Board of Education Annual Teachers' Training Conference, 1989.

3 George W. O'Connor, *Some Not So Random Thoughts on Police Improvement* (Troy, NY: Police Department Services, 1976).

4 Bureau of the Census, U.S. Department of Commerce, *Statistical Abstract of the United States, 1990* (Washington, DC: U.S. Government Printing Office, 1990), 273 and 274.

5 Bureau of the Census, U.S. Department of Commerce, *City Government Finances in 1987–88*, GF-88-4 (Washington, DC: U.S. Government Printing Office, 1990), 3.

6 Roy Bahl and Greg Lewis, "City-Suburban Variation in Police Expenditures," in *Metropolitan Crime Patterns*, ed. Robert M. Figlio, Simon Hakim, and George S. Rengret (Monsey, NY: Criminal Justice Press, 1986), 181–206.

7 Elinor Ostrom, Roger B. Parks, and Gordon P. Whitaker, *Patterns of Metropolitan Policing* (Cambridge, MA: Ballinger, 1978), chaps. 4 and 9 and p. 90.

8 American Bar Association, *Standards Relating to the Urban Police Function* (Chicago: American Bar Association, 1974).

9 Gordon P. Whitaker, Stephen Mastrofski, Elinor Ostrom, Roger B. Parks, and Stephen L. Percy, *Basic Issues in Police Performance* (Washington, DC: National Institute of Justice, 1982).

10 Commission on Accreditation for Law Enforcement Agencies, *Standards for Law Enforcement Agencies* (Fairfax, VA: CALEA, 1983).

11 O. W. Wilson and Roy C. McLaren, *Police Administration*, 3d ed. (New York: McGraw-Hill, 1972).

12 Gary T. Marx, *Undercover: Police Surveillance in America* (Berkeley: University of California Press, 1988).

13 Carl B. Klockars, "The Dirty Harry Problem," *The Annals* 452 (November, 1980): 33–47; and Edwin J. DeLattre, *Character and Cops: Ethics in Policing* (Washington, DC: American Enterprise Institute, 1989).

14 Wesley A. Carroll Pomeroy, "The Sources of Police Legitimacy and a Model for Police Misconduct Review: A Response to Wayne Kerstetter," in *Police Leadership in America: Crisis and Opportunity*, ed. William A. Geller (New York: Praeger, 1985).

15 For municipal departments: The total number of municipal police departments is from the 1989 UCR, appendix 3; ICMA's *Municipal Year Book 1990*, table 3, provides data on the type of government for 7,106 cities. The 3,000 police departments from municipalities that provide data to the UCR but are not included in the ICMA count are assumed to be small jurisdictions with mayor-council governments. The 418 town meeting governments and the 175 commission governments are included under direct election and rounded to 600. The 79 representative town meeting governments are included under mayoral government because citizens elect a legislature that appoints department heads.

For county departments: There are 3,042 counties in the United States. About 150 are sparsely populated rural counties and counties coterminous with a central city and are assumed to have no full-service law enforcement agency. The National Sheriffs' Association estimates that about 2,825 counties have a full-service sheriff's department headed by an elected office holder. In roughly 75 counties the department is headed by a chief appointed by an elected or appointed executive. The proportion is assumed to correspond to the national proportion of types of county government reported in the ICMA's *Municipal Year Book, 1990*, table 4.

16 Stephen D. Mastrofski, "Varieties of Police Governance in Metropolitan America," *Politics and Policy* (Summer 1988).

17 Donald Witham, *The American Law Enforcement Chief Executive: A Management Profile* (Washington, DC: Police Executive Research Forum, 1985), 64–68.

18 Police Executive Research Forum, "Elements of an Employment Agreement for Police Chief Executives" (Washington, DC: Police Executive Research Forum, 1980).

19 Bureau of Justice Statistics, U.S. Department of Justice, *Law Enforcement Management and Administrative Statistics, 1987* (a computer analysis prepared by Brian A. Reaves, 6 June 1990).

20 International City Management Association, *Municipal Government Year Book, 1989* (Washington, DC: International City Management Association, 1989).

21 FBI, *Uniform Crime Reports: Crime in the United States* (Washington, DC: U.S. Government Printing Office, 1970 and 1988).

22 Timothy J. Flanagan and Katherine M. Jamieson,

eds., *Sourcebook of Criminal Justice Statistics—1987* (Washington, DC: U.S. Government Printing Office, 1988).

23 New York Unconsolidated Laws, Title 3, chapter 11, para. 971.

24 Personal communication with Chief John Leyden, North Kingston, Rhode Island, who has served as president of the state IACP.

25 U.S. Advisory Commission on Intergovernmental Relations, *Significant Features of Fiscal Federalism*, 1989 ed., 1: M-163 (Washington, DC: ACIR, 1989), 13.

26 John K. Hudnik, *Federal Aid to Criminal Justice: Rhetoric, Results, Lessons* (Washington, DC: National Criminal Justice Association, 1984).

27 David L. Carter, Allen D. Sapp, and Darrel W. Stephens, *The State of Police Education: Policy Direction for the 21st Century* (Washington, DC: Police Executive Research Forum, 1989), 38.

28 Susan E. Martin, "Women on the Move?" *Police Foundation Reports* (Washington, DC: Police Foundation, 1989).

29 Bureau of Justice Statistics, U.S. Department of Justice, *Profile of State and Local Law Enforcement Agencies, 1987* (Washington, DC: U.S. Government Printing Office, 1989), table 7.

30 George W. Greisinger, Jeffrey S. Slovak, and Joseph J. Molkup, *Civil Service Systems: Their Impact on Police Administration* (Washington, DC: Law Enforcement Assistance Administration, 1979).

31 National Civil Service League, *A Model Public Personnel Administration Law* (Chevy Chase, MD: National Civil Service League, 1970).

32 Personal communication from Jerry L. Dowling, editor of *Police Labor Monthly*, 24 May 1989.

33 Steven A. Rynecki and Michael Morris, *Police Collective Bargaining Agreements: A National Management Survey* (Washington, DC: Police Executive Research Forum, 1981).

34 *Monell v. Department of Social Services* 436 U.S. 658 (1978).

35 Candace McCoy, "Survey Results: Police Legal Liability," in *Police Management* 2, no. 3 (June 1987): 11–12.

36 Patrick Gallagher, "Managing the Risks of Police Pursuit Policies," *Governmental Risk Management Reports* (Stamford, CT: Tillinghast, 1989).

37 Wayne A. Kerstetter, "Who Disciplines the Police? Who Should?" in *Police Leadership in America*, ed. Geller.

38 Whitaker et al. (*Basic Issues in Police Performance*) initially created similar criteria, which Dorothy Guyot (*Policing As Though People Matter* [Philadelphia: Temple University Press, 1991], chap. 10) developed.

39 John K. Hudzik, *Federal Aid to Criminal Justice: Rhetoric, Results, Lessons* (Washington, DC: National Criminal Justice Association, 1984) 148–61, 211–15, 242–44.

40 On relations between police and prosecutor, see Brian Forst, Frank J. Leahy, Jr., Jean Shirhall, Herbert L. Tyson, and John Bartolomeo, *Arrest Convictability as a Measure of Police Performance* (Washington, DC: National Institute of Justice, 1982).

41 Bureau of Justice Statistics, U.S. Department of Justice, *Report to the Nation on Crime and Justice: The Data* (Washington, DC: U.S. Government Printing Office, 1983), 81–5.

42 Bureau of Justice Statistics, U.S. Department of Justice, *Jail Inmates 1987* (Washington, DC: U.S. Government Printing Office, 1988), 4.

43 FBI, *Crime in the United States, 1988* (Washington, DC: U.S. Government Printing Office, 1989), 172.

44 Marvin E. Wolfgang, Robert M. Figlio, and Thornstein Sellin, *Delinquency in a Birth Cohort* (Chicago: University of Chicago Press, 1987); and Donna Martin Hamparian, Joseph M. Davis, Judith M. Jacobson, and Robert E. McGraw, "The Young Criminal Years of the Violent Few" (Washington, DC: Office of Juvenile Justice and Delinquency Prevention, Department of Justice, 1985).

45 Two articles summarize the advantages of consolidation: Leonard A. Matarese, "The Public Safety Concept Comes of Age," *New Jersey Municipalities* (May 1986); and Kenneth Chelst, "Police-Fire Merger: A Preimplementation Analysis of Performance and Cost," *Journal of Urban Affairs* 9, no. 2 (1987): 171–88.

46 Leonard Matarese, personal communication, 14 August 1989.

47 Gerald R. Murphy, *Special Care: Improving the Police Response to the Mentally Disturbed* (Washington, DC: Police Executive Research Forum, 1986).

16 External resources

Few, if any, police executives in the United States have more money than they think they need, or too big a labor force. Indeed, many police executives are exercising considerable ingenuity in making the available resources stretch far enough to guarantee the level of public safety and public service expected by the community. It is unfortunate, then, that many police executives are unaware of a whole range of unconventional funding sources. They do not know that every police headquarters is surrounded by a community of organizations and individuals with a vital interest in seeing that the police get what they need. The police manager who recognizes this and aggressively seeks help from the community stands a good chance of being rewarded.

Business

The nation's business community has a vested interest in law enforcement and crime prevention because crime has adverse effects on corporations. Crimes ranging from property theft to embezzlement affect a company's bottom line. In addition, in communities beset by crime, companies find it difficult to attract and retain high-caliber employees, and the communities themselves become less vital and less hospitable to commerce. Finally, high crime rates require companies to pay the high costs of maintaining their own security systems, which often duplicate services already provided by the public police.

The nation's business community has a vested interest in law enforcement and crime prevention.

But beyond the desire to prevent immediate economic loss and the encroachment of crime, the business community has several other reasons for lending support to law enforcement programs. Many companies have a sense of corporate responsibility and a commitment to the community from which they draw their viability and strength. By contributing to the community, the corporation enhances the environment in which it operates and promotes loyalty to, and respect for, the corporation on the part of community members. And whereas crime-ridden communities are not hospitable to commerce, stable communities benefit business by providing customers, employees, and an attractive environment.[1]

Funding

A direct way to obtain the business community's support is to apply to corporate giving programs for assistance. Under federal tax laws, corporations are able to donate up to 10 percent of their annual net profit to tax-exempt organizations or agencies. Among the types of funding that police executives may want to investigate are so-called small gifts, general support, corporate-sponsored projects, and—probably the most likely type of support—programmatic grants (that is, grants earmarked for a specific project). If the corporation has well-defined requirements, the police executive can identify reasonably clearly (especially after a preliminary meeting with members of the corporation's foundation or "corporate giving" unit) the types of projects the corporation is likely to support, the duration of funding, and evaluation criteria at the end of the grant period.

Corporate givers are generally sympathetic to local programs that can ultimately benefit company employees by upgrading certain aspects of life in the community. Because givers have special knowledge of the problems and the people in the community in which they have either headquarters or a branch office, they are better able to evaluate proposals designed to alleviate problems in this known territory. The dollar amount of these grants can vary considerably, depending on the project, the resources of the granting corporation, and the other causes competing for the company's support.

The police executive can find out more about which companies give grants and the nature and terms of those grants by consulting the *Taft Corporate Giving Directory*, published by The Taft Group in Washington, D.C. (Later this chapter discusses the more formal processes required to seek grants from large philanthropic foundations, which, unlike corporations that have only one or two staff members devoted to corporate giving programs, exist solely in order to fund various efforts and generally have large staffs; obtaining such funding requires more specialized skills on the part of successful grant applicants.)

Training

Corporations can provide other assistance besides direct funding. Many corporations have in-house training programs to teach management skills to their own employees. Although some of these skills are not generally taught—or not taught in a sophisticated manner—in traditional police executive training programs, they are nonetheless very important to the modern police department (for example, management, computer technology, and auditing). Many police departments are allowed to take advantage of these corporate training opportunities.

One vehicle for obtaining such training opportunities is Operation Bootstrap, established by the International Association of Chiefs of Police (IACP) in 1984. Bootstrap encourages businesses to welcome police officials into their in-house training programs.[2] It is designed to improve police administration by exposing police executives to state-of-the-art management theory and practice.

Under Operation Bootstrap, the IACP division of State Associations of Chiefs of Police (SACOP) asked a number of Fortune 500 companies to provide space for law enforcement personnel in management courses that could be considered relevant to police administration. Companies were asked to waive tuition costs; police agencies would be required to pay travel and per diem expenses, with some financial assistance provided by the National Institute of Justice. By 1988 dozens of Fortune 500 companies, including Boeing, The Hartford, Unisys, AT&T, A&P, Honeywell, Metropolitan Life, Tenneco, and Exxon were participating in Operation Bootstrap, offering training programs in finance, strategic management, communication, conflict resolution, and other subjects.[3] Program officials estimate that more than one thousand participants from more than five hundred police departments nationwide are trained annually.

In another corporate-sponsored training program, police managers in Philadelphia participated in management courses offered by twelve area companies. The police commissioner had personally appealed to the Greater Philadelphia First Corporation's board of directors, comprising executives from most of the region's major corporations. The board responded warmly, paving the way for senior police personnel to gain skills that might otherwise have been unavailable to them.[4]

In still another example of training assistance from the private sector, Security Pacific National Bank, which has several hundred branches in California, produced a film on the proper response to bank robberies for distribution throughout the California law enforcement community.

Programs like these not only provide needed training to the nation's police departments, but they also facilitate better relations between the police and community leaders. Such relationships can promote mutual understanding and lead to cooperative ventures to prevent crime and maintain order.

Loaned executive programs

Shared knowledge and exposure to other organizations can result, also, from loaned executive programs. The private sector uses such programs to allow one or more employees to work, with pay, for a not-for-profit or community organization for as long as a year at a time. Xerox, for instance, conducts a Social Service Leave Program; IBM has a Faculty Loan Program. A loaned executive program of the Baltimore County police department is also worth noting. In that program, companies lend local business executives to the county police department one or more days per week, sometimes for as long as several months. The executives have helped this department in a number of ways affecting administrative procedures, computer technology, needs assessments, and the corresponding budget requests.[5]

The number of executives available for such programs is limited; and not surprisingly, the number of agencies competing for the executive loan is relatively high.[6] The favorable exposure these programs have received, however, has led to the creation of variants of the loaned executive programs.

One variant is "resource sharing," by which companies release employees from work so they can perform volunteer service in programs of special interest to the company. Resource sharing allows workers not only to understand and contribute to corporate philanthropic goals but also to work together away from the office. Corporate giants such as Xerox, Bank of America, GTE-Sylvania, and Samsonite have sponsored this type of program.

Another variant of the loaned executive program is the IBM-sponsored Fund for Community Services, which provides financial support to community organizations for which IBM employees do volunteer work. Funding is initiated by an employee request that describes the project, the dollar amount, and the employee's involvement.[7]

These loaned executive and corporate volunteer programs are excellent ways for police to obtain services and gain useful knowledge and experience. In particular, through working with their corporate counterparts, police executives have an opportunity to see how management principles and techniques are used in the private sector, and may gain a new appreciation of their value.[8]

Other contributions

Businesses that may not be in a position to make grants or donate services but that are inclined to contribute to the community in some way can provide equipment, materials, or the use of space. This, of course, frees up funds that police managers would have spent for the donated items. This kind of help is especially useful in connection with computer technology.

Like the rest of society, police departments are becoming more and more automated—more and more dependent on efficient, effective communications and data processing systems. The modern police department harnesses the power of the computer to assist with many tasks that used to be done entirely by hand (for example, crime analysis, research, planning, dispatching, personnel administration, fingerprint identification, networking with other agencies, and training;

see the chapter on information management). But the cost of buying, implementing, and servicing automated systems is often prohibitive, especially for small departments. By obtaining help from an outside source, police executives can more easily stay abreast of technological advances and continue to participate in the "information society."

In addition, companies such as IBM, Unisys, NCR, AT&T, and Prime Computer, Inc., have developed computer-aided dispatch systems or management information systems for police departments (see the chapter on information management). To companies like these, the thousands of law enforcement agencies in the United States represent a sizeable market with special needs. With the proper approach, companies could tap that market—and if they did, police departments could benefit.

By obtaining help from an outside source, police executives can more easily stay abreast of technological advances and continue to be players in the "information society."

Other physical resources also may be obtained from the corporate community, and space is one of them. Computers are not very useful if there is no place to put them, and businesses may provide the space (if adequate security can be arranged). More commonly, businesses provide space for other purposes—for example, meetings, training, exercise. For departments pursuing community-oriented policing strategies, space can be provided for storefront police ministations (see the chapter on crime prevention). Or businesses may be willing to provide space free or at reduced rents in exchange for more police presence in certain locales. Clearly, of course, the willingness of companies to donate such physical plants cannot override the police responsibility to determine how law enforcement personnel should be allocated in the community.

The Repeat Offender Project (ROP) of the Washington, D.C., metropolitan police department consistently asks for and obtains other physical resources from the local business community: buildings, lots, cars, trucks, and surveillance vans. The Board of Trade, business associations, and other such organizations facilitate the arrangements. The only requirement is that the provider be informed of the outcome of the cases in which its contributions were used and of the role its contributions played.

Partnerships for planning

To obtain many of the external resources mentioned above, the police executive must identify an existing need and locate appropriate resources to meet that need. But the ultimate success of such efforts depends on an ongoing public-private partnership. Just as business councils assess corporate and consumer trends and attempt to adopt strategies that will allow stable growth, so law enforcement and its community partners must work together to assess the state of criminal justice and to construct plans for ensuring public safety and quality public services. No public agency should do its planning in a vacuum (see the chapter on research). Doing so is short-sighted and dysfunctional, can create unnecessary conflicts over municipal resources, and may ultimately be a disservice to the public that the police are pledged to serve.

Accordingly, progressive police executives are beginning to take an aggressive approach to community involvement. For example, the Washington [state] Association of Sheriffs and Police Chiefs, in an attempt to demonstrate that public safety is a community responsibility and not just a job for the police, formed the Washington Law Enforcement Executive Forum in 1981. Consisting of sheriffs, police chiefs, and business leaders, the forum attempts to approach public safety issues in the community rationally, thoughtfully, and inclusively. The forum has sponsored loaned executive, management-training, and legislative advocacy programs, and in so doing has reached out to other associations, public and private criminal justice agencies, the media, and major corporations. The forum was instrumental in bringing about the passage of a number of laws whose effect has been to improve law enforcement and public safety. It collaborated with the Washington state patrol, the state traffic safety commission, and a Seattle radio station to fund a toll-free hotline for catching drunk drivers. And it has cosponsored several programs designed to further professionalize the law enforcement community.[9]

As this section has suggested, there is no telling what help a police executive might get by asking. Yet it goes without saying that no assistance, no matter how great or small, should tempt the executive to compromise his or her professional decision-making processes. In creating partnerships with corporate organizations, the police manager should be sure that the ground rules are clear. Companies should not expect to be able to unduly influence police policy or practice simply because they have provided some service to the police department. Nor should they expect any favor in return.

By and large, corporate executives view these kinds of assistance as a corporate and civic responsibility. They give to help achieve a goal whose effects will be salutary for the community and, by extension, for their employees and their own corporate image.[10]

Police membership associations

Collegial association is important for any group of professionals, and the police are no exception. Police associations, like membership associations in general, are devoted to service and professional development. They provide a supportive, nurturing milieu for members and set standards of professional conduct. They promote the building, preservation, and dissemination of knowledge. They are interested in how the public can best be served by their profession.

Perhaps the best-known police membership association is the International Association of Chiefs of Police (IACP), with more than fourteen thousand individual and sixty-seven nation members. Headquartered in Arlington, Virginia, the IACP offers its members technical assistance, training, executive placement, research, publications, public relations and advocacy programs, and other developmental and organizational services.

The Police Executive Research Forum (PERF) was established in 1977 in Washington, D.C., with the help of the Police Foundation. A national organization of chief executives from large and medium-sized state, county, and city law enforcement agencies, PERF provides professional conferences and a range of management consultant services, including productivity analysis, workload assessment and beat planning, and technical assistance in communications, budgeting, information processing, internal affairs, and so forth. Among other programs, PERF established the Senior Management Institute for Police, a three-week course taught largely by faculty from Harvard's Business School and its John F. Kennedy School of Government.

The National Sheriffs' Association, also based in Arlington, Virginia, has approximately thirty-one thousand members, including sheriffs; deputy sheriffs; municipal, state, and federal law enforcement officers; and other professionals in the criminal justice system. It provides its members with consultation, technical assistance, publications, insurance programs, and professional conferences and sponsors a comprehensive victim assistance program.

Providing a forum for addressing the special concerns of black police executives, the National Organization of Black Law Enforcement Executives (NOBLE) admits into its membership black law enforcement executives above the rank of lieutenant, as well as black police educators, academy directors, and other interested individuals and organizations. Among its goals are an increase in minority participation at all levels of law enforcement, elimination of racism in the field of criminal justice, and the reduction of urban crime and violence. Headquartered in the nation's capital, NOBLE puts on professional conferences and provides technical assistance and consultation on a broad range of issues, including coordinated community efforts to prevent crime and to strike at its roots.

Parallel to NOBLE in purposes and services to its members is the Hispanic American Police Command Officers' Association. Its headquarters shifts, depending on the location of its incumbent elected officers.

Police executives faced with organizational challenges can also contact one or more of several police planning organizations that can provide information on

---

External resources　The following listing provides information for contacting resources cited in this chapter:

Organizations and programs

American Bar Foundation
750 N. Lake Shore Drive
Chicago, Illinois 60611

American Society for Industrial Security
1655 N. Fort Myer Drive
Suite 1200
Arlington, Virginia 22209

Association of Police Planners and
Research Officers International
910 Sleater Kinney, S.E.
Suite 187
Lacey, Washington 98503

Hispanic American Police Command
Officers' Association
P.O. Box 521103
Miami, Florida 33152

IBM Faculty Loan Program
IBM Corporation
Corporate Support Programs
2000 Purchase Street
Purchase, New York 10577

IBM Fund for Community Services
(see preceding address)

International City Management
Association
777 North Capitol Street, N.E.
Washington, D.C. 20002

International Association of Chiefs of
Police
1110 North Glebe Road
Suite 200
Arlington, Virginia 22201

National Association of Police Planners
1000 Connecticut Avenue, N.W.
Suite 9
Washington, D.C. 20036

National Conference of Christians and
Jews
71 Fifth Avenue
Suite 1100
New York, New York 10003

National Crime Prevention Council
1700 K Street, N.W.
2d Floor
Washington, D.C. 20006

National League of Cities
1301 Pennsylvania Avenue, N.W.
6th Floor
Washington, D.C. 20004

National Organization of Black Law
Enforcement Executives
908 Pennsylvania Avenue, S.E.
Washington, D.C. 20003

National Sheriffs' Association
1450 Duke Street
Alexandria, Virginia 22314

National Urban League
500 East 62d Street
New York, New York 10021

how other departments have solved their own management problems. These planning organizations include the Association of Police Planners and Research Officers International, with chapters in Florida, southern and northern California, and the Pacific Northwest (including Canada); the National Association of Police Planners (based in the police agency of the incumbent elected president); and the Ontario Police Forces Planning Association.

Any number of other associations can also be asked for assistance; the accompanying sidebar suggests sources of information.

Media

In the search for community resources, the media should never be overlooked. We live in a communications age. To the extent that police executives ignore one of society's chief instruments for public communication, they do themselves, and ultimately their communities, a disservice. And consider community-oriented policing: if good police work indeed requires good communication between

---

Ontario Police Forces Planning
  Association
c/o Constable Pattie Rumley
90 Harbour Street
Toronto, Ontario, Canada M7A 2S1

Police Executive Research Forum
2300 M Street, N.W.
Suite 910
Washington, D.C. 20037

Police Foundation
1001 22d Street, N.W.
Suite 200
Washington, D.C. 20036

U.S. Conference of Mayors
1620 I Street, N.W.
4th Floor
Washington, D.C. 20006

Xerox Social Service Leave Program
Xerox Foundation
P.O. Box 1600
Stamford, Connecticut 06904

Directories

Foundation Directory, Foundation
  Center, 79 Fifth Avenue, New York,
  New York 10003

Grants for Crime and Law Enforcement,
  Foundation Center (see preceding
  address)

IACP *Directory of Members* (see
  address above for International
  Association of Chiefs of Police)

*The Jeffers Directory of Law
  Enforcement Officials* (New York:
  Pace Publications, 1990)

*National Directory of Law Enforcement
  Administrators, Correctional
  Institutions and Related Agencies*
  (Stevens Point, WI: National Police
  Chiefs and Sheriffs Information
  Bureau)

*Scroggins National Law Enforcement
  Directory* (Montrose, CA: Scroggins
  National)

Taft Corporate Giving Directory, The
  Taft Group, 5230 MacArthur
  Boulevard, Washington, D.C. 20016

Taft Foundation Reporter, The Taft
  Group (see preceding address)

Government resources

Several resources cited in this chapter
  are housed in the U.S. Department of
  Justice:

Community Relations Service

Office of Justice Programs, which is
  home to the Bureau of Justice
  Assistance and the National Institute
  of Justice. NIJ houses the National
  Criminal Justice Reference Service.

police and community residents, why limit communication to personal contact in the neighborhood? Television, radio, video, and the print media are powerful communications tools.

Although the Federal Communications Commission has relaxed its requirements that radio and television stations provide public service spots, many stations do provide some time for public service announcements. These announcements may be helpful to the police.

That does not mean, however, that the police executive should expect consistently favorable news coverage. The news media's job is to cover police stories objectively—be that coverage positive or negative. Indeed, a key to success in dealing with media companies is to see them as businesses that, like any other corporations, must simultaneously meet complex, multiple objectives. What a television station does in fulfilling its public service obligations may be independent of its current news coverage of the police.

News coverage aside, media organizations can help the police reach either short-term practical goals or long-term strategic goals. Consider Crime Stoppers (discussed at greater length in the chapter on crime prevention), a nationwide crime control program that brings together media representatives, law enforcement officials, and citizens in order to encourage citizens to report crime. Crime Stoppers calls upon the media to educate the public about the program and to regularly publicize details of an unsolved "crime of the week" by presenting an account or reenactment of the offense. The messages encourage anyone who has knowledge of a crime to call Crime Stoppers to report that crime. People whose tips result in an arrest typically receive a cash reward.

News coverage aside, media organizations can help the police reach either short-term practical goals or long-term strategic goals.

Since 1976, when the first Crime Stoppers program was established, an estimated seven hundred programs have sprung up across the nation.[11] Through September 15, 1990, according to statistics released by Crime Stoppers International, the program had resulted in 309,696 cases solved, more than $1.8 billion in recovered narcotics and stolen property, and a 97 percent conviction rate.

Another cooperative venture with the media began when the metropolitan police department in Washington, D.C., enlisted the support of local government agencies, automotive and trade associations, and insurers in a campaign to raise public awareness about auto theft. The conference to launch the campaign received front-page coverage from the city's major daily newspaper, and periodic articles covered the campaign as it progressed. Program officials also appeared on talk shows and in news features. One area television station went beyond straight news coverage and agreed to produce a public service announcement and distribute it to other stations. The Committee of Police Chiefs of the Metropolitan Washington Council of Governments subsequently adopted a similar campaign for the entire metropolitan area.[12]

The potential benefits of working with the media are limited only by a police executive's creativity and willingness to build alliances with media organizations. Television stations can donate studio time or consultation with experts in video production. Radio stations can help produce public service announcements. (Radio advertising, it should be noted, is an inexpensive, effective means of reaching a great number of people.) A newspaper's editorial staff or columnists can be instrumental in raising community awareness or funds for special purposes, such as bulletproof vests, a memorial for a slain officer, or some other cause.

Cooperation involves two parties, and some media outlets may be less than willing. But more is lost by not trying to enlist their support than by trying and being rebuffed. It is important to realize that working with the media produces results that transcend the immediate goal (which may be to reduce auto thefts, identify criminals, and so forth). Working with the media by making knowledgeable police representatives available for attributable interviews on a timely basis helps establish rapport with media representatives, and that rapport may ultimately mean that news coverage of police matters gains in depth and understanding. Furthermore, news coverage raises public consciousness of the police and the challenges they face each day and, in the best scenario, teaches the citizenry that enlightened law enforcement requires public interest and participation. Finally, news coverage builds community cohesiveness and spirit.

Not-for-profit organizations

There are all manner of private, not-for-profit interest groups that can be of value to the police executive. They are found everywhere but tend to cluster in state capitals and Washington, D.C. They may have as their primary function research, advocacy, public education, or some combination thereof. Because their programs are not required to produce a profit, these organizations may be in a position to provide services free of charge or on a cost-recovery basis. They can therefore be a valuable source of assistance for police executives and managers.

One example is the National Crime Prevention Council (NCPC), sponsor of McGruff, the well-known animated crime dog, and the "take a bite out of crime" public service campaign. Funded by a mix of philanthropic organizations, government agencies, and major corporations, the council serves as a national focal point for citizen crime prevention activities and addresses issues ranging from property security to prevention of alcohol and drug abuse.[13] It operates a computerized information center with data on more than five thousand crime prevention programs, as well as a resource center with more than fifteen hundred books, reports, and audiovisuals. Referral information, standard computer searches, and many NCPC informational materials are free (see also the chapter on crime prevention).

Another nationally known nonprofit is the Police Foundation, created in 1970 with a grant from the Ford Foundation. In addition to its research program, discussed below, the Police Foundation has a technical assistance division that provides departments across the country with training and consultation on crime control and other police operations. It also sponsors conferences and other forums intended to promote examination of and debate on issues of pressing importance to the police community.

Nonprofit organizations that do not have a criminal justice focus can also be valuable resources, if their goals are relevant to the police mission. Among these are the National Urban League, the National League of Cities, and the NAACP. The International City Management Association (ICMA) and the U.S. Conference of Mayors (USCM) are interested in police service in the nation's cities and provide information and services useful to police managers. For instance, ICMA provides management information and urban data services and sponsors a training institute for city and county employees in various fields. USCM, whose members are the mayors of cities with more than thirty thousand people, conducts research and provides educational information, technical assistance, and legislative services. Both organizations also have publishing programs.

Another such organization is the National Conference of Christians and Jews (NCCJ), which for decades has provided considerable assistance to police departments seeking to promote better community relations. Founded in 1928, NCCJ is an ecumenical organization whose purpose is to work toward better human relations across all religions and races. It has approximately seventy regional offices nationwide, some of which provide human relations services to police departments in their area. The New York City and Los Angeles regional offices are two of the most active in this respect.

Local affiliates and organizations

Police executives looking for resources should also investigate the local affiliates of organizations such as Rotary International, the Kiwanis, Elks, and Lions clubs, and the Chamber of Commerce. These community service groups often award small grants for such things as police training. But sometimes they undertake much larger projects. In Evanston, Illinois, for example, the Kiwanis Club raised more than $36,000 to purchase safety vests for police officers and recruits.

Affiliate groups generally are interested in projects that enhance life in the community and projects that meet the needs of special populations.

Affiliate groups generally are interested in projects that enhance life in the community and projects that meet the needs of special populations, for example, young people, drug abusers, and elderly people. It is important for police executives and managers to get to know members of these groups, including local business leaders, lawyers, judges, and elected officials. Not only will members of these groups know how police can best use the resources of a given organization, but they also represent a rich network of community leaders that can contribute in various ways to the mission of policing. Once again, however, police officials should be cautioned that although relationships might be friendly, they should also be professional. The police executive should studiously avoid situations in which a conflict of interest might arise or appear to arise.

Neighborhood resources

There are other community groups that the police executive may not at first look on as a resource, because they may be relatively small. But such groups as homeowners' associations, neighborhood organizations, and church groups can be very important to crime control efforts. Their strength derives from the fact that they are such an integral part of the community. A police executive with a problem-oriented philosophy will find that these groups can help identify problems that require the attention of the department.[14]

More than that, however, regular communication between the police and neighborhood groups builds long-term, mutually beneficial relationships between police officials and members of the community. With the information and support supplied by members of these organizations, the police can be more effective. And although many of these organizations may be small, cumulatively they represent a significant force that can be mobilized on a given issue: as discussed at greater length in the chapter on crime prevention, many such groups are well organized and their members are highly motivated.

Neighborhood organizations are also a great source of volunteers—a natural resource to police departments faced with increasing workloads and pinched resources.[15] Volunteers can perform a broad range of support services that the police must otherwise provide instead of being out in the community. Volunteers who are properly screened, trained, and supervised can keep records, operate computers, conduct crime prevention surveys, provide telephone assistance, manage recovered property, or serve as translators in multilingual communities.

The Palo Alto (California) police department has scores of volunteers to help perform support or specialized duties. The department saved a significant amount of money by enlisting four retired executives to conduct a financial planning trends analysis for the department and the city. The volunteer program provides more than inexpensive labor, however. The Palo Alto volunteer program has reportedly enhanced department performance, lowered costs, and increased public support for the agency.

Unfortunately, many police both management and, particularly, organized labor—resist using volunteers. But although volunteer programs can create certain problems, steps can also be taken to avoid those problems:

1. Assign a staff member to manage the program.
2. Properly target all advertising for volunteers.
3. Conduct fingerprint and background checks.
4. Provide orientation and training.
5. Explain in detail the job to be done.
6. Provide volunteers with feedback and recognition.[16]

One of the largest volunteer programs, of course, is Neighborhood Watch. It has received wide acclaim as a means of involving citizens in a public safety effort. It differs from the kind of volunteer program that Palo Alto has, however, in that police are involved only peripherally. They attend organizing meetings and provide some training, but their primary responsibility in the Watch program is simply to respond to calls.

Neighborhood organizations are a great source of volunteers—a natural resource to police departments faced with increasing workloads and pinched resources.

There are thousands of Neighborhood Watch programs across the country. In some of these neighborhoods, the number of burglaries has decreased notably. In others, it has not. As discussed more fully in the chapter on crime prevention, this difference has been attributed to the disparity between the number of Watch groups that have been formed and the number that are truly active. Many citizens, after the initial enthusiasm wears off, simply do not participate.

Senior citizen volunteers The Asheville, North Carolina, police department has signed an agreement with the Land-of-Sky Regional Council on Aging to enlist the help of up to 20 senior citizen volunteers to work for the police department's Victim Call Back Program.

Members of the Retired Senior Volunteer Program (RSVP) will help the police telephone individuals who have been victims of a crime. Through this personal contact with the volunteers, the department hopes that the victim will be reassured that the police department does care about what has happened to them. Volunteers are also assisting the police department by entering pawn shop tickets into the computer hoping to find stolen property, doing shotgun maintenance, and helping to restructure the property control office. Others are helping to gather information for office cases over the phone. Volunteers complete training before assuming their duties.

Source: Cited in *The Guide to Management Improvement Projects in Local Government* (Washington, DC: International City Management Association, 1990).

Studies of Neighborhood Watch programs and related initiatives, such as "Cop-of-the-Block" programs, have suggested that they have a questionable effect on crime.[17] Nonetheless, funding agencies seem to believe that the potential for these programs is great enough to justify further efforts. The Bureau of Justice Assistance has made millions of dollars in block grants available for community crime prevention programs, and the Office of Justice Programs has established demonstration crime watch programs in cities such as Knoxville, Tennessee; Tucson, Arizona; Jacksonville, Florida; and New Haven, Connecticut. The programs provide crime prevention training to all officers, use data analysis to discover crime patterns and decide where citizen programs would help most, and make crime prevention "how-to" kits available to communities, schools, and businesses.[18]

As the chapter on crime prevention points out, the most successful community crime prevention programs have been created by organizations that have strong community ties and were created to achieve different public safety goals, for example, to improve driver awareness, plan for natural disasters, or prevent child abuse. Regardless of their goals—whether to reduce crime or to clean up a garbage-filled alley—programs like these, which bring people together for a cause deemed important to the common good, can only strengthen a community.

Clergy and other civic leaders

Civic leaders are directly or indirectly involved in many programs that enhance police department resources. Nonetheless it may be helpful to look at community leadership as a resource in its own right. A simple request from the department for a prominent citizen to serve on a task force, give a speech, testify on behalf of the police at a legislative hearing, or coordinate a community service program is often accepted with pleasure.

Members of the clergy are usually among the more informed and concerned citizens in the community vis-à-vis crime and social problems and are often willing to lend a hand in programs that touch upon their ministries in some way. Frequently they agree to participate in or lead community groups focusing on such issues as child abuse, crime, drug abuse, and homelessness. Churches are being used for hotline centers, drug awareness centers, shelters, and various other purposes.

Members of the clergy are usually among the more informed and concerned citizens in the community vis-à-vis crime and social problems.

When the mayor of Charleston, South Carolina, for example, created a task force on mentally ill homeless people, it was chaired by the director of the Charleston Interfaith Crisis Ministry, a nonprofit agency sponsored by the city and local churches and offering emergency services to homeless people. In another such program, an "Outreach Teams Coalition" was created in Santa Monica, California, to assist the area's homeless population. The coalition has two teams that offer food, clothing, shelter, and treatment to street people. Both the Charleston and the Santa Monica programs include members of the law enforcement community, and they train police in responding to street people.[19]

In another attempt to extend police resources, executives might want to consider forming a police-clergy team—a ride-along program for clergy of all denominations to be used in special situations, for example, family disturbances, death notifications, and other crises that may require counseling or mediation. Clergy can also be enlisted to counsel police officers and their families. Finally, clergy can volunteer the use of their churches for police-citizen meetings to work on a community problem or to air grievances.

Civic leaders can be found not only among the clergy but also in all other walks of life, and they are as varied in their skills, resources, and interests as the general population. They have one thing in common, however. They are doers. They see a problem and they try to do something about it. In that respect, they have something in common with the police. The extent to which police executives identify the civic leaders whose causes correspond to their own, and create mutually beneficial partnerships with them, helps determine the extent to which these executives can wisely invest their departmental resources.

It is important that departments collect and maintain data bases identifying the kinds of people and organizations that can be prevailed upon to help.

For this purpose, and for the purpose of tapping other resources described in this chapter, it is important that departments collect and maintain data bases identifying the kinds of people and organizations that can be prevailed upon to help. A list of civic leaders, their particular interests, and the resources at their command, for instance, makes it much easier to match requirements of the task to be done with the people who can be called upon to lend assistance.

Private security

The phenomenal growth of the private security industry has paralleled the relatively slow growth of public policing. A possible correlation between the two growth patterns may be irrelevant. What matters is the potential for some sort of partnership that will enhance the public's safety while observing clear jurisdictional boundaries and protecting the public's legal rights. Legal rights are an issue because the public is constitutionally protected from unnecessary police intrusion, but private police are not so constrained.

A few other potential difficulties might also stem from the indiscriminate use of private security personnel:

1. Without proper screening procedures, security companies may hire people who not only are unqualified to provide security services but may also have criminal records or otherwise be unfit to carry out their assigned duties.
2. Employment standards of security firms may be lower than those of police departments. Police are usually rigorously trained and tested for intelligence, psychological and social skills, and physical strength—all of which are needed for complex and sometimes dangerous police work.
3. The hiring of private security personnel who are not capable of handling serious criminal activity gives a false sense of security and therefore may do more harm than good.

If issues of rights protection, standards, and jurisdiction are resolved, however, public and private police can form a powerful law enforcement partnership. A study of the private security industry conducted under the auspices of the National Institute of Justice found that certain police tasks can sometimes be handled more efficiently by private security—tasks such as ensuring the security of public buildings, enforcing parking regulations, and maintaining court security. In addition, the study found that police and security managers agreed that some non-crime-related tasks could be contracted out to the private sector and that private security should respond to some minor criminal incidents occurring on the property it is protecting. Responding to minor criminal incidents would include responding to burglar alarms, investigating misdemeanors, completing official misdemeanor reports, and initiating preliminary investigations of other crimes.[20]

A public-private police partnership should also include exchanges of information and products. Police work can be facilitated if the police gain access to equipment and various investigative techniques developed by the private security industry. Private security, in turn, can benefit from police intelligence on criminals, including bad-chcck violators and con artists.[21]

The National Institute of Justice study mentioned above recommended that police departments become more familiar with private security operations. Departments can do so by appointing security liaison officers, keeping directories of security firms, providing training opportunities to private security personnel, and staying abreast of the professional literature.

The Dallas police department began an ongoing relationship with the private security industry in 1983, when representatives of the department and the private security industry formed the Dallas Police/Private Security Joint Information Committee, consisting of five private security officials and two members of the Dallas police department. The committee created a one-hour instructional program on private security for the police academy; published a newsletter on crime trends and prevention; and established a bulletin to provide private security companies with late-breaking news.[22]

If issues of rights protection, standards, and jurisdiction are resolved, public and private police can form a powerful law enforcement partnership.

Such cooperative efforts between the police and private security companies are becoming increasingly common and can be found in places as far-flung as New York City; Chicago; Tacoma, Washington; and Montgomery County, Maryland.

Police executives wishing to learn more about private security can get in touch with the American Society for Industrial Security (ASIS). The society's goals are similar to those of other trade and professional associations (establishing standards, providing for the members' professional development, and nurturing professionalism). ASIS has a certification program that requires candidates to meet experience and educational requirements and pass a one-day examination. The society also has promoted the need for cooperation between the police and private security.

Other public agencies

In addition to providing services to citizens, public agencies provide services to each other. Indeed, the police have much to gain from working with other agencies in the battle against crime and disorder (see also the chapter on the governmental setting). The most obvious source of assistance, of course, is other criminal justice agencies—at local, state, and federal levels. And among the most obvious means of collaboration are joint task forces for investigating crimes, joint training programs, and computer networks for information exchange (see the chapter on information management).

One example of computer networks for information exchange is the Regional Information Sharing Systems (RISS), sponsored by the Office of Justice Programs of the U.S. Department of Justice. The RISS program consists of seven multistate projects that support the exchange of information and provide related services to law enforcement agencies at every level throughout the nation. Drug trafficking, organized crime, and white-collar crime are all targets.[23]

The RISS program was set up to assist other public criminal justice agencies. But any number of other government agencies that were established for reasons entirely outside the realm of law enforcement nonetheless have enough in common with the police to make cooperation with them a mutually beneficial arrangement.

Consider Operation Brightside, a comprehensive community improvement project carried out in Washington, D.C., in 1984 and 1985. Brightside used the resources of several municipal agencies, including the police and fire departments, the Office of Business and Economic Development, and the departments of Consumer and Regulatory Affairs, Public Works, Housing and Community Development, and Human Services. Its goals were to reduce crime, bring all multifamily rental housing units and businesses into compliance with safety and health codes, and, in general, enhance the quality of life in the community.

The final assessment report for Operation Brightside claims that the project led to a significant decrease in the area's criminal activity, a goal-directed community economic plan, an improved physical environment, and better interdepartmental coordination in the D.C. government.[24]

Another model interagency program is Project DARE (Drug Abuse Resistance Education), a joint undertaking of the Los Angeles police department and the Los Angeles Unified School District. (The project is discussed in the chapters on local drug control and crime prevention.) The DARE curriculum was developed by health education specialists, and the police officers involved in DARE are carefully selected and given a two-week, eighty-hour seminar delivered by law enforcement and educational agencies.

Another multiagency program, this one developed by the police department and the executive school superintendent in Newark, New Jersey, created a truancy task force to deal with young people who shoplifted and snatched purses during school hours. In this program, which was admittedly controversial, the task force divided the city into four districts and assigned a bus to each. The bus carried a driver, two teachers who served as truancy officers, and a police officer. The task force stopped youngsters on the street and asked them for identification. If they were over sixteen, they were released. All others were taken to a central location and referred to social workers, who followed up on each youth's behavior. Follow-up procedures included contact with parents or guardians. If a youth continued to skip school, he or she risked being brought to court as a disorderly person.

In another interagency project, the counseling unit of the Youth Services Division of the Baltimore County police department established a special training program for youth offenders. Entitled JOINT (Juvenile Offenders in Need of Treatment), the program sends thirteen- to eighteen-year-olds to the Maryland Correctional Institution at Jessup to get a taste of what a life of crime might lead them to. Face-to-face meetings with specially trained volunteer inmates give the youths a vivid picture of prison life and suggest that there are much better alternatives. This version of a "scared straight" program seeks to delay a youth's return to delinquency and to buy enough time for him or her to outgrow delinquent tendencies.[25]

Projects like Brightside, DARE, and JOINT illustrate the potential of joint ventures between public agencies. The strength of these kinds of projects seems to be their systematic, multifaceted approach to problem solving—an approach that most agencies are not equipped to undertake alone.

The Washington, D.C., metropolitan police department has found that other law enforcement agencies (there are more than two dozen law enforcement agencies with one or another type of jurisdiction within the District of Columbia), as well as branches of the armed services, are willing to contribute resources that will serve mutually desirable goals, such as those embodied in the department's Repeat Offender Project (ROP). ROP has obtained confidential funds for firearms cases from the Bureau of Alcohol, Tobacco, and Firearms confidential funds for drug cases from the Drug Enforcement Agency (DEA); and sophisticated camera equipment for criminal investigations from the U.S. Navy.

The department has also availed itself of personnel and funds from the FBI, Army Intelligence, and the Immigration and Naturalization Service (INS), among other agencies.

Another kind of governmental service is available from a branch of the U.S. Department of Justice—the Community Relations Service (CRS)—to help police departments grapple with race relations, an important dynamic in community relations throughout the country. Established by Title X of the Civil Rights Act of 1964, CRS provides conciliation, mediation, and technical assistance services to communities experiencing (or in danger of experiencing) some sort of racial disturbance.

With ten regional offices nationally, CRS responds to requests for assistance, assesses a given problem, determines whether the problem is amenable to solution by CRS, and then employs dispute resolution techniques to resolve the conflict. Charges related to excessive use of police force are one of the most common sources of problems handled by CRS; others concern defamation, intimidation, and racially motivated assault of minorities.

CRS also tries to minimize the potential for civil disorder by identifying high-risk areas and providing assistance before disturbances occur. One way CRS tries to do this is by providing appropriate training to police departments. An additional advantage of this training is that, by employing panels of law enforcement personnel and community leaders to go on-site and help assess and address certain problems, CRS enriches the perspectives and skills of the participating panel members.

Finally, police managers should be aware of provisions of Title IV of the Intergovernmental Personnel Act of 1970 that allow funding for the temporary assignment of personnel between agencies of the federal government and agencies of state, local, and Native American tribal governments, institutions of higher education, and certain other organizations for work of mutual concern or benefit. The federal agency involved in the assignment may agree to pay all, some, or none of the costs of an assignment. An assignment agreement may be made for up to two years and may be extended by the head of the federal agency for up to two more years, given agreement among all parties. The emphasis, however, is on limiting the duration strictly to the time necessary for completing the assigned tasks.[26]

Academic institutions

The academic community and the police community have often been worlds apart on law enforcement issues. The growing professionalism in policing in recent years, however, has been accompanied by an increase in natural ties between police executives and academic institutions. These ties can be built upon to supplement police department resources.

Faculty of area schools can assist police managers in a variety of ways:

1. Training curriculum development
2. Identification of prospective police recruits and employable civilian professionals
3. Provision of college courses pertinent to the functional responsibilities of departmental personnel
4. Provision of classes, seminars, or workshops for recruits, incumbent officers, middle managers, and command personnel
5. Assistance in police department planning, research, and evaluation.

Assistance arrangements between police and faculty are varied. Although faculty services, like those of many other consultants, can be secured by contract, faculty members often donate their services or provide them in exchange for access to research data or the opportunity to develop publishable articles and studies. Police departments wishing to encourage executives, managers, or personnel in specialized areas to pursue graduate studies or acquire advanced degrees can negotiate with colleges and universities for appropriate classes or courses of study to be developed and provided. The police department can reciprocate by ensuring a certain number of students for the course, either by offering a tuition reimbursement plan or by requiring graduate credit as a prerequisite to advancement through the ranks.

The number and variety of cooperative arrangements existing between universities and police departments are very great. The Graduate School of Criminal Justice of Rutgers University, for instance, was represented on a planning task force for the landmark fear reduction study in Newark, New Jersey, conducted by the Police Foundation.

In Houston, universities and police cooperate in many ways. Area faculty members participate with other community members on the city's Police Advisory Committee. They are also appointed to special task forces addressing such issues as the revamping of the curriculum and structure of the police department's training academy. Faculty teach classes in the academy's recruit and in-service training programs and are frequently invited to speak at command staff meetings. The department contracts with faculty members to teach special courses such as conversational Spanish and Vietnamese. And the department's Office of Planning and Research occasionally uses faculty members to conduct community surveys or teach writing skills to sworn and civilian personnel.

The number and variety of cooperative arrangements existing between universities and police departments are very great.

The Chicago police department during the early 1980s appointed university faculty—as well as local staff of national organizations such as the Police Foundation, PERF, and the American Bar Foundation—to a review committee to help assess the value of proposed research and departmental changes. The committee was asked to determine how new programs might be evaluated and, in some instances, whether grant proposals should be written. The group was used as a sounding board and as a means of gaining *pro bono* access to the academic or research networks. Its members also worked directly with departmental staff in program development and research.

A similar review committee in Evanston, Illinois, provided the police chief with the opportunity to try out ideas and assess possible operational changes without frightening or upsetting departmental personnel. The committee disseminated information to staff about departmental progress and provided an environment in which department managers could freely discuss how they might go about handling particular issues.

As valuable as faculty may be, they are only one part of this assistance equation. Students in criminal justice programs at the university or high school level, for instance, are placed in police departments in paying jobs or on assignments for academic credit to introduce them to criminal justice operations. But it is essential that the police department provide these students with meaningful work and adequate supervision. And if a student intern is earning academic credit, he or she should be able to complete the assigned projects before the end of the school term. In particular, it is a serious mistake to underestimate the time and effort required for proper supervision and coordination between the school and the department. Such underestimation demoralizes the supervisor and the student, deprives the department of the full use of student resources, and, worst of all, gives the student a negative image of the department.

Police departments can also recruit student interns from criminal justice and

---

Tapping research resources   In 1985 the Evanston (Illinois) police department, with assistance from the Police Executive Research Forum, established a research advisory committee of prominent professors, researchers, and practitioners in the fields of law enforcement and criminal justice to advise on departmental questions. Most of the committee members were Evanston residents, so they provided a local as well as a professional perspective.

The ultimate purpose of the committee was to help the department improve its overall effectiveness. The department sought the committee's advice on the latest thinking about law enforcement policies and methods as well as on responses to specific local problems and service needs. The committee provided a forum for discussing issues, exchanging viewpoints, and brainstorming.

The committee provided insights on a number of questions for the department; among them were community-oriented policing, the use-of-force policy, computer-aided dispatch, a differential response program, program evaluation, and citizen surveys.

In return for this assistance, the department provided information that was useful to committee members for research or other purposes.

The success of such a program depends on the willingness of the chief to tap community resources, to discuss issues openly outside of police circles, and to accept constructive criticism as it is offered.

Source: William H. Logan, chief of police (retired), and Frank Kaminski, deputy chief, Evanston (Illinois) police department.

---

social work programs as direct service providers, for example, as community service workers, police or citizen counselors, and police-citizen group facilitators. Students in these two academic disciplines and others can also be enlisted to assist in research and evaluation projects. The Houston police department, for example, assigned a major research project to a University of Houston public policy class. The work was divided into parts, one for each student to research and write up during the semester. In the end, the police department got a quality research report written by the professor of the class; the students acquired valuable experience in conducting useful research; and the professor gained a publishable article.

Research institutions

With surging crime rates causing many to doubt the validity of traditional law enforcement theories and practices, police policy and procedure need empirical underpinnings more than ever before. Research is essential to the growing professionalism of the U.S. law enforcement community. In response to this perceived need, the Police Foundation was established in 1970.[27] A number of other organizations (such as the Police Executive Research Forum and the IACP) and academic institutions (such as the John Jay College's Criminal Justice Center, the Southwestern Law Enforcement Institute, and the Southern Police Institute) have ambitious research programs and thus contribute to the movement toward greater professionalism. But although many police departments have welcomed these developments, others have been slow to acknowledge the value of research and its potential effect on policing and community life.

The work of the Police Foundation illustrates the contributions such organizations can make to individual departments, to law enforcement in general, and to the community. In 1982, for instance, the National Institute of Justice awarded the foundation a grant for an empirical study of strategies to reduce citizen fear of crime, improve the quality of neighborhood life, and increase citizen satisfaction with police services. The study was based on the premise that fear of crime often exceeds the actual risk of being victimized and that this fear causes a deterioration in the quality of community life.

After studying several programs in Newark and Houston, researchers found that closer contact between the police and neighborhood residents did indeed reduce fear of crime and increase satisfaction with the police. The study recommended that the police avail themselves of every opportunity to improve relations with citizens, become good listeners, develop strategies to solve problems identified by citizens, and involve the citizens in crime-reduction strategies. It also recommended that police officers and supervisors be allowed to try new approaches even if there is some risk of failure.[28]

Further empirical research during the 1980s built on insights gleaned in the fear reduction research and in other projects and began to establish the value of formal adoption of problem-solving strategies (see the chapters on the patrol function, criminal investigations, and local drug control).

The single greatest supporter of empirical research in the criminal justice system is the U.S. Department of Justice. This federal department houses the National Institute of Justice (NIJ), the Bureau of Justice Statistics, the Bureau of Justice Assistance, and the Office of Juvenile Justice and Delinquency Prevention, all of which sponsor and publish criminal justice research. In addition to making grants available for policy-relevant research, these organizations are vast storehouses of information that police executives can use to build crime prevention and reduction strategies.

NIJ's National Criminal Justice Reference Service (NCJRS) is the chief repository of criminal justice studies and data in the country. It dispenses state-of-the-art research information free of charge to state and local agencies and publishes a *User's Guide* that briefly describes NCJRS products and services. For a nominal fee, NCJRS also prepares customized, annotated bibliographies on a wide range of criminal justice topics.

Consultants

Anyone who has had broad experience using consultants knows that they cannot cure all that ails us. But they can be helpful when the department lacks internal resources for solving a problem.

Using consultants

What services do consultants offer a police executive? They can provide expert analysis, practical advice, and useful information. They can identify problems. They can identify causes of problems. They can recommend solutions. They can provide the executive with skills and knowledge that are otherwise unavailable— or at least unidentified—within the department.

Most police executives are generalists. Over the years, each may have developed one or two areas of special expertise (for example, budget preparation, tactical planning, computer programming), but none may have the level of skill called for to address all pressing agency problems efficiently and effectively. A good manager recognizes a situation that is beyond the current capabilities of the department and knows when to hire an outside expert. Consultants cost money, but it may cost more in the long run if department staff try to do a job themselves with insufficient skills or time. For example, if a department has a computer networking problem and no computer systems expert on staff, it may be advisable to hire outside help rather than train a staff member to the level required to solve a complex problem.

There are other good reasons to consider consultants. They can, for instance, be brought in when a solution to a problem may already be evident to some but is difficult to implement because of political pressures or bureaucratic inertia. To those who oppose the solution or are undecided about which solution they favor, the objective, third-party opinion can sometimes make a tough decision more palatable. And for chiefs besieged by requests for more or better services but strapped by limited resources, consultants can serve as efficiency experts and can even help raise money. Management consulting firms may not know much about policing, but they know about organizational structure and philosophy and may be able to help a department apply the principles of good management (see the chapter on organization and management).

Consultants can be helpful when the department lacks internal resources for solving a problem.

An example of a specific consulting assignment would be to set up a program by which a department could charge others—such as neighboring towns—for ancillary police services such as traffic and crowd control. The consultants could conduct feasibility studies for such fee-for-service programs, set up fee schedules, devise implementation plans and marketing strategies, and serve as marketing agents for the department. Innovative programs of that sort often require changes in both procedures and attitude. Consultants can be a good means of bringing about change: they can bring fresh ideas to a staid department, or present old ideas in terms that motivate those who are asked to transform ideas into action.

In the area of finance and budgets, the advice of a financial consultant or the assistance of an auditing firm may enable the department to reduce persistent budget problems somewhat. Consultants can assess a department's cash flow and financial stability and set forth recommendations for improvement. Other assignments appropriate for consultants include, but are not necessarily limited to,

1. Organization, management, and staffing studies
2. Job analysis, position classification, and pay studies
3. Personnel selection and promotional testing
4. Computer and communications systems development
5. Computer-aided dispatching (CAD) systems
6. Crime and police service analysis
7. Performance measurement studies
8. Building and facilities planning and design
9. Accounting and purchasing systems development
10. Training program development
11. Program evaluation.[29]

Finding consultants

Having established a need, how does one find a consultant? A good place to start is local colleges and universities, particularly their criminal justice and business departments. Faculty at these institutions can bring their own knowledge of local conditions to bear upon a problem.[30] Executives should not, however, overlook the obvious (other police executives) or the only slightly less obvious (officials of state and national law enforcement organizations). These people can provide advice and counsel from their own experiences (providing they have learned from them), or they can refer the chief to a consulting firm or other source that has already proved helpful.

Sending out a request for proposals, often referred to as an RFP, is a common means of finding out approximately how well different consultants can meet a department's needs and how much the department will have to pay to have those needs met. It is not *always* best to choose the lowest bidder. High-quality service is the ultimate goal, even if one has to pay a little more to get it. Needless to say, references should be checked thoroughly and an effort made to ascertain whether a consultant is capable of meeting the demands of the job.

Once the selection is made, the consultant and the executive should sign a contract to include provisions covering each of the following:

The task, its scope, and its boundaries

Procedures that will be used, including (if applicable) a detailed description of all the interview samples that will be used and the kinds of documents that will be required

Personnel assigned to the job, and their qualifications

A timetable for each phase of the project

The amount of payment, and the payment schedule

A list of those who will receive the consultant's report, how and when they will receive it, and what level of confidentiality must be maintained and by whom.

During the course of the project, the department should closely guide and monitor the consultant's progress. The final result of a collaboration like this is not attributable solely to the consultant; it is the product of a give-and-take relationship between two parties intent on reaching the same goal. The quality of the consultant's work depends considerably upon the advice and consent of those for whom the work is being done.

Cautions

A few general cautions on the use of consultants are in order:

Don't expect too much at first. Consultants who have never worked with an organization probably know little about its structure or its culture. They need time to get up to speed.

Don't hire consultants on a long-term basis to perform functions that staff should be performing. If staff are either not sufficiently motivated or competent, hiring a consultant only serves to avoid the real problem and can even make it worse if staff feel they are being circumvented.

Give consultants definite goals and time limits; some charge by the hour.

Be sure the consulting firm's principal staff, whose credentials attracted you to the firm, will be available. The difference within firms may be as great as the differences between them.

Don't hire a consultant without first checking references thoroughly.

These cautions are simply that—cautions. There are many well-qualified, reputable consultants, but it is good to exercise a little care because mistakes in hiring consultants can be costly. Furthermore, the more homework the department does before hiring a consultant, the better the relationship is likely to be once the ink on the contract is dry.

Nonpolice professional associations

Many professions have a direct interest in certain types of crime and social dysfunction and have considerable resources at their command. Among these are the medical, legal, and social work professions. Illegal drug trafficking, fear of AIDS, and homelessness have provided common ground for a host of professions struggling to come to terms with difficult global problems.

The American Bar Association (ABA), for instance, through its research affiliate, the American Bar Foundation, conducts research on a number of issues of concern to police as well as to other professionals and broader segments of society—juvenile justice, rape case processing by police and prosecutors, the use of deadly force by and against the police, drunk driving, and search warrants, to name a few. The ABA Criminal Justice Section's Special Committee on Criminal Justice in a Free Society conducted a major study of the entire criminal justice system. The committee, consisting of a cross section of the criminal justice community, including police chiefs, held hearings in several locations around the country; witnesses from all parts of the criminal justice system testified. Most major criminal justice studies available were reviewed, and extensive telephone surveys were conducted. Not surprisingly, the committee found that "most criminal justice system participants identify lack of resources as the major obstacle to effective law enforcement."[31]

The Criminal Justice Section, whose staff is headquartered in Washington, D.C., also has established a task force of law enforcement officials and other professionals whose ultimate purpose is to increase citizen reports of drug crimes. It is a grass-roots program that counts on the participation of the local police and others willing to help make their communities better and safer places to live. In previous decades, the ABA played a powerful role in setting goals for the professionalization of policing, employing recognized police leaders to draft the still widely cited "Urban Police Function Standards."

Associations do not have to be as large, or as directly related to the criminal justice system, as the ABA to be of assistance to the police. The Pan American Trauma Association, an ad hoc committee of university-level trauma surgeons from throughout the United States, is a good example. These professionals are in the business of providing emergency medical care to millions of victims of violence, some of whom are police officers. They have joined with law enforcement groups backing gun control legislation and testified before Congress on the effect that the free flow of sophisticated weapons in this country has on the provision of emergency care and on the physical and psychological well-being of the community.

Any number of professional associations have developed training and technical assistance programs on AIDS, homelessness, and other subjects relevant to policing. The potential for sharing resources or receiving information and training gratis is tremendous. Not all associations, of course, have the potential to contribute money, materials, or staff to a given project. But collectively they are a huge source of information, and many are willing to dispense that information at little or no cost.

Philanthropic organizations

Sometimes we overlook the obvious. In the search for extra resources, we may find ourselves trying to elicit help from those who either have no resources to give or have no compelling reason to give them. Police executives sometimes forget that there are philanthropic organizations whose sole purpose is to provide funding to eligible tax-exempt nonprofit organizations and agencies with worthy causes. Unfortunately, gaining access to those funds is more complicated than just asking.

Foundations usually require would-be recipients to submit proposals outlining why the funding is needed and what it will be used for. This requirement has spawned the great art of proposal writing, which is almost an industry in itself, supporting thousands of consultants and how-to publications.

Most chiefs cannot afford the time—and many may lack the necessary skills—to write proposals themselves, although they certainly should be aware of the requisites of proposal development and should sign off on the final draft. In large departments, chiefs should entertain the idea of establishing a division whose sole purpose is to obtain grants and *pro bono* services for the police department. One cost-effective means of doing this is to create one's own foundation.

Police executives sometimes forget that there are philanthropic organizations whose sole purpose is to provide funding.

The Baltimore County Police Foundation, for example, was established in 1979. This private, nonprofit organization is sponsored by business and dedicated to improving the quality of police service in Baltimore County and strengthening the relationship between the police and the community. The foundation works with the community and the police department to develop innovative programs, publicize services, and, more important, fund projects that could not otherwise be funded under the county budget. The foundation funds special projects such as remodeling the police department to facilitate sensitive handling of abused children. Funding also supports seminars for police managers; other educational activities, such as police training course materials and videotapes; and programs as diverse as the Crime Prevention Fund and the Annual Foundation Awards Program.

It is advisable to include corporate and philanthropic community leaders on the board or among the members of a foundation. These leaders may have an inside track to the funds dispersed, or to services that can be provided, by their

---

The New York City Police Foundation The New York City Police Foundation is an example of the external resources that exist in some communities. The foundation was the brainchild of civic-minded business leaders and public officials who recognized the importance of the police to the community.

Since its formation as an independent nonprofit corporation in 1972, the foundation has raised over $4.5 million from corporations, individuals, and philanthropic organizations to support more than 140 initiatives not otherwise possible under the city's budget.

More than a quarter of the foundation's grants support scholarship and personnel development programs. Other projects have been in the areas of health and well-being, police proficiency, crime prevention, and community understanding. Some initiatives begin as experiments wholly funded by private dollars and then become institutionalized within the police department when they prove successful. Notable examples have been an executive development program and a work-site hypertension and cardiovascular fitness program. The foundation also helped save the NYPD mounted unit when it was threatened during the city's fiscal crisis in 1976.

One of the projects undertaken at the foundation's own initiative was production of the film *Safe Passage*, a drug prevention documentary that was prepared for elementary school children and then given to the police department and the board of education. The foundation also administers project grants, one of which—for example—funded a film series on constitutional law.

Source: Gerald W. Lynch, Chairman, New York City Police Foundation, and President, John Jay College of Criminal Justice.

own organizations. They have valuable contacts with other corporations or philanthropic organizations that may make a crucial difference in funds solicitation. And they have expertise in management or fund-raising or both.

Chiefs from small departments may find it more feasible to establish a position responsible for fund-raising, hire a consultant, or avail themselves of publications or training that will help them gain proficiency in proposal writing. Whatever route is taken, however, the approach must be tightly focused. Preparing a thoughtful, viable proposal takes considerable time, and that time can be saved if, with a little foresight, one can determine that the project is unlikely to be funded.

There are some simple ways to narrow the choices. By consulting recent editions of the *Foundation Directory* or the *Taft Foundation Reporter*, chiefs can find out which organizations give grants, to whom they give them, why they give them, and how much they give. The *Foundation Directory* is published by the Foundation Center, headquartered in New York City. The center also publishes *Grants for Crime and Law Enforcement*, which lists approximately one thousand grants of $5,000 or more made by hundreds of foundations. The grants cover projects to support crime prevention, victim aid, counseling of delinquents and ex-offenders, legal rights, prison reform, prisoner services, and legal research. Most important, the list includes grants to police and other law enforcement agencies. For a reasonable fee, the Foundation Center also undertakes a computer search of grants to identify foundations as possible sources of support.

Chiefs from small departments may find it feasible to establish a position responsible for fund-raising, hire a consultant, or avail themselves of publications or training that will help them gain proficiency in proposal writing.

Many public libraries or university libraries maintain a collection of the IRS 990 forms filed annually by foundations. This form reviews a foundation's income and expenditures, including its grant expenditures for recent years.

The Office of Development, Testing and Dissemination within the National Institute of Justice has published a reference work entitled *Strategies for Supplementing the Police Budget.* Chiefs can obtain this free of charge from NIJ's National Criminal Justice Reference Service, located in Rockville, Maryland.

Conclusion

Although this chapter encourages the police manager to be as creative as possible in pursuing resources that the department may use to achieve its objectives, the chapter should not be construed to mean that the task of obtaining such resources is easy or problem-free. Asking others for assistance, whether in the form of funding, services, or materials, most often requires hard work and persistence and may entail an ability to handle occasional rejections. Rejections may reflect negative images of the police or biases about what the police role should be. But persistence in the face of occasional rejection is advisable, to gain both the obvious short-term benefit of added resources and the not-so-obvious long-term benefit of improved relationships with the community.

This chapter does not cover every possible avenue of assistance available to the police executive; it serves to illustrate the possibilities. As a general rule, however, the police executive should remember that the police must be part of a community, not a separate entity standing alone and aloof. That is true not only of day-to-day operations but also of broader, strategic activities that ultimately facilitate police work and enhance life in the community. By reaching out to others, many of whom would be quite willing to help if only they were asked, police leaders can build a more closely knit community and improve their own ability to ensure public safety. Such an approach represents enlightened self-interest at its best.

1 Criminal Justice Center, John Jay College of Criminal Justice, *Private Funding for Police Training* (New York: Criminal Justice Center, 1983), 10. The discussion of business funding that follows draws in part on this publication.

2 Michael G. Shanahan, "Operation Bootstrap," *The Police Chief* (February 1987): 18. For a description of the program, see also Bill Bruns, "Operation Bootstrap: Opening Corporate Classrooms to Police Managers," *NIJ Reports*, no. 217 (November/December 1989): 2–6.

3 Michael T. Farmer, "IACP's Private Sector Liaison Committee in Action," *The Police Chief* (April 1988): 18.

4 Peter Binzen, "Philadelphia Police Find Management Classes an Arresting Idea," *The Philadelphia Inquirer*, March 28, 1988.

5 Michael G. Shanahan, "Private Enterprise and the Public Police: The Professionalizing Effects of a New Partnership," in *Police Leadership in America: Crisis and Opportunity*, ed. William A. Geller (New York: Praeger, 1985), 449–58.

6 For further information on loaned executive programs, see Criminal Justice Center, *Private Funding for Police Training*, 13.

7 Ibid.

8 Shanahan, "Private Enterprise and the Public Police."

9 Washington Law Enforcement Executive Forum, *Strategic Planning Annex: 1987–1990* (Olympia: Washington Law Enforcement Executive Forum, Washington Association of Sheriffs and Police Chiefs, 1987).

10 Criminal Justice Center, *Private Funding for Police Training*, 12.

11 Dennis P. Rosenbaum, Arthur J. Lurigio, and Paul J. Lavrakas, "Enhancing Citizen Participation and Solving Serious Crime: A National Evaluation of Crime Stoppers Programs," *Crime and Delinquency* 35 (1989): 401–20.

12 Maurice T. Turner, "Lock Out Car Theft: A Public Private Partnership," *The Police Chief* (April 1988): 47–49.

13 John A. Calhoun, "Rebuilding the Social Contract through Crime Prevention Efforts," *The Police Chief* (September 1987): 87.

14 Lee McGehee, Reuben Greenberg, Joseph Koziol, Ted Meyer, and Jerry Tesmond, "Workshop for Recently Appointed Chiefs," *The Police Chief* (March 1987): 90–94.

15 This discussion of the uses of volunteers draws heavily on Richard Bocklet, "Volunteer Aid to Better Policing," *Law and Order* (January 1988).

16 Ibid., 181.

17 Lawrence Sherman, *Neighborhood Safety: Crime File Study Guide* (Washington, DC: National Institute of Justice, U.S. Department of Justice, 1988), 3; Tony Pate, Marlys McPherson, and Glen Silloway, *The Minneapolis Community Crime Prevention Experiment: Final Evaluation Report* (Washington, DC: Police Foundation, 1988), 15.

18 Edwin Meese III, "Neighborhood Watch: A Crime Prevention Success Story," *The Police Chief* (February 1988): 10.

19 Peter Finn, "Dealing with Street People: The Social Service System Can Help," *The Police Chief* (February 1988).

20 William C. Cunningham and Todd H. Taylor, *The Growing Role of Private Security: Research-in-Brief* (Washington, DC: National Institute of Justice, U.S. Department of Justice, 1984).

21 Philip P. Purpura, *Security and Loss Prevention* (Boston: Butterworth Publishers, 1984).

22 John E. Driscoll and William B. Kolender, "Private Security: Complementing—Not Competing With—Law Enforcement," *The Police Chief* (March 1986): 101–2.

23 Richard B. Abell, "Effective Systems for Regional Intelligence Sharing," *The Police Chief* (November 1988): 58–59.

24 D.C. Department of Consumer and Regulatory Affairs, *Executive Report to the Mayor on Operation Brightside* (Washington, DC, 1985).

25 Jay K. Golomb, "Evaluating the Impact of Project T: A Comprehensive Youth Awareness Program" (November 1987, unpublished), 15.

26 Interested parties can get more information on this program from the Personnel Mobility Program/CEEDG, Staffing Operations Division, U.S. Office of Personnel Management, Washington, DC 20415.

27 Thomas J. Deakin, *Police Professionalism: The Renaissance of American Law Enforcement* (Springfield, IL: Charles C. Thomas, 1988).

28 Antony M. Pate, Mary Ann Wycoff, Wesley G. Skogan, and Lawrence W. Sherman, *Reducing Fear of Crime in Houston and Newark: A Summary Report* (Washington, DC: Police Foundation, 1986).

29 This list draws on material provided to the author by private security specialist William C. Cunningham.

30 Robert Trojanowicz, "A Consultant's View: What Chiefs Should Know about Our Role," *The Police Chief* (November 1988): 19.

31 "Study Finds Police Efforts Hindered by Lack of Resources, Drug Epidemic," *Crime Control Digest* (December 19, 1988): 1.

17 Forensic sciences

Crime laboratories in the United States have become increasingly important in law enforcement since their beginnings in Los Angeles in 1923 and Chicago in 1929.[1] They have grown from small fingerprint and photography units into large-scale scientific operations addressing a wide range of evidentiary problems. Forensic scientists, with the aid of increasingly sophisticated instruments, now provide police and courts of law with information that helps to answer crucial "who, what, when, and why" questions surrounding known or suspected criminal acts.

The number of crime laboratories in the United States has also expanded, especially since the late 1960s—as a result of increasing rates of violent and drug-related crime, the growing movement toward professionalism in law enforcement, and the criminal courts' receptivity to scientific evidence. But even with the increase in their scientific resources and in their numbers, laboratories still receive only a small percentage of total police resources and are barely able to keep pace with the rising demand for services.

As crime and evidence caseloads have grown, the effective and timely delivery of forensic science services has become increasingly important. For police chiefs to allocate financial resources for these services and direct these resources to areas of maximum benefit, they need to understand the basic principles of forensic science and laboratory management. The well-informed chief can help ensure that laboratory services are provided and used effectively to support investigators and other criminal justice decision makers in their attempts to solve crimes and prosecute offenders.

This chapter provides the law enforcement professional with overviews of the system of crime laboratories and the principles of forensic science; discusses management issues in crime scene investigations and in laboratory operations; reviews ongoing efforts to upgrade and professionalize the field of forensic science; and describes some new technologies, such as DNA typing. Whereas the 1970s and 1980s were marked by a rapid increase in the number and size of forensic operations, the 1990s promise to be distinguished by greater attention to quality assurance and the competence of personnel, more sophisticated techniques to link offenders to their crimes, and greater accountability of laboratories to the judicial system.

Overview of the system of crime laboratories

As of 1990, there were well over three hundred crime laboratories in the United States, or about three times the number that existed in 1967.[2] Several factors contributed to this rapid expansion: U.S. Supreme Court decisions restricting police interrogation practices, presidential crime commissions' calls for greater professionalism in law enforcement, increases in the rates of violent crime and drug abuse, and the availability of federal monies to upgrade law enforcement. More than 80 percent of the laboratories are housed within law enforcement agencies, with the great majority of these (about 90 percent) operating at the state or local level.

Until the 1970s, most crime laboratories were located in cities and counties with high rates of crime and the need for analysis of evidence. In the 1970s and 1980s statewide systems of crime laboratories became popular, with more than a dozen states (including large ones like California, Texas, Illinois, Michigan, Florida, New Jersey, and New York) adopting such configurations to deliver scientific services to medium- and small-sized communities not already served by local laboratories. Such state systems, characterized by a centralized main laboratory and additional satellite facilities geographically dispersed throughout the state, were created after "systems" studies found that the use of physical evidence varied inversely with the distance between the crime location and the laboratory.[3] These statewide systems now act in tandem with municipal and county facilities in many states and provide the great bulk of service to state and local law enforcement agencies.

The principal goal of most crime laboratories is to provide services to their parent law enforcement agency. The most commonly supplied services are the examination of drugs, trace evidence (defined below under "Exchange principle"), body fluids, firearms and toolmarks, and alcohol levels in blood or breath.[4] Caseloads being what they are, few of these laboratories accept evidence from non-law-enforcement officials or from agencies outside their immediate jurisdictions.

Federal laboratories, such as those operated by the FBI, Drug Enforcement Administration (DEA), and Bureau of Alcohol, Tobacco and Firearms (ATF), principally serve the needs of their own agents but will assist state and local agencies when the need arises. Whereas the FBI laboratory accepts a broad range of types of evidence, others, like the DEA, confine their examinations to those types of evidence that are routinely gathered in their own enforcement activities. The FBI maintains a single, centralized laboratory in Washington, D.C., plus a research and training facility in Quantico, Virginia. The DEA, the ATF, and the U.S. Postal Service operate main laboratories in the Washington, D.C., area and regional laboratories in locations around the country.

For investigations involving a death, crime laboratories must interact with medical examiner and coroner offices, which are another type of important forensic system (one not addressed in detail in this chapter). These facilities exist in a variety of configurations, ranging from unified statewide medical examiner systems to local (elected) coroner operations.[5] The medical examiner or coroner focuses on the investigation of violent, suspicious, or unattended deaths and may supply critical information to the police in their investigation of such cases. The medical examiner or forensic pathologist works with other specialists, depending on the circumstances of death. These other specialists include forensic toxicologists, who can help determine the role of poisons, drugs, and other toxic chemicals that may be ingested into the human system and contribute to death; and forensic anthropologists and odontologists, whom pathologists commonly call in to assist in identifying human remains and in determining the source of injuries, such as bitemarks, that may have been inflicted on a victim of homicide or sexual assault.[6]

Coordination between the crime laboratory and the medical examiner's office is an important requirement in death investigations. Evidence removed from the body, including bullets, clothing, body fluids, and a wide range of trace materials, is customarily secured and forwarded to the appropriate crime laboratory for examination. The results of these examinations are then integrated with the medical examiner's findings to produce a determination of the cause and manner of death. Although consolidation is by no means a national trend, some cities and counties (for example, Dallas County, Texas) have consolidated their medical examiner and crime laboratory functions. Those arguing for such a configuration emphasize cost savings in the laboratory plus superior coordination of examinations in death investigations. Those arguing against it point to the resultant overemphasis on death cases at the expense of investigations of other assaults and property crimes.

Overall, about two-thirds of crime laboratories' caseloads involve identification of suspected drugs and alcohol. Evidence related to violent crimes and property crimes makes up 12 percent and 15 percent, respectively, of caseloads.[7] In urban crime laboratories, a greater proportion of evidence examined is derived from violent crime, whereas in regional and state laboratories, drug caseloads are proportionately greater.

On average, individual examiners in the nation's crime laboratories handle between four hundred and five hundred cases per year, with examiners in municipal laboratories having the highest caseloads and examiners in federal labs the lowest. One must exercise great care in employing such caseload data as indicators of workload or productivity, however, and must take into account the types, volume, and analysis requirements of the evidence being examined. For example, the examination of a single suspected marijuana cigarette may only take a few minutes, whereas the complete analysis of a multi-ton seizure of marijuana may take days. The microscopic identification of sperm on a vaginal swab may be accomplished in a matter of minutes, whereas typing the genetic markers in the same sample may take several weeks.

Most of the growth of crime laboratories in the past two decades, in terms of both equipment and staff, has been in response to the rising caseload of drug-related crimes. Here, the introduction of sophisticated instrumentation (for example, gas chromatograph–mass spectrometers and fourier transform infrared spectrophotometers) has enabled laboratories to identify and quantify suspected drugs with speed, precision, and accuracy. Outside of instrumentation, the two other most notable technological breakthroughs in forensic examination have occurred in connection with fingerprints and serology (the identification and typing of blood, semen, and other tissues or body fluids), and these developments are discussed in more detail near the end of the chapter.

Principles of forensic science

Forensic scientists have a strict professional obligation to remain objective and to pursue "scientific truth" wherever it may lead. They are obliged to note and record both the strengths and weaknesses of the evidence under review insofar as it associates the suspect with the crime scene or victim under investigation. The police investigator, in contrast, views his or her primary goal as making arrests that result in convictions. Still, the investigator, like the forensic scientist, must be alert to evidence that absolves the suspect and must be mindful that a person's guilt or innocence is ultimately determined by a court of law.[8]

Forensic scientists have a strict professional obligation to remain objective and to pursue "scientific truth" wherever it may lead.

Forensic scientists must also refrain from reading into their results more than is present and, even in the face of overwhelming evidence from other sources, such as eyewitnesses, must testify only to results that may be reviewed and verified by other scientists. Their examinations are conducted as much for the defendant as for the police and prosecution. Nevertheless, forensic examiners recognize that the police and the prosecutor are their *primary* clients and that they are dependent upon the police for retrieving from crime scenes the physical clues that are ultimately examined in the laboratory. The police, in turn, should understand the basic concepts of forensic science and the examination procedures used.

Basic concepts

The three basic concepts of forensic science with which the police manager should be familiar are the exchange principle, absolute and comparative analyses, and individuality.[9]

Exchange principle First formulated by Edmund Locard, creator of the first police crime laboratory (in Lyons, France, in 1910), the exchange principle states that when two objects come into contact, there usually will be a transfer, or exchange, of small amounts of material from one to the other. Thus, when suspects make contact with victims or other objects at crime scenes, they leave behind traces of themselves and take with them traces of the things they have touched. Materials such as hairs, fibers, and small particulate matter are often referred to as *trace evidence*.

Absolute and comparative analyses Examinations in the crime laboratory are generally of two basic types: absolute and comparative. Absolute examinations are undertaken to identify an unknown or otherwise suspicious material—as when laboratories are requested to identify a suspected drug or to see whether they can detect an accelerant in fire debris recovered from the scene of a suspected arson. In a comparative analysis, characteristics of the evidence (material of unknown origin) are compared with those of a standard (material of known origin). Examples of such comparative examinations are the analyses of latent fingerprints, bullets and cartridge cases, toolmark impressions, and various trace materials to see whether they can be linked to their source.

Individuality The expression "everybody and everything is unique" is a basic guiding principle in collecting, analyzing, and interpreting physical evidence. The comparative analysis described above is a quest for these indicators of individuality. The forensic scientist first investigates whether items possess similar "class" characteristics, that is, whether they possess features shared by all objects or materials in a single class or category. (For firearms evidence, bullets of the same caliber, bearing rifling marks of the same number, width, and direction of twist, share class characteristics in that they are consistent with being fired from the same type of weapon.) The forensic scientist then attempts to determine an item's "individuality"—the features that make one thing different from all others similar to it, including those with similar class characteristics. The spatial relations among minutiae in fingerprints, indented or striated markings on toolmarks and firearms, physical matches of material broken or cut apart, and the special characteristics of an individual's handwriting that distinguish it from all others are examples of individualizing characteristics. As is discussed later, blood and other biological materials now also have the potential for establishing individuality.

When evidence in question has the same individual characteristics as does a material of known origin, the examiner may conclude that a conclusive association has been established. In some cases, the examiner may not find a sufficient number of individualizing characteristics to support a firm conclusion of identity and may report only that no significant differences were found or that a possible common origin is indicated. This conclusion does not exclude the possibility that the evidence and the material of known origin originated from different sources.

Examination procedures

Examiners in crime laboratories use a number of procedures in examining evidence. An understanding of these procedures can help police managers determine how the lab can best assist the department in criminal investigations.

Identifications   As explained above, the purpose of absolute analyses is to identify a material and place it in a category of like items with similar class characteristics. The identification of certain materials may provide evidence of a crime, as when a powder is identified as cocaine or when a sample of breath or body fluid is found to contain alcohol. In drug possession and driving-under-the-influence cases, the laboratory may also be called upon to establish the purity of the questioned substance or its concentration in the medium (blood, urine, and so forth) in which it is found. Identifying a material is also the first step in determining its origin.

An understanding of examination procedures can help police managers determine how the lab can best assist the department in criminal investigations.

Associations and disassociations   As discussed above, frequently an examiner cannot determine conclusively whether two or more items of evidence originated from the same source. Even in the absence of the necessary characteristics for a finding of true common origin, however, the examiner may offer valuable assistance to the investigator by describing one or more of the class characteristics of the evidence in question. This is the usual approach to the examination of such evidence as hairs, fibers, paints, and glass. Usually, the more class characteristics that two samples are found to have in common, the greater the likelihood that the materials originated from the same source. With most forms of physical evidence, these are qualitative judgments informed by the training and experience of the examiner and cannot be expressed in terms of statistical probability.

The reverse of an association—a *dis*association—may result when the examiner observes that the materials in question have dissimilar class or individual characteristics, indicating that two or more items could *not* have shared a common origin. For example, a spent .45-caliber bullet could not have been fired from a .38-caliber gun; or a bloodstain with A antigens could not have originated from an individual with only B antigens in his or her blood. The finding of such dissimilar characteristics may prove extremely important in removing suspicion from an innocent party and refocusing an investigation in a more productive direction.

Reconstructions   An examination of physical evidence may also help law enforcement officials reconstruct *how* a particular crime occurred, as when gunpowder residues or blood spatter patterns indicate the position and movements of a suspected shooter and his or her victim. Learning how the crime occurred may prove to be crucial to the investigator in determining the involvement of one or more individuals in the crime, deciding whether the event was accidental or intentional, and evaluating the truthfulness of statements given to police by victims, witnesses, or suspects.

Standards and controls   Investigators of evidence at the crime scene must also collect reference standards and controls so that evidence can be properly interpreted. A *standard*, as explained above, is a representative sample of material of known origin, to which the evidence is to be compared. A *control* is a sample of material that is from the same source as the material containing the evidence but that does not contain any evidentiary transfer (that is, the evidence has not been mixed with or deposited on the control sample).

Standards (materials of known origin) are needed for comparative analysis of the evidence (materials of unknown origin). Such standards may be obtained from persons, objects, or locations in an investigation or may be collected from manufacturers of products (paint, fibers, glass). In an assault for which a bloodstained knife has been secured as evidence, a standard of known blood will be drawn from the person or persons suspected of having been cut by the knife, as well as from the alleged assailant. When glass fragments are gathered as evidence from the soles of a burglary suspect's shoes, glass standards will be retrieved from the broken window at the burglar's point of entry.

Controls (uncontaminated material from the same source as the material containing the evidence) are particularly important in cases in which the transfer of biological fluids is suspected. For example, in a case in which an assault victim is thought to have shed blood on a suspect's clothing, it is necessary not only to gather the evidence and blood standards from the suspect and victim but also to collect a *control* sample—an unstained portion of the same fabric on which the bloodstain is found. The reason a control sample is needed is that clothing may routinely contain such substances as perspiration or urine that can interfere with the proper interpretation of results from the contaminated areas. The examiner needs to verify that he or she is reading the results from the questioned stain and not from the underlying garment on which the stain was deposited.

Occasionally, when a suspect claims that the origin of questioned evidence in his or her possession is from a legitimate source, alternative known or "alibi" samples are necessary.[10] For example, an individual may claim that the questioned fibers on his or her garment originated from other clothing in his or her closet, not from the victim. If the laboratory can show that the evidence is decidedly different from the so-called alibi source or location, the value of an association between the questioned evidence and known samples other than the alibi sample is much greater.

Crime scene investigation and evidence-handling operations

The effectiveness of a forensic operation rests on the ability of the police department's evidence recovery system to recognize, preserve, document, and retrieve relevant physical evidence. Obviously, the laboratory cannot work on samples that have not been recognized as significant at the scene and that have consequently been irretrievably lost. Likewise, sophisticated laboratory equipment and highly trained scientists cannot resurrect a sample that has been irreversibly damaged by improper collection and storage. Police department policies and procedures should stress the importance of investigation of the scene as an integral element of criminal investigation and should facilitate a close working relationship between the crime scene search, the detective, and the laboratory functions of the department.

Obviously, the laboratory cannot work on samples that have not been recognized as significant at the scene and that have consequently been irretrievably lost.

The chief executive of the department must recognize the fundamental importance of evidence recovery and provide resources to support this function. A 1984 study of four jurisdictions found that the norm for crime scene staffing was one crime scene technician for about every two thousand index crimes committed annually.[11] On average, there was one crime scene technician for about every ten investigators in the department, and two crime scene technicians for about every scientist in the crime laboratory examining evidence collected by these technicians.

Management of the crime scene search

Managing the crime scene search function is a challenging task. Most crimes generate some type of physical evidence,[12] but it is neither practical nor desirable for the police to attempt to collect and store all of it. (Nor is it necessary or possible for the crime laboratory to examine all of the evidence that the police collect.) The task of the police department is to maximize its resources by gathering (and analyzing) physical evidence that will be most useful in solving crimes and in assisting with successful prosecution of offenses having the highest priority.

Establishing an appropriate balance between the demand for crime scene processing and the available resources is particularly challenging, as the Commission on Accreditation for Law Enforcement Agencies (CALEA) recognizes in its standards.[13] The standards call for departments to prepare written guidelines governing the circumstances under which crime scene search officers are to be summoned and the comprehensiveness of search required.

In most departments, the deployment of crime scene search resources is greatly influenced by the perceived importance of the offense. The most intense crime scene investigations are generally conducted in cases of homicide, rape, and other violent crimes against persons. When budgetary constraints force crime scene investigations to be limited, property crimes such as auto theft or burglary may receive a more restricted examination, often limited to processing for latent prints.

The task of the police department is to maximize its resources by gathering (and analyzing) physical evidence that will be most useful in solving crimes and in assisting with successful prosecution of offenses having the highest priority.

Some departments develop a schedule of priorities for deployment of criminal investigators[14] and laboratory resources. In this situation, the department administration needs to guard against a possible tendency to relegate the crime scene search process in "low-priority" crimes to the status of a public relations tool. This tendency can subtly undermine both the crime scene search and the investigative functions, eventually eroding the quality of the overall operation.

Appropriate measures of performance are needed to evaluate both the effectiveness of the crime scene unit and the overall effectiveness of the department in using physical evidence in the investigative process. Supervisors will want to ascertain the responsiveness of technicians to calls for assistance, as well as the thoroughness with which they search for clues. Supervisors should verify that the proper evidence and standards are being recovered, preserved, and documented, and that this evidence is routed expeditiously to the appropriate laboratory for analysis. (It is here that the laboratory supervisor should take the leading role in critiquing the technicians' evidence collection skills.) The ultimate criterion of performance is whether evidence is discovered that can help solve cases and link suspects to crimes. To judge both the effect of collected evidence on a case and the performance of the technician in court as he or she recounts his or her crime scene procedures, the supervisor needs to consult both investigators and prosecutors.

Organizational questions

Because the crime scene search function is intimately related to several other important functional areas of the police department, the question of where it should be located within the department is a complex one. On the one hand, as an element of the preliminary investigation of a crime, crime scene search capability must be available around the clock and be dispatched and coordinated with functions normally carried out by patrol units (neighborhood canvass, scene security, and so forth). But on the other hand, as an element of the subsequent criminal investigation, the scene search must be coordinated with other investigative and follow-up activities (witness statements, interrogation of suspects, autopsy, and so forth) normally within the purview of the detective function. (In some departments, as the chapter on criminal investigations discusses, patrol officers conduct the complete investigation of at least certain types of crimes.) In addition, as an element of the scientific investigation of the crime, the scene search function must be coordinated with the laboratory evaluation of the evidence.

In large departments, it is generally recommended that the department have a core staff of specially trained crime scene investigators.[15] Regardless of the organizational placement of this unit, its functions should be well coordinated with the related department units. Although placement in patrol may be preferred for logistical purposes, the close functional relationship of the crime scene unit with the criminal investigation and the crime laboratory may make either of those two more suitable than patrol for purposes of providing appropriate technical supervision of the crime scene function. It is also appropriate to involve scientific staff from the laboratory in the scene investigation when their special expertise may be of value. To optimize the evidence collection function, the department should avoid assigning ancillary functions (for example, courier duties, traffic control, general photography) to the crime scene unit.

The initial officer on the scene must be sufficiently knowledgeable to determine whether a crime scene specialist should be called and to protect potentially valuable evidence until the specialist arrives.

Whether or not a specialized crime scene unit is available, the department must ensure that all police personnel have a basic understanding and appreciation of physical evidence. The initial officer on the scene must be sufficiently knowledgeable to determine whether a crime scene specialist should be called and to protect potentially valuable evidence until the specialist arrives. An appreciation of the potential value of the physical evidence at the scene will improve the quality of the preliminary investigation that the reporting officer conducts. In certain situations when crime scene resources are limited, the reporting officer may be required to perform basic evidence preservation and collection duties on his or her own.

Like the issue of organizational placement, the question of whether crime scene personnel should be civilian or sworn has no simple answer. Sworn personnel may be more effective by virtue of having had more extensive training and experience in law enforcement, criminal investigation, and courtroom testimony. The processes by which sworn staff are recruited and selected may also mean they have a higher level of baseline competence. An investment in developing sworn personnel's expertise in crime scene investigations also pays dividends when the personnel are promoted or transferred into other units.

But highly effectively crime scene units can also be staffed with properly trained and supervised civilian personnel. Civilian staff recruited and trained specifically for evidence collection tasks may be both more suited for and more dedicated to this work than sworn officers for whom crime scene work may be just another assignment. In addition, unlike sworn officers (who transfer out to other assignments), civilian staff may be more likely to remain within the unit, minimizing the need for constant retraining. Civilian staff may also prove more effective in that they are less likely than sworn officers to be assigned additional duties (such as routine patrol functions and report taking) that will distract them from the primary function of evidence collection.

However, if crime scene search units are staffed by civilians merely as an economy measure, the lower salaries may interfere with the goal of attracting and retaining qualified and dedicated personnel. The limited opportunities for career advancement may also work to the detriment of a civilian staff. Further, care must be taken that the civilian staff not be perceived as having lower status or importance than sworn staff performing the same function. When this perception exists, it affects the morale and performance of the civilian staff and ultimately can mean that, in the eyes of the civilians' sworn co-workers, the entire function of evidence collection is downgraded.

Selection, training, and supervision

Effective crime scene investigation requires a unique combination of skills. Crime scene personnel must couple a keen investigative inquisitiveness with a capacity for methodical attention to detail. The selection process for crime scene personnel should take into account both preparation and aptitude. It is helpful for the candidate to have some academic background or experience in criminal investigation and crime scene work, or a combination of study and experience.

Crime scene personnel must couple a keen investigative inquisitiveness with a capacity for methodical attention to detail.

The department should provide an in-service training program that covers law, rules of evidence, criminal investigation, report writing, and court testimony, as well as the fundamentals of recognizing, preserving, collecting, and documenting evidence. Skills in photography, diagramming, and fingerprint processing are of paramount importance. Formal in-service training should be supplemented by practical field training under the supervision of an experienced crime scene specialist.

To develop the full value of physical evidence as an independent source of information, the crime scene investigator needs to approach the scene in an objective, scientific fashion. He or she must also understand the potential value and limitations of various types of evidence and be aware of the appropriate standards and controls that may be required for laboratory analysis. For this reason, scientific personnel should be involved in designing and delivering the training provided to crime scene specialists.

A mechanism should be in place allowing supervisors to receive feedback from patrol officers, detectives, and laboratory specialists regarding the quality of the crime scene investigation.

The crime scene technician should not be relegated to collecting items at the direction of the investigator. Rather, the department should adopt a policy that places the crime scene technician in charge of the crime scene. But the technician should conduct the search for evidence in cooperation with the detective or other investigator in charge of the case and clearly should address issues that the officer considers significant.

It is advisable for the department, in consultation with scientific staff, to produce written guidelines for the crime scene unit covering procedures for processing crime scenes, packaging evidence, and preparing crime scene reports. In addition, supervisors should be required to review reports and to make periodic unannounced visits to the scenes to observe the caliber of the field work. A mechanism should be in place allowing supervisors to receive feedback from the patrol officers, detectives, and laboratory scientists regarding the quality of the crime scene investigation. The laboratory should also give feedback to the crime scene unit as to the results of laboratory examinations that were conducted on evidence collected by the crime scene unit.

Moreover, the department should develop performance measures for crime scene personnel that balance the need for productivity with the need for quality work. For example, not every crime scene provides latent prints that are of good enough quality for purposes of comparison—but the Oakland, California, police department found that approximately 70 percent of the burglary scenes processed over a four-year period resulted in the collection of latent prints and that approximately 60 percent of these prints were of usable quality. The department then used benchmarks such as these to evaluate the performance of individual crime scene technicians on an annual basis.

Management of evidence submitted to the laboratory

Managing the evidence submitted to the laboratory involves making four kinds of decisions: decisions about filtering the evidence, storing it, destroying it, and dealing with jurisdictional overlap.

Like the decision to gather evidence in the first place, the decision whether or not to conduct a laboratory examination of collected evidence can fundamentally affect the solution or successful prosecution of a case. At this point as at each point in the process, decisions are made—by crime scene officers, investigators, prosecutors, or laboratory personnel—to filter out evidence and restrict the number of examinations that are ultimately made.

Filtering is necessary for practical reasons. Much potential evidence collected early in an investigation will later be found to be irrelevant, as additional information is developed in the case. Or the potential value of laboratory examinations may be made moot by overwhelming information from a witness. In addition, laboratory resources will never be equal to the task of conducting all the analyses that might be possible in police investigations.

However, it is important to recognize that this filtration process has the potential for introducing significant bias into the otherwise objective process of scientific investigation. For example, potential evidence that could exclude a suspect may be overlooked at the scene if the crime scene examiner has prematurely focused on a particular theory of reconstruction. Or physical evidence capable of answering a critical investigative question may never be analyzed if an investigator is unaware of its potential value. Or, if the laboratory examiner is unaware of the nature of the investigatory problem, valuable laboratory time may be wasted on an insignificant analysis.

The agency's procedures for deciding what evidence will be examined and what tests will be conducted should take into account the need for close coordination between investigative and crime laboratory personnel. Although laboratory analysts must remain objective, they should also receive all relevant investigative information dealing with the physical evidence in a case and should participate in the decision as to which items should be examined. The necessary information can be exchanged in an initial conference between the laboratory analyst and the investigator, covering the crime report and the report of the crime scene investigation. Periodic contact should occur between the laboratory staff and the investigators to reevaluate case priorities as the investigation progresses.

Likewise, the department should develop standard procedures for the secure storage of evidence both before and after analysis—procedures that protect the evidence from loss, contamination, and deterioration.[16] Guidelines that meet relevant legal standards should be developed for the disposal of evidence after a specified period of time. If additional analysis may be contemplated at a later time, it is appropriate that the legal community (prosecutors, defense attorneys, judges, and so forth—any party with an interest in the case) be made aware of the department's procedure for storing and disposing of evidence.

Finally, in the investigation of deaths there is jurisdictional overlap between the police and the medical examiner or coroner. Physical evidence found on or near the body may, at least initially, be the responsibility of the medical examiner. Departments should have well-established guidelines for the division of labor and responsibility at death investigation scenes and autopsies, as well as for transfer of evidence between the medical examiner and the crime laboratory. Good lines of communication should be encouraged among the investigator, pathologist, and crime lab.

Special problems in handling evidence

The proper collection and preservation of biological evidence has been the focus of considerable research. Two issues are of particular concern to the police administrator: the potential hazard of infection from biological evidence and the need for special procedures to preserve these samples for testing.

It has been established that biological materials, particularly liquid blood and semen, have the potential for transmitting a variety of serious diseases, including hepatitis B and AIDS. The police department has a responsibility, on the one hand, to establish and enforce procedures that protect the health of those of its employees who deal with these potentially deadly agents and, on the other hand, to properly discharge its responsibilities to protect the public and investigate crime.

Simple and well-established industrial hygiene procedures exist for the safe handling of potentially infectious biological agents.[17] The department should publish written guidelines explaining the procedures and should provide all potentially affected personnel with protective materials (gloves, eye shields, disinfectants) and training in how to use them properly. Specifically, the primary safeguards against infectious hazards are proper hygiene and barrier protection. Personnel should always

1.   Wear gloves when handling items contaminated with body fluids
2.   Wash hands thoroughly after handling such contaminated evidence
3.   Avoid eating, smoking, or drinking in areas where evidence contaminated with biological fluids is being processed or stored
4.   Disinfect implements (e.g., scalpels, razor blades) and surfaces (desks, counters in the property rooms) that were used in the collecting and processing of biologically stained evidence
5.   Package sharp implements (e.g., hypodermic needles) in rigid containers to prevent them from causing injuries when subsequently handled.

At the same time that concern about the health hazard of biological evidence has grown, the potential value of this evidence for identifying and prosecuting criminal offenders has increased exponentially. Enzyme and protein genetic typing has become routine in the examination of blood and semen evidence. Tests can narrow the source of a bloodstain to a very small portion of the population (typically, to between one person in one hundred and one person in ten thousand) and, with the advent of DNA typing (discussed below), have the potential for truly individualizing a biological sample. But for biological evidence (such as blood and semen stains) to be usable for genetic typing, it must be properly preserved.

Proper preservation requires thorough drying, followed by frozen storage.[18] When dried stain samples are kept at room temperature, they become untypable within a few weeks or months. But when stored under freezer conditions, they can generally be typed after several years.[19] Similarly, vaginal swabs that will be untypable after being stored undried in a closed tube for only a few hours will produce good genetic typing results even months or years later if they are first thoroughly dried and then stored frozen. For this reason, at least one state (California) has enacted a protocol mandating the active drying of swabs collected from sexual assault victims.[20]

When the police department designs storage facilities for evidence and develops procedures for collecting and preserving biological evidence, it should consider the need for drying and freezing this type of evidence. The need for frozen storage is particularly acute when laboratory resources are not available to analyze all the collected evidence within a short time after collection. The ability to preserve samples for later analysis allows limited resources to be focused first on cases requiring the most urgent attention. It also allows evidence to be stored until such time as more discriminating tests—for example, DNA typing—become routinely available.

The crime laboratory: Selection and training of staff

The basic educational and training requirements for crime laboratory staff depend on the specific positions and tasks to which the individuals will be assigned. Drug chemists, serologists, and trace evidence examiners, for example, all need different types of education and training, although all are expected to have a common academic background in the chemical and biological sciences. In fact, police agencies almost universally require people working in these three disciplines to have a minimum of a bachelor's degree either in a natural or physical science or in criminalistics or forensic science; in addition, the new examiner's training must also include exposure to practical casework situations either through internships during academic training or through basic, on-the-job training.

Some specialties, notably the examination of documents, firearms, or latent fingerprints, are learned primarily on the job through an apprenticeship; few specific college-level courses in those specialties are available. Even so, groups that offer voluntary professional certification in these areas are tending more and more to require academic degrees. The American Society of Crime Laboratory Directors–Laboratory Accreditation Board (ASCLD-LAB) *requires* bachelor's degrees in science for drug analysts, serologists, toxicologists, and trace evidence examiners, and *recommends* that document, firearms, and latent print examiners also possess academic degrees with science courses.[21]

The state of the art in forensic science advances rapidly, and crime laboratory examiners must be afforded the opportunity to maintain and enhance their knowledge and skills through continuing education programs.

The state of the art in forensic science advances rapidly, and crime laboratory examiners must be afforded the opportunity to maintain and enhance their knowledge and skills through continuing education programs. Such advanced training is essential if examiners are to derive maximum information from the collected evidence. In addition, professional groups like the American Society of Crime Laboratory Directors *require* that laboratory executives provide their scientific staffs with such opportunities.

The issue of whether laboratory analysts should be sworn or civilian is parallel in many respects to the situation of crime scene specialists. The major differences in the two assignments are that the laboratory assignment generally involves much less field work and much more need for scientific training than the crime scene assignment. The trend has been toward a decrease in the proportion of sworn staff among crime lab analysts and managers. In a 1974 survey thought to be representative of the criminalistics profession, about 45 percent of respondents were sworn personnel; a 1983 survey of crime laboratories found that only about 30 percent of staff were sworn.[22]

An argument against using sworn staff in the laboratory is that, because of potential limitations on promotional opportunities, they may not view the laboratory as a desirable assignment. Conversely, the laboratory may become a dead-end haven for marginal sworn employees. In addition, finding staff who possess the physical, psychological, and intellectual aptitudes for both the police force and the laboratory environment is very difficult. Moreover, some members of the legal system may view sworn laboratory staff as less objective than civilian scientists.

On the other side, an argument against civilian staff is that they might not be as interested in or as dedicated to the investigative aspects of their work as sworn officers. That is, they may be far more interested in detecting or measuring a physical or chemical phenomenon than in applying the scientific study to actual casework. And if civilians are used mainly as an economy measure, salaries may not be competitive with those in industry and may result in problems of recruitment and retention. If civilian staff are not given appropriate status vis-à-vis their sworn colleagues, morale may suffer, and support for the entire laboratory function may weaken.

Professionalism in the forensic sciences

Both the popular and the scientific press have published numerous accounts describing new technologies developed by the forensic sciences to unlock the secrets of physical clues.[23] Those reports have been countered by others questioning the integrity and professionalism of expert witnesses.[24] The competency and impartiality of these experts have been challenged, as has their forthrightness in presenting their qualifications to the judicial system. A number of initiatives are under way in the field of forensic science addressing these concerns, and it is important that police managers be familiar with them.

For an occupational group to qualify as professionals, two requirements must be met: there must be a body of specialized knowledge, and the members of the group must acquire competency in applying that knowledge through an extensive period of academic study.[25] Members of a profession also engage in continual self-evaluation and self-regulation to monitor and maintain the competence of practitioners. In addition, professionals must be of high moral character, must practice collegiality, and must offer "value-free" service to society.[26] Collegiality implies harmonious, collaborative, cooperative relationships with fellow workers. Value-free service is service that a professional provides nonjudgmentally and without introducing his or her own biases into the review of the evidence or the opinions developed. Convincing arguments may be made that practitioners of criminalistics are engaged in a specialized field of inquiry, namely, the laboratory analysis and interpretation of physical evidence and the communication of pertinent results to legal fact finders. Furthermore, criminalists and other forensic scientists have addressed the matter of practitioner competency with great vigor.

Before the late 1960s, there were few examples of self-evaluation and self-regulation in criminalistics that met the test of adequately defining either the professional group as a whole or those qualified to practice. Several initiatives since then have addressed the qualifications and competence of individual practitioners as well as the procedures and facilities used by these individuals to carry out their work. These initiatives include codes of ethics, certification, accreditation, proficiency testing, and management guidelines.[27]

Codes of ethics

Most forensic scientists belong to one or more professional associations that articulate the codes of conduct their members are expected to adhere to. Two of the oldest forensic associations, the American Academy of Forensic Sciences (established in 1948) and the California Association of Criminalists (established in 1950), have devoted considerable effort to developing such codes. Although differences exist among the several codes—usually in terms of level of detail and rigor of enforcement procedures—almost all of them speak to similar obligations: to be technically competent and to follow the "scientific method"; to approach examinations and interpretations of results with complete objectivity; to prepare reports and to deliver expert testimony in a nonpartisan manner; and to pursue professional development.

Although membership in professional associations is voluntary, some crime laboratories have incorporated professional codes into their own guidelines and hold their employees accountable. Some laboratory managers have even elected to incorporate national or regional codes of conduct into their own personnel and disciplinary procedures because the parent department's rules usually fail to address the unique requirements of forensic examiners.[28]

Certification

A national certification committee composed of representatives from various forensic science professional groups developed a certification proposal that was presented to the profession at large in 1980 for ratification.[29] The proposal called for a voluntary peer-review process for recognizing those who had attained the minimum qualifications necessary to practice one or more disciplines of criminalistics (that is, drug identification, serology, firearms and toolmark examination, and trace evidence examination). The proposal was not supported by a majority of the members of the profession, and the concept was shelved for several years. In 1986 a regional forensic association, the California Association of Criminalists, resolved to establish minimum qualifications for individuals practicing criminalistics; the association administered its first written examination in May 1989.[30]

In 1988, the national certification committee was reestablished, and in 1989 it filed for incorporation as the American Board of Criminalistics. Its specific proposal for national certification would require a baccalaureate degree in a natural science or appropriately related field, two years' experience actively working in the field of criminalistics, and passing scores on at least two written examinations: a general examination in criminalistics and at least one specialty examination in serology, drug identification and toxicology, trace evidence examination, or firearms and toolmark examination. Recertification would require meeting specified continuing-education requirements.

Once the specific tests have been developed, criminalistics will join several other forensic specialty groups that have had established certification procedures for a number of years: forensic pathology, toxicology, anthropology, odontology, questioned-document examination, and latent-fingerprint examination.

Accreditation

ASCLD-LAB began accrediting laboratories in 1981. The purpose was to improve the quality of laboratory services offered to the criminal justice system by evaluating and identifying laboratories that meet or exceed criteria set by peers. This is a voluntary program in which inspection teams review crime laboratories' operations, management, physical plant, safety, and security. This program focuses on the *system* that should be in place to ensure that evidence is examined properly and reported completely.

Laboratories initially complete a self-evaluation form, using a checklist of standards and criteria developed by ASCLD. These criteria, deemed "essential," "important," or "desirable," reflect the extent to which a particular condition directly affects the "work product" of the laboratory and the "integrity of the evidence." Laboratories must satisfy all the essential criteria; a minimum of 70 percent of the important criteria; and 50 percent of the desirable criteria. Examples of *essential* criteria are (1) guaranteeing the security of the plant and integrity of the evidence; (2) using only laboratory procedures that are generally accepted in the field and are in writing; (3) employing analysts who have "education and experience commensurate with the analysis and testimony they provide"; and (4) having examiners complete ongoing proficiency tests.

The accreditation manual also requires that laboratories participate in one or more of the following programs to ensure the integrity of their results: periodic internal review of case notes and reports; both open and blind (that is, without the analyst's knowledge that it is a test) testing of the quality of examiners' results; and external proficiency testing (as is discussed below) to guard against the inbreeding of tests and procedures.

After the self-evaluation form is completed, ASCLD-LAB sends an inspection team to the applicant laboratory for an on-site review. A major portion of the inspection involves reviewing randomly selected case files, records of analyses, and notes and data generated by the examiners. The inspection team assesses the laboratory's conformance with the accreditation criteria described above. The team holds a summation conference with the laboratory director and appropriate staff and prepares a final report. The report is submitted to the Laboratory Accreditation Board, which makes the final decision to accredit.

As of 1990, approximately seventy-seven of the more than three hundred laboratories in the United States had been accredited under this program. Accreditation is good for a period of five years, after which the laboratory must reapply and undergo another evaluation and on-site inspection.

Proficiency testing

In 1974, a voluntary proficiency testing program was established under grants to the Forensic Sciences Foundation (FSF) from the Law Enforcement Assistance Administration.[31] Through this program, crime laboratories have the opportunity to see how well they can examine and interpret various types of physical evidence. Although proficiency testing is recognized as but one element of a comprehensive quality assurance program (see below), it has served to focus attention on the testing and the accuracy of examinations performed in the laboratory.

Although proficiency testing is recognized as but one element of a comprehensive quality assurance program, it has served to focus attention on the testing and the accuracy of examinations performed in the laboratory.

Under the initial proficiency testing grants, laboratories were issued simulated evidence samples—for example, bloodstains, hairs, paint or glass chips, or fibers—along with written scenarios that asked them either to identify substances or to determine whether two or more samples might have originated from the same source. The program revealed a wide range of proficiency levels in laboratories, with several types of evidence posing serious difficulties for the participants. Results also indicated a clear lack of uniformity among laboratories in examination and reporting procedures, as well as the need to continue proficiency testing.

When the government support ended, ASCLD, FSF, and a private organization (Collaborative Testing Services) continued working together to provide the testing on a fee-for-service basis. By 1990 about two hundred laboratories in North America were participating in the program. Although the majority of laboratories have been found to produce correct results, the program has revealed errors stemming from inadequate standard reference materials, inexperienced examiners, inappropriate tests, or misinterpretation of otherwise good data.

The proficiency testing program has not only provided participating crime laboratories with an objective external tool for monitoring their own performance, but it has also stimulated many other federal, state, and local laboratories to institute their own internal proficiency testing procedures. Forensic science has reached a stage at which it recognizes that laboratory proficiency cannot be *assumed* but must be positively *demonstrated* through programs such as this one.[32] Police managers should encourage their laboratories to participate in such testing programs and should provide the laboratories with the necessary financial support. The department administration should also regularly consult with scientific staff concerning their performance. When problems or deficiencies are detected, the police manager should be prepared to provide the necessary resources (personnel, equipment, training, and so forth) to correct the underlying problem.

Management guidelines

In September 1987, the ASCLD adopted a set of guidelines addressing the special obligations of laboratory managers "to safeguard the integrity and objectives of the profession and to ensure the faith of the public in the quality of its practice."[33] The guidelines are divided into five major sections, covering the responsibilities of the manager to the parent agency, to the employees, to the public, and to the profession, as well as the manager's obligation to implement a strong quality assurance program.

These guidelines are significant in that, if adopted by a department, they commit laboratory management to (1) using well-documented procedures for ensuring the validity and objectivity of work performed; (2) providing a proper scientific working environment for employees, including encouraging them to participate in the activities of professional societies; and (3) notifying bench-workers of the high standards expected of them and of the organization's willingness to provide them with the resources necessary to maintain such standards.

Managing the crime laboratory

An understanding of the management of the crime laboratory itself is also relevant to the police manager. Among the questions of interest are the position of the laboratory in the organization, the selection and background of the lab director, and issues of internal management and supervision.

Position of the laboratory in the organization

As a general rule, in a department with its own laboratory, the laboratory should be as high in the organization as possible, with direct access to the chief. Two of the primary reasons for such placement in the table of organization are the special budgetary requirements of a laboratory and the need for laboratories to maintain scientific independence. This placement is desirable so that the laboratory director can provide necessary justifications for suitable laboratory space, acquisition and maintenance of (expensive) scientific instrumentation, and the hiring (and continuing education) of scientifically qualified personnel. Moreover, although close coordination and good working relationships between the investigative units and the laboratory are essential, the laboratory's scientific objectivity and independence from undue influence by other units within or outside the department are equally essential—and ensuring that independence is management's responsibility. Management has a primary duty to see that staff are not pressured by anyone at any level, within the department, the judicial system, or the community, to give prejudiced testimony.[34] Failure to establish and maintain an appropriate separation of authority between laboratory and detective units may have dire consequences, as history has demonstrated.[35]

If the laboratory is housed in the same division as the investigators, the laboratory should be an independent unit that does not report to the commander of the detectives. But placing the laboratory in a part of the organization (patrol, for example, or support services) that may not recognize the significance of forensic science in the criminal investigation process may condemn the laboratory to a reduced level of budgetary support and may keep it from developing effective and necessary communications and rapport with investigative units.

Although close coordination and good working relationships between the investigative units and the laboratory are essential, the laboratory's scientific objectivity and independence are equally essential.

Housing the laboratory outside the department altogether has been recommended by some as a means of ensuring scientific objectivity.[36] To be sure, separation of the laboratory from the police function may reduce the likelihood of some types of institutionalized bias and may reduce even more the likelihood that others in the legal system will perceive the lab to be biased. To go even further in this direction, the crime laboratory's services could be made equally available to the prosecution and defense in criminal cases (as is done by the Institute of Forensic Sciences in Dallas).

However, increasing the laboratory's geographical or organizational remoteness can also be expected to limit the effectiveness of the laboratory's participation in the investigative phases of a case, when its scientific input may have the greatest chance of contributing to justice. Remoteness also makes the police department less able to direct the efforts of the laboratory toward the cases that the department considers most important and weakens the department's control over the criminal investigation process.

Background and selection of the laboratory director

The laboratory director should have an appropriate scientific background and experience in the forensic sciences. Formal training in management is also helpful. The ASCLD-LAB recommends that the laboratory director have a minimum of a bachelor's degree in a natural science or criminalistics, five years' experience in forensic science, and two years' supervisory experience. If the laboratory director is not technically trained, it is essential that supervisory scientific personnel have sufficient managerial rank and authority to supervise the technical aspects of the work effectively and that they have a strong voice in selecting analytical equipment and procedures and in establishing policies related to the scientific operation of the laboratory.

Most departments have recognized the importance of a strong scientific background to the management of a laboratory operation.

In many police departments, management positions have historically been reserved for sworn officers, and some laboratories are headed by uniformed commanders with little or no scientific training. However, most departments have recognized the importance of a strong scientific background to the management of a laboratory operation. The trend has been toward employing civilians for both management and bench staff and tightening the educational requirements.

Organization within the laboratory

The organization of units within laboratories varies widely and depends on a number of factors, including laboratory size, types of services offered, and relative workloads. Most laboratories, particularly those with large staffs, are organized along functional lines related to the types of evidence being examined—firearms, serology, drug evidence, latent prints, and so forth. In other laboratories, special sections may be devoted to particular types of analytical instruments (for example, the scanning electron microscope) that are exceptionally expensive and can be properly used only by people who have had highly specialized training.

Specialization, whether by type of evidence examined or by type of analytical instrument used, has both advantages and disadvantages. On the one hand, in high-volume units it supports the development of in-depth expertise in various areas and promotes efficiency, but on the other hand it may also produce a narrow view of casework and—when several different types of work are required on a single case—may result in poor communication among analysts. Specialization can also stifle the professional growth of staff if they are not given the opportunity to receive cross-training that would allow them to change career tracks. Analysts who have been trained in laboratories organized with specialized units may have difficulty developing the broad base of scientific knowledge necessary for a supervisor or coordinator of the larger operation.

Whatever the organizational structure, units in the lab frequently have overlapping responsibilities, and the manager has to allocate resources among units. For example, fiber evidence may be examined in the trace evidence section primarily by microscopy, but some samples may require further analysis using an instrument (such as an FTIR spectrophotometer) that is also used for examining other types of evidence, such as drugs. In this case, the manager needs to determine whether the volume of trace evidence cases requiring instrumental analysis warrants dedicating this expensive instrumentation to the trace evidence unit or whether it may not be a more efficient use of resources to share equipment, operator expertise, or both between the drug analysis and trace evidence sections.

The manager of the laboratory must strive to create an organizational structure that stimulates collaborative work, consultation, and shared decision making among the scientific staff.

Some laboratories prefer to rotate staff among units or to assign full responsibility for all aspects of a single case to one examiner. Rotation of staff provides the laboratory manager with greater flexibility in making case assignments and promotes a broad view of the entire case, with good coordination between the various specialties that may be required by the evidence in the case. However, placing a single examiner in charge of a case may result in superficial examination in those areas in which the examiner is technically weak and may create situations where the examiner is pressed to exceed the limits of his or her training and expertise.

Regardless of the basic philosophy the department adopts on organization and staffing, the manager of the laboratory must strive to create an organizational structure that stimulates collaborative work, consultation, and shared decision making among the scientific staff. In practice, therefore, most laboratories follow an intermediate path between the extremes of the "generalist" and "specialist" philosophies. Their goal is to provide staff not only with a reasonably broad understanding of the principles of forensic science and the requirements of its various subdisciplines but also with concentrated training and in-depth expertise in one or more specialty areas. Analysts trained in this way should be capable of recognizing the limitations of their expertise; of evaluating the need for, and coordinating, a variety of examinations in a complex case; and, eventually, of becoming effective supervisors and crime laboratory managers.

Service levels and case priorities

Like crime scene resources, laboratory services can rarely handle all of the potential demand. One national study found that only a fraction of the evidence submitted to laboratories is actually examined.[37] The chief and the laboratory manager may need to make difficult choices as to which categories of evidence or types of crime will receive the greatest attention. Here, as with crime scene processing, the task is to optimize resources by analyzing physical evidence that will be most useful in solving crimes and in assisting with successful prosecution of the most serious offenses.

As a service organization, the crime laboratory generally reacts to requests from other units, chiefly investigators and prosecutors, as part of the overall investigation and prosecution of the case. However, these outside parties may not fully understand the value and limitations of the available laboratory services or may overlook significant evidence that a more objective observer who is not as intimately involved with the case will readily perceive. The scientific units of the agency should therefore participate with the investigative unit in the decision as to what items in a case should be analyzed. Laboratory managers should be given the responsibility for evaluating requests for service to ensure that laboratory resources are used appropriately and should also be given the authority to reject requests for analyses that do not appear to play a significant role in the investigation or prosecution of the case.

Once the laboratory accepts the evidence, a variety of factors affect the priority with which the evidence is examined. These may include order of submission, legal deadlines (for example, filing deadlines or trial dates), perishability of the evidence, seriousness of the crime, perceived value of the evidence to the case, and the likelihood that the analysis will be productive. Laboratory managers should develop guidelines for setting priorities concerning cases—and specific items of evidence within particular cases—and should also establish a mechanism for obtaining feedback from the requestor as to changing priorities as the case progresses.

In the interests of efficiency, cases that can be rapidly concluded or handled as a group may be given priority over ones that are likely to be extremely time-consuming and complex. When laboratory resources are limited, the decision may be to concentrate on crimes against persons rather than property crimes or to eliminate work on cases with no known suspects. But it is also necessary to

---

Coping with the great number of drug identification cases　If the laboratory becomes overburdened with a high volume of routine drug identification cases, its capacity to assist in the investigation and prosecution of other crimes will diminish. The drug caseloads in many crime laboratories have skyrocketed as public awareness and funding have focused on drug-related problems. Close coordination between the narcotics investigator, the laboratory, and the prosecutor is necessary to optimize the efficient handling of drug cases and to prevent them from swamping the laboratory's ability to provide other critical analytical services.

Coordination between investigative units and the laboratory   Physical evidence can extend the department's ability to establish a link between a series of crimes and to eliminate or identify suspects. For example, development of a biological typing profile on a suspected rapist from semen samples collected in a series of cases can provide a means of rapidly screening and eliminating potential suspects who may come to the attention of the sex crime investigators. Identification of a previously unknown burglary suspect through a computer search of latent prints from one crime scene can lead to the clearance of dozens of additional cases and can contribute to investigators' efforts to address neighborhood problems that promote burglaries.

consider the degree to which laboratory analysis is essential to establishing the elements of the crime. Thus, although driving under the influence and possession of small amounts of drugs may not be considered as serious as assaults and homicides, the determination of blood alcohol level or the identification of controlled substances is essential if these cases are to be prosecuted at all. (Identification of drugs is a special problem—see sidebar.)

These decisions on priorities mirror the process frequently used to increase the effectiveness of overburdened investigative units (see the chapter on criminal investigations). In making these decisions, however, the police manager should not lose sight of the tendency of a relatively small number of offenders to commit a wide variety of crimes on a repeat basis. A crime analysis approach and coordination between investigative units and the laboratory may identify those cases with unknown suspects for which a concentrated effort by the laboratory would be worthwhile.

One approach to managing limited resources is to restrict the scope of routine services offered. The laboratory should provide a core level of services adequate to meet the majority of the department's needs in a timely fashion. However, the laboratory manager should determine whether the time and expense of acquiring and maintaining competence to analyze a particular type of evidence is justified by the number or significance of cases involving that evidence. It may be cost-effective for the laboratory to refer certain examinations (for example, trace metal analysis or soil comparisons) to an outside agency or private contractor that is better able to maintain the required expertise. With this approach, care must be taken lest the quality and responsiveness of the service suffer. Laboratory managers must also guard against the possibility that an excessive reliance on outside expertise may cause the technical capabilities of the laboratory staff to stagnate or wither.

Supervision of scientific personnel

To manage the scientific aspects of the crime laboratory operation effectively, administrators should not only pay attention to efficiency and work flow but should also carefully nurture the creative thinking, scientific objectivity, and independent professional judgment of the staff. The nature of the samples in forensic science demands that analysts be allowed to exercise discretion in choosing the analytical approaches most appropriate to the problem at hand. For instance, analysts may need to select methods capable of dealing with contamination, degradation, or other conditions that may jeopardize the sample. Analysts must be capable of defending their own test procedures and results in court; and in the process, as expert witnesses, they are frequently required to testify to broader, related scientific issues.

The ASCLD *Guidelines for Forensic Laboratory Management Practices* and the ASCLD-LAB *Accreditation Manual* outline issues that administrators should address in directing the technical aspects of the laboratory function. The tasks of the laboratory manager are to ensure that scientifically acceptable, reliable procedures and equipment are used, that the analysts are competent to perform the work they are assigned, and that their work in each case has been properly documented and can be relied on. These tasks require a delicate balance between control and flexibility: methods and procedures must be controlled, while analysts must be encouraged to exercise their scientific judgment intelligently.

The laboratory manager, with the full participation of the scientific staff, should establish a framework of well-understood and clearly articulated technical guidelines within which casework should be done. Routine technical procedures should be in writing and should include a description of the appropriate controls and standards required. If any sign of a technical problem appears, the laboratory must have mechanisms for reviewing the procedure and taking corrective action. Although forensic examiners may be given considerable latitude in choosing the methods to be used in particular situations, before new procedures and equipment can be used in casework they must be properly tested.

Proper documentation of casework is critical, both to allow for supervisory review and to provide a foundation for later testimony. Examiners must generate and maintain notes and other records (for example, sketches, photographs, charts) documenting the observations and analytical data upon which their conclusions are based.

Because laboratory reports usually "stand alone" (that is, are not accompanied by an examiner's oral explanations), they should contain both the testing results and the examiner's interpretations. Supervisors should routinely review reports and the supporting documentation to ensure that the conclusions of the analysts are reasonable, within the constraints of scientific knowledge, and supported by the data. If the laboratory manager and supervisory staff do not possess sufficient technical knowledge in a particular discipline to conduct an in-depth review, a mechanism for internal or external peer review should be established.

Because the testimony of an expert in court is often the most visible portion of a forensic scientist's efforts, the manager should periodically monitor this testimony as well as court transcripts of experts' court appearances. Experts must state their qualifications without distortion or puffery. Testimony should be limited to conclusions that can be substantiated by analyses documented in a laboratory report. Case adversaries (prosecutors and defense attorneys) should be queried about their interactions with examiners and their level of satisfaction with the scientists' interpretations of and opinions about the evidence. For example, the State of Illinois Bureau of Forensic Services has a procedure whereby examiners provide a postcard to each litigant and the judge in every case in which they testify. All parties are asked to evaluate the performance of the examiner and to return the card to the laboratory manager.

Training and research

As noted in an earlier section, entry-level professional staff should possess a solid academic foundation in the natural and physical sciences. However, the laboratory should also provide extensive in-service training to its new employees. The training period may last from a few months to several years, depending on the nature of the work. A written training program in each discipline is essential, and maintaining a training record for each analyst is important—both for professional development and for documentating the qualifications of examiners for court.

Basic training in the forensic sciences generally consists of reading; practical exercises; short courses offered in-house or by external organizations; apprenticeship on actual cases under the supervision of an experienced analyst; oral, written, and blind sample examinations; and moot court exercises. The analyst must be required to demonstrate proficiency in a series of practical tests before being assigned to independent casework.

Like other scientists, forensic professionals must engage in continuing education to remain current in their field. The proposed certification program of the American Board of Criminalistics outlines continuing education requirements for recertification. Formal short courses are available through state and federal agencies (such as the FBI Academy in Quantico, Virginia), although the demand far exceeds the supply. National and regional professional organizations present periodic workshops and annual scientific meetings at which current technology is presented. Private organizations and local universities also provide training courses.

Responsibility for continuing education should be divided between the department and the individual professional. The laboratory manager and the police chief should formally acknowledge the importance of professional development by supporting continuing education and participation in other professional activities whenever possible. The laboratory manager has the responsibility of providing appropriate in-service training to prepare the staff for assigned casework and should allot a reasonable amount of bench time for this purpose. The laboratory should provide access to a library of current professional journals and other technical literature. Individual analysts should be expected to maintain their scientific skills and knowledge by routinely reviewing current literature and regularly consulting professional colleagues.

Applied research is another responsibility of laboratory staff. Most of the methods and procedures used in forensic science are adapted from technology developed in other fields and adjusted to suit the demands of forensic science (for example, the need to handle small, contaminated samples). But because most academic institutions lack funding and forensic science expertise, much of the work to support this technology transfer is necessarily conducted in working crime labs. Therefore, it is important that the staff be encouraged to develop and maintain skill in designing and conducting applied research. The critical scientific thinking required in such research is the same as that required in analyzing and interpreting a complex forensic case. A case-related research project either in-house or in collaboration with outside colleagues is an excellent vehicle for continuing education and professional development.

Some experts have recommended that at least 10 percent of the examiner's bench time be reserved for training and research functions.[38] However, the heavy caseload demands in most crime laboratories create pressure to sacrifice these vital activities. Studies have found that examiners spend far less than 10 percent of their time on training and research.[39] The police chief and the laboratory manager should strive to balance the need for production with the need for staff members to maintain their technical competence and scientific credibility.

Quality assurance

Quality assurance is a primary responsibility of management and becomes an even greater challenge as the number of caseloads increases and the demand for rapid results intensifies. Quality assurance means that the concepts presented on the preceding pages are combined and integrated—that is, it includes steps to maintain and document the chain of custody of evidence from discovery through analysis to presentation in court; it also addresses the education, training, and proficiency of analysts, the reliability of the instruments and procedures used, the documentation of casework in laboratory notes, and the written reports and expert testimony of forensic examiners. The laboratory should have a formal quality assurance program that covers all these elements; it should also document its ongoing compliance with appropriate standards. Review of these records is one way in which the users of the laboratory (for example, the department and the courts) can judge the reliability of its work product.

Tests for routine proficiency are one of the most valuable components of a quality assurance program. The proficiency of the examiners in each analytical area in which they do casework should be tested periodically (the ASCLD-LAB recommends at least once every two years). Although proficiency samples can be produced in-house, external proficiency test samples are an ideal vehicle for this type of declared testing and serve the added purpose of providing a means for comparing performance between laboratories. As noted earlier, one source is the proficiency testing program conducted by Collaborative Testing Services in conjunction with the Forensic Sciences Foundation and ASCLD. In addition to declared testing, simulated cases may be submitted blind either by the laboratory manager or from external units to measure the laboratory's routine performance. For example, the narcotics investigation unit might occasionally submit a test sample of known drugs as if it were a routine case, to check the laboratory's performance.

The laboratory should have a formal quality assurance program and should document its ongoing compliance with appropriate standards.

Another extremely valuable quality assurance procedure is the inspection or audit. This review of the laboratory's procedures and work product may range from internal peer review (for example, review of one laboratory section by another, or review of the laboratory unit by the audit unit of the department) to a full-scale inspection by a team of external scientists such as the ASCLD-LAB accreditation inspection. The presence on the inspection team of persons external to the department helps to ensure an independent and objective evaluation.

Research on the value of laboratory evidence

In the early years of laboratory development, many laboratories were created as the result of a scandal in which cases went unsolved or a police department bungled an investigation and destroyed or contaminated evidence.[40] But although in the succeeding years many police managers have basically *assumed* the value of crime laboratory operations, there have been few reliable research data to support such a claim. Laboratory analyses are certainly the very foundation of drug prosecutions as well as of many driving-while-intoxicated cases, but what is the value of a laboratory in routine cases of homicide, rape, assault, and burglary in which physical clues are examined? Research has shed light on this question.

A study published by the British Home Office (a national government agency with responsibilities similar to those of the U.S. Department of Justice) sought to describe the value of forensic work performed by two of its English Forensic Science Service Laboratories to police officers submitting physical evidence.[41] Scientists working the cases were interviewed, as were a sample of investigators; all were asked questions about the purposes of the physical evidence submission as well as about the value of laboratory results. Practically 80 percent of requests from police were for the purpose of corroborating the identity of a suspect about whom ideas were "already well formed": evidence was sought linking the offender to the crime. The laboratory provided helpful information in about three-quarters of cases when suspects had been identified, but it did so in less than 40 percent of cases *without suspects*. Confirmation of the involvement of suspects who had been apprehended was produced in 60 percent of cases, whereas suspects were absolved in about 7 percent of submissions.

Another study, in the United States, examined the various uses and effects of physical evidence on the solution of serious crimes and the apprehension and prosecution of offenders.[42] This study, conducted at four sites nationwide, found that the rates of clearance for robberies and burglaries were significantly higher in cases for which physical evidence was examined than in cases for which it was not. In fact, on average, police were about three times as likely to clear cases (controlling for other factors) when scientific evidence was analyzed. Forensic evidence had its greatest effect in cases that traditionally have the lowest solution rates—cases with suspects neither in custody nor identified at the outset of the investigation. This study also found that, in cases with forensic evidence, a significantly higher percentage of persons arrested for crimes of burglary and robbery were convicted as charged.

The report accompanying these findings also presented a number of recommendations and policy options as to how police departments might enhance their use of physical evidence; specifically, policy recommendations focused on patrol and crime scene operations, investigative units, the crime laboratory, the prosecutor's office, and top-level police administration. Recommendations addressed ways in which limited police and scientific resources might be directed to those investigations in which physical evidence can make the greatest difference.

Technological advances

Two significant technological breakthroughs that promise to have a major effect on forensic science during the 1990s are automated fingerprint identification systems and DNA typing.

Automated fingerprint identification systems (AFIS)

Although fingerprints are regarded as the single most powerful type of physical evidence that can be used to identify suspects and link them to scenes of crimes, until recently this potential was seldom realized. In 1975, a Rand Corporation study found that fingerprints were used to identify suspects in only about 1 percent of burglaries and concluded that much more evidence and fingerprints were being collected from the scenes of crimes than could be effectively processed.[43] Traditionally, detectives submitted the names of likely suspects to identification technicians, who checked their fingerprints against latent prints found at a scene. The manual classification and filing systems used by police departments and the impracticality of searching large files of prints to compare with latent prints presented significant barriers to investigations.

Since the late 1970s, however, computer systems have permitted automated classification, storage, and searching of large files of fingerprints and have enabled departments to begin to exploit more fully the potential of latent fingerprint identifications. Departments now are able to take crime scene prints in cases without named suspects and conduct "cold searches" against fingerprint files. The rates of success when departments use these automated systems far exceed the rates when departments use the traditional methods of checking latent prints against the records of suspects. For example, the California Department of Justice's CAL-ID system reports a 15 percent "hit" rate on latent searches; the San Francisco police department also reports a 15 percent hit rate; Houston reports a hit rate of 13 percent.[44] In contrast, hit rates using traditional non-computerized card searching methods may be as low as 1 percent, although rates of cold hits vary widely from jurisdiction to jurisdiction.[45] It seems likely that, during the 1990s, most large urban and state law enforcement agencies will acquire such automated systems for in-house use.

Considerable headway has also been made in developing techniques that transcend the traditional dusting powders and chemical enhancement methods. Technologies now exist that improve the ability of laboratories to develop latent fingerprints from surfaces that resist conventional processing.[46] A "superglue" fuming technique has been used successfully to develop prints on porous objects such as styrofoam cups. Invisible fingerprints have also been made visible via laser light examination—a method that causes amino acids and other secretions in the print to luminesce. The laser may also be used to enhance prints on objects that have already been dusted or treated with chemicals.

DNA technology

The field of forensic serology was dramatically transformed in the 1970s and early 1980s as laboratories developed improved techniques to exploit information from protein genetic markers in biological evidence such as human blood and body fluids.[47] With the introduction of forensic DNA testing in the late 1980s, the value of biological evidence has taken another quantum leap forward.

DNA (deoxyribonucleic acid) is a double-stranded molecule that is present in the cellular material of all life forms and controls their genetically inherited characteristics. The particular combination of traits defined by the genetic code in DNA is unique for every individual. Molecular biologists have developed the technology for testing specific regions of DNA to determine a group of DNA types, or an individual DNA profile, from such biological samples as bloodstains, semen, hair, and bone. The forensic advantage of DNA over conventional blood grouping and protein genetic marker systems is the potential of DNA typing to link a blood or semen stain to one individual, excluding all others; similarly, DNA has the potential to exclude as potential sources of a stain all persons except the responsible party. Although the "uniqueness" of a DNA profile will vary depending on the specific tests employed, DNA typing laboratories are often able to distinguish a person from every other person in a group of several million individuals on the basis of their DNA typing profiles. Techniques are under development to amplify and type the extremely small amounts of DNA present in a single shed hair or a few sperm cells. This increased sensitivity will allow the application of DNA testing to samples that cannot be typed at all by conventional genetic marker testing.[48]

The DNA typing techniques used in forensic work originated in the practice of clinical medicine and genetics. But forensic specimens pose special analytical problems because they are frequently small in size and contaminated with extraneous material from the crime scene. Therefore, methods developed for use on clinical specimens must be validated to verify their reliability and sensitivity on forensic evidence samples. Extensive development and validation of DNA typing technology has been undertaken, primarily by commercial DNA testing laboratories and by the forensic laboratories of the British Home Office, the FBI, and the Royal Canadian Mounted Police.[49]

Initially, the bulk of the forensic DNA testing in the United States was conducted by commercial typing laboratories. In late 1988, the FBI laboratory began accepting cases from local departments for DNA typing; soon afterward, a few local crime laboratories (those in the state of Virginia were the first) followed suit. By mid-1989, DNA testing had been accepted in the courts of more than two dozen states, including courts at the appellate level in Florida and Virginia. The FBI Academy has a DNA training program for local crime lab analysts, and many local jurisdictions are beginning to provide DNA testing in their own laboratories. National consensus quality assurance standards have been developed for forensic DNA laboratories.[50] Laboratory administrators should strive to meet these standards in establishing their own DNA programs.

The full potential of DNA typing technology has not yet been realized. One proposal is that computerized files of DNA profiles on former offenders be constructed, much like automated fingerprint files, so that investigators can consult such data bases in cases in which they lack suspects. The benefits of being able to link a series of violent sexual crimes to one another and to develop information pointing to the identity of the offender are obvious. Several states (including California, Virginia, Colorado, Washington, Illinois, and Louisiana) are proceeding to collect blood samples from convicted sex offenders and other violent felons for the purpose of building such files, and the FBI is coordinating an effort to construct a national DNA data base. For DNA data files prepared by different jurisdictions to be useful regionally and nationally, they must contain compatible information. Agencies must coordinate their testing procedures with the national effort if DNA profiling is to have its maximum effect in solving violent serial crime.

Like other kinds of evidence, DNA typing must be used in ways that are compatible with the protection of individual citizens' rights and liberties. Some observers have raised concerns about potential misuse of data banks containing genetic information; and as this new technology is applied to criminal investigation, guidelines will need to be developed.[51]

Conclusion

The forensic sciences have made significant contributions to the criminal justice system throughout modern history, and such breakthroughs as DNA typing and automated fingerprint storage and retrieval systems hold additional promise for the future. Scientific evidence is frequently crucial in linking a suspect to a crime and establishing a case that will hold up in court.

This chapter has provided an overview of the basic principles a police chief needs to understand in order to make best use of the laboratory facilities available to the department. With a thorough understanding of the principles of evidence, the management issues in crime scene and laboratory operations, and the tools for professionalizing forensic sciences, the chief will be able to allocate resources intelligently, set sound and realistic priorities for crime scene investigation and lab work, and select the right personnel for forensic assignments.

Ultimately, the chief's responsibility is to see that forensic laboratory resources are available and applied competently in those situations when physical evidence can assist in an investigation.

1   John I. Thornton, "Criminalistics—Past, Present and Future," *Lex et Scientia* 11 (1975): 1–44.

2   Joseph L. Peterson, Steven Mihajlovic, and Joanne Bedrosian, "The Capabilities, Uses and Effects of the Nation's Criminalistics Laboratories," *Journal of Forensic Sciences* 30, no. 1 (January 1985): 10–23.

3   Walter Benson, John Stacy, and Michael Worley, *Systems Analysis of Criminalistics Operations* (Kansas City, MO: Midwest Research Institute, 1970).

4   *Summary of Survey Results: Crime Laboratories, 1988* (San Jose, CA: Pacific Western Information Systems, 1988).

5   Charles Petty and William Curran, "Operational Aspects of Public Medicolegal Death Investigation," in *Modern Legal Medicine, Psychiatry and Forensic Science*, ed. William Curran, A. Louis McGarry, and Charles Petty (Philadelphia: F. A. Davis Co., 1980).

6   William Eckert, ed., *Introduction to the Forensic Sciences* (St. Louis: C. V. Mosby Co., 1980).

7   Peterson, Mihajlovic, and Bedrosian, "Capabilities, Uses and Effects."

8   Charles Swanson, Neal Chamlin, and Leonard Territo, *Criminal Investigation*, 4th ed. (New York: Random House, 1988).

9   See, for example, John I. Thornton, ed., *Crime Investigation*, 2d ed. (New York: John Wiley and Sons, 1981); Peter R. DeForest, R. E. Gaensslen, and Henry C. Lee, *Forensic Sciences: An Introduction to Criminalistics* (New York: McGraw-Hill, 1983); Richard Saferstein, *Criminalistics: An Introduction to Forensic Science*, 3d ed. (Englewood Cliffs, NJ: Prentice-Hall, 1987); and Barry Fisher, Arne Svensson, and Oliver Wendel, *Techniques of Crime Scene Investigation*, 4th ed. (New York: Elsevier, 1986).

10 DeForest, Gaensslen, and Lee, *Forensic Sciences*.

11　Joseph L. Peterson, Steven Mihajlovic, and Michael Gilliland, *Forensic Evidence and the Police: The Effects of Scientific Evidence on Criminal Investigations* (Washington, DC: U.S. Government Printing Office, 1984).

12　Brian Parker and Joseph Peterson, *Physical Evidence Utilization in the Administration of Criminal Justice* (Washington, DC: U.S. Department of Justice, 1974).

13　Commission on Accreditation for Law Enforcement Agencies, "Collection and Preservation of Evidence," in *Accreditation Standards* (Fairfax, VA: Commission on Accreditation for Law Enforcement Agencies, 1987) 83-1 to 83-6. Hereafter referred to as CALEA, 1987.

14　John Eck, *Managing Case Assignments: The Burglary Investigation Decision Model Replication* (Washington, DC: Police Executive Research Forum, 1979).

15　Commission on Criminal Justice Standards and Goals, *Report on Police*, Standard 12.1 (Washington, DC: U.S. Government Printing Office, 1973); Peterson, Mihajlovic, and Gilliland, *Forensic Evidence*; and CALEA, 1987.

16　American Society of Crime Laboratory Directors, *Laboratory Accreditation Manual* (American Society of Crime Laboratory Directors, 1985). Hereafter referred to as ASCLD-LAB, 1985.

17　Theodore Hammett and Walter Bond, *Risk of Infection with the AIDS Virus through Exposures to Blood* (Washington, DC: National Institute of Justice, 1987).

18　CALEA, 1987.

19　Jan Bashinski and P. Kalish, "The Effectiveness of Long Term Freezer Storage of Bloodstains," *California Association of Criminalists Newsletter* (June 1980).

20　*California Medical Protocol for Examination of Sexual Assault and Child Sexual Abuse Victims* (Sacramento: California Office of Criminal Justice Planning, 1987), 18.

21　ASCLD-LAB, 1985.

22　Kenneth S. Field, Oliver Schroeder, Jr., Ina Curtis, Ellen Fabricant, and Beth Ann Lipkin, *Assessment of the Personnel of the Forensic Sciences Profession* (Washington, DC: U.S. Government Printing Office, 1977), vol. 2; and Peterson, Mihajlovic, and Bedrosian, "Capabilities, Uses and Effects."

23　Debra Moss, "DNA—The New Fingerprints," *ABA Journal* (1 May 1988): 66-70; and Gayle Golden, "Scientific Justice," five-part series appearing in the *Dallas Morning News* (3-7 Apr. 1988).

24　Peter Applebome, "As Influence of Police Laboratories Grows, So Does Call for High Standards," *New York Times* (22 Dec. 1987); Thomas Frisbie, " 'Expert' Witnesses Are on Trial," *Chicago Sun Times*, (8 Mar. 1987); and James Starrs, "Mountebanks among Forensic Scientists," in *Forensic Science Handbook*, ed. Richard Saferstein (Englewood Cliffs, NJ: Prentice-Hall, 1988), vol. 2.

25　Jan S. Bashinski, "Criminalistics: An Emerging Profession"; and John M. Hartmann, "Criminalistics: A Profession without Professionals?" (Paper delivered at the California Association of Criminalists Fall Seminar, Costa Mesa, CA, 1988).

26　Talcott Parsons, "The Professions and Social Structure," *Social Forces* 17 (May 1939): 457-67.

27　Jan S. Bashinski, "Laboratory Standards: Accreditation, Training and Certification of Staff in the Forensic Context," in *Proceedings of the Banbury Conference on DNA Technology and Forensic Science* (New York: Cold Spring Harbor Laboratory, 1989).

28　Joseph L. Peterson and John E. Murdock, "Forensic Science Ethics: Developing an Integrated System of Support and Enforcement," *Journal of Forensic Sciences* 34 (May 1989): 749-62.

29　Criminalistics Certification Study Committee, *Certification in Criminalistics: A Final Report to the Profession* (Rockville, MD: Forensic Sciences Foundation, 1979).

30　"Procedure for Certification," *California Association of Criminalists Newsletter* (April 1987).

31　Joseph L. Peterson, Kenneth S. Field, Ellen L. Fabricant, and John I. Thornton, *Crime Laboratory Proficiency Testing Research Program* (Washington, DC: U.S. Government Printing Office, 1978).

32　D. Lucas, C. Leete, and K. Field, "An American Proficiency Testing Program," *Forensic Science International* 27 (1985): 71-79.

33　"ASCLD Guidelines for Forensic Laboratory Management Practices," *Crime Laboratory Digest* 14, no. 2 (April 1987): 39-46.

34　Ibid., 40.

35　United States District Court, Northern District of Illinois, Eastern Division, *Report of the January 1970 Grand Jury* (Washington, DC: U.S. Government Printing Office, 1970).

36　L. W. Bradford, "Barriers to Quality Achievement in Crime Laboratory Operations," *Journal of Forensic Sciences* 25, no. 4 (October 1980): 902-7.

37　Peterson, Mihajlovic, and Gilliland, *Forensic Evidence*.

38　Bradford, "Barriers to Quality Achievement"; and California Association of Criminalists and California Bureau of Forensic Services, *Report of a Symposium on the Practice of Forensic Serology* (Sacramento, 1987).

39　George Sensabaugh, "Forensic Science Research: Who Does It and Where Is It Going?" in *Forensic Science*, 2d ed., ed. Geoffrey Davies (Washington, DC: American Chemical Society, 1986); and Peterson, Mihajlovic, and Bedrosian, "Capabilities, Uses, and Effects."

40　Thornton, "Criminalistics."

41　Malcolm Ramsay, *The Effectiveness of the Forensic Science Service* (London: Home Office Research and Planning Unit, 1987).

42　Peterson, Mihajlovic, and Gilliland, *Forensic Evidence*.

43　Peter Greenwood, Jan Chaiken, Joan Petersilia, and Linda Prusoff, *Observations and Analysis*, vol. 3 of *The Criminal Investigation Process* (Santa Monica, CA: Rand Corporation, 1975).

44　Thomas Wilson and Paul Woodard, *Automated Fingerprint Identification Systems: Technology and Policy Issues* (Washington, DC: U.S. Department of Justice, 1987).

45　Joan Petersilia, "Processing Latent Fingerprints: What Are the Payoffs?" *Journal of Police Science and Administration* 6, no. 2 (1978): 157-67.

46.　Robert J. Hazen, "Significant Advances in the Science of Fingerprints," in *Forensic Science*, ed. Geoffrey Davies, 2d ed. (Washington, DC: American Chemical Society, 1986).

47 R. E. Gaensslen, Peter J. Desio, and Henry C. Lee, "Genetic-Marker Systems: Individualization of Blood and Body Fluids," in *Forensic Science*, ed. Davies.

48 Office of Technology Assessment, U.S. Congress, *Genetic Witness: Forensic Uses of DNA Tests*, OTA-BA-438 (Washington, DC: U.S. Government Printing Office, 1990).

49 Program for an International Symposium on the Forensic Aspects of DNA Analysis, FBI, Quantico, VA, 19–23 June 1989.

50 Technical Working Group on DNA Analysis Methods, "Guidelines for a Quality Assurance Program for DNA Restriction Fragment Length Polymorphism Analysis," *Crime Laboratory Digest* 16, no. 2 (1989): 40–59. See also J. Bashinski, "Managing the Implementation and Use of DNA Typing in the Crime Laboratory," in *Forensic DNA Technology*, ed. Mark Farley and James Harrington (Boca Raton, FL: Lewis Publishers, CRC Press, 1990); and Office of Technology Assessment, *Genetic Witness*.

51 Office of Technology Assessment, *Genetic Witness*.

18 Arrestee and lockup management

Police lockups are immediate detention facilities designed to hold all arrestees from the jurisdiction or subregion until they can be processed for release, interrogated, or moved to a longer-term holding facility or a pretrial detention facility (usually the local jail). Many lockups are located inside police stations or substations.

Often the local judicial officer(s) responsible for setting bond or bail is located at this same site and can arrange a release (conditional or otherwise). Or when an arrestee must be questioned or distance makes it impractical to transport the prisoner to the county pretrial detention facility, the arrestee may be held in the lockup for a short period (less than seventy-two hours). The lockup may also be used to hold prisoners for several days. This may be done to allow the police to develop further information about arrestees—information such as warrants or involvement in other crimes—or to permit an investigation to continue. Holding periods may also be extended because of overcrowding in local jails, as discussed below. Basically, lockups give police a reasonable amount of time (a day or two) to sort things out, continue an investigation, identify the suspect, search for local and other warrants, reduce the trauma surrounding an arrest, provide medical assistance to injured prisoners, or allow arrestees to sleep off the effects of alcohol or drugs.

Police management of arrestees in a traditional lockup environment is a task that has always been outside the mainstream of police skills, resources, and managerial expertise.

Police management of arrestees in a traditional lockup environment is a task that has always been outside the mainstream of police skills, resources, and managerial expertise. But for a number of reasons, lockup and arrestee management is demanding more from police managers and has become hazardous duty to all involved.

One reason for this development is that court decisions have set higher standards for police care of arrestees. When something goes wrong in the lockup, courts have become increasingly critical of police management and are increasingly likely to hold the local government liable. (In addition, local citizens have been aroused by what sometimes appears to be deliberate police indifference to the needs of arrestees.)

A second reason is that the numbers of detainees are increasing, causing tensions inside lockups to rise and living conditions to deteriorate, and expanding the sheer volume of work faced by police lockup staff in housing, processing, and caring for arrestees. In these circumstances, even the day-to-day issues of who cleans the lockup becomes burdensome to the police manager, and it is not surprising that the constitutional rights of the pretrial detainees held in lockups may become secondary.

Third, holding periods are longer. Delays in moving arrestees to the local jails may occur because no personnel have been assigned to be "transportation officers," and officers cannot be spared from street duty. Further, with many local jails experiencing critical overcrowding and operating under court-imposed population caps, the police lockup represents the only remaining facility to house arrestees. Thus, prisoners may remain in lockups for several additional days until space can be found for them at the local jail. When this happens—as it frequently does in some localities—both practical and constitutional questions arise. Practically, holding prisoners for several days is troublesome unless the lockup has immediate access to a range of screening, professional, and supervisory services and resources. Constitutionally, there are serious concerns about whether the detention services generally required in jails must be provided in lockups as well.

Fourth, detainees are afflicted by an increasingly complex array of medical, psychiatric, or other problems. More and more the lockup is used to hold arrestees who will probably need mental health services or juvenile shelter care homes. With the deinstitutionalization of many troubled persons, the lockup also serves as a temporary shelter to hold people who are drunk or homeless or have mental health problems—to hold them both for their own protection and to keep them out of the view of the complaining public.

The lockup is one of a department's highest risks.

Yet the lockup staff are often ill equipped to handle such problems. Staff may have no access to medical and classification screening to determine arrestees' current condition. Local law enforcement staff often know little about some admittees (others, of course, are well known to police) and may not know if a person is on some sort of life-support medication. Staff may also have difficulty determining that an arrestee has a physical ailment when the symptoms resemble signs of alcohol or drug withdrawal.

It should not surprise managers of police lockups across the country that the lockup is one of a department's highest risks. If passive arrestees are lodged with aggressive arrestees, the passive ones may be attacked and injured. Or juveniles may be mixed with adults. Other nightmarish situations, too, may develop, for this is a psychologically high-risk time when arrestees may harm

---

Lockup data by size of city Comprehensive data on police lockup facilities throughout the nation are difficult to obtain. A 1989 report by the Bureau of Justice Statistics of the U.S. Department of Justice provided information on lockups in cities with populations of 250,000 or more (see table below). Just over 44 percent of the departments operated at least one lockup facility separate from a jail. The median total lockup capacity was fifty-eight.

Population served	Departments with lockups (%)	Median total departmental lockup capacity
Total of all cities	44.1	58
1,000,000 or more	75.0	499
500,000-999,999	46.7	174
350,000-499,999	28.6	39
250,000-349,999	46.7	30

Source: Bureau of Justice Statistics, U.S. Department of Justice, *Police Departments in Large Cities, 1987* (Washington, DC, 1989).

themselves—all too often fatally. Research has suggested that most arrestee deaths occur during the first forty-eight hours of incarceration,[1] with about 27 percent of such deaths occurring during the first three hours of incarceration.[2] Other studies have shown that 88.7 percent of those attempting suicide while in the custody of a criminal justice agency do so during detention in either a police lockup or a jail holding facility.[3]

A twenty-year study of inmate deaths in the Milwaukee area revealed that of the sixty-six deaths during that period, 46 percent were suicides, 38 percent resulted from "natural causes," 11 percent were accidents or accidental overdoses, 3 percent were deaths resulting from law enforcement actions, and 2 percent were deaths classified as undetermined.[4] Of these deaths, 54 percent occurred in temporary holding areas, although only 20 percent of the total inmate population was in these areas.

Not only is the management of arrestees in the lockup setting risky and full of problems, but it is also not an inherent part of the mission of most law enforcement agencies; it is often an unwanted sideline staffed by sworn personnel who have not "made it" in other areas of the department and by civilian detention aides. These staff members, sworn and civilian alike, are usually not trained to provide the level of care that many arrestees require. Thus the surprising thing, given alternatives to police lockups (discussed in a later section), is that police departments continue to manage lockups at all.

It is the responsibility of the police executive to stay informed about lockup conditions, to become more proficient in dealing with the operation of the lockup, and to develop and aggressively implement policies and procedures to address critical areas of vulnerability.

In most jurisdictions, of course, divesting local police departments of responsibilities for lockup management may not be feasible, at least in the short term. In the long term, proper planning across the entire criminal justice system is critical to alleviating a host of problems connected with the processing of arrestees and detainees. Proper mechanisms for coordination among the courts, police, and corrections agencies can help to expedite case processing. Construction of new facilities or renovation of existing ones should help address physical inadequacies—conditions that often contribute to managerial problems. In the short term, however, jail crowding is likely to make the role of the lockup increasingly important, and it is the responsibility of the police executive to stay informed about lockup conditions, to become more proficient in dealing with the operation of the lockup, and to develop and aggressively implement policies and procedures to address critical areas of vulnerability.

This chapter reviews relevant case law; summarizes the standards for incarceration facilities that various professional associations have developed; discusses issues related to personnel and training; surveys the major issues related to management of arrestees; explores strategies for divesting police departments of responsibility for lockup management; and proposes ways for police managers to develop better relations with local corrections agencies.

Case law

Litigation initiated by arrestees who were harmed or who allege they were harmed in lockups—or by such arrestees' families—has increased the courts' scrutiny of police short-term holding facilities.

Since the early 1970s, federal courts have issued a number of opinions about the constitutionality of conditions of detention. The scope and impact of judicial scrutiny of lockups has continued to broaden. The test that the courts will now apply in determining whether conditions of confinement are constitutional is "whether those conditions amount to punishment of the detainee." Loss of privacy, loss of freedom of choice, and loss of freedom of movement are not considered punishment.[5]

A list of some recent mandates set for the care of pretrial detainees in police holding facilities follows. This review is not exhaustive but merely suggests the kinds of situations that have given rise to the evolving case law. (Legal citations appear in the notes at the end of the chapter.)

1. Such detainees should have no less protection for personal security than is afforded convicted prisoners under the Fourteenth Amendment,[6] including protection from other arrestees.[7]
2. The level of medical care should be at least at the level required for convicted prisoners; indeed, pretrial detainees have greater rights to medical treatment than do prisoners.[8]
3. When officials know, or should know, of an inmate's particular vulnerability to suicide, they are obliged under the Fourteenth Amendment not to act with deliberate indifference to that vulnerability.[9]
4. Pretrial detainees' due process rights are at least as great as a convicted prisoner's Eighth Amendment rights.[10]
5. Officials have an obligation to act to address serious medical, psychological, or psychiatric needs of detainees.[11]
6. Arrestees must be protected from lockup policies, procedures, or actual practices—such as laxity in supervising and monitoring the cell area or in searching arrestees, or indifference to the medical needs of arrestees—that allow any of the above to occur.[12]
7. Arrestees must not be subjected to unsafe physical conditions.[13]

The standard for pretrial detainees most used by federal courts in reviewing police liability concerning events that occur in lockups is that set by *Bell v. Wolfish.*[14] The *Bell* decision applies the "legitimate governmental interest" test to determine whether conditions or restrictions of pretrial detainees are constitutional. That test was enunciated by the Supreme Court: "A court must decide whether the disability is imposed for the purpose of punishment or whether it is but an incident of some other 'legitimate governmental purpose.' "[15] Thus, *Bell* also established that no actions against a pretrial detainee are permissible if they have the effect of being "punishment."

The Fourteenth Amendment's due process guarantees have been interpreted as protecting the pretrial detainee population.

Although most courts have established that Eighth Amendment rights do not extend to pretrial detainees (because, by definition, these detainees are not to be subjected to any punishment at all), the Fourteenth Amendment's due process guarantees have been interpreted as protecting the pretrial detainee population. In *Roberts v. City of Troy*, the court noted that "the rights of the pretrial detainee under the 14th amendment are greater than the rights of a convicted prisoner under the 8th amendment."[16] As of 1991, this decision had not been reviewed by a federal appeals court.

Police lockup-management liability commonly involves arrestees who are emotionally distraught, intoxicated, or prone to violence. The police often know of an arrestee's condition, and such knowledge makes them vulnerable if the person harms himself or herself or is harmed by other detainees with whom he or she is held.

For example, in *Danese v. Asman*, the federal trial court found that a pretrial detainee has a Fourteenth Amendment right to personal security even though he is incarcerated.[17] In this case, the trial court ruled, the detainee was deprived of his liberty by the officers' failure to protect him from self-injury—for "the right to personal security under the Fourteenth Amendment is not extinguished by lawful confinement."

Further, the trial court found that this protection applied both to unsafe physical conditions in the city jail and to unsafe conditions that were exacerbated by the defendant officers' lack of action to protect the detainee "despite awareness of his threats of self-injury and his mental and physical condition."

The federal appeals court reversed this decision, noting that these specific rights were not clearly enough established for an official to know he or she is violating a rule. The appeals court noted that it is one thing to ignore an arrestee's condition (a practice that would cause liability) and another thing to be obliged to actively screen the arrestee to determine his or her condition. The appeals court rejected the notion that there is a right "to have the police diagnose one's condition as prone to suicide." The Supreme Court declined to review this case.

In many federal cases involving detainee suicides, the provision of medical care—or rather the lack thereof—is an important theme. Perhaps the most notable case concerning medical care in a pretrial detention facility is *Partridge v. Two Unknown Police Officers of the City of Houston*.[18] Here the appellate court established that the police had an obligation to provide appropriate care—whether this care was medical, psychological, or psychiatric. The court noted: "[J]ust as a failure to act to save a detainee suffering from gangrene might violate the duty to provide reasonable medical care absent an intervening legitimate government objective, failure to take any steps to save a suicidal detainee from injuring himself may also constitute a due process violation under *Bell v. Wolfish*."

This case is also of interest to police administrators because it highlights the need for arresting officers to pass along information to the lockup staff about an arrestee's behavior at the time of the arrest. In *Partridge*, the arresting officers had gained from the detainee's father specific information about the detainee's mental and physical history. They witnessed the detainee's aberrant behavior at the time of arrest and during transport. Yet they did not report this behavior to the lockup staff. In the *Partridge* decision the court noted the absence of a written policy and procedures manual and expressed concern about adequate staffing of the lockup.

Other cases have established the responsibility of the detaining agency to protect arrestees from one another. In *DeBow v. City of East St. Louis*, the state appellate court found that a detainee injured in a police lockup was entitled to damages because the detainees were inadequately supervised and because officers failed to monitor detainee conduct to keep violent detainees separate from other detainees.[19] In this case, the plaintiff sustained permanent brain damage when he was struck on the head by the boot of the detainee in the cell with him. The court noted: "[I]t is sufficient that the defendants acted recklessly by disregarding detainee safety. This disregard can be demonstrated either by deliberate acts or by failure to act."

Lest police managers become too apprehensive, emerging case law as it relates to federal civil rights actions under "Section 1983"[20] maintains a burden of proof for the plaintiff to show the defendant's "gross negligence" or "deliberate indifference" when the conduct in question occurs at the time of arrest. An employee's gross negligence exists when the employee "intentionally does something unreasonable with disregard to a known risk or a risk so obvious that he must be assumed to have been aware of it, and of a magnitude such that it is highly probable that harm will follow."[21] Deliberate indifference is "when action is not taken in the face of 'a strong likelihood, rather than a mere possibility,' that failure to provide care would result in harm to the prisoner."[22]

Put another way, "gross negligence" is "conduct," and "deliberate indifference" is a "state of mind."[23] The police manager of a lockup will need to ensure as a minimum level of performance that there is not gross negligence or deliberate indifference to any arrestee, as measured by the absence of care or the failure to take steps to keep arrestees from harming themselves or others.

Finally, the police administrator needs to ensure that the guidelines provided by the *Monell* decision are understood. The Supreme Court's *Monell* decision about immunity for local government officials notes:

[A] local government may not be sued under Section 1983 for an injury inflicted solely by its employees or agents. Instead, it is when execution of a government's policy or custom, whether made by its lawmakers or by those whose edicts or acts may fairly be said to represent official policy, inflicts the injury that the government as an entity is responsible under section 1983.[24]

Therefore, the police administrator should establish policy, train officers in that policy, and ensure that the policy is followed—rather than be caught in court with a defense limited to "this is what we say—but that is what we really do."

If the trend in court decisions continues, those developments plus the existing body of case law about the rights of pretrial detainees will transform the management of police lockups so that the task will begin to resemble the administration of the local county jail.

Professional standards

One striking difference between most police activities and the operation of holding facilities is that almost every element of detention and penal facility management is governed by formal state and national standards and their influence on operations is substantial. In most states jails and prisons are subject to standards developed and promulgated by legislatively created bodies or commissions. In some jurisdictions there are multiple layers of standard-generating bodies. These bodies often have staffs with the capacity to inspect and report on levels of compliance with standards. Failure to comply with standards can result in a range of actions, from a letter or telephone call to the closing of part or all of an institution. As already discussed, actions by federal courts also have had profound effects on the operation of jails and prisons and, by extension, on the operation of police lockups.

Most important, the police manager needs to be aware of any state standards for lockups, for these are typically mandatory and are usually linked with an inspection process for the facility. Because the physical plant is an important part of ensuring the safety of arrestees, the police manager ignores such standards at his or her peril. In the *Danese* case cited earlier, for example, the court noted that the Roseville, Michigan, city jail had failed to comply with state jail standards after a period of time and after notice. This led the court to agree that there existed a pattern of indifference supporting liability.[25]

Standards, model procedures, audit packages, and other helpful guidelines applicable to the management of police lockups have been promulgated by the American Jail Association, National Institute of Corrections, American Corrections Association's Commission on Accreditation for Corrections (CAC), Federal Bureau of Prisons, National Sheriffs' Association, Commission on Accreditation for Law Enforcement Agencies (CALEA), and National Commission on Correctional Health Care. Police administrators may use the standards to evaluate their lockup's current status and to develop recommendations relating to their continuing management of such facilities.

In 1973 the National Advisory Commission on Criminal Justice Standards and Goals addressed the management of the detention system by police. Its report recommended that the police divest themselves of corrections and detention facilities and maintain responsibility only for "those facilities necessary for short term processing of prisoners immediately following arrest."[26] The commission recommended that police departments operating such short-term facilities hire and train civilian personnel to perform the necessary functions. In addition, it urged departments to use state or county facilities so that arrestees can be transferred from (short-term) initial processing detention to (longer-term) arraignment detention.

When CALEA began its work, one of the first areas it targeted for standards development was the lockup. The initial standards, however, proved to be a significant financial burden for applicant agencies. Developed to parallel the standards set for local jails by the Commission on Accreditation for Corrections, the CALEA standards incorporated physical plant mandates as well as procedural requirements, and called for a physical plant condition superior to that existing in most lockups. Although these standards were professionally reasonable, they were an obstacle for a large number of agencies seeking accreditation.

Revised CALEA standards eliminating most of the standards pertaining to physical plant were published in 1987. Emphasis was placed, instead, on procedural, health, and safety matters. (The standards also indicate that all personnel assigned to holding facilities should receive training, with the type and level of training varying according to the nature of the assignment and the responsibilities attached to it.) A lockup that does not meet the current CALEA standards may pose significant health and safety threats not only to those detained but also to those working in the facility.

Personnel and training

Before activities are initiated to improve the lockup, both the police chief and other local government officials must be committed to making these changes. Most lockups will need, along with an increased budget, a commitment to place qualified and trained staff in the lockup. Raising the professional visibility of the arrestee management function will be an important first step in improving this operation. Employees should be made fully aware that the department is committed to operating a safe, secure, and clean lockup that preserves the constitutional rights of pretrial detainees and the safety of police personnel.

Staff members should have both a desire to be helpful and the wits to be careful. They must be trained to exhibit as little bias as possible, especially in matters that relate to race, ethnicity, gender, religion, and sexual orientation.

It is important to place the lockup management responsibility with one individual commander rather than with a series of watch commanders or sergeants. Clear accountability for lockup management will increase the likelihood that procedures will be followed and appropriate issues raised and resolved. In addition, responsibilities should be clearly assigned for searching, screening, observing, and monitoring arrestees.

No matter where the holding facility is located, the selection of a facility manager or managers and staff is crucial. Persons coming into custody have special physical and psychological needs. Physically, arrestees may have problems; in some localities, moreover, AIDS may be prevalent. Psychologically, the first few hours in custody are always the hardest and the period when most suicides occur. Physical and psychological factors such as drug withdrawal, alcohol- or drug-engendered hallucination, chronic illnesses that need attention, anger, severe depression, and other mental problems—all these can make detention facilities a management nightmare.

Not every employee is suited to these job responsibilities in such an environment. What is needed are employees who, although sensitive to the care that detainees may need, still have the judgment to recognize that many arrestees can be dangerous. Staff members should have both a desire to be helpful and the wits to be careful. They must be trained to exhibit as little bias as possible, especially in matters that relate to race, ethnicity, gender, religion, and sexual orientation. Most of all, it is helpful if personnel assigned to holding areas are tolerant by nature or by training. They must remember that it is for the judiciary and correctional staff, not for those responsible for pretrial custody, to determine and administer punishment. The job of a civilian or officer assigned to detention areas is to see to the care, custody, and control of arrestees.

Because of concern for arrestees and concern for organizational (and, in some cases for personal) liability for negligence or misconduct, the screening of detention personnel must be taken very seriously. Selection criteria must be based on the tasks to be performed. Any temptation to use the lockup assignment as a way of dealing with problem employees must be resisted.

Furthermore, staff should not work in the lockup if they do not know the procedures for screening arrestees, preserving the rights of pretrial detainees, and reacting to emergencies. Thus, if staff are normally rotated in and out of lockup assignment, such training should be provided to all personnel. This training can also serve to reaffirm the department's commitment to improved management of arrestees in the lockup.

The applicable standards of the Commission on Accreditation for Law Enforcement Agencies indicate the type of pre-service and in-service training that personnel assigned to holding facilities should receive. Among the topics that should be covered are the department's policies and procedures, processing of arrestees, use of tools for screening arrestees, rights of pretrial detainees, and emergency procedures (including emergency medical procedures and fire evacuation). CALEA standards also call for civilian staff who may work in the vicinity of the lockup or arrestee processing area to receive training.

Civilian lockup staff, New York City The New York City police department defines the duties of a civilian, nonsworn police attendant to include the following:

Searching prisoners

Lodging prisoners in cells and removing them from cells

Inspecting each cell for the well-being and security of prisoners

Attending to the personal needs of prisoners

Preparing such department forms as prisoner rosters, prisoner transfer sheets, and medical treatment statements

Making sure that the cleanliness of cells is maintained.

The total training time is 19 days; the areas covered include, among others, police science, law, self-defense, ethical awareness (responsibility, discrimination, ethical dilemmas, group cooperation, etc.), social science, and telephone techniques. In contrast, sworn recruits in the New York City correction department receive 35 days of training, and sworn recruits in the New York City police department receive 115 days of "vestibule" training.

Management of arrestees

Some holding facilities, or lockups, may have to hold detainees for substantial periods of time. Generally 72 hours or less is considered short term. Seventy-two hours may be required because the detainee is waiting to see a judge or to be transferred to a longer-term detention facility. Over weekends and holidays the period can extend to 120 hours. For this reason, lockup management may require attention to classification, medical care, physical facilities (including recreation and sanitation), security, fire safety, supervision of arrestees, the security of arrestees' property, food service, and other matters not usually a part of police concerns. Because such matters are routine in jails and prisons, much is already known to assist those who are planning for better management of holding facilities.[27] Written policies and procedures should cover all these areas and others.

Development of written policies and procedures

As part of its overall system of written directives, a police department that must manage a lockup should develop written policies and procedures for lockup management, incorporating the mandates of state or national standards and case law. Whether in the form of a general order, standard operating procedures, or a departmental directive, these written policies and procedures should cover

The legal basis for operating the lockup

The purpose of the lockup (short-term holding for detainees awaiting transport, holding of detainees for interrogation, holding of inebriants, and so forth)

Booking and/or processing requirements, if applicable

Screening and classification procedures

Emergency procedures (fire, medical, others as appropriate)

Procedures for visits by families, friends, attorneys

Food service, if provided

Security procedures and equipment, including key control

Periodic inspections, repairs, maintenance, and cleaning

Use of force

The handling of media inquiries and requests for interviews.

The CALEA standards provide a useful format in drafting such procedures, even if the agency is not seeking accreditation. Before completing the policies and procedures, the police manager may want to ask for a review by the department's legal advisor, its insurance carrier, representatives of the community's mental health services, emergency services coordinator, code enforcement personnel, budget personnel, and others whose assistance may be needed in implementing any procedures or in securing funds for implementation.

Screening and classifying arrestees

A system for routinely screening arrestees, no matter how general it is, can help a department defend against a claim that it is negligent, disregards the needs of injured, psychologically disturbed, or violent arrestees, or has failed to protect other detainees or police employees. The screening of arrestees who will be held in the lockup does not need to be lengthy or complicated. The procedure should include reviewing the arrestees' physical condition and recording cuts, scrapes, alertness, signs of intoxication, signs of drug abuse, pregnancy, and other readily observable conditions. A suitable screening form can be based on forms used by the local correctional facility and further refined through consultation with emergency medical personnel. The records of these screenings should be placed in the arrestee's file and forwarded to the local jail when he or she is transported there. To conform to relevant state laws, it is generally advisable to retain copies of screening records at the location of the lockup for future reference.

The department should consider incorporating psychological factors into the screening, again adapting approaches already in use. For example, when the arresting officer or the booking or lockup personnel note that an arrestee is hostile, violent, or unusually passive, they should include such observations in a written record. Officers bringing arrestees into the lockup should also be instructed to alert lockup staff to unusual behavior that occurred while the arrestee was in the officers' custody. (As discussed below, the department should ensure that a violent arrestee is not placed where he or she can victimize another arrestee.) Selection, training, and assignment of staff are critical in developing and implementing screening systems to keep predatory inmates from victimizing weak ones.

Use of force by staff—which, if it occurs at all, is especially likely at the initial stage of detainee processing, when the screening efforts are being made—must be documented, controlled, reported, investigated, audited, and managed. Each incident should be investigated by a superior officer, and serious cases should be investigated by command personnel from outside the lockup unit. Personnel who use force unnecessarily must be disciplined, retrained, or both. Written procedures must be developed that clearly define "force" and the circumstances under which it may be used. Clearly written, easily understood, workable operational guidelines specifying alternatives to the use of force must be developed.[28] Police assigned to lockup duty need the tools and skills to do their job, just as street officers do.

A good classification system identifies not only those who need special attention but also those who present threats to the orderly management of a facility.

The information obtained during screening should then form the basis for a decision about where the arrestee is to be held. In a facility with more than one holding cell or room, decisions about where to place high- or low-risk arrestees can be based on the need to monitor or observe detainees and, of course, on space availability. A good classification system identifies not only those who need special attention but also those who present threats to the orderly management of a facility. Contagious diseases and other health hazards must be recognized, and the weak and predatory should be separated. In other words, inmates must be separated in a logical (and legal) fashion so as to reduce risk to other inmates—and risks of escape. It is also necessary to separate by sex; and juveniles must be separated from adults.

Medical care

It is not enough, of course, merely to screen arrestees. Policies and procedures must be established to address what the lockup staff will do in the widely varied circumstances when an arrestee poses a physical, medical, or psychological risk. Departments should have in effect policies that prohibit bringing injured arrestees into a lockup before they receive medical attention. If an arrestee refuses medical attention, evidence from the medical center of such a refusal should accompany the arrestee and the arresting officer to the lockup.

The law enforcement agency should have a contract or a cooperative agreement with its local mental health service to provide emergency intervention when arrestees are judged to be at high risk psychologically. This intervention can take place in the lockup itself or at a local hospital or mental health center, whichever is appropriate and feasible.

Finally, the police manager should discuss with the officials who set bond or conditions of release the possibility of taking identified risk factors into account in their decisions. Procedures should be developed that allow the release of injured prisoners on bond or other conditional release, or the relocation of such high-risk individuals to the local jail as soon as possible.

Standards promulgated by the National Commission on Correctional Health Care may offer some useful guidelines for developing medical care programs. Procedures must be established for dealing with emergency medical situations. Written policies must exist for the delivery of medical, dental, and mental health services under the control of a designated health authority. At the very least, first aid kits must be available and easily accessible in the lockup facility, and staff must be trained in their use, as well as in basic first aid and CPR.

Physical facilities

The courts have repeatedly determined that holding prisoners in substandard conditions, where they do not have access to basic services, is unconstitutional. Substandard conditions are often associated with severe overcrowding, which compounds all service delivery difficulties and exacerbates all other management problems. Although courts are sympathetic to arguments about the costs of additional facilities, they have made it clear that the law does not permit any government to deprive its citizens of constitutional rights on a plea of poverty.

Courts have made it clear that the law does not permit any government to deprive its citizens of constitutional rights on a plea of poverty.

Detainees must be provided with toilets, wash basins, adequate air circulation, appropriate temperatures, access to telephones, access to drinking water, access to daily showers (depending on length of detention), and access to private interview space. If arrestees remain in a lockup for an extended period, other conditions may need to be addressed, such as noise levels and access to exercise facilities. Administrators should further provide for at least one sanitation inspection annually by local or state health officials; a written plan for controlling vermin; a written policy for the issuance of clean bedding; a written policy about possession of items for personal hygiene; and written plans for housekeeping and maintenance. In addition, at least weekly the department should conduct an inspection of the lockup to ensure that everything is in working order—toilets, sinks, locks, video monitors, and so forth. Such an inspection should include searches for contraband that may have found its way into the facility. Records should be kept documenting all inspections.

If the department identifies physical conditions that need to be corrected, the police chief should immediately ask that work be undertaken. If the requested changes are not made, the chief's liability will not be decreased, but at least in that case it might be shared with other units of local government as appropriate. Further, the department's annual budget submission to the local government should include provision for making improvements to the lockup facility over a five-year period. Such capital budgeting will help ensure that needed equipment and other physical improvements can be acquired.

Security

Security of inmates and personnel is essential. The department should conduct regular security inspections of the lockup. Such an inspection should assess the possibility of arrestee escapes, identify means of introducing contraband into the facility, and review the entire physical plant. The inspection should also flag any physical conditions that can contribute to arrestees injuring themselves. An overall "conditions" inspection should be completed at least annually.

The department also needs the following: routine, thorough searches for weapons and other contraband, regardless of the search done by the arresting officer; a lockup facility control center; a communications system; emergency alarms (personal alarms are especially useful); written procedures for door and key control; written policies for inmate movement; twenty-four-hour security posts for surveillance of inmates; weekly inspection of security facilities and devices; written procedures for counting detainees and searching; written procedures for storing chemicals and firearms and controlling all tools and utensils; a written hostage policy; and a comprehensive training program for selected staff in controlling disorders and using chemical agents.

To monitor arrestees (not only for security reasons but also to ensure their safety against other hazards), the department should consider installing, at a minimum, audio monitors; both audio and visual monitors would be preferable. Monitoring equipment should be used in such a way, of course, that attorney-client and other protected communications remain confidential. The presence of monitoring equipment can sometimes give staff a false sense of security, however, so the lockup supervisory staff must ensure that assigned staff view the monitors periodically. In any case, use of cameras and audio monitoring equipment should not eliminate periodic rounds by staff through the entire lockup to ascertain the condition of every arrestee. The lockup procedures should specify the intervals at which these checks are to be made and should provide for written documentation of the time, the name of the inspecting staff person, and any incidents or noteworthy condition of arrestees.

Although lockup security probably need not be as "hard" as security in a jail setting, the detainees are equally dangerous.

Security in the lockup area should ensure that arrestee escape is unlikely. In one local police lockup, security cameras clearly showed an arrestee escaping through the open vehicle sally-port. The arrestee (who was being held for questioning in a felony case) was apprehended after a few hours, but the incident resulted in some unpleasant attention from the news media. The camera had recorded more than a few breaches of procedure. Although lockup security probably need not be as "hard" as security in a jail setting, the detainees are equally dangerous. Therefore the security design and procedures at a lockup need serious attention by department management (see the chapter on equipment and facilities).

Other security issues that should be addressed include access by visitors and other nonpolice personnel; police weapons control; location of emergency equipment such as officer protection devices; and storage of caustic or flammable agents.

Safety procedures

A number of matters relating to fire and safety must be dealt with (the CALEA standards address many of these):

Independent documentation that the facility complies with applicable fire safety codes

Routine inspections by a qualified fire and safety officer

Written fire safety regulations

Automatic fire and smoke alarms, which are tested often

Materials and furniture with high fire safety performance

Power generators that are tested frequently

Regular fire and emergency drills

Written evacuation plan

Monthly testing of emergency equipment, and replacement as necessary.

All emergency plans must be in writing; and a primary and secondary release system must be in place for the prompt release of inmates from locked areas in an emergency.

Detainee rights and discipline

In the areas of detainee rights and discipline, there is a substantial body of knowledge with roots in statute, case law, and standards. Much of the knowledge was developed in the prison and jail settings, but it has considerable relevance to police lockups. Essentially, detainees must have access to courts, attorneys, medical care, and visits; the right to correspond with persons outside the institution; opportunities to exercise their religious freedoms; and protection from abuse—but all these rights are subject to limitations necessary to maintain order and security and subject, also, to length-of-detention considerations (see *Bell v. Wolfish*). In addition, insofar as jail overcrowding converts police lockups into pretrial detention facilities where inmates are held for more than a couple of days, written rules of inmate conduct must be established and must state the penalties that may be imposed for rule violations. Crimes committed by inmates while they are in custody (destruction of property, assault, and so forth) should result in arrest, and staff should be trained in pertinent procedures. All disciplinary hearings should result in written dispositions within clearly defined time frames (*Bell v. Wolfish*).

Records and arrestee property

Record management should ensure that all information necessary to process the arrestee is compiled in a timely fashion. All screening and other logs documenting activity within the lockup must be maintained according to procedure and stored securely. Misplaced arrestee property is a problem for most lockup managers. Thus, if arrestee property, including valuables, will remain in the lockup for any period of time, secure storage and receipts should be used. The insurer may be helpful in proposing ways to control losses. Secure property lockers, drop safes for money, and storage for seized evidence should be readily available to personnel assigned to lockups.

Food service

Although many lockups do not provide a full-scale food service, those that do must deal with several areas of concern:

A registered consulting dietitian should ensure compliance with nationally recommended food allowances.

Care should be taken to ensure that food is not withheld either as a result of indifference or as punishment.

Appropriate medical personnel should prescribe medically mandated diets.

Written policies should control religiously mandated diets and the preparation and review of all menus.

Written health and sanitation procedures should govern food preparation and service.

Frequent inspections should be conducted; to ensure disease prevention, the inspections should review, among other things, the temperatures of food storage areas and the condition of cooking appliances.

Most state standards for lockups incorporate these mandates. As with other issues presented here, assistance in implementing these procedures is generally available from the local correctional agency.

Divesting police departments of lockup responsibility

If a police department is managing a lockup, it should consider finding an appropriate agency to take over this function. Another facility such as a centralized booking facility may be used; or a booking capability may be designated or created within the local jail; or correctional personnel may manage the lockup while it remains physically in police department quarters.

If a police department is managing a lockup, it should consider finding an appropriate agency to take over this function.

However, legal considerations may make it difficult to shift responsibility for this function away from police departments. The police need to review their municipal and state laws and case law to determine their responsibilities for maintaining lockup facilities and should define the legal basis for this function. In some cases, the function of booking or processing prisoners has evolved into a detention role that has no legal basis. Or the desire to provide space to detain individuals during questioning or to hold public inebriants until they are sober may have grown into a lockup or quasi-lockup function. If the department determines that it wishes to divest itself of responsibility for lockup management, local or state legislation may be needed. The need for new legislative authority, however, should not be a strong deterrent to pursuing divestiture.

Another possible impediment to divesting the police of the lockup function may be the absence of an alternative facility. When a new police or local correctional facility is being planned, however, plans may also be made to move the booking and short-term detention facility. Or, at the site of the current facility, it may be possible to eliminate traditional constraints by modifying existing structures or using modular units or other new technology.

To facilitate the process of developing alternatives, the department should develop or update a detailed operational overview of the current facility (see also the chapter on equipment and facilities). This document can serve as a point of departure for local government managers, as the police executive begins to search for and negotiate with the appropriate agency to take over the lockup function.

Among the subjects that should be addressed in this document are the costs (in capital, personnel, and potential liability) associated with meeting state and national standards; staffing the facility properly; implementing policy changes; providing medical care and meals; training employees; ensuring the legal rights of detainees through access to phones, law libraries, their attorneys, and other resources; changing the physical plant; and adding security equipment (for example, cameras, noise sensors, "break-away" hooks, and appliances to deter would-be suicides).

The police chief may also wish to consider the regional implications of a centralized booking and processing facility. In a suburban or even a rural location, economies of scale may mean that a central facility presents the greatest potential for adequately and economically holding arrestees who come from the surrounding geographical area.

One perhaps unexpected resource at the police manager's disposal in preparing the documentation for divesting the department of the lockup is the department's insurance carrier. Insurance carriers, including the managers of self-insurance pools, are always eager to ensure that all appropriate steps are taken to reduce risk in police department operations.

An insurance review of the lockup may well confirm the police manager's contention that the lockup presents high risk. In addition, if the department must keep the lockup, recommendations from the insurance carrier can be used as the basis for a request to the local government for increased funds to correct deficiencies. The insurance carrier may also be in a position to recommend the level of training needed by staff, the availability to arrestees of prompt and qualified medical care, and means of improving fire safety and emergency planning in the lockup.

The chief, working with local criminal justice representatives, should ensure that every possible alternative to arrest is identified and, when possible, implemented.

With the assistance of the local government, the police chief should identify the agencies most appropriate to take over the lockup function and approach the directors of these agencies, if politically feasible. There may be alternatives to full divestiture. In some cases, arrangements have been made for correctional staff to replace police staff in lockups. In other cases, the police lockup has been closed, and prisoners have been taken directly to a facility specifically designed for the function. In still other cases, arrestees are detained in the police lockup only for a short time during which specifically designed transportation units "circle" the region picking up arrestees to be moved to the central facility.

Moreover, the chief, working with local criminal justice representatives, should ensure that every possible alternative to arrest is identified and, when possible (given other department objectives), implemented. Decreased use of police lockups will follow when public inebriants are appropriately diverted to a detoxification center; people are released on summons, when appropriate; and individuals are delivered, as needed, to emergency mental health services. Access to homeless shelters, battered spouse shelters, and similar community institutions will also decrease the need for holding those who need some care and attention but have no apparent resource other than the police.

Clearly, a divestiture effort requires planning that will call upon the resources, cooperation, and innovative ideas of all the involved criminal justice agencies.

The location where warrants or other legal documents are obtained and served on the arrestee will need study. (In this regard, the innovative use in some jurisdictions of closed circuit television, having prisoners "appear" before judges for arraignment without the necessity for time-consuming, expensive, and risky physical transportation, deserves consideration.)[29] The concerns of judges and prosecutors about divestiture will need to be identified. And if arrestees are to be moved from the custody of one entity to the custody of another, the record management function will need clarification.

Finally, the political reality of the situation must be addressed. It is naive to assume that police managers or other criminal justice officials will not be threatened by the removal of a function, even a troublesome one, from their agency. If possible, a strategy should be devised under which all agencies gain something by a change. This will require the trust and good faith of all involved.

It is naive to assume that police managers or other criminal justice officials will not be threatened by the removal of a function, even a troublesome one, from their agency.

When reviewing the obstacles to divesting police departments of lockups, one should also remember the three main advantages:

Legal (reducing potential police liability for arrestee injury; shifting to another agency the obligations to safeguard the rights of pretrial detainees)

Financial (avoiding the costs of meeting lockup standards, providing training, employing civilian detention aides, modifying physical plant, and so forth)

Managerial (redirecting police resources to meet the central missions of police—not diverting them to peripheral missions—in an era of tight budgets).

Police and local corrections

Most police, from line staff through management, tend to forget the local corrections function, or at least they take it for granted. Properly managed, local corrections is almost invisible; if not run correctly, the function is visible to the point of local embarrassment. But except when the police are working with the booking staff, arranging for lineups, or questioning inmates, they generally have few contacts with, little understanding of, and little appreciation for local corrections.

The plight of local corrections, and corrections in general, must be a prime concern of law enforcement. Overcrowding of facilities affects the ability of law enforcement to deal with crime in the community, especially if police operations lead to many arrests. Courts are intervening in local corrections and establishing population caps for some institutions, and in these situations, the jail administrator has no choice but to turn away police officers who come with "fresh" arrests.

In some local governments this has necessitated enlarging lockups or creating lockups from squad rooms, locker rooms, or offices. Some police officers may even have to keep arrestees in their vehicles until a space opens at the local jail.

Whereas the police are often frustrated with the inability of local corrections to "find room" for arrestees, correctional administrators are frustrated that the police have not included them in the planning of police operations designed to maintain public safety. Police procedures should require that, consistent with the need for confidentiality in many police operations, local correctional agencies be notified before major operations that may result in a larger than usual number of arrestees (operations such as mass arrests of violent demonstrators or drug abusers). If a police department will be serving warrants, the agency that must process or house prisoners should be notified at an appropriate time. In addition, police and corrections agencies should make joint contingency plans for addressing natural disasters, fires, riots, and other occurrences that will require collaboration.

The relationships between managers of police and local adult corrections agencies often are at a level not conducive to productive policy discussions. Each agency is faced with increasing demands for services, usually with no increased funding. This atmosphere prompts insular policy development and, at times, the placing of blame. In the scramble for local budget dollars and public goodwill, both sides often lose sight of the advantages of cooperation, such as increased flow of intelligence from incarcerated prisoners through corrections staff to police.

In the scramble for local budget dollars and public goodwill, both sides often lose sight of the advantages of cooperation.

Police managers and correctional managers at the local level must establish and maintain the kinds of relationships that will help both parties obtain the necessary resources and reach their goals. In most instances, local criminal justice coordinating councils or other less formal groups meet to discuss issues of concern to all elements of the local criminal justice system. If no means of formal communications exists, the police chief can provide the necessary leadership to establish suitable linkages.

Conclusion

The topics and concerns outlined in this chapter will be carefully examined by any court whose attention in an action is directed to the conditions at a facility. Currently the legal standards employed by the federal courts in evaluating the actions of administrators seem to concern the needs for security, order, and discipline more than the standards used in the 1970s did. Despite demonstrated judicial interest, however, serious vulnerability to suits in these areas persists. Another important problem area is the distinction between pretrial detainees and convicted persons. Although this distinction has become less important in terms of suits in the federal courts, many state and local minimum standards for facility operations continue to draw important distinctions between detention before trial and after conviction.

The most effective way for law enforcement personnel to ensure the adequacy of their short-term holding operations is to draw on the expertise of corrections professionals.

The management of any detention or holding facility must incorporate a comprehensive and detailed array of policies, procedures, standards, training, and evaluations of operations. The most effective way for law enforcement personnel to ensure the adequacy of their short-term holding operations is to draw on the expertise of corrections professionals, who already know a great deal about how to operate holding facilities, and the resources cited in this chapter. Resources are available on request from the closest local, state, or federal agency concerned with setting or enforcing standards for detention and from the U.S. Department of Justice.

Police resources should be devoted to law enforcement and community efforts that will reduce crime and increase public safety. When the police operate a lockup, the activity is secondary; thus it traditionally does not receive necessary resources, and both arrestees and police personnel are at risk in ways that this chapter has documented. Whenever possible, management of lockups should be assigned to the appropriate corrections agency in the jurisdiction. There are many models of consolidated regional booking facilities that can help adjoining police departments to divest themselves of lockup responsibilities.

Whether or not police retain responsibility for running lockups, legislative and political obstacles must be overcome if a locality is to develop an arrestee management and detention system that will meet the constitutional and legal rights of arrestees, put police fiscal and other resources to proper use, and provide a safe and secure environment for all involved.

1   Richard G. Zevitz and Susan R. Takata, "Death in Cellblocks: A Study of Inmate Mortality in Jail and Lockup Custody," paper presented at the American Society of Criminology conference, Montreal, 14 November 1987.
2   Lindsay Hayes, "And Darkness Closes In . . . A National Study of Jail Suicides," *Journal of Criminal Justice and Behavior* (1983):461–84.
3   Lindsay Hayes and Joseph Rowan, *National Study of Jail Suicides: Seven Years Later* (Alexandria, VA: National Center for Institutions and Alternatives, 1988).
4   Zevitz and Takata, "Death in Cellblocks."
5   *Bell v. Wolfish*, 441 U.S. 520 (1979).
6   *Colburn v. Upper Darby Township*, 838 F.2d 663 (3rd Cir. 1988).
7   *Davidson v. Cannon*, 474 U.S. 344 (1986). Although the court concluded in *Davidson* that prison officials are required under the due process clause of the Fourteenth Amendment to provide detainees with personal security from other arrestees, the court also held that prison officials would be found to have violated a prisoner's due process rights only if the officials' actions were "deliberate" or "callous[ly] indifferent" to a prisoner's rights. In contrast, when a prison official is merely negligent in allowing another inmate to injure a detainee, no procedure for compensation is constitutionally required (*Davidson*, 474 U.S. at 348–49). In short, the protections of the Fourteenth Amendment, whether procedural or substantive, are not triggered by the negligence of a corrections official who failed to protect a detainee from an attack by another inmate.
8   *Colburn v. Upper Darby Township*; dicta in *Anderson v. City of Atlanta*, 778 F.2d 678, 686 n. 12 (11th Cir. 1985).
9   *Colburn v. Upper Darby Township*, 838 F.2d 663 (3rd Cir. 1988); *Roberts v. City of Troy*, 773 F.2d 720 (6th Cir. 1985); *Madden v. City of Meriden*, 602 F.Supp. 1160 (Dist. Conn. 1985).
10 *Bell v. Wolfish*, 441 U.S. 520 (1979).
11 *Partridge v. Two Unknown Police Officers of City of Houston*, 791 F.2d 1182 (5th Cir. 1986).
12 *Partridge v. Two Unknown Police Officers of City of Houston*.
13 *Danese v. Asman*, 670 F.Supp. 709 (E.D. Mich. 1987), overruled on other grounds, *Danese v. Asman*, 875 F.2d 1239 (6th Cir. 1989), cert. denied,—U.S.—, 110 S.Ct. 1473 (1990).

14 *Bell v. Wolfish*, 441 U.S. 520 (1979).
15 Ibid. at 538.
16 *Roberts v. City of Troy*, 773 F.2d 720 (6th Cir. 1985).
17 *Danese v. Asman*, 670 F.Supp. 709 (E.D. Mich. 1987), overruled on other grounds, *Danese v. Asman*, 875 F.2d 1239 (6th Cir. 1989), cert. denied,—U.S.—, 110 S.Ct. 1473 (1990).
18 *Partridge v. Two Unknown Police Officers of the City of Houston*, 791 F.2d 1182 (5th Cir. 1986).
19 *DeBow v. City of East Saint Louis*, 510 N.E. 2d 1985 (Ill. App. 1987).
20 42 U.S.C. sec. 1983: "Every person who, under color of any statute, ordinance, regulation, custom, or usage, of any State or Territory or the District of Columbia, subjects, or causes to be subjected, any citizen of the United States or other person within the jurisdiction thereof to the deprivation of any rights, privileges, or immunities secured by the Constitution and laws, shall be liable to the party injured in an action at law, suit in equity, or other proper proceeding of redress."
21 *Nishiyama v. Dickson County, TN* (814 F.2d 277 [6th Cir. 1987]).
22 *Matje v. Leis* (571 F.Supp. 918 [S.D. Ohio 1983]).
23 *Doe v. New York City Department of Social Services* (649 F.2d 134 [2nd Cir. 1981]).
24 *Monell v. New York City Department of Social Services* (436 U.S. 658 [1978]).
25 See also *Strandell v. Jackson County, IL*, 634 F.Supp. 824 (S.D. Ill. 1986); and *Lightbody v. Town of Hampton*, 618 F.Supp. 6 (Dist. N.H. 1984).
26 National Advisory Commission on Criminal Justice Standards and Goals, *Police* (Washington, DC: US Government Printing Office, 1973), 313.
27 The various national institutes and associations noted earlier are excellent clearinghouses for current information and standards on jail management.
28 See William A. Geller and Michael S. Scott, *Deadly Force: What We Know—A Practitioner's Desk Reference on Police-Involved Shootings* (Washington, DC: Police Executive Research Forum, 1991).
29 See William A. Geller, *Videotaping Police Interrogations and Confessions: A Review of the International Literature*, an interim report to the National Institute of Justice (Washington, DC: Police Executive Research Forum, 1989).

Part six:
Continuity
in times
of change

19 Practical ideals for managing in the nineties: a perspective

No man is good enough to govern another man without that other's consent. I say this is the leading principle—the sheet anchor of American republicanism.
Abraham Lincoln[1]

What the Golden Rule seeks to convey is not that society is composed of a network of explicit bargains, but that it is held together by a pervasive bond of reciprocity.
Lon F. Fuller[2]

The philosophic expression of noble ideals and the application of those ideals to the most mundane and commonplace circumstances need to be understood by police managers. This chapter tries to show the intimate connection between the nation's constitutional foundations and the daily work of police. The genius of these foundations is the latitude they allow public servants in conscientiously fulfilling their duty. Thus, although there are no simple formulas, every generation of leaders need not reinvent the wheel.

When the Founders framed the Constitution of the United States, when they forged a constitutional republic as an experiment in ordered liberty, in fact they provided the foundation for the finest ideals and principles of modern policing. The Constitution, which took effect on June 21, 1788, together with the Bill of Rights, adopted December 15, 1791, provided a fresh roadmap for government leaders of the 1790s. That roadmap remains one of the fundamental tools available to police and other government leaders of the 1990s who are striving to blaze trails that will draw their agencies to the highest ideals of public service, even while the prevalence of crime, corruption, and other social and moral ills are tempting police to become cynical and to question or reject these ideals. Ideals and constitutional principles *can* be incorporated into both departmental policies and departmental practice.

The constitutional heritage and modern policing

The Preamble to the Constitution reads:

We the People of the United States, in Order to form a more perfect Union, establish Justice, insure domestic Tranquility, provide for the common defence, promote the general Welfare, and secure the Blessings of Liberty to ourselves and our Posterity, do ordain and establish this Constitution for the United States of America.

The most striking word in the Preamble is its first one: *We*. It is the people who "do ordain and establish this Constitution." It is the citizens who established a country governed and unified by laws, a country in which the laws apply to all, irrespective of station or office. The United States became a nation, constituted itself as a country, on the basis of these words and on the basis of a trust that men and women would honor these words in the future.

Implicit in the Constitution are two basic principles that flow from that first word. First, citizens must do much for themselves in their own daily behavior

---

The law applies to all In *Federalist No. 57*, James Madison emphasized that the uniform application of law to the governed and to appointed and elected officials alike "has always been deemed one of the strongest bonds by which human policy can connect the rulers and the people together. It creates between them that communion of interests and sympathy of sentiments . . . without which every government degenerates into tyranny."

Source: Alexander Hamilton, James Madison, and John Jay, *The Federalist Papers*, intro. Clinton Rossiter (New York: Mentor Books, 1961), No. 57.

---

and in educating the young. No police force can uphold or maintain justice, domestic tranquility, and general welfare if the public is determined to destroy them or lacks the courage to stand up for them.

Second, those who govern and those who are governed have to be joined in the common purpose of securing the blessings of liberty, and the law applies equally to both. The U.S. heritage denies that the relationship between governors and governed is adversarial—"us against them." The purpose of government is to serve the public good, and those who govern are expected to honor the trust of the public by serving faithfully. Thus, governors are called "public servants." The men and women who govern are citizens, too, and their interests are joined with those of the general population.

Every time a police officer interacts with citizens, every time a police leader establishes departmental policy, every time police officials make decisions about the judicious allocation of resources and personnel, every time a department reviews standards for recruitment and performance, those two basic principles should be kept in mind: citizens themselves share the responsibility for upholding constitutional ideals, and those with public authority are bound to serve the public good. These two principles provide the context for the not yet fully articulated police mission—to preserve ordered liberty. That police seek *ordered* liberty means that they try to respect the freedom of each person as much as is consistent with justice for every other person.

Police-community collaboration

Basic constitutional principles mean that the police and the community collaborate in the public interest. For when police and the citizenry work together for the common good, then schools, businesses, and the institutions of government can pursue their rightful purposes; the law-abiding can be protected and assisted when in need; and police have a chance of reducing criminal activities that threaten the innocent. Achieving domestic tranquility and securing the blessings of liberty then become realistic goals. Indeed, just as local government ideals and priorities guide police decision making, police dedication to the public welfare can have a ripple effect on other aspects of local government service.

Police dedication to the public welfare, reflecting basic constitutional principles, can have a powerful influence in shaping local definitions of the police mission—and in guiding police strategic and programmatic choices.

Police dedication to the public welfare, reflecting basic constitutional principles, can have a powerful influence in shaping local definitions of the police mission—and in guiding police strategic and programmatic choices. The shared purposes of our country as identified in the Constitution's Preamble—especially establishing justice, ensuring domestic tranquility, and promoting the general welfare—all figure prominently in the daily work of police, as four examples illustrate: (1) fear reduction programs; (2) traffic management decisions; (3) community decision making; and (4) drug abuse education.

Fear reduction programs The Citizen Oriented Police Enforcement (COPE) program in Baltimore County, Maryland, grew from recognition that the quality of people's lives is not only threatened but seriously impaired when they live in fear. When fear increases in neighborhoods, people do not leave their homes unguarded; and elderly people are afraid to go shopping, afraid to go to church, and unable to lead normal lives. Government, then, clearly falls short in its obligation to "ensure domestic tranquility."

A police department cannot allocate its resources to reduce fear—and the causes of fear—unless it becomes sufficiently involved with and concerned about the people to learn what they are afraid of.

But a police department cannot allocate its resources to reduce fear—and the causes of fear—unless it becomes sufficiently involved with and concerned about the people to learn what they are afraid of. Without such knowledge, the department may, for example, suppose that if it reduces the number of burglaries, fear will inevitably drop.

Surely, the reduction in number of burglaries matters, but one of the key contributions of COPE was to keep the police from making presuppositions about what types of problems generated the most fear among the community. As COPE unit officers asked the citizens about their fears, they discovered, sometimes to their surprise, that what produced the most fear among people was vandals on the streets, youths fighting at bus stops, tall hedges where assailants might lurk, poorly lit sidewalks, and traffic lights that changed too quickly for older people to get safely across the street.

By learning about the actual fears of the people, by having bus stops policed and hedges trimmed, and by showing citizens how to organize and petition their government, COPE reduced fear by reducing its causes. Rather than attempting to convince residents that their fears were misplaced or that change was impossible, officers respected citizen concerns, used specialized knowledge to help the community assess risks and gauge the appropriateness and efficacy of countermeasures, and worked jointly with the community to accomplish agreed-upon objectives. By taking cooperative steps to learn what they needed to know in order to achieve their mission, by trying to see things from the point of view of the people experiencing the problems, police were able to concentrate scarce resources at the "point of discontent" and, in the judgment of the community, improved the lives of the citizens.

As shown throughout this book, police agencies from coast to coast increasingly understand and act upon the insight that the way relationships among police and the public are structured and the way powers and responsibility are shared are crucially important for the success of the police mission.[3] A spirit of reciprocity makes a difference.

Traffic management decisions At first blush, the idea that asking fundamental questions about democracy can help guide traffic enforcement tactics may sound odd. Yet more people have first-hand contact with the police—and form impressions of them that may well influence public attitudes toward collaborations for public safety—in traffic-related matters than in any other circumstances. What do constitutional ideals have to do with traffic enforcement? Consider two persistent problems—speeding, and illegal parking at special events.

Where should the police set up speed checkpoints? In locations most convenient to the police—locations where police can most easily catch the largest number of speeders and write the most tickets? Or in locations where there have been accidents or complaints from the public and where speeding is clearly hazardous? If police operate from the premise that the purpose of traffic laws is to foster safety and efficiency in travel—in other words, if the purpose of traffic laws is to serve the public interest—the answer becomes clear.

Similar questions may be asked about how the police should use their traffic management energies in connection with special events that cause serious parking congestion—holy day services at churches, grand openings of stores, and so forth. Should the police ticket the numerous illegal parkers as an answer to the problem? If police operate from the premise that they and the community are not adversaries, they will try to find out how they can help the community hold its special event, help get people in and out of the area safely, and help find places for the cars to park that do not obstruct essential access points. If a parking violation truly presents a hazard, should the police issue a ticket and move on? Police who are working with citizens for the public good might make an announcement, if feasible, that the car is presenting a danger and ask that it be promptly moved, before deciding whether to issue a summons and, if need be, tow the car.

Community decision making Another application of the principle of working with citizens for the public good was demonstrated in a medium-sized U.S. community when a group of citizens sought city approval to establish a summertime farmers' market on a busy downtown street. Doing so would mean closing the street to vehicular traffic one day per week.

The mayor convened representatives from each of the municipal departments and asked for their opinions. The traffic engineering bureau said the presence of the market and the closing of the street would play havoc with traffic. The police commander for the affected area said he didn't have enough personnel to assign people to the market every Thursday. The sanitation department said it could not clean up—it had enough to do already. The litany of obstacles went on and on.

Following a long discussion, the mayor noted the police chief's uncharacteristic silence and asked him what he thought of the request. The chief replied that he had been sitting there musing about the purpose of the government. "That purpose," he said, "is to help people do what they want to do as long as it doesn't disrupt the common good and order."

"Well, that's true," replied the mayor.

The chief continued, "Let me ask some key questions. Do the business proprietors in this area object to this farmers' market coming in?" The answer was no. "Does anyone on the block that will be closed object?" The answer was that only one person objected to it. "Whose farmers are they?" It was established that 80 percent of the people who would sell their produce were farmers from the county in which the community was located.

After receiving these answers, the chief said, "I'm hearing that our people want the market, that they're going to get good produce at a cheaper price, and that virtually no one is objecting to it except the city government. What we should be doing here is not telling ourselves why this cannot be done but asking how we can help to make it possible. Once we put it in place, observe it. If it's disruptive, we can change it. But the main thing is, we should try to cooperate with what the people want."

The farmers' market became a reality and a success. The farmers clean up after themselves, traffic problems are nonexistent, community residents regularly come there to shop, and no complaints of any kind have been made about the market.

Sometimes, obviously, the desires of the public cannot be met with the police resources available, and greater resources cannot be secured. But this fact of life does not justify summarily dismissing proposals without considering them.

Drug abuse education   Still another police initiative based on the principle that police and the citizenry must collaborate in pursuit of public safety is the Drug Abuse Resistance Education (DARE) program. It was conceived by the Los Angeles police department and has been rapidly replicated by over two thousand departments in forty-nine states. (See also the discussions of DARE in the chapters on crime prevention and local drug control.)

DARE was designed in the belief that drug consumption and dependency corrode the quality of life in a society, destroying society's will and capacity for self-governance. With a pervasive problem like narcotics consumption and dependency, it is obvious that comprehensive programs must be mounted. Enforcement of the law is only one facet of the effort. For any measure to be effective, law enforcement must be combined with prevention, education, and treatment. For their part, police involved in drug education need to learn how they can be most helpful, especially with youths in high-crime areas; and they need to know the state of treatment research and the availability of treatment in their area.

Many DARE programs reflect the fact that police are listening to the students who say they do not want to hear only from former addicts and users whose lives have been largely destroyed by drugs. They want to hear from winners, not just losers. They want to meet people who have never used drugs and whose lives are happy and successful, to learn how they resisted peer pressure to get into drugs. In short, many youngsters are responding to the counsel "Just say no" with the correct question, "To what shall we say yes?"

Police understanding of what students need to know is as fundamental to effective DARE programs as police knowledge of citizens' fears was to the success of COPE. Understanding is not enough, of course. DARE programs depend on the willingness of police departments to assign officers to work with students. If for financial reasons the department seems unable to assign officers to such work, the chief should carefully reexamine the possibility of reallocating existing resources. Such willingness to explore alternative means hinges on a public-service–oriented conception of the police mission as well as the desire to mount an informed offensive against drugs.

This offensive may include educating the media so they understand that policing is more than law enforcement and that the demand side of narcotics consumption was never controllable by crime fighting alone.

Governing the governors

Policing as a profession should take care to remember one other underlying aspect of constitutional government—the obligation of the governors to govern *themselves*—and should hold before itself the words James Madison wrote in *Federalist* No. 55 to encourage his compatriots to ratify the Constitution:

What is government itself, but the greatest of all reflections on human nature? If men were angels, no government would be necessary. If angels were to govern men, neither external nor internal controls on government would be necessary. In framing a government which is to be administered by men over men, the great difficulty lies in this: you must first enable the government to control the governed; and in the next place oblige it to control itself.[4]

The Founders of the United States believed that public institutions and public servants could aspire to fulfill demanding missions for the public good and that they could exercise self-control—observe limits—in the process. The Founders knew, of course, that "power tends to corrupt, and absolute power corrupts absolutely,"[5] and so they established a form of government intended to prevent absolute power. But they did not believe that high purposes and deeply worthwhile ideals were beyond the abiding aspiration, or even beyond the reach, of human beings. Thus, the documents that established the fledgling U.S. government were based on enormous trust—trust that people in a democracy would choose able leaders and that those leaders would govern responsibly.

Policing as a profession should take care to remember one underlying aspect of constitutional government—the obligation of the governors to govern *themselves*.

Recognizing that such trust would always be essential, and understanding human beings as he did, Madison wrote in *Federalist* No. 57:

The aim of every political constitution is, or ought to be, first to obtain for rulers men who possess most wisdom to discern, and most virtue to pursue, the common good of the society; and in the next place, to take the most effectual precautions for keeping them virtuous whilst they continue to hold their public trust.[6]

As Madison saw, the most fundamental questions about values for public servants to ask themselves and their institutions are, first, "Am I trying to be the kind of person who has the wisdom to discern the common public good and the virtue to pursue it?" Second, "Are my colleagues and I taking effective precautions in our institution to secure the kinds of accountability that bring out the best in people and to minimize the effects of what is worst in them?"

Police executives who consider such questions seriously are in the vanguard of the growing movement toward "values-driven" police departments. They are drawing policing to higher standards of professional service by basing institutional policies and practices on clearly articulated and deeply believed ideals and principles as to who the police are and what they stand for, individually and institutionally.

The temptation to cynicism

It is commonplace for people to claim that life is more difficult and more complicated than ever before. We face more crises, it is said, more issues and dilemmas; children face more perplexities in choosing "life-styles"; we are beset by more terrifying problems of technology, more tribulations caused by rapid change. Given these realities, it is said, ideals are difficult if not impossible to uphold.

Police perform their duties for a public whose own behavior leaves much to be desired.

On reflection, however, it is clear that this view is shortsighted. Nobody today has difficulties any greater than those faced by Socrates, or Thomas More, or Horace Mann, or Robert E. Lee, or Abraham Lincoln, or Frederick Douglass, or Anne Frank, or Harry Truman, or Sojourner Truth, or Golda Meir.

It is true that every segment of the public contains predators, but this has always been the case, in every society. It is also true that many of our citizens fall short in character or judgment. There is nothing new about this either. Even so, it can be demoralizing for police officers and their chiefs to attempt to live up to the expectations set by the Constitution in the face of what they perceive as corruption and hypocrisy throughout the communities they serve. Police perform their duties for a public whose own behavior leaves much to be desired. Police often note that the country is faced with private-sector money launderers, inside traders, industrial polluters, and remorseless criminals. They point to self-centered and self-righteous individuals and groups who apparently will go to any lengths to gain their ends on abortion, nuclear policy, or other issues. They point to individuals and groups who act from suspicion or hatred of racial or ethnic groups.

Frequently it seems that the professionalism of police, attorneys, judges, and others has to be sustained even despite politicians who betray the public trust— that honorable public servants are left to contend with disruptive turf battles among elected and appointed officials whose ambitions may seem remarkably shallow.

Similarly, the police often find that they do their work under the scrutiny of video, audio, and print media whose commentators misrepresent what they do.

Finally, many police are dismayed that a portion of the public supports the decriminalization of drugs at a time when the rest of society is mounting a full-scale attack on the consumption and sale of illegal drugs. In short, our times offer a picture that is not altogether appealing.

But again, this is not new. In 1776 John Adams wrote to a friend that there was "so much rascality, so much venality and corruption, so much avarice and ambition [among men] *even* in America [that there might not be] virtue enough to support a republic."[7]

Conversely, the driving aspiration to excellence has historical roots as well. About 2,400 years ago, the Greek philosopher Socrates observed that nothing is so good for the soul as discussing human excellence every day. Between 46 and 43 B.C., the Roman statesman Cicero wrote, "The chief thing in all public administration and public service is to avoid even the slightest suspicion of self-seeking." He added "[N]othing is more commendable, nothing more becoming in a pre-eminently great man than courtesy and forbearance. Indeed, in a free people, where all enjoy equal rights before the law, we must school ourselves to affability and what is called 'mental poise.'"[8] He meant that good leadership requires generosity, self-control, and restraint, as well as unimpeachable integrity.

The articulation of ideals applies both to the individual police officer and to the department itself.

Similarly, in 1813 Thomas Jefferson wrote to John Adams about human excellence:

I agree with you that there is a natural aristocracy among men. The grounds of this are virtue and talents. . . . There is also an artificial aristocracy, founded on wealth and birth, without either virtue or talents. . . . The natural aristocracy I consider the most precious gift of nature for the instruction, the trust, and government of society.[9]

Leaders in our own century have also aspired to excellence, in policing and elsewhere. In 1931, August Vollmer wrote in the Wickersham Commission's *Report on Lawlessness in Law Enforcement* of the ways in which police must behave to earn the esteem of the public. O. W. Wilson drafted the "Square Deal Code" of Wichita, Kansas, that has since been adopted as a code of ethics by the IACP and many police departments. As that code shows, the articulation of ideals applies both to the individual police officer and to the department itself.

Others in policing have been and are currently concerned to achieve the highest levels of public service.

Principled men and women engage in work that is worth doing and dedicate themselves to excellence in public and private life.

The frailties and strengths of human beings, and the human condition itself, do not change fundamentally over the centuries. This is why it remains true, now as always, that principled men and women engage in work that is worth doing and dedicate themselves to excellence in public and private life. These people and the institutions they work in embody and articulate the ideals for which they stand.

From words to actions

By reflecting on their own behavior and asking pointed questions, individuals and institutions learn to identify ideals of human conduct and performance that deserve to be respected and cherished above all others. What principles and ideals matter so much that they are beyond compromise? What basic convictions must we hold dear so that we as individuals are worthy of self-respect—and so that we and our institutions are worthy of public confidence?

Many police executives and their colleagues are addressing such age-old questions forthrightly, and as a result the ideals their departments stand for and intend to live up to are usually framed in terms that have a long tradition of human dedication behind them.

Many police departments express allegiance to high ideals by appealing to the best in their personnel. Certainly, many people want to spend their lives doing things that are worthwhile. Most police officers want their efforts to help achieve things that deserve to be admired and even honored. From this it follows that human institutions need to be designed to provide opportunities for their members to do worthwhile work, and to do it in a climate of regard for individuals, their seriousness of purpose, and their highest aspirations.

Properly articulated departmental ideals, and the policies and practices that flow from them, affirm fundamental constitutional and moral values.

Thus, in articulating values or ideals and principles, police departments normally emphasize personal and institutional commitment to the following:

The highest ethical standards

The highest standards of integrity

The achievement of personal and professional excellence

The value of human life

The dignity of all individuals

The just, consistent, and equitable exercise of police powers and discretion

The accountability of all departmental personnel

The authority of law and the constitutional principles of the United States.

It is easy to put such noble words on paper. It is more difficult to explain and to teach in a department what they mean. It is an enduring challenge to give them vitality, to *embody them* in the public and private behavior of leaders and in the implementation of departmental policies, regulations, priorities, and practices that are faithful to the words on paper.

Properly articulated departmental ideals, and the policies and practices that flow from them, affirm fundamental constitutional and moral values. They instruct personnel about departmental expectations in both simple and complex matters. And they help to deter avoidable misconduct and avoidable ignorance of departmental expectations. But what does all this mean in practice?

Respect for human dignity

Suppose a police department commits itself to respect for the dignity of all individuals. What is it promising? To say that human beings have dignity is to say that they have worth, they are important, they matter, they deserve to be treated in particular ways *just because they are human beings*. Human beings should always be treated as valuable in themselves and not merely as a means to the achievement of someone else's desires or ambitions. Persons should not be treated as objects.

In practice, to respect the dignity of human beings is to believe that, all other things being equal, people ought to be allowed to live their lives by their own lights. This is to acknowledge that they should make decisions for themselves about how to conduct their lives; they should be free to establish their own principles of thought and action, to be masters of their own fate. This means that in our dealings with them we should, whenever possible, use reason and persuasion rather than coercion. We should also listen to what they think; being reasonable, after all, is a two-way street.

Ideals should be articulated through deliberation and communication within the department.

Obviously, when people abuse their freedom of choice and action by obstructing the freedom and well-being of others, it is appropriate, and often obligatory, to stop them—by persuasion or coercion in one form or another. Yet even when we interfere with the freedom of others, respecting their dignity means using no more coercion than is necessary to prevent their wrongdoing.

Respect for dignity is incompatible with needless confrontation, excessive force, or discrimination. So, too, individual dignity is slighted by departmental practices that spurn opportunities for the public and for departmental personnel to exercise judgment in conducting their affairs.

High ideals in themselves are not enough: they must be applied in complex cases in real and complex circumstances.

The implication for departmental strategy and policy is that this ideal (and all the other ones) should be articulated through deliberation and communication within the department. In addition, the judgment of the community about its needs and priorities should be sought and encouraged. Then both the police and the public should be told—and shown—in daily actions and in policies for training and supervision, treatment of complainants, discipline, discretion, use of force, and recruitment *what* the department means by respect for dignity and *that* it truly means what it says.

These are not very complicated matters. Respecting dignity means simple things like not being rude to colleagues, applicants, or complainants; listening carefully to what they are trying to say; having the humility to believe that what others are trying to say might be instructive. It means overcoming every temptation to be a bully, a bigot, or a tyrant.

That these basics of respect for people's dignity are uncomplicated does not mean, surely, that it is always easy to live up to high standards or always simple to decide how to apply fundamental principles. When citizens are invited to cooperate with police, some of them may behave rudely in public forums and monopolize time available for discussion. Finding ways to limit their disruption calls for imagination, patience, and decisiveness. Likewise, it is often difficult to decide—under pressure of the need for immediate action—just how much force is required to subdue a suspect. Making such decisions is not an exact science, and even principled people of good judgment cannot always reach answers that, on reflection, they find entirely satisfactory. What this shows is that high ideals in themselves are not enough: they must be applied in complex cases in real and complex circumstances.

High standards of integrity

Similar examples can be given for a department that expresses its commitment to the highest standards of integrity. Integrity means wholeness, being one person in both public and private, living up to high standards of decency even when no one else is watching. It is made up of habits of justice, temperance, courage, compassion, and honesty.

To stand for integrity, then, means calling on ourselves to do our best at all times in all circumstances, to become competent and trustworthy in action and judgment—whether as friends or as neighbors, parents, professionals, public servants, or in any other dimension of our lives—because we believe that it is beneath us to do anything less.

Integrity is inseparable from respect for justice, and respect for justice means treating everyone fairly. Thus our highest ideals are inevitably interwoven, and it is this fabric of sound choices and trustworthy judgment and behavior that underlies a department's dedication to personal and professional excellence.

Here, too, the implications for police leaders and departmental policies can be outlined. To stand for integrity means not compromising the well-being of the public or the department in response to the winds of political fashion. It means not placing individual career advancement ahead of the police mission, not behaving one way in front of the media and another way behind their backs. It means telling the truth, insofar as respect for confidentiality permits, and working conscientiously to discover the truth in all affairs of the department. Easy to say and not always easy to do, but if our actions belie our words, then our colleagues and subordinates will treat our noblest words as mere platitudes—powerless to inspire, at best trivial and at worst a contemptible lie.

Our highest ideals are inevitably interwoven, and it is this fabric of sound choices and trustworthy judgment and behavior that underlies a department's dedication to personal and professional excellence.

Integrity is far more than the absence of corruption. Yet too often well-meaning reformers inside and outside policing treat integrity as a vacuum—an absence of graft. Such confusion focuses remedial efforts on minimal standards of performance rather than on excellence, and it badly shortchanges police personnel and the public that relies on their best efforts. (See also the chapter on fostering integrity.)

The meaning of other ideals—for example, the value of human life; the just, consistent, and equitable exercise of discretion; and the authority of law and constitutional principles—can be inferred from what has already been said about dignity, integrity, and the nation's constitutional heritage. But a bit more explanation may be appropriate concerning respect for law and the accountability of all departmental personnel.

The authority of law

On the subject of lawfulness among the police, departments should emphasize that public service places no one above the law and that a department that respects the law will oppose (for example) not issuing traffic citations to police out of "professional courtesy" as surely as it will oppose police brutality, discriminatory hiring, falsified reports, and perjured testimony. The last of these—perjury—provides a good set of examples for explaining a department's respect for law.

Law enforcement personnel sometimes ask whether it is right to falsify reports and commit perjury in order to convict a guilty, known criminal when the admissible evidence to convict is lacking. The answer is that perjury is *always* wrong. It is not only illegal but also a betrayal of all oaths of public office and a betrayal of oneself.

That this question is occasionally raised suggests that some people consider the Constitution to be mere advice rather than the fundamental law of the land and believe law to be not binding on those who serve good causes. These people seem not to understand that those who are sworn to defend the Constitution and the law are, above all others, in a position to harm and even to destroy the Constitution and the law.

Many criminal justice personnel have betrayed the public, destroyed their careers, and devastated their families by persuading themselves that serving a good cause is a license to go beyond the law.

Police oaths of office and oaths to give honest and complete testimony are not conditional promises. Swearing or affirming to tell the truth, the whole truth, and nothing but the truth puts one's entire self on the line as credit, collateral, for what one says. This credit is destroyed by perjury. Thus, perjury corrodes character. Some who ask whether perjury is ever acceptable do not understand this—do not understand what it does to those who commit it. Perhaps they do not know that the corruption of Bob Leuci, the "Prince of the City," began with illegal wiretaps designed to gain evidence against the "bad guys" or that the thefts by the Buddy Boys in the seventy-seventh precinct in Brooklyn were rationalized as punishment of dealers.[10] Countless public officials have engaged in similar patterns of self-deception and self-righteousness. Many criminal justice personnel have betrayed the public, destroyed their careers, and devastated their families by persuading themselves that serving a good cause is a license to go beyond the law. Their rationalizations of wrongdoing have led them down a steep path to base and selfish public corruption. All of this is incompatible with respect for law and therefore with the mission of police.

Still, most questions about falsification of reports and perjury are asked by officers who care very much about high ideals and fulfillment of the police mission. They stress that dangerous criminals remain at large because of highly technical evidentiary requirements for prosecution and conviction. They ask how they are to protect the public if they have no lawful way to take such criminals off the streets.

Such questions deserve a careful answer. That perjury is wrong must be emphasized, but this leaves open the question, "Well, if that is not the way, what *should* we do?" The response to this question should be framed in terms of all the *legitimate* methods and resources for protecting the public that are at the disposal of police. And the response is not complete without acknowledgment that acting out of respect for law, or any other fundamental principle, may sometimes limit our ability to accomplish other highly worthwhile purposes. The human condition is such that doing the right thing is not always altogether satisfying.[11]

It may be helpful to explain, as several police executives have put it, that perjury makes you suspicious of yourself. It also destroys your credibility with colleagues and with the suspect whose rights you have betrayed. That suspect will tell other people, "The cop did me wrong," and that truthful accusation can undermine the reputation for honesty that is essential to long-term effectiveness in policing. This point can be reinforced by asking police how they would feel if internal affairs officers lied about them—even if they lied only by asserting police innocence when police actually were guilty of wrongdoing. Finally, it bears remembering that all of us are fallible, and in false testimony we risk convicting suspects for actions they did not commit—thereby clearing the case and leaving the actual perpetrator at large.

Accountability

Respect for accountability as a fundamental ideal is a bit more complex, partly because many textbooks treat accountability as a strictly negative dimension of police management, involving only criticism, discipline, and punishment but not praise and rewards. Such textbooks tend to obscure the fact that accountability implies that each individual in an institution is obliged to perform in accordance with its highest ideals and fundamental mission, while the institution itself is obliged to assess its effectiveness in fulfilling its public mission.

In practice, accountability includes responsible training and supervision; an active internal affairs unit or function properly directed by the chief; consistent, timely, and justifiable discipline; appropriate delegation; and responsiveness to demonstrated merit in promotion and assignment. Rewarding fine performance is as basic to accountability as disciplining and correcting unacceptable performance.

Equally fundamental, a department's accountability is demonstrated by its willingness to ask whether its mission is being accomplished as well as possible, and what the leadership can do to make the department the most effective servant of the public good. When things go wrong, often the reason is not that the police involved were incompetent or corrupt but that they were trying to do a good job and were hasty, or a bit overzealous, or too caught up in the demands of the moment. Finding out why they went wrong may enable better teaching within the department, better service to the public—and recognition and reinforcement of the good intentions of the police involved.

Often things go right because of skilled professionalism, but sometimes because the police were lucky. Accountability means reviewing *how* things were accomplished as well as *whether* they were, and trying to make the methods of police as dependable as possible, leaving nothing to chance or luck. As a practical matter, the police should not overlook the golden opportunities to learn from mistakes that did *not* have catastrophic consequences. In the case of out-of-policy shots that produced no injuries, for example, an agency has the great advantage that officers can cooperate because they face no prospect of a civil lawsuit or indictment for a wrongful death, even if they may still face internal discipline.[12]

A comprehensive respect for accountability also recognizes that police are not at war with citizens but, instead, are accountable to them in the sense of being responsible for meeting their needs. It is therefore difficult, if not impossible, to carry out the police mission unless officers on the front line can respond to community needs in a creative and timely way. Thus, those officers must be empowered to exercise discretion and to use imagination and take responsible risks. Otherwise, police service on site is limited to carrying messages of public discontent back to headquarters.

It is difficult, if not impossible, to carry out the police mission unless officers on the front line can respond to community needs in a creative and timely way.

If a department really intends to advance this kind of creativity and assumption of responsibility by its personnel, then it should be very careful in how it treats intelligent and reasonable good-faith mistakes made in a spirit of respect for the expressed ideals of the institution. An honorable mistake made by a conscientious and dedicated public servant is far different from a willful abuse of authority, a deliberate betrayal of departmental policy and regulations, or a demonstration of incompetence. Departments concerned for accountability ought to keep those differences very much in mind and should help educate the public about the distinctions, too. By recognizing these differences in daily practice, police departments come to embody the aspirations they say they respect and encourage. That is, they achieve integrity when their deeds match their words.

Permanent ideals and changing conditions

A clear sense of fundamental ideals serves as a moral and professional compass. A commitment to respect for the dignity of others, to integrity, to authority of law, and to accountability can keep an institution or an individual on the right course, just as a helmsman's compass keeps a ship on course.

But a compass is not enough. In addition, a helmsman must know the waters, the tides, the currents, the shifting shoals and sands beneath the waters, the weather and the climate, the winds, the channels, and the rules of the sea. A helmsman cannot secure the safety of the ship and its passengers, crew, and cargo without attention to changes in the environment and in the conditions of their voyage.

Though the highest ideals are permanent, they must be applied and strategically implemented with a clear eye for the changing problems the public faces, the corresponding changes in needs for service, and fluctuations in the condition of the department itself.

So, too, with a police department. Though the highest ideals are permanent, they must be applied and strategically implemented with a clear eye for the changing problems the public faces, the corresponding changes in needs for service, and fluctuations in the condition of the department itself.

If, for example, newly recruited police are exposed to academy training that is at odds with field training, making their preparation for duty internally inconsistent, then policy and strategy must be revised to give the overall training wholeness and consistency—in a word, integrity. If there have been recurring problems in the use of force by police, then priority should be given to articulating policy and standards that can be drawn not only from law but from a fundamental respect for dignity. If there are persistent problems of attrition, low expectations, a sense of futility, and estrangement from mission in a police department, then early attention should be given to implementing methods of seeking—and acting upon—employee input about job effectiveness and satisfaction. Without that information and lines of communication that will produce it, a department cannot hope to achieve real professional excellence.

Fidelity to ideals cannot be achieved, however, if attention to circumstance and change is random rather than systematic. The highest executives in any police or law enforcement institution need to establish procedures that can routinely alert them to problems, to opportunities, to changes—as surely as a helmsman needs systematic methods for determining water depth, impending weather conditions, and so on. (See also the chapters on performance measurement and research.) And if the department expects to elicit the information it needs, then it must provide to others—police and public alike—the information *they* need in order to achieve as fully as possible the common good.

It is for such reasons that police departments have committed themselves to policies intended to involve their own members, other public service agencies, corporations, and the community itself in advancing the public good. In Houston, for example, promises have been made to

Involve the community in all policing activities that directly affect the quality of community life

Structure service delivery in a way that will reinforce the strengths of the city's neighborhoods[13]

Seek the input of employees in matters that affect employee job satisfaction and effectiveness.[14]

Other departments have developed training programs for their officers that explain their department's commitment to specific ideals. The communication of those ideals to the public and to police personnel alike yields benefits such as the following:

A framework for policy making and decision making

An impetus for genuine respect between police and the public that can help improve officer safety

The outline for a comprehensive plan of accountability and performance evaluation

A reduction in unpleasant surprises, as the community is informed of what it can expect in the way of treatment and services.

The desirability of these results never changes, even though the circumstances and methods of achieving them may vary over time.

Departments that have sought these results have not only labored to express their basic convictions but have also implemented methods for achieving their ideals. That is essential. At the same time, a slavish devotion to process without an overarching concern for results is folly. Always, those seeking to live up to the highest ideals must face hard questions of evaluation: did we accomplish the goals we set, did we do so using appropriate means, did we do so without creating as many problems as we solved? Unless the police have the wisdom, honesty, courage, and skill to ask and answer evaluative questions routinely, their statements of "values" are likely to become forgotten pages gathering dust or polished plaques mocking the department's daily habits.

Realistic idealism

To successfully incorporate worthwhile values into the policies and practices of their departments, police managers must simultaneously be both realists and idealists. They must be realists because they work in an imperfect world. Yet a realist, properly understood, is not a cynic. Rather, a realist is a person who determines what is possible on the basis of facts and evidence. A cynic, by contrast, is a person who believes—in spite of all the contrary evidence—that every human being has a price, that no one can ever really be trusted. Such a person believes, with Machiavelli, that fear is the only durable bond among people.

Nor is an idealist an innocent. An idealist is a person who realizes that we must aspire to high principles, high purposes, for our lives to be fully worth living. An innocent, by contrast, naively believes that every person is trustworthy and altruistic.

To successfully incorporate worthwhile values into the policies and practices of their departments, police managers must simultaneously be both realists and idealists.

Innocence is dangerous. Cynicism is perhaps even more so. Avoidance of both by achieving realism *and* idealism is the antidote to the danger on both sides. Realism and idealism must be achieved together, for if we know the ideals that deserve our esteem but have no sense of how to deal with the facts of our condition, we will be powerless to achieve our purposes. And if we know how to accomplish things but are without faith in ideals, we will have no idea of what is worth accomplishing. Realistic idealism is therefore the only fruitful approach to the conduct of individual and institutional life.

A chief can scarcely lead an organization responsibly without knowing the meaning of respect for human dignity, integrity, accountability, personal and professional excellence, and related ideals. He or she cannot bring the ideals to life or sustain their vitality without abiding personal devotion to them in private life and in the establishment of departmental policy, strategy, tactics, and practice. At the same time, a chief must know and heed the realities of the institution and engage in activities that make ideals both clear and inspiring.

As a realistic idealist, a new chief can turn around a department that is in disarray, without any sense of shared mission, its spirit of accomplishment and aspiration withered away, its employees distrustful and bitter. Under such circumstances, the chief will need to take decisive, concrete, visible steps to restore belief that things can be improved and that confidence in the prospect of improvement is not naive and foolish. Only when tangible results have encouraged people—literally, *given them courage*—are they likely to be ready, let alone willing, to focus their energies on the well-being of the institution as a whole, on the overall quality of its service, on the nature of its entire mission, and on the ideals that are inseparable from a genuine aspiration to fulfill that mission.

In a sense, timing is everything. A department corroded by cynicism will reject or ridicule efforts to articulate ideals. Such efforts are perceived as ploys to manipulate personnel, con the public, snow the media, or seduce political superiors into increasing the department's budget allowances.

This does not mean that chiefs should conceal or underplay their personal commitment to the ideals they seek to uphold. Just the opposite: chiefs should set the stage for departmental articulation of fundamental ideals by showing from the outset that when they speak of selfless service and dedication to the public good, they mean it. Furthermore, they must show that their words are not self-aggrandizing, self-righteous, a screen for deception and manipulation, or a sign of innocence. Only then can their subsequent work on ideals and policy implementation ring true.

Not all of this is a matter of talk, of course. Chiefs who speak of selfless public service must show by their actions their awareness that men and women are not angels and that a naive trust in all people to do their best in the face of temptation is a childish mistake. So, too, they must show by their actions their awareness that men and women are not beasts and can often be reached more powerfully by appeals to their hopes and dreams than by intimidation.

Chiefs should set the stage for departmental articulation of fundamental ideals by showing from the outset that when they speak of selfless service and dedication to the public good, they mean it.

With such concerted effort, chiefs can reduce obstacles to progress placed in their way by critics who dismiss them as "idealistic." Critics who use this word as an insult actually mean "unrealistic." At the same time, a chief's efforts in this regard can show convincingly that realism leaves no place for cynicism and despair.

There are additional benefits besides organizational improvement. Chiefs whose efforts to change a department are discernibly selfless may be spared accusations that their "real" motives are selfish. In some cases, chiefs survive in office because efforts to impugn their motives cannot be made plausible. Thus, there may be nothing so prudent as virtue.

Furthermore, when leaders stand resolutely on the high ground of mission and professional dedication, they give the lie to the cynicism that ruins so many lives in policing and elsewhere. It is cynicism that tempts people to believe the worst: "Everybody is out for himself. Wall Street is dirty, Congress is dirty, judges are dirty; everybody lies. Why should I be different? Why should I hold myself to a higher standard?" The conduct of honorable leaders exposes that for what it is—self-deceptive and self-indulgent rationalization of behavior that is everywhere and always beneath us. People who see others at work and at home who are not selfish, not dishonest, can become realistic idealists in their own right.

It is by such realistic idealism that our Constitution came into being, that the purposes of the Preamble were articulated, and that our form of government was fashioned. If police now and in the future are to stand, in their turn, for that vision of the public good, that vision of public service, they will do so by paying similar attention to the facts and giving similar heartfelt devotion to the ideals.

The work of the Founders was imperfect. But they pressed on—for themselves and their posterity. So it should be with the police. The police, too, will make mistakes, but a great deal depends on them. If the police fail in their mission of advancing ordered liberty and are unable to protect citizens from predation, citizens may trade away freedoms for security. They may risk vigilantism or totalitarian government in order to be safe on the streets and in their homes.

Against these dangers stand the men and women who have made policing their life's work. To "secure the blessings of liberty," today's police leaders must conduct their private and professional lives in accordance with high ideals—and must do so confidently and clearly, providing others with inspiration. They have to express these ideals not only in their conduct but also in words that everyone can trust and must show by their actions that they are willing to stake everything on their ideals. This, too, never changes.

1   B. C. Brymer, *Abraham Lincoln in Peoria, Illinois* (Peoria, IL: Edward J. Jacob, Printer, 1926), 103.

2   Lon L. Fuller, *The Morality of Law*, rev. ed. (New Haven: Yale University Press, 1975), 20.

3   See Albert J. Reiss, Jr., "Shaping and Serving the Community: The Role of the Police Chief Executive," and Lee P. Brown, "Police-Community Power Sharing," both in *Police Leadership in America: Crisis and Opportunity*, ed. William A. Geller (New York: Praeger, 1985), 61–69 and 70–83.

4   Alexander Hamilton, James Madison, and John Jay, *The Federalist Papers*, intro. Clinton Rossiter (New York: Mentor Books, 1961), No. 51, 322, 324.

5   Lord Acton, *Essays on Religion, Politics and Morality*, ed. J. Rufus Fears (Indianapolis: Liberty Classics, 1988), 519.

6   Hamilton, Madison, and Jay, *The Federalist Papers*, No. 57, 351.

7   John Adams to Mercy Warren, 8 January 1776, in *Warren-Adams Letters, Being Chiefly a Correspondence among John Adams and James Warren*, 1743–1814, 2 vols. (Boston: The Massachusetts Historical Society, 1917–1925), 1:201, 202.

8   Cicero, *De Officiis*, trans. Walter Miller, in *Cicero* (Cambridge, MA: Loeb Classical Library, vol. 21, 1975), 1.25.8g, 90; 2.21.251.

9   Thomas Jefferson to John Adams, 28 Oct. 1813, in *Three Thousand Years of Educational Wisdom*, 2d ed., ed. Robert Ulich (Cambridge: Harvard University Press, 1954), 474.

10   See Edwin J. Delattre, *Character and Cops: Ethics in Policing* (Washington, DC: American Enterprise Institute, 1989), 9, 78, 79; and Mike McAlary, *The Buddy Boys: When Good Cops Turn Bad* (New York: G. P. Putnam's Sons, 1987).

11   See Delattre, *Character and Cops*, 190–214.

12   See William A. Geller, "Officer Restraint in the Use of Deadly Force: The Next Frontier in Police Shooting Research," *Journal of Police Science and Administration*, 13 (1985):153, 166.

13   John P. Bales and Lee P. Brown, "The Philosophy of Neighborhood Oriented Policing," in *Developing Neighborhood Policing*, ed. IACP (Arlington, VA: International Association of Chiefs of Police, 1988), 8.

14   Robert Wasserman and Mark H. Moore, *Values in Policing*, Perspectives on Policing (National Institute of Justice, U.S. Department of Justice, and Program in Criminal Justice Policing and Management, John F. Kennedy School of Government, Harvard University, November 1988), 4.

Bibliography

1 The evolution of contemporary policing

Bittner, Egon. "The Impact of Police-Community Relations on the Police System." In *Community Relations and the Administration of Justice*, edited by David Patrick Geary. New York: John Wiley and Sons, 1972.

Fogelson, Robert. *Big-City Police*. Cambridge: Harvard University Press, 1977.

Fyfe, James J., ed. *Police Practice in the '90s*. Washington, DC: International City Management Association, 1989.

Goldstein, Herman. *Policing a Free Society*. Cambridge, MA: Ballinger, 1977.

————. "Improving Policing: A Problem-Oriented Approach." *Crime and Delinquency* 25 (1979): 236–58.

Kelling, George L., and Mark H. Moore. *The Evolving Strategy of Policing*. Perspectiveness on Policing, no. 4. Washington, DC: National Institute of Justice and Harvard University, 1988.

Miller, Wilbur R. *Cops and Bobbies: Police Authority in New York and London 1830–1870*. Chicago: University of Chicago Press, 1973.

Repetto, Thomas. *The Blue Parade*. New York: Free Press, 1978.

Skolnick, James. *Justice without Trial*. New York: John Wiley and Sons, 1966.

Walker, Samuel. *A Critical History of Police Reform*. Lexington, MA: Lexington Books, 1977.

Westley, William H. *Violence and the Police*. Cambridge: MIT Press, 1970.

Wilson, James Q. *Varieties of Police Behavior*. Cambridge: Harvard University Press, 1968.

Wilson, James Q., and George L. Kelling. "The Police and Neighborhood Safety." *Atlantic Monthly* (March 1982): 29–38.

Wilson, O. W. *Police Administration*. New York: McGraw-Hill, 1950.

2 Organization and management

Bryson, John M. *Strategic Planning for Public and Non-Profit Organizations*. San Francisco: Jossey-Bass, 1988.

Couper, David. *How to Rate Your Local Police*. Washington, DC: Police Executive Research Forum, 1983.

Eck, John E., and William Spelman. *Problem-Solving: Problem-Oriented Policing in Newport News*. Washington, DC: Police Executive Research Forum, 1987.

Geller, William A., ed. *Police Leadership in America: Crisis and Opportunity*. New York: Praeger, 1985.

Goldstein, Herman. *Policing a Free Society*. Cambridge, MA: Ballinger, 1977.

————. *Problem-Oriented Policing*. New York: McGraw-Hill, 1990.

Kelling, George L., and Mark H. Moore. *The Evolving Strategy of Policing*. Perspectives on Policing, no. 4. Washington, DC: National Institute of Justice and Harvard University, 1988.

Ouchi, William G. *Theory Z: How American Businesses Can Meet the Japanese Challenge*. Reading, MA: Addison-Wesley, 1981.

Peters, Thomas J., and Robert H. Waterman, Jr. *In Search of Excellence: Lessons from America's Best-Run Companies*. New York: Harper and Row, 1982.

Sherman, Lawrence W. "Policing Communities: What Works." In *Crime and Justice: A Review of Research*, Vol. 8, edited by Albert J. Reiss, Jr., and Michael Tonry. Chicago: University of Chicago Press, 1986.

Sherman, Lawrence W., et al. *Repeat Calls to the Police in Minneapolis*. Washington, DC: Crime Control Institute, 1987.

Skogan, Wesley, "Fear of Crime and Neighborhood Change." In *Crime and Justice: A Review of Research*, Vol. 8, edited by Albert J. Reiss, Jr., and Michael Tonry. Chicago: University of Chicago Press, 1986.

Sparrow, Malcolm K., Mark H. Moore, and David M. Kennedy, *Beyond 911: The New Era of Policing*. New York: Basic Books, 1990.

Wasserman, Robert, and Mark H. Moore, "Values in Policing." Working papers series no. 88-05-15. Cambridge: Program in Criminal Justice Policy and Management, John F. Kennedy School of Government, Harvard University, 1988.

Wilson, James Q. *Bureaucracy*. New York: Basic Books, 1990.

3 The patrol function

Block, Peter B., and James Bell. *Managing Investigations: The Rochester System*. Washington, DC: Police Foundation, 1976.

Eck, John E., and William Spelman. *Problem-Solving: Problem-Oriented Policing in Newport News*. Washington, DC: Police Executive Research Forum, 1987.

Gay, William G., Theodore H. Schell, and Stephen Schack. *Routine Patrol*. Vol. 1 of *Improving Patrol Productivity*. Washington, DC: U.S. Government Printing Office, 1977.

Goldstein, Herman. *Problem-Oriented Policing*. New York: McGraw-Hill, 1990.

Kelling, George L., Tony Pate, Duane Dieckman, and Charles E. Brown. *The Kansas City Preventive Patrol Experiment: A Technical Report*. Washington, DC: Police Foundation, 1974.

McEwen, J. Thomas, Edward F. Connors III, and Marcia I. Cohen. *Evaluation of the Differential Police Response Field Test*. Washington, DC: U.S. Government Printing Office, 1986.

Levine, Margaret J., and J. Thomas McEwen. *Patrol Deployment*. Washington, DC: National Institute of Justice, U.S. Department of Justice, 1985.

New York City Police Department. *The Community Patrol Officer Program: Problem Solving Guide*. New York: New York City Police Department, 1988.

Oettmeier, Timothy N. *An Evaluation of the Houston Police Department's D.A.R.T. Program*. Houston: Houston Police Department, 1985.

Reiner, G. Hobart, Thomas J. Sweeney, Raymond V. Waymire, Fred A. Newton, Richard G. Grassie, Suzanne M. White, and William D. Wallace. *Integrated Criminal Apprehension Program Crime Analysis Operations Manual*. Washington, DC: Law Enforcement Assistance Administration, U.S. Department of Justice, 1977.

Schack, Stephen, Theodore H. Schell, and William G. Gay. *Specialized Patrol*. Vol. 2 of *Improving Patrol Productivity*. Washington, DC: U.S. Government Printing Office, 1977.

Sherman, Lawrence W., Patrick R. Gartin, and Michael E. Boerger. "Hot Spots of Predatory Crime: Routine Activities and the Criminology of Place." *Criminology* 27 (1989): 27–55.

Spelman, William, and Dale K. Brown. *Calling the Police: Citizen Reporting of Serious Crime*. Washington, DC: U.S. Government Printing Office, 1984.

4 Crime prevention, fear reduction, and the community

Eck, John E., and William Spelman. *Problem-Solving: Problem-Oriented Policing in Newport News*. Washington, DC: Police Executive Research Forum, 1987.

Goldstein, Herman. *Problem-Oriented Policing*. New York: McGraw-Hill, 1990.

Hope, T., and M. Shaw. *Communities and Crime Reduction*. London: Her Majesty's Stationery Office, 1988.

International Association of Chiefs of Police. *Reducing Crime by Reducing Drug Abuse*. Washington, DC: International Association of Chiefs of Police, 1988.

Lavrakas, P. J., and S. F. Bennett. "Thinking about the Implementation of Citizen and Community Anti-Crime Measures." In *Communities and Crime Reduction*, edited by T. Hope and M. Shaw. London: Her Majesty's Stationery Office, 1988.

Moore, M. H., and R. C. Trojanowicz. *Policing and the Fear of Crime*. Perspectives in Policing, no. 3. Washington, DC: National Institute of Justice, 1988.

Pennell, S., C. Curtis, and J. Henderson. *Guardian Angels: An Assessment of Citizen Responses to Crime*. Vol. 2. Technical report to the National Institute of Justice. San Diego, CA: San Diego Association of Governments, 1985.

Reiss, A. J., Jr., and M. Tonry, eds. *Communities and Crime*. Crime and Justice Series, vol. 8. Chicago: University of Chicago Press, 1986.

Rosenbaum, D. P. "Community Crime Prevention: A Review and Synthesis of the Literature." *Justice Quarterly* 5 (1988): 323–95.

_____, ed. *Community Crime Prevention: Does It Work?* Beverly Hills, CA: Sage, 1986.

Skogan, Wesley G. *Disorder and Decline.* New York: Free Press, 1990.

---

5 Criminal investigations

Brown, Michael K. *Working the Street: Police Discretion and the Dilemmas of Reform.* New York: Russell Sage Foundation, 1988.

Critchley, T. A. *A History of Police in England and Wales.* London: Constable, 1979.

Eck, John E. *Solving Crimes: The Investigation of Burglary and Robbery.* Washington, DC: Police Executive Research Forum, 1983.

Eck, John E., and William Spelman. *Problem-Solving: Problem-Oriented Policing in Newport News.* Washington, DC: Police Executive Research Forum, 1987.

Goldstein, Herman. *Problem-Oriented Policing.* New York: McGraw-Hill, 1990.

Martin, Susan E., and Lawrence W. Sherman. *Catching Career Criminals: The Washington, D.C. Repeat Offender Project.* Police Foundation Reports 3. Washington, DC: Police Foundation, 1986.

Marx, Gary T. *Undercover: Police Surveillance in America.* Los Angeles: University of California Press, 1988.

Moran, Frank. *"The Eye That Never Sleeps": A History of the Pinkerton National Detective Agency.* Bloomington: Indiana University Press, 1982.

Porter, Bernard. *The Origins of the Vigilant State: The London Metropolitan Police Special Branch before the First World War.* London: Weidenfeld and Nicolson, 1987.

Skolnick, Jerome H. *Justice without Trial: Law Enforcement in a Democratic Society.* New York: John Wiley and Sons, 1975.

Spelman, William, et al. *Repeat Offender Programs for Law Enforcement: New Approaches to an Old Problem.* Washington, DC: Police Executive Research Forum, 1990.

Williams, Gerald. *Law Enforcement Accreditation: An Effort to Professionalize American Law Enforcement.* Ph.D. diss., University of Colorado at Denver, 1988.

---

6 Traffic services

Anacapa Sciences. *Guide for Detecting Drunk Drivers at Night.* Washington, DC: National Highway Traffic Safety Administration, 1982.

Baker, J. Stannard, and Lynn M. Fricke. *The Traffic Accident Investigation Manual.* Vol. 1. Evanston, IL: Northwestern University, Traffic Institute, 1986.

International Association of Chiefs of Police. *Model Police Traffic Services (Policies).* Gaithersburg, MD: International Association of Chiefs of Police, 1976.

_____. *Model Police Traffic Services (Procedures).* Gaithersburg, MD: International Association of Chiefs of Police, 1976.

Lacey, John H., et al. *Enforcement and Public Information Strategies for DWI General Deterrence.* DOT-HS-807-066. Washington, DC: National Highway Traffic Safety Administration, 1986.

National Committee on Uniform Traffic Laws and Ordinances. *Uniform Vehicle Code and Model Traffic Ordinance.* Rev. ed. Evanston, IL: National Committee on Uniform Traffic Laws and Ordinances, 1987.

National Highway Traffic Safety Administration. *Alcohol and Highway Safety 1984: A Review of the State of Knowledge.* DOT-HS-806-569. Washington, DC: National Highway Traffic Safety Administration, 1985.

_____. *Improved Sobriety Testing Battery.* DOT-HS-806-512. Washington, DC: National Highway Traffic Safety Administration, 1986.

Northwestern University Traffic Institute. *PTS Performance Measures.* Washington, DC: National Highway Traffic Safety Administration, 1991.

Presidential Commission on Drunk Driving. *Final Report.* Washington, DC: Presidential Commission on Drunk Driving, 1983.

---

7 Local drug control

Botvin, Gilbert J. "Substance Abuse Prevention: Theory, Practice, and Effectiveness." In *Drugs and Crime,* edited by Michael Tonry and James Q. Wilson. Chicago: University of Chicago Press, 1990.

Chaiken, Jan, and Marcia Chaiken. "Drugs and Predatory Crime." In *Drugs and Crime,* edited by Michael Tonry and James Q. Wilson. Chicago: University of Chicago Press, 1990.

DeJong, William. *Arresting the Demand for Drugs: Police and School Partnerships to Prevent Drug Abuse.* Washington, DC: National Institute of Justice, 1987.

Moore, Mark H. *Buy and Bust.* Lexington, MA: D. C. Heath, 1977.

Musto, David F. *The American Disease: Origins of Narcotic Control*. New York: Oxford University Press, 1987.

Polich, J. Michael, Phyllis L. Erickson, Peter Reuter, and James P. Kahan. *Strategies for Controlling Adolescent Drug Use*. Santa Monica, CA: Rand Corporation, 1984.

Reuter, Peter, and Mark Kleiman. "Risks and Prices: An Economic Analysis of Drug Enforcement." In *Crime and Justice: An Annual Review of Research*, edited by Michael Tonry and Norval Morris. Chicago: University of Chicago Press, 1986.

Sherman, Lawrence W. "Police Crackdowns: Initial and Residual Deterrences." In *Crime and Justice: A Review of Research*, edited by Michael Tonry and Norval Morris. Chicago: University of Chicago Press, 1990.

Weisel, Deborah Lamm. "Playing the Home Field: A Problem-Oriented Approach to Drug Control." *American Journal of Police* (1990).

———. *Tackling Drug Problems in Public Housing: A Guide for Police*. (Washington, DC: Police Executive Research Forum, 1990.

8 Organized crime

Abadinsky, Howard. *Organized Crime*. 3d ed. Chicago: Nelson Hall, 1990.

Andrews, Paul P., Jr., and Marilyn B. Peterson. *Criminal Intelligence Analysis*. Loomis, CA: Palmer Enterprises, 1990.

Cressey, Donald R. *Theft of the Nation*. New York: Harper and Row, 1969.

Cummings, John, and Ernest Volkman. *Goombata*. Boston: Little, Brown and Company, 1990.

Dintino, Justin, and Frederick T. Martens. *Police Intelligence Systems and Crime Control*. Springfield, IL: Charles Thomas, 1983.

Edelhertz, Herbert, ed. *Major Issues in Organized Crime Control*. Washington, DC: U.S. Government Printing Office, 1987.

Kelly, Robert, ed. *Organized Crime: A Global Perspective*. Totawa, NJ: Rowman and Littlefield, 1987.

Kwitny, J. *Vicious Circles: The Mafia in the Marketplace*. New York: Norton, 1979.

Peterson, Virgil W. *The Mob: 200 Years of Organized Crime in New York*. Ottawa, IL: Green Hill Publishers, 1983.

President's Commission on Organized Crime. *The Impact: Organized Crime Today*. Washington, DC: U.S. Government Printing Office, 1986.

Reuter, Peter. *Racketeering in Legitimate Industries: A Study in the Economics of Intimidation*. Santa Monica, CA: Rand Corporation, 1987.

Salerno, Ralph, and John Tompkins, *The Crime Confederation*. Garden City, NY: Doubleday, 1969.

9 Fostering integrity

Delattre, E. *Character and Cops*. Lanham, MD: University Press of America, 1989.

Goldstein, Herman. *Police Corruption*. Washington, DC: The Police Foundation, 1975.

———. *Policing a Free Society*. Cambridge: Ballinger, 1977.

International Association of Chiefs of Police. *Building Integrity and Reducing Drug Corruption in Police Departments*. Arlington, VA: IACP and Bureau of Justice Assistance, U.S. Department of Justice, 1989.

Muir, W. *Police: Streetcorner Politicians*. Chicago: University of Chicago Press, 1977.

Philadelphia Police Study Task Force. *Philadelphia and Its Police: Toward a New Partnership*. Privately printed, 1987.

Punch, M. *Conduct Unbecoming*. 1985.

Rubinstein, Jonathan. "The Dilemma of Vice Work." In *Police Corruption: A Sociological Perspective*, edited by Lawrence W. Sherman. Garden City, NY: Anchor Books, 1974.

10 Human resource management

In addition to the references cited below, the following publications are useful: *Fire and Police Personnel Reporter*, *Crime Control Digest*, *Public Personnel Management*, and *NIJ Reports* from the National Institute of Justice.

Ayers, Richard, and Paul Coble. *Meeting Law Enforcement's Responsibilities by Safeguarding Management's Rights*. Gaithersburg, MD: International Association of Chiefs of Police, 1987.

Bopp, William J., and Paul Whisenand. *Police Personnel Administration*. Boston: Allyn and Bacon, 1980.

Carter, David C., Allen D. Sapp, and Darrel W. Stephens. *The State of Police Education: Policy Direction for the 21st Century*. Washington, DC: Police Executive Research Forum, 1989.

Cayer, N. Joseph. *Managing Human Resources: An Introduction to Public Personnel Administration. New York: St. Martin's Press, 1980.

Goldstein, Herman. "Progress in Policing." Chap. 2 in *Problem-Oriented Policing*. New York: McGraw-Hill, 1990.

Moore, Perry. *Public Personnel Management: A Contingency Approach*. Lexington, MA: Heath and Company, 1985.

More, Harry W., and W. Fred Wegener. *Effective Police Supervision*. Cincinnati: Anderson Publishing Company, 1990.

Public-Sector Bargaining. Edited by Benjamin Aaron, Joyce M. Nakita, and James L. Stern. 2d ed. Washington, DC: BNA Books, 1988.

Reinke, R. *Selection through Assessment Centers: A Tool for Police Departments*. Washington, DC: Police Foundation, 1977.

Territo, Leonard, et al. *The Police Personnel Selection Process*. Indianapolis: Bobbs-Merrill, 1977.

11 Information management

Applegate, Lynda M., James I. Cash, and Quinn Mills. "Information Technology and Tomorrow's Manager." *Harvard Business Review* (November/December 1988): 128–36.

Colton, Kent W., Margaret Brandeau, and James M. Tien. *A National Assessment of Police Command, Control and Communication Systems*. Washington, DC: National Institute of Justice, 1983.

Kolesar, Peter, and Arthur J. Swersey. "The Deployment of Urban Emergency Units: A Survey." *Delivery of Urban Services with a View towards Applications in Management Science and Operations Research*. Edited by Arthur J. Swersey and Edward J. Ingall. New York: Elsevier North-Holland, 1986.

Larson, Richard. "The Future of Police Emergency Response Systems." *NIJ Reports* (Washington, DC: National Institute of Justice, March 1985): 2–4.

———. "The New Crime Stoppers." *Technology Review* 92, no. 8 (Cambridge: Massachusetts Institute of Technology, November/December 1989): 26–31.

Moran, John, and Karen Layne. "Enhanced 911/CAD: Interfacing New Technology to Fight Crime." *Police Chief* (August 1988): 25–29.

Office of Technology Assessment, U.S. Congress. *Criminal Justice, New Technologies, and the Constitution*. Washington, DC: U.S. Government Printing Office, 1988.

The Police Chief 57, no. 3 (March 1990): 22–53 (special focus on computers and communications).

The Police Chief 57, no. 4 (April 1990): 20–56 (special focus on state-of-the-art policing).

Software Reference Guide. Washington, DC: International City Management Association. Published annually.

Spelman, William. *Beyond Bean Counting: New Approaches for Managing Crime Data*. Washington, DC: Police Executive Research Forum, 1988.

12 Research, planning, and implementation

Bardach, Eugene. *The Implementation Game: What Happens after a Bill Becomes Law*. Cambridge: MIT Press, 1977.

Cook, Thomas D., and Donald T. Campbell. *Quasi-Experimentation: Design and Analysis Issues for Field Settings*. Chicago: Rand-McNally, 1979.

Cordner, Gary W. "Police Research and Police Policy: Some Propositions about the Production and Use of Knowledge." In *Police Leadership in America: Crisis and Opportunity*, edited by William A. Geller. New York: Praeger, 1985.

Eck, John. *Using Research: A Primer for Law Enforcement Managers*. Washington, DC: Police Executive Research Forum, 1984.

Garner, Joel H., and Christy A. Visher. "Policy Experiments Come of Age." *NIJ Reports* no. 211 (September/October 1988).

Hudzik, John K., and Gary W. Cordner. *Planning in Criminal Justice Organizations and Systems*. New York: Macmillan, 1983.

Sparrow, Malcolm. *Implementing Community Policing*. Perspectives on Policing. Washington, DC: National Institute of Justice, November 1988.

Stewart, James. K. "Research and the Police Administrator: Working Smarter, Not Harder." In *Police Leadership in America: Crisis and Opportunity*, edited by William A. Geller. New York: Praeger, 1985.

Wildavsky, Aaron, and Jeffrey L. Pressman. *Implementation*. Berkeley: University of California Press, 1973.

Wilson, James Q. "Police Research and Experimentation." In *Progress in Policing: Essays on Change*, edited by Richard A. Staufenberger. Cambridge, MA: Ballinger, 1980.

Wilson, O. W. *Police Planning.* 2d ed. Springfield, IL: Charles C. Thomas, 1971.

13 Personnel and agency performance measurement

Bayley, David H., and Egon Bittner, "Learning the Skills of Policing." In *Critical Issues in Policing: Contemporary Readings*, edited by Roger G. Dunham and Geoffrey P. Alpert. Prospect Heights, IL: Waveland Press, 1989.

Berk, Ronald A., ed. *Performance Assessment: Methods and Applications*. Baltimore: Johns Hopkins University Press, 1986.

Bittner, Egon. *The Functions of Police in Modern Society*. Washington, DC: U.S. Government Printing Office, 1970.

Cohen, Bernard, and Jan Chaiken, *Investigators Who Perform Well*. Washington, DC: U.S. Department of Justice, 1987.

DeVries, David L., Ann M. Morrison, Sandra L. Shullman, and Michael L. Gerlach. *Performance Appraisal on the Line*. New York: John Wiley and Sons, 1981.

Eck, John E. *Using Research: A Primer for Law Enforcement Managers*. Washington, DC: Police Executive Research Forum, 1984.

Greene, Jack R., and Stephen D. Mastrofski, eds. *Community Policing: Rhetoric or Reality*. New York: Praeger, 1988.

Iannone, N. F. *Supervision of Police Personnel*. 4th ed. Englewood Cliffs, NJ: Prentice-Hall, 1987.

Landy, Frank J., and James L. Farr. *The Measurement of Work Performance*. New York: Academic Press, 1983.

Mastrofski, Stephen D. "Police Agency Accreditation: The Prospects of Reform." *American Journal of Police*, vol. 5, no. 2 (Fall 1986): 45–81.

Muir, William Ker, Jr. *Police: Streetcorner Politicians*. Chicago: University of Chicago Press, 1977.

Posavac, Emil J., and Raymond G. Carey. *Program Evaluation: Methods and Case Studies*. 2d ed. Englewood Cliffs, NJ: Prentice-Hall, 1985.

Rossi, Peter H., and Howard E. Freeman. *Evaluation: A Systematic Approach*. 4th ed. Newbury Park, CA: Sage, 1989.

Whitaker, Gordon P., Stephen Mastrofski, Elinor Ostrom, Roger B. Parks, and Stephen L. Percy. *Basic Issues in Police Performance*. Washington, DC: U.S. Department of Justice, 1982.

Williams, Gerald L. *Making the Grade: The Benefits of Law Enforcement Accreditation*. Washington, DC: Police Executive Research Forum, 1989.

14 Equipment and facilities

American Institute of Architects. *The Architect and Client*. Pamphlet 5. Washington, DC: AIA, 1975.

Commission on Accreditation for Law Enforcement Agencies. *Standards for Law Enforcement Agencies*. Fairfax, VA: CALEA, 1987.

Dibner, David R. *You and Your Architect*. Washington, DC: American Institute of Architects, catalog no. 4N802, rev. 1978.

Geller, W. A., and M. Scott. "Deadly Force: What We Know." In *Thinking about Police: Contemporary Readings*, ed. Carl Klockars. 2d ed. New York: McGraw-Hill, 1990.

Sweetman, Sherri. *Report of the Attorney General's Conference on Less Than Lethal Weapons*. Washington, DC: National Institute of Justice, 1987.

15 The governmental setting

Advisory Commission on Intergovernmental Relations. *Significant Features of Fiscal Federalism, 1989 Edition*. Vol. I M-163. Washington: ACIR, 1989.

American Bar Association. *The ABA Standards for Criminal Justice*. 2d ed. Vol. 1. Chicago: ABA, 1980.

Bureau of Justice Statistics, U.S. Department of Justice. "Profile of State and Local Law Enforcement Agencies, 1987." *Bulletin* (March 1989).

Center for Research in Criminal Justice. *The Iron Fist and the Velvet Glove: An Analysis of the U.S. Police*. 2d ed. Berkeley, CA: Center for Research on Criminal Justice, 1977.

Deakin, Thomas J. *Police Professionalism: The Renaissance of American Law Enforcement*. Springfield, IL: Charles C. Thomas, 1988.

Greisinger, George W., Jeffrey S. Slovak, and Joseph J. Molkup. *Civil Service Systems: Their Impact on Police Administration*. Washington, DC: Law Enforcement Assistance Administration, 1979.

Guyot, Dorothy. *Policing As Though People Matter*. Philadelphia: Temple University Press, 1991.

Jacob, Herbert, Robert Lineberry, and Anne Heinz. *Crime in City Politics*. New York: Longman, 1983.

Kerstetter, Wayne. "Who Disciplines the Police? Who Should?" In *Police Leadership in America: Crisis and Opportunity*, edited by William A. Geller. New York: Praeger, 1985.

Mastrofski, Stephen. "Police Agency Accreditation. The Prospects of Reform." *American Journal of Police*, vol. 5, no. 2 (Fall 1986): 45–81.

Ostrom, Elinor, Roger B. Parks, and Gordon P. Whitaker. *Patterns of Metropolitan Policing*. Cambridge, MA: Ballinger, 1978.

President's Commission on Law Enforcement and Administration of Justice. *Task Force Report: The Police* Washington: U.S. Government Printing Office, 1967.

Rynecki, Steven A., and Michael Morris. *Police Collective Bargaining Agreements: A National Management Survey*. Washington: Police Executive Research Forum, 1981.

Scheingold, Stuart A. *The Politics of Law and Order*. New York: Longman, 1984.

U.S. Civil Rights Commission. *Who Is Guarding the Guardians?: A Report on Police Practices*. Washington, DC: U.S. Government Printing Office, 1981.

Walker, Samuel. *A Critical History of Police Reform: The Emergence of Professionalism*. Lexington: D. C. Heath and Company, Lexington Books, 1977.

———. "The Politics of Police Accountability: The Seattle Police Spy Ordinance as a Case Study." In *The Politics of Crime and Criminal Justice*, edited by Erika Fairchild and Vincent Webb. Beverly Hills, CA: Sage, 1985.

Williams, Oliver. "A Typology for Comparative Local Government." *Midwest Journal of Politics*. Vol. 5, no. 2 (May 1961): 150–64.

Witham, Donald. *The American Law Enforcement Chief Executive: A Management Profile*. Washington, DC: Police Executive Research Forum, 1985.

16 External resources

For a list of external resources, see pages 468–69.

17 Forensic sciences

"ASCLD Guidelines for Forensic Laboratory Management Practices." *Crime Laboratory Digest* 14, no. 2 (April 1987): 39–46.

Bashinski, Jan S. "Laboratory Standards: Accreditation, Training and Certification of Staff in the Forensic Context." In *Proceedings of the Banbury Conference on DNA Technology and Forensic Science*. New York: Cold Spring Harbor Laboratory, 1989.

Commission on Accreditation for Law Enforcement Agencies. "Collection and Preservation of Evidence." In *Accreditation Standards*. Fairfax, VA, 1987.

DeForest, Peter R., R. E. Gaensslen, and Henry C. Lee, *Forensic Sciences: An Introduction to Criminalistics*. New York: McGraw-Hill, 1983.

Fisher, Barry, Arne Svensson, and Oliver Wendel. *Techniques of Crime Scene Investigation*. 4th ed. New York: Elsevier, 1986.

Office of Technology Assessment, U.S. Congress. *Genetic Witness: Forensic Uses of DNA Tests*. OTA-BA-438. Washington, DC: U.S. Government Printing Office, 1990.

Peterson, Joseph L., Kenneth S. Field, Ellen L. Fabricant, and John I. Thornton. *Crime Laboratory Proficiency Testing Research Program*. Washington, DC: U.S. Government Printing Office, 1978.

Peterson, Joseph L., Steven Mihajlovic, and Michael Gilliland. *Forensic Evidence and the Police: The Effects of Scientific Evidence on Criminal Investigations*. Washington, DC: U.S. Government Printing Office, 1984.

Saferstein, Richard. *Criminalistics: An Introduction to Forensic Science*. 3d ed. Englewood Cliffs, NJ: Prentice-Hall, 1987.

Technical Working Group on DNA Analysis Methods. "Guidelines for a Quality Assurance Program for DNA Restriction Fragment Length Polymorphism Analysis." *Crime Laboratory Digest* 16, no. 2 (1989): 40–59.

Thornton, John I. "Criminalistics—Past, Present and Future." *Lex et Scientia* 11 (1975): 1–44.

———, ed. *Crime Investigation*. 2d ed. New York: John Wiley and Sons, 1981.

Wilson, Thomas, and Paul Woodard. *Automated Fingerprint Identification Systems: Technology and Policy Issues*. Washington, DC: U.S. Department of Justice, 1987.

18 Arrestee and lockup management

Commission on Accreditation for Law Enforcement Agencies, Inc. "Holding Facility." Chapter 72 in *Standards for Law Enforcement Agencies*. Fairfax, VA: Commission on Accreditation for Law Enforcement Agencies, Inc. 1987.

Geller, William A. *Videotaping Police Interrogations and Confessions: A Review of the International Literature.* An interim report to the National Institute of Justice. Washington, DC: Police Executive Research Forum, 1989.

Hayes, Lindsay. "And Darkness Closes In . . . A National Study of Jail Suicides." *Journal of Criminal Justice and Behavior* (1983, vol. 10, no. 4): 461–84.

Hayes, Lindsay, and Joseph Rowan. *National Study of Jail Suicides: Seven Years Later.* Alexandria, VA: National Center for Institutions and Alternatives, 1988.

Thompson, Joel A., and G. Larry Mays, eds. *American Jails: Public Policy Issues.* Chicago: Nelson-Hall Publishers, 1991.

Zevitz, Richard G., and Susan R. Takata. "Death in Cell-Blocks: A Study of Inmate Mortality in Jail and Lockup Custody." Paper presented to the American Society of Criminology, Montreal, Canada, 14 November 1987.

19   Practical ideals for managing in the nineties: a perspective

Acton, Lord. *Essays on Religion, Politics and Morality.* Edited by J. Rufus Fears. Indianapolis: Liberty Classics, 1988.

Bittner, Egon. *The Functions of the Police in Modern Society.* Rockville, MD: National Institute of Mental Health Center for Studies of Crime and Delinquency, 1970.

Cicero. *De Officiis.* In *Cicero.* Translated by Walter Miller. Cambridge, MA: Loeb Classical Library, 1975, vol. 21.

Delattre, Edwin J. *Character and Cops: Ethics in Policing.* Washington, DC: American Enterprise Institute for Public Policy Research, 1989.

Erasmus. *The Education of a Christian Prince.* Translated by Lester K. Born. In *Three Thousand Years of Educational Wisdom.* Edited by Robert Ulich. 2d ed. Cambridge: Harvard University Press, 1954.

Fuller, Lon L. *The Morality of Law.* Rev. ed. New Haven: Yale University Press, 1975.

Goldwin, Robert. "Of Men and Angels: A Search for Morality in the Constitution." In *The Moral Foundations of the American Republic.* Edited by Robert H. Horwitz. Charlottesville: University Press of Virginia, 1979.

Hamilton, Alexander, James Madison, and John Jay. *The Federalist Papers.* Introduced by Clinton Rossiter. New York: Mentor Books, 1961.

McDonald, Forrest. *Novus Ordo Seclorum: The Intellectual Origins of the Constitution.* Lawrence: University Press of Kansas, 1985.

Meyers, Marvin, ed. *The Mind of the Founder: Sources of the Political Thought of James Madison.* Rev. ed. Hanover, NH: The University Press of New England, 1981.

Story, Joseph. *A Familiar Exposition of the Constitution of the United States.* Lake Bluff, IL: Regnery Gateway, 1986.

U.S. National Commission on Law Observance and Enforcement. *Report on Police,* No. 14. Washington, DC: U.S. Government Printing Office, 1931. Also known as *The Wickersham Report,* after the commission's chairman.

Vollmer, August. *The Police and Modern Society.* Berkeley: Bureau of Public Administration, University of California, 1936. Reprint. College Park, MD: McGrath Publishing Company, 1969.

List of contributors

Persons who have contributed to this book are listed below with the editor first and the authors following in alphabetical order. A brief review of experience and training is presented for each. Because many of the contributors have published extensively, books, monographs, articles, and other publications are omitted here. Numerous works by these individuals appear in the bibliography and in endnotes to chapters.

William A. Geller (Editor) is Associate Director of the Police Executive Research Forum. Previously, he served as Project Director of the American Bar Foundation, Executive Director of the Chicago Law Enforcement Study Group, Special Counsel for Public Safety and Internal Security to the Chicago Park District, and Law Clerk to Justice Walter V. Shaefer of the Illinois Supreme Court. He has written, lectured, and consulted widely on police leadership, risk reduction, and racial equity for units of federal, state, and local government, community groups, universities, police training institutes, and law enforcement equipment manufacturers. He has served as project manager for the Harvard Executive Session on Drugs and Community Policing; Commissioner of the Wilmette, Illinois, Fire and Police Commission; and liaison to the American Bar Association Committee that wrote the "Urban Police Function" standards. Mr. Geller was awarded the City of Chicago's Richard J. Daley Police Medal of Honor and the New York City Police Commissioner's Certificate of Commendation. He is a graduate of the University of Chicago Law School and the recipient of its 1975 Casper Platt Award for Excellence in Writing.

Jan S. Bashinski (Chapter 17) is Manager of the California Department of Justice DNA Laboratory. Previously, she directed the Oakland Police Department Crime Laboratory. She has served as a consultant reviewer of forensic science research for the National Institute of Justice and has been extensively involved in developing crime laboratory management and quality assurance standards through her service on the American Society of Crime Laboratory Directors Laboratory Accreditation Board and through her activities in the American Academy of Forensic Sciences and the California Association of Criminalists. She holds a bachelor's degree in chemistry and a master's degree in criminalistics, both from the University of California at Berkeley.

Cornelius J. Behan (Chapter 19) has served as Chief of the Baltimore County (Maryland) Police Department since 1977. Prior to his appointment, he completed a thirty-one-year career with the New York City Police Department, rising from patrolman to Chief of Field Services, the second highest rank in the department. Active in over a dozen professional law enforcement organizations, he has served as president of the Police Executive Research Forum, the National Executive Institute, and the Maryland Chiefs of Police Association. He has been a participant in the Executive Sessions, John F. Kennedy School of Government, Harvard University, and with the National Law Enforcement Steering Committee. He holds an A.A.S. degree from the Bernard Baruch School of Business of the City University of New York and a B.S. from John Jay College of Criminal Justice and has done extensive graduate work in management and criminal justice.

William H. Bieck (Chapter 3) is an urban policy planner in the Field Operations Command, Houston Police Department. He has been engaged with others in developing ways to more effectively manage patrol and investigative operations. Previously he worked on the Kansas City Preventive Patrol Experiment, was principal investigator in the Kansas City (Missouri) Police Department's Response Time Analysis Study, and provided technical assistance for the Law Enforcement Assistance Administration's Integrated Criminal Apprehension Program. He has served on several national advisory boards to evaluate law enforcement programs and assess research direction. He has also consulted for federal, state, and city agencies as well as private corporations, universities, and research institutitions.

Noel C. Bufe (Chapter 6) is Director of The Traffic Institute at Northwestern University. He has also held positions as Governors' Highway Safety Representative of the state of Michigan; Administrator of Michigan's Office of Criminal Justice Programs; Deputy Administrator of the National Highway Safety Administration (NHTSA), U.S. Department of Transportation; Executive Secretary of the Michigan Law Enforcement Officers Training Council; Management Consultant with the International Association of Chiefs of Police; and Administrative Assistant to the Secretary of the Board, St. Louis (Missouri) Police Department. He holds a B.S. degree in police administration, an M.S. degree in criminal justice administration, and a Ph.D. in education, all from Michigan State University.

Gerald Caplan (Chapter 9) is professor of law at the George Washington University. He has served as general counsel to the Metropolitan Police Department of the District of Columbia, director of the National Institute of Justice of the Department of Justice, and director of the Philadelphia Police Study Commission. He has written extensively on police and criminal justice issues.

Gary W. Cordner (Chapter 12) is Associate Professor of Police Studies at Eastern Kentucky University and Editor of the *American Journal of Police*. He began his police career in Ocean City, Maryland, and later served as police chief in St. Michaels, Maryland. He lectures regularly in the Texas Law Enforcement Management Institute, the Ohio Police Executive Leadership College, and the Kentucky Command Decisions School and has consulted for police agencies in several states. He received a B.S. degree from Northeastern University and M.S. and Ph.D. degrees from Michigan State University.

Sylvester Daughtry (Chapter 4) is Chief of Police in Greensboro, North Carolina, where he began his law enforcement career as a uniformed patrol officer. He holds a bachelor's degree from North Carolina A&T State University, is a graduate of the Southern Police Institute at the University of Louisville, and is a graduate of the FBI National Academy. He is currently (1991) the Fourth Vice President of the International Association of Chiefs of Police, and is on the Board of Commissioners for the Commission on Accreditation for Law Enforcement Agencies. He also has served widely as an assessor for the Accreditation Commission and has served as panelist and lecturer on crime prevention topics internationally.

Edwin J. Delattre (Chapter 19) is Olin Scholar in Applied Ethics, Professor of Education, and Adjunct Professor of Philosophy at Boston University; Adjunct Scholar, American Enterprise Institute, Washington, D.C.; and president *emeritus* of St. John's College in Annapolis, Maryland, and Santa Fe, New Mexico. He is the author of two books and of numerous articles on ethics in law enforcement, in government, in business, and in higher education. He is a frequent lecturer at the FBI Academy on principles of leadership and on integrity, character excellence, and corruption in public and private life. He holds a B.A. degree from the University of Virginia and a Ph.D. in philosophy from the University of Texas at Austin.

John E. Eck (Chapters 5 and 7) is associate director of research at the Police Executive Research Forum (PERF). Since joining PERF in 1977, he has conducted studies on improving the management and effectiveness of criminal investigations. He has written an introduction to research for law enforcement managers and published a number of reports that are used extensively in police and criminal justice courses in colleges and training academies. Mr. Eck has also served as a consultant on investigations management to the London Metropolitan Police and has taught research methods to police managers at the Canadian Police College. He holds a master's degree in public policy from the University of Michigan. Mr. Eck is currently a doctoral student at the Institute of Criminal Justice and Criminology at the University of Maryland, College Park.

Terry Eisenberg (Chapter 10) is Commander of the Employee Development Bureau of the United States Capitol Police. He is also President of Personnel Performance, Inc., a law enforcement human resources consulting firm. He was formerly employed by Westinghouse Electric Corporation's Defense and Space Center as Director of Psychological Services, by the International Association of Chiefs of Police as a staff member of the Professional Standards Division, and by the San Jose (California) Police Department as a police officer. Dr. Eisenberg has served as an instructor in a number of colleges and universities and as an expert witness and litigation consultant in many civil cases pertaining to public safety personnel and organizational practices. He has also published over fifty articles, manuscripts, and book chapters. Dr. Eisenberg is a former National Aeronautics and Space Administration (NASA) Fellow and holds a Ph.D.

degree in industrial/organizational psychology from the University of Maryland.

Deborah Y. Faulkner (Chapter 14) is a Captain with the Metropolitan Nashville Police Department. She has a B.A. degree in journalism from Memphis State University, an M.S. in criminal justice from Middle Tennessee State University, and an Ed.D. in human development counseling from Vanderbilt University. She is a graduate of the FBI National Academy and a past president of the Tennessee chapter of Academy graduates. Currently, she is the police department's Accreditation Manager and is President of the Tennessee Accreditation Network. She is a member of PERF and has served on numerous police oral boards.

David Fogel (Chapter 18) is Professor of Criminal Justice at the University of Illinois at Chicago. He has served as Superintendent of Juvenile Hall and was Director of Institutions for Marin County, California; Commissioner of Corrections in Minnesota; Executive Director of the Illinois Law Enforcement Commission; and Director of the Office of Professional Standards, Chicago Police Department. He has been a German Marshall and Fullbright Fellow. He holds a B.A. degree in history from Brooklyn College, an M.S.W. from the University of Minnesota, and a doctorate in criminology from the University of California (Berkeley).

Craig B. Fraser (Chapter 12), is Planning and Budget Manager for the Santa Ana (California) Police Department. Previously he served as Director of Training, Education, and Accreditation for the Metropolitan Police in Massachusetts, taught at Boston University, directed the Management Information Division of the Winston-Salem (North Carolina) Police Department, held appointments at the School of Criminology at Florida State University, at Washburn University, and at the University of Kansas, and worked as a Project Director and Analyst in the Kansas City Evaluation Office of the Police Foundation. He has broad experience in training and consulting in law enforcement planning, crime analysis, and resource allocation. He holds a bachelor's degree from Duke University and a master's degree and a doctorate in political science from Purdue University.

Sheldon F. Greenberg (Chapter 14) is Associate Director of the Police Executive Research Forum, directing management services operations. Previously, he served as Director of Research and Planning, Assistant to the Chief of Police, and Commander of the Administrative Services

Bureau with the Howard County (Maryland) Police Department. He started as a police officer in 1969. In addition, he has served as an instructor for the U.S. Border Patrol, U.S. Marshals Service, Senior Management Institute for Police, and numerous police academies. He has directed PERF programs in police agencies throughout the United States and internationally in Cyprus, Jordan, Panama, Kenya, and Eastern Europe. He has written texts on stress management and numerous articles on subjects such as police planning, police officer fitness, and police agency management. He holds a Ph.D. degree from Union College, an M.Ed. from Johns Hopkins University, and a B.A. from Loyola College of Baltimore.

Charles A. Gruber (Chapter 11) was appointed Chief of Police for Elgin, Illinois, in June 1990. Prior to this appointment, he served as Chief of Police in Shreveport, Los Angeles, for almost four years and in Quincy, Illinois, for eleven years. Chief Gruber is past president of the International Association of Chiefs of Police. He was appointed by the governor to the Illinois State Law Enforcement Training Board. He was recognized by the U.S. Marshals Service in Washington, D.C., as the Law Enforcement Officer of the Year for 1989, and by the Shreveport Bar Association, which awarded him the Liberty Bell Award. Chief Gruber holds a bachelor's degree in psychology and a master's degree in police administration. He is a graduate of the FBI National Academy and its National Law Enforcement Executive Development program and the National Executive Institute. He is also a graduate of the University of Louisville Administration Officers Course, Southern Police Institute.

Dorothy Guyot (Chapter 15) is a faculty member of St. John's College, Annapolis, a community of learning where she engages students in thinking through fundamental questions. Her research into issues in upgrading the quality of police service began when she taught at John Jay College of Criminal Justice, continued at Rutgers School of Criminal Justice, and has culminated in a book published in 1991. She holds a B.A. in political science from the University of Chicago and a doctorate from Yale.

Eusevio "Ike" Hernandez (Chapter 4) is President of Hernandez and Associates Management Consultants. Formerly, he was Deputy Chief of Police for the San Jose Police Department. He is founder of the Hispanic American Police Command Officers Association and a Paul Harris Fellow of Rotary. Previously, he served as a consultant to various public agencies, including the Community Relations Service, Atlanta University, and local police departments. He holds a B.A. degree in police administration from San Jose State University and an M.P.A. from Golden Gate University.

Clifford Karchmer (Chapter 7) is associate director of program development at the Police Executive Research Forum (PERF), where he has directed projects on white collar crime, asset forfeiture, and illegal money laundering involving organized crime and narcotics traffickers. Prior to joining PERF in 1986, he served as a research scientist with the Battelle Memorial Institute in Seattle and Washington, D.C. Mr. Karchmer has also served as special investigator for the Pennsylvania Crime Commission, coordinator of program development for the Massachusetts Committee on Criminal Justice, and director of the Massachusetts Organized Crime Control Council. He received a master's degree in public administration from Harvard's John F. Kennedy School of Government, a master's degree in political science from the University of Wisconsin, and a bachelor's degree from Princeton University.

George L. Kelling (Chapter 1) is a Professor in the College of Criminal Justice at Northeastern University and a fellow in the Program of Criminal Justice in the John F. Kennedy School of Government at Harvard University. While working for the Police Foundation from 1971 to 1980, he directed the teams that conducted and published the results of the Kansas City Preventive Patrol Experiment and the Newark Foot Patrol Experiment.

Richard J. Koehler (Chapter 18) is Professor of Law and Criminal Justice at John Jay College of Criminal Justice, City University of New York. Previously he served as Commissioner of Correction (1986–90), and first Deputy Commissioner of Correction (1981–83) for New York City. He also served as Chief of Personnel for the New York City Police Department and held positions as commanding officer of the Office of Planning and Management Analysis and Director of Communications, NYPD. He has been a member of the Board of Directors of the American Jail Association and has been active in the American Correctional Association and the International Association of Chiefs of Police. He holds a B.A. degree in social science from John Jay College of Criminal Justice, an M.A. in urban affairs from Hunter College, and a J.D. from Fordham University School of Law in New York City.

Peter A. Lupsha (Chapter 8) is a Professor of Political Science at the University of New Mexico. He is the author of numerous articles on organized crime, drug trafficking, terrorism, and intelligence. He has been a speaker at the FBI Academy and the national convention of the LEIU. He has been a consultant to a number of agencies and governments on issues of international drug trafficking and organized crime. He is a member of the International Association for the Study of Organized Crime and the International Association of Law Enforcement Intelligence Analysts. Currently he is working on intelligence driven analytical models for interdicting international drug trafficking groups in the Southwestern Border region. He holds a B.A. degree from Oklahoma State University, an M.A. from the University of California (Berkeley) and a Ph.D. from Stanford University.

Kai R. Martensen (Chapter 15) is a Principal Associate with the Jefferson Institute for Justice Studies. He is on the Board of Directors of the Baltimore County Police Foundation. Previously he was a member of the Baltimore County (Maryland) Police Department (1979–89) and the Oakland (California) Police Department (1957–65) involved in planning, implementing, and evaluating police programs. As a member of several research and consulting firms, he has conducted numerous police management studies and provided technical assistance to federal, state, and local government agencies on police, criminal justice, and public safety subjects. He holds a B.A. degree in criminology from the University of California, Berkeley, and an M.A. in public administration from the University of Southern California.

Stephen D. Mastrofski (Chapter 13) is Associate Professor of Administration of Justice at the Pennsylvania State University. He holds a bachelor's degree from the University of Iowa and a doctorate in political science from the University of North Carolina. He has authored a variety of publications on performance measurement of police, police organization and behavior, and police reform. He serves on the editorial board of several criminology and criminal justice journals and as a peer reviewer for the National Institute of Justice. He has been a consultant to several law enforcement agencies. He and a colleague recently completed an evaluation of drunk-driving enforcement for the Pennsylvania Department of Transportation.

Susan W. McCampbell (Chapter 18) is Assistant Sheriff for the Alexandria (Virginia) Office of Sheriff, a position she has held since 1984. Prior to that, she worked for the Police Executive Research Forum as the Law Enforcement Accreditation Manager, developing standards and accreditation procedures for the Commission on Accreditation for Law Enforcement Agencies, Inc. She holds a bachelor's degree in political science from The American University, and a master's degree in city and regional planning from The Catholic University of America.

Jerry Eugene Mechling (Chapter 11) is Director of the Strategic Computing and Telecommunications in the Public Sector Program and Adjunct Lecturer in Public Policy of the John F. Kennedy School of Government at Harvard University. In addition, Dr. Mechling is a Principal in Hayes-Mechling-Kleiman, Inc., a management and systems consulting company. Formerly, Dr. Mechling served as an Aide to the Mayor and Assistant Administrator of the Environmental Protection Administration for Mayor John V. Lindsay of New York City, and as Director of the Office of Management and Budget for Mayor Kevin H. White of Boston. He holds an A.B. degree in physical sciences from Harvard University and M.P.A. and Ph.D. degrees from the Woodrow Wilson School at Princeton.

Mark H. Moore (Chapter 2) is the Guggenheim Professor of Criminal Justice Policy and Management at Harvard's John F. Kennedy School of Government. In 1974 and 1975, he served as Chief Planning Officer for the U.S. Drug Enforcement Administration. He is the author of numerous books and articles in the fields of criminal justice and public sector management. Since 1985, he has led Harvard's Executive Session on Community Policing. He has also taught in the Senior Managers in Policing Program operated by the Police Executive Research Forum since its inception. Dr. Moore holds a B.A. (summa cum laude) from Yale University and M.P.P. and Ph.D. degrees in public policy from the Kennedy School at Harvard University.

Patrick V. Murphy (Chapter 9) is Director of the Police Policy Board of the U.S. Conference of Mayors. He has served as police chief executive in New York, Detroit, Washington, and Syracuse; president of the Police Foundation; and administrator of the Law Enforcement Assistance Administration. He holds a B.A. degree from St. John's University and an M.P.A. from the City College of New York.

Dennis E. Nowicki (Chapter 10) is Chief of Police in Joliet, Illinois, and retired Deputy Superintendent of the Chicago Police Department. He holds a B.S. degree in personnel administration from Northwestern University and an M.S. in management public service from DePaul University. He has certificates from the Senior Management Institute for Police of the Police Executive Research Forum and Harvard University and from the Northwestern University Traffic Institute.

Joseph L. Peterson (Chapter 17) is Associate Professor of Criminal Justice at the University of Illinois at Chicago. He received a doctor of criminology degree from the University of California at Berkeley in 1971, specializing in criminalistics/forensic science. He has managed the forensic science research program of the National Institute of Justice and has directed the Criminal Justice Center at John Jay College of Criminal Justice, the Forensic Sciences Foundation in Rockville, Maryland, and the Center for Research in Law and Justice at the University of Illinois at Chicago. He has published extensively on the uses and effects of forensic science on the investigation and prosecution of criminal cases.

Glenn L. Pierce (Chapter 11) is Director of the Center for Applied Social Research at Northeastern University, where he has directed studies on the character of demand for police services, the social and economic status of American families, the impact of legislative change on individual and organizational behavior, and the strategic role of information technology in public sector institutions. He has undertaken studies for a variety of municipal, state, and federal agencies and he has also conducted research for private-sector organizations and private foundations. His research has been published in a variety of professional journals, edited volumes, and monographs. Mr. Pierce holds a Ph.D. degree in sociology from Northeastern.

Dennis P. Rosenbaum (Chapter 4) is Director of the Center for Research in Law and Justice and Associate Professor of Criminal Justice at the University of Illinois at Chicago. He holds a B.A. degree in psychology from Claremont McKenna College and a Ph.D. in psychology from Loyola University of Chicago. He has directed a wide range of research and evaluation projects focusing on police and community crime control programs, and has served as an advisor to many local, state, and national organizations in the criminal justice field. His published books and articles give primary attention to citizen participation in neighborhood anti-crime and anti-drug activities.

William Spelman (Chapter 3) is Assistant Professor at the Lyndon B. Johnson School of Public Affairs, University of Texas at Austin, where he teaches courses on urban policy and management. Before coming to Texas in 1988, Dr. Spelman was Senior Research Associate with the Police Executive Research Forum, where he conducted studies of citizen reporting of serious crimes, repeat offender programs, and problem-oriented policing. He holds an A.B. degree in political science and economics from UCLA, an M.P.P. from the John F. Kennedy School of Government, and a Ph.D. in public policy from Harvard University.

Darrel W. Stephens (Chapter 2) is executive director of the Police Executive Research Forum. Since beginning his career as a police officer in Kansas City, Missouri, in 1968 he has served as assistant chief in Lawrence, Kansas (1976–79), and as police chief in both Largo, Florida (1979–83), and Newport News, Virginia (1983–86). Stephens, who also spent a year early in his career as a National Institute of Justice Fellow, has written extensively about police issues. He holds a master's degree in public services administration from Central Missouri State University and a bachelor's degree in the administration of justice from the University of Missouri–Kansas City.

James K. "Chips" Stewart (Chapter 1) is a Principal with the consulting firm of Booz-Allen & Hamilton, Inc., serving as Director of Justice Systems Technology. Previously, he served for eight years as Director of the National Institute of Justice, the principal research agency for the Justice Department. Mr. Stewart's awards and recognitions include election to the Directory of Distinguished Americans. He has engaged in policy-relevant research in all aspects of criminal justice and has been a consultant on using state-of-the-art management and technology to improve justice agency effectiveness. He is a member of the FBI National Academy Associates, a board member of the White House Fellows Foundation, and a principal for the Council for Excellence in Government. He is a graduate of the University of Oregon and holds an M.P.A. degree from California State University.

John Sturner (Chapter 14) is Deputy Chief of the Saint Paul (Minnesota) Police Department. He has served as commander of the Patrol, Detective, and Support Services Divisions. He chairs the committee on Police Support Services of the International Association of Chiefs of Police and has served as a consultant to the National Institute of Jus-

tice and to the Commission on Accreditation for Law Enforcement Agencies as an assessor. He is President of the Northwest Chapter of the Federal Bureau of Investigation National Academy Associates and is a member of the Police Executive Research Forum. He holds a B.A. degree in public administration and is completing a master's degree in management, both from Metropolitan State University in Saint Paul. He is a graduate of the Federal Bureau of Investigation National Academy, the Senior Management Institute for Police, Command and General Staff College of the United States Army. He currently holds the rank of Lieutenant Colonel in the Military Police Corps of the United States Army National Guard.

Thomas J. Sweeney (Chapter 3) is Chief of Police in Bridgeport, Connecticut. He has previously served as Deputy Commissioner of the Westchester County Department of Public Safety and Director of Staff Services for the Yonkers Police Department. In an earlier capacity with the Kansas City (Missouri) Police Department, he developed and implemented studies on preventive patrol and response time. In the wake of that research, he guided the formulation of directed patrol concepts that became the basis for extensive patrol development activities under ICAP and MPO.

Gary W. Sykes (Chapter 10) is Director of the Southwestern Law Enforcement Institute, a division of The Southwestern Legal Foundation on the campus of The University of Texas at Dallas. Previously he served as Associate Professor and Professor of Justice Administration, College of Urban and Public Affairs, University of Louisville, where he also taught in the Southern Police Institute. Prior appointments include assistant professor of criminal justice and political science at the University of Wisconsin–Superior and Berea College, Berea, Kentucky. He holds B.A., M.A., and Ph.D. degrees in political science from The Pennsylvania State University. He has served on several criminal justice related boards and commissions and has published numerous articles, book chapters, and research studies in major criminal justice publications. While teaching at the University of Wisconsin–Superior, he served as a sworn officer for a year in the Superior Police Department.

Larry N. Thompson (Chapter 6) is Bureau Chief of the Highway Patrol Bureau of the Arizona Department of Public Safety. He has served in all ranks within the police agency and as bureau chief in both the Administrative and Criminal Investigation Bureaus. In addition, he is chairman of the Advisory Committee on Highway Safety with the International Association of Chiefs of Police (IACP), where many standards for police equipment and the certification criteria for drug recognition technicians are in development stages. He holds a bachelor's degree in public management from St. Mary's College of California and has completed numerous upper-management-level seminars and courses. Affiliations include the AAMVA, CARE, IACP, FOP, and the Associated Highway Patrolmen of Arizona.

Robert C. Wadman (Chapter 13) was appointed Chief of Police for Aurora, Illinois, in 1989. Previously, he was Chief of Police for Omaha, Nebraska; Deputy Commissioner of Public Safety for the State of Utah; and Chief of Police for Orem, Utah. Other law enforcement experience includes employment as a federal agent for the U.S. Department of Justice and patrolman/police sergeant in San Diego, California. Chief Wadman has an M.P.A. degree from Brigham Young University. He has written several manuals and articles dealing with law enforcement and crime prevention.

Chuck Wexler (Chapter 12) is Special Assistant, the President's Drug Advisory Council, Washington, D.C. He was formerly with the Office of National Drug Control Policy. He has served as the Director of the Professional Development Division at the International Association of Chiefs of Police and has been a consultant to city managers and mayors across the country in the selection of police executives. He was Operations Assistant to the Police Commissioner of the Boston Police Department, where he also was head of the Community Disorders Unit and Director of Planning and Research. He is a graduate of Boston University and received a master's degree from Florida State University. He earned a Ph.D. from the Massachusetts Institute of Technology, where he also was an instructor.

Gerald L. Williams (Chapter 5) has been Chief of Police in Aurora, Colorado, since July 1986. He began his career in criminal justice as a patrol officer in 1969 in Arvada, Colorado, and worked his way up through the ranks to become Arvada's Chief of Police. Dr. Williams holds a B.A. degree in sociology from Metropolitan State College and a Master of Criminal Justice Administration and a Doctorate in Public Administration from the University of Colorado. He also is a graduate of the FBI National Academy. Professional accomplishments include appointments to various state boards and councils by the governor of Colorado, adjunct assistant professor status at the University of Colorado Graduate School of Public Affairs, and publication of research projects, papers, and articles relating to police administration. Dr. Williams is Chairman for the Commission on Accreditation for Law Enforcement Agencies and has served as a working group member of the Executive Sessions on Policing at Harvard University's John F. Kennedy School of Government, a trainer for the Police Executive Research Forum, and an exchange representative in Israel for the Anti-Defamation League.

Hubert Williams (Chapter 16) is President of the Police Foundation. He served as police director of Newark, New Jersey, from 1974 to 1985. Mr. Williams has a bachelor's degree from John Jay College of Criminal Justice and a juris doctorate from Rutgers University. He was a research fellow at Harvard Law School's Center for Criminal Justice and was founding president of the National Organization for Black Law Enforcement Executives (NOBLE). He currently serves on the U.S. Sentencing Commission's Advisory Committee on Alternatives to Imprisonment, the Harvard Executive Sessions on Policing, and the Advisory Committee on Innovations in State and Local Government.

Illustration credits

Chapter 3   Figure 3–1: Alfred Blumstein, Jacqueline Cohen, Jeffrey A. Roth, and Christy A. Visher, *Criminal Careers and "Career Criminals,"* vol. 1 (Washington, DC: National Academy Press, 1986); James F. Nelson, "Multiple Victimization in American Cities: A Statistical Analysis of Rare Events," *American Journal of Sociology* 85 (1980): 870–91; and Glenn L. Pierce, Susan Spaar, and LeBaron R. Briggs, *The Character of Police Work: Strategic and Tactical Implications* (Boston: Center for Applied Social Research, Northeastern University, 1986).

Chapter 6   Figure 6–2: District of Columbia Department of Highways and Traffic, *Highway and Traffic Safety Improvement Program for the District of Columbia* (Washington, DC: District of Columbia Department of Highways and Traffic, n.d.), 20.

Chapter 8   Figure 8–2: President's Commission on Law Enforcement and Administration of Justice, *The Challenge of Crime in a Free Society* (Washington, DC: U.S. Government Printing Office, 1967), 194; Figure 8–3: Office of National Drug Control Policy, 1989.

Chapter 15   Figure 15–1: *Statistical Abstract of the United States* (Washington, DC: U.S. Government Printing Office, 1988), 25; Figure 15–2: David C. Couper, *How to Rate Your Local Police* (Washington, DC: Police Executive Research Forum, 1983); Figure 15–3: Adapted from Stephen D. Mastrofski, "Varieties of Police Governance in Metropolitan America," *Politics and Policy* (Summer 1988).

Index

Page numbers in *italics* refer to sidebars or illustrations.

Municipal Management Series

**Local Government
Police Management,
Third Edition**

Text type
Times Roman, Helvetica

Composition
EPS Group Inc.
Baltimore, Maryland

Printing and binding
Arcata Graphics/Kingsport
Kingsport, Tennessee

Design
Herbert Slobin